www.wadsworth.com

www.wadsworth.com is the World Wide Web site for Wadsworth and is your direct source to dozens of online resources.

At *www.wadsworth.com* you can find out about supplements, demonstration software, and student resources. You can also send e-mail to many of our authors and preview new publications and exciting new technologies.

www.wadsworth.com
Changing the way the world learns®

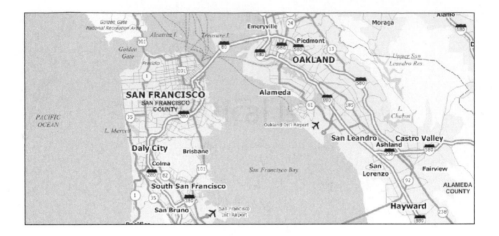

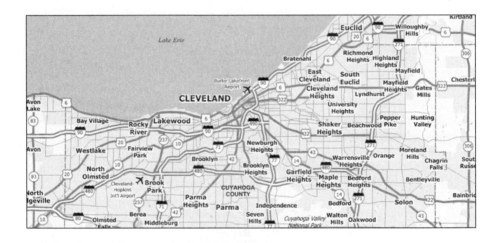

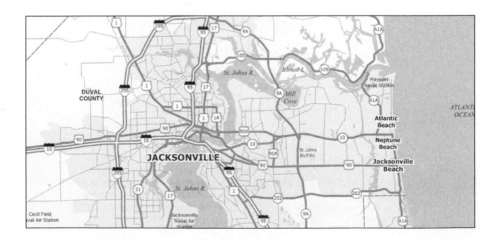

URBAN POLITICS

·

Power in Metropolitan America

SEVENTH EDITION

BERNARD H. ROSS
American University

MYRON A. LEVINE
Albion College

THOMSON
WADSWORTH

Australia ■ Brazil ■ Canada ■ Mexico ■ Singapore
Spain ■ United Kingdom ■ United States

THOMSON

✷ ™
WADSWORTH

Executive Editor: *David Tatom*
Associate Development Editor: *Rebecca F. Green*
Editorial Assistant: *Cheryl C. Lee*
Technology Project Manager: *Michelle Vardeman*
Senior Marketing Manager: *Janise Fry*
Marketing Assistant: *Teresa Jessen*
Marketing Communications Manager: *Kelley McAllister*
Project Manager, Editorial Production: *Candace Chen*
Creative Director: *Rob Hugel*
Art Director: *Maria Epes*
Print Buyer: *Karen Hunt*

Permissions Editor: *Kiely Sisk*
Production Service: *Interactive Composition Corporation*
Photo Researcher: *Cheri Throop*
Copy Editor: *Joel Rosenthal*
Illustrator: *Interactive Composition Corporation*
Cover Designer: *Brian Salisbury*
Cover Image: *Chicago Skyscraper,* © *Alex L. Fradkin/Getty Images*
Compositor: *Interactive Composition Corporation*
Cover and Text Printer: *Webcom*

Thomson Higher Education
10 Davis Drive
Belmont, CA 94002-3098
USA

For more information about our products, contact us at:
**Thomson Learning Academic
Resource Center
1-800-423-0563**

For permission to use material from this text or product, submit a request online at
http://www.thomsonrights.com.
Any additional questions about permissions can be submitted by e-mail to
thomsonrights@thomson.com.

Library of Congress Control Number:
2005925536

ISBN 0-534-60487-0

This book is dedicated to
Marlene Ross and
Nancy Levine for their
patience, support,
love, and faith.

——————————■——————————

BRIEF CONTENTS

CONTENTS

CHAPTER 6

MACHINE POLITICS   173

CHAPTER 7

REFORM POLITICS   197

CHAPTER 16
THE FUTURE OF URBAN AMERICA   513

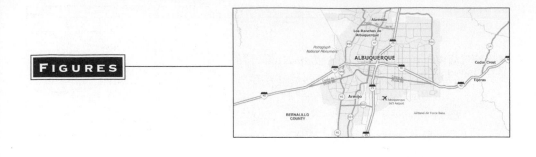

FIGURES

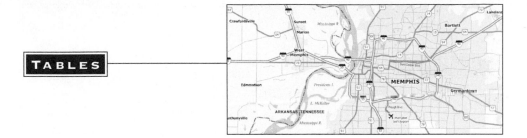

TABLES

The seventh edition of *Urban Politics* highlights two relatively new factors that have exerted a strong influence on urban affairs. The first is globalization. In a world increasingly without borders, cities are buffeted by economic investment decisions and immigration and labor patterns over which they exert little control. The second is the rise of the security city after the terrible events of 9/11. Patterns of public spending, intergovernmental aid, private investment, and urban development have all been altered as the nation and its cities grapple with the threat posed by terrorism.

Yet despite these important contemporary trends, the story of American urban politics is characterized as much by continuity as by change. The shift of population and wealth from the cities to the suburbs continues unabated. Recent evidence of urban reinvestment, gentrification, and a downtown "renaissance" does little to offset the flow of population and resources to suburbia. Suburban sprawl and the political fragmentation of the metropolis provide a setting that acts to impede the realization of equitable and sustained patterns of growth.

To a great extent, suburban populations control many state houses. Yet suburbia is no monolith. The concepts of "inner-rings suburbs," "edge cities," "edgeless development," "privatopias," and "disaster communities" only begin to point to the diversity and complexity of a suburban nation.

Cities and suburbs also compete with one another for local economic development. The heightened intercommunity, interregional, and global competition for business serves to provide businesses with leverage to obtain tax concessions, subsidies, and other favors from state and local decision makers.

Population, economic investment, and power also continue to flow from the Frostbelt to the Sunbelt. With reapportionment, the Sunbelt's growing political clout will be reflected in both Congress and the Electoral College, power bases that over the years will reshape national policies toward cities. Politics in U.S. cities, particularly in the Southwest, also continues to reflect the growing size and political power of the nation's Hispanic population. The 2005 election of Antonio Villaraigosa as mayor of Los Angeles underscores the growth of Latino voting power.

In recent decades, concern for local economic development has tended to dominate the politics of a great many cities and suburbs. Yet urban politics in the United States is to a great degree also the politics of race. Recent census data documents the increased entry of new population groups into the suburbs. But that piece of good news is offset by evidence that points to the continuing racial disparities among communities, the impact of exclusionary zoning, and the troubling resegregation of local school systems. Continued attention must be paid to the equitable funding and quality of schools and other important municipal services.

We persist in our belief that a thorough understanding of urban politics requires an analysis of both the formal structures of local government and the more informal, behind-the-scenes exercise of political power. The formal rules of the game affect "who gets what" in the urban arena. Yet the formal rules do not dictate the outcomes of urban politics. Informal power greatly constrains the actions of local government.

In writing this book, we do not assume that "urban politics" is a world with which most citizens and college students are greatly familiar. Even active, engaged citizens often have little knowledge of significant events that occur in other communities—both in neighboring communities as well as in communities across the nation. Newspapers do a poor job of reporting urban affairs; events outside a community's borders are presumed to be of no interest to a paper's readership. Even within a metropolitan region, "news doctors" urge the editors of major dailies to devote greater space and attention to thematic issues, such as highway development, that affect a broad range of communities. Important local news stories that affect a single community are either downplayed or ignored.

To help remedy this lack of knowledge, in this edition of *Urban Politics* we have tried something new, to draw on the images of American cities and suburbs that have become a part of the popular culture. In "boxed" features placed throughout the book, we point to where Hollywood films offer insights into the workings of urban politics. We are careful to note just where cinematic portrayals aid—and distort—our understanding of urban affairs.

Every chapter of the seventh edition of *Urban Politics* has been thoroughly rewritten. A totally new chapter, Chapter 3, is devoted to gentrification and globalization. Chapter 10, "Women and the Gendered City," was written by Robyne Turner, the Schutte Professor of Urban Affairs at the University of Missouri–Kansas City. It is our good fortune to be joined once again by Professor Turner, whose work helps to increase our understanding as to just whose needs are met—and ignored—in the urban arena. Chapter 11 includes important new material on the Smart Growth and New Urbanism movements.

We are indebted to friends and colleagues who have contributed to our understanding of the city. Professor Ross wishes to thank his colleagues in Public Administration for their support and for their reviews and bits and pieces of information that were worked into the draft chapters as the manuscript progressed. Special thanks go to Howard McCurdy, David Rosenbloom, and the rest of The American University faculty who were willing to engage in free-flowing discussions about the issues of the day. Kristin McDonald-Casson and Josh Franzel, students in the Department of Public Administration at

The American University, were also noteworthy in their efforts in fact gathering and footnote/endnote checking.

Myron Levine extends special thanks to Bill Peterman, Janet Smith, and Bob Waste, good friends who helped to keep him abreast of continuing developments in the city. Vicky Grant was extremely helpful in numerous ways, both large and small. A dedicated, tireless worker, she did invaluable work on the manuscript. Albion College's Faculty Development Committee also provided much-appreciated support.

We would like to thank the reviewers of this edition: Yonn Dierwechter, University of Washington, Tacoma; Eric Anthony Johnson, University of North Carolina, Greensboro; and Matt Lindstrom, Siena College.

Previous editions of this book were published by F.E. Peacock Publishers. We are grateful for the faith that Thomson Wadsworth showed us in picking up the manuscript after Ted Peacock's retirement. We are particularly thankful for the work of David Tatom, Candace Chen, and Rebecca Green. Kiely Sisk was quite helpful with permissions, as was Cheri Throop in researching photographs. The efforts of Michael Ryder, the project editor at Interactive Composition Corporation, and Joel Rosenthal, the copyeditor, helped to make the manuscript more readable.

THE 9/11 ATTACKS AND THE DEBATE OVER THE REBUILDING OF LOWER MANHATTAN

On the morning of September 11, 2001, Al Qaeda terrorists slammed a jetliner, loaded with passengers and fuel, into the 91st floor of the north tower of the World Trade Center (WTC) in New York's Lower Manhattan. Eighteen minutes later, a second Boeing 757 hit the south tower between the 78th and 84th floors. Within an hour, a third plane dove and crashed into the Pentagon in Washington. Terrorists highjacked a fourth plane, United Flight 93, which was likely targeted for the Capitol in Washington; it crashed in the fields of Pennsylvania as heroic passengers fought the highjackers.

Fueled by the massive amounts of office paper, the fire at the World Trade Center was as hot as 2,000 degrees Fahrenheit. The intensity of the fire barred escape from the upper floors of the 110-story twin towers. Onlookers watched in horror as office workers in the upper stories, with no possibility of escape, jumped to their deaths to the pavement below.

The horror intensified when the support structures of the towers melted. First the south tower and then the north tower imploded, crumbling to the ground. Onlookers ran in panic, seeking to escape the cloud of dust and debris that obliterated the daylight.

In all, 3,000 people died in the day's attacks, 2,749 at the World Trade Center.[1] All seven buildings in the World Trade Center complex, including the monumental twin towers, collapsed. Nearby buildings suffered severe smoke, water, and structural damage. The area also suffered ecological contamination as the fires and the massive dust cloud spread asbestos, heavy metals, PCBs, and other toxins.[2]

In the midst of the crisis, New York City Mayor Rudy Giuliani rushed to the scene and established his authority. He took to the airwaves to reassure the nation that someone was in charge. In the days and weeks that followed, he testified to the nation's grief and the respect that the nation gave the firefighters, the police, rescue workers, and other "first responders" and fallen heroes. Giuliani's popularity soared, and the national news media proclaimed him "America's mayor."

Term limits barred Giuliani from pursuing and winning a third term in office. Somewhat reluctantly, Giuliani passed the torch to a successor, backing Wall Street financier Michael Bloomberg against Giuliani's political nemesis, Democrat Mark Green. Bloomberg won the mayoralty, spending $75 million of his own money, a record for local elections anywhere.[3]

The attacks unified New Yorkers as never before, papering over class, ethnic, and racial divisions. Yet, in the months and years that followed, those political fault lines would reemerge.

There was serious debate over what should be built on the Ground Zero site. Some enthusiasts urged the rebuilding of the twin towers or the construction of an even taller skyscraper as a testament to America's perseverance and spirit. Wall Street interests pushed for the urgent replacement of the large volume of lost office space destroyed by the attacks, repairing the hole that had been made in the heart of the nation's financial center. They opposed demands that a large portion of the site be set aside as a memorial; instead, they argued for the national urgency of rebuilding lower New York as a vital economic, transportation, and telecommunications hub.

Critics countered that there was no need to maintain such a large volume of office space and to build new monumental skyscrapers. Even before the 9/11 attacks, advances in telecommunications had weakened the real estate market in Lower Manhattan, with firms increasingly seeking less expensive office sites elsewhere in the city and metropolitan area. New skyscrapers would only drain tenants away from other areas of the city. Super-tall buildings could also conceivably be the target of future terrorist attacks.

The families of the 9/11 victims lobbied against rebuilding visions that sought to restore the dense commercial character of the World Trade Center area. As thousands had died in the attacks, families argued that a large portion of the site should be devoted to a park-like memorial.

Community activists and the residents of nearby Battery Park City argued for the construction of new residential areas with parks and walkways. They wanted a Lower Manhattan of human scale with mixed-use activities. They did not want to rebuild Lower Manhattan exclusively for modernistic skyscrapers and global commerce.[4]

The debate over the rebuilding of the World Trade Center was highly contentious and emotional, marked by the interplay of public and private interests. Private power, not just public authority, shaped the rebuilding at Ground Zero, just as private power had fused with public authority in the city's decision in an earlier era to construct the original World Trade Center.

PRIVATE POWER AND THE LIMITS OF URBAN GOVERNMENT

An examination of the events surrounding 9/11 reveals much about who holds the power in the urban arena. In fact, the particular focus of this book is on power—how it is distributed and how it is exercised in the urban political arena. A focus on power leads us to look beyond the formal institutions of local government. The power to get things done is not always held by local mayors, managers, and councils. In U.S. cities and suburbs, private individuals and corporations often possess, or at least share, the power to make key decisions. Private power constrains the actions of public officials.

Urban government in the United States is essentially "limited" government; municipal officials are highly constrained in their ability to solve problems. The U.S. Constitution limits local authority, making municipalities highly dependent on the actions of state and national officials. In fact, as local governments are not even mentioned in the Constitution, they lack constitutional powers of their own.

Just as important, local officials have only the most limited ability to influence private actors, whose investment decisions go a long way toward determining the growth and decline of cities. As a result of globalization, important investment decisions are made in corporate boardrooms that sometimes even lie outside U.S. borders, beyond the control of municipal officials.

The urban condition and the limited ability of local governments to solve urban problems are revealed in a summation of the larger events surrounding 9/11: New York's initial decision to construct the World Trade Center, the trends that made the World Trade Center vulnerable to attack; an identification of the victims; the politics surrounding plans for the post-9/11 rebuilding and memorialization of the Ground Zero site; and the impact the attack has had on New York and other cities. As we shall see, New York City's elected officials have had the most limited ability to determine the plans for the rebuilding of the World Trade Center. The war on terror has placed new and costly burdens not just on New York City, but on cities and suburbs nationwide, further limiting local abilities to combat other pressing urban problems.

JUST HOW POWERFUL WAS MAYOR RUDY GIULIANI?

It is easy to overstate the formal authority and power of local governing officials. Oftentimes, news stories make it appear that elected leaders are in control of their cities. But this is far from the truth.

Amid the national publicity that surrounded Mayor Rudy Giuliani as he responded to the events of 9/11, it might appear that the mayor possessed the power to run New York City. But this would be far from the truth. As capable as he was, Mayor Giuliani could not dictate the city's affairs. Indeed, the events of 9/11 were an exception, a crisis that allowed the capable Giuliani to momentarily seize the media's attention. In economic development and other critical policy areas, in contrast, Giuliani did not dominate but had to share power with corporate officials and other governmental and nongovernmental actors who made key decisions critical to New York's health.

Giuliani's post-9/11 aura obscures the general weakness of the mayoral office and local public authority in general. As a result of his highly visible 9/11 actions, Giuliani appeared powerful. But as seen in the criticisms he suffered as mayor prior to September 11, Giuliani clearly was not all-powerful.

Nor was he overwhelmingly popular. According to early 2000 public opinion polls, Giuliani had even fallen behind Democrat Hillary Clinton in his attempt to win New York's open U.S. Senate seat. Suffering from prostate cancer, Giuliani withdrew from the very difficult race, ceding the Republican Party nomination to a little-known Long Island Congressman, Rick Lazio.

As mayor, Giuliani had noteworthy successes in instituting new managerial reforms and in reestablishing New York City as a good place for business.[5] However, his actions were largely deferential to, and did not challenge, the priorities of the city's big corporations. Giuliani provided large corporations with tax reductions and other desired subsidies. He did not pay similar attention to concerns for housing affordability or to the plight of the city's welfare and homeless populations.[6]

When Giuliani left office, the weakness of the city's mayoralty was again exposed. His successor, Michael Bloomberg, lacked the magnetic persona of his high-profile predecessor. Bloomberg's poll ratings continued to sink as he attempted the impossible, to broker the competing needs of New York's diverse constituencies in a city that was being forced to confront new security concerns in the face of an already severe budgetary crisis. Bloomberg was roundly criticized for his attempt to impose business-like performance and managerial reforms on the city schools.

POWER: A DEFINITION

As forceful and dynamic as Mayor Giuliani was, he possessed only a limited ability to get things done. The ability to get things done is precisely the meaning of **power.**

Power is too often misunderstood and viewed solely as **social control,** the ability of a political actor to force others to comply with his or her wishes.[7] Under this elementary definition, power denotes the ability of an actor to use threats or sanctions to achieve compliance.

But social control does not fully capture some of the most important aspects of urban power. In city politics, a person with power can get significant things done. The cooperation of a person of power is often essential to the accomplishment of important objectives; the refusal of a person of power can frustrate the actions desired by others. Power, then, denotes the ability to do important things. As Clarence Stone observes, power entails not just social control but also **social production:** power *to*, not just power *over.*

The exercise of power does not always denote a situation of conflict. Power can also be exercised quietly when effective cooperative arrangements are organized. Defined as the capacity to act or get things done, power is exercised when actors successfully arrange cooperation in the pursuit of goals.[8]

In the urban arena, we need to find out who has the power to get things done and who has the ability to stop or thwart proposed changes. Whose cooperation is essential to the realization of important urban outcomes? Whose interests are served? Political power determines whose perceptions of urban problems dominate and which solutions are pursued while others are ignored.

An examination of power requires that we go "behind the scenes" of urban government. Of course we must look at the formal procedures and institutions of government, but we cannot end our examination there. While a study of the formal rules will reveal who has the right to make important decisions, such a formal structural analysis is an insufficient method for the study of political power. Governmental officials make decisions, but they are often severely constrained by the influence of business groups and other private sector actors—and by the decisions, rules, and regulations set by state and national officials.

PRIVATE POWER AND THE BUILDING OF THE WORLD TRADE CENTER

Why was the WTC initially built in Lower Manhattan? A brief review of the decision to build the WTC will underscore the importance of private power in determining patterns of urban growth, decline, and development.

Like many older mercantile and manufacturing cites, by the middle of the twentieth century, New York was exhibiting clear symptoms of decline and distress. Private decisions had served to undermine New York's economy. Home buyers sought, and developers built, new housing in the suburbs, weakening the city's tax base. The city lost tens of thousands of manufacturing and port jobs as technological innovations, including the rise of trucking, the automobile, and jet travel, enabled corporate CEOs to shift production facilities to sites in the suburbs and the Sunbelt. Federal subsidies for highway construction, home mortgages, and new business investment further served to accelerate the shift to the suburbs and the Sunbelt.

By the 1970s, New York City was caught in the depths of a fiscal crisis and teetered on the edge of bankruptcy. The city had a population in need of social services. However, the region's middle-class residential and industrial tax base largely lay in the suburbs, beyond the city's taxing reach.

Although it was not fully appreciated at the time, the construction of the World Trade Center proved to be a critical part of New York City's economic renaissance. By the late-1980s and 1990s, New York had clearly recovered; it had come back as a headquarters city for global firms, with command-and-control offices concentrated in close proximity to one another in Lower Manhattan. The office space provided by the World Trade Center and the nearby World Financial Center helped accommodate the economic renaissance.

Private power lay behind the original decision to build the WTC complex, a project that was willed into existence largely as the result of the vision and political muscle of one man, Chase Manhattan Bank president David Rockefeller. In the middle of the twentieth century, Rockefeller saw that the economic condition of Lower Manhattan was becoming increasingly desperate. New office construction had drifted to the city's mid-town area. As Rockefeller's own office building at the time was the only modern skyscraper constructed in the vicinity of Wall Street, Rockefeller feared for the future of the city's financial district. He sought to clear the area of its many small buildings and antiquated warehouses to build a massive, new office complex that would spur the economic takeoff of all of Lower Manhattan.[9]

David Rockefeller, working hand in hand with his brother, New York Governor Nelson Rockefeller, pushed for the construction of the World Trade Center. The WTC was built despite the organized protests of the area's "Radio Row" electronics storeowners and other small merchants who were about to be evicted to make room for the project. Community activists scored the towers' bleak modernism and further objected that such a large-scale urban renewal project would be destructive of neighborhood life. The superblocks of the project broke the city's historic street grid. Street life in the area was further drained as the WTC routed pedestrian traffic to the large underground commercial arcade located beneath the complex.

As formidable as he was, Rockefeller could not bring about the rebirth of Lower Manhattan by himself. Despite his massive wealth, he needed the legal authority possessed by government for evictions, land assembly, various planning and construction approvals, and continued financial support. Rockefeller found a willing partner in the Port Authority of New York and New Jersey and its executive director Austin Tobin.[10] The Port Authority was an independent agency created to manage the affairs of the bi-state port area. Tobin and the Port Authority continued to support the construction of the WTC well after changes in New York's economy made it clear that the complex's new towers would not house port-related trading firms; instead, the WTC became the home for financial firms spilling over from nearby Wall Street.

PRIVATE POWER AND THE REBUILDING AT GROUND ZERO

Just as private actors played a dominant role in the initial decision to build the World Trade Center, they also had considerable say in determining what would be rebuilt in New York after the 9/11 attacks. The city was not free to rebuild anything it wanted, even at Ground Zero. Indeed, neither the mayor nor the city council possessed the authority to decide what would be constructed at the WTC site. Instead, major decisions regarding the rebuilding effort were lodged in the hands of narrow-based governmental agencies dominated by downtown corporate interests.[11]

The Port Authority owned the World Trade Center site. Just weeks before the 9/11 attacks, the Authority had leased the towers and their underground shopping complex to Larry Silverstein and his partner in return for $120 million per year in rental payments, payments that Silverstein was legally obligated to continue even after the Center's destruction.[12] After the devastation, Silverstein argued that he had a legitimate interest in getting a proper return on his investment; he had the legal right under the terms of the lease to determine the rebuilding plan. Silverstein possessed still additional power as he, not government, controlled much of the money that would pay for the new construction; as the leaseholder of the towers, he stood to receive $3.5 billion or more in insurance money as a result of the destruction of the WTC.[13]

Landov

The proposed 1,776-foot high Freedom Tower, as originally conceived by Daniel Libeskind. Libeskind's design,
despite its popularity, was soon altered considerably as a
result of continuing concerns regarding terrorism and
security. The site's leaseholder also did not fully accept
Libeskind's design plan. By 2005, it appeared that even
the project's off-center, twisting spiral tower would be
redesigned.

Silverstein resisted the most expansive memorial visions for the site and,
instead, fought for designs with as much office and commercial space as possible.
He brought in his own architect, Richard Childs, to modify the designs of world-
renowned architect Daniel Libeskind. The Lower Manhattan Development Corporation had chosen Libeskind, the designer of Berlin's celebrated Jewish
Museum, as the winner in the international design competition for the rebuilding
at Ground Zero. Libeskind's site-design plan included a below-ground memorial
and a monumental 1,776-foot Freedom Tower with an asymmetrical spire soaring above 70 floors of offices. Silverstein, who would be paying for the building,
did not believe that Libeskind, who had never constructed a skyscraper before,
had the experience to construct a commercially viable office tower.

Silverstein and the Port Authority also advanced plans for a vast underground
arcade of shops connected to the complex's New York–New Jersey train hub. Such
a vast subterranean shopping mall would enrich the developer but would drain
substantial life from the city's streets and foot traffic away from nearby stores.

Although Silverstein's position was formidable, his power was not absolute.
For the rebuilding to proceed, he would need the financial support and cooperation of the Port Authority, various other public agencies, and New York's

governor. While Silverstein preferred his own architect, Childs, political pressure forced him to work with Libeskind as well. Silverstein ultimately accepted a project with more public design features and less commercial space than he had initially wanted.

Two months after the attack, New York Governor George Pataki and Mayor Rudy Giuliani created the Lower Manhattan Development Corporation (LMDC) to oversee the rebuilding efforts, not just at the Ground Zero site but across all of Lower Manhattan. Pataki, a skilled politician, wanted to ensure that all participants in the process were heard and that the rebuilding plans did not offend the sensibilities of the victims' families and the general public. The LMDC was given the power to distribute federal aid, condemn land, and override local zoning. While the LMDC was charged with pooling together all the stakeholders concerned with the project, critics charged that the agency was more responsive to the demands of the Wall Street business community than to the needs of the residents of surrounding neighborhoods.

The LMDC hosted numerous forums for public comments on its rebuilding plans. Critics attacked the LMDC for its lack of racial diversity and its lack of transparency in making decisions behind closed doors[14] Public sentiment led Governor Pataki and the LMDC to reject all six of the plans that were initially chosen as the "finalists" in the design competition for World Trade Center rebuilding. The rejected plans all lacked certain grandeur; Silverstein and the Port Authority had brought forth plans with new, box-like buildings to restore as much of the area's lost office space as possible. The public's outrage led the LMDC to hold a second round of competition with a greater emphasis on innovation and architectural distinction. It was in the second round that Daniel Libeskind's overall design for the site, with its monumental Freedom Tower and the preservation of the twin towers "footprints," emerged as the winner.

As this review of post-9/11 decisions has shown, the key agencies in the rebuilding effort at Ground Zero gave considerable say to business interests. New York City had good reason to be sensitive to business needs. As a result of the devastation and disruption brought by 9/11, a number of WTC and other Lower Manhattan businesses relocated, some temporarily and some permanently, to other areas both inside and outside the city. Some corporations consolidated their offices in suburban commercial centers just across the river in New Jersey. Decisions made in corporate boardrooms would decide the extent to which the city would bounce back from the post-9/11 economic recession. Municipal officials could only attempt to influence these critical private sector decisions.

PRIVATISM: LIMITING THE POWER OF GOVERNMENT

Private business interests played a large role in the initial decisions concerning the building, and in the post-9/11 decisions regarding the rebuilding, of New York's World Trade Center. Private interests play an important role in municipal affairs; the only unusual aspect of the WTC case studies, especially in the post-9/11 reconstruction, was the degree to which business' actions were played out on the front pages of the city's newspapers.

Cities in the United States are greatly dependent on decisions made by private individuals and corporate officials. U.S. cities, unlike cities in Europe, do not enjoy a tradition of strong governmental planning that helps to counterbalance private power.

In Europe, government officials possess a much greater ability to guide private investment to ensure the achievement of public purposes. European planners can enact strong measures to build affordable housing, preserve the city streetscape, curb urban sprawl, promote mass transit, and protect green areas, actions that are largely unthinkable in the United States. Farmers in Europe are even given substantial subsidies so that they will not sell their land to residential developers. European city and regional planning officials promote mixed-income housing; they even have the ability to insist that the developers of a new commercial project provide subsidized housing units for the poor.[15] Private developers and the free market in Europe do not dictate the geography of urban development to the extent they do in the United States.

On the whole, Americans are an antigovernment people who resist strong urban planning requirements and see land-use restrictions as violations of their individual and property rights. Under the American political culture of **privatism,** private sector freedom is equated with liberty, government intrusions and regulations are kept to a minimum, and private sector actors are allowed great leeway to develop and dispose of their property as they see fit.[16]

The essential decisions that determine a city's health and decline are in the hands of private actors, not government officials. Municipal officials in New York, for instance, can do little to guarantee the city's economic well-being if the top officials in private corporations decide to locate production and headquarters facilities elsewhere—in the suburbs, in the Sunbelt, and overseas. Municipal officials can try to influence, but they do not control, private sector decisions.

New York, of course, is not unique. Faced with the devastation of the 1992 riots, Los Angeles similarly had little alternative but to rely on private actors in its attempts to rebuild the city's riot-torn areas. The private sector, not the government, controlled the investment resources necessary to build new facilities and bring new jobs to the community. Privatism, however, meant that the rebuilding effort would go only as far as the private sector was willing to take it. The private-led strategy produced only the most limited results. (See "Privatism and L.A.: Can the Private Sector Rebuild the Riot-Torn Inner City?" on p. 10.)

In reality, neither business nor government alone has the capacity to solve the urban crisis. The American culture of privatism means that government must attempt to mobilize the private sector for the public good. Effective urban problem solving requires the forging of effective partnerships between public and private sector actors.

Such partnerships, as we shall see in this book, are often difficult to maintain. Public-private partnerships also tend to give great respect to the concerns of business actors; they do not always fully respond to the needs and demands of a city's more disadvantaged residents.

The deadly 1992 civil disturbances in Los Angeles began after an all-white, sub-urban jury cleared four Los Angeles police officers of criminal charges in the beat-ing of a black motorist, Rodney King. The officers had pursued King for speeding. The entire nation was shocked by video footage, recorded by a nearby resident, which revealed that a circle of police officers repeatedly clubbed and kicked King, who, apparently under the influence of drugs, tried to get up from the ground.

The trial was moved from the heated L.A. environment to nearby Simi Valley, a predominantly white, suburban community in Ventura County. The all-white Simi County jury acquitted three of the four officers of criminal charges; a mis-trial was declared in the case of the fourth.[17] The acquittals helped to touch off a conflagration that began in the poor South Central section of Los Angeles and quickly spread to the downtown and to other parts of the city. Fifty-eight per-sons died in the most costly, peace-time, civil disorder in United States history.

After the riots, the federal government refused to provide massive assistance for Los Angeles' recovery. As a result, the city turned to a strategy designed to promote private investment in riot-torn neighborhoods. Peter Ueberroth, the former baseball commissioner and successful organizer of the 1984 Los Angeles Olympic Games, led the private sector initiative **Rebuild L.A.** (or, more simply, **RLA**) to bring jobs and new economic opportunity to the inner city, especially to ghetto youths.

RLA sought to convince corporate executives to invest in the city. But ulti-mately, RLA produced relatively little, except for a few notable construction projects and new inner-city supermarkets. Six years after the riots, the inner city remained riot-scarred. One-third of the buildings destroyed in the disturbance still had not been replaced, and some 200 lots in the riot area remained vacant.* Teenage unemployment in the area remained high. In 1993, Ueberroth stepped aside. In December 1996, RLA itself faded from existence. After Ueberroth's departure, RLA gave greater emphasis to a bottom-up approach to renewal, working more closely with neighborhood businesses and community organizations.**

The poor track record and short life of RLA underscore the severe limita-tions of urban strategies that allow private officials to make decisions critical to the health of cities and their neighborhoods. Private actors are constrained by considerations of profit and risk. Most private businesses did not deem the inner city, with its shortage of trained labor and its high crime rates and insur-ance costs, a desirable location.

RLA was roundly criticized for the limited nature of its actions. In fairness, however, the public sector, too, deserved blame. In a privatist nation, the gov-ernment was unwilling to provide the resources necessary for rebuilding inner-city Los Angeles.

* Hector Tobar, "Riots' Scars Include 200 Still-Vacant Lots," *Los Angeles Times*, April 21, 1997; Rene Sanchez, "Economic Boom Is a Distant Rumble in South Central L.A.," *The Washington Post*, August 31, 1999.

** Cynthia Jackson-Elmoore, "RLA in Retrospect: One Nonprofit's Efforts to Effect Change," *National Civic Review* 89, 1 (Spring 2000): 67–86.

THE THEMES OF THIS BOOK

The major focus of this book is on the interrelationship of private power and public authority in the shaping of the city. In addition, six important sub-themes guide this book's study of the politics of America's cities and suburbs:

1. Globalization is a relatively new force that is acting to shape patterns of development and power in America's cities and suburbs.

2. Despite the importance of private power, the formal rules and structure of American cities and suburbs remain important as they continue to exert significant influence on local affairs.

3. Federal and state actors and intergovernmental relations have a crucial impact on the politics of the *intergovernmental city*.

4. Sunbelt cities suffer from serious urban problems despite the general distinction that can be made between Frostbelt and Sunbelt communities.

5. Urban politics in the United States is largely the politics of race, not just a politics of economic development and municipal service delivery. Citizens in the United States have not been willing to confront fully the continuing patterns of racial imbalance in the American metropolis. A "new immigration" has added to the diversity found in U.S. communities, adding to the complexity of ethnic and race relations.

6. New gendered interpretations are essential for a more complete understanding of who exercises power and whose needs are met in the urban arena.

1. THE IMPORTANCE OF GLOBALIZATION AS A RELATIVELY NEW FORCE IN SHAPING CITIES AND SUBURBS.

Supranational economic structures and advances in telecommunications have eroded the local and national borders of old. The terrorists chose the World Trade Center as the target of the 9/11 attacks because New York City and Wall Street were seen as a pivotal control center of the global economy. The WTC towers were a symbol of that control. As new telecommunications technology carried American ideals and images around the world, U.S. foreign policy and economic advances served to fuel resentments overseas, resentments that were unleashed in the WTC assault.

Globalization denotes the increased permeability of cities to international economic forces, global corporate decision making, new population movements, and other forces outside their borders—even terrorist attacks conceived from abroad. In Chapter 3, "Recent Trends: Gentrification and Globalization," we look more closely at the impact of global forces on cities and suburbs.

In brief, New York is a command-and-control city, a nodal concentration of the headquarters of multinational corporations and financial services firms in the new world economy. Los Angeles is another U.S. city that plays a similar role on the world economic stage. Cities such as Chicago and Miami can be seen as global, too; although less important than New York or Los Angeles on the global stage, they occupy important positions as national and regional financial centers.

New York, Los Angeles, and Chicago were once port and manufacturing centers. However, as a result of deindustrialization and globalization, the character of these cities was transformed. They became less centers of manufacturing and more centers of corporate headquarters, financial services, and entertainment.

Not all cities have been able to find a niche in the new global economy. Across the country, cities lost the good-paying manufacturing jobs that characterized the urban economies of an earlier era. Advances in transportation, communications, and computerization all enabled corporations to shift their manufacturing, data-processing, and record-keeping jobs overseas to low-wage countries with less stringent labor and environmental protection regulations.

Globalization also entails the trans-border movement of populations. According to the 2002 U.S. Census estimates, 36 percent of New York's population was born outside the United States. In a global age, New York City, more than ever, is a city of immigrants.

A full look at the victims of the WTC attacks shows the diversity of a global city; their homelands ranged from the Dominican Republic to Canada to Poland.[18] Among the dead were legal immigrants and undocumented workers who worked as window washers, custodial and food service staff, and deliverymen from nearby cafés and delicatessens. Also among the dead were Latin Americans, primarily from Mexico, who worked in the WTC's offices, the below-ground eateries, and the top-floor world-renowned Windows on the World restaurant. Mexicans had become New York's most quickly growing minority.

In a global age, immigration is an important factor in the politics of many big cities. Twenty-four large- and medium-sized cities have a population that is over one-fifth foreign born (see Table 1-1). Over 60 percent of the population in Miami was born outside the United States, as was nearly half the population of Santa Ana (California) and over 40 percent of Los Angeles and Anaheim. In immigration **gateway cities** such as Los Angeles, New York, San Francisco, Miami, Chicago, Washington, Houston, San Diego, Boston, Dallas, Philadelphia, and Seattle, newcomers represent both a source of urban vitality and a strain on local resources.

The arrival of the new immigrants helped to mask the continuing weakness of many central cities. Some observers looked at the 2000 U.S. Census and took satisfaction in the small population gains reported by central cities, gains that, in some cases, reversed decades of urban decline. Yet, suburban growth continued to outpace that of central cities (see Figure 1-1). In cities such as Atlanta, the disparity was overwhelming; from 1990 to 1996, Atlanta gained only a 2-percent increase in its population while its suburbs grew by 22.3 percent.[19] Were it not for the arrival of new immigrants, a number of large cities would have suffered continuing population decline.

■ **TABLE 1-1**

CITIES RANKED BY PERCENT OF POPULATION THAT IS
FOREIGN BORN, 2002, TOP 30 CITIES

Rank	Place	Percent	Rank	Place	Percent
1.	Miami city, FL	60.6	16.	El Paso city, TX	24.9
2.	Santa Ana city, CA	48.4	17.	Stockton city, CA	24.2
3.	Los Angeles city, CA	41.3	18.	Riverside city, CA	23.9
4.	Anaheim city, CA	40.3	19.	Fresno city, CA	22.7
5.	San Francisco city, CA	36.7	20.	Chicago city, IL	22.6
6.	San Jose city, CA	36.5	21.	Newark city, NJ	22.4
7.	New York city, NY	36.0	22.	Phoenix city, AZ	21.1
8.	Long Beach city, CA	30.9	23.	Las Vegas city, NV	21.1
9.	Houston city, TX	28.1	24.	Denver city, CO	20.2
10.	San Diego city, CA	27.9	25.	Austin city, TX	19.6
11.	Oakland city, CA	27.1	26.	Aurora city, CO	17.7
12.	Boston city, MA	27.0	27.	Minneapolis city, MN	17.6
13.	Dallas city, TX	26.5	28.	Seattle city, WA	17.2
14.	Sacramento city, CA	26.4	29.	Arlington city, TX	16.6
15.	Honolulu CDP, HI	25.5	30.	St. Paul city, MN	16.3

SOURCE: Extracted from U.S. Census Bureau, American Community Service Office, "Percent of Population that is Foreign Born," September 2, 2003.
Available at: www.census.gov/acs/www/Products/Ranking/2002/R15T160.htm.

2. THE CONTINUING IMPORTANCE OF THE FORMAL RULES AND GOVERNMENTAL STRUCTURE OF AMERICAN CITIES AND SUBURBS.

Despite the significance of private power, the rules and formal procedures of government count. The formal rules and structures of urban government help to determine whose voices are heard and "who gets what" from politics.

Our brief review of post-9/11 rebuilding efforts in New York reveals a **fragmentation of decision-making authority** that is typical of metropolitan areas nationwide. No one government governs the metropolitan New York region, coordinating actions for the public good. Nor does New York City's mayor or city council possess the legal authority to guide the 9/11 reconstruction effort. Instead, the formal structure of government acts to fragment or balkanize decision making by creating numerous, independent decision-making forums.

It bears repeating: New York City's elected officials did not possess the formal authority to decide what would be built at Ground Zero. Instead,

SUBURBAN POPULATION IS GROWING TWICE AS FAST
AS CITIES (PERCENT CHANGE IN METROPOLITAN
POPULATION AND FAMILIES, 1990–1997)

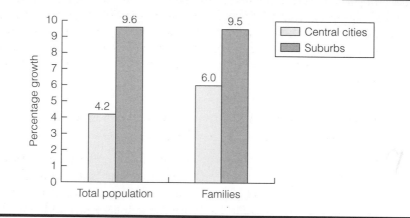

SOURCE: DHUD, *The State of the Cities* 1998, p. 7. The HUD study is based on the U.S. Bureau of the U.S. Census Current Population Study.

extensive decision-making power was placed in the hands of narrow-based, public entities, including the Port Authority of New York and New Jersey and the Lower Manhattan Development Corporation (LMDC). When it came to the rebuilding of the WTC, the formal rules fragmented authority even further, giving the developer, Larry Silverstein, certain prerogatives to make decisions that were at odds with the rebuilding visions of the governor, the mayor, the LMDC, and even the Port Authority. Although most Americans do not realize it, independent bodies such as the Port Authority and the LMDC occupy important positions in local affairs.

Political scientists often point to the potential for undemocratic decision making when the public is unaware of the existence of such independent bodies and does not elect their directors. As seen in the WTC rebuilding controversy, such bodies tend to represent the needs of organized special interests, including the business community, rather than the general public. Mayors and other elected officials find it difficult to lead a city when formal authority is divided among so many autonomous bodies.

The WTC case also points to the importance of structuring rules for citizen participation to increase the democratic nature of the decision making. In Chapter 8, "Citizen Participation and Decentralization," we describe efforts aimed at heightening the influence of citizen and neighborhood groups. Yet, it is not always easy to assess the degree to which formal participatory processes influence decision making. In the WTC rebuilding controversy, sharply critical public comments at public forums did lead the LMDC to dismiss the initial six site-design finalists and begin the search for a more grandiose rebuilding plan. Public sentiment also helped force Larry Silverstein to work with architect Daniel Libeskind on the architectural design for the Freedom Tower. Yet, despite these examples of public influence, many important rebuilding decisions, including the decision to build an underground shopping mall that would maximize the commercial value of the project while diverting pedestrian traffic away from nearby stores, were made in relative secrecy. The general public and neighborhood groups had no real opportunity to challenge the overall commercial thrust of the WTC rebuilding effort.

3. THE IMPORTANCE OF INTERGOVERNMENTAL RELATIONS AND THE RISE OF THE DEPENDENT CITY.

Troubled cities lack the means to solve urban problems on their own. State laws, in particular, limit municipal freedom in important ways. Cities and suburbs are not free to tax however they see fit, nor does a city council have the power to freely borrow money or to enact whatever laws and regulations it wishes. Instead, cities are dependent on the grants of authority allowed them by the states.

State and federal actions exert a great influence on municipal affairs. New York City's financial well-being was weakened when the state legislature in 1998, prodded by Republican Governor George Pataki, ended the city's ability to tax stock transfers. The legislature also took away the city's ability to tax suburban commuters who worked in the city and used the city's facilities. City advocates argued that the loss of the commuter tax cost the city $400 to $500 million per year.[20]

New York State law also mandated that New York City pay for half the state share of the federal Medicaid program for poor people, the largest such requirement in the nation. In 2002, this mandate cost New York City taxpayers a whopping $3.1 billion.[21] No other state in the nation burdened its cities with such extensive Medicaid expenses.

Big cities especially lack the formal power to raise the revenues necessary to solve complex social problems. Interlocal competition for business further serves to constrain a municipality's ability to raise needed revenues. A municipality that raises taxes runs the risk of driving businesses to locate in competing cities and suburbs. As a consequence, cities seek to limit taxes, which, in turn, limits the ability of cities to finance important schooling and social services.[22] More distressed cities are dependent on state and federal assistance to provide an adequate level of basic services.

New York's post-9/11 ability to rebuild was greatly dependent on state and federal support. Even before the 9/11 attacks, the city was facing great budget difficulties. The attacks of 9/11 led to a severe local economic recession and a further loss of local tax revenues, all at a time when the city needed to find new revenues to pay for the rebuilding at Ground Zero and new security and antiterrorism measures.

In the wake of 9/11, the State of New York did not respond with a significant package of new state aid to the city.[23] Instead, the city was largely forced to rely on its own revenues and to constrict services to cope with rebuilding costs.

The federal government promised New York $21 billion in rebuilding assistance, with another $5 billion going to victims' families. The money was a great help. However, it fell far short of compensating the city for the extensive losses that it suffered as a result of the attacks, an economic loss that through 2004 was estimated at $83 billion to $95 billion.[24]

In his proposed 2005 budget, President George W. Bush increased the amount of antiterrorism money for high-risk cities. Such aid was greatly needed. But Bush also proposed broadening the number of cities eligible to receive the $1.4 billion in assistance from 7 to 50. This **spread effect** reduced the money that would be made available to New York and the nation's biggest cities.[25]

While New York and other big cities received new federal homeland security monies, they suffered a loss of federal aid in related policy areas. The Bush administration proposed cuts in assistance for local police, firefighters, and public housing. New York City stood to lose 139 police officers as a result of Bush's efforts to terminate the Community Oriented Policing Services (COPS), a program initially intended as a short-run demonstration program.[26]

During the 1980s, the Reagan administration had slowed the growth of federal aid to states and cities. In certain fiscal years, Reagan was even able to effect a cut in federal aid, expressed in inflation-adjusted constant dollars (see Table 1-2). Yet, as Table 1-2 also shows, neither Reagan nor his Republican successors were able to choke off the stream of federal aid to states and cities. For a while, new congressional budget procedures slowed the rate of growth. Yet, even expressed in constant dollars, federal intergovernmental assistance has continued to rise over the years. Federal and state aid programs, together with their accompanying rules and regulations, remain a prominent influence on the administration of the **intergovernmental city**.

As we shall see in Chapter 2, "The Evolution of Cities and Suburbs," federal and state actions have not always been helpful to cities. Many important federal and state programs have constituted a "hidden" urban policy that has worked, often inadvertently, to exacerbate urban ills.

4. THE CONTINUED EXISTENCE OF URBAN PROBLEMS IN SUNBELT CITIES DESPITE THE GENERAL DISTINCTION THAT CAN BE MADE BETWEEN FROSTBELT AND SUNBELT COMMUNITIES.

Over the last half century, the urban crisis acquired a regional tint. The 2000 Census documented the continuing shift of population from the Northeast and the Midwest to the South, the Southwest, and the West (see Figure 1-2). The transition to a postindustrial economy led to the decline of both jobs and population in the older, "smokestack" cities of the Frostbelt—the Northeast and Midwest. Metropolitan areas centered on declining industries shrank in size and lost population and jobs to other parts of the country. In contrast,

■ TABLE 1-2

**FEDERAL GRANTS-IN-AID TO STATE AND
LOCAL GOVERNMENTS (IN BILLIONS)**

Fiscal Year	Federal Grants (in current $)	Percent Increase or Decrease over Previous Year	Amount in Constant $ (1992 $)	Percent Increase or Decrease over Previous Year
1955	3.2	4.9	17.9	3.5
1960	7.0	8.6	33.4	7.1
1965	10.9	7.3	48.2	5.2
1970	24.1	19.3	86.9	11.8
1975	49.8	14.8	126.6	3.3
1980	91.4	9.6	155.7	−1.1
1981	94.7	3.6	146.5	−5.9
1982	88.1	−6.9	127.5	−13.0
1983	92.4	4.9	127.7	0.2
1984	97.6	5.5	129.5	1.4
1985	105.9	8.5	135.6	4.7
1986	112.3	6.1	139.7	3.0
1987	108.4	−3.5	130.4	−6.7
1988	115.3	6.4	133.9	2.7
1989	121.9	5.7	136.2	1.7
1990	135.3	11.0	144.7	6.2
1991	154.5	14.2	158.6	9.6
1992	178.1	15.2	178.1	12.3
1993	193.6	8.7	188.7	6.0
1994	210.5	8.8	201.3	6.7
1995	225.0	6.8	209.7	4.2
1996e	255.0	8.3	n.a.	n.a.
1997e	275.2	7.9	n.a.	n.a.

e Office of Management and Budget estimate.
n.a. Not Ascertained.
SOURCE: Advisory Commission on Intergovernmental Relations, *Significant Features of Fiscal Federalism
1995, Volume 2: Revenues and Expenditures* (Washington, DC: ACIR, 1997), p. 60, and other ACIR reports.

Houston, San Diego, Dallas, San Antonio, Phoenix, San Jose, and a great
many other cities in the **Sunbelt**—the South (especially the Southwest) and the
West—gained substantial population and economic activity.

Data from the 2000 Census confirms the continuing growth of Sunbelt communities. Twenty-three of the 25 counties experiencing the largest population

■ FIGURE 1–2

PERCENT POPULATION CHANGE BY STATE: 1990 TO 2000

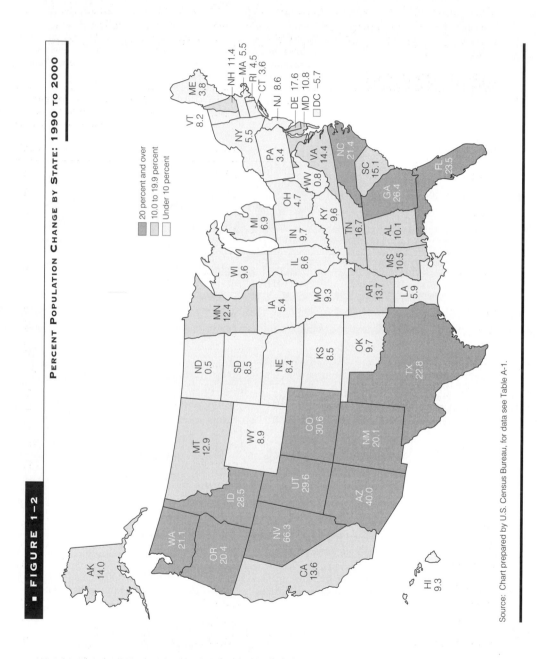

20 percent and over
10.0 to 19.9 percent
Under 10 percent

ME 3.8
NH 11.4
MA 5.5
RI 4.5
CT 3.6
NJ 8.6
DE 17.6
MD 10.8
DC -5.7

VT 8.2
NY 5.5
PA 3.4
WV 0.8
VA 14.4
NC 21.4
SC 15.1
GA 26.4
FL 23.5

OH 4.7
KY 9.6
TN 16.7
AL 10.1
MS 10.5
LA 5.9

MI 6.9
IN 9.7
IL 8.6
MO 9.3
AR 13.7

WI 9.6
IA 5.4
MN 12.4

ND 0.5
SD 8.5
NE 8.4
KS 8.5
OK 9.7
TX 22.8

MT 12.9
WY 8.9
CO 30.6
NM 20.1

ID 28.5
UT 29.6
AZ 40.0

WA 21.1
OR 20.4
NV 66.3
CA 13.6

AK 14.0

HI 9.3

Source: Chart prepared by U.S. Census Bureau, for data see Table A-1.

growth were in the South and the Southwest; a 24th (King County or greater Seattle) was in the Pacific Northwest. Only one of the top 25 growing communities, Joliet, Illinois, outside Chicago, was in the Frostbelt (see Table 1-3). Instead, Frostbelt counties suffered the most severe population decline during the 1990s. Only three of the top 25 "losers" in terms of population were

■ TABLE 1-3

TOP 25 COUNTIES IN THE U.S. RANKED BY LARGEST
POPULATION GROWTH, 1990–2000

County, State	Number	Rank
Maricopa, AZ	950,048	1
Los Angeles, CA	656,286	2
Clark, NV	634,397	3
Harris, TX	582,477	4
Orange, CA	435,621	5
Riverside, CA	374,974	6
Broward, FL	367,487	7
Dallas, TX	366,208	8
Dade, FL	316,168	9
San Diego, CA	315,817	10
San Bernardino, CA	291,054	11
Queens, NY	277,781	12
Tarrant, TX	276,116	13
Cook, IL	271,697	14
Palm Beach, FL	267,681	15
Travis, TX	235,873	16
Gwinnett, GA	235,538	17
King, WA	229,729	18
Collin, TX	227,639	19
Orange, FL	218,853	20
Bexar, TX	207,537	21
Wake, NC	201,535	22
Hidalgo, TX	185,918	23
Santa Clara, CA	185,008	24
Mecklenburg, NC	184,243	25

SOURCE: U.S. Census Bureau, *County and City Data Book: 2000*, Table B-1, prepared by the Geospatial and Statistical Data Center University of Virginia Library, Charlottesville VA. Available at: http://fisher.lib.virginia.edu/collections/stats/ccdb/documents2000/rankings2000/cc00_rnk_HN06.html

clearly situated in the Sunbelt: Norfolk (Virginia), and Orleans and Vernon (Louisiana) (see Table 1-4).

A look at recent population changes in the nation's largest cities confirms the general regional pattern of Sunbelt growth and Frostbelt decline. Frostbelt cities—Chicago, Philadelphia, and Detroit—lost population. In contrast, Sunbelt cities—Phoenix, San Diego, San Antonio, Los Angeles, Houston, and

■ TABLE 1-4

TOP 25 COUNTIES IN THE U.S. RANKED BY LARGEST POPULATION DECLINE, 1990–2000

County, State	Number	Rank
Baltimore IC, MD	−84,860	1
Philadelphia, PA	−68,027	2
Allegheny, PA	−54,783	3
Wayne, MI	−50,525	4
St. Louis IC, MO	−48,496	5
Washington, DC	−34,841	6
Norfolk IC, VA	−26,847	7
Hamilton, OH	−20,925	8
Milwaukee, WI	−19,048	9
Erie, NY	−18,319	10
Cuyahoga, OH	−18,162	11
Oneida, NY	−15,367	12
Montgomery, OH	−14,747	13
Aroostook, ME	−12,998	14
Orleans, LA	−12,264	15
Broome, NY	−11,624	16
Onondaga, NY	−10,637	17
Cambria, PA	−10,464	18
Vernon, LA	−9,430	19
Luzerne, PA	−8,899	20
McDowell, WV	−7,904	21
Kanawha, WV	−7,546	22
Lucas, OH	−7,307	23
Mahoning, OH	−7,251	24
St. Clair, IL	−6,770	25

Available at http://fisher.lib.virginia.edu/collections/stats/ccdb/documents2000/rankings2000/cc00_rnk_HN08.html

■ TABLE 1-5

POPULATION CHANGE, 10 LARGEST U.S. CITIES,
APRIL 1, 2000 TO JULY 1, 2002

Rank	Place	July 1, 2002	April 1, 2000	Numerical Change	Percentage Change
1	New York, N.Y.	8,084,316	8,008,278	76,038	0.9
2	Los Angeles, Calif.	3,798,981	3,694,742	104,239	2.8
3	Chicago, Ill.	2,886,251	2,896,047	−9,796	−0.3
4	Houston, Texas	2,009,834	1,953,633	56,201	2.9
5	Philadelphia, Pa.	1,492,231	1,517,550	−25,319	−1.7
6	Phoenix, Ariz.	1,371,960	1,321,190	50,770	3.8
7	San Diego, Calif.	1,259,532	1,223,416	36,116	3.0
8	Dallas, Texas	1,211,467	1,188,589	22,878	1.9
9	San Antonio, Texas	1,194,222	1,151,268	42,954	3.7
10	Detroit, Mich.	925,051	951,270	−26,219	−2.8

SOURCE: U.S. Census Bureau, "Large Suburban Cities in West Are Fastest-Growing, Census Bureau Reports," press release, July 10, 2003.
www.census.gov/Press-Release/www/2003/cb03-106.html

Dallas—exhibited the greatest population growth (see Table 1-5). The nation's most quickly growing communities were in the Southwest. In just two years, from 2000 to 2002, Gilbert, Arizona, a suburb south of Phoenix, saw a population increase of 23 percent. North Las Vegas and Henderson, Nevada, each gained over 17 percent; Chandler and Peoria, Arizona, gained 14 and 13 percent respectively; and Irvine, Rancho Cucamonga, and Chula Vista, California each experienced a population growth of 12 percent or more—all in just two years.[27]

The term **Sunbelt** denotes those areas of the American South, Southwest, and West that have experienced a general growth of population and economic activity during the past few decades. Yet there is no clear consensus as to the precise boundaries of this region.[28] There is a substantial consensus that the Sunbelt includes, at the very least, the states south of a line from North Carolina running west through Oklahoma and southern California.

Still, different authors have used different definitions when talking about the Sunbelt (see Figure 1-3). A number include Virginia within the region. Others look at the growth of population and economic activity as the defining characteristics of the region and even include Colorado, northern California, and the Pacific Northwest—forming a "Sunbelt" that in some places is rather cool, cloudy, rainy, and even snowy.[29]

THREE VIEWS OF THE SUNBELT

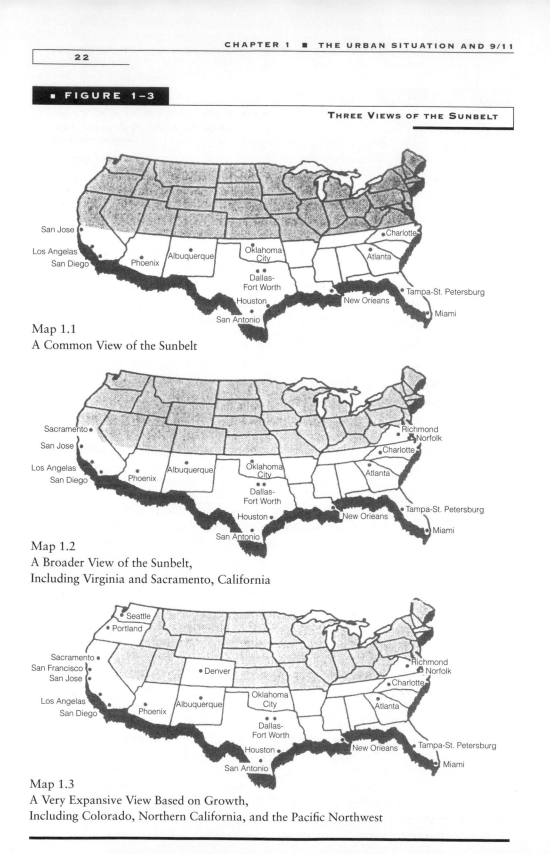

Map 1.1
A Common View of the Sunbelt

Map 1.2
A Broader View of the Sunbelt,
Including Virginia and Sacramento, California

Map 1.3
A Very Expansive View Based on Growth,
Including Colorado, Northern California, and the Pacific Northwest

Ann Markusen uses the term **gunbelt** to underscore the importance of defense-related expenditures to Sunbelt communities, especially in California, Florida, and the Southwest. The gunbelt, however, clearly extends beyond the more traditional borders of the Sunbelt to include Seattle, Colorado Springs, Washington, DC, high-tech suburbs of Boston, and other centers of defense-related prosperity.[30]

Yet, there is a great analytical danger in dividing the United States into two such large and loosely defined regions as Frostbelt and Sunbelt. Such a rough regional division may hide and distort as much as it reveals.

Frostbelt cities are not all suffering unmitigated decline. Detroit, Bridgeport (Connecticut), and Newark (New Jersey) are among the Frostbelt cities that continue to suffer severe economic structural problems and fiscal distress. Yet, others—notably Baltimore, Boston, Cleveland, New York, and Pittsburgh—have exhibited signs of resurgence and renaissance, despite the continued existence of severe urban problems. In the 1990s, numerous cities in the Northeast and Midwest enjoyed a substantial economic recovery, with new downtown construction and, in some cases, new population growth.

The extent of the "renaissance" of these northern cities, however, should not be overstated. The rebound of downtowns did not always lead to improved economic conditions for city residents; in some cases, neighborhood conditions became even worse.[31] Philadelphia, for example, faced an escalating crime rate, an austerity budget, the curtailment of many municipal services, and the imposition of new taxes—all despite impressive new construction in the city's central business district. New York, too, enjoyed a dynamic downtown boom that in many ways had only a marginal impact on life in the city's poorer outer-borough neighborhoods.

Nor is there uniform growth and prosperity throughout the Sunbelt. Parts of the South—notably Alabama, Louisiana, Mississippi, and Arkansas—did not experience the rapid economic and population growth enjoyed by other parts of the Sunbelt. In a number of Old South states, growth and prosperity were largely confined to resort and retirement communities. In important ways, New Orleans more closely resembles a troubled city of the Frostbelt than it does the more dynamically growing cities of the American Southwest. New Orleans and Baton Rouge (Louisiana), Galveston (Texas), and Biloxi and Gulfport (Mississippi) are among the southern cities that have turned to casino gambling in an effort to find new sources of revenue for local services.

The dynamic population growth of the Sunbelt also helps to mask the continuing poverty in the region. Half of the 20 poorest cities in the nation are found in the Sunbelt, with Miami exceeding Cleveland and Newark in terms of local poverty (see Table 1-6).

The 1992 Los Angeles riots underscore the continued severity of urban problems despite Sunbelt growth. Los Angeles enjoyed a strategic Sunbelt location that allowed the city to take advantage of a growing trade with Asia. With the arrival of investment capital from overseas, Los Angeles became a dynamic center of new construction. Compared to declining economies of Rustbelt communities, Los Angeles seemed quite fortunate; the city gained both jobs and population.

■ TABLE 1–6

ESTIMATES OF THE PERCENT OF PEOPLE BELOW POVERTY LEVEL, BY CITY, 2002

Rank	Place	Percent	Lower Bound	Upper Bound
1	Miami city, FL	31.2	24.6	37.8
2	Newark city, NJ	30.6	24.8	36.4
3	Cleveland city, OH	26.3	21.7	30.9
4	El Paso city, TX	26.1	22.1	30.1
5	Atlanta city, GA	25.9	21.3	30.5
6	St. Louis city, MO	24.0	19.7	28.3
7	Detroit city, MI	23.3	20.2	26.4
8	Cincinnati city, OH	23.2	18.9	27.5
9	Minneapolis city, MN	22.9	19.3	26.5
10	Long Beach city, CA	22.6	17.3	27.9
11	Memphis city, TN	22.5	19.0	26.0
12	Milwaukee city, WI	22.0	19.0	25.0
13	New Orleans city, LA	21.7	17.9	25.5
14	Corpus Christi city, TX	21.7	17.4	26.0
15	Philadelphia city, PA	21.2	19.1	23.3
16	Dallas city, TX	20.9	18.4	23.4
17	Buffalo city, NY	20.8	15.7	25.9
18	Baltimore city, MD	20.6	17.6	23.6
19	Fresno city, CA	20.2	15.7	24.7
20	Stockton city, CA	20.1	13.8	26.4

SOURCE: U.S. Census Bureau, *American Community Survey,* revised September 2003.
www.census.gov/acs/www/Products/Ranking/2002/R01T160.htm

However, globalization proved to be a mixed blessing for L.A. Many of the new jobs that were created in Los Angeles paid low wages and benefits in order to compete with overseas producers.[32] The influx of new populations into the region also increased intergroup tensions, as new immigrants competed with African Americans in the low-wage job sector.[33]

Economic restructuring has also hurt Sunbelt urban economies. The 1980s decline in oil prices and collapse of the savings and loan industry brought new economic problems to Houston and other once-dynamic "oil patch" cities in the Southwest. In southern California, jobs had increased by 27 percent during the 1980s, but the end of the Cold War soon brought with it spending reductions and layoffs in the region's defense-related and aerospace industries. The dot-com explosion of the 1990s helped fuel the economic boom of San Francisco and other Bay Area and Pacific Northwest cities, sending property prices soaring. Later in the decade, however, the "bust" or shakeout of web-based creative firms hurt the economics of these very same cities.

Sunbelt growth also brought with it rising land prices, higher office rents, and increased traffic congestion. As a result, cities in California and other Sunbelt states lost some of the competitive edge they enjoyed in previous decades.[34]

In studying cities and suburbs, we must take special care to observe the ways in which patterns in Sunbelt communities are similar to, and diverge from, patterns in their Frostbelt counterparts.

5. THE RELUCTANCE OF AMERICANS TO CONFRONT THE ISSUE OF RACE.

Americans are ambivalent on matters of race. While the 2000 Census revealed some encouraging news regarding the decline of residential racial segregation,[35] many blacks, Hispanics, and Asians still face discrimination in the housing market and do not enjoy the same housing opportunities available to whites. In some metropolitan areas, minorities must earn $60,000 to live in neighborhoods that are roughly equivalent to what white families earning half that amount can afford.[36]

While recent decades have shown some improvement in terms of residential integration, there has been little serious effort to alleviate the segregation of public schools. Americans overwhelmingly disapprove of *de jure* **segregation**; that is, segregation mandated by law, as existed in the South through the early 1960s. In 1954, the Supreme Court in **Brown v. Board of Education** decision began the prolonged process of bringing an end to the *de jure* segregation of public schools.

Yet, many big cities today have schools with no, or only a handful of, white students. The United States shows no great willingness to eliminate *de facto* **segregation**, the continuing residential and school segregation that exists "in fact" but is not mandated by law.

The Supreme Court's ruling in **Millikin v. Bradley** (1974) effectively brought an end to many big-city school desegregation efforts. In *Millikin,* the Court ruled that Detroit's suburbs did not have to participate in a metropolitan busing plan even if their participation represented the only effective way to desegregate central-city schools. According to the Court, absent a finding that a suburb had purposely taken an action that segregated its schools, it was not required to participate in any effort to mitigate the concentration of racial minorities in central-city schools.

In Boston, 30 years of court-ordered school desegregation efforts produced little. The city's neighborhoods remain largely separated by race, and the city's minority children are largely excluded from suburban neighborhoods and the more advantaged suburban schools.[37] By the end of the 1990s, the Court allowed local school districts new leeway to retreat from earlier desegregation plans.

The existence of school segregation a half century after *Brown* points to the continuing racial divide in the American metropolis. Today, however, the racial cleavage is no longer simply "black" versus "white." Instead, the arrival of new immigrant groups has added to the complexity of race relations. In post-1992 riot Los Angeles, African Americans, Hispanics, Asians, and whites all fought over jobs at the central-city rebuilding sites. In addition, most of the more than 150 Korean-owned liquor stores burned during the city's 1992 disturbances never reopened. African-American activists objected that the liquor stores were a blight on their community, and the Los Angeles city council restricted the operation of liquor stores in the riot areas. Korean Americans complained that they were being scapegoated unfairly, and were denied their fair share of reconstruction assistance.[38]

The 1992 riots were not the first, nor the last, episodes of violent explosion to rock urban America. The **President's National Advisory Commission on Civil Disorders** (more popularly known as the **Kerner Commission,** after Illinois Governor Otto Kerner, the chairman of the group) sought to discover the root causes of the chain of riots that swept across U.S. cities during the 1960s. The Kerner Commission concluded that the fundamental cause of the violence lay in the fact that the United States had become "two societies, one black, one white—separate and unequal."[39] A powder keg of inner-city poverty, discrimination, and racial resentment had exploded. Whites tended to speak of "riots" and "civil disturbances"; many African Americans referred to the same events quite differently as an **urban uprising** or an **urban rebellion,** terms denoting a political response to continuing segregation and inequality. The Commission warned of the dire consequences that would follow if the United States failed to bridge the racial gulf.

Over the years, though, American society has taken few serious steps to avoid the Kerner Commission's **"two societies" prophecy.** Even though racial minorities have succeeded in gaining increased entrance into suburbia, the process of inner-city ghettoization proceeds unabated. The United States has not pursued the goals of increased racial integration and de-ghettoization; instead, it has opted for a strategy of "mild ghetto enrichment," dispensing governmental aid while maintaining the continued racial separation and inequalities of the metropolis:

> The white-dominated U.S. society has clearly chosen to create and maintain two racially separate and unequal societies, as the Kerner Commission feared it might. In spite of all the pious statements to the contrary, the leaders and citizens of nearly all parts of U.S. society have no intention whatever of changing that deliberate policy.[40]

During 1992 in Los Angeles, a variety of urban groups rebelled, rioted, and looted for different reasons. (See "Los Angeles' 'Rainbow Riots,'" on p. 27.) Urban ills have become so complex that no single interpretation can capture the complexity of the 1992 violence.

After the Rodney King trial verdict was announced, there was no single "riot" that occurred in Los Angeles in 1992. Rather, in Los Angeles in 1992, there were multiple riots; different outbursts with somewhat different causes that occurred more or less simultaneously.*

Some rioters sought material gain by pilfering goods from local stores. Other young rioters found fun in the exuberance and lawlessness in the streets. Still other participants saw the explosion as an expression of black rage against white oppression.

The precipitating factor that started the 1992 Los Angeles riots was the failure of the all-white jury to convict the four officers for the Rodney King beating. The destruction or "trashing" of governmental buildings in downtown Los Angeles was probably the most organized and overtly political action in a sea of more spasmodic outbreaks of violence and theft.

Not all of the events that occurred during the riots were organized. Nor could all of the violence be justified as political, as a voice of protest against discrimination, police brutality, and political repression. The initial outbreak in South Central L.A. began with the robbery of a liquor store. Local gang members also brutally beat white truck driver Reginald Denny, a malicious act that cannot be justified as a political protest.

Much of the property violence was directed against Koreans, other Asian Americans, and Hispanics, a new generation of inner-city, small-store proprietors. Korean-owned stores were a particular focus of the destruction and the arson, suffering an estimated 45 percent of the total riot property damage. First-generation Korean families had sought opportunity by running small shops in urban areas that larger chain stores had abandoned.** Here, again, much of the violence can be seen as political. The acts of arson were directed against businesses that residents saw as having a record of exploitive practices; oftentimes, businesses that maintained a good relationship with local residents were spared.[†] Yet, some African-American business owners, too, suffered losses in the riots; not all the violence was targeted or political.

Significantly, over half of those arrested during the disturbance were Latino, not African American.[‡] Whatever the reasons for the looting in the city's Latino neighborhoods, it certainly cannot be viewed as an expression of protest against the Rodney King trial verdict. The 1992 Los Angeles **rainbow riots** were clearly multiracial in character.

* Harlan Hahn, "Los Angeles and the Future: Uprisings, Identity, and New Institutions," in *The Los Angeles Riots: Lessons for the Urban Future*, ed. Mark Baldassare (Boulder, CO: Westview, 1994), p. 81.

** Pyong Gap Min, *Caught in the Middle: Korean Communities in New York and Los Angeles* (Berkeley, CA: University of California Press, 1996), pp. 1–4 and 90; Nancy Abelmann and John Lie, *Blue Dreams: Korean Americans and the Los Angeles Riots* (Cambridge, MA: Harvard University Press, 1995), especially pp. 1, 90, and 119–148.

[†] See Regina Freer, "Black-Korean Conflict," in *The Los Angeles Riots*, pp. 175–203.

[‡] Joan Petersilia and Allan Abrahamse, "A Profile of Those Arrested," in *The Los Angeles Riots*, pp. 135–147; Raphael J. Sonenshein, *Politics in Black and White: Race and Power in Los Angeles* (Princeton, NJ: Princeton University Press, 1993), pp. 210–226.

Today, the Kerner Commission's "two societies" warning appears deficient, as it does not capture the complexity of racial tensions resulting from urban America's new diversity. In Los Angeles, new population groups from Asia, Mexico, and Central America—Salvadorians, Caribbean blacks, Chinese, Japanese, Iranians, Indians, Filipinos, Vietnamese, Koreans, and others—entered into a struggle with older Latino and African-American groups over the shrinking inner-city economic pie.[41]

Since 1992, U.S. cities have been relatively calm. There have been race-related outbursts in Miami, Cincinnati, and a few other cities since 1992, but there have been no disorders of the magnitude of the riots of the 1960s and 1992.

Given the severity of urban inequalities, it might be a bit too optimistic to view the 1992 Los Angeles riots as an event from the distant past. Riots and rebellions are a periodic part of the American urban scene. As Robert Waste has observed, even during periods of relative calm, America's cities are less at peace than they are "between riots."[42]

6. THE "GENDERED CITY" AND THE IMPORTANCE OF GENDERED INTERPRETATIONS OF URBAN POLITICS.

Much new work in recent years has been done in the fields of women's and gender studies as applied to cities. Cities and suburbs are settings that create—and limit—the opportunities available to women. Viewing cities through the lens of gender helps to enhance our understanding of urban phenomena, yielding alternative perspectives on urban problems and what should be done.[43]

A gendered perspective on urban problems, for instance, highlights the **feminization of poverty**: being female or living in a female-headed family increases a person's chances of winding up in poverty. Women who work often occupy low-wage manufacturing or service positions that do not pay enough to provide for a family. In addition, families with only one breadwinner—normally female-headed families—live in a very fragile economic situation; they are likely to be reduced to poverty in the event of a job layoff or major health problem. Programs that fail to address the needs of poor women and their children will fail to solve the crises of urban poverty and the inner city.

The devastation of 9/11 was so great that reaction cut across gender lines. Yet, a gendered perspective helps to elucidate the debate over reconstruction. The "male" perspective emphasized plans for rebuilding monumental skyscrapers, reestablishing the nation's symbols of strength, and restoring a vigorous Wall Street financial district and a powerful national economy. An alternative "female" perspective, however, gave greater emphasis to reshaping Lower Manhattan as a livable community with quality residences, parks, playgrounds, walkways, and a place for the arts—a vision distinctly different from rebuilding a zone dedicated so exclusively to the modern cathedrals of global business.

While different rebuilding orientations can be labeled male and female, of course, men and women do not line up neatly on the opposing sides of this or any other urban issues. Neither men nor women are united in their opinions as to what should be the future of Lower Manhattan.

A gendered perspective also helps to give new insight as to how globalization is related to inner-city problems in places such as southern California. Globalization brought an influx of poorly paid, labor intensive manufacturing jobs to Los Angeles. Women who had recently arrived from Latin America and Asia dominated job positions at the bottom rungs of the Los Angeles labor market in such fields as clothing, textiles, and high-tech assembly. The surge of immigration and the feminization of the labor force produced a strong downward pressure on wages, especially in industries that faced competition from Third-World producers.[44]

A gender-informed response to the Los Angeles riots would not rely so heavily on RLA-style corporate deal making for inner-city economic development. An approach focused on the needs of poor women would also emphasize raising the minimum wage, protecting immigrant workers from exploitation at the hands of employers, funding new educational and job training opportunities, increasing affordable housing for female-headed families, and providing adequate child care, health services, and income supports for low-wage working women.

In New York, a gender-sensitive view of urban problems led to the distribution of post-9/11 rebuilding assistance to the garment factories of nearby Chinatown. These factories, reliant on the labor of immigrant women, were closed for weeks and months as a result of disruptions caused by the 9/11 attacks. A gendered perspective recognized the needs of Lower Manhattan's residential communities; it did not seek simply the construction of new office towers.

METAPHORS FOR URBAN AMERICA

It is not easy to grasp the full dimensions of the contemporary urban condition. As a result, urbanists use metaphors to highlight some of the most significant urban trends and problems.

Robert Waste points to America's **shooting-gallery cities**, where inner-city residents live in "kill zones" and are subject to absurdly high probabilities of violent harm. High-rise public housing and distressed urban neighborhoods such as Watts and South Central in Los Angeles can also be viewed as **urban reservations**, areas in which the poor and unwanted are shunted aside and separated from the rest of American society.[45]

Los Angeles and New York are also typical of America's **urban citadels** or **fortified cities**, where the fear of crime has led the residents of high-rise luxury towers to live behind locked doors and security-guarded entrances; suburbanites seek the safety of gated communities and "defensible enclaves."[46] In response to the terrorist threat, both public authorities and private property owners have increased surveillance, security, and other aspects of the fortified city.

In the worst-case scenario, America's big cities can be seen as slipping toward a **Blade Runner future**. In the science fiction movie *Blade Runner,* daily life entails an ever-present and increasingly violent battle between the technologically competent, affluent "haves" and the low-skilled, urban poor.[47]

Even during the 1990s, a time of soaring national economic prosperity, many cities faced "the triple threat of concentrated poverty, shrinking populations, and middle-class flight that began two decades ago."[48] Good-paying manufacturing jobs, once the backbone of central-city economies, had largely disappeared, only to be replaced by unstable, low-paying service work. The notion of **dual cities** refers to the increasing gulf between two quite different urban Americas—the technological competent part of the city that is growing and prospering while disadvantaged residents and more technologically superfluous and obsolescent neighborhoods are left behind.

A number of cities have adapted to the loss of manufacturing jobs by carving out new roles as tourism, sports, and convention centers. The rise of **tourist cities** or **entertainment cities** denotes the post-industrial transformation and adaptation of big-city economies.[49] As we discuss in Chapter 4, "Who Has the Power? Decision Making and Urban Regimes," cities that devote increased levels of services for visitors risk neglecting the needs of the city's disadvantaged residents and poorer neighborhoods.

The phrase **"chocolate city, vanilla suburbs"** refers to the continuing racial imbalance of most American metropolises.[50] Yet this simple characterization misses the new diversity of America's cities and suburbs as new immigrant populations have added to the multiethnic mosaic of urban America. Even America's black population is increasingly diverse with new arrivals from the Caribbean (from such places as Jamaica, Haiti, and the Dominican Republic) and West Africa and Sub-Saharan Africa (including Nigeria and Senegal). These black groups have somewhat distinct social and cultural norms and remain somewhat segregated from one another.[51] The chocolate-city–vanilla-suburbs dichotomy also fails to capture the recent rise in the numbers of racial minorities in suburbia, an uneven process that we describe in more detail in Chapter 11, "Suburban Politics and Metropolitan America." America's suburbs are not quite as vanilla as they once were.

The phrase **edge cities** points to the new concentrations of offices, technology parks, college campuses, and shopping galleries in the suburbs.[52] Such nodes or clusters of dynamic growth often yield the impression that suburbs have gained their independence from the central city, hiding the deeper ties and dependencies among communities in a metropolitan area. As we discuss in Chapter 11, the new focus on suburban edge cities also tends to obscure the continuing spread of low-rise suburban sprawl with its harmful effects on urban ecosystems.

The modern metropolis can no longer be understood simply in terms of suburban development, central-city decline, and black-white racial tensions. America's postindustrial, **postmodern cities** are marked by ever more complex and chaotic social, economic, racial, and political polarizations.[53]

9/11 AND THE URBAN CONDITION

The attacks of 9/11 ushered in a new age of terrorism in which cities across the United States have had to pick up the substantial costs of additional security responsibilities. In a national survey, 275 city officials reported increases in security-related spending. Nearly all cities told of the need to protect such vulnerable facilities as nearby water supplies, government buildings, stadiums, information technology infrastructure, power plants, ports, and airports. Half the cities reported significant increases in public spending due to terrorism.[54]

The new security agenda greatly strained the budgets of municipalities already operating under conditions of severe fiscal distress. In the two months following the 9/11 attacks, Atlanta spent $15 million on overtime pay. In the year following 9/11, Seattle paid an extra $6 million in overtime to police officers and firefighters for training, the protection of key facilities, and emergency coordination with surrounding communities. Philadelphia estimated that it would pay an additional $60 million for new security measures, including related capital improvements.[55]

The costs to New York, of course, were greater still. In fiscal 2002, New York spent over $365 million on overtime, with the Police Department accounting for 70 percent of the WTC-related figure. The city estimated that it would cost nearly $22 billion to just replace the buildings and infrastructure lost in the attacks.[56]

Cities attempted to cope with these new burdens at a time when they were facing a constriction of state aid. The states faced budget problems of their own. The states, too, had to undertake new and costly security responsibilities. But state officials also faced the reluctance of voters to raise taxes. Caught in their own fiscal bind, state after state reduced aid to cities in more traditional program areas.

Big-city economies were also hurt as a result of the new vulnerabilities revealed by 9/11. New York lost 131,000 jobs, including 25,000 jobs that moved outside the city during the 2001 recession year.[57] Much of this loss came as a result of 9/11.

In the most vulnerable cities, corporations began to consider the convenience of suburban locations and the advantages inherent in dispersing their headquarters personnel and key functions among various cities and suburbs. After the devastation suffered on 9/11, the brokerage firm of Goldman Sachs decided to move its entire equity trading department from New York to Jersey City, reversing the company's earlier decision to cluster its employees in Manhattan. Morgan Stanley, the largest securities company in Manhattan, moved a number of its operations to suburban Westchester. New York City officials responded by offering tax breaks and other incentives in an effort to keep businesses downtown.[58]

The fear of terrorism further helped to spur the decentralization of secondary or "back-office" functions to more secure and lower cost small-city, suburban, and rural sites. The implosion of the twin towers raised new concerns about the safety of working in skyscrapers. Escalating insurance premiums charged on downtown high-rise structures that could be possible targets of a terrorist attack also served to drive office development to suburban office parks.

The climate of terrorism also worked to alter the character and mode of operations of central-city businesses. Office buildings, especially in big cities, took on aspects of urban fortresses, with building access strictly controlled through limited, security-guarded entrances. While a great many corporations have simply adapted to the new post-terrorist environment, the new inconveniences of doing business in the fortress city has led some firms to seek less onerous suburban sites.

The impact of the 9/11 attacks was felt by cities across the United States. Federal anti-terrorism laws added to the time of business travel, impeding the speedy movement of both freight and personnel. Such laws have the potential for lessening the competitive position of U.S. cities in the global economy. The **USA Patriot Act of 2001** strengthened border screening in an effort to weed out terrorists; but such intensive screening also had the effect of making non-U.S. nationals feel less than welcome. Global gateway cities were expected to be particularly hard hit as a result of the new obstacles to commerce. Jobs losses as a result of 9/11 were expected to exceed 73,000 in metropolitan Los Angeles, 63,000 in the Chicago area, and 50,000 in the Seattle region. The disruption of maritime movements also resulted in local job losses in port cities such as Long Beach, California.[59]

The new terrorism environment has hurt cities economically; yet, predictions that 9/11 marked the "end of cities" are clearly overstated. Globalization, immigration, technology, and the need for efficient business locations will continue to influence the development of cities and suburbs. Where demographic and economic conditions dictate, cities will continue to grow despite the ongoing threat of terrorism.[60]

New York exhibited an amazing resilience in the wake of the terrorist destruction. Tenants displaced by the devastation of 9/11 did not so much leave New York as move to other parts of the city. Over two-thirds of the tenants of the World Trade Center relocated to sites elsewhere in Manhattan. Other former WTC tenants found sites in the city's outer boroughs, not just the suburbs.[61]

As we discuss in Chapter 2, the loss of population and jobs to the suburban rim has been a fact of life for cities since at least as far back as the end of World War II. In more recent years, changes in telecommunications and transportation, the transition to post-industrialism, and the growth of a global economy have served to further weaken the economic position of many cities and older suburbs. Even before 9/11, cities and suburbs were already facing difficult financial and social conditions and severe economic distress. The new post-9/11 terrorism environment has only compounded an already difficult urban situation, adding new pressures toward suburbanization and draining revenues from municipal coffers.

The future is not easily predicted. In case of a future terrorist attack, fears will likely reach new heights, accelerating the flight of businesses to the suburbs and diverting still more monies to security-related activities.

CONCLUSIONS

The 2000 Census revealed that after decade of decline, cities in the Midwest—and in the South—during the 1990s had gained renewed vitality. But the 1990s economic boom did not solve the urban crisis. Statistical indicators pointed to continuing conditions of urban distress, distress that would be compounded as urban resources would soon be diverted to security-related spending after 9/11.

In 2002, the poverty rate in central cities (16.7%) was still nearly twice that of the suburbs (8.9 percent).[62] One of every six central-city families lived in poverty. Miami (31.2 percent), Newark (30.6 percent), Cleveland (26.3 percent), El Paso (26.1 percent), Atlanta (25.9 percent), St. Louis (24.0 percent), Detroit (23.3 percent), Cincinnati (23.2 percent), Minneapolis (22.9 percent), and Long Beach (22.6 percent) were among the large numbers of American cities that reported debilitating rates of poverty despite a decade of national economic growth.[63] Slightly earlier figures report overwhelming poverty rates in "disaster" cities: Benton Harbor, Michigan (64.3 percent); Camden, New Jersey (44.2 percent); and East St. Louis, Illinois (44.3 percent).[64]

Yet suburbs, too, have begun to feel the new impact of poverty. As the 2000 Census revealed, poverty rates in suburbia actually edged up during a decade in which central-city poverty rates fell slightly.[65]

The boom of the 1990s was followed by an economic downturn that hurt cities and regions across the nation. In the recession year of 2001, the Detroit metropolitan area lost 55,000 jobs; Cleveland 19,000; Chicago 16,000; St. Louis 12,000; and Greensboro 13,000. Even high-tech metropolitan areas were affected: Seattle lost 15,000 jobs; San Jose 13,000; and San Francisco 11,000. The impact of 9/11 served to prolong the recession, with New York, Chicago, Atlanta, San Jose, Boston, and Seattle metropolitan areas each losing more than 40,000 jobs in 2002.[66]

According to a number of important indicators, the economic gap between central cities and suburbs widened during the 1990s as middle-class families continued to desert the city for the suburbs. Unemployment remained a greater problem in central cities than in the suburbs, differences that continued through the post-9/11 economic recession (see Table 1-7). Central cities were not generally the winners in the nation's transition to a service economy; the bulk of high-skill job creation was found in the suburbs. Job growth rates in central cities lagged behind those of the suburbs. Central cities continued to lose private-sector employment market share to the suburbs.[67]

Cities dependent on declining manufacturing industries continued to be hard hit by the process of economic transformation. Even in growing Sunbelt cities and Frostbelt "renaissance" cities, the benefits of economic growth were spread unevenly and did not filter down to poorer residents and more disadvantaged neighborhoods. Drug problems, gang violence, globalization, and the arrival of a new immigration all acted to compound the urban crisis.

Urban problems spread to the suburbs, so suburbia no longer offered a refuge. Many inner-ring suburbs exhibited deterioration and decline. Rapidly

■ **TABLE 1-7**

JOBLESSNESS REMAINS HIGHER IN CENTRAL CITIES THAN IN SUBURBS (UNEMPLOYMENT RATE BY PLACE OF RESIDENCE FOR 20 LARGEST METROPOLITAN AREAS), NOVEMBER 2003

Total Employed by Place of Residence

City	MSA/PMSA			City			Suburbs*		
	Dec 2000	Dec 2004	Change	Dec 2000	Dec 2004	Change	Dec 2000	Dec 2004	Change
New York	4,170,581	4,177,982	0.2%	3,531,716	3,507,435	−0.7%	612,524	643,543	5.1%
Los Angeles	4,522,490	4,597,457	1.7%	1,797,131	1,826,921	1.7%	2,396,620	2,436,348	1.7%
Chicago	4,154,897	4,038,388	−2.8%	1,285,496	1,220,990	−5.0%	2,629,757	2,577,576	−2.0%
Houston	2,124,915	2,240,481	5.4%	1,001,440	1,047,086	4.6%	1,067,314	1,133,419	6.2%
Philadelphia	2,487,023	2,544,268	2.3%	633,355	633,487	0.0%	1,825,392	1,882,140	3.1%
Phoenix	1,643,018	1,807,816	10.0%	753,289	828,371	10.0%	442,070	487,166	10.2%
San Diego	1,371,879	1,472,774	7.4%	628,691	674,928	7.4%	672,337	721,784	7.4%
Dallas	1,945,613	1,937,091	−0.4%	665,368	647,968	−2.6%	1,106,941	1,117,008	0.9%
San Antonio	759,463	808,007	6.4%	516,524	547,624	6.0%	222,867	238,170	6.9%
Detroit	2,273,779	2,069,704	−9.0%	370,408	333,210	−10.0%	1,810,374	1,652,094	−8.7%
San Jose	1,006,484	815,982	−18.9%	508,735	412,444	−18.9%	284,617	230,747	−18.9%
Indianapolis	843,305	850,236	0.8%	412,021	405,824	−1.5%	403,312	417,202	3.4%
San Francisco	974,561	874,342	−10.3%	432,196	385,402	−10.8%	542,365	488,940	−9.9%
Jacksonville	564,583	587,183	4.0%	374,901	385,317	2.8%	189,682	201,866	6.4%
Columbus	850,477	844,844	−0.7%	397,459	390,766	−1.7%	409,018	410,042	0.3%
Austin	743,967	743,473	−0.1%	400,749	390,178	−2.6%	320,891	330,124	2.9%
Baltimore	1,257,999	1,290,365	2.6%	269,101	266,584	−0.9%	968,602	1,002,858	3.5%
Memphis	545,395	549,981	0.8%	304,665	303,295	−0.4%	227,815	233,310	2.4%
Milwaukee	793,491	796,073	0.3%	260,522	256,877	−1.4%	494,487	500,233	1.2%
Boston	1,830,344	1,777,856	−2.9%	302,617	291,596	−3.6%	1,379,293	1,342,829	−2.6%

* Suburbs are the remainder of the Metropolitan Area less all central cities for which BLS publishes data. "City" of ALL MSAs are the 512 of 542 central cities for which BLS publishes data. ALL MSAs exclude Puerto Rico.

SOURCE: Bureau of Labor Statistics. as presented by HUD User.

Available at: http://socds.huduser.org/BLS_LAUS/emplstat.pdf.

growing, working- and middle-class suburbs lacked the resources to build the schools, roads, and other facilities required by the quick pace of urban development. A new generation of Americans concerned about the environment began to question the desirability of sprawled development, with its reliance on road building and its destruction of green space.

By the end of the twentieth century, the public lost faith in "big government" and its problem-solving abilities. Republican presidents did not give the same priority to urban spending as did Democrats. States across the nation faced a taxpayers' revolt and state budgetary constraints that led to a new stringency in urban aid. In California, severe state budget deficits threatened reductions in aid to cities and school districts. Governor Arnold Schwarzenegger won the state's special recall election and promptly repealed, as he promised he would, his predecessor's increase in the state's motor vehicle registration tax, a fee that his predecessor had tripled. Schwarzenegger's move resulted in an additional loss of $3 billion a year in anticipated state revenues, further constricting state spending and the prospects of state assistance to cities.

The new security costs borne by cities in the face of terrorism aggravated the already difficult fiscal position for many cities. New York and other cities complained about the paucity of state assistance that did not match the scope of city problems in the post-9/11 world. Security concerns also resulted in heightened "fortress city" security arrangements. In major cities, security concerns had the potential for accelerating the decentralization of businesses to suburbia, although it remained to be seen just how substantial that exodus would be.

How cities would respond to these challenges would depend on power—public power, private power, and the power of intergovernmental actors. The focus of this book is on power: Who has the power to get things done in local politics? Whose cooperation is essential for effective governance? This book seeks to determine whose demands are being met in the urban arena and whose are ignored.

Major themes—the importance of private power, the impact of globalization, the continuing significance of formal governmental structure and formal rules, the importance of the state and federal governments as players in urban affairs, Sunbelt-Frostbelt regional variations, and the continuing significance of race and gender—will guide our exploration of the politics of American communities. In Chapter 2, we examine the various influences on the evolution of cities, suburbs, and metropolitan areas in the United States.

NOTES

1. The death toll for the World Trade Center is up to date as of January 2004. See "Rebuilding At a Glance," The Gotham Gazette. Available at: www.gothamgazette.com/rebuilding_nyc/at_a_glance.shtml.
2. Megan D. Nordgrén, Eric A. Goldstein, and Mark A. Izeman, The Environmental Impacts of the World Trade Center Attacks: A Preliminary Assessment, a report of

the National Resources Defense Council, February 2002. Available at: www.nrdc.org/cities/wtc/wtc.pdf.

3. In Chapter 7, we discuss in greater detail the inability of campaign finance laws to restrain Bloomberg's record-breaking spending in the 2001 mayoral campaign.

4. This last perspective is offered by a number of the essays in Michael Sorkin and Sharon Zukin, ed., *After the World Trade Center: Rethinking New York City* (New York: Routledge, 2002).

5. Rudolph W. Giuliani, *Leadership* (New York: Miramax Books, 2002).

6. For examples of the literature that is sharply critical of Giuliani, see: Andrew Kirtzman, *Emperor of the City* (HarperCollins, 2001); and Wayne Barrett, *Rudy! An Investigative Biography of Rudy Giuliani,* rev. ed. (Basic Books, 2001).

7. Clarence N. Stone, Regime Politics: Governing Atlanta, 1946–88 (Lawrence: University Press of Kansas, 1989), pp. 222–226.

8. Ibid., pp. 8–9 and 289.

9. The story of David Rockefeller's actions in bringing about the birth of the World Trade Center is told by Eric Darton, *Divided We Stand: A Biography of New York City's World Trade Center* (Basic Books, 2001); James Glanz and Eric Lipton, City in the Sky: The Rise and Fall of the World Trade Center (Times Books, 2003).

10. Jameson W. Doig, *Empire on the Hudson* (New York: Columbia University Press, 2001).

11. Glenn Pasanen, "Finance," Gotham Gazette, September 11, 2002. Available at: www.gothamgazette.com/finance/91102.shtml.

12. Charles V. Bagli, "A Memorial, Yes, but Battle Lines Form for Everything Else," *The New York Times,* February 29, 2003.

13. Silverstein argued that he should receive not $3.5 billion but $7 billion in insurance awards for the rebuilding efforts, as, in his point of view, insurance companies were obliged to compensate him for two separate attacks on the towers. The details of Silverstein's views are expressed in a January 21, 2003 letter he wrote to the chairperson of the Lower Manhattan Development Corporation. A copy of the letter is available at: www.wirednewyork.com/forum/topic.cgi?forum=4& topic=422. In December 2004, a federal jury ruled that the insurance companies were obligated to compensate Silverstein for two separate attacks. As a result of earlier out-of-court settlements, the ruling, if allowed to stand, would allow Silverstein up to $4.65 in insurance funds, money that was critical to financing the Freedom Tower and other aspects of the WTC rebuilding effort. For details of the continuing conflict between Silverstein, the LMDC, the Port Authority, and Governor Pataki and other players, see: Devin Leonard, "Freedom Tower: Tower Struggle," Fortune, January 26, 2004; and Charles V. Bagli, "Towers' Insurers Must Pay Double," *The New York Times,* December 7, 2004.

14. "Six Months Later," Gotham Gazette, March 11, 2002, available at: www.gothamgazette.com/iotw/911_sixmonths/; Herbert Muschamp, "An Agency's Ideology Is Unsuited to Its Task," *The New York Times,* July 17, 2002; Michael Sorkin, "Bring It On: In Search of Democracy at Ground Zero," Slate, January 15, 2003, available at: www.slate.msn.com/id/2077010/.

15. Pietro S. Nivola, *Laws of the Landscape: How Policies Shape Cities in Europe and America* (Washington, DC: Brookings Institution, 1999); Michael Keating, "Local Economic Development Politics in France," *Journal of Urban Affairs* 13, 4 (1991): 443–459; Myron A. Levine, "The Transformation of Urban Politics in France: The Roots of Growth Politics and Urban Regimes," *Urban Affairs*

Quarterly 29 (March 1994): 383–410.; Myron A. Levine and Jan Van Weesep, "The Changing Nature of Dutch Urban Planning," *Journal of the American Planning Association* 54 (Summer 1988): 315–323; and Elizabeth Strom, "In Search of the Growth Coalition: American Urban Theories and the Redevelopment of Berlin," *Urban Affairs Review* 31, 4 (March 1996): 455–481.

16. Sam Bass Warner, Jr., *The Private City* (Philadelphia: University of Pennsylvania Press, 1968).

17. The jury seemingly accepted the defense attorneys' contentions that the officers had acted acceptably, that they had followed departmental policy governing the use of their batons, and that they had used no undue force in subduing King. The jurors viewed the entire tape, including earlier scenes of King charging police officers, not just the dramatic clips of the baton blows inflicted by the police against King. The public, though, was outraged by the verdict. Federal authorities brought the police officers to a second trial, this time on federal charges for having violated Rodney King's civil rights. For a discussion of the issues involved in the change of venue and the jury selection, see Hiroshi Fukurai, Richard Krooth, and Edgar W. Butler, "The Rodney King Beating Verdicts," in *The Los Angeles Riots: Lessons for the Urban Future*, ed. Mark Baldassare (Boulder, CO: Westview, 1994), pp. 73–102. Lou Cannon, *Official Negligence: How Rodney King and the Riots Changed the LAPD* (New York: Times Books/Random House, 1997), pp. 258–259, also provides a more detailed discussion of these complex events.

18. Steven Greenhouse and Mireya Navarro, "The Hidden Victims," *The New York Times*, September 17, 2001.

19. DHUD, The State of the Cities 1999, Exhibits 7 and 8.

20. William C. Thompson, Jr., New York City Comptroller, remarks presented at the "State of the City's Economy Conference," Federal Reserve Bank, New York, January 14, 2003, available at: www.comptroller.nyc.gov/press/speeches/ state_of_city_conference_1-14-03.shtm.

21. Ibid.

22. Paul E. Peterson, *City Limits* (Chicago: University of Chicago Press, 1981).

23. Center for an Urban Future, "Sympathy, But No Support: Even after 9/11, Albany Continues a Decade-Long Pattern of Shortchanging New York City," New York, April 2002. Available at: www.nycfuture.org.

24. Thompson, remarks presented at the "State of the City's Economy Conference." Erica Pearson, "Money for Rebuilding," Gotham Gazette, February 3, 2003. Available at: www.gothamgazette.com/article/issueoftheweek/20030203/200/271.

25. Raymond Hernandez, "Antiterror Budget Rises, but Critics Say City is Shortchanged," *The New York Times*, February 3, 2004.

26. Elaine S. Povich, "NYers Feel Pinch of Bush's Budget," *The New York Times*, February 3, 2004.

27. U.S. Census Bureau, "Large Suburban Cities in West Are Fastest-Growing, Census Bureau Reports," press release, July 10, 2003. Available at: www.census.gov/Press-Release/www/2003/cb03-106.html. These were the quickest growing of the nation's 242 communities with a population of 100,000 or more.

28. Richard M. Bernard and Bradley R. Rice, eds., *Sunbelt Cities* (Austin: University of Texas Press, 1983); Robert Kerstein, "Sunbelt Regimes: Past, Present and Future: A Review of the Literature" (paper presented at the annual meeting of the Urban Affairs Association, New Orleans, March 1994).

29. Carl Abbott, *The New Urban America,* rev. ed. (Chapel Hill: University of North Carolina Press, 1987).

30. Ann Markusen, Peter Hall, Scott Campbell, and Sabina Diedrick, *The Rise of the Gunbelt; The Military Remapping of Industrial America* (New York: Oxford University Press, 1991). Also see David L. Carlton, "The Sunbelt Debate Revisited," *Urban Affairs Quarterly* 20 (November 1993): 114–122.

31. Harold L. Wolman, Coit Cook Ford III, and Edward Hill, "Evaluating the Success of Urban Success Stories," *Urban Studies* 31 (June 1994): 835–850.

32. Stuart A. Gabriel, "Remaking the Los Angeles Economy: Cyclical Fluctuations and Structural Evolution," pp. 27–28; and Gary A. Dymski and John M. Veitch, "Financing the Future in Los Angeles: From Depression to 21st Century," p. 47, both in *Rethinking Los Angeles,* ed. Michael J. Dear, H. Eric Schockman, and Greg Hise (Thousand Oaks, CA: Sage Publications, 1996).

33. Allen J. Scott, "The Manufacturing Economy: Ethnic and Gender Divisions of Labor," pp. 215–244; and Paul Ong and Abel Valenzuela, Jr., "The Labor Market: Immigrant Effects and Racial Disparities," pp. 165–191, both in *Ethnic Los Angeles,* ed. Roger Waldinger and Mehdi Bozorgmehr (New York: Russell Sage Foundation, 1996).

34. Annette Steinacker, "Economic Restructuring of Cities, Suburbs, and Nonmetro-politan Areas, 1977–92," *Urban Affairs Review* 34, 2 (November 1998): 231.

35. Edward L. Glaeser and Jacob L. Vigdor, "Racial Segregation in the 2000 Census: Promising News," a report of The Brookings Institution Center on Urban and Metropolitan Policy, Washington DC, 2001. Available at: www.brookings.edu/dybdocroot/es/urban/census/freyfamiliesexecsum.htm.

36. John R. Logan, "Separate and Unequal: The Neighborhood Gap for Blacks and Hispanics in Metropolitan America, a report of the Lewis Mumford Center for Comparative Urban and Regional Research, University at Albany, Albany, New York, October 2002. Available at: http://mumford1.dyndns.org/cen2000/SepUneq/SUReport/SURepPage1.htm.

37. John R. Logan, Deirdre Oakley, and Jacob Stowell, "Segregation in Neighbor-hoods and Schools: Impacts on Minority Children in the Boston Region," a report of the Lewis Mumford Center for Comparative Urban and Regional Research, University at Albany, Albany, New York, September 2003. Available at: http://mumford1.dyndns.org/cen2000/colorlines/colorline01.htm.

38. Min, *Caught in the Middle,* pp. 91–92. Also see Raphael I. Sonenshein, "The Battle Over Liquor Stores in South Central Los Angeles: The Management of an Interminority Conflict," *Urban Affairs Review* 31, 6 (July 1996): 710–737.

39. Report of the *National Advisory Commission on Civil Disorders* (New York: Bantam Books, 1967). For similar analysis of the causes of the 1980 riot in the Liberty City section of Miami, Florida, see United States Commission on Civil Rights, Confronting Racial Isolation in Miami (Washington, DC, June 1992).

40. Anthony Downs, "The Future of Industrial Cities," in *The New Urban Reality,* ed. Paul E. Peterson (Washington, DC: Brookings Institution, 1985), p. 293.

41. The press, too, has had difficulty in reporting the complexity of the new urban race relations, and instead has distorted events by "framing" them in the older black-versus-white conflict terms. For an interesting article on how the media misrepresented the conflicts and riots in New York in the early 1990s, see Carol B. Conaway, "Crown Heights: Politics and Press Coverage of the Race War That Wasn't," *Polity* 32, 1 (Fall 1999): 93–118.

42. Robert J. Waste, *Independent Cities: Rethinking U.S. Urban Policy* (New York: Oxford University Press, 1998), p. 144.

43. See, for instance, two important collections of articles: Judith A. Garber and Robyne Turner, eds., *Gender in Urban Research, Urban Affairs Annual Review,* vol. 42 (Newbury Park, CA: Sage, 1994); and Kristine Miranne and Alma Young, eds., *Gendering the City Women, Boundaries, and Visions of Urban Life* (Lanham, MD: Rowman and Littlefield, 2000).

44. Scott, "The Manufacturing Economy: Ethnic and Gender Divisions of Labor," pp. 223–230.

45. Waste, *Independent Cities,* pp. 12–17.

46. Mike Davis, "Fortress Los Angeles: The Militarization of Urban Space," in *Variations on a Theme Park: The New American City and the End of Public Space,* ed. Michael Sorkin (New York: Hill and Wang, 1992); and Peter Marcuse, "The Enclave, the Citadel, and the Ghetto: What Has Changed in the Post-Fordist City," *Urban Affairs Review* 33, 3 (November 1997): 228–264. Also see Michael Dear and Steven Flusty, "The Iron Lotus: Los Angeles and Postmodern Urbanism," *Annals of the American Academy of Political and Social Science* 551 (May 1997): 158; and Edward I. Blakely and Mary Gail Snyder, *Fortress America: Gated Communities in the United States* (Washington, DC: Brookings Institution, 1997).

47. Waste, *Independent Cities,* p. 111.

48. U.S. Department of Housing and Urban Development, The State of the Cities 1999, Exhibit 11.

49. Dennis R. Judd and Susan R. Fainstein, eds., *The Tourist City* (New Haven, CT: Yale University Press, 1999); Dennis R. Judd, *Building the Tourist City* (M. E. Sharpe, 2002); Heywood T. Sanders, "Convention Center Follies," *The Public Interest* 132 (Summer 1998): 58–72; Heywood T. Sanders, "Convention Myths and Markets: A Critical Review of Convention Center Feasibility Studies," *Economic Development Quarterly,* 16, 3 (August 2002): 195–210.

50. Reynolds Farley, et al., "Continued Racial Residential Segregation in Detroit: 'Chocolate City, Vanilla Suburbs' Revisited," *Journal of Housing Research* 4, 1 (1993): 1–38.

51. John R. Logan and Glenn Deane, "Black Diversity in Metropolitan America," a report of the University of Albany's Lewis Mumford Center for Comparative Urban and Regional Research, Albany, NY, August 2003. Available at: http://mumford1.dyndns.org/cen2000/BlackWhite/BlackWhite.htm.

52. Joel Garreau, *Edge City: Life on the New Frontier* (New York; Doubleday, 1991).

53. Dear and Flusty, "The Iron Lotus," p. 156.

54. Christopher Hoene, Mark Baldassare, and Christiana Brennan, "Homeland Security and America's Cities," National League of Cities Research Brief on America's Cities, Washington, DC, December 2002.

55. Elizabeth Becker, "A Nation Challenged: The Mayors; Ridge Deflects Pleas to help the Cities Pay Security Costs," *The New York Times,* October 26, 2001; Charles Pope, "War on Terrorism: Security Costs Weigh Heavily at Local Level," *Seattle Post-Intelligencer,* February 10, 2003.

56. William C. Thompson, Jr. (New York City Comptroller), One Year Later: The Fiscal Impact of 9/11 on New York City, New York, September 2002. Available at: http://comptroller.nyc.gov/bureaus/bud/reports/impact-9-11-year-later.pdf.

57. Fiscal Policy Institute, "The Employment Impact of the September 11 World Trade Center Attacks: Updated Estimates Based on the Benchmarked Employment Data,"

New York, March 8, 2002. Available at: www.fiscalpolicy.org/Employment%
20Impact%20of%20September%2011_Update.pdf. Three-fourths of the total job
loss came after the 9/11 attacks.

58. Charles V. Bagli, "Seeking Safety, Manhattan Firms Are Scattering," *The New
York Times,* January 29, 2002; Leslie Eaton, "Attack Gave a Devastating Shove to
the City's Teetering Economy," *The New York Times,* September 8, 2002.

59. This paragraph is based on James H. Johnson, Jr. and John D. Kasarda, "9/11 and
the Economic Prospects of Major U.S. Cities," *Planning & Markets* 6, 1 (September
2003). Available at: www-pam.usc.edu/volume6/v6ilalsl.html. The numbers on the
expected loss of jobs are from Ross C. DeVol, et al., "The Impact of September 11
on U.S. Metropolitan Economies," a report of The Milken Institute, Santa Monica,
CA, January 2002. Available at: www.milkeninstitute.org/publications/
publications.taf?function=detail&ID=161&cat=ResRep.

60. Alice Rivlin and Alan Berube, "The Potential Impacts of Recession and Terrorism
on U.S. Cities," a report of The Brookings Institution Center on Urban and Metropolitan Policy, Washington, DC, 2002.

61. Jack Lyne, "NYC Report: Most Displaced Tenants Pick Manhattan, but Available
Space Up in All Markets," Online Insider, November 26, 2001. Available at:
www.conway.com/ssinsider/snapshot/sf011126.htm.

62. U.S. Census Bureau, "Poverty 2002," Table 5. Available at: www.census.gov/hhes/
poverty/poverty02/r&dtable5.html.

63. U.S. Census Bureau, "Rankings Tables 2002: Percent of People Below Poverty
Level," American Community Survey Office, September 02, 2003. Available at:
www.census.gov/acs/www/Products/Ranking/2002/R01T160.htm.

64. U.S. Department of Housing and Urban Development, The State of the Cities
1999, Exhibit 15. The figures are from 1995.

65. Alan Berube and William H. Frey, "A Decade of Mixed Blessings: Urban and
Suburban Poverty in Census 2000," a report of The Brookings Institution Center
on Urban and Metropolitan Policy, Washington DC, 2002. Available at:
www.brookings.edu/dybdocroot/es/urban/publications/berubefreypoverty.pdf.

66. United States Conference of Mayors, "Weak Growth Prospects After Heavy Job
Losses in 2001 and 2002," City Mayors, on-line publication. Available at:
www.citymayors.com/gratis/us_mayors.html.

67. Steinacker, "Economic Restructuring of Cities, Suburbs, and Nonmetropolitan
Areas," p. 229; and John Brennan and Edward W. Hill, "Where Are The Jobs?
Cities, Suburbs, and the Competition for Employment," The Brookings Institution
Survey Series, November 1999. Available at: www.brookings.edu/es/urban/
hillfa.pdf.

In this chapter, we describe three different views as to why cities and suburbs have evolved as they have. As we shall see, urban growth and decline are not totally natural phenomena. Contrary to what many Americans think, the economic and racial segregation of the metropolis is not purely the result of a free

market that reflects differences in wealth and consumer tastes. Nor has the regional migration of jobs and population to the Sunbelt been solely the result of natural factors. Individual choice and the free market are not the only factors that have determined the shape of modern metropolitan America. Often unrecognized, two other forces—"hidden" governmental policies and private sector power—exerted great influence in shaping patterns of local growth and decline.

THE GROWTH AND EVOLUTION OF METROPOLITAN AMERICA: NATURAL FACTORS

According to Edward C. Banfield, metropolitan growth throughout history has primarily been the product of natural forces—forces so strong that Banfield has called them "imperatives."[1] The first imperative is **demographic:** Population increases force a city to expand. The second is **technological:** The available transportation and communications technology determines just how far outward the expansion of a metropolitan area will go. Obviously, cities in the age of the automobile can grow outward much farther than cities of the horse-and-buggy and streetcar eras. Technology also determines if a city can develop upward—through the construction of high-rise buildings and skyscrapers—and not just outward. The third factor is **economic:** Persons of affluence who can afford the costs of new housing and the commute to the city will seek to escape the older sections of the city, with their noise, traffic congestion, and decayed and cramped housing, for a "better life" in more desirable areas on the urban fringe.

The importance of transportation to the development of cities helps to explain the location of urban centers. The original settlement of most

American cities occurred near a major locus of transportation—a harbor, river, canal, or important railroad or trail junction. American cities developed in areas that were easily accessible, where commerce would be made easy. Only a few cities in the United States, such as Fort Worth, developed from an army settlement that provided protection in a hostile environment.

Initially, North American cities, especially in the 1700s and early 1800s, were relatively small in size. These commercial centers had not yet experienced the influx of population with industrialization and immigration. The primitive nature of technology also acted to limit the geographical size of the city; people had to live close to their work. As walking was a major form of urban transportation, historian Kenneth Jackson has labeled these pre-industrial communities **walking cities**.[2] Indeed, a person could easily traverse the entire distance of the city on foot, and there was a clear distinction between the relatively small built-up city and the rural countryside located not too far away. Due to the primitive nature of transportation, the relatively small cities of this period contained a full mixture of functions and a cross section of the population. Working spaces were often located in the same neighborhood as living spaces, and merchants, shippers, laborers, the rich, and the poor all lived inside the city. The limitations of transportation technology constrained suburbanization, precluding the loss of wealth and industry to the surrounding countryside.

In fact, most of the rural hamlets and farm villages that existed around the city at that time could not be considered suburban, as residents had little inter-action with the city. Transportation difficulties imposed strict limitations as to how far a person could reasonably travel.

The cities were centers of opportunity. The result was a process of **urbanization,** where poorer migrants left the countryside and went to the American city in search of jobs and wealth. However, urban growth soon led to overcrowding and congestion. The living conditions in the growing American city were not always desirable, especially as residences were often located in close proximity to stockyards, tanneries, lumberyards, and other urban nuisances. In the growing city, streets were often unpaved. With primitive sanitation and overcrowded housing, the city was also the site of major public health epidemics. In 1793, yellow fever killed 5,000 people in Philadelphia; St. Louis in 1849 lost one-tenth of its population to cholera. Four years later, yellow fever led to a loss of 11,000 lives in New Orleans.[3] The industrial age, with its smoke-belching factories and cinder-throwing train engines, would only exacerbate the environmental problems of urban living.

Persons who could afford it sought refuge from city life in residences on the edge of urbanized areas, far from the unsanitary conditions and deteriorated housing stock of the central city. Each successive transportation innovation— the horse-pulled streetcar, the electric trolley, and the steam railroad—extended the urban population farther and farther outward from the city center. Although we can trace the beginning of suburbanization in the United States to about 1815, suburbs did not gain significant populations until the latter half of the nineteenth century.[4] Even then, suburbs were primarily the bastion of more affluent workers, or at least workers who had the means to buy housing far from the congestion of the city and still be able to commute to work.

Most people in the early American city either had to remain within walking distance to their jobs or could move only as far out as a horse-pulled streetcar could take them. It would take innovations in transportation technology to redefine the urban landscape. But even with the introduction of new transit systems, urban areas in the United States remained very compact as compared to the sprawling megalopolises of today. New technology in building construction also reinforced the urban core. By the 1880s and 1890s, advances in architectural technology saw the construction of the first skyscrapers (or, at least, the predecessors of modem skyscrapers), allowing the city to expand upward before it greatly expanded outward.

For a long while, the city simply extended its boundaries with each new outward movement of the population. Cities often used their **annexation** powers to adjoin neighboring areas to the city. Residents in these rapidly growing and underdeveloped outlying areas, where streets in some cases were barely paved, gave their approval to annexations in order to receive public water, drainage, gas, street lighting, road paving, and other municipal services that the more established cities could provide. In other cases, annexation proceeded by legal force, as the result of permissive state annexation statutes.

However, resistance to annexation accelerated in 1873 when the growing suburb of Brookline, Massachusetts, surrounded on three sides by the city of Boston, refused to be incorporated into it. Residents of Brookline had come to see themselves as apart from Boston and, despite the promise of service improvement, were happy with the way things were. By the latter part of the 1800s, "Boston was something to be feared and controlled," and opponents of annexation portrayed Brookline as a "refuge" from an industrial Boston and its corrupting influences. They charged that "the high levels of city services maintained by Boston meant higher taxes, and, further, they frankly stated that independent suburban towns could maintain native American life free from Boston's waves of incoming poor immigrants."[5]

The **streetcar suburbs** of the era grew beyond the jurisdictional reach of the central city. Brookline's resistance to annexation was the beginning of a wave; soon, more and more suburbs asserted their independence and refused incorporation with the central city. As historian Sam Bass Warner, Jr. has observed, "[T]he metropolitan middle-class abandoned their central city."[6]

The rural poor continued to pour into **industrial cities** in search of jobs. In need of labor, the mills and foundries of the North in the early 1900s even sent recruiters to the South to hire poor black tenant farmers. The mechanization of agriculture and the phasing out of the sharecropper system in the South displaced many of the rural poor, spurring the migration to cities. The pace of this migration was accelerated by the labor needs of city factories during and after World Wars I and II. Rail lines also brought southern blacks to Chicago, Pittsburgh, and other big cities of the North. In the **Great Migration**, millions of poor African Americans from the rural South made their way northward in search of civil rights, jobs, and prosperity.[7]

The **automobile revolution** truly reshaped the metropolis. Suburban residents no longer needed to live in close proximity to the streetcar and railroad tracks; suburban homes could now fill in the spaces between the "fingers" or spokes of the rail and streetcar systems. The automobile also allowed residents to live farther and farther away from the old center city.

Industrial and commercial enterprises followed the move of their better quality workforce to the suburbs. Manufacturing firms sought suburban locations where land was cheaper and sites were more suitable to new, land-intensive **assembly-line technology.** New transportation technology, in the form of the trucking industry, enabled the movement of warehousing and distribution activities to the suburbs. Older industrial and warehousing sections of the city, such as New York's SoHo and Lower East Side, began to decline as their small manufacturing lofts could no longer compete with spaciousness offered by suburban assembly lines and warehousing. By the 1970s, advances in **containerization** would put a further premium on suburban sites; city streets were too congested, and older warehouse loading docks too antiquated to handle the new shipping technologies.

The retail and entertainment industries, too, soon followed the exodus of population to the suburbs. The growing suburban middle class had the buying power and did not want to be bothered with long commutes, traffic jams, and the search for parking downtown. As a result, developers built plaza-type shopping centers and, later, enclosed shopping malls at the intersections of major highways with the urban rim highway or beltway. Retail activity in the older downtown shopping districts dropped off markedly. By the mid-1980s, Hudson's department store, long associated with Detroit, closed the doors of its downtown store after having opened new stores at various suburban shopping malls throughout the metropolitan area. Detroit gained the dubious distinction of being the largest city in the nation not to have a major department store within its borders. Baltimore, Toledo, and Fort Worth were soon among the nation's big cities that also saw their major downtown department stores close their doors.

By the latter part of the twentieth century, technological advances in the field of **telecommunications** freed white-collar offices from sites in the old downtown. Suburban office parks competed with central-city downtowns for new office development. Outside Chicago, the office towers of Schaumburg and other northwestern suburbs constituted a virtual second downtown. Orange County, California witnessed an office boom south of Los Angeles. Similar growth occurred on the rim of a great many metropolitan areas, including the Route 128 area outside Boston; White Plains, New York; Rosslyn and Crystal City, Virginia (just across the river from Washington, DC); Troy and Southfield, Michigan; the corridor between Dallas and Fort Worth, Texas; the Perimeter Center north of Atlanta's Beltway; and the Silicon Valley region between San Francisco and San Jose, California—to name only a few. These new developments redefined suburbia; high-technology suburbs or **technoburbs** duplicated the white-collar job, retailing, and entertainment functions traditionally associated with central cities and became attractive sites for globally oriented, high-tech companies and foreign-owned firms.[8]

These full-fledged technoburbs, also referred to as **edge cities** or **new suburban downtowns,** were modernized and seemingly vastly improved versions of suburbia, especially when compared to the relatively tranquil "bedroom" communities of the 1950s. Functions and services once found only in central cities now were commonly found in suburbia. The **multicentered metropolis** had become a reality, displacing the more traditional conceptualization of a metropolis as having only a single core center.[9] For a great many people, daily life revolved around the corporate office parks, shopping malls, entertainment complexes, chain restaurants, and cultural centers of these new suburban villages. Suburbs were at the cutting edge of technology, and life on the city's rim no longer seemed "sub" to central cities in any way.[10] The new perimeter cities, though, did not contain a fair share of affordable or public housing. Nor were they fully open to the region's poor and minority citizens, populations that remained concentrated in the central city and some of the region's older and now declining inner-ring suburbs.

Advances in communications, computerization, and data technology allowed firms to decentralize further. Fax machines, satellite communication, and digital technology were only a few of the advances that allowed businesses to move data entry and other clerical functions to less costly sites that were distant from corporations' central-city headquarters. **Back-office clerical functions** could now be located in the suburbs, in far-off small towns, and even overseas. Rosenbluth Travel, one of the nation's largest travel agencies, moved its 200-employee reservations center from downtown Philadelphia to low-wage Linton, North Dakota; American Airlines moved its ticket-processing center from Tulsa to Barbados. New York Life and a number of other insurance companies moved their life insurance processing operations overseas to Ireland, where workers are well educated but relatively poorly paid by American standards.[11]

As already hinted, not all suburbs prospered as the United States was transformed from an urban to a suburban nation. While the technoburbs, edge cities, and more affluent residential rim communities prospered, older, inner-ring, blue-collar suburbs began to exhibit some of the same social and fiscal problems typically associated with declining central cities. In many ways, the conditions of the most troubled older suburbs, including East Cleveland, East St. Louis, and East Palo Alto (California), were almost indistinguishable from those of the urban core.

As suburban growth boomed, metropolitan areas were reconfigured, losing much of their older central-city focus. The nation's shift to a service economy served only to further the decline of big-city industrial centers: "The industrial city has become an institutional anachronism."[12] In the transition to a postindustrial era, New York, Philadelphia, Detroit, Cleveland, St. Louis, and numerous other large- and medium-sized cities were hard hit by the erosion of their economic base. By the last third of the twentieth century, the political economies of these cities were characterized by a loss of jobs, a declining fiscal base, severe budgetary cutbacks, increased racial conflict, a hovering threat of fiscal insolvency, and a desperate search for new businesses.

Of course, not all central cities suffered such extensive economic and population decline. Generally speaking, Sunbelt cities (with some exceptions) continued to grow. In the Frostbelt, too, some cities were able to attract new office development to help compensate for the loss of manufacturing jobs. "World class" cities[13] such as New York and Los Angeles maintained vital downtowns capable of attracting international corporate headquarters and sustaining convention activity even while large portions of the city suffered through the economic transition. Other cities, too, saw their downtowns begin to rebound beginning with the 1990s post-recession economic boom.

New York, Los Angeles, Chicago, San Francisco, Houston, and Denver are among the major cities that have greatly changed over the past half century; they essentially have lost their older industrial character and have become **postindustrial cities** with a new focus on corporate offices, conventions, and tourism. Manufacturing jobs, once the backbone of the city economy, had migrated to the suburbs and overseas, or had been lost to automation, robotics, and recession.

By the end of the twentieth century, a number of cities were able to carve a new niche for themselves as centers of international banking, finance, and corporate headquarters activity in a **global economy.** As we shall discuss more fully in Chapter 3, "Recent Trends: Gentrification and Globalization," city after city invested in its telecommunications infrastructure to be more competitive in attracting new multinational corporations and their support firms. Yet, globalization brought uneven benefits to cities. While some cities experienced new multinational investment, others could not find a place for themselves in the new national economy. **Urban dualism** was also exacerbated; while some trendy neighborhoods experienced significant upgrading, other city areas saw their needs ignored as the city sought to make itself attractive to new corporate investors.

By labeling as "imperatives" the three factors that shape metropolitan growth—population pressures, transportation technology, and the distribution of income—Banfield has essentially taken the position that government can do relatively little to reshape the urban landscape or ameliorate urban problems: "The argument is not that nothing can be done to improve matters. Rather, it is that only those things can be done which lie within the boundaries— rather narrow ones, to be sure—fixed by the logic of the growth process."[14] According to Banfield, city-suburban, intersuburban, and interregional inequalities will continue to exist, as no government in a free society can easily reverse the free-market choices of its people.

However, do Banfield's three factors constitute "imperatives" that dictate the shape of metropolitan areas? While Banfield's three factors explain much of the pressure for urban growth, they do not dictate the exact pattern of metropolitan growth that will occur. The present-day shape of metropolitan areas in the United States was neither purely natural nor inevitable. Urban growth and decline has not been purely the result of unhindered, free market choice.

Political scientist Clarence Stone has criticized Banfield's thesis, "[T]he market does not operate in isolation from government policy."[15] Government actions, too, have helped to determine just where people live and which communities grow and which decline. Decisions made by banks and other private institutions of power have promoted urban transformation, accelerating suburbanization and regional job and population shifts while guaranteeing central-city disinvestment and decline. Banfield's notion of demographic "imperatives" slights the roles played by government policy and private power in shaping the modern metropolis and the "urban crisis."

GOVERNMENTAL INFLUENCES ON METROPOLITAN DEVELOPMENT

Altogether, demographic pressures, affluence, and technological advances provide only a partial explanation of how America's cities and suburbs wound up in their present condition. Government policies, too, played a crucially important role in determining the shape of metropolitan America and the health of America's communities.[16]

The federal programs with the greatest impacts on metropolitan America were not explicitly urban in their orientation. These programs had other quite laudable objectives. They sought to help Americans buy homes of their own; they sought the construction of an interstate highway system; and they sought to subsidize the construction of much-needed hospitals and sewage plants during a period of rapid suburban growth in the post-World War II era. It was not until much later that urban analysts clearly recognized the negative impacts that these programs had on cities. These programs produced adverse effects so great that, even if unintended, they can be said to constitute a **hidden urban policy.**

In this section, we identify some of the more significant components of the federal government's hidden urban policy. We also look at the most significant actions of local governments that have served to produce unbalanced metropolitan growth.

FEDERAL HOUSING POLICY: THE FHA AND VA

Many middle- and working-class families would not have been able to buy homes of their own in the absence of federal assistance. The 1934 Housing Act created the **Federal Housing Administration (FHA)** with the goal of helping families to acquire homes of their own. The FHA provided loan insurance for up to 80 percent of the value of an approved property. In the event that an FHA-insured homeowner defaulted on a loan, the FHA essentially guaranteed that it would repay 80 percent to the creditor. The risk of making home loans was thereby reduced. As a result, financial institutions were willing to finance homes for millions of Americans who otherwise would never have received credit. Facing reduced risk, lenders could also lower down payment requirements and interest rates; home buying thus became increasingly affordable.

The federal government provided similar assistance to the millions of veterans returning home after World War II. Under the GI Bill of Rights of 1944, the **Veterans Administration (VA)** was authorized to insure home mortgages to veterans. The legislation made buying a home easy; no down payment was required from the buyer.

As "the VA very largely followed FHA procedures and attitudes . . . the two programs can be considered as a single effort."[17] Together, the VA and FHA programs offered prospective homebuyers a very attractive package of low or no down payment, easy credit, and a 25- to 30-year period of relatively small monthly payments. The programs also put the federal government heavily into the mortgage market, where it has remained to this day.

These programs helped promote the purchase of new homes, spurring suburban development; the programs gave little attention to the purchase of apartments or the renovation of older housing stock in the central city. The FHA **redlined** large portions of the city, refusing to insure loans in the inner city. In the case of Camden, New Jersey, the FHA redlined the entire city "as unacceptably risky, and consequently mortgage money dried up almost completely."[18]

As can easily be seen, through much of their history, the FHA and VA programs subsidized the growth of suburban areas and largely wrote off central cities, assuring the **disinvestment** in, and decline of, inner-city neighborhoods. This anti-city bias was written into the agency's 1939 *Underwriting Manual*. The *Manual* instructed FHA underwriters to minimize credit risks and homeowner defaults on their obligations by looking for "economic stability" when making neighborhood evaluations; as the *Manual* continued, "crowded neighborhoods lessen desirability."[19]

The FHA and VA programs helped young marrieds to buy homes of their own. The working and middle classes took advantage of FHA and VA loans and fled the city. The graying neighborhoods of the central city became available for occupancy by lower income residents, including African Americans and Hispanics. The federal housing finance programs had contributed to the growing racial and financial divide separating the central city from its suburbs.

FHA policy was even more pernicious when it came to racial segregation. Until the 1950s and 1960s, the FHA pursued a policy of explicit racial segregation in insuring home loans. As the agency's *Underwriting Manual* warned, "If a neighborhood is to retain stability, it is necessary that properties shall continue to be occupied by the same social and racial classes."[20] The *Manual* instructed federal underwriters to give a low rating to mortgage applications that would lead to the "infiltration of inharmonious racial or nationality groups" into a neighborhood.[21] The FHA even endorsed the use of **restrictive covenants,** legally binding agreements that prohibited a buyer from reselling a home to someone of a different race!

As a consequence of these rules, very few FHA-insured loans were given to black families; only 2 percent of the housing built in the postwar period under FHA mortgage insurance was sold to minorities, and half of that was for housing built in all-minority subdivisions.[22] The FHA would not approve loans to minority applicants seeking to move into all-white suburbs. In Detroit in the 1940s, the FHA withheld approval for the financing of an all-white subdivision until after the developer first agreed to build a six-foot-high, half-mile-long concrete wall to separate his property from a bordering black neighborhood.[23]

How could a federal agency so explicitly endorse segregation? The FHA was essentially a decentralized program where important lending decisions were made by local lending institutions. Consequently, the FHA "incorporated into national housing policy the perspectives of the bankers and the mortgage lenders who participate in its local implementation."[24] FHA administrators "were drawn from the ranks of the housing and banking industries"; they "shared the real estate industry's view that segregation was preferable to integration."[25] They also feared that integrating a neighborhood would jeopardize local property values. The National Association of Real Estate Boards endorsed this philosophy in its code of ethics; the FHA subscribed to a similar set of principles.

Eventually, the FHA would change its policy. By 1949, the FHA finally dropped its references to "racial groups" and "infiltration." But, by then, it was largely too late; the harm had already been done, as the FHA had underwritten the decline of central cities and the racial homogeneity of thousands of suburbs.

After the urban riots of the 1960s, the FHA faced new pressures to reverse its pro-suburban bias and guarantee home loans inside central cities.[26] However, even in attempting to help, the FHA once more inadvertently hastened the decline of central-city neighborhoods. Unscrupulous lenders and realtors helped marginally qualified persons to obtain the newly available FHA-insured loans, knowing that the FHA would fully pay off the loan when the borrower defaulted on the loan. As a result, many FHA-insured properties wound up in default, boarded up, and abandoned.

THE HIDDEN URBAN POLICY OF THE FEDERAL TAX CODE

As we have seen, the FHA and VA programs helped promote suburban growth and a racially segregated metropolis. However, the impact of these two programs pales by comparison to that of yet another hidden federal urban policy: the **federal tax code's provisions for homeowners.**

Homeowners have historically been allowed to deduct mortgage interest and property taxes from their taxable gross income. The billions of dollars in tax benefits allowed homeowners each year dwarfs the amount the federal government allocates to low-income housing programs. According to the bipartisan Joint Committee on Taxation, in fiscal 2002 alone, tax expenditures for homeowners totaled a whopping $88 billion—$66.5 billion in tax revenues lost due to the deduction allowed for mortgage interest, and another $21.4 billion in deductions for local property taxes.[27] The mortgage deduction alone totaled approximately three times the entire budget of the Department of Housing and Urban Development.[28]

These tax deductions give great benefits to wealthy and middle-class home-owners, not to renters (who get no direct tax break under these programs) or the poor (who rent or who have homes of low value and who seldom itemize their deductions). The more expensive the house and the greater the mortgage payments and local taxes, the more these federal tax breaks mean to a home-owner. In fiscal 2001, homeowners with incomes over $100,000 received 62.7 percent of the mortgage deduction; in contrast, families earning less than $50,000 received less than 6 percent of the benefits.[29]

These tax write-offs have enabled millions of middle-class Americans who could not otherwise afford to do so to buy a home of their own. In effect, the government helps homeowners pay the costs of the home. The result has also been a tax-subsidized flight to the suburbs, with central cities losing much of their middle-class tax base.

In more recent years, these same tax provisions have acted to stimulate **condominium and cooperative apartment conversions,** where tenants buy a living unit in a multifamily building. Once again, an individual gets a generous tax break if he or she owns a home, condominium, or cooperative; no subsidy is given to renters. Given this set of tax incentives, it often makes good sense for a family to buy a living unit, and a market is created whereby landlords convert apartment buildings into condominiums and cooperatives. The result of such conversions, though, is to deprive a city of its rental housing stock and to displace tenants who cannot afford to buy their apartments in a building that is "going condo." The victims of the conversion process too often are the elderly and the poor, tenants on limited incomes who suddenly find themselves ousted from their long-time dwellings.

THE FEDERAL HIGHWAY PROGRAM AS ANTI-URBAN POLICY

In the midst of the Cold War, advocates for a strong national defense urged the completion of a national highway network that would enable the quick and efficient transport of military personnel and materiel. The National Defense Highway Act of 1956 increased the federal share of funding highway construction projects from 50 percent to 90 percent.

The new program provided a major impetus for suburban development. The interstate highway program did not just seek to link cities across the nation; it also built new freeways in urban areas, major commuting roads that opened metropolitan areas to extensive suburbanization.

Federal highway construction had the further effect of destroying viable neighborhoods in city areas. Urban highways divided neighborhoods, displac-ing tenants and cutting off residents from local stores and their friends; such areas quickly declined. Highway construction also pushed citizens to move outside the city. In New York, the 1950s construction of the Cross Bronx Expressway uprooted a solid working-class, Jewish neighborhood; displaced from their homes, many of the residents left the city, never to return.

In Miami and other cities, highway construction not only destroyed viable neighborhoods; it was also used as a tool for **Negro removal.** In Miami, the building of I-95 "ripped through the center of Overtown," a large African-American community of at least 40,000 people, displacing residents who were forced to resettle in more distant black neighborhoods, most notably Liberty City. With the completion of the expressway, there was little left to Overtown, once known for its vitality as the "Harlem of the South."[30]

The federally subsidized urban highways have become the new "main streets" of a growing suburban America.[31] The new highways and beltways built around cities expedited commuting trips into the city, and facilitated trips from one suburb to another. Huge shopping centers—and later enclosed malls—were constructed at the intersections of major highways. The decentralization of manufacturing, warehousing, distribution, and retailing activities soon followed. The urban freeways even enabled **reverse commuting,** where residents of the central city travel to the "good" jobs in edge cities on the city's rim. The roads south of San Francisco, for instance, are jammed with San Francisco residents traveling to jobs in Silicon Valley.

THE IMPACT OF MILITARY SPENDING AND OTHER FEDERAL PROGRAMS

Military and defense policy, too, promoted suburbanization as decision makers sought spread-out production sites that could not easily be bombed by the enemy. During World War II, the War Production Board (WPB) "did no less than reconstruct America's capital plant by investing enormous sums of federal monies to build new production facilities for America's industries."[32] The WPB was staffed by corporate executives on leave; they preferred the cost advantages of factory sites in suburban and Sunbelt locations—sites that had the advantages of cheap labor and land and which were located at a distance from the union activists of the central city. Instead of simply relying on Detroit's existing facilities, they built new plants outside the city.[33] Government war production helped to shift the sites of future production from the central cities to the suburbs. As we shall later discuss in further detail, military and aerospace spending also helped to catalyze the growth of the Sunbelt.

Other federal programs also encouraged suburbanization. Generous federal grant programs helped to pay the cost of much-needed **hospitals and sewage processing facilities.** These programs helped to underwrite the infrastructure costs of new suburban development.

Government **tax incentives to businesses** helped pay for the costs of new physical plant and equipment investment in the suburbs; equivalent tax write-offs were not always offered to rehabilitate aging plants in the central city. The federal government's investment tax credit, for instance, sought to provide incentives for firms to invest in more modern business and industrial equipment. However, in doing so, it gained the reputation for being an "urban disinvestment tax credit" as it spurred business to abandon aging central-city plants for new facilities in the suburbs.[34]

Even **urban renewal** in the 1950s and 1960s, a program that was intended to redevelop cities, helped to "push" businesses and residents out of the cities and into the suburbs. Urban renewal cleared large parcels of land, razing homes and apartment buildings in working-class and poorer neighborhoods to make way for new upper-income apartments, modern university and hospital campuses, and expanded central business districts. Forced out of their homes, displaced families with the means often chose to leave the city altogether for a new life in the suburbs, far away from the city and its problems.

THE ACTIONS OF LOCAL GOVERNMENT

Local governments, too, have played a major role in contributing to present-day metropolitan imbalances. Each local jurisdiction has been able to use its control over **zoning and land-use policy** to determine just which forms of development may or may not take place within its borders. (See "Zoning and Its Impact: The New York Metropolitan Area" below.) Suburbs often use these powers to keep out less fortunate residents. Many suburbs severely limit or ban the construction of subsidized housing for the poor, apartment buildings, and even townhouses. A suburb can also sharply drive up the price of buying a house within its borders by requiring that new houses be built only on excessively large lots and that they meet expensive construction requirements exceeding any reasonable concern for health and safety.

ZONING AND ITS IMPACT: THE NEW YORK METROPOLITAN AREA

In 1916, New York became the first city to adopt a zoning ordinance, a move so revolutionary and potentially beneficial that it was hailed as opening "a new era of civilization."* New York's zoning ordinance regulated the use, height, and bulk of all new buildings. It was passed as a result of the influence of the city's realtors, business interests, and prominent property owners who feared that the continued construction of skyscrapers would act to depress the value of their surrounding properties.

But the zoning ordinances did more than protect the interests of the business community. Zoning helps to assure orderly land development by preventing incompatible land uses. No homeowner, for instance, wants to see a factory or an automobile service station built next to his or her home. Zoning prevents that by designating different sections of a community for different uses. Certain land parcels are designated for industrial and commercial uses; other parcels are reserved for residential development. Light industry can be kept separate from heavy industry. Multifamily dwellings are allowed in certain areas but are zoned out of others.

The idea of zoning soon spread like wildfire. Zoning is now the primary land-use control tool employed by cities and suburbs throughout the nation.

continued

ZONING AND ITS IMPACT: THE NEW YORK METROPOLITAN AREA (CONT.)

Suburbs have used zoning to keep both nuisance industrial activities and lower income people outside their borders. Communities in Westchester County, New York, north of New York City, have used zoning and other land-use restrictions in an attempt to prevent the "Bronxification" of their area: "their goal was to attract 'class' not 'mass' to Westchester." Zoning restrictions typically prevent or sharply limit the construction of apartment buildings and high-density development. Poorer people and even many middle-class families are excluded when local zoning ordinances require that homes be built on large lots and that new homes have exceedingly large-size rooms and other expensive construction features.

Not all communities in the greater New York region used exclusionary zoning as aggressively as did Westchester. In Nassau County on Long Island, pressures from large-scale developers were more intense, and local political leaders generally took less interest in limiting development. Still, certain Long Island communities—for example, Oyster Bay—did adopt land-use barriers every bit as strict as those used in Westchester.

What would happen if a city had no stringent zoning laws to guide and control new development? One hint of an answer is provided by the 1964 opening of the Verrazano Narrows Bridge, which connected Staten Island to the New York City mainland. The bridge's construction touched off a building boom in relatively undeveloped portions of the island. As Staten Island was not a suburb but part of New York City, it possessed no legal authority to enact zoning restrictions of its own: "Compared with the region's typical suburb, Staten Island has been a paradise for the home building industry." Planning and environmental values were ignored as the private sector "produced housing on Staten Island that is smaller, less expensive, more crowded, and less attractive than that built during the same period in the suburbs of the New York region."[**] In 2003, the New York City Council responded with a massive rezoning to limit the pace of new construction to protect greenspace and "the suburban neighborhood character" of Staten Island.[***]

Zoning, then, has its virtues. But as we have also seen, zoning is also employed by suburbs as a potent weapon of exclusion that lessens the supply of affordable housing in a region and prices less-advantaged people out of their communities. We discuss the debate over zoning in greater detail in Chapter 11, "Suburban Politics and Metropolitan American."

[*] Robert M. Fogelson, *Downtown: Its Rise and Fall, 1880–1950* (New Haven, CT: Yale University Press, 2001, p. 160. See Fogelson's larger discussion, pp. 160–166.

[**] Michael N. Danielson and Jameson Doig, *New York: The Politics of Urban Regional Development* (Berkeley, CA: University of California Press, 1982), pp. 79 and 106–107.

[***] "New York City Council Stated Meeting Report, December 3, 2003," *The Gotham Gazette*, December 3, 2003: www.gothamgazette.com/searchlight/council.2003.12.03.shtml.

Control over land uses allows more fortunate suburbs to effectively lock out poor and working-class families. Racial minorities, too, have a problem gaining access to more exclusive suburban communities; only wealthier minority families have the ability to buy houses in communities in which decision makers have enacted exclusionary land-use and zoning practices. Through their use of exclusionary zoning, better-off suburbs restrict the production of affordable housing units. As a result, central cities and inner-ring, aging suburbs wind up with populations that are disproportionately poor, minority, and in need of government services.

For much of their history, central cities themselves, responding to the political power of white voters, quite often undertook policies that **segregated public housing** and promoted the formation and expansion of racial ghettos. The deference that the federal government showed local governments in slum clearance and public housing helped to assure that local preferences for segregation would prevail.[35]

From the 1940s through the 1960s, governmental policy in Chicago actively sought to reinforce segregated residential patterns. The Chicago Housing Authority did not simply award an available public housing unit to the next family on a waiting list; instead, assignments to different buildings were based on race. Each city council member was also allowed a virtual veto over the placement of new public housing in his or her ward, thereby guaranteeing that no public housing for minorities would be built in white neighborhoods. Instead, new public housing was built in minority areas and reinforced the ghetto. The city also used urban renewal programs to remove African Americans from areas targeted for revitalization, resettling displacees in new, segregated, high-rise housing projects. For all intents and purposes, the city of Chicago had undertaken a policy of explicit segregation in constructing and maintaining a new and enlarged, high-rise **second ghetto,** a ghetto much different from those portions of the city that had large minority populations in the pre–World War II era.[36]

It is only today that these high-rise towers of hopelessness are being torn down. The federal government's **HOPE VI** has helped to pay for the demolition of the distressed public housing buildings in a number of cities. The goal is deconcentration, to allow tenants to find residences in less poverty-impacted communities.

Yet, it has often proven difficult to find new housing for the displacees. HOPE VI provides tenants with vouchers that they can use to find housing in other neighborhoods. However, as landlords are often reluctant to rent units to former public housing residents, many of the HOPE VI dispacees have little choice other than to move into substandard housing in their old neighborhoods. As citizens in other neighborhoods continue to oppose the construction of public housing in their areas, public officials often wind up building replacement housing on the site of, or near, the former public housing "projects." To a great extent, both federal and local governments have acted to reinforce segregation by allowing the reconcentration of very poor, minority residents in troubled, minority communities.[37]

Chicago is not alone in its history of local segregative action. New York City admitted to having violated the federal Fair Housing Act by setting racial quotas on certain public housing projects and by steering black and Hispanic applicants away from largely white projects. The city also gave preferential treatment to applicants who lived in a neighborhood surrounding a project, thereby giving white families in a neighborhood priority in gaining entrance to predominantly white housing projects.[38]

Some suburbs have similarly used urban-renewal-type programs in an effort to oust unwanted families from their jurisdictions. In 1997, the Chicago suburb of Addison agreed to pay $1.8 million to Hispanic families who had been pushed out of a designated renewal area. The village razed nearly a dozen apartment buildings, in some cases structures that were far from blighted: "It was Mexican removal in the guise of urban renewal," said the lead attorney representing the Leadership Council for Metropolitan Open Communities.[39]

THE GOVERNMENT'S ROLE ASSESSED

In his review of the history of government programs that have affected American urban development, Kenneth Jackson asks, "Has the American government been as benevolent—or at least as neutral—as its defenders claim?"[40] The answer must be a resounding "No!" Urban problems are not purely the result of natural ecological evolution; they are also the consequences of government actions.

Even the contemporary comeback of many big cities is as much the result of government policy as the product of natural market forces. Over the past 40 years, federal assistance has focused on the construction of stadiums, convention centers, aquariums, and other projects designed to enhance the rejuvenation of downtowns. In New Orleans, for instance, federal monies complemented local efforts in building the Convention Center, Riverwalk, Canal Place, and Sheraton Hotel projects. By comparison, much more narrow and limited federal efforts were made to rejuvenate New Orleans neighborhoods, efforts that were further scaled back over the years in the wake of federal spending cutbacks. The "tilt" of federal urban policies has been in favor of downtowns and away from neighborhood revitalization.[41]

Government policy has clearly played a great role in shaping the metropolis. A bold proponent of this perspective might also argue that the government has an obligation to remedy the problems it helped to create.

THE IMPORTANCE OF CORPORATE AND PRIVATE POWER

Government actions, while crucially important, are still not the only influence on urban growth and decline. Powerful private and corporate actors seek to influence development decisions that enhance profit maximization. As Joe R. Feagin and Robert Parker observe in their book *Building American Cities: The*

Urban Real Estate Game, "the most powerful players on the urban scene" include the "array of visible real estate decision makers in industry, finance, development, and construction."[42]

PRIVATE POWER AND SUBURBAN GROWTH

If we look back in history, we can see that natural factors by themselves did not fully determine suburbanization. In the early twentieth century, certain industries moved to sparsely populated sites on the edge of the urban area *before* developments in transportation technology made those sites easily accessible, before trucks became an effective substitute for rail transport, and before a substantial suburbanization of residences occurred:

> Between 1899 and around 1915, corporations began to establish factory districts just beyond the city limits. New suburban manufacturing towns were being built in open space like movie sets. Gary, Indiana, constructed from 1905 to 1908, is the best-known example. Other new industrial satellite suburbs included Chicago Heights, Hammond, East Chicago, and Argo outside Chicago; Lackawanna outside of Buffalo; East St. Louis and Wellston across the river from St. Louis; Norwood and Oakley beyond the Cincinnati limits; and Chester and Norristown near Philadelphia.[43]

What motivated the move of industry to the urban rim during the pre-suburban era? The move was not simply a consequence of new transportation technology or the desire of industrial owners to locate their factories close to an already suburbanized workforce. Rather, factory owners sought suburban plant sites that would allow them to control workers and **to contain labor militancy.**

The late 1880s and 1890s was a period of labor conflict in central cities: "Employers quickly perceived an obvious solution. Move!"[44] The owners of industry sought suburban plant sites to escape the union organizing and labor unrest of the industrial city. In manufacturing suburb of Pullman, south of Chicago, industrial magnate George Pullman, inventor of the railway sleeping car, could control his workforce, offering good company-owned cottages as an inducement to workers, while evicting union organizers and other "trouble-makers" from both their housing and their jobs.

In the mid-twentieth century, private entrepreneurs also played a key role in promoting the growth of suburbia. Landowners and other real estate interests marketed suburbs as the "American dream," as idealized, segregated living environments.[45] The demand for suburban homes was created, at least in part, by the marketing plans and sales pitches of property developers.

The role played by private developers is most clearly revealed in the growth of Los Angeles. The sprawl of the Los Angeles region is often attributed to the region's rapid development during the age of the automobile. Yet, Los Angeles actually began its development as a "spread city" *before* the automobile gained popularity, before the region's famed freeways were built.

The growth of Los Angeles' suburbs in the early 1900s was made possible by the machinations of a private streetcar company, Henry Huntington's

Pacific Electric Railway. Huntington's interest was in real estate, and the railway was simply his way of bringing buyers to his new suburban home sites. Perhaps the finest mass transit system of its day, Huntington's Red Cars (featured in the cartoon movie *Who Framed Roger Rabbit?*) traveled along at speeds of 45 to 55 miles per hour. Huntington's electric railway was over-built and operated at a loss, but the losses did not matter, as the mass transit system was essential to the success of his real estate investments:

> The Pacific Electric lost millions of dollars extending lines far ahead of demands for service, but the loss was compensated many times over by the profits from land sales by the Huntington Land and Improvement Company. In fact, the system was built not to provide transportation but to sell real estate.[46]

The dispersed settlement pattern of Los Angeles was established well before the arrival of the automobile; it was produced by the needs of real estate speculation.

PRIVATE INSTITUTIONS, RACIAL STEERING, AND CENTRAL-CITY DISINVESTMENT

The actions of private institutions also help to explain patterns of racial segregation and neighborhood growth and decline. Under **racial steering,** realtors help guide white home seekers to one neighborhood and minority home seekers to another. As we have already seen, the racial steering of the FHA was reflective of practices prevalent among private realtors.

In many cities, the resegregation and quick decline of urban neighborhoods were also the result of the **blockbusting and panic selling** tactics employed by unscrupulous realtors and mortgage lenders. These realtors and financiers sought the fees and profits that could be made from the quick turnover of housing. To prompt white owners to sell their homes, agents would prominently introduce a black family into the neighborhood; white owners would then be counseled to rush and sell their homes before the neighborhood declined and the investment value of their homes would be diminished.

Today, racial steering, blockbusting, and other similar techniques are no longer legal. Yet these practices still exist in modified form, especially as violations of the law are hard to detect and prove in court.

The power and practices of private credit institutions also go a long way to determining neighborhood prosperity and decline. Private institutions ultimately determine which neighborhoods receive an injection of cash for housing rehabilitation and new construction, and which, receiving no such investment, suffer accelerated deterioration and decline.

Redlining refers to the practice whereby credit institutions make few if any loans in areas of a city or community that credit officers see as posing greater-than-desired financial risks. The red line denotes an area within which home loans are seen to be too risky an investment. At one time, banks and other credit institutions actually drew a line on a map to indicate those parts of the city in which they would make no investments. The result of such **disinvestment** was to take away the money necessary for the potential rehabilitation and growth of declining urban areas. In effect, redlining cut off the economic blood for new construction and community upkeep.

Public law now prohibits redlining; banks and other financial institutions can no longer draw a red line on a map or otherwise write off entire sections of a city when dispensing loans. Yet redlining, too, can be seen to continue in a greatly modified form. In troubled neighborhoods, mortgage finance institutions extend loans for condominium and cooperative conversions while denying financing to landlords who wish to rehabilitate affordable apartment buildings and to inner-city homeowners who wish to make major home repairs.

Evidence points to continuing discrimination in lending patterns despite the protections offered by federal law. One study found that black-owned firms received smaller loans than did white applicants with similar characteristics.[47] A Richmond, Virginia jury in 1998 ordered Nationwide Insurance to pay $100.5 million in damages to a local housing group that sued the company for being reluctant to insure homes in black neighborhoods. Although Nationwide did not refuse all loan applications from black neighborhoods, the company still used race as a consideration when making loans, instructing its agents to avoid "black urbanite households with many children."[48]

Federal law has sought to end redlining and put lending institutions under pressure to provide home and small business loans in underserved areas of the city. The **Community Reinvestment Act (CRA) of 1977** seeks to ensure that banks make loans in communities, including poorer communities, from which they receive deposits. The CRA requires that mortgage finance institutions disclose where they make their loans; community groups can then use this information to pressure credit institutions that fail to make loans to minority applicants in inner-city neighborhoods.

In the late 1980s and early 1990s, housing advocacy groups used the CRA to induce credit institutions to make new loans in disadvantaged communities. The CRA even gave community organizations the right to challenge bank mergers if a bank had failed to meet its obligations under the CRA. In various cities across the nation, ACORN (the Association of Community Organizations for Reform Now) and other community groups threatened to oppose specific bank mergers, and by doing so convinced financial institutions to commit millions of dollars in new loans for inner-city businesses and low-income mortgages.

Some banks look upon the requirements of the CRA as an opportunity to make new loans, strengthen the community, and, in the process, strengthen the bank. These banks advertise the availability of residential and commercial loans. They work with—and even help fund—community groups such as ACORN to identify potential home buyers, screen loan applicants for the banks, and counsel low-income prospects as to how to budget their funds. In Cleveland, Chicago, and Pittsburgh, the CRA agreements helped lead banks to "'rediscover' the inner city as a viable and profitable market."[49]

Other credit institutions, however, continue to drag their feet and are reluctant to make loans to applicants who are not deemed "credit-worthy." Evidence of continued redlining persists despite the mandates of the CRA. Mortgage lenders' determinations of "creditworthiness" continue to be influenced by the race of loan applicants and not just by economic factors.[50]

The CRA has helped to produce tens (if not hundreds) of billions of dollars in loans to low-income and minority households in communities that might otherwise have been overlooked. Still, the public disclosure requirements of the CRA are not much of a threat except in those few neighborhoods where active community organizations are vigilant in monitoring the practices of local credit institutions. Banks have little difficulty satisfying the CRA requirements; in 1998, only 15 banks of the 772 examined, or about 2 percent, received less than a satisfactory grade from regulators.[51]

Despite the CRA's successes, mortgage institutions and free-market conservatives complain about the costs of compliance. In the mid-1990s, the Republican majorities in Congress began consideration of bills that would relax the CRA's requirements, exempting nearly 88 percent of the nation's banks from the CRA's provisions.[52] Republican Senator Phil Gramm of Texas argued that "professional protest groups" such as ACORN had used the CRA to extort benefits from financials institution and to force those institutions to cede to quotas for both lending and hiring.[53] In 1999, the Gramm-Leach-Bliley Act modified the CRA, easing the requirements of the Act as they applied to small banks and savings institutions. The result has been to weaken the CRA, as a large percentage of home lending is done by credit institutions that either are not annually reviewed or are not subject to the CRA's community reinvestment requirements.[54]

PRIVATE POWER AND URBAN RENEWAL

Urban renewal was a program in the 1950s and 1960s that sought to rebuild slum neighborhoods. Yet, in a number of ways, urban renewal worsened the living conditions of the urban poor; The program often responded more to the desires of corporate officials than to the needs of inner-city residents.

Urban renewal tore down more housing than it built; displaced residents were crowded into other impoverished neighborhoods. In numerous cities, urban renewal became synonymous with **Negro removal,** as "the federal bulldozer" was used to remove minorities from sections of the city near more exclusive white neighborhoods.[55]

How did a program aimed at the elimination of slums and urban blight go wrong? Private sector and governmental actors shaped the program to achieve their own ends. Downtown business owners used the program to acquire land to build an expanded central business district that could compete with the lure of suburban malls. Local hospitals and universities, too, sought room for expansion and modernization. Corporate and institutional elites and their political allies used urban renewal to clear out the poor and minorities who lived in the path of commercial and institutional expansion. The new housing that was built in renewal areas was often too expensive to be afforded by the former residents of the neighborhood; downtown business leaders backed plans that built housing for persons with good buying power, not the poor.

All these problems associated with urban renewal were apparent in Chicago at mid-century.[56] Downtown oriented business officials designed a redevelopment plan to attract customers back to the city's economically troubled downtown. Michael Reese Hospital and the Illinois Institute of Technology sought expanded campuses. Corporate and institutional leaders needed the city's help in acquiring desired land and in clearing the poor from the targeted renewal areas. The city exercised its power of **eminent domain** to take (with appropriate compensation) the land from private owners for public purposes. The renewal sites were then turned over to developers at a fraction of their real costs. Many of the displaced minority residents were often rehoused in a long row of massive public housing projects, known in Chicago as "The Wall." The University of Chicago helped shape an urban renewal program that effectively constructed a buffer zone between the campus and the surrounding black community, an effort designed to maintain the University's attractiveness to faculty and students. The University not only opposed construction of public housing in the immediate renewal area, it actually demolished sound buildings and displaced existing tenants.

PRIVATE POWER AS A CAUSE OF HOMELESSNESS

There are numerous reasons why people go homeless. Some individuals are drug users and alcoholics. Others are former mental patients who have been left to wander the streets as a result of deinstitutionalization. Still others are unable to pay the rent because of low pay, the loss of a job, marital breakup, or a family crisis.

Yet it is too simplistic to view contemporary urban homelessness solely as the consequence of individual failings. Homelessness also results from the actions taken by private sector actors and public officials. The "shortage of low-income housing, the impact of changing technology on work, the globalization of the economy, and the labor market that dooms certain kinds of workers to economic marginality"[57] all act to create homelessness. Government policies, including the deinstitutionalization of psychiatric patients and the cutback in social welfare and public housing assistance, too, increase the number of the homeless.

The **single room occupancy (SRO) hotel** once offered the poor one last refuge from the streets. SROs are not what tourists would consider hotels. Instead, SROs are run-down and decrepit facilities, often in undesirable parts of town, where a poor person with a few dollars can find a place to sleep for the night. Today, however, in many cities, SRO hotels and the flophouses of **skid row** have all but disappeared as private developers and public redevelopment officials have built new office and retail complexes, convention centers, and luxury apartment buildings in areas that were once the site of SRO housing. With the destruction of a city's stock of SRO housing, its poorest residents have lost their last alternative to the municipal shelter and the streets.[58]

Homelessness is also a result of the restructuring of American industry. As corporations have moved production facilities overseas, the good-paying industrial jobs once found in cities in the United States have disappeared. In the face of rising rents, the loss of a job or any disruption in the income stream can leave a family homeless.[59]

Economic restructuring has acted to make families headed by women especially vulnerable to homelessness. "Women's jobs" pay low wages, are often part time, and lack economic security. Homelessness among women and children also results because young men facing economic uncertainty do not always make good partners; women and their children must leave the home to escape abusive relationships and bad marriages. Divorced or single poor women with children are especially prime candidates for homelessness.[60]

THE SHIFT TO THE SUNBELT

Historically, urban development patterns in the United States have been shaped by two great waves of migration: the poor migrated to the cities, and the middle class moved to the suburbs. A third and more recent demographic wave has seen the shift of population and jobs from the Frostbelt to the Sunbelt. By 1980, the regional shift had already become quite pronounced. Almost all those cities that gained population over the previous decade were located in the South and the West; those that lost population were mostly in the Northeast and North Central regions of the country (see Table 2-1).

THREE EXPLANATIONS OF SUNBELT GROWTH

As we saw in Chapter 1, "The Urban Situation and 9/11," there is no exact consensus as to just what states or areas constitute the Sunbelt. Still, there is general agreement that the term *Sunbelt* denotes those areas of the South and West that have enjoyed a general increase of population and economic activity over the past few decades.

We must exert a bit of caution in making generalizations that characterize such a broad and diverse region. Not all parts of the South and the West share fully in the region's new-found growth. Periods of national recession coupled with the collapse of savings and loan institutions and post-Cold War cutbacks in military spending all hurt local Sunbelt economies. By the late 1990s, some Sunbelt cities lagged behind municipalities in the Northeast and Midwest in terms of employment and economic growth.

■ TABLE 2-1

GROWING AND DECLINING CITIES BY REGION:
CITIES OVER 100,000 POPULATION, 1980

U.S. Region	Number of Cities with 100,000 Plus Population	Number of Cities Gaining Population	Number of Cities Losing Population
Northeast	23	—	23
North Central	39	8	31
South	60	46	14
West	47	39	8
Total	169	93	76

SOURCE: Bureau of the Census, U.S. Department of Commerce News (Washington, DC: June 3, 1981). p. x.

Still, in spite of these downturns, the Sunbelt can generally be viewed as a region of long-term population and economic growth. From 1970 to 1996, annual population growth in metropolitan areas in the West (2.6 percent) and South (2.3 percent) outpaced that in the Northeast (where there was no growth) and the Midwest (where growth averaged a mere 0.3 percent). In terms of employment, the slowest-growing metropolitan areas—New York, Buffalo, Pittsburgh, and Cleveland—were in the Northeast and Midwest; the fastest-growing metropolitan areas—Las Vegas, Austin, Phoenix, Boise, and Santa Ana (California)—were all in the Sunbelt.[61]

What are the reasons that underlie the long-term growth of the Sunbelt? The three general factors that we used to explain suburban growth can also be applied to Sunbelt growth. Sunbelt growth is not simply the result of natural factors; it is also the product of government policies and of corporate and private sector power.

NATURAL FACTORS.   Sunbelt growth can be seen as a natural demographic trend resulting from affluence, innovations in technology, and citizens' preference for the good life. Citizens moved to the Sunbelt in search of warm weather, sunny skies, and good beaches. Florida and Arizona had climates that were especially hospitable to retirees. Other newcomers sought to flee the congestion, overcrowded conditions, crime, and social problems of the cities of the Northeast and Midwest. The arrival of immigrants from Mexico, the Caribbean, Central America, and the Pacific Rim further fueled the growth of Sunbelt cities. Business came, too, when technology permitted, as a. result of the availability of cheap land.

Technological advances made possible the regional shift in jobs and population. The development of the interstate highway system and jet plane travel, and breakthroughs in telecopying and telecommunications enabled businesses and people to locate in new regions of the country. Branch firms could be sited in the Sunbelt; corporate executives could fly to meetings as required. Face-to-face meetings could be dispensed with altogether as executives can "meet" by teleconference and fax documents around the country as needed.

Air conditioning is one often-overlooked technological innovation that made possible the growth of the Sunbelt. With the marvel of machine-cooled air, no longer was much of the South a "hot belt," inhospitable to office work. With air conditioning, people were increasingly willing to move to a city like Miami, which had been built on a swamp.

GOVERNMENT POLICY.   Government programs also assisted the growth of Sunbelt communities. Most important among these programs was **spending by the Defense Department** and the government-supported defense industry. World War II production provided a major stimulus to Sunbelt growth as "the armed forces made deliberate efforts to relocate their personnel and training facilities around the country and to spread out defense contracts in order to make bombing and even invasion more difficult for the enemy."[62] Warm-weather cities provided ideal sites for port activities, troop training, and airplane testing. New Orleans, Atlanta, Fort Worth, Oklahoma City, San

Antonio, Albuquerque, Phoenix, Los Angeles, and San Diego all witnessed great expansion as the site of aircraft production facilities and military bases.[63] Production in many of these facilities continued through the Cold War. The massive expenditures on the **space program** further spurred the economies of Florida (with launches at Cape Canaveral) and Texas (with NASA's Johnson Space Center located in Houston).

Military **procurement**—the buying of military materiel—further abetted Sunbelt growth. From 1951 to 1981, the amount spent by the Defense Department on prime contracts increased by 810 percent in the South and 402 percent in the West; during the same period the amount allocated to the Midwest decreased by 1.5 percent.[64] The military simply sought to buy supplies from contractors conveniently located near its installations. Often, southern suppliers also proved to be cheaper because of the low levels of unionization and the low wage structure in the region. Aircraft carriers were retrofitted in the naval yards of Norfolk, Virginia, and not in Philadelphia or New York City.

National defense and aerospace spending was also the fuel that propelled Silicon Valley's vigorous growth. The region's educational infrastructure (anchored by Stanford University) and the spirited entrepreneurship of cyberspace engineers cannot by themselves explain the region's phenomenal takeoff. Silicon Valley was a national leader in terms of government contracts for missile guidance systems and other electronic components and production devices. Defense contracts even helped to pay for the expensive recruitment and relocation of engineers to the region.[65]

The **regional bias of the programs of the Federal Housing Administration** also worked to promote new home construction in the region. The FHA sees its job as helping people to obtain mortgages wherever they want to buy a home. If people want to buy homes in the Sunbelt, the FHA is only too willing to guarantee loans made to qualified buyers. As a result, communities in California, Florida, Texas, and Arizona have been prime beneficiaries of the home loan guarantees provided by the FHA. In the absence of the FHA, a much smaller number of families would have been able to move to the Sunbelt.

The **federal tax code**, especially its provisions for homeowners, similarly helped facilitate home purchases in the region. Such tax write-offs as the investment tax credit and accelerated depreciation on the purchase of new facilities and equipment also subsidized the shift of new commercial activity to the region. Tax incentives given to the oil, gas, and energy industries further spurred economic development in the South and West. Houston's growth is in part due to the favorable tax treatment given to the petrochemical industry. Over the years, the federal government further assisted Houston's growth with grants for infrastructure development, notably for port development and highway construction, and spending related to the space program.[66]

While the 1993 **North American Free Trade Agreement (NAFTA)** postdates much of the regional shift to the Sunbelt, it may prove to be another federal policy that boosts the economies of a number of Sunbelt cities. Scholars, however, are still attempting to study the exact regional effects of NAFTA. It appears that NAFTA has had some positive effect on the growth of such border communities as Brownsville, Laredo, El Paso, and San Antonio.

CORBIS

The Port of Houston in Deer Park, Texas. Federal assistance helped to build a ship channel running 50 miles inland from the Gulf of Mexico to Houston. The channel was critical to Houston's growth and economic development.

Reports point to increases in jobs in the manufacturing, financial services, legal, and hotel and restaurants sectors in border communities as NAFTA eased cross-border trade. Nearly 31,000 new jobs were created in El Paso from 1993 to 2000; while much of this growth may be due to a bullish national economy, some of the gain can be reasonably credited to NAFTA.[67] Representatives from the Northeast and the Midwest also complain that NAFTA unfairly steers economic development assistance and funds for pollution cleanup to the U.S.-Mexico border while slighting similar concerns in the Great Lakes region along the Canadian border.

Yet NAFTA also brought new problems to border communities. Cities along major truck routes to Mexico experienced new traffic congestion and pollution. Border communities in Texas and Arizona also suffered a loss of jobs to the extent that lifting of tariffs allowed corporations to shift production factories across the Rio Grande.[68]

Aggressive action by local governments has also been essential to the dynamic emergence of a number of Sunbelt cities. The municipal governments of Houston, San Antonio, and San Jose all incurred vast debts in order to undertake the sewer, street, highway, and other infrastructure improvements necessary for Sunbelt expansionism. In the post-World War II period, Houston boosted its debt by a factor of eight in order to finance the city's public construction boom. As Heywood Sanders observes, "Contrary to the notion that Houston's development was built on a *limited local state,* or a form of urban development fully dominated by free enterprise, the city's public sector actively fueled and sustained the urban development process with public dollars"[69] (emphasis in the original). San Jose's boom in the 1960s was similarly brought about by an unprecedented level of public capital investment.

Public investment programs undertaken by local officials were likewise essential to Los Angeles' growth as the nation's number-two city. L.A.'s preeminence was not pre-ordained by its climate and Pacific location. Instead, **local statism,** an aggressive and expensive program of local government investment in the region's port, airport, and rail facilities, remade Los Angeles as a dynamic hub of industry and global trade. Sustained public spending was the key to improving the region's air, sea, and rail connections, enabling L.A. to emerge as a global center of containerization and the intermodal transfer of cargo.[70]

PRIVATE POWER. The actions of private sector actors similarly help to explain much of the shift of commerce and industry to the South and West. Factory owners sought locations in the low-wage states of the Sunbelt, states that had laws that enabled owners to undercut workforce unionization, minimize taxes, and reduce the costs of complying with state and local environmental and social regulations. In the middle of the twentieth century, the textile industry moved from New England to the South to escape the militancy of unionized workforces in the North. States in the South had **right-to-work laws** that weakened labor unions; as workers in the South could not be forced to join a union, employers could discourage unionization by hiring nonunion workers. A general antiunion climate of state and local governments in the South coupled with lower wage rates soon acted to attract other industries to the region.

Sunbelt cities also attracted business as a result of a civic attitude that can be labeled **economic boosterism.** Historically, in northern cities, powerful coalitions of Democratic Party politicians, their ethnic constituencies, vocal minority groups, and powerful municipal labor unions all posed a challenge to business priorities. In southwestern municipalities, in contrast, the political terrain was much less contested; the business community was able to rule essentially without challenge. As a result, municipal governments in the Southwest reflected the desires of the business community; tax burdens were lower, and spending was less oriented toward social problems as contrasted to cities in the Northeast and the Midwest.[71] Only in recent years have minority and neighborhood groups begun to challenge the business community's hold on public affairs in Sunbelt cities.

URBAN PROBLEMS IN THE SUNBELT

Growth in the Sunbelt brought with it numerous problems, not just advantages. The growing cities of the Sunbelt have to find the means to pay for new highways, schools, and other improvements in infrastructure.

Cities such as Dallas, Houston, and Los Angeles suffer monumental automobile congestion problems. Numerous communities in California and the Southwest suffer from water shortages. Homes built near combustible foliage in drought-plagued areas have led to the problem of chronic fires (especially in California communities where fires are whipped by the seasonable, hot Santa

Ana winds).[72] Houston faces the problem of land **subsidence;** parts of the city are actually sinking because water was pumped out of the ground to make way for development.

Coping with overcrowded schools in fast-growing cities is a particularly difficult problem. Constitutional and statutory limitations on taxing and borrowing often make impossible the construction of new school facilities. In overcrowded districts, students are too often shunted off to makeshift class-rooms in annexes and trailers. In Los Angeles, the school board has considered year-round schooling—having students attend schools on different overlap-ping schedules throughout the entire 12 months of the calendar year, thereby relieving classroom overcrowding without having to incur the huge expense of building new schools.

Growth also compounds environmental problems. Florida's rapidly grow-ing urban areas have led to the disturbance of wildlife habitats and a reduction in the acreage devoted to agriculture. In the Los Angeles basin, air pollution has become so severe that very drastic solutions have been proposed. At one time, the South Coast Air Quality Management District and the Southern California Association of Governments even urged the adoption of a quite rad-ical plan to reduce emissions where residents "may be forced to buy methanol and electric cars, ride to work in van pools, mow their lawns by hand, and spray their underarms with manually pumped deodorant."[73] The plan also sought to improve the jobs-housing balance in the region by discouraging commercial development near the coast and encouraging businesses to locate nearer to inland population centers and affordable housing, reducing the length of daily automobile commuting trips.

The stereotype of Sunbelt prosperity also overlooks the fact that growth has been unevenly distributed in the region. The new prosperity has not reached every small and mid-sized city. Fresno (California) and New Orleans suffer fiscal and social problems so severe that in many ways these communities appear to have more in common with Frostbelt cities than with their Sunbelt neighbors. Even the more economically dynamic, large cities of the Sunbelt contain substantial **pockets of poverty,** with hundreds of thousands of people living below the poverty line, despite the region's general prosperity.

The Sunbelt's economic bubble burst in the 1980s. The region lost many of its textile mills to low-wage competition in Taiwan and Singapore, oil prices tumbled, and defense spending was cut back as the Cold War came to an end. By 1989, nine of the ten metropolitan areas with the highest rates of unemploy-ment were in the Sunbelt: McAllen, Laredo, Brownsville, and El Paso in Texas; Shreveport, Houma-Thibodaux, and Alexandria in Louisiana; Modesto, California; and Mobile, Alabama. Flint, Michigan, was the only Frostbelt representative among the 10 cities on the list.[74]

A new division among Sunbelt communities also emerged as a function of a city's position in a globalized economy. While Los Angeles, Dallas, Miami, Atlanta, and other internationally connected communities have emerged as centers of global information and corporate headquarters, other Sunbelt communities have seen their economies slow or stagnate.[75]

Low tax rates by themselves may no longer be sufficient to guarantee the continuing economic competitiveness of Sunbelt communities. The 1990s economic resurgence of a number of Frostbelt communities is instructive. Cities in high-amenity states such as Michigan, Wisconsin, Minnesota, and Massachusetts provided the services and a quality of life that succeeded in attracting new business development despite relatively high tax rates. Sunbelt cities were beginning to find that they could no longer simply rely solely on their low-tax, low-wage, antiunion reputations. They would have to make the investments in education, human resource development, and the community amenities that many business leaders expect.

CONCLUSIONS

The contemporary urban condition cannot be traced to "natural" factors alone. "Hidden" government urban policies and private sector power are also responsible for producing a contemporary urban condition marred by suburban sprawl, deep racial and class divisions, and regional shifts of population and jobs. In recent years, economic elites have shifted production to Latin American and Pacific Rim nations, further weakening local economies. The "bright spots" of the contemporary urban story—the downtown revival, the renaissance of Frostbelt cities, and the upgrading of gentrified neighborhoods—all do little to offset the long-term trends. The urban crisis continues in a good many ways.

What are the implications of the demographic trends, government policies, and private sector actions discussed in this chapter? The evolution of metropolitan areas has produced the following important patterns:

1. **The fragmentation of metropolitan areas.** Each metropolitan area comprises an integrated economic entity.[76] Cities and suburbs are interdependent and cannot prosper without one another. The economic interdependence of municipalities is clearly evident in commuting patterns. Many suburbanites commute to central-city workplaces; city residents increasingly "reverse commute" to the growing number of jobs in the suburbs; the residents of one suburb drive to work in other suburbs.

   Yet when it comes time for governance, there is little recognition of this economic interdependence. For purposes of governance, the metropolitan area is fragmented or divided into numerous smaller, independent units—cities, counties, townships, suburbs, and special districts—that owe little legal responsibility to one another. Each can afford to pursue those actions in such areas as land use and taxing that are of greatest benefit to its residents. The negative impacts of such actions on surrounding communities need not be considered.

2. **The separation of resources from need.** The evolution of U.S. cities and suburbs has resulted in an unbalanced metropolis. In a pattern that can be called **dual migration,** the poor and racial minorities continue to move into cities while the well-to-do middle class moves out to the suburbs. Suburban land-use and zoning practices coupled with

discriminatory housing practices help to reinforce the unbalanced nature of the American metropolis. Central cities have become centers of populations in need of expensive services in such areas as public education, language instruction, mental health, and social welfare. Taxable resources, however, increasingly lie in suburban jurisdictions beyond the reach of central-city governments.

Unbalanced development also characterizes suburbia. Not all suburbs are bastions of wealth and prosperity. Instead, many suburbs are the sites of overcrowded schools, antiquated industrial plants, aging infrastructure, and populations in need. The situation for such troubled suburbs is the same as it is for troubled central cities; both lack the ability to tap the taxable resources of the metropolis to provide for their populations in need.

3. **Racial imbalance in the metropolis.** Dual migration, exclusionary land-use practices, racial steering, and discriminatory lending practices have acted to create a distribution of population across the metropolis that is marred by severe racial imbalance. The arrival of new immigrant groups, especially from Latin America and Asia, has added to the numbers and diversity of the minority population of "gateway" cities."[77]

   Not all suburbs can be characterized as "vanilla" communities. Some suburbs have experienced substantial integration. Others, such as Baldwin Park in suburban Los Angeles, are minority-dominated. Minority suburbanization has increased in recent years. Yet, minority families still do not find all suburbs equally open to them. The result is severe racial imbalance and isolation, in both residential neighborhoods and in the public schools.

4. **Prospects for minority power in the central city.** In one respect, the growing numbers of racial minorities in central cities offers minorities a certain advantage—a heightened chance of political power. Over the years, growing black populations have helped elect black mayors in a number of cities, including New York, Chicago, Cleveland, Detroit, Gary, Philadelphia, Newark, Oakland (California), San Francisco, New Orleans, Charlotte, Atlanta, and Birmingham (Alabama). Among the cities that have seen the election of Hispanic mayors are Los Angeles, Miami, San Antonio, and Denver. Yet, as we shall see later in this book, prospects for minority power are dependent not only on the size of a group's population but on the abilities of its leaders to construct workable intergroup alliances.

5. **The changing position of cities in the postindustrial, globalized economy.** Heavy industry no longer dominates the American economy. The United States has moved to a postindustrial economy marked by increased levels of education, a shift to service industries, and technological breakthroughs in such areas as communications and information processing.

The effect of this economic transformation on cities has been immense. Advances in communications and transportation have increased the viability of suburban and Sunbelt commercial sites. In contrast, numerous communities that were dependent on manufacturing suffered a long-term decline. Some have undergone a difficult but successful transition; others have been unable to diversify their economic base or find a new role for themselves in a changed national economy. The long-term decline of Detroit, with its undiversified economy and reliance on the automobile industry, stands out as a case in point.

Urban-sociologist John Kasarda argues that cities must find new roles in a service economy if they are to prosper. According to Kasarda, headquarters offices, finance, marketing, research, and communications are the new growth industries for cities. To be competitive, cities must invest in rewiring and other infrastructure improvements to meet the needs of modern information-processing offices. They must also spend funds on quality-of-life amenities that will make a city attractive to higher-income residents and corporate personnel.[78]

Mayor John Street sought to increase Philadelphia's attractiveness to business and technologically competent workers when he announced his plans to make his entire city a wireless "hot spot." Philadelphia planned to install 4,000 wireless antennas on street poles in order to offer all citizens subsidized, high-speed internet access. The mayor argued that the municipal program would also span the "digital divide" by bringing increased Internet access into poorer neighborhoods. Critics, however, pointed to the costs of the program and the difficulties that the city would have in keeping its system state of the art. Philadelphia was not the only city to go wireless. Cleveland offered free Internet access via 4,000 transmitters to anyone in the city's Midtown, University Circle, and lakefront areas.[79]

The poor occupy a precarious position in the information-age, postindustrial city. Even where cities find a new "fit" in the global economy, the jobs available in a technology-based age may be beyond the skills of the poor. Municipal investment in facilities and services designed to attract global businesses and their workforces may also mean that less money is available for social services for the poor.

Strategies for long term economic adaptation also offer no guarantee of local fiscal health. In a global economy, American cities face increased competition from low-wage nations in Latin America and the Pacific Rim. Assembly and data processing services once based in U.S. cities are now increasingly being provided by low-wage workers in South Asia.

The decisions of multinational corporations exert a strong influence on a city's health. The growth and decline of cities is also dependent on larger economic cycles and forces over which localities can exert little control. The sudden downturn in economic vitality of Sunbelt cities in the 1980s and 1990s, the economic "bust' of the Texas "oil patch," and the sudden loss of interest of Japanese corporations in Los Angeles real estate all remind us of the tenuous character of local economic health in a global age.

The impact of globalization and the continued transformation of American cities are the subjects of our next chapter.

NOTES

1. Edward C. Banfield, *The Unheavenly City Revisited* (Boston: Little, Brown, 1974), pp. 25–51.

2. Kenneth T. Jackson, *Crabgrass Frontier: The Suburbanization of the United States* (New York: Oxford University Press, 1985), pp. 14–15. Also see Sam Bass Warner, Jr., *Streetcar Suburbs: The Process of Growth in Boston, 1870–90,* 2nd ed. (Cambridge, MA: Harvard University Press, 1978), pp. 15–16.

3. David R. Goldfield and Blaine R. Brownell, *Urban America: A History,* 2nd ed. (Boston: Houghton Mifflin, 1990), p. 152.

4. Jackson, *Crabgrass Frontier,* pp. 12–45, especially p. 13.

5. Warner, *Streetcar Suburbs,* pp. 164–65. Also see Ronald Dale Karr, "Brookline Rejects Annexation, 1873," in *Suburbia Re-examined,* ed. Barbara M. Kelly (New York: Greenwood Press, 1989), pp. 103–110.

6. Warner, *Streetcar Suburbs,* p. 165.

7. Joe William Trotter, Jr., ed., *The Great Migration in Historical Perspective: New Dimensions of Race, Class, and Gender* (Bloomington: University of Indiana Press, 1991).

8. Robert Fishman, *Bourgeois Utopias: The Rise and Fall of Suburbia* (New York: Basic Books, 1987), pp. 184–187.

9. Leonard I. Ruchelman, *Cities in the Third Wave: The Technological Transformation of Urban America* (Chicago: Burnham, 2000), pp. 43–44.

10. Joel Garreau, *Edge City: Life on the New Frontier* (New York: Doubleday, 1991).

11. Robert D. Atkinson, "Technological Change and Cities," *Cityscape: A Journal of Policy Development and Research* 3, 1 (1998): 135–136.

12. Paul E. Peterson, "Introduction," in *The New Urban Reality,* ed. Paul E. Peterson (Washington, DC: Brookings Institution, 1985), p. 1.

13. John D. Kasarda, "Urban Change and Minority Opportunities," in *The New Urban Reality,* pp. 33–42.

14. Banfield, *The Unheavenly City Revisited,* p. 26.

15. Clarence Stone, "The Politics of Urban Restructuring: A Review Essay," *Western Political Quarterly* 43 (March 1990): pp. 219–231; the quotation appears on p. 222.

16. Janet Rothenberg Pack, ed., *Sunbelt/Frostbelt: Public Policies and Market Forces in Metropolitan Development* (Washington, DC: Brookings Institution, 2005), traces the continuing impact of government spending and regulatory actions on the health of local communities.

17. Jackson, *Crabgrass Frontier,* p. 204.

18. David L. Kirp, John P. Dwyer, and Larry A. Rosenthal, *Our Town: Race, Housing, and the Soul of Suburbia* (New Brunswick, NJ: Rutgers University Press, 1997), p. 27.

19. Quoted in Jackson, *Crabgrass Frontier,* p. 207.

20. Ibid., p. 208.

21. Citizens Commission on Civil Rights, *A Decent Home...A Report on the Continuing Failure of the Federal Government to Provide Equal Housing Opportunity* (Washington, DC: 1983), reprinted in *Critical Perspectives on Housing,* ed. Rachel G. Bratt, Chester Hartman, and Ann Myerson (Philadelphia: Temple University Press, 1986), p. 299.

22. Ibid., p. 301.

23. Thomas J. Sugrue, *The Origins of the Urban Crisis: Race and Inequality in Postwar Detroit* (Princeton, NJ: Princeton, University Press, 1996), p. 64.

24. Benjamin Kleinberg, *Urban America in Transformation* (Thousand Oaks, CA.: Sage Publications, 1995), p. 114.

25. Dennis R. Judd, *The Politics of American Cities,* 3rd ed. (Glenview, IL: Scott, Foresman, 1988), p. 281.

26. Rachel G. Bratt, *Rebuilding a Low-Income Housing Policy* (Philadelphia: Temple University Press, 1989), pp. 123–130.

27. Kenneth R. Harney, "Federal Tax Code Favors Home Owners," *Los Angeles Times,* February 10, 2002.

28. Peter Dreier and John Atlas, "The Mansion Subsidy: Why Should Our Tax Code Underwrite the Lifestyles of the Rich and Famous?" *The New Democrat* (January/February 1997): www.dlcppi.org/tnd/9701/essay2.html.

29. Harney, "Federal Tax Code Favors Home Owners."

30. Raymond A. Mohl, "Race and Space in the Modern City: Interstate-95 and the Black Community in Miami," in *Urban Policy in Twentieth-Century America,* ed. Arnold R. Hirsch and Raymond A. Mohl (New Brunswick, NJ: Rutgers University Press, 1993), p. 102.

31. For a discussion of the impact of federal transportation policy on urban areas, see Schneider, *Suburban Growth,* pp. 13–34 and 233–245.

32. Paul Kantor with Stephen David, *The Dependent City: The Changing Political Economy of Urban America* (Glenview, IL: Scott, Foresman, 1988), p. 99.

33. John H. Mollenkopf, *The Contested City* (Princeton, NJ: Princeton University Press, 1983), pp. 103–109.

34. Michael P. Smith *City, State, and Market* (New York: Blackwell, 1988), p. 55, cited by Kleinberg, *Urban America in Transformation,* p. 237.

35. Arnold R. Hirsch, "Searching for a 'Sound Negro Policy'": A Racial Agenda for the Housing Acts of 1949 and 1954," *Housing Policy Debate* 11, 2 (2000): 393–441.

36. Arnold R. Hirsch, *Making the Second Ghetto: Race and Housing in Chicago, 1940–60* (Chicago: University of Chicago Press, 1983 and 1998).

37. Susan J. Popkin, et al., "The Gautreaux Legacy: What Might Mixed-Income and Dispersal Strategies Mean for the Poorest Public Housing Tenants?" *Housing Policy Debate* 11, 4 (2000): 911–942; Brian Turetsky, "The Lack of Affordable Housing and Its Impact on Minorities" (Washington, DC: Lawyers' Committee for Civil Rights Under Law, 2003).

38. Robert Pear, "New York Admits to Racial Steering in Housing Lawsuit," *The New York Times,* July 1, 1992.

39. Melita Marie Garza and Flynn McRoberts, "Addison Settles with Hispanics," *Chicago Tribune,* August 8, 1997.

40. Jackson, *Crabgrass Frontier,* p. 191.

41. Mickey Lauria, Robert K. Whelan, and Alma H. Young, "The Revitalization of New Orleans," in *Urban Revitalization: Policies and Programs,* ed. Fritz W. Wagner, Timothy E. Joder, and Anthony J. Mumphrey, Jr. (Thousand Oaks, CA: Sage Publications, 1995), pp. 102–127.

42. Joe R. Feagin and Robert Parker, *Building American Cities: The Urban Real Estate Game,* 2nd ed. (Englewood Cliffs, NJ: Prentice-Hall, 1990), p. 16.

43. David M. Gordon, "Capitalist Development and the History of American Cities," in *Marxism and the Metropolis,* 2nd ed., ed. William K. Tabb and Larry Sawers (New York: Oxford University Press, 1984), p. 40.

44. Ibid., p. 41.

45. Judd, *The Politics of American Cities,* pp. 169–172.

46. David L. Clark, "Improbable Los Angeles," in *Sunbelt Cities: Politics and Growth Since World War II*, ed. Richard M. Bernard and Bradley R. Rice (Austin: University of Texas Press, 1983), pp. 271–272. Also see David Brodsly, *L.A. Freeway* (Berkeley: University of California Press, 1981), pp. 68–71.

47. Timothy Bates, "Unequal Access: Financial Institution Lending to Black- and White-Owned Small Business Start-ups," *Journal of Urban Affairs* 19, 4 (1997): 487–495

48. Joseph P. Treaster, "Insurer Must Pay $100.5 Million in Redlining Case," *The New York Times,* October 27, 1998.

49. Alex Schwartz, "The Limits of Community Reinvestment: The Implementation of Community Reinvestment Agreements in Chicago, Cleveland, New Jersey, and Pittsburgh" (paper presented at the annual meeting of the Urban Affairs Association, Fort Worth, Texas, April 22–25, 1998).

50. For a business journal article that points to the continued racial disparities in mortgage lending and insurance practices, see "The New Redlining," a *U.S. News* Investigative Report, *U.S. News & World Report,* April 17, 1995, pp. 51–58.

51. Allan J. Fishbein, General Counsel for the Center for Community Change, testimony before the Senate Committee on Banking, Housing, and Urban Affairs, Hearings on the "Financial Services Act of 1998," June 24, 1998.

52. "The New Redlining," pp. 51 and 56–58.

53. Christi Harlan, "Why Gramm Strangled Bank Bill," *Austin American-Statesman,* October 23, 1998.

54. William C. Apgar and Mark Duda, "The Twenty-Fifth Anniversary of the Community Reinvestment Act: Past Accomplishments and Future Regulatory Challenges," *FRBNY (Federal Reserve Bank of New York) Economic Policy Review* (June 2003): p. 174. For analyses of more recent proposed program revisions that would weaken the Act, see: Robert E. Rubin and Michael Rubinger, "Don't Let Banks Turn Their Backs on the Poor," *The New York Times,* December 4, 2004; and the National Community Reinvestment Coalition, "NCRC Memo on the New CRA Proposal by FDIC, OCC, FRB," 2004, available at www.ncrc.org/pressandpubs/press_releases/documents/NCRC_analy_FDICOCCFRB_prop.doc.

55. Martin Anderson, *The Federal Bulldozer: A Critical Analysis of Urban Renewal, 1949–62* (Cambridge, MA: MIT Press, 1964), pp. 6–8; Theodore J. Lowi, *The End of Liberalism* (New York: W. W. Norton, 1969), pp. 251–266; June Manning Thomas and Marsha Ritzdorf, eds., *Urban Planning and the African American Community* (Thousand Oaks, CA: Sage Publications, 1997).

56. The story is told by Hirsch, *Making the Second Ghetto*, pp. 100–170.

57. Doug A. Timmer, D. Stanley Eitzen, and Kathryn D. Talley, *Paths to Homelessness: Extreme Poverty and the Urban Housing Crisis* (Boulder, CO: Westview Press, 1994), p. 5.

58. Charles Hoch and Robert A. Slayton, *New Homeless and Old: Community and the Skid Row Hotel* (Philadelphia: Temple University Press, 1989).

59. Joel Blau, *The Visible Poor: Homelessness in the United States* (New York: Oxford University Press, 1992), pp. 34–47. Martha R. Burt, *Over the Edge: The Growth of Homelessness in the 1980s* (New York: Russell Sage Foundation, 1992).

60. Timmer, Eitzen, and Talley, *Paths to Homelessness,* pp. 26–28; Peter Rossi, *Without Shelter: Homelessness in the 1980s* (New York: Twentieth Century Fund, 1989), pp. 34–36.

61. Wyly, Glickman, and Lahr, "A Top 10 List of Things to Know About American Cities," p. 15.
62. Richard M. Bernard and Bradley R. Rice, eds., Introduction to their book *Sunbelt Cities: Politics and Growth Since World War II*, p. 12.
63. Ibid.
64. Virginia Mayer and Margaret Downs, "The Pentagon Tilt: Regional Biases in Defense Spending and Strategy," a publication of the Northeast-Midwest Institute, Washington, DC, January 1983, p. 9.
65. Mia Gray, Elyse Golob, Ann R. Markusen, and Sam Ock Park, "The Four Faces of Silicon Valley," in *Second Tier Cities: Rapid Growth Beyond the Metropolis*, ed. Ann R. Markusen, Yong-Sook Lee, and Sean DiGiovanna (Minneapolis: University of Minnesota Press, 1999), pp. 293–299.
66. Joe R. Feagin, *Free Enterprise City: Houston in Political and Economic Perspective* (New Brunswick, NJ: Rutgers University Press, 1988), pp. 54–55, 63–71, 186–188, 203–204. Also see Mollenkopf, *The Contested City*, pp. 242–251.
67. Lucinda Vargas, *Maquiladoras: Impact on Texas Border Cities*, a report of the Federal Reserve Bank of Dallas, June 2001: www.dallasfed.org/research/border/tbe_vargas.html.
68. See Sam Howe Verhovek, "Benefits of Free-Trade Pact Bypass Texas Border Towns," *The New York Times*, June 23, 1998, and two articles in the September 1993 *Northeast-Midwest Economic Review*, a publication of the Northeast-Midwest Institute (Washington, DC): "Coalition Leaders Protest Focus of NAFTA on Southwest," pp. 3ff., and Eric Hartman and Allegra Cangelosi, "Borderline Case: NAFTA Plan Steers Clean-up Funds to Southwest Only," pp. 9–11.
69. Heywood T. Sanders, "The Political Economy of Sunbelt Urban Development: Building the Public Sector" (paper presented at the annual meeting of the American Political Science Association, New York, September 2–5, 1994).
70. Steven P. Erie, *Globalizing L.A.: Trade, Infrastructure, and Regional Development* (Stanford, CA; Stanford University Press, 2004).
71. Mollenkopf, *The Contested City*, pp. 242–253.
72. Mike Davis, *Ecology of Fear: Los Angeles and the Imagination of Disaster* (Vintage, 1998), pp. 93–148.
73. Robert Reinhold, "Sweeping Changes Weighed to Reduce Los Angeles Smog," *The New York Times*, December 19, 1988.
74. Hilary Stout, "Jobless Aren't Migrating to Boom Areas: Great Disparity in Living Costs Is Major Deterrent," *Wall Street Journal*, February 24, 1989.
75. Carl Abbott, "Through Flight to Tokyo: Sunbelt Cities and the New World Economy, 1960–90," in *Urban Policy in Twentieth-Century America*, ed. Hirsch and Mohl pp. 183–212.
76. Anthony Downs, *New Visions for Metropolitan America* (Washington, DC: Brookings Institution, 1994), pp. 45–59; William R. Barnes and Larry C. Ledebur, *The New Regional Economies: The U.S. Common Market and the Global Economy* (Thousand Oaks, CA: Sage Publications, 1998), pp. 19–48 and 83–100.
77. Audrey Singer, "The Rise of New Immigrant Gateways," a report of The Brookings Institution Living Cities Census Series, Washington, DC (February 2004), available at: www.brook.edu/dybdocroot/urban/pubs/20040301_gateways.pdf.
78. John D. Kasarda, "Urban Change and Minority Opportunities," in *The New Urban Reality*, ed. Peterson, pp. 33–68. Also see "'Cyberopolis': The Cybernetic City Faces the Global Economy," in *The City and the World: New York's Global*

Future, ed. Margaret E. Crahan and Alberto Vourvoulias-Bush (New York: Council on Foreign Relations Press, 1997), pp. 51–69. A city can also promote the fine arts in an effort to build an "amenity infrastructure" that would help make it an attractive site for a high-tech workforce; see Williams S. Hendon and Douglas V. Shaw, "The Arts and Urban Development," in *The Future of Winter Cities. Urban Affairs Annual Review,* vol. 31, ed. Gary Gappert (Newbury Park, CA: Sage Publications, 1987), pp. 209–217. Newark, New Jersey, a city that has faced numerous crises, had built a downtown arts center as the focal point of its revitalization efforts.

79. James Dao, "Philadelphia Hopes for a Wireless Lead," *The New York Times,* February 17, 2005; David P. Caruso, "Philadelphia Joins List of Cities Mulling Wireless Internet for All," AP wire story appearing in *The Detroit News,* September 2, 2004.

RECENT TRENDS: GENTRIFICATION
AND GLOBALIZATION

3

The evolution of metropolitan areas is a never-ending process. Two important new trends are gentrification and globalization. Cities that have adapted to a changed global economy have shown evidence of a rebound and renaissance. The adaptation, though, points to the continuing influence of private actors—real

estate interests and multinational corporations, among others—in reshaping the city to their liking. Gentrification and the city's response to globalization are not determined by economics alone. They also reflect the impact of governmental policy decisions and private power.

GENTRIFICATION: IS THE URBAN CRISIS OVER?

Many United States cities evidenced a renewed vitality after they hit the depths of the urban fiscal crisis of the 1970s. Most visible is the rebirth of once-troubled central business districts. There has also been substantial new housing construction and rehabilitation in sections of cities that previously suffered extensive disinvestment and deterioration.

When the beginnings of neighborhood reinvestment were first observed in the late 1970s and 1980s, newspaper commentators glorified a "back to the city" movement. The movement is also popularly referred to as *gentrification*, as it denotes the rediscovery of city life by young workers, the well-to-do urban "gentry."

Gentrification does not always denote a white "invasion" of poor minority neighborhoods. Chicago's South Side near Lake Michigan has been rediscovered by middle-class and professional African Americans. New York's historic Harlem, too, has seen an influx of black professional and middle-class citizens, in what has sometimes been referred to as Harlem's "Second Renaissance."[1] Local activists warned that the nature of their community was being changed without meeting the needs of the poor and the jobless. Starbucks had even located coffeehouses in both neighborhoods.

THE REDISCOVERY OF THE INNER CITY

Gentrification refers to the upgrading of deteriorated urban neighborhoods that occurs when middle-class families, particularly singles and young marrieds, place new value on city living. Gentrification is especially likely to occur when declining property values make certain inner-city neighborhoods, especially areas that are close to the work and entertainment opportunities of an active downtown, ripe for development. In the early stages of gentrification, such neighborhoods offered houses at bargain prices to young home seekers. Where the inner-city neighborhoods were "discovered" and became fashionable, they attracted professionals and other people capable of paying the soaring price of housing. As the neighborhoods continued to evolve, they lost some of the bohemian and entrepreneurial character of the first wave of gentrification.

Gentrification is an imprecise term that refers to a broad phenomenon. *Urban regeneration, inner-city revitalization, neighborhood renewal and rehabilitation, neighborhood reinvestment, back-to-the-city,* and *urban reinvasion and resettlement* are all among the many terms and phrases that writers have used as synonyms for gentrification.[2] Writers have even used the term broadly to refer to the opening of new suburban-style shopping malls and entertainment centers in once-abandoned core downtowns.

More strictly defined, gentrification does not refer to new commercial ventures or the comeback of a city's central business district. The essence of gentrification is a transformation process that "operates in the residential housing market."[3] Precisely used, gentrification denotes a process of class (and often racial) succession in a neighborhood, where the poor are displaced by more upscale home seekers.

THE BENEFITS AND COSTS OF GENTRIFICATION

Only a couple of decades ago, gentrifying neighborhoods were seen as relatively rare and unique, as interesting exceptions to the more general pattern of central-city decline. Gentrifying neighborhoods were "islands of renewal in seas of decay."[4] Today, however, gentrification is clearly more widespread and is no longer exceptional. As a number of major cities have experienced gentrification, one team of city observers has asked if perhaps the urban crisis should be looked at as "islands of decay in seas of renewal."[5]

Some casual observers have looked at the new construction and investment activity in "reclaimed" areas of cities and have concluded that the urban crisis is over. Gentrification does more than just bring a sense of new vitality to previously declining neighborhoods. Gentrifying neighborhoods attract technologically competent residents who make the city a more competitive site for firms in the high-tech, legal, and financial service sectors. Gentrification also brings new upscale taxpayers to the city, expanding the municipal tax base. Rising property values in neighborhoods on an upward trajectory result in greater tax contributions to the city's coffers. Gentrifying neighborhoods also bring new shops and restaurants to a city, increasing the quality of daily urban life.

Yet, such a paean to the benefits of gentrification overstates both the extent of gentrification and its positive impact on cities. Not all cities across the country have experienced substantial residential resettlement. Gentrified neighborhoods are more typical of corporate headquarters cities with attractive downtowns and tight housing markets. Gentrification is also more likely to occur in those cities with a stock of housing of interesting architectural character located close to an active downtown offering professional job, cultural, and nightlife opportunities. New York, Boston, Philadelphia, Washington, DC, Atlanta, Chicago, Denver, Los Angeles, San Francisco, Seattle, and Portland are among the cities that have witnessed substantial residential reinvestment. The private reclamation of residential areas is much more limited in Detroit, Cleveland, Newark, and numerous cities of the old South.[6]

Even in cities where it does occur, gentrification does not necessarily lead to a better life for all city residents. The conditions of gentrifying neighborhoods can improve without having much effect on the lives of people who live in a city's low-end residential districts. Not too surprisingly, one study of gentrification in New York City in the mid-1980s concluded that "if there are neighborhoods that are revitalizing, they are improving in the midst of a continuing decline for the inner city as a whole."[7] Gentrification is least likely to occur in those worst-off poor and minority neighborhoods with the greatest concentrations of poverty and the highest rates of social disorganization.[8]

Nor does gentrification necessarily draw a wealth of new taxable resources that can be used to improve education and other public services in the city. Study after study has shown that the "back to the city" nature of gentrification is somewhat exaggerated. Gentrification does not really represent a great return of well-off suburban households to the central city; instead, a majority of the gentrifiers are people who moved to a comeback neighborhood from other parts of the city, not from the suburbs. A large number of the new inner-city investors are also people who moved from other parts of the city but had spent their childhoods in the suburbs.[9] Gentrifying neighborhoods are not filled with well-off people who suddenly returned to the city from the suburbs.

On the whole, gentrification does little to offset the long-term migration of population and wealth from the central city to suburbia. Over 80 percent of new homes are built in the suburbs, not in central cities:[10] "Many cities are still starved for new residents and revenues. The movement of new middle-class residents into U.S. cities is a small counter-trend; the dominant trend, by far, is movement away from central cities and towards the suburban periphery."[11] Gentrifying neighborhoods provide impressionistic evidence of city rebirth that masks the continuing nature of the urban crisis.

Even where neighborhood revitalization does occur, new residents are not always willing to support improved services in other parts of the city. Gentrifiers demand service improvements for their own neighborhoods; they want to protect the substantial investment in their homes. Nor are they always willing to support higher taxes for public education.[12] A large number of these new residents either have no children or move to the suburbs as soon as their children are of school age. Others simply choose to send their children to private schools, not the city's relatively poor-quality public schools.

Finally, gentrification also results in a substantial problem of **displacement** as existing residents are pushed out to make way for the newcomers. Even

"Stop Gentrification" graffiti. Graffiti on a wall in New York City's East Village depicts someone about to kick a person sleeping on the street in front of a boutique, a protest against the continuing gentrification occurring in the neighborhood.

where the disadvantaged are not directly pushed out by home buyers and upscale renters, the rising land values and rents in gentrifying neighborhoods make housing increasingly unaffordable to the poor.

Gentrification entails "a process that is fundamentally rooted in class" and "class transformation."[13] Lower-income residents who are displaced must bear the burden of moving; often they can find housing elsewhere only at higher prices than that they were already paying. The burden is especially troublesome for the poor, the elderly, and those on fixed incomes. Due to the higher rates of poverty among female householders, gentrification results in the disproportionate displacement of women and female-headed families.[14]

Gentrification entails the reshaping of neighborhoods for more affluent and technologically competent residents. Urban geographer Neil Smith sees gentrification as a process of neighborhood "invasion" where, in the contest over city space, the so-called "better" classes expropriate poorer and minority areas for their own use.[15]

NEW-STYLE GENTRIFICATION: CORPORATE-LED SUPERGENTRIFICATION

Gentrification was once thought of as a process that commenced when a few "urban pioneers" bought and rehabilitated property in troubled neighborhoods. In some cases, artists moved to distressed areas, taking advantage of the substantial workspace that was offered at low rents. Their arrival signaled the opening of an area to further resettlement. In the "take off" phase of gentrification that followed, the artists and urban pioneers were followed by other newcomers who found value in living in the newly discovered, suddenly trendy areas of the city.

The picture of pioneer-led gentrification dominated perceptions of neighborhood transformation in the 1970s and 1980s. But it no longer describes the spate of inner-city home buying and new construction that has taken place since the economic boom of the 1990s. Gentrification can no longer be viewed as being precipitated by the venturesome actions of a few urban pioneers. Today, gentrification is often corporate-led, with real estate agents and developers buying up concentrations of properties in neighborhoods ripe for new, upscale development.[16] In other cases, already gentrified neighborhoods are undergoing still more extensive change as successful members of the corporate and financial communities buy up property, displacing the first wave of urban gentrifiers.

In SoHo in Lower Manhattan, the artists who in the 1970s converted abandoned manufacturing lofts into working and living spaces were themselves eventually displaced as landlords and developers sought still more profitable uses for properties in a "hot" neighborhood.[17] As SoHo evolved, it became the site of upscale residential buildings and chain department stores; the area has lost much of its 1970s "artsy" flavor. Elsewhere in New York City, successful members of the city's financial community used their abundant wealth to buy into already-gentrified areas such as Brooklyn Heights and Park Slope.

Loretta Lees uses the terms **financifiers** and **supergentrifiers** to denote the quite different character of this second wave of neighborhood invasion and transformation.[18] When asked why they chose to move to the inner city, the initial urban pioneers often claimed to value their new neighborhood's ethnic and racial diversity. The new financifiers, however, do not place a similar value on diversity and local community life. In some cases, the supergentrifiers even constructed large, fortified dwelling units out of character with the neighborhood's housing stock; the new dwellings were of a scale that dwarfed previous residential conversions. The supergentrifiers value a neighborhood because of its convenient location and its cachet, not its prior racial and ethnic mix. They also cherish upscale amenities and shopping. In the super-gentrified areas of the **boutique city,** spiraling housing prices act to drive out the middle- and working-class, not just the poor.[19]

GOVERNMENT ACTION, PRIVATE POWER, AND GENTRIFICATION

It is too simple to view gentrification as solely resulting from the free-market actions of urban pioneers and other home seekers who find new value in urban life. Gentrification also results from the decisions made by private business elites and governmental actors.

The turn-around of Philadelphia's Society Hill area was not a natural phenomenon; it was the result of a conscious marketing strategy and of the joint actions taken by the city's downtown real estate community and governmental planners. A civic elite willed a renewed and trendy Society Hill area into being. All but a few of the residents already living in the area were expelled to make way to create a new, socially homogeneous neighborhood that could be marketed to a higher class of tenant. Society Hill's revitalization serves as evidence of "the undeniable impact that a small number of individuals can have in guiding—or even partly reversing—established urban trends."[20]

New York has witnessed similar machinations in its suddenly "hot" neighborhoods. The rise of "Silicon Alley" was not simply the result of the decisions of web-based creative artists and "technobohemians" to live and work in a relatively small enclave of old offices and warehouses in Lower Manhattan. The city's real estate interests discovered the profits that could be made from land speculation and from the "selling of a new media district," charging accountants, lawyers, and financiers for offices and residences in newly fashionable areas of the city. Real estate firms even "rebranded" a section of nearby Chinatown as "SoHo East," charging dot-com firms $30 per square foot for space that had previously been rented to garment manufacturers at only $7.25 per square foot.[21]

The revitalization of New York's DUMBO ("Down Under the Manhattan Bridge Overpass") was largely brought about by the actions of a single firm, David Walenta's Two Trees Development Corporation. Walenta purchased nearly the entire stock of industrial lofts in this portion of Brooklyn, just across the river from Manhattan, ousting the more marginal artists who had earlier moved into the area with its low rents. Supported by municipal zoning changes, Walenta rehabilitated the buildings, with their glorious views of Manhattan, for upscale residential use. In place of the former machine shops, Walenta established a high-amenity community with expensive restaurants and fashionable art galleries.[22]

Private power has often worked hand-in-hand with government to promote gentrification. Global corporations have an interest in assuring that a city will be able to house a pool of high-quality, technologically competent, professional labor. As a result, municipal governments have taken steps to promote neighborhood change as part of their strategy of recruiting global businesses and maintaining their city's economic competitiveness.

Gentrification and the resulting displacement of the urban poor and minorities cannot be attributed solely to the workings of a "free" market.[23] Instead, corporate-dictated actions and government policy have expedited and altered the process of neighborhood transformation. Extensive corporate investment financed the demolition of older buildings and the construction of new luxury townhouses and condominiums. The result was **supergentrification,** a process that produced a neighborhood much different in character than did the earlier pioneer wave of gentrification.

Corporate developers bought up clusters of properties in inner-city neighborhoods in order to provide a critical mass of development that would add to the sense of comfort and safety of upscale home seekers. In Chicago's West Town area, including Wicker Park and Humboldt Park, realtors and developers vigorously lobbied against efforts by a nonprofit group to acquire and upgrade housing units for the community's poor. The city's growth coalition feared that efforts to maintain the presence of poor people would interfere with development efforts, impeding the ability of developers to command high housing prices in an upward-trajectory community.[24] In some gentrifying neighborhoods, developers have promoted panic selling. The most unscrupulous developers have even been charged with resorting to arson in order to oust marginal tenants in order to make way for newer, more profitable projects.

Local governments, too, have facilitated gentrification, with rezoning and tax breaks for developers, as part of the effort to increase a city's attractiveness to national and world-class firms. In Chicago, at the behest of the real estate industry and its allies, the government awarded historic landmark status to Wicker Park, a move that both contributed to the marketing of the community and provided new tax credits for housing rehabilitation.[25]

In Chicago and other cities, federal programs such as **HOPE VI** promoted gentrification by helping local governments to demolish intimidating public housing structures that once stood as a barrier to housing construction for upper-status groups.[26] The relaxation of federal rules governing mortgage insurance for luxury housing helped catalyze the development of new luxury housing in Long Island City, a section of Queens just across the East River from Manhattan.[27]

DEALING WITH GENTRIFICATION

Gentrification increases the value of a neighborhood to its residents.[28] But residents who are forced out of a neighborhood do not benefit from a neighborhood's revival. Policymakers concerned with equity thus face an important question: Can neighborhood upgrading be encouraged while minimizing the displacement of poorer citizens?

Grassroots organizing and community action can help to mitigate some of the ill effects that accompany gentrification. In the Washington Heights neighborhood of New York's upper Manhattan, a multiethnic coalition of community groups fought to ensure that the housing opportunities for the poor would be included in plans for the upgrading of the area. In contrast, in the Park Slope neighborhood of Brooklyn, community action was largely absent; market forces and the unchecked actions of developers led to more extensive cooperative and condominium conversions and greater displacement.[29]

In San Francisco, grassroots action led to the enactment of **restrictions on the conversion of single room occupancy (SRO) hotels.** This was an attempt to lessen displacement in the city's Tenderloin, a low-income area with a large transient population, on the border of the city's burgeoning downtown.[30] Political action by San Francisco nonprofit groups effectively forestalled development plans that would have extended the city's financial district into the Tenderloin, displacing the residents of the area's SRO hotels.

In the southern part of San Francisco, in Bernal Heights, local citizen groups pursued an alternative strategy. They pressured the city to acquire land and build public housing so that the neighborhood would retain its income mix despite market pressures for transformation.[31]

In a number of cities, **community development corporations (CDCs)** have focused on the forging of financial partnerships for the development of affordable housing. As we describe in more detail in Chapter 8, these groups work with bankers, public officials, and other partners to assure that at least some housing units will be provided for the poor in neighborhoods threatened by new development.[32] In Chicago's largely poor Humboldt Park area, the Bickerdike Redevelopment Corporation assembled the funding necessary to rehabilitate good-quality, affordable housing units for the poor in the face of development pressures spilling over from neighboring, gentrified Wicker Park. Community groups such as Bickerdike have also fought for mandatory **setasides,** where new residential developments in hot housing markets are required to include a certain percentage of affordable units.

Boston requires the developers of new downtown commercial office structures to pay **linkage fees** that will be used to help finance affordable housing elsewhere in the city. Community groups in Boston and other cities have argued for balanced development, including the continued provision of affordable housing, as opposed to patterns of developer-dictated investment and rapid neighborhood transformation.

In Chicago, the African-American community has stressed **heritage tourism and development** as part of their strategy to claim a share of the jobs and other benefits form the revitalization of the city's historic Bronzeville neighborhood. South Side Chicago groups do not control gentrification; but they have the ability to influence perceptions of which groups and development projects have an "authentic" right to be in the neighborhood. In South Side Chicago, the arrival of middle and upper class African Americans is seen as "much more palatable" than the prospect of continued displacement by whites.[33]

GLOBALIZATION AND ITS IMPACT ON CITIES

The forces underlying gentrification can be found, to a large degree, in global economic restructuring. Multinational corporations have discovered the value of "density" in facilitating interaction and in allowing for the convenient access to financial, legal, and other support services. As a result, international corporations have located many of their headquarters and financial services operations in "nodes" of command and communication. New York, London, and Tokyo have become the command-and-control and financial centers in the new global economy. Subcenters of corporate control exist in Chicago and numerous other cites. Even in an age of fast-paced, international business transactions, face-to-face communication remains of value. In global cities and other communities that have become corporate headquarters, well-paid workers put new pressures on the local housing market, buying up homes in newly discovered neighborhoods in close proximity to workplaces and the city's nightlife and cultural facilities.

THE DEFINING CHARACTERISTICS OF GLOBALIZATION

With the continuing advance of telecommunications and transportation technology, cities and suburbs became increasingly subject to the influence of forces beyond their borders. The economic health of a city, for instance, may be greatly dependent on the decisions made in the boardrooms of multinational corporations about where to expand or contract a corporation's offices and production facilities. Manufacturing in the United States is also highly dependent upon the supply of parts that are manufactured and pre-assembled in overseas plants. European and Asian interests have also invested heavily in real estate in American cities. As a result, the economic base of many communities in the United States has become increasingly linked to decisions made by overseas corporate actors and the actions of global financial markets.

Everyone agrees that globalization is important. But just what is meant by globalization?

Globalization implies a permeability of borders, that cities are not in control of their own fates but are on the receiving end of decisions and processes that occur outside their borders, especially in the offices of multinational corporations. While there is no consensus on a precise definition, a survey of the literature highlights the following aspects of globalization as the process affects United States cities:

- **The concentration of corporate headquarters and firms that provide financial, legal, and other support services.** In the new global economy, a number of major U.S. cities experienced an economic rebound as the headquarters sites of international, national, and regional firms. New York, today, is a truly global city with businesses that make decisions that reach into the far corners of the world. In New York, corporate, legal, and financial services jobs took the place of the manufacturing, warehousing, and port-related jobs of old New York. Once-industrial Cleveland similarly experienced a partial rebound as a regional center for office headquarters, although the city continues to be dominated by its manufacturing job base. Cleveland, like New York, has come back economically. However, the city's long-term decline is still evident in its shrinking population size. Cleveland, which in the early twentieth century was the nation's fifth largest city, had fallen to 33rd place.[34]

  Los Angeles, like New York, saw its central business district grow as a result of new investment from overseas. In a global world, capital knows no borders. Los Angeles' downtown prospered when currency exchange rates made investment in U.S. land and buildings an attractive proposition for Japanese financiers. L.A.'s real estate bubble burst, however, when the Japanese economy slowed significantly, and many Japanese firms no longer saw new investment in U.S. facilities as financially viable.

- **Innovations in transportation and telecommunications.** Advances in transportation and telecommunications technology—from fax machines to satellites, computer technology, fiber optics, and teleports (locations where advanced telecommunications technology is made available to a variety of customers)—have given firms a new ability to locate their headquarters and financial service divisions at some distance from the production facilities. Many firms have chosen to maintain their command or headquarters functions at prestigious addresses in big cities even while locating their manufacturing divisions in lower-cost small cities and suburbs, or even overseas.

- **The increased mobility of international firms.** Freed by technological advances from the need to be situated in any single area, firms have an increasingly large choice of locations. As a result of advances in telecommunications, a firm can choose New York, London, Tokyo, Paris, Frankfurt, or another great urban center as the site of its international headquarters. Manufacturing, too, is similarly mobile as plants can be sited in any number of cities, states, and nations, with their products transported and assembled in the United States as necessary. As a result, a locality today finds that it is in competition—regionally, nationally, and globally—with a number of cities and suburbs for firms that have a choice of geographic locations. While the mobility of international firms can easily be overstated, it is nonetheless undeniable that firms have a greater variety of geographic options before them today than at any time in the past.

- **The growing importance of technology and the knowledge industry.** In a postindustrial economy, cities can no longer afford to stake their economic future on "smokestack chasing" alone. With the decline of manufacturing, there are simply too few factories available to assure a city's economic health. **Smart cities** and suburbs pursue an alternative strategy; they seek to enhance their attractiveness by upgrading their telecommunications infrastructure and by providing the education, training, and housing necessary to attract global headquarters and service firms with their upscale workforces. In California's **Silicon Valley,** the location of Stanford University, a concentration of professional workers in the computer and knowledge-based industries proved to be a key to the continuing economic dynamism of the San Jose and peninsula area. Just to the north, San Francisco responded with its own effort to facilitate the start up of entrepreneurial or "dot-com" firms. Austin, Texas, is another city that has similarly grown as a result of government policies that built on the advantages provided by the University of Texas and Dell Computer Corporation. New York City, too, invested in a teleport and other telecommunications infrastructure in order to promote the development of **Silicon Alley,** the take-off area of software, web advertising, and other Internet and "new media" firms in Chelsea and the former Garment District, just north of Greenwich Village.[35]

- **The importance of leisure, artistic, and cultural activities to a city's economic life.** In a world in which national and world-class corporations and their productive workers have a choice of locations, cities cannot rely solely on the policies that proved effective during their industrial past. Smart cities no longer rely on the tax incentives and subsidies of old. Instead, they also seek to attract business though policies that offer a good quality of life and create an attractive living environment.

- **The rise of new immigration.** If capital in the age of globalization is increasingly mobile, so too is labor. Advances in transportation and technology have only heightened immigration pressures as laborers from Mexico, the rest of Latin America, South Asia, and East Asia have increasingly sought opportunity in the United States. The United States' global foreign policy has also worked to produce this new immigration, with people from Korea, Vietnam, the Philippines, Russia, Cuba, El Salvador, and numerous other nations having sought refuge in the United States as a result of U.S. foreign policy actions.

Globalization entails recognition that economic and political decisions and events that take place outside a city's (and even a nation's) borders potentially have great influences on a city. Globalization implies the impersonal workings of the marketplace, where such factors as currency rates, international flare-ups, and the attractiveness of other global investment opportunities all influence the level of investment in a community. *New York Times* columnist and globalization expert Thomas Friedman uses the label "the electronic herd" in pointing to the impersonality, rapid speed, and relative uncontrollability of global marketplace transactions as they impact national and local economies.[36]

One often unrecognized characteristic of globalization is the increased **vulnerability** of cities.[37] The horrible events of 9/11 serve as witness to the openness of cities to terrorism. But the vulnerability of cities to transnational forces extends beyond terrorism. With modern jet travel, diseases such as AIDS, too, can quickly cross from one continent to another.[38] Local economies, too, are increasingly vulnerable as the banking and currency actions in one

CORBIS

Shanghai Mayor Han Zheng shakes hands with visiting Chicago Mayor Richard M. Daley after a signing ceremony as part of the first "Chicago-Shanghai Dialogue" in the business capital of China. In an age of globalization, a mayor must market the city to potential investors overseas.

economy can exert a sudden detrimental effect on a local economy an ocean away. International crises can create waves of immigration that flood into a city, adding to municipal service burdens and changing the nature of the city polity. Many cities further suffer an increased sense of economic vulnerability as telecommunications advances allow global firms to locate regional head-quarters and production facilities in technoburbs and edge cities.

Over the past three or so decades, all cities can be seen to have been increasingly subject to influences from beyond their borders. Should we then refer to all cities as "global cities"? Some urban commentators would answer "no!" They prefer to reserve the phrase "global city" to refer only to the small hand-ful of cities that represent a true concentration of international finance and command-and-control headquarters firms. (See "Globalization and Global Cities: Is There a Difference?" below.)

GLOBALIZATION AND GLOBAL CITIES: IS THERE A DIFFERENCE?

Since the 1970s, all cities have been affected to some degree by globalization, by forces beyond their borders. Yet, only a select handful can be said to be "global cities" or centers where international businesses have chosen to concentrate their command-and-control headquarters, financial services, and legal functions.

New York, London, and Tokyo clearly meet anyone's definition of a global city. But is Los Angeles, the second largest city in the United States, truly a global city? To a great many observers, the answer is an obvious yes. Los Angeles' downtown has grown as the center of Pacific Rim banking. Japanese and other overseas firms have invested heavily in real estate in the greater Los Angeles region. The city is also one of the largest trading cities in the world. It has expanded its airport facilities to accommodate increased international commerce. It is also a multicultural city where the civic flavor has been enriched by new arrivals from Mexico, El Salvador, Guatemala, China, Korea, Japan, and a large number of other Latin American and Pacific Rim nations.

But urban sociologist Michael Peter Smith argues that, despite this seemingly impressive array of evidence, Los Angeles should still not be regarded as a global city as it is "a receiver rather than a sender of global commands and con-trols."* Smith observes that L.A. has been more of a victim than a master of global forces. Changes in U.S. immigration laws beginning in the 1980s opened the city to a flood of new immigration. U.S. foreign policy also swelled immi-gration to the region as foreign policy friends sought political refuge in the United States. The new arrivals provided the basis for the city's burgeoning new sweatshop economy, where textile production is fueled largely by immigrant (including illegal immigrant) labor. The depression of wages and the feminiza-tion of the workforce employed in marginal industries are clearly symptomatic of a globalized economy but not necessarily of a command-and-control city.

continued

GLOBALIZATION AND GLOBAL CITIES: IS THERE A DIFFERENCE? (CONT.)

Los Angeles also lost much of its high-wage manufacturing jobs as international corporations shifted automobile assembly and other production facilities to such low-wage, anti-union countries as Mexico, Brazil, and Turkey. With the end of the Cold War, Los Angeles was on the receiving end of yet another set of externally made decisions, as cutbacks in national defense spending adversely affected employment in the region's many aerospace and defense-related facilities.

Perhaps our focus is a bit too constricted if we fail to classify a city such as Los Angeles as a global city just because it lacks the concentration of command-and-control headquarters of a London or a New York. As Saskia Sassen correctly observes, "there is no such entity as a single global city."** Globalization does not have similar effects across cities. Instead, we must begin to think of different types or levels of global cities.

As already noted, New York, Tokyo, and London clearly belong in the top tier of cities that are truly world centers of communications and finance.*** Los Angeles (a center not just of Pacific Rim banking but of media and international and multicultural communications) would be in a second tier of global cities, as would Chicago (an important national-level headquarters city) and Washington, DC. A third tier would consist of those cities that have a more limited or specialized position in the world economy, including Houston (with its ties to Mexico and Latin America), Miami (with its Cuban enclave and its emergence as a center of Caribbean banking and finance), and San Francisco (offering Los Angeles new competition as a Pacific Rim finance center). Boston, Dallas, and Philadelphia would be in a fourth tier of cities with more limited international ties. A fifth tier would likely include Atlanta, Rochester, Columbus, and Charlotte (an important regional banking center), cities that through aggressive entrepreneurship have begun to carve out a niche for themselves in the global economy.

Writers such as urban geographer Edward Soja worry that such categorizations and rankings give too much weight to the presence of command-and-control industries in downtown financial districts.† Soja argues that once an observer looks beyond London, New York City, and Tokyo, other aspects of globalization gain importance and should not be slighted. Los Angeles, with about 40 percent of its population foreign born, is a global city where many of its citizens have maintained bicultural identities. Issues of multiculturalism often dominate the local arena.

Former Los Angeles mayors Tom Bradley and Richard Riordan saw Los Angeles as the "gateway for the Pacific Rim." Mayor James Hahn attempted to build even greater bridges to Mexico. These mayors also led high-profile trade missions overseas. Hahn also sought to encourage small business

continued

GLOBALIZATION AND GLOBAL CITIES:
IS THERE A DIFFERENCE? (CONT.)

start-ups in Los Angeles by having local entrepreneurs build on contacts they maintained with friends in their countries of origin.[‡]

* Michael Peter Smith, "Looking for Globality in Los Angeles," in *Articulating the Global and the Local,* eds. Ann Cvetkovich and Douglas Kellner (Boulder, CO: Westview, 1997), pp. 55–71; the quotation appears on p. 55.

** Saskia Sassen, *The Global City,* 2nd ed. (Princeton, NJ: Princeton University Press, 2001), the quotation appears on p. 341.

*** The listing of cities by tiers is largely based on Paul K. Knox, "Globalization and Urban Economic Change," *Annals of the American Academy of Political and Social Science* (May 1997): pp. 22–23. Also see Anthony M. Orum and Kiangming Chen, *The World of Cities* (Oxford, UK: Blackwell, 2003), pp. 98–99.

† Edward W. Soja, *Postmetropolis: Critical Studies of Cities and Regions* (Malden, MA: Blackwell, 2000), pp. 222–232.

‡ Steven P. Erie, *Globalizing L.A.: Trade, Infrastructure, and Regional Development* (Stanford, CA: Stanford University Press, 2004), pp. 224–227.

GLOBALIZATION AND THE CHANGING CITY

A quick review of New York City's contemporary evolution reveals the influence of globalization. In the mid-1970s, New York was near bankruptcy, and the city lost jobs as a result of deindustrialization. Population and wealth were moving to the suburbs. The city could not repay its debts, and a fiscal crisis ensued, forcing cutbacks in municipal services. Since then, the city has rebounded as a center of global finance and corporate services. Gentrification brought new life to once fading neighborhoods—and with it the problems of housing affordability and displacement. The Gotham that emerged was, economically and socially, quite different from the industrial New York that existed at mid-century:

> While always important as a headquarters city, New York's single largest social stratum in the mid-1950s was blue-collar white ethnics. Turn-of-the-century immigrants and the children they bore before World War II constituted an industrial working class of considerable proportions. Today, few white blue-collar workers remain; many once categorized this way are now elderly. New groups have replaced them, ranging from white professionals and managers to minority and female clerical workers, to immigrant service workers. Office workers in corporate, social service, and government settings vastly outnumber production workers.[39]

Globalization did not affect all areas in the city in the same way. While Wall Street, Silicon Alley, Midtown, and gentrifying neighborhoods such as Brooklyn Heights and Park Slope all evidenced a new prosperity, the benefits of the economic rebound were only faintly felt in other neighborhoods, especially in the outer reaches of the boroughs with their growing immigrant populations.

New York suffered uneven development. The city's gains in jobs went beyond the financial services and creative-work sectors. Typical of a globalized city, New York's economy was also marked by a new **informalization or casualization of work,** where unregistered or off-the-books activity was often performed by immigrant labor.[40] Global New York suffered a new degree of polarization and dualism, with gentrifying, well-to-do areas flourishing amid continued poverty and ghettoization.

New York was only one of a great many cities that began to reshape its neighborhoods in an attempt to court firms in the biotechnology and other technology-related fields. The City of Baltimore announced a dramatic proposal to transform the run-down area bordering Johns Hopkins University. Homeowners and renters were being moved out as 20 city blocks were to be razed in order to make way for a $1 billion bioscience park that city leaders claimed "will transform the east side of Baltimore into a shiny new corporate Mecca for prescription drug developers, medical device makers and gene decoders."[41] The project sought to transform the entire neighborhood by generating new jobs, housing, and retail development.

Nor did globalization have the same effect across cities. Pittsburgh, once America's steel city, underwent a difficult transformation before emerging as a regional corporate office center. But even Pittsburgh's new office economy proved vulnerable to corporate downsizing and decisions made by executives with no loyalty to the city. In contrast, Philadelphia, Detroit, St. Louis, Newark, Buffalo, and even Cleveland continued to suffer long-term decline as new office startups could not offset the losses incurred when large corporations shifted their production facilities elsewhere. Transportation and telecommunications innovations even enabled corporations to shift production to facilities in low-wage and low-regulation areas overseas.

Central cities also lost both headquarters and high-tech firms to the burgeoning technoburbs or edge cities. In these "self-contained high-end suburbs," or **nerdistans,** as Joel Kotkin has labeled them, the "raw material is not ports, coal, iron, or even highway locations, but concentrations of skilled workers."[42]

Technological changes also allowed corporations to establish back offices in cheaper and more efficient sites in small cities—as well as overseas—as opposed to high-cost, major American cities. American Express moved its back offices from New York to Salt Lake City; Metropolitan Life relocated its back offices to Greenville (South Carolina), Scranton (Pennsylvania), and Wichita (Kansas).[43]

In 2003, Salt Lake City and 17 other Utah communities announced plans to build the nation's largest ultra-high-speed digital network. The $470 million digital infrastructure project would enable access to high-speed data, which is critical to the region's continued ability to attract an educated workforce and technology-oriented businesses. As the project's director boasted: "The best network in the U.S. will be in Utah—not in New York, not in Chicago, not in Los Angeles."[44]

Cities of the industrial age have been superseded by the post-industrial global city. Even General Motors, with its roots in Detroit, no longer maintains its headquarters solely in that city. GM has established a second headquarters in Manhattan to handle all of the specialized financial work that a multinational corporation requires.[45]

THE NEW IMMIGRATION AND THE AMERICAN CITY

In 1970, 17 percent of New York City's population was foreign born. By 1980, just ten short years later, the percentage increased dramatically; over a third of the city's population were immigrants.[46] Changes in U.S. law beginning in the 1960s opened the doors of the American city to a **new immigration** from the Caribbean, Latin America, and the Pacific Rim—as opposed to the waves of immigration from Europe that had swelled the populations of East Coast and Midwestern cities during the earlier mercantile and industrial eras.[47]

The 1965 amendments to the Immigration Reform and Control Act began a process of change that **liberalized U.S. immigration laws.** By 1980, reforms virtually abolished the old system of per-country quotas that had favored immigration from Europe and sharply limited the number of arrivals from other parts of the world.[48] Changes in the law also eased family reunification, allowing workers to bring their families from overseas. The **amnesty** provision of the Act, which sought the humane goal of regularizing the status of undocumented residents, also appears to have spurred the arrival of new undocumented workers, especially from Mexico.[49] U.S. political commitments also led the nation to welcome the arrival of Soviet Jews and Vietnamese, Cambodian, Laotian, and Cuban refugees, among others. Additional immigration slots are awarded to persons with valued occupational skills. A 1990 provision, designed to promote diversity, awarded an additional 55,000 additional permanent residency visas to aliens from countries with low immigration rates to the United States.

The actions of important global financial institutions, including the World Bank and the International Monetary Fund (IMF), at times have also served to spur events that led to the immigration to U.S. cities. The World Bank's insistence that the French-speaking nations of West Africa devaluate their currency left West African traders with inventories of limited worth. Many of these traders decided to seek new opportunity in the United States, particularly in New York City. IMF pressures that forced the Dominican Republic to adopt new measures of fiscal stringency led to an increase in the Dominican migration to the United States. The immigration of Dominicans to the United States doubled in the 1980s and quadrupled in the 1990s.[50]

The new immigration affected life not only in big cities but also in numerous small- and medium-sized cities and suburban communities. Immigrant populations increased in such heartland cities as Denver, Nashville, Oklahoma City, and Wichita. St. Paul (Minnesota) and Milwaukee and a number of smaller Wisconsin cities—Wausau, Green Bay, Sheboygan, Appleton, LaCrosse, and Eau Claire—saw the resettlement of the Hmong, an ethnic group from Laos that came to the U.S. as a result of the Vietnam war.

The 2000 census also confirmed a trend that was already becoming visible a decade earlier: the foreign-born population living in suburbia was quickly growing.

Los Angeles was ringed by various Mexican, Korean, Chinese, and Vietnamese suburbs. Westminster, a town south of Los Angeles, was popularly known as "Little Saigon."[51] On the east coast, Hicksville, New York, became a virtual "Little India," a center of the large professional Indian community living on Long Island. While these suburbs had to bear the costs of schooling and absorbing a growing immigrant population, the immigrants also greatly contributed to the local economies.

In one important way, the pattern of new immigrant settlement today differed quite a bit from the immigration of old. The older waves of immigrants from Europe flowed into the nation's big cities. In today's decentralized metropolitan economies, the new arrivals are increasingly skipping the central city and moving directly to the suburbs. Many of the new immigrants also had family already living in the suburbs.[52] The nation's six **immigrant magnet metros**—the greater New York, Los Angeles, San Francisco, Chicago, Washington, and Miami areas—gained over three million migrants from abroad in the 1990s.[53]

Despite the new stream of immigrants to the suburbs, immigrants nonetheless continue to be found disproportionately in central cities, especially in highly distressed cities. Immigrant populations were especially concentrated in five port-of-entry or **gateway cities**: Miami (with an amazing 60 percent of its population foreign-born in 1990); Santa Ana, California (51 percent); Los Angeles (38 percent); San Francisco (34 percent); and New York (19 percent). San Jose, San Diego, Boston, Newark, Houston, and Chicago are other cities with large immigrant concentrations.[54] (See "Are Cities Better Off As a Result of Immigration? Chicago's Killer Heat Wave and 'Little Village'" below.)

ARE CITIES BETTER OFF AS A RESULT OF IMMIGRATION? CHICAGO'S KILLER HEAT WAVE AND "LITTLE VILLAGE"

Does immigration add to a city's overall health? In some cases, the answer is clearly yes, as demonstrated in Chicago's 1995 killer heat wave.

That summer, over 485 people died in the city due to heat-related causes. The mortality of the elderly was especially high. Yet, the deaths were not distributed equally throughout the city. People in certain neighborhoods were more likely to die than in other neighborhoods. In Chicago, the mortality rate was quite low in the predominantly poor Mexican-American South Lawndale or "Little Village" neighborhood. In contrast, in nearby North Lawndale, an equally poor African-American neighborhood, the death rate skyrocketed.

Why did the elderly of Little Village fare so well compared to the elderly of North Lawndale? Continuing immigration from Mexico made Little Village a lively neighborhood, with an active shopping district with many open stores and a healthy and well-supported network of churches. The elderly in Little

continued

ARE CITIES BETTER OFF AS A RESULT OF IMMIGRATION?
CHICAGO'S KILLER HEAT WAVE AND "LITTLE VILLAGE" (CONT.)

Village escaped the heat by frequenting air-conditioned stores. Elderly residents were not afraid to venture out onto the crowded sidewalks of the 26th Street shopping district, with its many stores, bakeries, restaurants, and pushcart vendors selling juices and churros. The well-financed churches of the neighborhood also provided caring networks that looked out for the more vulnerable elderly.

North Lawndale, by contrast, was a much different neighborhood with many boarded-up buildings, abandoned lots, and drug dealing on the streets. In North Lawndale, there were few stores for the elderly to frequent. The elderly also lived in fear of violence and refused to venture out into the streets or, in some cases, even to open the door to municipal officials who were inquiring as to their health. As a result, many of the elderly died behind their chain-locked doors, with windows bolted shut, in apartments that became virtual furnaces in the heat. The elderly in North Lawndale also lived in virtual isolation, with no family members to check up on them as their families had moved away to other areas of the city. Even the churches of North Lawndale exhibited distress, lacking the membership and finances to provide the networks of support evident in Little Village.

Both Little Village and North Lawndale are poor neighborhoods. Yet there is a vast difference between the two. Continuing immigration gave Little Village a vital street life and active churches that added to community safety. Nearby North Lawndale, receiving no equivalent immigration, suffered an exodus of population that led to empty streets, boarded-up housing, and depleted local social institutions. Globalization replenished community life in Little Village. North Lawndale, without new arrivals, suffered advanced abandonment and decline.

Source: Eric Klinenberg, *Heat Wave: A Social Autopsy of Disaster in Chicago* (Chicago: University of Chicago Press, 2002), chap. 2.

New York City's Chinese population grew so large that it spilled over the traditional borders of Chinatown into Little Italy and the Lower East Side. The old Chinatown of Lower Manhattan was joined by new Chinatowns in Jackson Heights and Flushing (Queens) and Sunset Park (Brooklyn).[55] In Chicago, far from the city's long-established south side Chinatown, a new, north side Chinatown along Argyle Street has emerged as a gate-of-entry for Vietnamese, Thai, and Chinese immigrants.

The new immigrants from Latin America and Asia faced great difficulty in finding good-paying, entry-level jobs in the high-tech, corporate economy of the post-industrial metropolis.[56] In port-of-entry cities, low-paid, predominantly female, clerical work has replaced the good-paying jobs of the docks and factories that characterized the industrial cities of old. A new **informalization of the economy** has seen the rise of small migrant-owned shops and even the reemergence of piece work, sweatshops, and home manufacturing.[57] The large number of Asian, Mexican, and other Latino immigrants in Los Angeles contributed to the city's resurgence as a low-wage, textile manufacturing center. (See "Film Review: *Real Women Have Curves*," below.)

FILM IMAGES OF THE CITY–IMMIGRANT LOS ANGELES: *REAL WOMEN HAVE CURVES* AND *BREAD AND ROSES*

Director Patricia Cardoso's film *Real Women Have Curves* (2002) focuses on the struggle of Ana, an 18-year-old Latina (played by America Ferrera) living in Los Angeles, to find her own way amid the conflicting demands of her Mexican and U.S. worlds. Should she take a scholarship and attend far-off Columbia University in New York City in defiance of the expectations of her family, especially those of her mother? Or should she stay in Los Angeles and play the traditional supportive role expected of Latina women both in the home and the workplace? Circumstances force Ana, at least for a while, to bow to her mother's wishes and take a job in the dressmaking sweatshop run by her sister.

The film reveals the hard-working and strong family values of the Mexican-American community. It also points to the feminization and the low-wage nature of work in the more casual side of L.A.'s new global economy. Despite the camaraderie and loyalty of the women, their small factory is literally a sweatshop where the ladies are forced to strip down to their underwear in order to cope with the suffocating heat. Ana, the more independent and politicized of the sisters, rants against the exploitation of these immigrant women by the multinational corporations that pay only a pittance for the women's hard labor and then retail the beautiful, hand-sewn gowns for hundreds of dollars.

Whereas *Real Women Have Curves* is a comedy that attempts to reveal big-city conditions through its soft-edge of humor, director Ken Loach's *Bread and Roses* (2000) is a more harsh and strident political work, an unvarnished indictment of the social and work conditions of immigrant Los Angeles. Loach shows the dangers (including possible rape) that illegal immigrants face when Maya (Pilar Padilla), is forced to depend on "coyotes" to smuggle her (and others) into the United States. The coyotes charge high fees to smuggle their human cargo into the country; in many cases, they also "rip off" their customers.

Maya is lucky to escape the coyotes and, with the help of her sister, find a job cleaning offices in one of Los Angeles' downtown towers. The film shows the low-wage, no-benefit, insecure jobs that make up the underside of L.A.'s glitzy, glowing, global economy. The women put up with all sorts of abuse on the job from fear of losing their economic security. The contracting firm, which is run by Mexicans, stands as an intermediary between the laboring women and the

continued

FILM IMAGES OF THE CITY IMMIGRANT LOS ANGELES:
REAL WOMEN HAVE CURVES AND *BREAD AND ROSES* (CONT.)

city's giant corporations. In the film, the men who run the cleaning service, including the crew manager (played by George Lopez) demand a portion of the women's wages (and, in some cases, sexual favors) for giving them their jobs. By contracting out their cleaning and janitorial jobs, L.A.'s major corporations preserve their "deniability"—they claim a lack of knowledge of the work conditions and poor pay of their largely Hispanic janitorial workforce.

Maya falls in love with a union organizer (Adrien Brody). In the long tradition of films about labor unionism, worker solidarity is presented as the critical key to worker protection and advancement in a harsh, exploitive, corporate world. Loach underscores the dualism of the global city by contrasting the harsh lives of the workers with the flamboyant wealth of a lavish Hollywood party.

Immigration is no longer confined to traditional gateway cities. New arrivals have altered the nature of politics in southwestern cities and even in cities in the Great Plains and the Mountain States. One-fifth of the Phoenix's population in 2000 was foreign-born; over a third of its population was of Hispanic origin. In Denver, one-fifth was foreign-born; immigrants from Mexico accounted for virtually all of the city's population growth during the 1990s. During the same decade, Kansas City saw its immigrant population double, a growth that helped to compensate for the continuing exodus of city residents to the suburbs. Dallas grew rapidly as it gained over 200,000 residents, mainly from Mexico but also from Asia. The new arrivals made Dallas one of the most diverse cities in the nation.[58]

The immigrant population includes noncitizens as well as citizens. In order to increase the legitimacy of government in foreign-born communities, a small handful of cities, including Takoma Park (Maryland) and Cambridge (Massachusetts) have taken steps to allow noncitizens to vote in local elections. As early as the 1960s, Chicago permitted noncitizens to vote in school board elections. New York City allowed legal migrants to vote for, and serve on, community school boards, until the boards were abolished in 2003. In 2004, San Francisco voters narrowly defeated a city charter amendment to give noncitizen parents and guardians the vote in school elections; opponents had argued that the measure would be in conflict with a provision of the state's constitution. Critics of such measures point to the importance of maintaining voting as a privilege of citizenship. Advocates argue for the essential fairness of the changes, as noncitizens pay taxes and their children attend public schools and are affected by the policy decisions made by local government.[59]

Proposals for voting by noncitizens were also a response to the refusal of some new immigrants to surrender their old national identities as previous generations of immigrants to the United States had done. Advances in communications (including cheap telephone calling cards and e-mail) and transportation allow the new immigrants to maintain frequent contacts with family and friends back home, feeding their sense of bicultural identity. Globalization has redefined citizenship, challenging the older view that "immigration involves the crossing of rigid, territorial national boundaries." Today's "back-and-forth migration" has led to a more fluid, **transnational sense of citizenship** in which migrants who come to the United States in search of economic opportunity continue to maintain their identity as the loyal sons and daughters of another nation. The Mexican "hinterland" is increasingly "meshed together" with Los Angeles as a growing number of people maintain transnational identities.[60]

Even in the Mexican communities of such far-off cities as Chicago and Detroit, new immigrants maintain their ties to Mexico. Workers in Chicago's Pilsen and Little Village neighborhoods and in Detroit's Mexicantown send parts of their paychecks to families back home and return to Mexico for frequent visits.

CONCLUSION: GLOBALIZATION, DEMOCRACY, AND POLITICAL POWER

Globalization raises fundamental questions of democracy and fairness. As Robin Hambleton, Hank Savitch, and Murray Stewart observe, "Economic pressures can force cities into a competitive mode within which economic goals dominate social goals and locally expressed aspirations succumb to wider forces. . . ."[61] Thomas Friedman puts it even more provocatively, that in the face of global pressures, "Your politics shrinks." Countries and communities put on a "Golden Straightjacket," pursuing growth by confining decisions to the core rules dictated by investors.[62]

At times, the undemocratic tendencies of globalization have resulted in a backlash. Anti-globalization protests on the streets of Seattle, Miami, New York, Montreal and numerous other cities were an attempt to call attention to the influence of the World Trade Organization, the World Bank, the International Monetary Fund, and other corporate-oriented global entities at the expense of local, grassroots power.

How can cities pursue more equitable policies in the face of antidemocratic global pressures? Must a big city experience unabated gentrification—and the accompanying problem of displacement—as the price that has to be paid in order to be attractive to national- and world-class businesses?

Susan Clarke and Gary Gaile observe five alternative strategies that U.S. cities have taken in response to globalization.[63] Of course, a great number of cities rely on **classic locational approaches,** attempting to lure business with subsidies and **tax abatements** (that is, lowering taxes on a business to the extent allowed under state law). This strategy, while popular, cannot assure a city success as more and more communities are offering businesses essentially the same package of benefits.[64] Even when a community "wins" by luring a big firm, the benefits of winning are diminished by the costs of the incentives that were provided.

Other communities have moved beyond "smoke-stack chasing" and do not rely on the mere offering of subsidies in an effort to attract business. Instead, these communities have attempted to upgrade their physical and telecommunications infrastructure (with improvements to fiber-optic networks, teleports, wireless access to the Internet, among other innovations), billing themselves as **world-class communities.** These communities also provide the resources and facilities to support business research and development activities and to aid small business start-ups.

Other communities have been even more creative in their response to competitive global pressures. St. Paul Mayor George Latimer pursued the vision of a Homegrown Economy, **building on a city's indigenous assets.** The citizens of St. Paul sought to "grow what we have,"[65] emphasizing the expansion of local and employee ownership of business. Other communities have entered into partnerships with **community development corporations (CDCs)** in an effort to build housing and provide jobs for neighborhood residents.[66]

Many communities have also begun to see the wisdom of **investing in human resources,** of building a more educated, technologically-competent, and adaptable workforce. As work in the global era is increasingly knowledge-based, cities and suburbs that can offer firms an educated, quality workforce will increase their prospects of being chosen as the sites of global-age development. Cities such as Portland, Oregon have made development assistance contingent on a firm's willingness to be linked with local job-training efforts.

Finally, certain cities have opted for a **sustainable development** strategy. These cities respond to the quality-of-life concerns of their citizenry. Such communities do not "go after" all new economic development but instead try to seek out growth that is compatible with environmental and equity values. Such communities recognize that a high quality of life attracts skilled, professional workers, making an area increasingly attractive to high-tech firms.[67]

The Cascadia Alliance in the Pacific Northwest is an example of an organization that has sought to promote growth and land-management policies consistent with goal of conserving the region's natural beauty.[68] In communities as diverse as St. Paul, Jacksonville, San Diego, Chattanooga, Seattle, and Vancouver, sustainability has been a prominent issue on the local agenda.[69] Citizens in these communities have become increasingly worried about the costs of unmitigated growth, including increased pollution, traffic congestion, the loss of open space, and the overcrowding of schools.

In a global age, the "work of cities" has changed. Cities can no longer afford to provide the same programs and undertake the same economic development strategies that worked so well in the past. More and more cities have begun to recognize the primacy that they must give to both human resource development and new investments in a city's telecommunications infrastructure.[70] (See "Responding to Globalization: The Arts- and Technology-Based Strategy of Tacoma, Washington," on p. 97.) By themselves, traditional economic development subsidies are insufficient to the task of attracting global-age business.

RESPONDING TO GLOBALIZATION: THE ARTS- AND TECHNOLOGY-BASED STRATEGY OF TACOMA, WASHINGTON

Tacoma, Washington has taken a highly entrepreneurial approach in developing a renewal strategy that is both technology-oriented and arts-based. Facing deindustrialization, this old port and lumber city had to find a way to diversify its economic base. The central business district could not compete with suburban retail. City planners sought a novel way to bring people back to the downtown, by developing the downtown as an arts, cultural, and education center. Planners also sought to create a new milieu with the educational and cultural facilities hospitable to technology-oriented development.

The city revitalized its aging theaters and took advantage of tax credits for the rehabilitation of buildings. New galleries opened. The city also needed to redevelop its downtown waterfront, which had become an eyesore blocking new investment. The State of Washington stepped in by expanding the local University of Washington campus and establishing a Technology Institute to aid the development of technology-related businesses. Tacoma Power vigorously promoted the capacity of its new fiber-optic system to businesses. City and county development agencies began to market the Tacoma area to technology-related firms.

Tacoma's strategic choices were constrained by the city's strong traditions of community (and labor union) activism, citizen participation, and public accountability. The arts and education were nonpolluting industries that met with public approval. The city also made additional commitments to public health, affordable housing, children's issues, and other quality-of-life concerns.

Sources: Susan E. Clarke and Gary L. Gaile, *The Work of Cities* (Minneapolis: University of Minnesota Press, 1998); Paul Sommers and Deena Heg, "Spreading the Wealth: Building a Tech Economy in Small and Medium-Sized Regions," a discussion paper prepared for The Brookings Institution Center on Urban and Metropolitan Policy," Washington, DC, October 2003, available at www.brookings.edu/es/urban/publications/200310_Sommers.htm. For an interesting comparison of the economic development strategies pursued by Tacoma and Cleveland, see Clarke and Gaile pp. 116–132 and 163–177.

Competitive pressures act to constrain a city's choices; yet a city is not simply the prisoner of global economic forces.[71] A city has a choice of strategies. A city can offer expensive subsidies to business, upgrade and market local assets, invest in human resources and education, or rely on a strategy of providing high levels of community amenities. In communities where racial minorities, neighborhood activists, and environmentalists have gained power, political leaders are increasingly willing to challenge the subsidies and development priorities demanded by business.[72]

As we will discuss in greater detail in the next chapter, the heightened mobility of capital in the global age has increased the power of business relative to that of municipal governments. But economics forces, by themselves, do not determine a community's response. While economics is important, so too, are the forces exerted by local democracy and local leadership.

We shall describe the continuing tension between the forces of local democracy and elite control in our next chapter, where we attempt to answer the question: "Who has the power in America's cities?"

NOTES

1. Rivka Gerwitz Little, "The New Harlem," *The Village Voice,* September 18–24, 2002. For an exploration of the class conflicts in Harlem that have resulted from gentrification, see Monique M. Taylor, *Harlem between Heaven and Hell* (Minneapolis: University of Minnesota Press, 2002).

2. All of these terms have slightly different connotations. See Bruce London, "Gentrification as Urban Reinvasion: Some Preliminary Definitions and Theoretical Considerations," in *Back to the City,* ed. Shirley Bradway Laska and Daphne Spain (New York: Pergamon Press, 1980), pp. 77–92; and Neil Smith and Peter Williams, "Alternatives to Orthodoxy: Invitation to a Debate," in *Gentrification of the City,* ed. Smith and Williams (Boston: Allen and Unwin, 1986), pp. 1–3.

3. Smith and Williams, "Alternatives to Orthodoxy," p. 1.

4. Brian J. L. Berry, "Islands of Renewal in Seas of Decay," in *The New Urban Reality,* ed. Peterson, pp. 72–95.

5. E. K. Wyly and D. J. Hammel, "Islands of Decay in Seas of Renewal: Housing Policy and the Resurgence of Gentrification, *Housing Policy Debate,* 10, 4 (1999), 711–771.

6. Berry, "Islands of Renewal in Seas of Decay," pp. 72–76, 86, and 95; Maureen Kennedy and Paul Leonard, "Dealing with Neighborhood Change: A Primer on Gentrification and Policy Choices, a discussion paper prepared for The Brookings Institution Center on Urban and Metropolitan Policy, Washington, DC, 2001. www.brookings.edu/urban.

7. Mark Baldassare, "Evidence for Neighborhood Revitalization: Manhattan," in *Gentrification, Displacement and Neighborhood Revitalization,* ed. J. John Palen and Bruce London (Albany: State University of New York Press, 1984), p. 91.

8. George Galster et al., "The Fortunes of Poor Neighborhoods." (paper presented at the conference on "Upward Neighbourhood Trajectories: Gentrification in a New Century," Glasgow, Scotland, September 26–27, 2002).

9. See the collection of articles in Shirley Bradway Laska and Daphne Spain, eds., *Back to the City,* particularly Phillip L. Clay, "The Rediscovery of City Neighborhoods: Reinvestment by Long-Time Residents and Newcomers," pp. 13–26. Also see Richard T. LeGates and Chester Hartman, "The Anatomy of Displacement in the United States," in *Gentrification of the City,* ed. Smith and Williams, pp. 180–181; Berry, "Islands of Renewal in Seas of Decay"; Mario D. Zavarella, "The Back-to-the-City Movement Revisited," *Journal of Urban Affairs* 9 (1987), pp. 375–390; and David P. Varady and Jeffrey A. Raffel, *Selling Cities: Attracting Homebuyers Through Schools and Housing Programs* (Albany: State University of New York Press, 1995), pp. 117–118.

10. Elvin K. Wyly, Norman J. Glickman, and Michael L. Lahr, "A Top 10 List of Things to Know About American Cities," *Cityscape: A Journal of Policy Development and Research,* 3, 3 (1998), p. 21; Alexander van Hoffman, "Housing Heats Up: Home Building Patterns in Metropolitan Areas," The Brookings Institution Survey Series, December 1999, www.brookings.edu/es/urban/hoffman.pdf.

11. Kennedy and Leonard, "Dealing with Neighborhood Change: A Primer on Gentrification and Policy Choices," p. 1.

12. Berry, "Islands of Renewal in Seas of Decay," p. 80; and Phillip L. Clay, *Neighborhood Renewal* (Lexington, MA: Lexington Books, 1979), p. 63.

13. Wyly and Hammel, "Islands of Decay in Seas of Renewal." p. 716.

14. Daphne Spain, "A Gentrification Research Agenda for the 1990s," *Journal of Urban Affairs* 14, 2 (1992): 128–129, 131.

15. Neil Smith, "New City, New Frontier: The Lower East Side as Wild, Wild West." In *Variations On a Theme Park*, ed. Michael Sorkin (New York: Hill and Wang, 1992), pp. 61–93. Also see Neil Smith, *The New Frontier: Gentrification and the Revanchist City* (London: Routledge, 1996).

16. Jason Hackworth, "Post-Recession Gentrification in New York City," *Urban Affairs Review,* 37, 6 (2002): 815–843; John J. Betancur, "The Politics of Gentrification: The Case of West Town in Chicago," *Urban Affairs Review* 37, 6 (July 2002): 780–814.

17. Neil Smith, "Gentrification Generalized: From Local Anomaly to Urban Regeneration as Global Urban Strategy." (paper presented at the conference on "Upward Neighbourhood Trajectories: Gentrification in a New Century," Glasgow, Scotland, September 26–27, 2002).

18. Loretta Lees, "A Reappraisal of Gentrification: Towards a 'Geography of Gentrification.'" *Progress in Human Geography* 24, 3 (2000): 389–408. Also see Hackworth, "Post-Recession Gentrification in New York City."

19. Joel Kotkin, *The New Geography: How the Digital Revolution is Reshaping the American Landscape* (New York: Random House, 2000), pp. 78–79.

20. Roman A. Cybriwsky, David Ley, and John Western, "The Political and Social Construction of Revitalized Neighborhoods: Society Hill, Philadelphia, and False Creek, Vancouver," in *Gentrification of the City,* ed. Neil Smith and Peter Williams (Boston: Allen & Unwin, 1986), p. 119. Also see Smith, *The New Frontier,* pp. 119–139.

21. Michael Indergaard, *Silicon Alley: The Rise and Fall of a New Media District* (New York: Routledge, 2004), pp. 26–27, 102–112. The Chinatown example appears on p. 110.

22. Hackworth, "Post-Recession Gentrification in New York City;" pp. 835–838.

23. Ibid. Betancur, "The Politics of Gentrification." pp. 806–808.

24. Betancur, "The Politics of Gentrification," pp. 787–789, 801–803.

25. Ibid., p. 790.

26. Wyly and Hammel, "Islands of Decay in Seas of Renewal."

27. Hackworth, "Post-Recession Gentrification in New York City;" p. 134–135.

28. Lance Freeman and Frank Braconi, "Gentrification and Displacement: New York City in the 1990s," *Journal of the American Planning Association* 70, 1 (Winter 2004): 39–52.

29. Joyce Gelb and Michael Lyons, "A Tale of Two Cities: Housing Policy and Gentrification in London and New York," *Journal of Urban Affairs* 15, 4 (1993): 345–366.

30. Tony Robinson, "Gentrification and Grassroots Resistance in San Francisco's Tenderloin," *Urban Affairs Review* 30, 4 (1995): 483–513.

31. Kennedy and Leonard, "Dealing with Neighborhood Change: A Primer on Gentrification and Policy Choices," p. 30.

32. Susan S. Fainstein, "Developing Success Stories," in *Affordable Housing and Urban Redevelopment in the United States, Urban Affairs Annual Review,*

vol. 46, ed. Willem Van Vliet (Thousand Oaks, CA: Sage Publications, 1997), p. 26.

33. Michelle Boyd, "Reconstructing Bronzeville: Racial Nostalgia and Neighborhood Redevelopment," *Journal of Urban Affairs* 22, 2 (2000): 107–122. The "palatable" comment appears on p. 118.

34. U.S. Census Data. Also see *Cleveland in Focus: A Profile from Census 2002*, a "Living Cities" report of The Brookings Institution, Washington, DC, November 2003.

35. For a description of the meteoric rise and eventual "bust" of New York's Silicon Alley, see Michael Indegaard, *Silicon Alley: The Rise and Fall of a New Media District* (New York: Routledge, 2004).

36. Thomas L. Friedman, *The Lexus and the Olive Tree: Understanding Globalization* (New York: Anchor Books, 2000), pp. 13–14, 112–142.

37. Hank V. Savitch and Paul Kantor, *Cities in the International Marketplace: The Political Economy of Urban Development in North America and Western Europe* (Princeton, NJ: Princeton University Press, 2002), pp. 14–15.

38. Randy Shilts, *And the Band Played On: Politics, People, and the AIDS Epidemic* (New York: St. Martin's, 1987).

39. John Hull Mollenkopf, *A Phoenix in the Ashes: The Rise and Fall of the Koch Coalition in New York City Politics* (Princeton, NJ: Princeton University Press, 1992), p. 47.

40. Saskia Sassen, *The Global City*, 2nd ed. (Princeton, NJ: Princeton University Press, 2001), pp. 294–300.

41. Michael Barbaro, "Baltimore Makes a Bold Bid to Transform Neighborhood," *Washington Post*, December 1, 2003. Also see Gady A. Epstein and Eric Siegel, "City, Hopkins Weigh Plan for East-side Development," *Baltimore Sun*, January 11, 2001.

42. Kotkin, *The New Geography*, p. 9.

43. Leonard I. Ruchelman, *Cities in the Third Wave: The Technological Transformation of Urban America* (Chicago: Burnham, 2000), p. 91.

44. Matt Richtel, "In Utah, Public Works Project in Digital," *New York Times*, November 17, 2003.

45. Saskia Sassen, *Cities in a World Economy*, 2nd ed. (Thousand Oaks, CA: Pine Forge Press, 2000), pp. 55 and 347.

46. Nancy Foner, "Introduction: New Immigrants in a New New York," in *New Immigrants in New York*, ed. Nancy Foner (New York: Columbia University Press, 2001), p. 1.

47. James M. Lindsay and Audrey Singer, "Changing Faces: Immigrants and Diversity in the Twenty-First Century," in *Agenda for the Nation*, eds. Henry J. Aaron, James M. Lindsay, and Pietro S. Nivola (Washington, DC: Brookings, 2003), especially pp. 217–225.

48. For an overview of the changes made in U.S. immigration laws and how they affected cities, especially New York, see Ellen Percy Kraly and Ines Miyares, "Immigration to New York: Policy, Population, and Patterns," in *New Immigrants in New York*, pp. 33–43.

49. Robert C. Smith, "Mexicans; Social, Educational, Economic, and Political Problems and Prospects in New York," in *New Immigrants in New York*, p. 280.

50. Paul Stoller, "West Africans: Trading Places in New York," in *New Immigrants in New York*, pp. 233–234; Patricia R. Pessar and Pamela M. Graham, "Dominicans:

Transnational Identities and Local Politics," in *New Immigrants in New York,* p. 254.

51. Janet L. Abu-Lughod, *New York, Chicago, Los Angeles: America's Global Cities* (Minneapolis: University of Minnesota Press, 1999), p. 374; Seth Mydans, "A Fallen Saigon Rises Again in the West," *New York Times,* April 5, 2002.

52. Richard P. Greene, "Chicago's New Immigrants, Indigenous Poor, and Edge Cities," *The Annals of the American Academy of Political and Social Science* 551 (May 1997): 178–190.

53. William H. Frey, *Metropolitan Magnets for International and Domestic Migrants,* report of The Brookings Institution's Center on Urban and Metropolitan Policy, Washington, DC, 2003.

54. Franklin J. James, Jeff A. Romine, and Peter E. Zwanzig, "The Effects of Immigration on Urban Communities," *Cityscape: A Journal of Policy Development and Research* 3, 1 (1998): 174–176; Abu-Lughod, *New York, Chicago, Los Angeles,* p. 413.

55. Min Zhou, "Chinese: Divergent Destinies in Immigrant New York," in *New Immigrants in New York,* pp. 152–167.

56. Mollenkopf, *A Phoenix in the Ashes,* pp. 44–68. Also see 69–76.

57. Sassen, *Cities in a World Economy,* 2nd ed., pp. 124–125.

58. See the following November 2003 reports of the Living Cities Project: *Dallas in Focus: Profile from Census* 2000; *Denver In Focus: A Profile From Census 2000; Kansas City in Focus: A Profile form Census 2000; Phoenix in Focus: A Profile from Census 2000,* all published in Washington, DC by The Brookings Institution.

59. Ronald Hayduk, "Noncitizen Voting: Expanding the Franchise in the U.S." (paper presented at the annual meeting of the American Political Science Association, Philadelphia, Pennsylvania, August 28–31, 2003); Michael Huang, "Citizenship and Voting," *Gotham Gazette* (August 25, 2003), available at: www.gothamgazette.com/article/feature-commentary/20030825/202/503; John Wildermuth, "Jones Rips Giving Noncitizens a Vote in School Elections," *San Francisco Chronicle,* July 27, 2004.

60. Jerome Straughan and Pierrette Hondagneu-Sotelo, "From Immigrants In the City, to Immigrant City," in *From Chicago to L.A.: Making Sense of Urban Theory,* ed. Michael J. Dear (Thousand Oaks, CA: Sage Publications, 2002), pp. 199–203. The quotations are from p. 201.

61. Robin Hambleton, Hank V. Savitch, and Murray Stewart, "Globalism and Local Democracy," in *Globalism and Local Democracy: Challenge and Change in Europe and North America,* eds. Hambleton, Savitch, and Stewart (London: Palgrave Macmillan, 2003).

62. Friedman, *The Lexus and the Olive Tree,* pp. 104–106.

63. The typology and discussion in the paragraphs that follow are largely based on Susan E. Clarke and Gary L. Gaile, "Local Politics in a Global Era: Thinking Globally, Acting Locally," *The Annals of the American Academy of Political and Social Science* 551 (May 1997): 28–43; and, Susan E. Clarke and Gary L. Gaile, *The Work of Cities* (Minneapolis: University of Minnesota Press, 1998), pp. 107–214.

64. Theodore J. Gilman, *No Miracles Here: Fighting Urban Decline in Japan and the United States* (Albany, NY: State University of New York Press, 2001), describes the limited benefits that can be expected when cities fail to innovate and simply copy the no-longer-novel economic development strategies of other cities.

65. Clarke and Gaile, "Local Politics in a Global Era," p. 39.

66. David L. Imbroscio, "Overcoming the Neglect of Economics in Urban Regime Theory," *Journal of Urban Affairs* 25, 3 (2003): 271–84, argues for the increased use of community development corporations as well as greater resort to community ownership and community land trusts in establishing "local-statist regimes" and "community-based regimes." In Chapter 8 of this book we examine in greater detail the potential of CDCs.

67. Kotkin, *The New Geography,* p. 7.

68. For an earlier overview of the Cascadia region's economic development efforts focused around the concept of sustainability, see Alan F. J. Artibise, "Achieving Sustainability in Cascadia: An Emerging Model of Urban Growth Management in the Vancouver-Seattle-Portland Corridor," in *North American Cities and the Global Economy,* ed. Peter Karl Kresl and Gary Gappert, *Urban Affairs Annual Review* 44 (Thousand Oaks, CA: SAGE Publications, 1995), pp. 221–250.

69. Clarke and Gaile, "Local Politics in a Global Era," p. 42.

70. Clarke and Gaile, *The Work of Cities,* pp. 4, 9–10, 184–185.

71. Savitch and Kantor, *Cities in the International Marketplace,* pp. 344–45. Also see their larger discussion on pp. 313–345.

72. Ibid., pp. 20–21.

Who Has the Power? Decision
Making and Urban Regimes

4

"Who has the power in local government?" To answer this question, we must look behind the formal structures of government to discern if there are off-stage actors who influence or constrain urban decision making. An examination of urban decision making will also allow us to assess the state of local democracy. Do suburbs and cities generally respond to the demands of the powerful few? Or is municipal government generally open and responsive to diverse interests and constituencies?

For many decades, the debate over local democracy was essentially dominated by two competing schools of thought: **Power elite theorists** saw the urban political system as relatively closed and dominated by business interests. **Pluralists,** in contrast, saw the political system as more open to a diversity of groups.

Yet in recent years, many urban theorists have come to see both the power elite and pluralist theories as failing to accurately describe the nature of urban political power. Business leaders do not simply dictate to a city, as elite theorists often contend; there are simply too many cases in which suburban and city officials fail to cater to the demands of business leaders. Yet local communities appear to be more sensitive to business interests and less responsive to neighborhood groups and citizen demands than pluralist theory contends.

A newer school of thought, that of **urban political economy,** argues that economic factors (including business concerns) act to constrain, but do not eliminate, a city's leeway in decision making. Economics counts, but so does politics. Still, as we shall see, business interests often occupy a special place in the local arena as city officials tend to cater to those projects that contribute to a city's economic growth and development.

POWER ELITE THEORY

Many of the early field studies of community power, often conducted by sociologists, came to the conclusion that business elites controlled local decision making. Helen and Robert Lynd, for instance, concluded that "Middletown" (Muncie, Indiana) was effectively controlled, in all important respects, by a business elite dominated by the "X Family."[1]

Probably the most notable power elite study was provided by Floyd Hunter in his analysis of the power structure of 1950s Atlanta (which he called "Regional City"), results he reaffirmed in 1980 after his "revisit" to the city.[2] Hunter used a **reputational approach,** asking knowledgeable observers to identify the most important decision makers in various policy arenas in the city. The same names of powerful figures came up on list after list. Hunter concluded that Atlanta was dominated by a private business elite whose leaders lived in the best parts of the city, frequented the same social clubs, and who met behind closed doors. (See "Urban Films—Power Elite Politics: *Roger and Me* and *Chinatown*".)

URBAN FILMS POWER ELITE POLITICS: *ROGER AND ME* AND *CHINATOWN*

There is probably no clearer statement of power elite theory than Michael Moore's "guerilla" documentary, *Roger and Me* (1989). Moore, a native of Flint, Michigan, traces the decline of his beloved city as it passes from an auto factory worker's paradise to a city marred by extensive abandonment, poverty, and helplessness. There are clear villains in Moore's film: General Motors and its CEO Roger Smith closed automobile plants in Flint in favor of production in low-wage plants in Mexico and overseas. Flint's decline is the result of its loss of good-paying jobs. Tens of thousand of workers in Flint lost their jobs as a result of plant closings.

Moore presents Smith as the power behind the scenes, isolated in corporate boardrooms and elite clubs, and protected by private security, with no first-hand knowledge of the misery that GM's policies are bringing the people of Flint. Indeed, Smith is a member of a private, corporate elite that is so aloof that Moore cannot even get to interview him. Smith is accountable to his stockholders; he is not answerable to the people of Flint. Moore shows Smith celebrating the Christmas season while the members of a poor Flint family are evicted from their home as they cannot pay the rent. It is Smith's and GM's decisions, not those of the mayor or the city council, that have doomed Flint and its hard-working people.

A similar elite-theory interpretation of urban development is presented in Roman Polanski's classic *Chinatown* (1974), starring Jack Nicholson and Faye Dunaway. *Chinatown* is a bit of historical fiction, based loosely on Los Angeles' 1908 land and water grab scandal. This *noir* detective-crime film presents a fictionalized account of the epic story of the growth of Los Angeles. A rich and powerful brute, Noah Cross (played by John Huston), resorts to both violence and behind-the-scenes manipulations to pave the way for both his own land development schemes and the growth of L.A. He orchestrates an artificial

continued

> ### URBAN FILMS POWER ELITE POLITICS:
> ### *ROGER AND ME* AND *CHINATOWN* (CONT.)
>
> water shortage by having the city turn off the supply of water to the San Fernando Valley, driving the area's orchard owners off their land so that their acreage can be opened to new development. Los Angeles' future is shaped by a labyrinth of unscrupulous and illegal land deals that are invisible to outside authorities. No one knows what is really going on behind the closed doors of elite circles.
>
> A closer look at *Chinatown* reveals that private actors did not by themselves possess the power to bring to consummation their plans for land speculation and the growth of Los Angeles. Noah Cross finds a willing partner in Hollis Mulwray, the head of the Department of Water and Power, who shares the visions of a dynamic, glorious Los Angeles of the future. *Chinatown* points to the power of the shared vision that mobilized both public officials and private powers in Los Angeles' long-enduring growth regime.

THE PLURALIST CHALLENGE

Political scientists closely associated with the school of pluralism attacked the sociologists' conclusions. They argued that Hunter and others employed a flawed methodology, using biased questions that presupposed the existence of a unified elite.[3] In reality, a city's business community is often divided, not unified, on key issues. In cities as diverse as Atlanta, Boston, Denver, Fort Worth, and San Diego, different factions of the business community have fought one another over such matters as the construction and location of a new convention center.[4]

The sociologists also confused reputation with reality; they discovered only who had the reputation for being powerful, not who actually influenced important local decisions. A person's reputation for being powerful might be undeserved and may simply reflect local mythology. In a small town, for instance, everyone might assume that the local college president is an all-controlling local actor when he or she might in reality be quite disinterested in most local matters. Similarly, while often reputed to be powerful, local business groups are not always active in civic affairs. In smaller- and medium-sized communities, in particular, economic development decisions are often left to the city manager and the professional staff at city hall.[5]

The pluralists argued that urban power researchers must do more than ask questions focused on building a list of a community's reputed power brokers. Instead, researchers must attempt to trace who actually did, and who did not, influence key city decisions.

In the classic statement of pluralism, *Who Governs?*, Robert Dahl found no evidence to support the view that a power elite ruled New Haven, Connecticut. Instead, Dahl found that power resources, while unequally distributed in the city, were not all concentrated in one set of hands.[6] Dahl's review of New Haven's history showed that industrialization and immigration acted to disperse wealth and voting power. New business entrepreneurs challenged the older business and social elite that once ruled American cities. Immigrants from Europe, too, possessed the advantage of numbers, an important resource at the ballot box.

No one elite group controlled politics in all issue areas. Instead, Dahl found a **specialization of influence** in which different groups are interested and active in different issue areas. The people active in school issues were different from the realtors and developers who dominated urban renewal and from the political activists involved in political party nominations. The larger citizenry, while fairly passive, still exerted considerable **indirect influence** over the process, as public officials, who could be denied reelection, had to anticipate the public's concerns.

Pluralist studies essentially replicated Dahl's findings in other cities. According to the pluralists, no covert elite ruled. Instead, power in the local arena was unequally, but widely, shared.

THE INADEQUACIES OF THE PLURALIST VIEW

The pluralists tried to trace how local decisions were actually made. Their critics charged that such methodology blinded analysts to behind-the-scenes exertions of power that do not take place in public forums. Public officials in New Haven, for instance, may have bent over backward in anticipation of the needs of Yale University and the city's business community; yet such influence is not readily traceable.[7]

The pluralists examined only the most visible "face" of power when they traced who actively influenced municipal decisions. Such an approach misses an equally important second face of power, that power is also exercised when a group is able to keep a threatening issue off the decision-making table. A potentially troublesome issue can be kept from developing and reaching city government; in essence, it is relegated to the rank of a **nonissue** or **nondecision** and is ignored.[8] But as there is no public decision to make, there is no public decision and bias for the pluralists to observe.

How does a nondecision work? A corporation's power may be so mighty that its executives can influence local affairs without having to lobby municipal officials in public. Municipal officials in Gary, Indiana, for instance, were relatively late in implementing air pollution controls as they feared offending U.S. Steel, the city's major employer. U.S. Steel did not have to publicly press the mayor or the city council who knew, as did everyone in the city, that the giant corporation could cut back production at its Gary mills and move jobs elsewhere should the city decide to impose and enforce costly pollution-reduction requirements on its Gary plants.[9]

Pluralist theory is further suspect in its assertion that every group can mobilize and be "effectively heard" when it feels threatened and when its urgent interests are at stake. Study after study has reported instances of poor-people's and community groups that, even when quite active, have little to show for their efforts. As protest actions by the poor are difficult to sustain over long periods of time, the target of an action often can simply outwait the protest.

Municipal officials can also deflect the power of a protest by dispensing only token or symbolic benefits instead of meaningful policy change.[10] Pluralism does not accurately portray the relative powerlessness of the poor.

SUNBELT CITIES: ELITE DOMINANCE IN TRANSITION

Throughout much of their history, Sunbelt cities have been governed by a "commercial-civic elite"[11] characterized by "the close relationship between the private economic community and the public decision-making community."[12] In Houston, the penetration of government by local business elites was so considerable that the borderline between business and government was not clearly discernible:

> As Houston grew during the 1950s and 1960s, the growth coalition held sway over local government. Oscar Holcombe, a land dealer and developer, was mayor for 22 of the years between 1921 and 1957. In 1981, the mayor was a developer; one-third of the city council was in real estate or closely related fields, and the planning commission was composed mostly of developers, builders, and others tied to the real estate industry field.[13]

Houston's priorities reflected those of its business leaders. The city invested considerable sums into the capital outlays demanded by business while keeping tax rates and social services to a minimum.

In other Sunbelt cities, business leaders formed strong civic groups that dominated the local political arena. Among the more notable were the Citizen's Charter Association in Dallas, the Good Government League in San Antonio, and the Phoenix 40.[14]

For much of the South's and Southwest's history, the dominance of local commercial-civic elites went virtually unquestioned. However, by the latter part of the 1900s, demographic changes in the Sunbelt and a new social awareness began to alter traditional patterns of power. The heightened activism of racial minorities, middle-class homeowners, taxpayer associations, and environmentalists all produced new challenges to elite rule.

San Antonio has seen a growing Chicano population challenge the hold of the traditional Anglo-business civic elite.[15] Houston maintains its pro-growth orientation, but the growing number of minority voters has led to the election of mayors with a commitment to job training and social service programs.[16] In San Jose, California, homeowners and environmentalists have begun to question the traffic congestion and overcrowding that accompanied the growth-oriented policies of the local civic elite.[17]

Demographic and economic changes have altered patterns of power in Sunbelt cities. Contemporary Atlanta no longer matches the elite power structure reported by Floyd Hunter. Today in Atlanta, traditional local business and social elites find that their hold on the city is challenged by the executives of national firms who lack the local loyalties of the city's more established elite groups. African-American elected representatives, too, are now key civic actors in majority-minority Atlanta.

San Jose and Charlotte are two cities where rapid economic growth has similarly resulted in a more diversified business community. The corporate managers of national and global firms do not always share the perspectives and interests of the older, locally rooted downtown elite. In San Jose, power has passed from the old local business elite to the executives of the national corporations that have sited new facilities in the area.[18]

In the dynamic Sunbelt, the power of the local business elite varies from community to community. In Fort Lauderdale, Florida, for instance, the influence of the private sector remains strong. Municipal decision makers pursued a business-oriented growth policy, building Fort Lauderdale's Riverwalk esplanade, a performing arts center, and other downtown facilities. The city did relatively little to aid its more disadvantaged residents. In Orlando, in contrast, local policies exhibited greater balance; city officials used development as a source of revenues to help finance low- and moderate-income housing.[19] In St. Petersburg, growth-oriented business elites have faced new counterpressures from minority groups and taxpayers upset that vast sums of money had been spent on the Suncoast Dome baseball stadium and the Pier Point waterfront aquarium while neighborhood needs went unmet.[20]

"CITY LIMITS": HOW ECONOMIC COMPETITION SHAPES POWER IN THE MODERN CITY

THE ECONOMIC ROOTS OF CITY LIMITS

Why is it that cities tend to cater to business needs even if there is no small cabal of business leaders who control a city's actions from behind closed doors? Paul Peterson, in his important book *City Limits*, articulates one possible explanation.[21] According to Peterson, local officials must deal with the problems posed by the **mobility of capital.** As the owners of a business can locate their facilities in another town or state, a municipality's officials, fearing the loss of a city's job and tax bases, have little real choice other than to pursue those actions that will attract business and ensure a city's economic good health.

The mobility of capital—the ability to locate their facilities elsewhere—gives business leaders substantial leverage in securing public subsidies and other considerations. Local officials often—but not always—respond with a sense of urgency to the threat of a business departure. (See "Bear Sterns, CIGNA, and the New York/New Jersey/Philadelphia Bidding Wars" on p. 109.) Local action can be embarrassingly quick when the owner of a sports franchise threatens to move a team elsewhere. Just days after Ross Perot, Jr., the then-majority owner of the Dallas Mavericks basketball team, began aerial site tours with suburban officials, the city of Dallas sweetened its offer to build the team a new downtown arena.[22] When Brooklyn, New York developers revealed plans for a new basketball arena to lure the Nets away from New Jersey, New Jersey Governor James McGreevey immediately countered by announcing a new state $150 million commitment to build a new rail line to the Nets' current home in the Meadowlands.[23]

BEAR STEARNS, CIGNA, AND THE NEW YORK/NEW JERSEY/ PHILADELPHIA BORDER WARS

The executives of large corporations have learned to play one community against another in the search for new tax abatements and other subsidies. As Petersonian theory predicts, local public officials will seldom risk offending business executives who threaten to locate a firm elsewhere. Only on rare occasions do local political leaders exhibit the political skill and daring to confront major corporations.

In 2002, the investment bank Bear, Stearns & Company demanded millions of dollars in additional tax breaks from New York City. The company complained of rising rents at its Brooklyn global operations site and threatened to move up to 1,000 of its employees across the river to the firm's regional offices in New Jersey. New Jersey officials had also offered the company tens of millions of dollars in tax breaks in their efforts to land an expanded share of the firm's operations.

New York development officials were outraged, given the concessions that the city had provided Bear Stearns over the years. A decade previous, in 1991, the company had made a similar threat to move its employees to its new office park in Whippany, New Jersey. New York City Mayor David Dinkins responded with more than $36 million in assistance. In return, the company agreed to move 1,500 back-office jobs to the new MetroTech development in the downtown Brooklyn section of New York, just across the bridge from Lower Manhattan. Only a half dozen years later, in 1997, Mayor Rudolph Giuliani gave Bear Stearns an additional $75 million in incentives and subsidies to aid the investment bank as it constructed its new headquarters building on Madison Avenue in midtown Manhattan. In return, the firm agreed to keep at least 5,700 employees in the city for the next 50 years.

New York officials saw Bear Stearns' 2002 announcement as an attempt to extract still additional assistance from the city. This time, though, the city faced a $5-billion budget deficit, and Mayor Michael Bloomberg refused. The mayor insisted that the city would hold the company to its past agreement.

After a public standoff, however, Bloomberg helped to arrange a package that would be acceptable to the corporation. Bear Stearns was allowed to convert $4.8 million of unused sales tax breaks from the 1991 agreement into new property tax exemptions for its Brooklyn development. The firm also negotiated new rents and agreed to a 20-year lease, assuring that the jobs would be kept in Brooklyn.

Jonathan Bowles, research director of the Center for an Urban Future, complained that the "ridiculous border war" between New Jersey and New York allowed major corporations such as Bear Stearns to play the two states against one another.

New York, however, was not the only city engaged in a bidding war with New Jersey. As part of its Camden Recovery Act, New Jersey Governor

continued

BEAR STEARNS, CIGNA, AND THE NEW YORK/NEW JERSEY/ PHILADELPHIA BORDER WARS (CONT.)

James E. McGreevey offered new tax incentives intended to lure thousands of jobs from CIGNA and other Philadelphia firms to locations in New Jersey. The new law offered a firm new tax advantages for each job that was created in New Jersey or moved to the state from another state. New Jersey offered a 75-percent reduction in state-corporate business taxes for any firm that moved to Camden. State officials argued that such generous provisions were necessary to bring a new economic renaissance to that much-troubled city. Pennsylvania officials decried the ratcheting up of an interstate bidding war.

The potential mobility of capital gives major firms a considerable strategic edge as they seek to secure advantageous tax provisions and other subsidies from states and localities. Critics complain of the inequities that result from such "corporate welfare." Homeowners and other businesses, especially smaller businesses, face the prospect of increased taxes to make up the costs of subsidies and foregone revenues. Schools and other community services also face the prospect of cutbacks as a result of the revenues that were negotiated away in economic development packages.

Sources: Jack Lyne, "$4.8M Incentives Shift Helps Keep 1,500 Bear Stearns Workers in New York," *Site Selection Online Insider,* April 2003, available at: www.conway.com/ ssinsider/incentive/ ti0304.htm; Charles V. Bagli, "Bear, Stearns Threatens to Leave City and Seeks Third Set of Deals to Stay," *The New York Times,* December 11, 2002; Henry J. Holcomb, "New Jersey Spurs Talk of Philadelphia Job War," *Philadelphia Inquirer* (September 3, 2003); Robert Moran, "Tax Break With Lure for CIGNA Is Signed," *Philadelphia Inquirer* (November 22, 2003).

Local authorities have provided team owners with new sports arenas (with luxury skyboxes) and lucrative tax concessions and benefits despite the cost overruns that often plague such projects and evidence that points to such investments as a very expensive and inefficient way to create new (and often low-paying) jobs. Cities may gain a sense of prestige and other intangible benefits from hosting a major-league team, and city officials also fear being blamed for the loss of a sports franchise. But strictly speaking, in economic terms, cities get little return for providing lavish subsidies to successful corporate owners.[24]

Our quick review of local policies in support of new stadiums and arenas is consistent with Peterson's theory. Whenever a local decision has an impact on a particular development project or the city's business climate, municipal officials quite often anticipate what business wants. No city can afford to adversely affect its business climate. The city as a whole is led to act as if it possessed a **unitary interest** in pursuing economic development; it is almost as if the pluralist politics within the city does not matter, as if there were no contending local groups pressing for different policies.

Such a unitary perspective was evident when Chicago's two newspapers, despite their normally conflicting partisan orientations, came together in support of the mayor's initiatives for school reform. News stories in both papers highlighted the underperformance of city schools and the importance of Mayor Richard M. Daley's initiatives in providing an educated workforce that will allow the city to pursue continued economic growth. Both newspapers focused on the mayor and his actions, portraying the measures as being in the public interest while downplaying the objections of community voices.[25] The city's interest in continued economic growth helped to crowd out normal politics even in the usually contentious arena of school politics.

PETERSON'S POLICY TYPOLOGY

Business considerations do not dominate all aspects of city politics. Not every municipal decision affects businesses directly or even has an impact on a city's business climate. Peterson sees three types of city policies: developmental, redistributive, and allocation. Business considerations tend to dominate the first two, but not the third.

When it comes to **developmental policy,** matters that directly affect the economic position of the city, governmental officials anticipate business needs. Municipal offices provide subsidies, land-use plans, and the roads and other infrastructure demanded by business leaders. Cities also cannot afford to impose a level of taxes that will drive businesses to competing communities.

Redistributive policy, which encompasses social welfare, health, housing, and other programs of assistance to poor people, is similarly affected by the fear that extensive social welfare spending will require an increase in tax levels, adversely affecting a city's attractiveness to business:

> [T]he pursuit of a city's economic interests, which requires an efficient provision of local services, makes no allowance for the care of the needy and unfortunate members of the society. Indeed, the competition among local communities all but precludes a concern for redistribution.[26]

For Peterson, New York City's mid-1970s fiscal crisis underscores the disastrous consequences that can result when a municipality ignores "city limits" and attempts to initiate broad social welfare policy.

But there is a third area of local policy that does not have a bearing on a city's competitive position or business climate. These are issues that are largely neutral in their economic effects. Business leaders have no direct concern with **allocation policies,** decisions that deal, for instance, with how library books and fire stations are distributed throughout the city. In this arena, a city is relatively free to react to the demands of citizen and neighborhood groups.

Do cities really prefer economic development programs over social welfare policy? One survey of the nation's mayors found that their policy attitudes roughly matched what Peterson's theory predicted. The mayors expressed a greater willingness to spend on programs for economic development; they were somewhat less willing to spend on allocative services. They were least willing to commit city resources to social welfare and other redistributive services.[27]

THE PETERSONIAN MODEL UNDER ATTACK

Peterson's notion of interlocal economic competition helps to explain the primacy of economic development policies on big-city agendas. Yet Peterson has numerous critics who are unhappy with his contention that a locality has little real alternative other than to cater to the needs and demands of business.[28] Peterson's theory borders on economic determinism in its reasoning that cities, acting on their need to maintain their economic viability, are led to cater to their business community while neglecting welfare, health, and housing services.

The pressures for a city to respond to the needs of business are never ending. Yet there is no simple economic determinism. Local politics and leadership choices remain important as a city decides just how it will respond to the threat posed by capital mobility.

In fact, there may be more than one way for a city to be economically competitive. Low taxes and the offering of special incentives represent one popular route for attracting businesses. But businesses will not always find low-tax, low-service communities attractive. Good schools, an educated workforce, ample parks and recreational space, and high quality-of-life amenities may also attract businesses, especially firms with a professional workforce who demand a high-quality lifestyle.

Peterson sees increased spending on education as counterproductive to a community's economic health as a result of the taxes that are required to pay for such a redistributive benefit. But a creative mayor or policy entrepreneur could reframe or "sell" increased spending on schools as a means of local economic development; high-technology businesses will be more willing to locate in a city with a better-educated labor force. Educational spending, which Peterson sees as redistributive, may have positive developmental effects.[29] Subsidized day care, too, is not just a redistributive program for women and children; it is also a program that increases a city's attractiveness to business by increasing the availability of low-cost labor in a community.[30]

The link between low tax rates and a community's attractiveness to business may also be looser than Peterson's theory assumes. Businesses are not fully free to move to those sites offering the greatest package of tax reductions and incentives. Transportation and accessibility to suppliers, quality labor, and markets are more prominent factors than low taxes in determining a business' siting decisions.[31] As businesses are not totally mobile, cities often can pay for housing and redistributive health, education, and social services without suffering an outmigration of business.

Peterson's assertion that "policies of benefit to the city contribute to the prosperity of all residents"[32] is clearly overstated. Municipal actions that lead to the maximization of land values work to the benefit of landowners and developers while displacing the poor, the elderly, and small businesses.[33] When it comes to downtown development projects, the owners of shops in other sections of the city may well object to having to pay for projects from which they do not directly benefit. In Kalamazoo, Michigan, plans for center-city revitalization stalled when the city's "larger community of business firms" objected to the costs entailed by higher taxes and the rerouting of traffic.[34]

Evidently, there is no unitary city interest in pursuing growth. Economic development can be highly contentious; economic development policy cannot be viewed as "groupless" or consensual as Peterson contends. Elected officials may well find it in their political interest to back neighborhood groups in their opposition to controversial economic development projects. In such a case, the "political logic" of opposing growth may cancel out Peterson's "economic logic" of supporting growth.[35]

Peterson errs in that his theory borders on economic determinism. Nonetheless, despite this overstatement, Peterson points to an extremely strong and important tendency in contemporary municipal affairs: In their efforts to preserve a city's competitiveness, local officials tend to initiate policies that cater to the needs of the business community and of tax-paying, upscale residents. As a result, city politics is essentially a limited politics. All but the nation's most affluent and countercultural communities tend to pursue local agendas that favor new economic growth and development.

REGIME THEORY: GETTING THINGS DONE THROUGH GOVERNING COALITIONS

SYSTEMIC POWER

Clarence Stone asks: "Why, when all of their actions are taken into account, do officials over the long haul seem to favor upper-strata interests, disfavor lower-strata interests, and sometimes act in apparent disregard of the contours of electoral power?"[36] For Stone, the answer lies in the limited ability of city officials to get important things done. City officials are systemically drawn to recognize the demands of the business community, as they need the cooperation of business leaders in order to carry major city projects to fruition.

While business leaders do not have the raw power to dictate a course of action to the city, they nonetheless possess the ability to frustrate projects they dislike. It is private leaders, not city officials, who determine where investments are made; their decisions determine the success or failure of downtown revitalization, neighborhood renewal, youth hiring, and many other important undertakings desired by municipal officials.

Officials in city hall do not always share the perspectives of business leaders and may even oppose the changes desired by the business community. Still, municipal officeholders sooner or later come to see the importance of forging a viable, working arrangement with key private interests.

REGIME THEORY AND THE IMPORTANCE OF GOVERNING COALITIONS

According to Stone, *power* is not simply the control of A over B; rather, **power** denotes the ability to get things done. Public and private actors often find that they need each other and that it is in their mutual interest to cooperate and work together. As a result, informal governing alliances often emerge in a city over time. The long-term, informal public-private governing arrangement that can be found in many cities is known as an urban **regime.**

Private actors who control critical resources usually occupy a privileged position in a city's governing regime. In some cities, business cooperation is so crucial to the success of public projects that the business community can be seen to possess **preemptive power;** their noncooperation can effectively doom a project. Business leaders protect their interests by parceling out selective benefits or rewards to political actors who chose to "go along."[37]

Regime theory points to the importance of looking at *governance,* and not just at elections, when determining who has power in a city. The membership of a **city's governing regime,** the people whose cooperation is essential for getting important things done, may be quite different from the **electoral coalition** that put the mayor and city council into office. During the election, a mayoral candidate courts support and votes from just about anyone who can help secure victory. But election does not guarantee the ability to deliver on important things once in office. In office, a mayor must build a new governing coalition. The mayor must reach out beyond his or her electoral base to forge a working alliance with whoever has the resources necessary for carrying plans to completion. As a result, governing coalitions frequently include actors who were not participants in the mayor's election campaign. A governing regime can be said to exist if an informal public-private alliance, based on mutual cooperation, carries over from one administration to the next.

Regime theory points to the limits of electoral politics when it comes to black and Hispanic power. Even in cities with an African-American majority, the election of a black mayor and a black city council does not guarantee that local government has the power to pursue strong policies that would work to the advantage of the city's African-American population and the poor. Instead, black officials in city hall must reach an accommodation with business officials who control key investment resources.[38]

The concept of a regime points to the relatively *durable* alliances that emerge among elected officials, their supporters, development interests, property owners, and professional bureaucrats in the day-to-day running of a city. In cities such as Atlanta, a growing black majority has dominated municipal elections, leading some observers to conclude way too quickly that black power has displaced the old civic business elite that once ran the city. A closer examination reveals a quite different story, that despite black electoral victories, local business leaders were still able to maintain their privileged position in the biracial regime that governed the new Atlanta. (See "Atlanta's Biracial Governing Regime" on pp. 115–117.)

ATLANTA'S BIRACIAL GOVERNING REGIME

Regime theory underscores the importance of coalition formation in the governing of a city. For most of the mid- and late 1900s, Atlanta was governed by a biracial governing regime, an effective working alliance between local business leaders and the city's African-American middle-class leaders. The existence of this informal, biracial governing coalition even helps to explain why Atlanta responded with more moderation, and with less racial violence, than did other southern cities to the changes brought by the civil rights movement.

Clarence Stone's study of Atlanta points to the importance of looking beyond elections to discern just whose cooperation is essential to the governing of a city. During the civil rights years, the city's downtown business elite took steps to avoid the protests and civil unrest that could tarnish the city's good-place-for-business image. As Clarence Stone describes, in "The City Too Busy to Hate," white business leaders and elected officials forged a working arrangement with middle-class black allies. The city's business leaders and African Americans did not share exactly the same interests; rather, they learned to work with one another.*

As blacks gained voting rights, a focus only on election results alone would lead to the mistaken conclusion that the city's black majority was able to take effective control of Atlanta. In reality, the picture is much more complex. The business community maintained a position of influence in the governance of Atlanta despite the growing dominance of African-American voters. The city's first black mayors, Maynard Jackson (elected in 1973) and Andrew Young (1981), came to see the value of working with the downtown business community.

Maynard Jackson was a political outsider who initially challenged Atlanta's traditional system of elite-led accommodation. He sought to reshape the planning process to allow neighborhoods a veto over growth projects favored by the downtown elite. He insisted on strong affirmative action policies, awarding 20 percent of contracts on development projects to minority firms. He also sought to reform the police department.

But Jackson soon discovered that he could not achieve his major objectives without business support. The mayor and the city's business elite eventually reached an accommodation. Atlanta's business leaders got the new international airport they badly desired; in return, they finally ceded to the strong affirmative action measures in hiring and contracting that Jackson had demanded. In reaching a new accommodation with business leaders, the mayor cut back his support of the neighborhood planning system, resisted the wage demands of the city's labor unions, and gave business leaders greater access to city hall. Many business leaders greatly disliked Jackson, but realized that they would benefit from a cooperative working relationship with city hall.

continued

ATLANTA'S BIRACIAL GOVERNING REGIME (CONT.)

Jackson's successors, Andrew Young and Bill Campbell (elected 1993), were even more supportive of economic growth. Young, in contrast to Jackson, was an Atlanta political insider who from the very beginning sought a cooperative relationship with the local business community. Young believed that economic growth would bring new jobs and business opportunities to the African-American community. His focus on economic development, including extensive subsidies for the revitalization of Underground Atlanta and his efforts to bring the 1996 Summer Olympics to Atlanta, won the enthusiastic endorsement of the city's business leaders. The Olympic Games provided justification for a massive investment in the region's communications infrastructure; 150 miles of fiber-optic cable was laid in the Olympic Village alone.**

Protests by neighborhood activists in Atlanta could not stop the city as it demolished homes and small businesses in a low-income area to build a park and gathering area for visitors to the Olympics. Neighborhood groups failed in their efforts to minimize the displacement of minorities and the homeless by bringing to a halt the construction of a new stadium (which was turned over to the Atlanta Braves baseball team after the summer games) and other facilities.***

Mayor Bill Campbell initially won great business support for his reduction in the size of the city workforce and for his Renaissance Program that sought to build on the energy of the Olympics. But the Renaissance Program floundered when business and elected leaders could not agree on specific projects. The city's newspapers and good-government civic forces also attacked the Campbell administration for corruption and bribery.

In 2001, Shirley Franklin, a black woman, was elected mayor. Having served as a policy advisor to the Atlanta Committee on the Olympic Games and as Mayor Andrew Young's chief administrative officer, Mayor Franklin came to office with the expectation that she would continue, not challenge, the working relationship between the city and business interests.†

This review of the political evolution of Atlanta reveals that, for much of its contemporary history, a biracial coalition has coalesced around economic development projects of mutual interest. At times, tensions marred the working relationship. In recent years the coalition has shown strain as its different members do not share the same values or fully trust one another.

Today, the governing ability of Atlanta's biracial regime is very much in doubt.‡ Suburbanization and globalization have brought new corporate executives to the region, managers who lack the interest in civic affairs and the loyalty of the home-grown, downtown leaders of the 1950s and 1960s. African-American unity, too, has been weakened by an increasing sense of distance between upper-strata and poorer black citizens.

The capacity of Atlanta's regime for serious problem solving has been undermined. For a long period of time, business involvement in city school policy all but disappeared. When business leaders finally did pick up the banner of school

continued

ATLANTA'S BIRACIAL GOVERNING REGIME (CONT.)

reform, continuing tensions between leaders from white suburbs and the more disadvantaged central-city neighborhoods precluded the formation of a workable biracial alliance.

* Clarence N. Stone, *Regime Politics—Governing Atlanta: 1946–88* (Lawrence: University of Kansas Press, 1989), especially pp. 77–159.

** Drew Whitelegg, "Going for the Gold: Atlanta's Bid for Fame," *International Journal of Urban and Regional Research* 24, 4 (2000): 801–817, especially 806 and 810.

*** Cynthia Horan, "Racializing Urban Regimes," *Journal of Urban Affairs* 24, 1 (2002): 25–27; Harvey K. Newman, "Race and the Tourist Bubble in Downtown Atlanta," *Urban Affairs Review* 37, 3 (January 2002): 301–302; Matthew J. Burbank, Charles H. Heying, and Greg Andranovich, "Antigrowth Politics or Piecemeal Resistance? Citizen Opposition to Olympic-Related Economic Growth," *Urban Affairs Review* 35, 3 (January 2000): 334–357; Matthew J. Burbank, Gregory D. Andranovich, and Charles H. Heying, *Olympic Dreams: The Impact of Mega-events on Local Politics* (Boulder, CO: Lynne Rienner, 2001); Larry Keating, *Atlanta: Race, Class and Urban Expansion* (Philadelphia, PA: Temple University Press, 2001).

† Michael Leo Owens and Michael J. Rich, "Is Strong Incorporation Enough? Black Empowerment and the Fate of Atlanta's Low-Income Blacks," in *Racial Politics in American Cities,* 3rd ed., eds. Rufus P. Browning, Dale Rogers Marshall, and David H. Tabb (New York: Longman, 2003), pp. 212–214.

‡ Clarence Stone and Carol Pierannunzi, "Atlanta's Biracial Coalition in Transition" (paper presented at the annual meeting of the American Political Science Association, Washington, DC, August 31–September 3, 2000).

DIFFERENT REGIME TYPES

As we have just seen, the business community controls key resources and usually occupies a privileged position in city affairs. Yet there is no guarantee that a business-oriented regime will always emerge and govern a city. In New York, a city much larger and more diverse than Atlanta, the business community has been less cohesive and has enjoyed less sustained dominance over municipal affairs. In New York, progressive mayors, public sector officials, labor unions, and community and reform political groups have been able to offer a relatively strong counterweight to corporate elites.[39]

Different regimes or governing alliances have emerged in different cities and at different periods in a city's history. Corporate-oriented regimes may be the norm in most big cities; yet not all cities are dominated by such growth coalitions. In some cities, a more neighborhood-oriented regime, organized around community issues and social services, has emerged, at least for short periods of time. In "good government" small- and medium-sized communities, the local political culture may mitigate against the active involvement of business officials in development decisions, leaving those decisions in the hands of the city manager and professionally trained municipal officials.[40] In other communities, there is no apparent regime or stable governing coalition; instead, each new election brings a new set of actors and interests who enjoy special access to city hall.[41]

What are the possible different regime types?[42] A **corporate regime** (also called a **development regime**) promotes continued growth, reflecting the interests of a city's major corporations. City governments governed by a corporate regime tend to slight equity concerns, especially the interests of poor people and the residents of a city's more distressed neighborhoods. Even in a corporate regime, business does not possess command power; the business community does not get everything it wants. Still, in a corporate regime, business leaders and elected officials find that they need to work with one another, despite their differences, to get things done.

However, not all cities are so growth oriented. Especially in small- and medium-sized cities, a **caretaker regime** (also referred to as a **maintenance regime**) will be reluctant to undertake the large-scale development projects demanded by major corporations. In a caretaker city, the small-business community and homeowners often join together in opposing big undertakings that will increase taxes and disrupt established patterns of life in the city. Caretaker governments focus on the provision of routine services, not the initiation of major renewal and development projects.

The rarest urban regime type of all is the **progressive regime,** in which a city responds to the demands of its lower- and middle-class citizens and environmentalist groups rather than pursuing corporate-oriented growth projects. In fact, there are two variants of the progressive regime: A **middle-class progressive regime** represents the concerns of environmentalists and homeowners who are opposed to costly and disruptive growth projects.[43] **A regime devoted to lower-class opportunity expansion,** by comparison, is not committed primarily to slow growth and environmental protection; instead, it seeks the greater provision of jobs and assistance in a city's poorer neighborhoods. In a progressive regime, nonprofit entities, community-based organizations, and community development corporations (CDCs) gain the access to city hall that is more normally reserved for business.[44]

Progressive coalitions built around resource redistribution are often unstable and short-lived. Harold Washington, the first African American to be elected mayor in Chicago, embraced a program of neighborhood equity and empowerment.[45] For a short period of time, Harold Washington was able to hold this lower-class-opportunity regime together through the force of his own charisma and leadership. However, the regime virtually dissolved with his death, and a corporate regime was reestablished in Chicago under the guidance of Mayor Richard M. Daley.

The fate of Boston's progressive regime tells a somewhat similar story. In 1983, community activists helped to elect the self-styled progressive Raymond Flynn as mayor. Flynn was committed to growth restrictions, affordable housing, and job training for the poor. But, again, such a progressive regime was short-lived. The economic recession and federal aid cutbacks of the early 1990s led Flynn and his successor, Thomas Menino, to give a new priority to growth projects.[46]

Similarly, in New York, community groups helped to elect David Dinkins, a mayor who was sympathetic to neighborhood needs. But no progressive regime was established, and Dinkins was succeeded in office by the more corporate-oriented Rudy Giuliani and Michael Bloomberg. Despite the city's liberal reputation, over the last half century New York has generally pursued a development policy favored by powerful market actors.[47]

The Chicago, Boston, and New York examples reveal how difficult it is for a broad-based progressive regime to maintain its support over time. Governing coalitions that exist for such short periods of time may not even merit the label "regime." The progressive coalition often withers because middle-class home-owners, environmentalists, and minority activists do not share a common agenda. Progressive regimes that impose regulation on private development also lose support, as they are blamed for retarding a city's economic growth by intruding on the workings of a free market.[48]

INTERGOVERNMENTAL REGIMES

Regime theory points to the need of public and private actors to build cooperative networks to get things done. Yet local regimes are also affected by intergovernmental influences. State and federal programs offer tax incentives, subsidies, and requirements for citizen participation that create and shape opportunities for local coalition formation.[49]

In the nation's most financially troubled and mismanaged cities, key decisions are increasingly made not in city hall but in the state house. In such cities, an **intergovernmental regime** exists, with the governor and key state legislators as important regime players.

Despite the protests of school administrators and civil rights/community activists, the State of New Jersey in 1995 took over Newark's distressed school system, removing the elected school board, the local school superintendent, and other top school administrators. State educational officials secured new contributions from businesses to the local schools, giving business leaders a new chance to shape school policy.[50] The State of Connecticut's takeover of the much-troubled, patronage-ridden Hartford school system created a similar governing bias. The regime was not elected by, nor accountable to, Hartford's citizens.[51]

In Chicago, Cleveland, Milwaukee, Phoenix, Pittsburgh, San Jose, and Seattle, state government officials acted to allow new stadiums and arenas to be built after local voters had previously gone to the polls and rejected funding measures for the projects. The states set up new and creative funding plans for the stadiums, administered by special agencies and authorities that were not directly accountable to local elected officials and voters.[52]

THE DEBATE OVER CITY POWER:
TWO CASE STUDIES

The study of community power is an inexact science. Different observers of city events often come to different conclusions. As the following case studies of San Francisco and Detroit help show, there continues to be great debate as to just how much influence the business community exerts on city affairs.

SAN FRANCISCO: MANHATTANIZATION
AND ANTIREGIME POLITICS

In recent decades, the San Francisco political arena has shown an openness to newly emergent political groups, including Chinese, African-American, Hispanic, and gay and lesbian voters. Yet elite influence continues to be felt in a number of key policy areas, especially on issues of local economic development.

The construction of the Yerba Buena Center, a large development project that includes the Moscone Convention Center, was a successful effort "by the city's ruling forces to expand the city's downtown boundaries" across Market Street into the low-income South of Market area. The growth coalition over-estimated the number of jobs and other benefits that the project would gene-rate. Operation of the convention center was not self-sustaining but required annual subsidies. Growth advocates also glossed over the project's displace-ment of 723 businesses and 7,600 jobs. Rising land values and rents led to further displacement in the neighboring area.[53]

Construction of the Center was endorsed by Mayor Dianne Feinstein, who would later be elected to the U.S. Senate. Her willingness to support the expan-sion efforts of downtown business interests was reinforced by the fact that her campaign war chest "came primarily from downtown corporations and big business." In her successful fight against a recall effort, a campaign where the city's normal $1,000 limit per contributor was not applicable, "(n)early half a million dollars came in within a few weeks, almost all from large corporate contributions garnered at a February 14 fund-raising dinner."[54]

Still, despite their success in the Yerba Buena project, big-money interests did not generally rule San Francisco. Various advocacy groups—racial mino-rities, gays and lesbians, and environmentalists—helped to offset the power of big business; neighborhood and environmental groups fought against the continued transformation or "Manhattanization" of their beloved city. They gained the adoption of measures that controlled rents, limited condominium conversions, protected the city's stock of low-income residential hotels, and restricted new high-rise construction.

In 1987, community groups helped elect a mayor, Art Agnos, who promised to protect neighborhoods from unfettered development. Agnos came to office and "slowly, systematically turned over the keys of City Hall to people who in the past often had the door slammed in their face."[55] Yet Agnos disappointed his grassroots supporters when he endorsed a number of major growth pro-jects favored by business elites, including new waterfront development and a downtown ballpark for the Giants baseball team.[56]

Anti-growth forces could not keep control of city hall. Agnos was suc-ceeded by the more conservative "ex-cop" Frank Jordan, who promised to reverse the city's "anything goes" philosophy and take back the city's streets from panhandlers.

Liberals regained control of city hall in 1995 with the election of legendary California House Speaker Willie Brown, an African American and a Democrat, as mayor. But Brown, an old-style politician, had many ties to development interests. In 1999, with support from business interests, labor unions, the Democratic party, and even the local Republican party, the development-enthusiast Brown handily squashed a 1999 challenge by radical-populist Tom Ammiano, an openly gay San Francisco Supervisor who had vowed to "declare war" on gentrification and the city's continued transformation. Brown outspent his opponent by more than 10 to 1, easily winning the December runoff. In office, Brown faced a city council committed to slow-growth values.[57]

In 2003, "socially connected entrepreneur" Gavin Newsom won a run-off election for the city's mayoralty against his Green Party opponent, "[s]haggy-haired Matt Gonzalez, darling of the young, the hip and the non-propertied classes."[58] Gonzales was backed by Agnos, Ammiano, and the actor and political activist Martin Sheen. Newsom promised to expedite the construction of affordable housing in the downtown and near the waterfront, an initiative that pleased growth interests and the city's construction unions. Gonzales, in contrast, emphasized tenants' rights and sought to put limits on the ability of chain stores to move into residential neighborhoods.[59]

As this brief recounting of the city's political history reveals, no stable regime governs San Francisco. Conservative, growth-oriented mayors have alternated in office with more progressive and liberal executives possessing a greater commitment to neighborhood, environmental, and minority concerns. Despite San Francisco's liberal reputation, no progressive regime emerged with a capacity to govern. Anti-growth and neighborhood forces constituted not a governing regime but an **anti-regime**—a loose alliance of groups that were able to block many of the big projects they disliked but were unable to take control of government.[60]

DETROIT: THE DESTRUCTION OF POLETOWN

Detroit today has a black voting majority, a black mayor, and a black-dominated city council. Yet Detroit's African-American community does not fully possess the power of governance. The city's elected leaders do not control the resources necessary for the city's economic rebirth, but instead must seek the cooperation of the leaders of industry.

The nature of power in Detroit is revealed in the controversy that surrounded the construction of a new General Motors assembly plant in the city's so-called Poletown neighborhood. In 1980, General Motors announced the closing of two older Detroit factories with the intention of building a new, more automated facility at a "greenfield" site elsewhere in the country. Detroit officials quickly scrambled to find General Motors an acceptable alternative site. The city, already devastated by a considerable loss of jobs and population, felt that it could not afford the consequences of a GM pullout.

City officials offered GM nine possible sites; GM found suitable only the site in the mixed African-American and Polish community adjacent to the old Dodge Main plant. Poletown residents protested. But the corporation refused to consider alternative site design and parking plans that would minimize the destruction of homes. A "quick take" procedure allowed the city to acquire and demolish homes before final compensation was arranged.

The costs, in both human and dollar terms, were substantial:

> This facility, the infamous "Poletown" plant, involved the destruction of a neighborhood. It was industrial urban renewal on a grand scale: within 18 months of the announcement of the project, 1,500 homes, 144 businesses, two schools, a hospital, 16 churches, and an abandoned reinforced concrete automobile assembly plant whose demolition cost alone was estimated at $12 million were gone, and 3,438 citizens had to be relocated.[61]

Site preparation was estimated at $200 million, but court settlements drove the costs of land assembly much higher.[62] By 1996, the city had paid $100 million in excess of revenues and still owed nearly $50 million on the project.[63] The city used general fund revenues and diverted federal Community Development Block Grant money from neighborhood projects to help pay the Poletown project costs.

The new plan added little in terms of municipal revenue that could be used immediately to improve services for the people of Detroit. GM was given the maximum property tax reduction allowed under state law, a 50-percent tax abatement for a period of 12 years. Furthermore, under the **tax increment financing** plan for the project, any gains in property tax revenue derived from the plant could be used only to repay the initial loans on the project and to make further improvements in the project area. The creation of the TIF district actually lessened the property tax revenue available to local school districts.[64]

While the city was legally obliged to give GM the full range of tax reductions and subsidies, GM was not obligated to deliver the full number of jobs that the corporation said the plant would bring the city. For a time, GM ran only one shift at the plant, halving the 6,000 jobs the plant was supposed to provide. The agreement between GM and the city was one-sided:

> The people of the City of Detroit assumed all the expenses and took all the risks. GM managed to maintain the option of when and under what conditions the proposed plant would be completed, and to determine the level of employment at the plant when and if it began operating.[65]

There had been no real bargaining between the city and GM: "There was, in a word, no policy discretion; there was only capitulation."[66] The city did not even attempt to discover just what tax subsidies GM needed to make a Detroit plant viable. Instead, the city gave GM what it had requested, the "maximum allowable tax abatement" under state law.

The costs to the city soon multiplied when the Chrysler Corporation threatened to close its aging plant on the east side of the city. Chrysler demanded, and was given, a virtual carbon copy of the Poletown deal. The city incurred still additional costs and liability in the expensive environmental cleanup of the contaminated site.[67]

Detroit was not quite GM's passive pawn. The city itself had initiated the action in response to the corporation's announced intention to leave. Mayor

Coleman Young was an adept leader who got his bureaucracy to quickly formulate, and his city council to approve, a plan that would avert GM's departure. Despite his radical and "black power" reputation, Young, the city's first elected black mayor, had established a working relationship with the leaders of the "Big Three" automakers. While Young was a dependable friend of business on the Poletown and Chrysler projects, he was a less dependable partner in other policy areas.[68]

Young acted to protect the future economic prospects of his city and its African-American population. Young saw the controversy in racial terms as "part of a continuing black/white struggle."[69] He dismissed the complaints of white Poletown residents who fought to keep their homes. According to Mayor Young, the white residents of Poletown would be displaced for the good of the city, just as the city's white-dominated government had displaced African-American residents from urban renewal districts beginning in the 1940s. Coleman Young "kept faith with the 'forgotten citizen' of Poletown: the black majority of the neighborhood."[70]

Mayor Young's actions reveal the continuing importance of political leadership. Young used his skills and power to gain the necessary state and city approvals for the controversial project. Yet he was a leader whose actions on the Poletown project were kept within the considerable constraints that GM had imposed on the city.

Young was succeeded in office by Dennis Archer, a more moderate African-American mayor who established a much smoother working relationship with corporate leaders. Archer reduced business taxes, built a downtown baseball stadium and football stadium, helped bring new casinos to the city, and cleared a site in the downtown for a new national headquarters park for Compuware.[71] Archer's successor, Kwame Kilpatrick, the nation's youngest big-city mayor, acted to expedite casino-related and other downtown development plans in his effort to make Detroit a tourist destination, possibly even to begin its growth as a world-class city.[72]

Despite Detroit's overwhelming African-American majority, Detroit cannot really be viewed as a black-power city. The city's African-American officials find that they can govern only by first courting private capital, especially the leaders of the automobile industry. Nor can Detroit's mayors be accurately viewed merely as puppets whose strings are pulled by the corporate elite.

Instead, Detroit has been governed by a long-standing corporate regime. In majority-black Detroit, there was a surprisingly good, long-term working relationship between city officials and corporate leaders. Despite periods of tension, the city's mayors generally worked with business leaders to increase corporate investment in the city and to bring jobs to the city's black community. The mayors needed the cooperation of business leaders. Corporate leaders, in turn, needed the cooperation of the city's political leaders. Mayoral endorsement was crucial to the legitimacy of downtown economic development projects.[73]

CONCLUSIONS: TOWARD A VIEW OF CONSTRAINED LOCAL POWER

The debate over the nature of power in U.S. cities goes on and on. Elite theorists believe that a relatively small group of business leaders and people of high social status control the key decisions that are made in a community. In contrast, the pluralists argue that power is more widely spread and that a wider number of groups and influence city decision making. Yet, as "antipluralists" point out, local political systems are seldom as open and penetrable as the pluralists presume.

In part, the debate continues because the exact distribution of power varies from one city to the next. Power in one city might be highly structured, while in another it might be more widely spread.

Pluralists and elite theorists can find evidence to support their outlooks in the recent histories of San Francisco and Detroit. Pluralists point to the empowerment of newly insurgent groups in both cities: neighborhood, gay and lesbian, racial minority, and environmental groups in San Francisco and the city's black majority in Detroit. Pluralists further argue that neighborhood groups in San Francisco have been able to implement numerous growth restriction measures over the strident opposition of the city's business community. In Detroit, Mayor Coleman Young acted from a strong sense of racial justice to ensure continued economic development and the provision of jobs to the city's overwhelmingly black population.

Elite theorists counter by pointing to the long-run success that corporate forces have had in expanding San Francisco's downtown and in transforming the nature of the city. They also underscore how political officials in Detroit were led to level housing in the Poletown neighborhood, displacing the area's elderly residents, in order to build a heavily subsidized manufacturing plant for GM.

The San Francisco and Detroit case studies also provide evidence that supports more contemporary perspectives on urban political power. Public officials in Detroit and San Francisco pursued economic growth projects in Petersonian-type fashion. In the Poletown case, Detroit had to match the economic development incentive packages that other cities were dangling before GM. Mayor Young was led to the distasteful act of destroying a neighborhood to save Detroit as a whole, a confirmation of Peterson's view that public officials act in the "unitary" interest of the city as a whole. In San Francisco, even a progressive mayor such as Art Agnos was eventually led to initiate policies favorable to corporate leaders. By the end of the twentieth century, San Francisco gave an even greater emphasis to corporate-oriented policies as public leaders tried to reenergize the local economy in the wake of the crash of the city's many dot-com firms.

Business elites are not all-powerful. Still, despite occasional setbacks, development favored by elites generally continues. Cities are not in a strong position to challenge business. Capital mobility imposes severe constraints on municipal decision makers. City officials cannot determine whether a business is serious in its threats to move to another city or to locate a new facility elsewhere. Nor can municipal officials accurately assess just what concessions a business really requires to locate, or stay, in a city.[74]

Regime theory underscores the importance of politics as well as economics in the governance of a city. Yet regime theory, too, also points to the limited prospects that neighborhood, community, and environmentalist forces have in challenging the priorities of the big-city business community. While antigrowth groups may succeed in deflecting the costs of a specific development project, they seldom succeed in convincing the city's leaders to adopt a sustained antigrowth agenda.[75]

Regime theory underscores the importance of looking beyond election results when seeking to identify how things get done. Regime theory also underscores the fact that even when a racial minority dominates municipal elections, there is no guarantee that city government will be able to pursue a policy agenda that reflects the needs of its citizens, especially its more disadvantaged citizens. In order to govern effectively, a mayor must build a governing coalition that goes beyond the alliance that helped win the election. Business interests usually enjoy a privileged position in such governing coalitions.

Yet despite its influence, the business community does not enjoy a command position over city affairs. Politics, too, remains important. Skilled political leaders can effectively challenge or alter the policy priorities favored by a city's growth coalition.

In our next chapter, we will continue our in-depth look at the prospects for leadership in the contemporary city. We will explore how the formal structure of local government affects the possibilities of leadership.

NOTES

1. Robert S. and Helen M. Lynd, *Middletown* (New York: Harcourt, Brace, 1929) and *Middletown in Transition* (New York: Harcourt, Brace, 1973).
2. Floyd Hunter, *Community Power Structure* (Garden City, NY: Anchor Books, 1963); the book was originally published in 1953. Floyd Hunter, *Community Power Succession: Atlanta's Policymakers Revisited* (Chapel Hill: University of North Carolina Press, 1980).
3. Nelson W. Polsby, Community *Power and Political Theory* (New Haven, CT: Yale University Press, 1963), pp. 21–24. For an overview of the debate between pluralists and their critics, see Robert J. Waste, ed., *Community Power: Future Directions in Urban Research* (Newbury Park, CA: Sage Publications, 1986).
4. Heywood T. Sanders, "Revisiting Atlanta: Reconsidering Regime, Space, and Development Outcomes." Paper presented at the annual meeting of the Urban Affairs Association, Cleveland, OH, March 26–29, 2003.
5. For an updated version of these observations, based on study of small- to medium-sized Michigan, Ohio, and Cleveland communities, see Laura A. Reese and Raymond Rosenfeld, "Reconsidering Private Sector Power: Business Input and Local Development Policy." *Urban Affairs Review* 37, 5 (May 2002): 659–663.

6. Robert A. Dahl, *Who Governs? Democracy and Power in an American City* (New Haven, CT: Yale University Press, 1961).
7. G. William Domhoff, *Who Really Rules? New Haven and Community Power Reexamined* (Santa Monica, CA: Goodyear Publishing, 1978), p. 113.
8. Peter Bachrach and Morton S. Baratz, "The Two Faces of Power," *American Political Science Review* 56 (December 1962): 947–952. Also see Bachrach and Baratz, *Power and Poverty: Theory and Practice* (New York: Oxford University Press, 1970), pp. 43–46.
9. Matthew Crenson, *The Un-Politics of Air Pollution: A Study of Non-Decision-making in the Cities* (Baltimore: Johns Hopkins Press, 1971), pp. 55–82 and 107–109.
10. Michael Lipsky, *Protest in City Politics* (Chicago: Rand McNally, 1972).
11. Blaine A. Brownell, "The Urban South Comes of Age, 1900–40," in The *City in Southern History,* ed. Blaine A. Brownell and David R. Goldfield (Port Washington, NY: Kennikat Press, 1977), pp. 142–143.
12. Peter A. Lupsha and William J. Siembieda, "The Poverty of Public Services in a Land of Plenty: An Analysis and Interpretation," in *The Rise of the Sunbelt Cities,* ed. David C. Perry and Alfred J. Watkins (Beverly Hills, CA: Sage Publications, 1977), p. 185.
13. Arnold Fleischmann and Joe R. Feagin, "The Politics of Growth-Oriented Urban Alliances: Comparing Old Industrial and New Sunbelt Cities," *Urban Affairs Quarterly* 23 (December 1987): 216.
14. Lupsha and Siembieda, "The Poverty of Public Services in a Land of Plenty," p. 185.
15. David R. Johnson, "San Antonio: The Vicissitudes of Boosterism," in *Sunbelt Cities: Politics and Growth Since World War II,* eds. Richard M. Bernard and Bradley R. Rice (Austin: University of Texas Press, 1983), pp. 235–254; and David R. Johnson, John A. Booth, and Richard J. Harris, eds., *The Politics of San Antonio: Community, Progress and Power* (Lincoln: University of Nebraska Press, 1983).
16. Fleischmann and Feagin, "The Politics of Growth-Oriented Urban Alliances," p. 216. For a more detailed examination of the extent to which population changes and a changing economic situation have, and have not, altered Houston's commitment to growth, see Igor Vojnovic, "Governance in Houston: Growth Theories and Urban Pressures," *Journal of Urban Affairs* 25, 5 (December 2003): 589–624.
17. Philip J. Trounstine and Terry Christensen, *Movers and Shakers: The Study of Community Power* (New York: St. Martin's Press, 1982), pp. 99–108.
18. Stephen Samuel Smith, "Hugh Governs? Regime and Education Policy in Charlotte, North Carolina," *Journal of Urban Affairs* 19, 3 (1997): 247–274; Trounstine and Christensen, *Movers and Shakers,* pp. 127 and 162–192.
19. Robyne S. Turner, "Growth Politics and Downtown Development: The Economic Imperative in Sunbelt Cities," *Urban Affairs Quarterly* 28 (September 1992): 3–21.
20. Platon N. Rigos and Darryl Paulson, "Urban Development, Policy Failure, and Regime Change in a Manager-Council City: The Case of St. Petersburg, Florida," *Urban Affairs Review* 32, 2 (November 1996): 244–263. For a discussion of the pluralization of politics in suburban Tampa, see Robert Kerstein: "Suburban Growth Politics in Hillsborough County: Growth Management and Political Regimes," *Social Science Quarterly* 74 (September 1993): 614–620; "Growth Politics in Tampa and Hillsborough County," *Journal of Urban Affairs* 13 (1991): 55–76.

21. Paul E. Peterson, *City Limits* (Chicago: University of Chicago Press, 1981).

22. Todd J. Gillman, "Dallas Boosts Offer for Arena," *Dallas Morning News,* September 12, 1997.

23. Charles V. Bagli, "A Grand Plan in Brooklyn for the Nets' Arena Complex," *The New York Times,* December 11, 2003. Despite New Jersey's offer, Bruce Ratner, real estate developer and owner of the Nets, continued to pursue his plans for a 21-acre commercial-residential Brooklyn project, anchored by a Frank Gehry-designed 19,000-seat basketball arena.

24. The literature on this subject is vast. See: Mark S. Rosentraub, *Major League Losers: The Real Cost of Sports and Who's Paying For It* (New York: Basic Books, 1997); David Swindell and Mark S. Rosentraub, "Who Benefits From the Presence of Professional Sports Teams? The Implications for Public Funding of Stadiums and Arenas," *Public Administration Review* 58, 1 (1998): 11–20; Ian Hudson, "Bright Lights, Big City: Do Professional Sports Teams Increase Employment?" *Journal of Urban Affairs* 21, 4 (1999): 397–408; Peter Eisinger, "The Politics of Bread and Circuses: Building the City for the Visitor Class," *Urban Affairs Review* 35, 3 (January 2000): 316–333; Phillip A. Miller, "The Economic Impact of Sports Stadium Construction: The Case of the Construction Industry in St. Louis, MO," *Journal of Urban Affairs* 24, 2 (2002): 159–173.

25. Kenneth K. Wong and Pushpam Jain, "Newspapers as Policy Actors in Urban School Systems: The Chicago Story," *Urban Affairs Review* 35, 2 (November 1999): 210–246.

26. Peterson, *City Limits,* pp. 37–38.

27. Martin Saiz, "Mayoral Perceptions of Developmental and Redistributive Policies" A Cross-National Perspective," *Urban Affairs Review* 34, 6 (July 1999): 832–834 and 838. Also see the earlier work by Thomas Longoria, Jr., "Empirical Analysis of the City Limits Typology," *Urban Affairs Quarterly* 30 (September 1994): 102–113.

28. Clarence N. Stone and Heywood T. Sanders, eds., *The Politics of Urban Development* (Lawrence: University of Kansas Press, 1987). For an exchange of views between Peterson and his critics, see Heywood T. Sanders and Clarence N. Stone, "Developmental Politics Reconsidered," pp. 521–539; Paul E. Peterson, "Analyzing Development Politics: A Response to Sanders and Stone," pp. 540–547; and Sanders and Stone, "Competing Paradigms: A Rejoinder to Peterson," *Urban Affairs Quarterly* 22 (June 1987): 548–551.

29. Robert J. Waste, "City Limits, Pluralism, and Urban Political Economy," *Journal of Urban Affairs* 15, 5 (1993): 445–455. Peterson, *City Limits,* p. 52, acknowledges that education policy is difficult to classify, as it spills over into more than one policy area.

30. Jeffrey R. Henig, "Defining City Limits," *Urban Affairs Quarterly* 27 (March 1992): 384.

31. Swanstrom, "Semisovereign Cities," pp. 88–96. Also see David L. Birch, "Who Creates Jobs?" *The Public Interest* (Fall 1981): pp. 3–14.

32. Peterson, *City Limits,* p. 147.

33. John R. Logan and Harvey L. Molotch, *Urban Fortunes: The Political Economy of Place* (Berkeley, CA: University of California Press, 1987).

34. Heywood T. Sanders, "The Politics of Development in Middle-Sized Cities," in *The Politics of Urban Development,* ed. Clarence N. Stone and Heywood T. Sanders, pp. 182–198 (the quotation appears on p. 192).

35. Todd Swanstrom, "Semisovereign Cities: The Politics of Urban Development," *Polity* 21 (Fall 1988): 96–110.

36. Clarence N. Stone, "Systemic Power in Community Decision Making: A Restatement of Stratification Theory," *American Political Science Review* 74 (December 1980): 978.

37. Clarence N. Stone, *Regime Politics—Governing Atlanta: 1946–88* (Lawrence: University of Kansas Press, 1989) p. 242.

38. Cynthia Horan, "Racializing Urban Regimes," *Journal of Urban Affairs* 24, 1 (2002): 23.

39. John Hull Mollenkopf, *A Phoenix in the Ashes: The Rise and Fall of the Koch Coalition in New York City Politics* (Princeton, NJ: Princeton University Press, 1992), pp. 201–202.

40. Laura A. Reese and Raymond A. Rosenfeld, *The Civic Culture of Local Economic Development* (Thousand Oaks, CA: Sage Publications, 2001).

41. See, for instance, Mark S. Rosentraub and Paul Hemke, "Location Theory, a Growth Coalition, and a Regime in the Development of a Medium-sized City," *Urban Affairs Review* 31, 4 (March 1996): 482–507.

42. Clarence N. Stone, "Summing Up: Urban Regimes, Development Policy, and Political Arrangements," in *The Politics of Economic Development*, ed. Stone and Sanders, pp. 272–273; and Clarence N. Stone, "Urban Regimes and the Capacity to Govern: A Political Economy Approach," *Journal of Urban Affairs* 15, 1 (1993): 18–22.

43. See, for instance, Terry Nichols Clark and Ed Goetz, "The Antigrowth Machine: Can City Governments Control, Limit or Manage Growth?" in *Urban Innovations: Creative Strategies for Turbulent Times*, ed. Terry Nichols Clark (Thousand Oaks, CA: Sage Publications, 1994), pp. 105–145.

44. David L. Imbroscio, *Reconstructing City Politics: Alternative Economic Development and Urban Regimes* (Thousand Oaks, CA: Sage Publications, 1997), pp. 97–138; David L. Imbroscio, "Overcoming the Neglect of Economics in Urban Regime Theory," *Journal of Urban Affairs* 25, 3 (2003): 271–284, esp. 279–282; Pierre Clavel, Jessica Pitt, and Jordan Yin, "The Community Option in Urban Policy," *Urban Affairs Review* 32, 4 (March 1997): 435–458; Richard C. Hula, Cynthia Y. Jackson, and Marion Orr, "Urban Politics, Governing Nonprofits, and Community Revitalization," *Urban Affairs Review* 32, 4 (March 1997): 459–489.

45. Pierre Clavel and Wim Wiewel, eds., *Harold Washington and the Neighborhoods: Progressive City Government in Chicago, 1983–87* (New Brunswick, NJ: Rutgers University Press, 1991).

46. Alan DiGaetano, "Urban Governing Alignments and Realignments in Comparative Perspective: Developmental Politics in Boston, Massachusetts, and Bristol, England, 1980–96," *Urban Affairs Review* 32, 6 (July 1997): 852–854, 856–660 and 864–866.

47. William Sites, "The Limits of Urban Regime Theory: New York City Under Koch, Dinkins, and Giuliani," *Urban Affairs Review* 32, 4 (March 1997): 536–557; John Mollenkopf, "New York: Still the Great Anomaly," in *Racial Politics in American Cities*, 3rd ed., ed. Rufus P. Browning, Dale Rogers Marshall, and David H. Tabb (New York: Longman, 2003), pp. 115–141.

48. Barbara Ferman, *Challenging the Growth Machine: Neighborhood Politics in Chicago and Pittsburgh* (Lawrence: University Press of Kansas, 1996), pp. 145–151; Imbroscio, *Reconstructing City Politics*, pp. 40–162.

49. Stone, *Regime Politics*, p. 164.

50. Peter Burns, "Regime Theory, State Government, and a Takeover of Urban Education," *Journal of Urban Affairs* 25, 3 (2003): 285–303.

51. Peter Burns, "The Intergovernmental Regime and Public Policy in Hartford, Connecticut," *Journal of Urban Affairs* 24, 1 (2002): 55–73. For details as to the economic development orientation of state actors in city affairs and the strains that can develop between state and local actors pursuing different agendas, see Peter Eisinger, "Partners for Growth: State and Local Relations in Economic Development," in *Governing Partners: State-Local Relations in the United States,* ed. Russell L. Hanson Boulder, CO: Westview, 1998), pp. 93–107.

52. This paragraph is based on Eisinger, "The Politics of Bread and Circuses: Building the City for the Visitor Class."

53. Chester Hartman and Rob Kessler, "The Illusion and Reality of Urban Renewal: San Francisco's Yerba Buena Center," in *Marxism and the Metropolis,* ed. William K. Tabb and Larry Sawers (New York: Oxford University Press, 1978); especially pp. 154 and 168. San Francisco's experience is typical, as many civic convention centers operate at a loss. While cities continue to build convention centers as part of their economic development strategies, these projects seldom earn a return or attract sufficient new business to justify the huge expense. The market for revenue-producing conventions and trade shows has become increasingly competitive as more and more cities have built convention facilities. As a result, no city is assured that its new center will capture a large share of the trade show business. Cities also find that they often must offer discounts to attract trade shows. See Heywood Sanders, *Space Available: The Realities of Convention Centers As Economic Development Strategy,* a report of The Brookings Institute Metropolitan Policy Program, Washington, DC, January 2005, available at www.brookings.edu/metro/pubs/20050117_conventioncenters.htm.

54. Chester Hartman, *The Transformation of San Francisco* (Totowa, NJ: Rowman and Allanheld, 1984); the quotations appear on pp. 169 and 174.

55. Dawn Garcia, "Who Holds the Keys to Power in S.F. Under Agnos?" *San Francisco Chronicle,* July 11, 1988.

56. Richard Edward DeLeon, *Left Coast City: Progressive Politics in San Francisco, 1975–91* (Lawrence: University of Kansas Press, 1992), p. 12.

57. Richard E. DeLeon, "San Francisco: The Politics of Race, Land Use, and Ideology," in *Racial Politics in American Cities,* 3rd ed., ed. Rufus P. Browning, Dale Rogers Marshall, and David H. Tabb (New York: Longman, 2003), pp. 168–169 and 186–193.

58. John Ritter, "Green Win Could Have Impact Beyond City Race," *USA Today,* December 4, 2003.

59. (Editorial) "Election 2003, On the Issues: How the Candidates Deal with Business Concerns," *San Francisco Chronicle,* December 2, 2003; Rachel Gordon, "Newsom's Housing Initiative Warms Up: Mayor-elect Plans Strategy to Pass March Measure," *San Francisco Chronicle,* December 12, 2003.

60. DeLeon, *Left Coast City,* pp. 7–8, 132–133, and 142–149.

61. Bryan D. Jones and Lynn W. Bachelor, "Local Policy Discretion and the Corporate Surplus," in Urban Economic Development, *Urban Affairs Annual Review,* vol. 27, ed. Richard D. Bingham and John P. Blair (Beverly Hills, CA: Sage Publications, 1984), p. 245.

62. Ibid., p. 253; also Bill McGraw, "Poletown Land Costs Double, and Are likely to Climb Higher," *Detroit Free Press,* March 1, 1988.

63. Bryan D. Jones and Lynn W. Bachelor, *The Sustaining Hand: Community Leadership and Corporate Power,* 2nd ed., revised (Lawrence: University of Kansas Press, 1993), pp. 107–108 and 115–127.

64. For evidence on the impact of tax increment financing on local school districts in Illinois, see Rachel Weber, "Equity and Entrepreneurialism: The Impact of Tax Increment Financing on School Finance," *Urban Affairs Review* 38, 5 (May 2003): 619–644.

65. David Fasenfast, "Community Politics and Urban Redevelopment: Poletown, Detroit, and General Motors," *Urban Affairs Quarterly* 22 (September 1986): 114.

66. Jones and Bachelor, "Local Policy Discretion and the Corporate Surplus," p. 246.

67. Ibid., pp. 217–232.

68. Marion E. Orr and Gerry Stoker, "Urban Regimes and Leadership in Detroit," *Urban Affairs Quarterly* 30 (September 1994): 48–73.

69. Jones and Lynn W. Bachelor, *The Sustaining Hand,* p. 161.

70. Ibid., pp. 161–162.

71. June Manning Thomas, *Redevelopment and Race: Planning A Finer City in Postwar Detroit* (Baltimore: Johns Hopkins University Press, 1997); Alan DiGaetano and Paul Lawless, "Urban Governance and Industrial Decline: Governing Structures and Policy Agendas in Birmingham and Sheffield, England, and Detroit, Michigan, 1980–97," *Urban Affairs Review* 34, 4 (March 1999): 559–563.

72. Peter Eisinger, "Reimagining Detroit," *City and Community* 2, 2 (June 2003): 85–101. Also see Fred Siegel, "The Death and Life of America's Cities," *The Public Interest* (Summer 2002): pp. 3–22.

73. Wilbur Rich, *Coleman Young and Detroit Politics* (Detroit: Wayne State University Press, 1989).

74. Jones and Bachelor, "Local Policy Discretion and the Corporate Surplus," p. 265.

75. Matthew J. Burbank, Charles H. Heying, and Greg Andranovich, "Antigrowth Politics or Piecemeal Resistance? Citizen Opposition to Olympic-Related Economic Growth," *Urban Affairs Review* 35 (January 2000): 334–357.

The formal structure and rules of government help to determine who gets what in the local arena. In this chapter, we shall examine the city's formal position in the American constitutional system. We shall also examine the various forms or structures of local government. Finally, we shall seek to determine the prospects of lead-

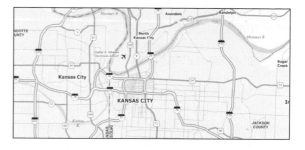

ership in cities and suburbs—to determine whether effective leaders can act informally to surmount the formal limitations of local government.

STATE GOVERNMENT AND LOCAL
GOVERNMENT STRUCTURE

More than is commonly recognized, the formal rules and structure of local government are largely shaped by the states, a privilege they enjoy as a result of their status under the United States Constitution. State constitutions, state laws, and state provisions for city charters all spell out the jurisdiction, structure, and formal powers of municipal government. A state's constitution and statutes largely determine whether a community may adapt a strong-mayor, weak-mayor, council-manager (city manager), or commission form of government.

State provisions set the requirements for **incorporation,** the conditions that an unincorporated area must meet if its residents want to establish it as a village or city with certain rights of self governance. Each state also sets the procedures that a city must follow if its leaders want to expand by **annexation,** that is, by absorbing neighboring communities into its borders. State provisions also detail the requirements for **secession** if residents of a section of a city want to detach their section from the larger city.

California statutes posed a severe obstacle to San Fernando Valley residents who wanted to break away from Los Angeles and establish their own city, a city that would have been the sixth largest in the nation in terms of population. California state law required secession be "revenue neutral" in its effects. This meant that the citizens in a newly created Valley city faced the daunting prospect of having to pay millions of dollars in "alimony" to Los Angeles, compensating the city both for services provided to the Valley and for revenue losses suffered as a result of detachment. Efforts by Staten Island to secede from New York City were similarly stymied by provisions of the state constitution that gave the larger city the power to veto detachment efforts.[1]

As we shall soon discuss, state law also largely defines local government service obligations and program authority. Each state can also set limits as to the amount of money that a municipality may tax or borrow.

The reform movement, which first gained substantial victories during the Progressive Era early in the twentieth century, sought to alter the structure and operations of city, state, and national governments. (See "The Reform Movement and the Progressive Era" below.) At the local level, the reformers initiated numerous new governing arrangements in their efforts to weaken the old political party machines. Two particular reform innovations, the council-manager and commission forms of government, sought to alter the structure of local government.

Yet the victory of the reformers, while quite substantial, was not complete. In a great many cities, reformed institutions coexist side by side with numerous

THE REFORM MOVEMENT AND THE PROGRESSIVE ERA (1890–1920)

At the beginning of the twentieth century, "good government" reformers sought to rid big cities of the political party "machines" with their corruption and partisanship. As we will discuss in greater detail in Chapter 7, the reformers believed cities could be run more efficiently by professionally trained managers dedicated to serving the public interest. The reformers argued for the merit selection of municipal personnel, ridding the city of the **patronage** systems under which political machine captains dispensed municipal jobs to their supporters with little concern for their competence. The reformers also wanted a professional city manager to direct the administration of a city's affairs.

While some reformers focused on restructuring local government, others pursued a broader agenda, including the enactment of social reforms and antitrust laws to curb the power of big businesses. Crusading journalists, popularly known as the **muckrakers**, exposed price-fixing by giant corporations, unsafe working conditions in factories, and corruption in city government. Lincoln Steffens' *Shame of the Cities* (published in 1904) revealed the misery of life in the tenement slums of the industrial era. Upton Sinclair's *The Jungle* (1906) exposed the scandalously unsanitary conditions in the meat-packing industry in Chicago, revelations that led to the creation of the U.S. Food and Drug Administration.

In California the Progressives came to power when a local prosecutor, Hiram Johnson, helped secure the conviction on bribery charges of Abraham Reuf,

continued

THE REFORM MOVEMENT AND THE PROGRESSIVE ERA (1890–1920) (CONT.)

the boss of San Francisco's political machine. The trial gained great public notoriety when one prosecutor was shot in the courtroom and a witness was found dead in his jail cell. The trial catapulted Johnson, a Progressive Republican, to the governorship in 1910. Johnson had also won popular support as a result of his ceaseless attacks against the power exerted by the Southern Pacific Railroad in California's affairs. Johnson was later elected United States Senator.

The Progressives in California and in other states, especially in the American West, enacted the instruments of direct democracy—the direct primary, initiative, referendum, and recall (all of which we will discuss in Chapter 7). The Progressives amended the California constitution to make all local elections nonpartisan. Across the nation, in city after city, progressive reformers introduced at-large and nonpartisan voting systems, civil-service or merit hiring practices, and the council-manager form of government.

Wisconsin's Robert M. ("Fighting Bob") La Follette succeeded in instituting a number of workplace and social reforms, including the establishment of workman's compensation. La Follette ran as the Progressive party's candidate for president in 1924, capturing 16 percent of the national vote. Many of the Progressive social reforms were later embraced by the national government during Franklin Delano Roosevelt's New Deal.

unreformed elements. Some cities have at-large and nonpartisan elections but weak merit-system protections for their employees; other cities have nonpartisan city council elections conducted on a district-wide—as opposed to a city-wide—basis. Some cities are more reformed in their structures and processes than are others.

DILLON'S RULE: STATE POWER AND THE LIMITS OF CITY GOVERNMENT

The U.S. Constitution mentions only two levels of government: the national government and the states. Nowhere is there a mention of local governments. Constitutionally speaking, cities, counties, special districts, school districts, and all other forms of local governments fall under the authority of the states. No city, county, township, or other local subdivision of the state has an inherent right to exercise governmental powers. Instead, such powers must be conferred on the local unit either by the state's constitution or by an act of the state legislature. In effect, local governments are considered **municipal corporations** with only those privileges and powers given to them by the state, their chartering authority.

The limited legal position of municipal governments was set forth most clearly in an 1868 ruling by Iowa Judge John F. Dillon. **Dillon's Rule,** as the constitutional doctrine has become known, denotes a hierarchical, superior-subordinate relationship between a state and its local governments. According to Judge Dillon, municipalities are mere "creatures of the states" and possess only those powers expressly delegated to them by the states.

The state's legal authority over local governments is total. As Judge Dillon notes, a state enjoys the power of life and death over local governments; as a state creates, it may destroy. The state's power is so complete that "the Legislature might, by a single act, if we can suppose it capable of such great a folly and so great a wrong, sweep from existence all municipal corporations in a state."[2] Consequently, a state may abridge, amend, or take away any power it has given to a city.

Under Dillon's Rule, the powers delegated to local government are to be strictly interpreted. If there is any doubt as to whether local government possesses the right to act in a certain policy area, that power is denied to the local government. As Judge Dillon explained:

> It is a general and undisputed proposition of law that a municipal corporation possesses and can exercise the following powers, and no others: First, those granted in express words; second, those necessarily or fairly implied in or incident to the power expressly granted; third, those essential to the accomplishment of the declared objects and purposes of the corporation—not simply convenient, but indispensable. Any fair, reasonable substantial doubt concerning the existence of power is resolved by the courts against the corporation and the power is denied.[3]

In 1903 and again in 1923, the United States Supreme Court upheld the principle established by Judge Dillon. Constitutionally, local governments are subunits of the states.[4]

Strictly speaking, under the American legal system, cities "are powerless to act on their own initiative."[5] They require a grant of authority from the states before they can act.

Yet as cities have evolved, they have generally gained greater leeway to act than a strict reading of Dillon's Rule would seem to allow. States find it impossible to oversee all of the actions of their cities, and citizens expect local governments to respond to local needs. Political considerations also offer protection to cities. Legislators from the city can be expected to fight off any state legislative attempt to interfere in city affairs. Governors, looking toward reelection, must consider the sensitivities of city voters. Considerations of fairness and due process further limit the arbitrariness of states in dealing with their localities.

As we shall soon discuss in greater detail, virtually every state has enacted some version of **home rule,** allowing municipalities at least some aspects of self-governance. In some states, constitutional provisions and court rulings have even determined that the powers given local government must be liberally construed. In these states, Dillon's Rule is not fully applicable, and local governments may perform a broad range of functions not expressly denied by state action.

Local governments have clearly accrued policymaking powers over the years. Yet, Dillon's Rule remains the dominant doctrine of municipal law. By limiting the ability of localities to tax, borrow, and spend, states severely constrain the ability of cities to meet the needs of their populations. As school districts, in legal terms, are a form of local government, they too are limited by state law in their ability to tax and spend, even in response the needs of growing school populations.

Dillon's Rule points to the importance of the state role in empowering local governments to take strong action in response to local problems. North Carolina, for instance, gives Charlotte and other cities liberal powers of annexation, the ability to grow and absorb taxable property by extending the city's boundaries. Charlotte and other North Carolina cities can even preserve land for future annexation, as state law gives them the power to veto attempts by neighboring areas to incorporate as independent municipalities. State annexation rules even give Charlotte the power to swallow up contiguous land without the owner's consent.[6]

STATE POWER AND "ACADEMIC BANKRUPTCY" LAWS: RESPONDING TO LOCAL SCHOOLS IN CRISIS

In recent years, the ability of the states to reach into local affairs is most clearly seen in the new actions that states have undertaken in response to troubled public school districts. By the year 2002, 24 states had enacted **academic bankruptcy laws** that allowed state officials to intervene in the operations of poorly performing local school systems.[7] A state, if it decides, can even take over troubled local schools, removing elected school officials and replacing them with state-appointed managers. Among the states that have actually taken over local school districts are New Jersey (which placed the Jersey City, Paterson, and Newark schools under its control), Connecticut (Hartford), Maryland (where the state in 1997 gave itself broad oversight power over a state-appointed Baltimore school board), California (Compton, Oakland, and West Fresno), New York (where the state appointed a management team for Roosevelt, Long Island schools, reducing the school board to an advisory role), Massachusetts (Lawrence), Pennsylvania (where the state in 2001 took over the management of Philadelphia's schools), and South Carolina (Allendale). Massachusetts also gave Boston University new managerial authority in the running of the troubled Chelsea school district.

In 2004, Michigan Governor Jennifer Granholm, a Democrat, signed legislation that ended the state takeover of Detroit's schools, a move that had been initiated by her Republican predecessor. The new legislation reversed the national trend of state takeovers and reestablished the authority of Detroit's locally elected school board.

The states have also acted to give the mayors of Chicago, Boston, Cleveland, Baltimore, Detroit, Oakland, and Harrisburg (Pennsylvania) direct control over city schools, breaking with the long-standing American tradition of insulating public schools from politics.

The Chicago case provides an especially vivid portrait of how state intervention has altered local authority in an effort to improve school performance. Chicago had previously tried community boards and other educational reforms, all to little avail. In 1995, the Republican-led Illinois legislature gave Democratic Mayor Richard M. Daley full appointment powers over Chicago's failing school system and total control over the schools' $3 billion annual budget. Daley appointed his own chief executive and chief financial officer to head the school system; he also replaced the city's elected school board with his own hand-picked five-member board of trustees. Daley gave the new board enormous powers to impose new economies and otherwise shake up the schools' failing performance. In the city's most troubled schools, large numbers of teachers were dismissed. Municipal unions objected to Daley's actions, but the state act stripped the local teachers' union of many of its bargaining rights.[8]

PREEMPTION

Under Dillon's Rule, states possess the power of **preemption**; they can deny local government the authority to act and can override those local actions that have taken place. States, for instance, can preempt the local income tax, barring municipalities from tapping into this important revenue source.

Oftentimes, preemptive action is taken at the bequest of powerful state interest groups. In response to a campaign mounted by the National Rifle Association, more than 40 states prohibit the local enactment of gun control ordinances.[9] In approximately 40 states, influential pesticide manufacturers and agricultural interests have won the passage of state laws that bar the local regulation of pesticide use. In other states, the tobacco lobby has pushed for the preemption of local antismoking laws. In Massachusetts, landlords won the passage of a state law that ended local rent control ordinances. California, Georgia, and Tennessee are also among the states that have preempted local rent control laws.[10]

CITY CHARTERS

The specific powers allowed a city by the state are laid out in a **city charter,** roughly the equivalent of a city's constitution. Until about 1850, the normal practice was for the legislature to incorporate or charter a city by passing a special act. A **special act charter** detailed the exact structure and powers that the new municipality would possess.

But it soon became too cumbersome for the state legislature to write a detailed charter for each individual city. As a result, over the years, states have tended to rely on **general-act charters** (also called **classified charters**) that put cities into different general categories or classes according to population (and, in some cases, the value of the local tax base). The state then imposes different service responsibilities on different classes of cities. The formal powers and taxing and borrowing authority also vary by city size and class. Larger cities are more likely to be granted a fuller range of governmental powers than are smaller incorporated towns and villages.

Grouping cities in a system of classes helps to protect any individual city against arbitrary treatment by a state. Yet, the classification system does not always guarantee protection.[11] Over the years, states have still been able to single out their major city for special action. If there is only one very large city in a state, the legislature can simply impose new obligations on its highest class of cities. Baltimore, Boston, Chicago, Des Moines, New Orleans, and New York are among the cities that states have singled out over the years despite having classified charter systems.

States can also alter the powers allowed a class of cities in a way that helps their largest communities. Oklahoma took action to permit the state's two largest counties to levy a sales tax for the purpose of constructing facilities for lease to the federal government. The legislation was designed to help Oklahoma and Tulsa counties in their efforts to become the site of a new Department of Defense record-keeping center.[12] The State of Maryland enacted a **quick-take law** that enhanced the ability of Baltimore to acquire tax-delinquent, abandoned property as the city pursued efforts to promote new development in blighted neighborhoods.[13]

HOME RULE AND HOME-RULE CHARTERS

As we have already observed, cities may not be as limited in their formal powers as a strict, legalistic reading of Dillon's Rule would suggest. Many states give their cities substantial functional authority under a concept known as *home rule*. Only in Alabama, Idaho, Nebraska, Nevada, Virginia, and West Virginia is Dillon's Rule strictly applied; in other states, cities possess a fair degree of latitude in their taxing and spending powers. In Alaska, Colorado, Illinois, Louisiana, and Wyoming, state constitutional provisions require a **liberal construction** or broad reading of home-rule powers.[14] In Utah, the state supreme court even rejected Dillon's Rule as "archaic."[15]

Home rule is an imprecise concept open to a variety of interpretations. Generally, home rule gives cities and counties the powers of self-governance, the greater leeway to undertake a variety of actions without first having to obtain express state permission for each action. Home-rule cities and counties are free to enact laws, just so long as these local laws do not contradict existing state statutes and are not preempted by state action. Texas grants its home-rule cities all powers of self-government not expressly denied by the state legislature.

Under a **home-rule charter,** a city can rewrite and alter the provisions in this basic governing document without having to seek a vote of the state legislature or of whatever state agency or charter commission the legislature has normally charged with the task. Under **structural home rule,** a locality is given the autonomy to determine its form of government—whether, for instance, it will have a mayor-council or manager-council system.

The concept of home rule is popular. A survey of states in the 1990s showed that 48 states gave their cities at least some measure of home-rule authority; Alabama and Vermont were the only exceptions. Home rule for counties was somewhat less popular, with 37 of the 50 states providing some local autonomy to counties.[16]

Yet just how much real authority a city and county possesses under home rule varies from state to state.[17] Twenty-eight states allow **broad functional home rule,** in which cities are permitted broad discretionary power in a range of policymaking and service responsibilities. Seventeen states allow cities what can be called **limited functional home rule,** in which local governmental powers are greatly circumscribed, and only limited local discretion is permitted.[18] In New Jersey, for instance, municipalities are viewed as "creatures" of the state and generally possess only those powers explicitly granted to them by the state. The State of New Jersey has not been reticent at all in establishing commissions and offices to oversee local affairs.[19] Kansas is another state where the courts have chosen to keep Dillon's Rule alive by interpreting home-rule powers quite narrowly.[20]

Some municipalities have interpreted their home-rule powers quite broadly and have gotten involved in policy areas not seen as traditional areas of municipal responsibility. Morton Grove, Illinois gained national prominence when it became the first locality in the nation to use its home-rule authority to enact a handgun control ordinance. New York City and Seattle led cities by instituting the partial public funding of local election campaigns, despite the fact that neither city had been given express permission by the state to enact such a law.[21] A handful of municipalities have enacted rent-control ordinances without explicit state authorization.

While home rule allows cities more control over their affairs, it is still the state that ultimately decides just what powers a city does and does not possess. In 39 states, Dillon's Rule remains the prevailing legal doctrine.[22] Yet states abridge home rule when a policy matter has an impact on surrounding communities and is not exclusively a matter of local concern.[23] Despite the liberal construction of home rule in Michigan, the Republican-controlled state legislature in 1999 was still able to overturn a City of Detroit residency law for municipal workers. The new state law simply prohibited localities from requiring municipal workers to live in the city in which they work.

State court rulings that protect citizens' rights also serve to restrict a locality's home-rule authority. The Supreme Judicial Court in Massachusetts, for instance, declared that despite home rule, cities in the state do not possess the authority to enact legislation limiting the ability of landlords to convert their properties into condominiums.[24]

Home-rule cities, like all cities, are also constrained by state-imposed limitations on local taxing, borrowing, and spending. In California, a citizens' "tax revolt" led to a series of state constitutional initiatives and new laws that undercut local taxing and spending authority. A new constitutional provision required a two-thirds vote by citizens for a locality to enact new local taxes, fees, and user charges; the two-thirds threshold impaired the ability of cities to fund key programs. As the tax limitations measures also impaired the ability of school districts to raise funds, the California legislature sought to correct the problem by mandating the reallocation of billions of dollars in local property taxes to support local school systems. This move helped schools but drained funds from other municipal services. Home rule has a "hollow ring" to it when a state such as California denies local governments much of their authority to raise and spend revenue.[25]

POWER AND POLITICS IN CHARTER REFORM

Different groups seek modifications in a city's charter in order to increase their influence in city hall. Charter revision is never simply a question of creating the "best" government for a municipality; charters help to determine who holds the power in the local arena.

New York Mayor Rudy Giuliani sought to rewrite the city charter to his advantage. A Republican in an overwhelmingly Democratic city, Giuliani suggested that the charter be changed to provide for nonpartisan elections, a change that would be helpful to Republican candidates. Giuliani's appointed charter revision committee also showed great interest in eliminating the Public Advocate's Office and the Independent Budget Office, two municipal agencies that had been highly critical of Giuliani policies. As one journalist reported, Giuliani could not "abide" New York Public Advocate Mark Green; the charter reform effort was an effort "to nuke the Public Advocate's office, and thus throw Mr. Green out of work."[26] Giuliani's successor, Michael Bloomberg, who also won office as a Republican, similarly called for nonpartisan elections as part of his charter reform campaign. Bloomberg's proposal was seen as self-serving and was opposed by a coalition of good-government organizations, racial-minority groups, and the Democratic party; it was rejected at the polls.

In Los Angeles, charter reform was intertwined with concerns over secession, governmental responsiveness, minority influence, and power.[27] Mayor Richard Riordan sought to defuse secessionist sentiment by restructuring the government of his vast 467-square-mile city so that it would be more effective and more responsive to neighborhood concerns. Downtown and regional business interests saw decentralization through new charter reform provisions as a more acceptable alternative to neighborhood secession.[28]

Contending interests led to the creation of two competing commissions to propose changes in the city's charter. One charter commission, an elected panel, was launched by Republican Mayor Richard Riordan; the other was appointed by the Democratic-controlled city council. The mayor's commission proposed to set up a system of elected neighborhood councils. The city council's charter commission, however, opposed the creation of elected neighborhood councils. City council members felt threatened; they feared that the elected neighborhood boards would nurture the birth of new political rivals.

Riordan also used charter reform as a vehicle to increase mayoral authority over the city's traditionally highly independent agencies. Riordan wanted a revised charter that would give the mayor sole authority to fire city department heads. However, so-called "good government" groups, public employee unions, and city hall's professional staff, including highly respected Chief Administrative Officer Keith Comrie, all objected to changes that would increase the mayor's power in budgetary and managerial matters.

In 1999 voters overwhelmingly approved a new charter for Los Angeles that gave the mayor's office a bit more power. A new system of neighborhood councils was also created in an effort to increase governmental responsiveness. The new neighborhood councils, however, were given far less power than neighborhood advocates had originally demanded.

THE FORMAL STRUCTURE OF CITY GOVERNMENT

In the United States there are three principal forms of city government: the mayor-council plan (with its weak-mayor and strong-mayor variants), the commission plan, and the council-manager plan. The mayor-council and the council-manager plans dominate. Very few communities are governed by the commission arrangement.

Over half of the nation's communities operate under the council-manager plan with its appointed chief executive. A 2001 survey of municipalities with a population over 2,500 showed that 53 percent had the council-manager plan, 38 percent the mayor-council form, and only 1 percent the commission arrangement. A number of smaller communities (5 percent of the respondents) reported that they were governed by a **town meeting** where all citizens are entitled to appear and participate in the making of local decisions.[29] The council-manager plan dominates in mid-sized communities and cities in the Pacific Coast states. However, in the nation's biggest cities and in small towns of population of 5,000 or less, the mayor-council arrangement prevails.[30]

WEAK-MAYOR SYSTEM

From the beginning of this country's history until about 1870, local mayors were truly quite weak. They were given few administrative powers; they seldom possessed the power to veto city council action. The country still regarded its colonial experience under George III as sound enough reason to minimize executive power.

By the mid-1850s, the growth of cities led to new municipal service responsibilities. State legislatures initially responded by creating a series of boards and commissions with service responsibility in such areas as education and law enforcement. In some cases, the members of these boards and commissions were elected by the local citizenry; in other cases, their members were appointed by state officials. The existence of numerous boards and commissions served to fragment power in the city. By 1870, new local charters were drafted, which for the first time provided for increased mayoral authority.

Under the weak-mayor form of government, the administrative authority of the city's chief executive is quite limited because the mayor lacks the power to appoint and dismiss administrative personnel. In weak-mayor cities, the mayor shares administrative power with a variety of other officials, including other elected executive officials (such as the local prosecutor or the city's financial controller), council appointees, and the members of numerous independent boards and commissions over whom the mayor possesses no direct authority (see Figure 5-1).

In some cities, the members of boards and commissions are elected by the voters. In other communities, they are appointed by the city council. In still other cities, key mayoral appointees are subject to confirmation by the city council; in some communities, the mayor cannot dismiss an appointee without council approval. In important policy areas, the boards and commissions may even be established by state law that gives the governor, not the mayor, the authority to name commission members. The members of these various boards and commissions often serve long, fixed terms of office that effectively insulate them from direct control by the mayor.

Madison, Wisconsin provides an example of a weak-mayor city. In Madison, the mayor does not directly control the operations of such city agencies as the police, fire, and welfare departments. Personnel matters, including the appointment and dismissal of top agency administrators, are handled by the independent boards and commissions, including the Police and Fire Commission and the Public Welfare Commission. The members of these commissions serve rotating fixed terms; in the absence of resignations, a mayor gets to appoint only one member a year to a commission.

San Francisco is another city where executive authority has historically been "divided, dispersed, and decentralized."[31] Reformers limited the powers of the mayoralty as a response to the corruption and scandals that plagued the office during days of the city's political machine. As a result, although the mayor of San Francisco possessed some of the aspects of a strong mayor, he or she faced the difficulty of sharing executive power with an independently elected assessor and city attorney and a variety of independent boards and commissions. For much of the twentieth century, the city's chief administrative officer (CAO), not the mayor, had direct control over the city bureaucracy in key policy areas. Appointed to a 10-year term, the CAO could resist a mayor's demands. The mayor also shares authority over fiscal matters with a city controller. Although appointed by the mayor, the CAO and controller enjoy considerable autonomy as they can be removed only by a two-thirds vote of the Board of Supervisors (San Francisco's name for its city council). In 1995, San Francisco voters changed the city charter, giving the mayor increased control over the CAO and decreasing independence of municipal boards and commissions.

TWO VARIATIONS OF THE WEAK-MAYOR STRUCTURE

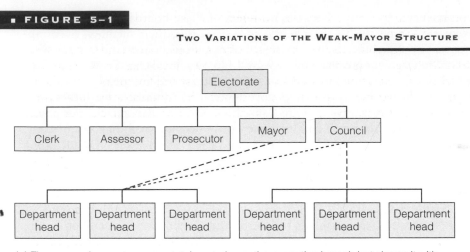

(a) The mayor does not possess total control over the executive branch but shares it with independently elected officials. Other departmental heads are subject to city council confirmation or are appointed directly by the council.

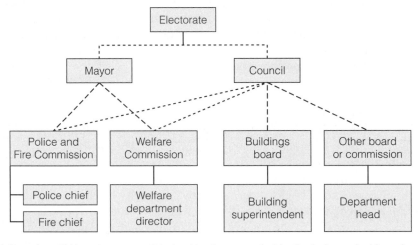

(b) Departmental heads are appointed not by the mayor but by the independent boards and commissions. The members of these boards and commissions serve long, fixed terms and are appointed directly by the council or by the mayor, subject to council confirmation.

----- Appointment power   ------- Confirmation power

Strikingly, in the vast majority of cities, the mayor lacks control over budget preparation, which is commonly made the responsibility of the city council or an independent appointive official. Only 11.6 percent of cities report that the power of budget development is placed in the hands of their chief elected executive.[32]

In many communities, mayors also find themselves without adequate staff and without the power to veto council-passed ordinances. In Houston, the mayor possesses fairly strong budgetary preparation, appointment, and removal powers, but no veto power.

The advantage of the weak-mayor city is simple: it provides numerous safeguards against the potential misuse of executive power. The existence of independent boards and commissions and the presence of council checks serve to insulate departments from improper political encroachment by the mayor.

Yet the disadvantages of the weak-mayor form of government are considerable. Just as no private business could be run efficiently without vesting significant power in the hands of its central executive, so too must sufficient power be vested in the head of the municipal corporation. Multiple executives and independent boards and commissions pose problems when it comes to shared direction and coordination.

The weak-mayor form also blurs accountability as city voters do not know whom to blame when things go wrong. If parks services are not being adequately provided, is it the fault of the mayor, the parks superintendent, the independent parks commission, or the budget chief? In a strong-mayor system, in contrast, the lines of accountability are clear: Blame the mayor!

On the whole, the weak-mayor form is inadequate to the task of governing large cities. Critics of Minneapolis' and Portland's weak-mayor system argue that it fragments power and fails to provide for effective leadership.[33] Today, the weak-mayor form is most often found in smaller communities, particularly in the rural South, where the demands upon government are more modest.

STRONG-MAYOR SYSTEM

As Figure 5-2 shows, the strong-mayor plan gives the elected mayor substantial control over the workings of city departments. Just as the president of the United States has the right to appoint various cabinet and agency officials, the mayor

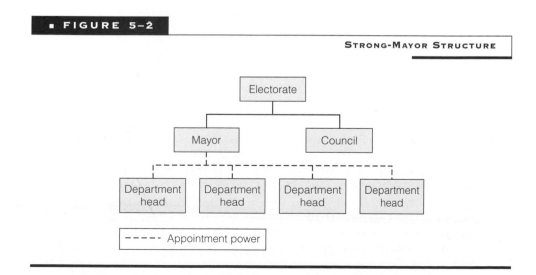

■ FIGURE 5-2

STRONG-MAYOR STRUCTURE

in a strong-mayor city maintains the right to name the heads of the various municipal departments and agencies. In contrast with the weak-mayor system, the strong mayor does not contend for administrative power with a multitude of independently elected officials, council appointees, and citizen boards and commissions.

Of course, even strong-mayor charters do not grant unlimited authority to the mayor. Most city charters include checks and balances on executive power. Councils often have the authority to confirm the mayor's appointments and to limit his or her power to remove agency heads. City councils also usually control the budget and appropriations processes awhile reviewing purchasing authority and contracting. They can also request audits and investigations of executive department activities. In cities in which the mayor is given veto authority over city council actions, the council can vote to override the mayor's veto. Civil service or merit systems of appointment place further restraints on a mayor's executive power.

Even a strong-mayor charter, then, does not guarantee a mayor sufficient power for effective leadership. Many strong-mayor cities have had ineffective mayors. No mayor can afford to rely solely on the formal powers and preroga-tives of the office; even in strong-mayor cities, a mayor has to learn how to build power in order to govern effectively.

The strong-mayor system is the dominant form of government in the nation's largest cities. Baltimore, Boston, Detroit, New York, Philadelphia, Pittsburgh, and St. Louis are all have strong-mayor systems. Large cities need a mayor who can mobilize public sentiment and mediate among the conten-ding interests in the city.

Yet a strong mayor can also infringe on the professionalism of city agencies. Mayors who govern from a partisan perspective can use their appointment pow-ers as patronage to incur favors and repay political debts. A department head or top administrator who fails to do the mayor's partisan bidding could easily be fired.

There also is no assurance that an elected mayor will be a capable adminis-trator. A mayor may be a good political campaigner and may even possess excellent media skills; but he or she may lack the necessary planning, budge-tary, financial, civil engineering, and managerial knowledge necessary for the effective running of a modern city.

COMMISSION GOVERNMENT

When Galveston, Texas, operating under the mayor-council plan, proved unable to respond to the disastrous hurricane and flood of 1900, Galveston citizens secured permission from the State of Texas to create a new form of government, the city commission. Initially, the new government in Galveston proved so successful that it was widely imitated. Houston received a similar charter in 1905, and by 1917 some 500 cities were operating under the plan. But since that time, Houston and numerous other cities abandoned the commis-sion plan as its disadvantages became apparent.

■ FIGURE 5-3

COMMISSION STRUCTURE

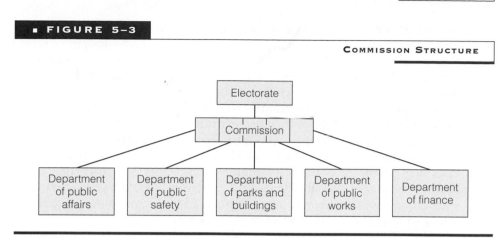

Today the commission structure tends to be concentrated in smaller communities. Tulsa and Portland are the nation's two largest cities with a commission government. Forest Park, Illinois, a suburb of Chicago, is another notable community with commission government.

Under the commission form of government, the five-to-nine members of the city council (referred to under the plan as the **city commission**) also serve as the heads of major city departments (see Figure 5-3). Normally, the commission members are chosen in citywide elections on a nonpartisan ballot. One commissioner is given the title of mayor, but possesses few prerogatives other than ceremonial powers and the right to preside over commission meetings. The mayor enjoys no more authority than any other commissioner.

In theory, the commission form concentrates the powers of government. There is no separation between legislative and executive powers that can act as a barrier to quick and effective service delivery. The legislators and the department heads are one and the same.

Yet for most cities, the disadvantages of the commission plan are overwhelming. Instead of providing quick action, commissions are often deadlocked. Each commissioner tends to represent only the narrow view of his or her own department. Commission members may also be reluctant to cut the budget requests of other departments, as such efforts will likely result in retaliation by other commissioners. Voters also rarely take a candidate's administrative skills into great account when casting their ballots. Minority groups further object that the at-large election feature of the commission plan works to dilute minority voting power.[34]

COUNCIL-MANAGER (CITY MANAGER) GOVERNMENT

In 1908, Staunton, Virginia became the first city to establish the position of a general city manager with extensive administrative authority. The success of Staunton's innovation led Richard Childs, president of the National Municipal

League, a leading reform organization, to tout the virtues of the council-manager government. The League in its *Model City Charter* promoted adoption of the council-manager arrangement. By 1920, over 100 cities had adopted the council-manager plan. The council-manager plan had become a central element in municipal reform ideology.

Today council-manager government is most commonly found in middle-sized cities and suburbs. Small towns often spurn the plan as they often find it too expensive to hire a full-time, professional manager. Big cities—including New York, Los Angeles, Chicago, Houston, Philadelphia, and Detroit—have populations that are too diverse and heterogeneous to permit easy leadership by an appointed manager, Instead of managerial leadership, these cities rely on a mayor who can deal with competing political factions and who can claim the legitimacy conferred by public election, both important resources for leadership.

The council-manager arrangement is the dominant form of government in Sunbelt cities, including Phoenix, San Diego, Dallas, San Antonio, San Jose, Sacramento, Long Beach, Las Vegas, Tucson, Austin, Fort Worth, Oklahoma City, Jacksonville, Charlotte, Memphis, and Virginia Beach. Kansas City and Wichita also employ the city manager system of government.

Under the council-manager plan, the city council appoints a professionally trained manager who is given responsibility for running the daily affairs of the city (see Figure 5-4). The city council retains the right to dismiss or replace a city manager whose appointment proves disappointing. Under the governing arrangement, the council enacts new laws, but their administration falls totally within the domain of the city manager. The manager is directly in charge of departmental heads and supervises their performance. City agencies are subject to managerial, not mayoral, direction.

■ FIGURE 5-4

COUNCIL-MANAGER PLAN

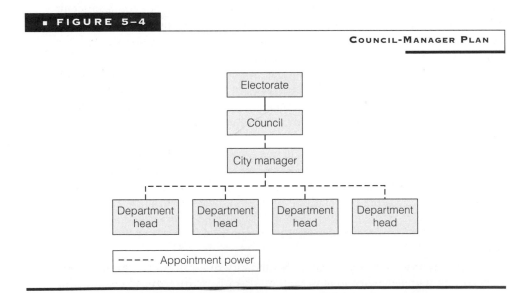

The mayoralty in a council-manager plan is largely titular and ceremonial in nature. The mayor in a council-manager city possesses no meaningful administrative, appointive, or veto powers. Usually, the mayor is chosen by the council from among its own membership. Dallas is an exception where the mayor is elected citywide and serves as the presiding officer of the city council. But, even in Dallas, it is the city manager, not the mayor, who controls city administration.

LEADERSHIP ROLES IN COUNCIL-MANAGER CITIES. City managers no longer tend to be narrowly trained in business administration or civil engineering. Instead, modern-day city managers are often policy generalists who are just as concerned with maintaining the quality of local schools and a city's economic vitality as with keeping tax rates low.[35]

One problem with the council-manager system is that the line that separates policy formulation (the job of the city council) and administration (the job of the city manager) is never quite clear. The most successful managers have always been initiators of policy, even if only in subtle ways. An effective city manager must do more than simply direct the municipal bureaucracy. As city council positions are often part-time, poorly paid, and understaffed, council members are often quite dependent on the research, options, and policy advice presented by the manager. Yet the wise manager must be careful in how he or she chooses to exercise influence, for the manager serves at the pleasure of the council and may be discharged by the council at any time.

City managers do not always choose to play an aggressive role in policy making. Most managers see their role as that of an *expert adviser* whose job is to provide information and recommendations to the city council. Such managers spurn playing the alternative role of the *political activist* who attempts to build a power base in order to get the council to follow his or her policy leads.[36] One survey of city and county managers in North Carolina found that over half of the respondents preferred to confine their activities to administration, leaving policy matters to the councils.[37] The effort by city managers to preserve a line between policy making and administration may be the result of their professional training. In those cities that elect a mayor citywide, the city manager may also look to the mayor for vision, for setting the overall direction of city affairs and knowing the desires of citizens.[38]

As already noted, the separation between policy making and administration is not clear-cut. Just what matters fall in the separate domains of policy and administration? More than one city manager has tended to "define 'policy' and 'administration' in a manner in which 'administration' loomed very large and 'policy' loomed very small."[39] Managers are not purely neutral. They have policy goals of their own and initiate actions that reflect their political beliefs.

Recent studies have reported the increased willingness of city managers to engage in policy-making activities. Policy-related activities are an unavoidable part of the city manager's job. The managerial profession has accepted the fact that its members by necessity will be involved in such policy-making activities as agenda setting, proposal development, and advocacy.[40] The older dichotomy that divided politics from administration has given way to a new vision of the city manager as a dynamic executive leader who helps forge a policy consensus.[41] A new breed of city managers has come to recognize the importance of taking action across a range of policies. Such leadership transcends the narrow concern for efficiency that once dominated the city manager profession.[42]

One survey of over 1,400 suburban communities found that a minority of city managers have acted as entrepreneurial leaders who propel dynamic policy change in response to citizens' demands and changed local conditions. These city managers are especially likely to seize the opportunity to act when other local elected officials fail to initiate innovative policy. Still, even activist managers prefer, whenever possible, to handle issues quietly, working behind the scenes.[43]

Not surprisingly, in a number of cities, the mayor and manager wind up being competitors for influence. Even in a council-manager city, the mayor is still the most visible public official; the public expects the mayor to lead, especially if he or she is elected citywide. Mayors accuse the city manager of improperly straying beyond matters of administration. City managers, in turn, often charge the mayor and council members with improperly overreaching into matters of administration.

Who dominates a council-manager city: the mayor, the manager, or the city council? James Svara has found that the city council tends to be dominant when it comes to determining a city's overall *mission* or sense of direction, for instance, establishing the city's general philosophy regarding taxing, spending, and growth. The council and city manager are both active when it comes to making specific decisions of *policy*, deciding exactly what programs and services will be provided. City managers, however, dominate the actual program *administration* or implementation; the manager regards it as his or her prerogative to make decisions regarding the daily workings of municipal programs. Council members tend to intrude in administration only when prompted by citizen complaints. Broad issues of *management*—personnel, budgeting, purchasing, contracting, and data processing—are also primarily left up to the city manager. In sum, in council-manager cities, the mayor and part-time council members tend to focus on determining a city's overall policy direction while leaving the more technical tasks of administration and management in the hands of the professionally trained manager.[44]

The relationship between the mayor and city manager varies from city to city and from personality to personality. Oftentimes, the relationship between the council and manager approximates the smooth working relationship of a private corporation's board of directors and its chief executive officer. Yet in other cities, conflict develops. In some cities, the manager dominates passive councils. In still others, the manager is victimized by an activist council or an ambitious mayor.

ADVANTAGES OF THE COUNCIL-MANAGER PLAN. Under the council-manager plan, a trained professional is hired to deal with the increasingly complex and technical tasks of running a city. City managers have the expertise in such areas as accounting, budgeting, personnel management, and civil engineering. They are also committed to the high ethical standards of their profession. Their decisions are not based on short term partisan considerations, and they abstain from involvement in local electoral campaigns. City managers see themselves as problem solvers willing to help elected officials to realize their priorities.

Trained executives bring greater efficiency and enhanced performance to a city. One study of 1,400 suburban communities showed that city managers were more aggressive than mayors in pushing for pay-for-performance systems, the privatization of municipal services, and other reforms to "reinvent" or modernize government.[45] Modern-day city managers tend to utilize a facilitative leadership style that emphasizes decentralized decision making, the delegation of responsibility, team building, and citizen participation.[46]

The council-manager plan tends to produce governance based on cooperation rather than conflict. The council-manager system predisposes actors to work together. City-council selection of a manager can also create a sense of a shared mission in the city.[47] Managers also act as mediators and facilitators. A new generation of city managers has been taught the arts of conflict resolution; city managers are no longer schooled narrowly just in budgeting and planning.[48]

CRITICISMS OF THE COUNCIL-MANAGER PLAN. The council-manager plan does not always work in reality as it does in theory. Some city councils tend to choose a local administrator to serve as manager, compromising the ideal of professional training and competence. Also, some city councils are reluctant to dismiss a manager who is not performing well; a municipality that gains a reputation as being "hostile" to city managers will find it very difficult to recruit a truly talented manager. In smaller cities, in particular, part-time council members working with a limited budget may be reluctant to undertake the time-consuming tasks and expenses involved in advertising for, screening, and interviewing new manager candidates.

Constant turnover in the manager's position is also disruptive to municipal operations. Successful city managers are constantly looking for opportunities to "move up" by assuming the chief executive position in a bigger city. Larger cities attract more experienced executives; smaller communities get younger and newer managers. A city manager may resign as a result of frustrations caused by continuing conflict among council members.[49] The election of a new dominant faction to a city council can also lead to a manager's resignation.[50]

Politically savvy city managers cultivate important constituencies that make it nearly impossible for elected officials to fire them. Miami Mayor Maurice Ferre learned this lesson too late when, in 1985, he dismissed city manager Howard Gary, an African American. Ferre, a Puerto Rican, had won 97 percent of the black vote in the previous election; but after his dismissal of Gary, his support among black voters fell to a mere 10 percent. He lost the next election to Xavier Suarez, a candidate Ferre had defeated two years previously. Suarez was the first Cuban American to be elected mayor of Miami.[51]

The political insulation of the city manager's office also leads to concerns regarding the manager's public responsiveness. Not having to face the public in a general election, a manager may not always respond to citizens' demands for services. A corporate-oriented manager, for instance, may pursue new business development and the city's continued growth despite citizen concerns over increased traffic congestion and environmental destruction.

In large cities, an elected mayor is more likely than an appointed manager to possess the public visibility and the campaign and public-relations skills necessary to rally public support and build effective coalitions. In Toledo, Ohio, the absence of energetic civic leadership was attributed to the city's long-term experience with a council-manager system. The city's mayors were often amateur politicians content with performing the ceremonial aspects of their jobs. In 1993, Toledo voters finally broke with the city's fabled "good government" tradition by casting their ballots for the strong-mayor plan. Cincinnati similarly responded to concerns about the lack of effective local leadership by abandoning features of its manager-council system; beginning in 2001, voters in Cincinnati chose their city's leader at the polls. El Paso, however, switched in the other direction, getting rid of its strong-mayor system and selecting its first city manager in 2004.

MODIFYING THE COUNCIL-MANAGER SYSTEM: SAN DIEGO AND OTHER CALIFORNIA CITIES.   The limitations of the council-manager model were most readily apparent in San Diego, the nation's second largest council-manager city. During his 11-year (1971–82) tenure as mayor, Pete Wilson (who would later be elected governor and U.S. senator) virtually "created" the office of mayor, taking it upon himself to deal with the emerging conflicts that the city manager was unable or unwilling to resolve. The city manager's office was the traditional ally of the business community, backing business' proposals for continued city growth, much to the displeasure of neighborhood and taxpayer groups.

When Wilson tried to walk a middle line between booster and antigrowth factions, he found that the city's council-manager form of government was a "structural straitjacket" that severely limited his power.[52] Wilson tried to reform the city charter, but voters overwhelmingly rejected the proposal to bring a strong-mayor system to San Diego.

Despite the charter reform defeat, Wilson succeeded in strengthening the power of the mayoralty. New rules in San Diego gave the mayor the right to name the members and chairs of the city council's standing committees. Several new positions in the mayor's office, including a consultant for each council committee and an independent fiscal analyst, decreased the mayor's and council's reliance on the information provided by the city manager. The mayor also gained the power to determine what issues would go before the full council as well as the right to name appointments to various city boards and commissions.

Wilson transformed the nature of city government in San Diego. Although San Diego still formally retained the council-manager structure, "knowledge-able people" recognized that Wilson was in charge. In San Diego, the may-oralty was strengthened, as "Leadership that is visionary, active, and responsible to the voters has become the preferred form."[53]

Wilson's successors, Mayors Roger Hedgecock and Maureen O'Connor, however, confronted a city manager and city council intent on regaining their prerogatives. The city council took away some of the mayor's appointive powers. In the absence of city charter provisions to institutionalize the mayor's power, the gains that Wilson had made as mayor could not all be sustained.

Like San Diego, other California cities, too, have acted to strengthen the mayor's office in order to provide more effective executive leadership. San Jose voters sought a mayoralty that would be able to deal with the problems brought on by rapid growth. Oakland strengthened its mayoral office in an attempt to bring greater capacity to a political system once characterized as leaderless.[54] A new black-liberal coalition sought to increase the problem-solving abilities of Oakland's government. In Oakland, the office of the mayor, once a poorly paid and part-time position, became a better paid and full-time position. Former California Governor Jerry Brown, elected mayor in 1998, strengthened the mayor's office even further. However, he lost a 2002 referendum that would have made some of his changes permanent. Brown nonetheless was able to use his newfound authority to dismiss Oakland's city manager.

Oakland, San Jose, Sacramento, and Hayward are all California cities that switched to the direct election of mayors. In these and other cities, racial minorities and homeowner groups sought to create offices that would redirect city priorities away from those of city managers tied to the old business-oriented governing regimes.[55]

THE CAO: HELPING ELECTED OFFICIALS

The Progressive Era reformers could not convince all cities to adopt the council-manager plan. In mayor-council cities, they sought the establishment of a chief administrative officer (CAO) to provide the mayor with the technical com-petency and administrative expertise of a career professional. Like a city manager, a CAO is the city's top administrative professional; but unlike a city manager, the CAO reports to the mayor, not to the city council.

The exact powers and workings of the CAO position vary from city to city. The primary responsibilities of the CAO tend to be in the areas of budgeting, fiscal affairs, and personnel. In some cities, the CAO is charged solely with advising the mayor, handling whatever responsibilities the mayor chooses to assign. In other cities, the CAO is given specific responsibility for supervising certain departments.

In some cities, the CAO is a permanent position that continues from administration to administration. In these cities, the CAO represents a valuable source of institutional memory and continuity in city affairs; a new mayor has an insider from whom he or she can learn about the budget, the administrative processes, and the power realities within city hall. Sometimes, however, a newly elected mayor may distrust a CAO as being too closely tied to the policies of the outgoing administration.

In most cities, the CAO is not a permanent position but is subject to mayoral appointment. The average tenure for CAOs is only two to three years.[56] New York City formally abolished its City Administrator position in the 1970s only to create a new system of deputy mayors that embodies much of the original CAO concept. However, appointment by the mayor may infringe upon the professional independence of the CAO, making the office quite different from that of a city manager. The CAO also tends to have less education and general-government experience than does the city manager of a big city.[57]

In some cities, the CAO has duties so extensive that they approximate those of a city manager. In Los Angeles, the duties of the office were so vast that in 1987 one national organization chose CAO Keith Comrie as its "city manager" of the year.[58]

CITY GOVERNMENTS EVOLVE: THE RISE OF THE "ADAPTED CITY"

The formal structures of a city's government are not fixed but are "malleable."[59] Over time, cities adapt by modifying elements of their government in response to new problems and criticisms. Consequently, there are few truly pure mayor-council and council-manager cities.

Mayoral cities have increased their professionalism and administrative competence. Nearly all have adopted merit-system hiring practices and requirements for competitive bidding on contracts offered by the city. A number of mayoral cities have increased the CAO's budgetary and appointment responsibilities and strengthened accounting procedures and local ethics laws. For their part, managerial cities, as our review of San Diego underscored, have sought to strengthen the leadership potential inherent in the mayor's office. They have also instituted the direct election of the mayor, district elections for at least some council members, and new procedures for citizen participation, all in an attempt to increase the public's voice in city affairs and to diminish the insulation of managerial government.

The structure of the modern city no longer represents a dichotomous choice between "politics" and "administration." Instead, cities have fused elements of both the council-manager and strong-mayor systems in order to promote a balanced government capable of effective problem solving while maintaining a clear responsiveness to citizens.[60] Even in mayor-council cities, mayors have generally spurned more partisan orientations in favor of a professional approach to city governance.[61]

CITY COUNCILS

In the vast majority of cities, service on a city council is a part-time job. Only half of the nation's cities with populations greater than 500,000 even hold weekly council meetings. In smaller communities, councils meet less frequently, usually every other week or once a month.[62]

In mid-sized cities, approximately a third of the councils serve full time. Half the mid-sized cities compensate members moderately well.[63] Only in the largest cities in the United States is service on a city council full-time and well paid.

In contrast to the United Sates Congress and the nation's state legislatures, city councils are seldom organized along party lines. Also in contrast to the U.S. Congress, committee deliberation is a less significant feature of local governance. Compared to the Congress, city councils conduct fewer public hearings on proposed legislation, and they attempt no great oversight of executive branch activity. Not serving full-time, council members lack the time to devote to ongoing committee sessions.

City councils are also generally too small in size to allow for the development of an effective committee system. Only in those few big cities with large councils can a significant portion of a council's business be assigned to committees. But even in these cities, committees have no consistent impact on policy outputs. In manager-council cities, the city manager briefs council members on policy options, leaving little role for council committee hearings.[64]

Part-time councils reflect the grassroots ideal of a citizen legislature, but they are poorly equipped to handle the complex job of directing the business of a big or medium-sized city. Part-time council members have little choice but to rely on the advice and analyses provided by support staff. Oftentimes, though, councils are not provided with sufficient support staff for the job. The frequent turnover of council members, which is partly the result of the poor pay and the demanding nature of the job, also diminishes a city council's ability to develop the necessary knowledge base to do its job.

Amateur and inexperienced part-time legislators are in a poor position to oversee city administration and to challenge the reports and recommendations of the mayor, city manager, and municipal department heads. As one local government commentator has observed, many council members are "befuddled policy makers, overly engaged implementers, and near-sighted overseers who ignore their supervisory role."[65]

Mayors and managers do not always dominate their city councils. In some cities, council factionalism and polarization pose an obstacle to getting anything done.[66] Where a city's charter permits, mayors have taken an "end run" around obstructionist councils by issuing **executive orders** to direct the actions of city agencies.

In the controversial issue area of gay and lesbian rights, mayors have sometimes resorted to executive order when the city councils had failed to act. In Houston in 1998, Mayor Lee Brown issued an executive order banning discrimination in city government on the basis of sexual orientation. Critics argued that the mayor had unlawfully bypassed the authority of the city council, but the Texas Supreme Court dismissed the lawsuit on a technicality, as the plaintiffs lacked the legal standing to bring the suit to court. New York Mayor David Dinkins faced similar criticism for his 1993 order that gave pension benefits and other rights to the domestic partners of city workers.

In 2004, Mayor Greg Nickels issued an executive order for Seattle to recognize same-sex marriages. Later that same year, the California Supreme Court ruled that San Francisco Mayor Gavin Newsom overstepped his authority permitted under state law when he directed the local clerk's office to issue marriage licenses to same-sex couples.[67]

Unlike the United States Congress, city council members do not make legislative service a long-term career. Only about half of a newly-elected council class will still be on the council five years later. Council members seldom face defeat at the hands of voters; in many cities, council elections are not very competitive. Yet there is a substantial voluntary turnover; council members often choose not to run for a new term as a result of the toll that council service takes on family life and business careers.[68]

Despite the evidence of substantial turnover, opinion polls point to continuing public support for **term limitations** as a means of bring new blood to the city council. Throughout the 1990s, an ever-growing number of states and localities placed strict limits on the number of consecutive terms a person could serve on a city council. As we discuss in more detail in Chapter 7, term limitations inhibited the development of the council's political skills and knowledge by forcing the relatively few experienced city legislators to retire from office.

What can be done to increase the quality of council performance? First, city councils need greater staff support if their members are to participate as an informed and independent voice in governmental affairs. Second, legislators must be given adequate compensation if they are to be expected to devote the considerable time necessary to do the public's business. Third, cities that have two-year terms for council members might consider shifting to four-year terms. As the evidence of council member reelection success underscores, two-year terms do not greatly increase the likelihood that incumbents will be defeated. Instead, frequent elections pose an additional burden on part-time public servants, leading some of the more talented and capable council representatives to retire voluntarily from office.[69] In cities where big-money donations have become part of increasingly costly council races, campaign finance reform may also help to ensure the independence and integrity of city council members.

Despite the shortcomings of city council operations, prospects for city council leadership and action have improved over the years: "Resurgent city councils have become more diverse, conflictual, and even more defiant of chief executives, reflecting trends in the polity at large."[70] Councils have increased their professional staffs and taken steps to form legislative committees in order to cope with the complex nature of city affairs. A number of cities, especially in the South, have also enlarged their councils in order to promote the increased representation of racial minorities and women.[71]

WOMEN: A NEW FORCE IN LOCAL POLITICS?

Women are underrepresented in the local arena but enjoy a bit better representation there than in national politics. As of January 2005, 13 of the nation's largest 100 cities had women mayors. In cities of over 100,000 people, 15.6 percent had women mayors; in cities of over 30,000, 16 percent were women.[72] Data from the mid-1990s shows that women held over 20 percent of the council seats in medium and large cities, a figure that falls far short of gender parity but is still better than in the U.S. Congress, where female membership in recent years has been 15 percent or less.[73]

Why are women somewhat more participant in local than national government? In part it is a reflection of family duties. Service at the local level poses less interference with child care and the other family responsibilities borne by women. Women may also have difficulty raising considerable sums of money necessary for electoral viability in congressional campaigns. In local races, in contrast, women can take advantage of their history of civic activity and draw on crucial bases of support from community groups, civic associations, and women's organizations.[74]

Women's participation in local affairs also reflects the importance of municipal issues to their lives:

> In the not-too-distant past, local politics was, for many women, the only avenue to which they had access. For many women today, it is still the most accessible. Moreover, the local level is where many of the problems that are of most concern to women are addressed, and consequently where many women are introduced to political gladiatorial combat.[75]

Women's style of political participation differs a bit from that of men. Compared to men, female city managers were more likely to emphasize communication and leadership strategies based on conciliation—bringing a city's officials together. The women managers tended to try to resolve disputes rather than relying on their authority to fire an agency head who had lost the council's confidence.[76] Another study found that female city council members devoted more time to their legislative work than did their male counterparts. Compared to men, women also had lengthier careers of council service. All of this evidence points to the possible emergence of women as a new force in city politics.[77]

FORMAL VERSUS INFORMAL POWER: ROOM FOR LEADERSHIP

By itself, any detailing of the formal structure, powers, and procedures of local government can provide only a partial understanding of how things get done in the urban arena. Leadership is the product of an individual's personal initiative and style and not just the formal powers of office.

City charters do not reveal everything when it comes to power and leadership. Chicago, for instance, is technically a weak-mayor city under its city charter. Yet despite the paucity of the formal powers of his office, Mayor Richard J. Daley, the legendary "boss" of Chicago in the 1950s and 1960s, was able to wield considerable power as head of the city and county Democratic machine. Four decades later, his son, Mayor Richard M. Daley, governing in a setting that was even less conducive to leadership, was similarly able to wield power, skillfully fusing together elements of both the machine and reform political styles.

City leaders cannot rely on their formal authority alone to get things done. The formal structures and rules of city government often constrain and fragment power, making it difficult for civic officials to undertake major policies and projects. Although not spelled out in the formal procedures of city government, mayors, managers, and other public officials find that if they are to be effective leaders, they must mobilize key actors through coalition-building strategies.

THE DIFFICULT TASK OF MAYORAL LEADERSHIP

In order to exercise effective leadership, a mayor first requires several resources: legal authority over key program areas, the assistance of a sufficient personal and budgetary staff, a salary that allows the mayor to serve as a full-time executive, and access to friendly media and political organizations.[78] Direct election is another critical resource; mayors who are appointed by the city council cannot claim any great legitimacy in speaking for the community.

In a great many cities, mayors are denied the preconditions for effective leadership. Part-time, poorly paid mayors who lack staff assistance are in a poor position to challenge managerial and city council policy recommendations, supervise administration, and lobby state and national officials and business CEOs. In only about 15 percent of America's communities does the mayor serve full-time; in nearly half of the nation's municipalities, the mayor is just another member of the city council; fewer than a third of the nation's mayors possess the power to veto a council ordinance.[79] Only in the nation's largest cities is there a tendency to give a mayor the resources necessary for leadership; but even in those cities, effective leadership often proves quite elusive.

City problems are so voluminous and complex that the modern city is often considered to be "ungovernable."[80] Yet some mayors have been able to lead. Leadership depends on a mayor's skill, orientation, and personality. (See "Is Mayoral Leadership Possible? The Post-Liberal, Pragmatic, Big-City Mayors" on pp. 157–158.)

IS MAYORAL LEADERSHIP POSSIBLE?
THE POST-LIBERAL BIG-CITY MAYORS

A list of more successful big-city mayors in more recent years would likely include New York's Rudy Giuliani, Los Angeles' Richard Riordan, Chicago's Richard M. Daley, and Philadelphia's Ed Rendell, all popular mayors who pursued a prudent mix of fiscal conservatism and more populist policy initiatives embraced by large portions of the urban community.

These mayors did not share the same commitment to redistributional policy that characterized the liberal mayors of the preceding era. Cutbacks in federal aid acted to dim the hopes of a more progressive urban agenda. These mayors had to make tough choices and have their cities do more with less.

Giuliani, Riordan, Daley, and Rendell were the most newsworthy of the "new progressives" intent on reforming municipal government for greater efficiency and improved service delivery. Cleveland's Michael White, Indianapolis' Steven Goldsmith, and Milwaukee's John Norquist were other prominent mayors who sought new ways to deliver services more efficiently in their cities. They pursued the privatization of services in order to save money and to foster a new competitive environment that would shake up the municipal bureaucracy. These mayors also emphasized the pursuit of business investment and the need to create an urban environment that would attract middle-class customers and residents back to the city.

These mayors also focused on improving the "quality of life" in their cities. In accordance with the "broken windows" theory of policing, in which small crimes and disorder serve only to beget more severe illegal activity, New York's Giuliani cracked down on subway turnstile jumpers, squeegee windshield washers, aggressive panhandlers, and even jaywalkers. New York hired additional police officers, and crime fell. Giuliani's critics argued that the fall in crime rates was a nationwide phenomenon, not solely the result of the mayor's policies. They also scored the mayor for undermining the city's tradition of liberal tolerance, for hassling the homeless and minority youth, and for giving too much attention to the business community's agenda and too little to affordable housing. After the police shooting of an unarmed immigrant working man, Giuliani's policies became a focal point of controversy.

As New York became more livable, Giuliani's popularity rose, despite his abrasive, arrogant, and caustic governing style. The events of 9/11 brought Giuliani to the nation's attention.

The new progressive mayors endorsed fiscal reform and policy priorities that favored the city's middle-class and business constituencies. Yet, Giuliani, Riordan, and the other "new breed" of mayors could not be stereotyped simply as "conservatives." Riordan won the plaudits of liberals for his support of affirmative action and gay rights. Riordan, a Republican, even endorsed the reelection of Democratic Senator Dianne Feinstein. Giuliani, also a Republican,

continued

**IS MAYORAL LEADERSHIP POSSIBLE?
THE POST-LIBERAL BIG-CITY MAYORS (CONT.)**

similarly endorsed a Democratic candidate for governor, earning the wrath of party activists. Giuliani, ever unconventional, even appeared in a dress on *Saturday Night Live*. Giuliani and Riordan also distanced themselves from national Republicans who called for school prayer and who attacked immigration and abortion. Both mayors proved popular among Latino and Jewish constituents. In his reelection, Riordan won a stunning 71 percent of the normally Democratic Jewish vote. Ed Rendell, after leaving office, served as the head of the national Democratic Party before becoming Governor of Pennsylvania.

The "new populist" mayors were successful, but their agenda was largely confined to policies that the local and global business communities could support. Their successors had a much more difficult time in governing. In New York, Mayor Michael Bloomberg, lacking Giuliani's public relations flare, faced enormous criticisms for his attempt to bring business-style reforms to the city's underperforming schools. Los Angeles' Mayor James Hahn alienated Latinos in his 2001 election victory over Antonio Villaraigosa and could not reassemble the multiethnic, liberal coalition of former Mayor Tom Bradley. Hahn's refusal to appoint Police Chief Bernard Parks, an African American, to a second term lost him considerable support in the city's black community. Hahn narrowly survived elimination in the city's 2005 mayoral primary, winning only 23.7 percent of the vote before losing to Villaraigosa in the May runoff.

In Philadelphia, Ed Rendell was succeeded in office by John Street, whose governance was hampered by federal anti-corruption probes. However, Mayor Street skillfully used the investigations as a tool to rally the support of black voters and Democrats; the mayor argued that he was the victim of a racially motivated attack by Republican forces in Washington who were attempting to influence Philadelphia's 2003 mayoral election. Only weeks after the investigation was made public, Philadelphia voters returned Street to office.

A TYPOLOGY OF LEADERSHIP STYLES

One useful study of mayoral leadership identifies five different types of mayors:

- The **Ceremonial** mayor attempts few policy initiatives and is for the most part content to deal with the ceremonial aspects of the job.

- The **Caretaker** mayor focuses on short-term issues and "what comes up." This mayor is essentially a troubleshooter who lacks a long-term vision or agenda for the city.

- The **Individualist** is a mayor who attempts to make some changes in the city but goes about it through personal appeals instead of trying to build broader coalitions, alliances, or networks.

- The **Executive** is a project-oriented mayor who attempts to get things done primarily by relying on his or her managerial skills and the authority of the mayor's office.

- The **Entrepreneur** has clear program goals and attempts to have a major impact on the city. The entrepreneur engages in a full range of public and coalition-building activities in order to amass broad community support for his or her program goals.[81]

In council-manager cities, effective mayors tend to play the role of coordinator or director. They are team builders and facilitators who seek to work cooperatively with both the city manager and city council. Compared to mayoral cities, leadership in council-manager cities tends to be less conflictive and more cooperative.[82]

MINORITY MAYORS: BUILDING BIRACIAL (AND MULTIRACIAL) COALITIONS AND THE DEBATE OVER DERACIALIZATION

Effective leadership is especially difficult for racial minority mayors, especially if they must govern in polarized situations. Minority mayors face a difficult choice: Should they attempt to use city resources in an all-out effort to redress racial discrimination? Or should they emphasize more broad policy goals in an attempt to build biracial (and, where possible, multiracial) coalitions?

DERACIALIZATION STRATEGIES: COALITION BUILDING IN CLEVELAND AND SAN ANTONIO

Carl Stokes won Cleveland's mayoralty in 1967, becoming one of the nation's first big-city black mayors, by putting together a **biracial coalition** of black voters and white liberals. In office, Stokes found that he could maximize policy change only at the cost of alienating some of the white people who had helped to elect him. When Stokes chose not to run for reelection, the fragile biracial coalition proved difficult to maintain, and for two decades African Americans lost their handle on Cleveland's mayoralty, an office they would not regain until Michael White's 1989 victory.

Michael White won reelection in 1993 and 1997. He did so by pursuing a deracialized strategy of attempting to do what was good for Cleveland as a whole, a strategy that he felt would deliver disproportionate benefits to the city's overwhelming black majority. Under **deracialization**, black candidates for citywide office tone down their racial appeals, deemphasize their redistributional agenda, and instead emphasize issues that cut across racial lines.

As mayor, White took a number of policy stances that were unconventional for a black urban leader, at times angering the local NAACP, municipal union officials, and members of his own Democratic party. He backed an end to forced school busing. He supported a Republican school choice plan that offered students vouchers that could be used at private and parochial—as well as public—schools. He privatized garbage collection and other municipal services and even forced the city's road repair unit to compete with private companies.[83] He also built new housing in an attempt to reclaim ghetto areas.

White's administration serves as an example of the continuing debate over deracialized leadership strategies. Mayor White's critics in the black community argue that he and other minority mayors embrace a deracialized approach at the price of failing to push for more extensive policy changes that would be of greater benefit to their primary constituency.

San Antonio's Henry Cisneros provides an example of a Hispanic mayor who successfully governed by forming a coalition that crossed racial lines. Cisneros' 1981 election marked a decisive victory for the city's emerging Mexican-American community. Cisneros acted to mute hostilities between the city's Anglo and Latino communities as he sought to forge a new sense of civic unity. Cisneros was an outspoken advocate of both Chicano interests and the necessity for reforming the city to meet the needs of business in a high-tech society. Cisneros argued that job opportunities for the city's Latino population were dependent on the city's ability to attract high-technology business.

Cisneros was a broad-based coalition builder, but his formal power was limited by the city's classic council-manager system of government. Activist groups also charged that the mayor focused too much of his efforts on revitalizing the city's central business district to the neglect of the city's neighborhoods. COPS (Communities Organized for Public Services), a neighborhood organization in the city's poorer Latino sections, criticized a number of Cisneros' downtown development projects, including his support of a new 65,000-seat domed stadium. Cisneros served four successful two-year terms as mayor, and declined to seek a fifth term. In 1993, he became U.S. Secretary for Housing and Urban Development in the Clinton Administration.[84]

CAN BIRACIAL AND MULTIRACIAL COALITIONS BE SUSTAINED? NEW YORK AND LOS ANGELES COMPARED

Why do biracial and multiracial coalitions emerge at certain points of time in some cities and not at other times and in other cities? A comparison of Los Angeles and New York will help us to discern the answer.[85]

In Los Angeles, a biracial coalition helped produce the five-term, 20-year governing regime of Mayor Tom Bradley, an African American. In New York, liberal mayors had a more difficult time in gaining office despite the city's fabled liberal political tradition. The multiracial coalition that elected David Dinkins the city's first African American as mayor in 1989 was short-lived. The coalition fractured as Dinkins could not handle a number of racially explosive incidents. The tensions between the black and Jewish communities that exploded in the Crown Heights section of Brooklyn led to the disaffection of a number of his Jewish and more moderate white voters, leading to Dinkins' defeat at the hands of the more conservative Rudy Giuliani.

New York's biracial coalition fell apart as the city's African Americans and white liberals (especially Jewish citizens) found themselves on different sides of polarizing issues. In the 1960s, black demands for the community control of schools and minority ownership of neighborhood stores came over the objections of Jewish teachers and store owners. Three decades later, memories of these antagonisms served as a barrier that prevented the formation of a stable, intergroup alliance.

In Los Angeles, in contrast, African Americans and Jews historically found themselves on the same side of community issues. As both groups were outsiders seeking to enter the then-conservative municipal political system of Los Angeles, both had something to gain from forming an alliance.

The quality of the local political leadership is another crucial factor that explains why a dominant biracial coalition was able to emerge for such a long period of time in Los Angeles but not in New York. Los Angeles' Tom Bradley was a "tough cop" who lived in a middle-class neighborhood. Even in the early stages of his political career, he built alliances with white liberal groups. He was not a street radical; he did not demand a redistributional agenda that offended potential white allies. Bradley pulled people together. In New York, in contrast, more divisive leaders emerged in both the black and Jewish communities.

Bradley's critics charge that his coalition focused too greatly on the needs of developers and the building of a new glass-tower downtown to the neglect of poorer neighborhoods. The outburst of violence in South Central Los Angeles served as testimony to the declining conditions of the city's worst areas during the Bradley era. Over the years, Latinos and Asian Americans were integrated into an expanded political coalition, but their loyalty, too, was strained as a result of the riots that occurred in the wake of the Rodney King verdict.

In the 1993 election that followed Bradley's retirement, liberals lost control of the mayoralty as the city turned to Republican Richard Riordan. Mayoral candidate Michael Woo could not fully piece the multiracial coalition back together. Woo built bridges to the African-American community, but these ties lost him support among moderate white and Latino voters in the racially charged atmosphere of post-riot Los Angeles; "the image of a rainbow Los Angeles evaporated."[86]

In 2001, James Hahn, with moderate-to-liberal Democratic roots, won the mayoralty by appealing to white voters and building on his family's ties to the African-American community. Latinos, however, charged that the Hahn campaign resorted to racially charged appeals in its late television advertising in order to mobilize voters and defeat a more progressive candidate, Antonio Villaraigosa, who would have been the first Mexican American to be elected mayor of Los Angeles.[87] Hahn was more liberal than his Republican predecessor. Yet lingering bitterness, resentment, and antagonisms helped to hem in Hahn's governing abilities. Mexican Americans were especially critical of what they saw as racial stereotypes in Hahn's campaign advertising. Hahn also lost support in the black community when he refused to reappoint Police Chief Bernard Parks, an African American. Los Angeles' multiracial governing coalition had clearly fractured. Yet, Villaraigosa would reassemble much of this fragile interracial alliance in his 1995 landslide election victory.

THE FUTURE OF BLACK AND HISPANIC MAYORS

In cities where African Americans are not a clear majority of the electorate, "The new black politics must be broader in its appeal and both deracial and transethnic if it is to be successful."[88] New York's David Dinkins, Los Angeles' Tom Bradley, Philadelphia's Wilson Goode, Seattle's Norman Rice, and Charlotte's Harvey Gantt are all noteworthy African Americans who used a deracialized electoral strategy to win the mayoralty.[89]

Denver's Federico Peña (who would later serve as U.S. Secretary of Transportation in the Clinton Administration), a Latino, also won office in a city where the size of the minority population at the time was relatively small. As did Bradley and Rice, Peña ran on a platform that emphasized managerial competence, economic development, improved police-community relations, and increased city responsiveness to homeowner and neighborhood concerns. Peña's election, however, did not signal a true arrival of minority political power; in office, his coalition was "dominated by white political and business elites."[90]

Peña was succeeded in office by Wellington Webb, the first African American to be elected mayor of Denver. Despite the city's rapidly growing Latino population, it was uncertain whether Denver would see the formation of a white-black-Latino governing coalition organized around a clear policy agenda.[91]

Even in cities where African Americans enjoy an electoral majority, deracialization may prove to be an important strategy in determining which of competing African-American candidates will win the allegiance of white swing voters and emerge as the victor. In New Orleans in 1986, Sidney Barthelemy's moderate appeal allowed him to win enough white votes to defeat an opponent who had stronger roots in the poor, black sections of the city. Barthelemy's cross-racial appeal was crucial to his 1990 reelection.[92] Similarly, in Atlanta in 1989, Maynard Jackson beat back other black contenders and won a third nonconsecutive term as mayor by stressing quality-of-life issues that gained him support from white voters.[93]

Does deracialization represent a pragmatic political strategy for blacks and Hispanics? Or is it a sellout of the African-American and Latino communities? Much of the answer to these questions depends on whether or not deracialization in a political campaign leads to deracialization in governance.[94] Does moderation in the pursuit of a broad electoral coalition necessarily impose severe constraints on the agenda that a black or Hispanic mayor can pursue upon winning office?

Advocates argue that deracialization strategies represent a maturation of black and Hispanic politics, allowing racial minorities to win office in communities where they do not comprise a clear majority of the active electorate. A candidate who campaigns on broad themes can, upon winning office, institute programs that will begin to address the socioeconomic problems of inner-city communities. New Orleans' Sidney Barthelemy instituted a vigorous affirmative action and contract compliance program as mayor despite the deracialized nature of his campaign for office.[95]

Critics of deracialization strategies respond that a mayor cannot easily switch to a redistributional and race-focused governing agenda after having stressed only more moderate appeals during the election campaign. Moderate black mayors "have generally pursued policies of fiscal conservatism and downtown development" rather than a more redistributive agenda.[96] Critics see such deracialization as a denial of the historical context of black politics:

> Black politics is a group struggle for race-specific empowerment in order to exercise some degree of independence and self-determination. If campaign behavior is a predictor of governance style and behavior, then deracialization is an anathema to the essence of black politics.[97]

As one critic of deracialization concluded, "Black politics is not maturing and may be degenerating."[98] In Los Angeles, Latino candidates who took a deracialized approach to their election campaigns largely pursued deracialized agendas after they gained their seats on the city council.[99]

Yet, Birmingham's Richard Arrington and Chicago's Harold Washington were two black mayors who were able to pursue policies of racial justice while also reaching out to liberal white voters. Their attempts to form a biracial coalition did not lead them to sacrifice the concerns of their primary constituency.[100]

In cities where the high degree of racial polarization make the formation of a progressive interracial alliance nearly impossible, a minority candidate may do well to pursue a strategy that seeks to unify and mobilize the mayor's primary constituency. Memphis Mayor W.W. Herenton relied on "black unity" conventions and crusade-like appeals to mobilize blacks to register and vote, even though these efforts initially alienated white liberals.[101]

CONCLUSIONS

The formal powers and structure of local government are spelled out in a city's charter and vary from community to community across the United States. The city charter determines whether a city has a strong-mayor form of government or whether the mayor must share executive authority with an appointed city manager.

The strong-mayor plan suffers notable shortcomings: elected mayors do not necessarily possess essential administrative skills; they may also run municipal affairs on a partisan basis. The council-manager plan offers the advantages of nonpartisan, trained, and professional administration. Governance under the council-manager arrangement emphasizes cooperation more than conflict. However, council-manager cities have often been criticized for failing to produce effective leadership—for not having an elected mayor who can mobilize the city polity. For a long period, city managers were also criticized as being part of the city's growth coalition, acting as a channel for the plans of local business elites.

Over the years, cities have adapted their structure by moving away from the pure mayor-council and council-manager forms. Mayors have been given professional assistance, including, in a number of cities, the help of a CAO. The features of managerial cities have been modified to allow for the direct election of the mayor, increased responsiveness to district concerns, and heightened citizen participation.

While a number of cities have increased the resources provided to the mayor and the city council, many still do not provide officials with the necessary pre-conditions for effective leadership. Mayoral leadership, however, is not simply dependent on the formal powers of office; leadership also derives from an individual's skills, style, and coalition-building abilities. Effective mayoral leadership remains quite elusive given the intractable nature of many urban problems, continued racial polarization, and the impact of formal governance structures that disperse power in most big-city governments.

African-American and Hispanic mayors have had a particularly difficult time in maintaining cross-racial political coalitions without compromising important parts of their political agenda. The arrival of Asians and other new immigrants makes the formation of stable multiracial coalitions even more difficult.[102] In Miami, the tensions between Cuban Americans and African Americans run particularly deep, making a coalition all but impossible. The gulf between the two communities is even reflected in their partisan affiliations; Cubans are very Republican while African Americans vote Democratic.[103]

The reforms first commenced during the Progressive Era continue to affect city governance today. The reformers sought to diminish the role that political party organizations and party "bosses" would play in city affairs. The reformers gave new authority to professionally trained administrators capable of increasing the effectiveness and efficiency of municipal operations. But these administrators, insulated from political pressures, were not always responsive to citizen demands and minority voices.

The next three chapters will reveal how the struggle between the political machine and the urban reformers continues to shape access, influence, and power in the present-day city.

NOTES

1. Miguel Bustillo, "Alimony Law Could Handicap a Fledgling Valley City," *Los Angeles Times*, January 10, 1999; Dean E. McHenry, Jr., "The State's Role in Urban Secession: The Impact of Procedures on the Success of Urban Movements" (paper presented at the annual meeting of the American Political Science Association, San Francisco, August 30–September 2, 2001).
2. *City of Clinton v. Cedar Rapids and Missouri Railroad Company*, 24 Iowa 455 (1868).
3. John F. Dillon, *Commentary on the Law of Municipal Corporations*, 5th ed. (Boston: Little, Brown, 1911), vol. 1, sec. 237.
4. *Atkins v. Kansas*, 191 U.S. 207 at 220–221 (1903); and *Trenton v. New Jersey*, 262 U.S. 182, 67LEd93j, 43 SCt 534 (1923).

5. Gerald E. Frug, *City Making: Building Communities without Building Walls* (Princeton, NJ: Princeton University Press, 2001), p. 5. See Frug, pp. 47–51, for a discussion of the continuing importance of Dillon's Rule despite the introduction of home rule.

6. David R. Berman, "State-Local Relations: Authority, Finance, and Regional Cooperation," *Municipal Year Book 1998* (Washington, DC: International City/County Management Association, 1998), p. 69.

7. Kenneth K. Wong and Francis X. Shen, "City and State Takeover as a School Reform Strategy," *ERIC Digest* 174 (July 2000). Available at: www.ericfacility.net/databases/ERIC_Digests/ed467111.html.

8. Rene Sanchez, "Mayor Daley Takes Turn at the Board as Schools' Revolt Hits Chicago," *Washington Post,* July 13, 1995.

9. Jon S. Vernick and Lisa M. Hepburn, "Twenty Thousand Gun-Control Laws?" (Research brief of The Brookings Institution Center on Metropolitan and Urban Policy, Washington, DC, December 2002). Available at: http://www.brookings.edu/es/urban/publications/gunbook4.pdf.

10. David R. Berman, "State-Local Relations: Authority, Finance, and Regional Cooperation," p. 66; Berman, "State-Local Relations: Devolution, Mandates, and Money," *The Municipal Year Book 1997* (Washington DC: International City/County Management Association, 1997), p. 44.

11. Frug, *City Making,* pp. 50–51.

12. David R. Morgan and James T. LaPlant, "State Requirements Affecting Local Government Structure: The Case of Oklahoma" (paper presented at the annual meeting of the American Political Science Association, Washington, DC, September 2–5, 1993).

13. John Kromer, "Vacant-Property Policy and Practice: Baltimore and Philadelphia" (Discussion paper prepared for The Brookings Institution Center on Urban and Metropolitan Policy, Washington, DC, October 2002). Available at: www.brookings.edu/es/urban/publications/kromervacant.pdf.

14. Dale Krane and Platon Rigos, "Municipal Power and Choice: An Examination of Frug's 'Powerlessness Thesis'" (paper presented at the annual meeting of the American Political Science Association, Washington, DC, August 31–September 3, 2000).

15. Jesse J. Richardson, Jr., Meghan Zimmerman Gough, and Robert Puentes, *Is Home Rule the Answer? The Influence of Dillon's Rule on Growth Management* (Discussion paper prepared for The Brookings Institution Center on Urban and Metropolitan Policy, Washington, DC, January 2003), p. 18. Available at: www.brookings.edu/dybdocroot/es/urban/publications/dillonsrule.pdf.

16. Advisory Commission on Intergovernmental Relations, *State Laws Governing Local Government Structure and Administration* (Washington DC: ACIR, 1993), pp. 20–23.

17. For a detailed discussion of the exact taxing and functional powers permitted cities under home rule in each of the 50 states, see Dale Krane, Platon N. Rigos, and Melvin B. Hill, eds., *Home Rule: A Fifty-State Handbook* (Washington, DC: Congressional Quarterly Press, 2000).

18. Advisory Commission on Intergovernmental Relations, *State Laws Governing Local Government Structure and Administration,* pp. 17 and 20–21.

19. Alma Joseph, "State-Local Relations in New Jersey: Is There Home Rule?" (paper presented at the annual meeting of the Urban Affairs Association, New York, March 14, 1998).

20. Advisory Commission on Intergovernmental Relations, "State-Local Relations: Authority, Finance, and Regional Cooperation," p. 64.

21. Richard Briffault, "Taking Home Rule Seriously: The Case of Campaign Finance Reform," in *Restructuring the New York City Government: The Reemergence of Municipal Reform*, eds. Frank J. Mauro and Gerald Benjamin, a special issue of the *Proceedings of the Academy of Political Science*, 37, 3 (1989), 35–42.

22. Richardson, Gough, and Puentes, *Is Home Rule the Answer?*

23. Frug, *City Making*, p. 51.

24. Ibid., p. 81.

25. Alvin D. Sokolow, "The Changing Property Tax and State-Local Relations," *Publius: The Journal of Federalism* 28, 1 (Winter 1998): 165–187. For more details of the "hollowing out" or weakening of local government in California, see: Peter Schrag, *The End of Paradise: California's Experience, America's Future* (New York: The New Press, 1998), pp. 163–167; David B. Magleby, "Ballot Initiatives and Intergovernmental Relations in the United States," *Publius: The Journal of Federalism* 28, 1 (Winter 1998): 147–163; and J. Fred Silva and Elisa Barbour, *The State-Local Fiscal Relationship in California: The Changing Balance of Power* (San Francisco: Public Policy Institute of California, 1999), available at: www.ppic.org/content/pubs/R_1299FSR.pdf.

26. Bob Herbert, "One-Man Feud," *The New York Times*, June 28, 1998.

27. The contending interests that surrounded Los Angeles' charter reform effort are described by a number of *Los Angeles Times* articles, including: Marc B. Haefele, "Is L.A. Charter Reform Headed for a Crash Landing?," September 20, 1998; Jim Newton, "Elected Commission Unveils its Version of Charter," December 29, 1998; Jesus Sanchez, "L.A. Developers Have Mixed Feelings on Charter Reform," May 25, 1999; and Xandra Kayden, "Charter Fight Reveals City Council's Power," June 3, 1999.

28. Mark Purcell, "The Decline of the Political Consensus for Urban Growth: Evidence from Los Angeles," *Journal of Urban Affairs* 22 (2000): 85–100; Tom Hogen-Esch, "The Coalition Dynamics of Secession in Los Angeles" (paper presented at the John Randolph Haynes and Dora Haynes Foundation conference on "Reform, L.A. Style: The Theory and Practice of Urban Governance at Century's Turn," University of Southern California School of Policy, Planning and Development, Los Angeles, September 19–20, 2002), available at: www.haynwww.haynesfoundation.org/WordDocs/hogen-esch.doc.

29. International City/County Management Association, "Municipal Form of Government, 2001." Available at: www.economiccouncilpbc.org/clientuploads/Documents/municpal_form_survey.pdf.

30. Tari Renner and Victor S. DeSantis, "Municipal Form of Government: Issues and Trends," *The Municipal Year Book 1998* (Washington, DC: International City/County Management Association, 1998), pp. 30–41.

31. Richard Edward DeLeon, *Left Coast City: Progressive Politics in San Francisco, 1975–91* (Lawrence: University of Kansas Press, 1992), p. 21

32. International City/County Management Association, "Municipal Form of Government, 2001."

33. See, for instance, John Gunyou, "'Weak Mayor' Model Is a Serious Handicap," [Minneapolis-St. Paul] *Star Tribune*, December 5, 2004.

34. In Chapter 7, "Reform Politics," we examine the biases of citywide, at-large elections in greater detail.

35. Tari Renner, "The Local Government Management Profession at Century's End," *The Municipal Year Book 2001* (Washington, DC: International City/County Management Association, 2001), p. 34–46.

36. William F. Fannin and Don Hellriegel, "Policy Roles of City Managers: A Contingency Typology and Empirical Test," *Urban Affairs Quarterly* 13 (April 1985): 212–226.

37. James H. Svara, "The Complementary Roles of Officials in Council-Manager Government," *The Municipal Year Book 1988* (Washington DC: International City Management Association, 1988), pp. 30–31. John Nalbandian, "The Manager as Political Leader," *National Civic Review* 90, 1 (Spring 2001), 63–73, reports a similar, self-effacing style of Dennis Hays, the chief administrative officer of Wyandotte County, Kansas. Hays was an important part of the leadership team that brought NASCAR to Kansas City. Yet he was reluctant to take the stage in public or engage in any activity that could be seen as political.

38. Poul Erik Mouritzen and James H. Svara, *Leadership at the Apex: Politicians and Administrators in Western Local Governments* (Pittsburgh, PA: University of Pittsburgh Press, 2002), p. 68.

39. Jeffrey Pressman, *Federal Programs and City Politics* (Berkeley: University of California Press, 1975), p. 36.

40. Tari Renner, "Appointed Local Government Managers: Stability and Change," *The Municipal Year Book 1990* (Washington, DC: International City/County Management Association, 1990), pp. 41 and 49–53; David N. Ammons and Charldean Newell, "'City Managers Don't Make Policy': A Lie; Let's Face It," *National Civic Review* 77 March/April 1988: 124–132; and Charldean Newell and David N. Ammons, "Role Emphasis of City Managers and Other Municipal Executives," *Public Administration Review* 47 (May/June 1987): 252.

41. John Nalbandian, "Tenets of Contemporary Professionalism in Local Government," *Public Administration Review* 50 (November/December 1990): 654–662. Also see Robert T. Golembiewski and Gerald T. Gabris, "Today's City Managers: A Legacy of Success-Becoming-Failure," *Public Administration Review* 54 (November/December 1994): 525–530.

42. Svara, "The Complementary Roles of Officials in Council-Manager Government," pp. 30–31; John Nalbandian, *Professionalism in Local Government: Transformations in the Roles, Responsibilities, and Values of City Managers* (San Francisco: Jossey-Bass, 1991).

43. Paul Teske and Mark Schneider, "The Bureaucratic Entrepreneur: The Case of City Managers," *Public Administration Review* 54 (July/August 1994): 331–340. Also see David Morgan and Sheilah Watson, "Policy Leadership in Council-Manager Cities: Comparing Mayor and Manager," *Public Administration Review* 52 (September/October 1992): 438–446.

44. James H. Svara, *Official Leadership in the City: Patterns of Conflict and Cooperation* (New York: Oxford University Press, 1990). Also see: James H. Svara, "The Roles of the City Council and Implications for the Structure of City Government," *National Civic Review* 91, 1 (Spring 2002): 5–23; and, David N. Ammons and Charldean Newell, *City Executives: Leadership Roles, Work Characteristics, and Time Management* (Albany: State University of New York Press, 1989), pp. 61–69.

45. Anirudh V.S. Ruhil, Mark Schneider, Paul Teske, and Byung-Moon Ji, "Institutions and Reform: Reinventing Local Government," *Urban Affairs Review* 34, 3 (January 1999): 433–455.

46. Doyle W. Buckwalter and Robert J. Parsons, "Local City Managers' Career Paths: Which Way to the Top?" *The Municipal Year Book 2000* (Washington, DC: International City/County Management Association, 2000), p. 20.

47. Svara, *Official Leadership in the City,* pp. 51–58.

48. William J. Pammer, Jr., Herbert A. Marlowe, Jr., Joseph G. Jarret, and Jack L. Dustin, "Managing Conflict and Building Cooperation in Council-Manager Cities: Insights on Establishing a Resolution Framework," *State and Local Government Review* 31, 3 (Fall 1999): www.cviog.uga.edu/slgr/1999ce.pdf.

49. James B. Katz, P. Edward French, and Hazel Prentiss-Cooper, "City Council Conflict as a Cause of Psychological Burnout and Voluntary Turnover among City Managers," *State and Local Government Review* 31, 3 (Fall 1999): 162–171. Available at: www.cviog.uga.edu/slgr/1999cb.pdf.

50. Tari Renner and Victor S. DeSantis, "City Manager Turnover: The Impact of Formal Authority and Electoral Change," *State and Local Government Review* 26, 2 (Spring 1994): 104–111; Renner, "The Local Government Management Profession at Century's End," pp. 39–40.

51. T.D. Allman, *Miami: City of the Future* (Boston: Atlantic Monthly Press, 1987), pp. 355–356.

52. The story of the transformation of San Diego government under Pete Wilson is told by Glen Sparrow, "The Emerging Chief Executive: The San Diego Experience," *National Civic Review* (December 1985): pp. 538–547. The quotation appears on p. 542. The description of developments during the post-Wilson years is taken from Glen W. Sparrow, "The Emerging Chief Executive 1971–91: A San Diego Update" in *Facilitative Leadership in Local Government: Lessons From Successful Mayors and Chairpersons,* ed. James H. Svara (San Francisco: Jossey-Bass, 1994), pp. 187–199.

53. The quotations in this paragraph are from Sparrow, "The Emerging Chief Executive: The San Diego Experience," p. 546.

54. Pressman, *Federal Programs and City Politics,* p. 32.

55. Rufus P. Browning, Dale Rogers Marshall, and David H. Tabb, *Protest Is Not Enough: The Struggle of Blacks and Hispanics for Equality in Urban Politics* (Berkeley: University of California Press, 1984), pp. 201–202.

56. Svara, *Official Leadership in the City,* p. 180.

57. Kimberly L. Nelson, "Assessing the CAO Position in a Strong-Mayor Government," *National Civic Review* 91, 1 (Spring 2002): 44–62; Svara, *Official Leadership in the City,* pp. 180–184.

58. Ammons and Newell, *City Executives,* pp. 58–59.

59. H. George Frederickson, Gary A. Johnson, and Curtis H. Wood, *The Adapted City: Institutional Dynamics and Structural Change* (Armonk, NY: M.E. Sharpe, 2004).

60. This section is based on Frederickson, Johnson, and Wood, *The Adapted City: Institutional Dynamics and Structural Change,* especially pp. 3–11, 52–82, and 118–138.

61. Mouritzen and Svara, *Leadership at the Apex,* p. 72.

62. Tari Renner and Victor S. DeSantis, "Contemporary Patterns and Trends in Municipal Government Structures." *The Municipal Year Book 1993* (Washington, DC: The International City/County Management Association, 1993), p. 66.

63. Peter J. Haas, "An Exploratory Analysis of American City Council Salaries," *Urban Affairs Review* 31, 2 (November 1995): 255–265.

64. John P. Pelissero and Timothy B. Krebs, "City Council Legislative Committees and Policy-making in Large United States Cities," *American Journal of Political Science* 41, 2 (April 1997): 499–518.

65. Svara, *Official Leadership in the City,* p. 153.

66. This was the case of Philadelphia in the 1980s. See Carolyn Adams. David Bartelt, David Elesh, Ira Goldstein, Nancy Kleniewski, and William Yancey, *Philadelphia: Neighborhoods, Division, and Conflict in a Postindustrial City* (Philadelphia: Temple University Press, 1991), pp. 146–153.

67. *Lockyer v. San Francisco* (2004), Available at: www.news.findlaw.com/nytimes/docs/glrts/lckyrsf81204opn.pdf.

68. Timothy Bledsoe, *Careers in City Politics: The Case for Urban Democracy* (Pittsburgh: University of Pittsburgh Press, 1993), pp. 113–119 and 126–128.

69. Ibid., pp. 18–82.

70. Susan MacManus, "The Resurgent City Councils," in *American State and Local Politics: Directions for the 21ˢᵗ Century,* eds. Ronald E. Weber and Paul Brace (New York: Chatham House Publishers of Seven Bridges Press, 1999), p. 166.

71. Ibid., pp. 168 and 176–177.

72. "Women in Elective Office 2005," a fact sheet prepared by the Center for American Women in Politics, The Eagleton Institute of Politics, Rutgers, The State University of New Jersey. Available at: http://www.cawp.rutgers.edu/Facts/Officeholders/elective.pdf.

73. In 2005, women were 15.0 percent of the U.S. House of Representatives and 14.0 percent of the Senate. Women were also 22.5 percent of the state legislative membership. See "Women in Elective Office 2005." Also see Bledsoe, *Careers in City Politics,* pp. 46, 122, and 177–178.

74. R. Darcy, Susan Welch, and Janet Clark, *Women, Elections, and Representation* (New York: Longman, 1987), pp. 33–34.

75. M. Margaret Conway, Gertrude A. Steuernagel, and David W. Ahern, *Women and Political Participation* (Washington, DC: CQ Press, 1997), p. 113.

76. Robert A. Schumann and Richard L. Fox, "Women Chief Administrative Officers: Perceptions of Their Role in Government," *The Municipal Year Book 1998* (Washington, DC: International City/County Management Association, 1998), pp. 116–122.

77. Bledsoe, *Careers in City Politics,* pp. 46, 122, and 177–178.

78. Jeffrey L. Pressman, "Preconditions of Mayoral Leadership," *American Political Science Review* 66 (June 1972): 512.

79. Renner and DeSantis, "Municipal Form of Government," pp. 35–37.

80. Douglas Yates, *The Ungovernable City* (Cambridge, MA: MIT Press, 1977).

81. John P. Kotter and Paul R. Lawrence, *Mayors in Action: Five Approaches to Urban Governance* (New York: Wiley Interscience, 1974).

82. Svara, *Official Leadership in the City,* pp. 81–121.

83. Peter Beinart, "The Pride of the Cities," *The New Republic* (June 30, 1997): pp. 16–18.

84. Kemper Diehl and Jan Jarboe, *Cisneros: Portrait of a New American* (San Antonio, TX: Corona Publishing, 1985), pp. 81–123; Henry Flores, "Structural Barriers to Chicano Empowerment," in *Latino Empowerment: Progress, Problems, and Prospects,* eds. Roberto E. Villarreal, Norma G. Hernandez, and Howard D. Neighbor (Westport, CT: Greenwood Press, 1988), pp. 28–35 and 39. Flores also observes the limitations of the deracialized economic development agenda pursued by Los Angeles Mayor Tom Bradley, an African American.

85. Raphael J. Sonenshein, *Politics in Black and White: Race and Power in Los Angeles* (Princeton, NJ: Princeton University Press, 1993). On the importance of organized labor to the Bradley coalition, see James A. Regalado, "Organized Labor and Los Angeles City Politics: An Assessment in the Bradley Years, 1973–89," *Urban Affairs Quarterly* 27 (September 1991): 87–108.

86. Raphael J. Sonenshein, "Is This the End? Biracial Coalition in the 1993 Los Angeles Mayoral Election" (paper presented at the annual meeting of the American Political Science Association, Washington, DC, September 1–4, 1994).

87. Matea Gold and Tina Daunt, "L.A. Takes a Turn to the Left with Democrat in Charge," *Los Angeles Times,* June 6, 2001; Anthony York, "Los Angeles' Dirty Little Election," *Salon.com,* June 7, 2001, available at: http://dir.salon.com/ politics/feature/2001/06/07/hahn/index.html; Jonathan Wilcox, "Why Moderate Angelinos and L.A. Republicans Made Hahn Mayor," *CalNews.com,* June 13, 2001, available at: www.calnews.com/archives/wilcox2.htm.

88. Huey L. Perry, "Exploring the Meaning and Implications of Deracialization in African-American Urban Politics," *Urban Affairs Quarterly* 27 (December 1991): 185. Also see Joseph P. McCormick II and Charles E. Jones, "The Conceptualization of Deracialization: Thinking Through the Dilemma," in *Dilemmas of Black Politics: Issues of Leadership and Strategy,* ed. Georgia Persons (New York: HarperCollins, 1993), pp. 66–84.

89. Huey L. Perry, ed., *Race, Politics, and Governance in the United States* (Gainesville FL: University Press of Florida, 1997) describes in greater detail the election and governing approaches of a number of black mayors, especially New York's David Dinkins, Baltimore's Kurt Schmoke, Seattle's Norman Rice, and New Haven's John Daniels. For a discussion of the changing nature of Philadelphia's biracial coalition, from the "good government" coalition that elected Wilson Goode the city's first black mayor in 1983 through the more conservative, machine-oriented variant led by Mayor John Street, see Richard A. Keiser, "Philadelphia's Evolving Biracial Coalition," in *Racial Politics in American Cities,* 3rd ed., eds. Rufus P. Browning, Dale Rogers Marshall, and David H. Tabb (New York: Longman, 2003), pp. 77–112. Also see Keiser, *Subordination or Empowerment? African-American Leadership and the Struggle for Urban Political Power* (New York: Oxford University Press, 1997), pp. 90–131.

90. Carlos Munoz, Jr., and Charles P. Henry, "Coalition Politics in San Antonio and Denver: The Cisneros and Peña Mayoral Campaigns," in *Racial Politics in American Cities,* 1st ed., eds. Rufus P. Browning, Dale Rogers Marshall, and David H. Tabb (White Plains, NY: Longman, 1990), pp. 179–190. Also see Rufus P. Browning, Dale Rogers Marshall, and David H. Tabb, "Has Political Incorporation Been Achieved? Is it Enough?" in *Racial Politics in American Cities,* pp. 212–230.

91. Rodney E. Hero and Susan E. Clarke, "Latinos, Blacks, and Multiethnic Politics in Denver: Realigning Power and Influence in the Struggle for Equality," in *Racial Politics in American Cities,* 3rd ed., eds. Browning, Marshall, and Tabb, pp. 309–330.

92. Huey L. Perry, "The Reelection of Sidney Barthelemy as Mayor of New Orleans," *PS: Political Science and Politics* 23 (June 1990): 156–158.

93. Carol A. Pierannunzi and John D. Hutcheson, Jr., "Deracialization in the Deep South: Mayoral Politics in Atlanta," *Urban Affairs Quarterly* 27 (December 1991): 192–201.

94. Huey L. Perry, "Deracialization as an Analytical Construct in American Urban Politics," *Urban Affairs Quarterly* 27 (1991): 181–191.

95. Ibid., pp. 187–189.

96. David C. Smith, "Recent Elections and Black Politics: The Maturation or Death of Black Politics?" *PS: Political Science and Politics* 23 (June 1990): 161.

97. Robert T. Starks, "A Commentary and Response to 'Exploring the Meaning and Implications of Deracialization in African-American Urban Politics,'" *Urban Affairs Quarterly* 27 (December 1991): 221.

98. Smith, "Recent Elections and Black Politics: The Maturation or Death of Black Politics?", p. 160.

99. Katherine Underwood, "Ethnicity Is Not Enough: Latino-Led Multiracial Coalitions in Los Angeles," *Urban Affairs Review* 33, 1 (September 1997): 3–27. The quotation is from p. 23.

100. See Keiser, *Subordination or Empowerment?*, especially pp. 159–172.

101. Marcus D. Pohlmann and Michael P. Kirby, *Racial Politics at the Crossroads: Memphis Elects Dr. W.W. Herenton* (Knoxville: University of Tennessee Press, 1996).

102. Edward J.W. Park and John S.W. Park, "Korean Americans and the Crisis of the Liberal Coalition: Immigrants and Politics in Los Angeles," pp. 91–108, and Paula D. McClain and Steven C. Tauber, "Racial Minority Group Relations in a Multiracial Society," pp. 111–136, both in *Governing American Cities: Inter-Ethnic Coalitions, Competition, and Conflict,* ed. Michael Jones-Correa (New York: Russell Sage Foundation, 2001).

103. Guillermo J. Grenier and Max Castro, "Blacks and Cubans in Miami: The Negative Consequences of the Cuban Enclave on Ethnic Relations," in *Governing American Cities: Inter-Ethnic Coalitions, Competition, and Conflict,* pp. 137–157.

Throughout much of the nineteenth century and the first half
of the twentieth century, strong
political party organizations or
political machines controlled
many facets of local government,
especially in major northeastern
and mid-western cities. For significant periods of time, local
party leaders, popularly known

as **bosses,** dominated politics in New York, Boston, Philadelphia, Pittsburgh,
Jersey City, New Haven, Albany, Chicago, Kansas City, and Cincinnati. Not as
commonplace in the South and West, "boss rule" also emerged in Lexington,
Memphis, New Orleans, San Antonio, Tampa, and San Francisco.[1]

The existence of political machines underscores the importance of behind-
the-scenes power in the city. In New York City, none of the famous bosses of
Tammany Hall, the fabled Democratic Party organization, served as mayor;
William Marcy Tweed, Richard Croker, John Kelly, and Charles F. Murphy all
operated from offstage. Deals were cut in private and played out in public.

Important business entrepreneurs reached an accommodation with machine
leaders, receiving important approvals, permits, franchises, and licenses in
return for their support. In Chicago, the legendary Mayor Richard J. Daley
built a long-lasting governing regime that fused the interests of the city's
downtown business community and its white ethnic neighborhoods.[2] Years
later, his son, Richard M. Daley, won the mayoralty, receiving the financial
backing of developers, manufacturing interests, and local labor unions.[3]

Today, the boss-dominated, highly disciplined party machines have largely
disappeared from the urban landscape. Yet certain machine-style practices
persist. In Philadelphia's "pay-to-play" scandal, political associates of Mayor
John Street were accused of having awarded millions of dollars of city bond
work in return for lavish gifts and political contributions. In Newark, New
Jersey, municipal workers were expected to make contributions to the Sharpe
James reelection campaign and to buy tickets to the mayor's annual birthday
bash. James' critics also accused the mayor of punishing backers of his opponent. Nonprofit agencies that supported James' rival lost city assistance;
businesses with ties to the losing candidate were confronted with municipal
summonses for building and health code violations.[4]

In a number of big cities, one-party dominance allows party leaders to determine who will hold office.[5] Democratic party leaders in the Brooklyn section of

New York still practice the machine art of **slating,** determining who will be the party's candidates for civil court. Judges, lawyers, and law clerks buy $300 tickets for party fundraisers. Lawyers who do not contribute complain of being "frozen out of receiverships and other lucrative work awarded by the court."[6]

The machine-style practice of ethnic **ticket balancing** also continues, in which a party seeks to broaden its support by offering a slate of candidates who can appeal to the city's diversity of ethnic groups. In New York, even Rudy Giuliani, a self-styled anti-machine reformer, engaged in ticket balancing. Giuliani, an Italian, won the mayoralty in 1993 by having Herman Badillo, the city's first Puerto Rican member of Congress, join him as his running mate for city comptroller. Giuliani's campaign also broadcast appeals by the noted actor Ron Silver in an effort to reach Jewish voters.

The nature of municipal government today cannot be fully understood without reference to the battle between the political machine and the reformers. The **reform movement** sought "good government" practices in place of the political machine's parochialism and corruption. Although it took many decades, the reformers eventually won their war with the political machine. Today, reforms such as nonpartisan and at-large elections and merit-based municipal hiring systems are common features of municipal government.

The urban political machine offered immigrants a route to empowerment. More recent studies, however, have come to question the degree to which the urban machines helped or hindered the political advancement of the new arrivals to America's shores. Today, we must discern the degree to which machine-style politics offers a new generation of urban immigrants an appropriate route to political power.

New York Mayor Michael Bloomberg, who is Jewish, conspicuously wears green in the city's annual St. Patrick's Day parade. Ethnic appeals remain an inherent part of city politics even in the post-machine era.

MACHINE POLITICS AT WORK

Machine politics is essentially an **exchange process.** To win elections, the political machine traded favors and benefits for votes. The machine gave its supporters such **material benefits** as emergency assistance (including food and shelter), help with immigration exams, and, most important, jobs. The machine's ward and precinct leaders also "fixed tickets" (by getting friendly judges to dismiss minor violations of the city code) and posted bail, all in response to constituent requests. Machine captains also aided business owners desiring a building permit, zoning variance, or the award of a city license, franchise, or construction contract. In return, the grateful business head was expected to provide the machine with either a cash kickback or a number of jobs that the machine could then dispense to its supporters in return for their votes.

The machine rewarded its friends and punished its enemies. The machine dispensed **specific benefits** that it could deny to people who failed to support the machine. Under the **patronage** or **spoils system,** the winning party in an election distributed government jobs, contracts, and other benefits to its supporters, following the old adage: "To the victors belong the spoils." The backers of the losing party risked being denied municipal jobs and favors.

In many ways, machine politics resembled a **brokerage system.** The classic machine politician was interested only in keeping himself in power and did not seek to advance broad public policy goals of his own. Machine leaders generally did not want to risk making unnecessary enemies and losing votes. Instead, machine leaders preferred the politically "safe" route of waiting for established civic actors and groups to reach a consensus. Then the machine assisted all concerned in achieving their agreed-upon goals, earning their obligations, a sort of "broker's fee," in the process.[7]

The political machine, though, was far from a fair or neutral broker. It was not equally responsive to all groups in the city. The Irish-dominated big-city machines often gave lesser benefits to Italians, East-European ethnics, and racial minorities.[8] The Chicago machine dispensed patronage jobs and services to its African-American supporters, but was reluctant to put blacks into positions of real authority or to push for housing and school desegregation.[9]

The urban machine also dispensed nonmaterial or **nontangible benefits** to its followers. In the 1800s and early 1900s, recently arrived immigrants from overseas found themselves all alone in a strange new land. There were few, if any government programs to assist them. The machine captain who came to their aid was their friend. In the cramped, overcrowded, immigrant wards of the city, machine politicians also won the loyalty of impoverished immigrants by sponsoring picnics and social and youth clubs. Practicing a form of **retail politics,** the machine's precinct captains sought to develop a close personal relationship with voters.[10] George Washington Plunkitt, the famed turn-of-the-century Tammany Hall district leader in New York, bragged of his relationship with the people of his district:

> To learn real human nature you have to go among the people, see them and be seen. I know every man, woman, and child in the Fifteenth District, except them that's

been born this summer—and I know some of them, too. I know what they like and what they don't like, what they are strong in and what they are weak in, and I reach them by approachin' at the right side.[11]

Plunkitt used his personal relationships with voters to build organizational loyalty:

I hear of a young feller that's proud of his voice, thinks that he can sing fine. I ask him to come around to Washington Hall and join our Glee Club. He comes and sings, and he's a follower of Plunkitt for life. Another young feller gains a reputation as a baseball player in a vacant lot. I bring him into our baseball club. That fixes him. You'll find him workin' for my ticket at the polls next election day.[12]

Precinct and block captains took note of as many birthdays and anniversaries as they possibly could. They provided families with help in emergencies. The machine captain paid for funerals, providing private carriages and impressive floral arrangements that no immigrant family could afford, saving "indigent families from the unimaginable horror of having one of their own buried by the county."[13] Machine leaders attended weddings, funerals, Irish wakes, and Jewish bar mitzvahs. The legendary South Side of Chicago Congressman William Dawson, a machine sub-leader, gained his constituents' support through an organization that functioned as much as a social club as a political organization. Every Friday night Dawson addressed a meeting at his headquarters:

Then the group adjourned to the nightclub in the basement and listened to the music of Jimmie Noone, the man who taught Benny Goodman how to play the clarinet. "It was a great social thing," John Stroger recalls. "Parties on Friday nights, then more meetings on Saturday morning." The Dawson machine was an important social institution as well as a political one.[14]

At its peak of power, the classic machine was characterized by **central control.** The boss and his associates made all the major decisions and dictated to party subordinates. As one analysis of the Hague organization, which ruled Jersey City well into the late 1940s, makes clear: "Complete obedience is necessary from the bottom to the top; officials are not supposed to have ideas on public policies, but to take orders."[15] In Chicago, the city council served more as a "rubber stamp" than an independent policy maker.[16] The **hierarchical** or **pyramidal structure** of the classic machine was also reflected in its detailed territorial organization (see Figure 6-1). Block captains (and in some cities even building captains) ministered to the needs of their constituents and reported to a precinct leader, who in turn reported to a ward or district leader, who, in turn, reported directly to the party boss or the boss' close assistants.

Not all party machines were so tightly disciplined. In many cities, local party organizations were marred by in-fighting and **factionalism.** In New York, a more "reformed" machine faction sought to tame Tammany Hall's blatant corruption, fearing that exposés of corruption would lead to the machine's ouster at the polls.[17] (See "Is There Such a Thing as 'Honest Graft'? Corruption and Machine Politics," on pp. 177.)

■ FIGURE 6-1

POLITICAL MACHINE ORGANIZATION CHART

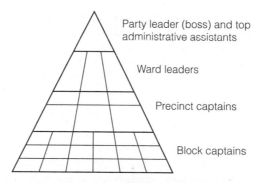

Party leader (boss) and top administrative assistants

Ward leaders

Precinct captains

Block captains

IS THERE SUCH A THING AS "HONEST GRAFT"? CORRUPTION AND MACHINE POLITICS

Political machines were often, but not always, notoriously corrupt. Dishonest machine politicians took substantial **graft** or payoffs in exchange for political favors. The costs of municipal projects rose, depleting municipal treasuries. The corruption of New York's Tweed Ring in the late 1800s took the city to the brink of bankruptcy.

Tammany district leader George Washington Plunkitt, who made a fortune in politics, defended the seemingly indefensible practice of taking graft. Plunkitt claimed that no Tammany official ever made a penny through "dishonest graft," by blackmailing saloon keepers or stealing from the public treasury. Instead, Tammany politicians simply displayed good business foresight, taking advantage of insider knowledge, a process that he called "honest graft":

> There's an honest graft, and I'm an example of how it works . . . . My party's in power in the city, and it's goin' to undertake a lot of public improvements. Well, I'm tipped off, say, that they're going to lay out a new park at a certain place.
>
> I see my opportunity and I take it. I go to that place and I buy up all the land I can in the neighborhood. Then the board of this or that makes its plan public, and there is a rush to get my land, which nobody cared particular for before.
>
> Ain't it perfectly honest to charge a good price and make a profit on my investment and foresight? Of course, it is. Well, that's honest graft.*

Plunkett was an outrageous character who even asked that the epitaph on his headstone should say: "He Seen His Opportunities and He Took 'Em." Plunkitt's protestations to the contrary, "honest graft" is not really very honest. Public officials today can be prosecuted for using their official positions and insider knowledge for their personal enrichment.

* William L. Riordan, *Plunkitt of Tammany Hall,* edited by Terrence J. McDonald (Boston: Bedford Books of St. Martin's Press, 1994), p. 49.

THE FUNCTIONS OF POLITICAL MACHINES

Despite their corruption, the political machines attracted support as they helped meet a variety of needs, responding to problems that, at the time, were ignored by the rest of society.[18] The machine served a **welfare function**, extending help to newly arrived immigrants and the needy. The machine provided assistance at a time before the welfare state was established, before there were strong government agencies to provide emergency assistance to persons in need.

During the severe winter of 1870–71, New York boss William Marcy Tweed "spent $50,000 of his personal funds in his own ward and gave each of the city's aldermen [another term for city council members] $1,000 out of his own pocket to buy coal for the poor."[19] Between 1869 and 1871, the Tammany-controlled city treasury also gave an estimated $1.4 million to the Roman Catholic Church and lesser amounts to other religious denominations and charities.[20] Of course, Tweed's main concern was in winning votes, not in helping those in need.

The machine also assisted in the naturalization of many new citizens and provided America's new arrivals with a highly symbolic **channel of social mobility.** The immigrants may have been barred from the upper rungs of society and the business world, but their voting numbers assured them of an important place in the political arena. Members of an ethnic group took pride as "one of their own" advanced up the ladder of political power.

Yet the actual social mobility that the machine offered its supporters was often quite limited. There were simply too few good-paying municipal jobs to go around. In order to preserve rewards for their kinsmen, Irish political leaders such as Boston's legendary Michael J. Curley dispensed only limited jobs and opportunities to the members of other ethnic groups. In Chicago, the city's Poles were not fully incorporated into the city's Democratic machine, as the organization's Irish leaders hoarded the lion's share of benefits for members of their own ethnic group.[21]

Nor did the big-city machine greatly help the advancement of racial minorities. In the post-World War II era, the urban machine often represented the views of the city's politically conservative, middle-class home owners. These more conservative machines sought to keep taxes low.[22] They also resisted housing and school integration.

The political machine also provided substantial **assistance to business.** In return for financial contributions and the control over jobs that could be used as patronage, the machine offered business owners exclusive contracts, licenses, and other preferential treatment. By working with the machine, business leaders gained a "sphere of influence" over economic development policy.[23]

In old New York, "good government" elements of the business community sharply criticized the city's growing debt and the Tweed Ring's scandalous schemes and payoff methods. But speculators such as Jay Gould, Jim Fiske, Cornelius Vanderbilt, and John Jacob Astor all enriched themselves by having corrupt government officials issue the necessary approvals of their business projects.[24] In Chicago, both Richard J. Daley and Richard M. Daley pursued a growth agenda that won the support of the city's business and civic leaders.[25]

The machine **centralized power.** Businesses often faced difficulty in getting a whole host of licenses, zoning variances, and various other inspections, permissions, and approvals from a myriad of city boards, agencies, and committees. A behind-the-scenes agreement between a business owner and a party boss served to assure that all needed clearances would be granted quickly.

The centralization of power facilitated **city growth.** Rapidly growing cities in the 1800s and early 1900s required new streets, sewers, housing, streetcar lines, and other facilities. The political machine abetted such growth projects by ensuring that all the necessary permissions were granted. The Tweed Ring in the 1860s pursued an ambitious development program for upper Manhattan that entailed the construction of new streets, water mains, sewers, parks, and streetcar lines.[26] The city expanded, businesses and real estate developers profited, and machine politicians took payoffs and distributed thousands of new patronage jobs. Boss Tweed even bought the votes of alderman in order to gain municipal approval for the construction of the Brooklyn Bridge; the construction offered Tammany additional opportunities for job patronage and kickbacks from contractors.[27]

In some cities, the machine also responded to a more disreputable community: **racketeers, organized crime, and illegal gambling.** The machine received payoffs from the "mob" in return for assuring that the city would not interfere unduly in the mob's activities.[28] In Chicago in the 1940s, William Dawson, the African-American boss of the city's South Side, protected the illegal "numbers game" of a black cartel that contributed huge sums of money to Dawson's ward organizations. Any police officer who harassed the protected "policy wheels" (or numbers games) was transferred. After a competing crime organization bought connections to the dominant machine faction, Chicago police cracked down on the policy wheels operated by African Americans but allowed the wheels run by the white crime syndicate to keep spinning.[29]

The political machine also played a **conciliating function,** helping to mute social conflict and class warfare. By dispensing benefits, the machines helped to undermine class-based action and support for trade union and socialist party politics.[30] Party officials even protected the owners of tenement buildings and sweatshops from whom they took payoffs. The political machine won the votes of lower-class workers but showed no interest in eradicating sweatshops and slum conditions: "Irish bosses turned their backs on more radical forms of working-class politics. The machine ultimately tamed Irish voters as well as leaders."[31]

IMMIGRATION, ETHNIC POLITICS, AND THE POLITICAL MACHINE

Strictly speaking, an immigrant base was not necessary to the life of a political machine. Patronage-based political organizations existed in the nineteenth-century American city even before the arrival of the massive waves of immigration from Europe.[32] (See "Film Review: *Gangs of New York:* The Tammany Machine and the Civil War Draft Riots" on pp. 180–181.) Denver,

FILM REVIEW:
GANGS OF NEW YORK: THE TAMMANY MACHINE
AND THE CIVIL WAR DRAFT RIOTS

Tammany leader William Marcy Tweed was a prominent character in Martin Scorsese's *Gangs of New York* (starring Leonardo DiCaprio, Cameron Diaz, and Daniel Day-Lewis). Scorsese's portrayal of the political machine and its development is largely accurate, even though the film distorts numerous aspects of New York's history.

The film shows Tweed in the mid-1800s, before he was able to fully consolidate his power and become the political boss of New York. In this early stage of the machine's development, rival political organizations and machine factions contested for votes. They even formed competing volunteer fire companies, racing to fires in order to win the loyalty of voters.

As the film reveals, Tammany was not initially built upon the votes of immigrants. Tammany started out as a social club and soon evolved into a political group that reflected the anti-immigrant concerns of nativist groups. But Tammany needed votes wherever it could find them. Tammany "worked the docks" to build its support among immigrants only when it was no longer possible for the organization to ignore the potential voting power of the unstoppable tide of new arrivals.

The film documents the extreme deprivations suffered by the new arrivals, showing why they would turn to machine leaders. The machine's leaders are not caring individuals; instead, their main interest is in winning votes and remaining in power. Scorsese's film portrays machine officials as violent and corrupt. Gangs and saloons served as recruiting grounds for the machine.

Gangs of New York depicts the city as a seething cauldron of ethnic animosities. America is seen to have its birth in the outcome of that ethnic struggle. As a filmmaker, Scorsese is interested in powerful visuals and in making a dramatic film. His portrayal of the degree of the ethnic violence and bloodshed is exaggerated, virtually hallucinatory.

Even the film's depiction of the very violent Civil War draft riots is exaggerated. The draft riots are a result of the extreme competition between the city's Irish and African Americans. In the film, both "out" groups were fighting for the same jobs and turf. The impoverished Irish rebelled when the imposition of conscription (the "draft") meant that they would be forced to fight and die in order to free black slaves. The conscription system was particularly unfair, as wealthier people were allowed to buy their way out of the draft.

The mobs in Civil War New York first attacked rich whites and then turned to killing and lynching African Americans. One large group of rioters even burned the Colored Orphan Asylum, from which the 237 children escaped. New York was engulfed in a race war.

It took thousands of Union Army troops, fresh from their victory at Gettysburg, to put down the riot: "Troops assaulted 'infected' districts,
continued

FILM REVIEW:
GANGS OF NEW YORK: THE TAMMANY MACHINE
AND THE CIVIL WAR DRAFT RIOTS (CONT.)

using howitzers loaded with grapeshot and canister [primitive fragmentation bombs] to mow down rioters and engaged in fierce building-by-building fights." Yet, despite the bitter violence, nowhere is it recorded that the Union ships in the harbor opened fire on the city, blasting the poor Irish sections of the city to smithereens, as depicted in the fantastical closing scenes of Gangs.

Source: Edwin G. Burrows and Mike Wallace, Gotham: A History of New York City to 1989 (New York: Oxford, 1999), pp. 315–316, 512–515, 822–826, and 877–899. The quotation appears on p. 895.

Memphis, Kansas City, New Orleans, Nashville, and Richmond all had political machines at a time when the immigrant population comprised only a small portion of the total population of each city.[33]

Yet, "It was the succeeding waves of immigrants that gave the urban political organizations the manipulable mass bases without which they could not have functioned as they did."[34] The political machine's block and precinct captains were only too happy to provide the new arrivals with help. Many of the immigrants, arriving from traditional and autocratic countries, were unfamiliar with the workings of democracy. They willingly accepted proffered jobs and services in exchange for their vote. It was a trade few could afford to pass up; it must have appeared to be one of the best bargains imaginable.

The political machine operated in a setting marred by bitter ethnic clashes and nativist resentment of the new arrivals. The prejudices were deep and salient. In Chicago in 1931, Republican Mayor "Big" Bill Thompson attempted to rally support by slurring the Czech (Bohemian) heritage and immigrant roots of his Democratic opponent, Anton "Tony" Cermak: "Tony, Tony, where's your pushcart at? Can you imagine a World's Fair Mayor with a name like that? I won't take a back seat from that Bohunk—Chairmock, Chermack or whatever his name is."[35]

The political machine was not above exploiting ethnic divisions and prejudices. Yet it still provided benefits to those immigrant groups whose votes it needed. Compared to more established elements of "Yankee" society that scorned the newcomers, the political machine, whatever its flaws, was the newcomers' friend.

Still, we must be cautious—the benevolence of the machine should not be overstated. The machine gave immigrants much-needed jobs and benefits. But the political organization did not aggressively fight for progressive legislation to improve tenement housing and eliminate sweatshop work conditions.[36]

MACHINE POLITICS—SUNBELT STYLE

For a long period in American history, political machines were a recognized feature of northeastern and mid-western cities with large immigrant populations from Europe. Yet the West had Boss Abraham Reuf's San Francisco organization, and the Pendergast organization dominated Kansas City politics for many years. In the South, notable statewide organizations included the Byrd machine in Virginia, the Long organization in Louisiana, and the Talmadge organization in Georgia.

Many rural areas in the South found their county governments controlled by local political machines or **courthouse gangs.** The most infamous of all county machines was that of the Parr family in Duval, Texas. In 1948, future president Lyndon B. Johnson won that state's senatorial primary by a margin of only 87 votes; he won Duval County by a lopsided 4,662 to 40 margin. The Duval machine had helped Johnson steal the election.[37]

The corrupt practices of the local Texas machines were extensive:

> On Election Day, Mexican Americans were herded to the polls by armed pistoleros, sometimes appointed "deputy sheriffs" for the day . . . In some precincts, these voters were also handed ballots that had already been marked . . . In other precincts, matters were managed less crudely: the voters were told whom to vote for, but were allowed to mark their own ballots; of course, the guards accompanied them into the voting cubby-holes to ensure that the instructions were followed.[38]

Bossism and political machines were features of politics of a number of southern cities, including New Orleans, Memphis, Charleston, Savannah, Augusta, Jacksonville, Chattanooga, Montgomery, Lexington, Louisville, Covington (Kentucky), and San Antonio.[39] Undoubtedly, the most famous big-city organization in the South was that of E. H. Crump, which dominated Memphis from the 1920s through the late 1940s. Crump provided an annual boat ride for orphans and shut-ins,[40] kept his organization relatively free from corruption, and maintained good relations with the city's business community.

As Memphis lacked a mass base of immigrant voters, Crump recognized that black voters could be the key to his political power. Blacks were not permitted to vote in much of the Deep South. But in Tennessee, the state's relatively small black population posed less of a threat to white control, and blacks voted in limited numbers. Crump offered African Americans a subordinate position in his machine. He appointed African Americans to positions in the municipal bureaucracy. Memphis even named monuments after prominent local black citizens, a rarity in the Old South. Crump's captains encouraged African-American registration, paying the poll tax for a selected number of blacks and carefully instructing them how to vote on election day. By challenging the Ku Klux Klan in the municipal election of 1923, "Crump simultaneously appealed to blacks and white ethnics as a friendly ambassador from a hostile outside world."[41] Once Crump cemented his power, though, he had less need for black votes; fewer blacks were allowed to register, and the benefits given the black community diminished.[42]

Tampa is another southern city where the local organization found it useful to appeal to black votes. In Tampa, Nick Nuccio, the son of Sicilian immigrants, gained power by fusing together the votes of Italians with those of the city's growing Hispanic and black communities. As a black newspaper publisher remembered, "He was the first public official who would come regularly to our meetings in our community—he was calling blacks 'mister' when most politicians were still saying 'boy' or 'nigger.'"[43] Once again, though, blacks were accorded only subordinate, junior partner status in the political machine. As we shall see, this was a pattern that was typical of big cities in the North as well as in the South.

WHY DID POLITICAL MACHINES DECLINE?

There are a number of reasons why political machines withered away. Changes initiated by the **reform movement** (which will be discussed in greater detail in the next chapter) took their toll on the political machine. Particularly damaging to the machine was the enactment of **merit systems** (also referred to as local **civil service systems**) that regulated the hiring, promotion, and dismissal of municipal employees, limiting patronage. Today, almost every city in the country uses the principles of merit-system hiring.

The impact of civil service on political machines was devastating. With fewer jobs to offer, the machine could no longer recruit an army of canvassers and voters. Little wonder that Tammany captain George Washington Plunkitt imagined all sorts of evils that would follow from "the curse of civil service reform":

The boys and men don't get excited any more when they see a United States flag or hear "The Star-Spangled Banner." They don't care no more for firecrackers on the Fourth of July. And why should they? What is there in it for them? They know that no matter how hard they work for their country in a campaign, the jobs will go to fellows who can tell [in the answers to civil service examinations questions] about the mummies and the bird steppin' on the iron . . .

Say, let me tell of one case. After the battle of San Juan Hill, the Americans found a dead man with a light complexion, red hair and blue eyes. They could see he wasn't a Spaniard, although he had on a Spanish uniform . . . Then a private of the Seventy-first Regiment saw him and yelled, "Good Lord, that's Flaherty." That man grew up in my district, and he was once the most patriotic American boy on the West Side. He couldn't see a flag without yellin' himself hoarse.

Now, how did he come to be lying dead with a Spanish uniform on? . . . Well, in the municipal campaign of 1897, that young man, chock full of patriotism, worked day and night for the Tammany ticket. Tammany won, and the young man determined to devote his life to the service of the city. He picked out a place that would suit him, and sent in his application to the head of department. He got a reply that he must take a civil service examination to get the place . . . He read the questions about the mummies, the bird on the iron, and all the other fool questions—and he left that office an enemy of the country that he had loved so well. The mummies and the bird blasted his patriotism. He went to Cuba, enlisted in the Spanish army at the breakin' out of the war, and died fightin' his country.

That is but one victim of the infamous civil service.[44]

The Chicago political machine was able to rely on patronage for decades after civil service rules meant the disappearance of vast patronage sources in other cities. Chicago officials classified numerous municipal jobs as seasonal or temporary in order to keep them exempt from civil service rules; somehow, though, the "seasonal" jobs lasted the full year and "temporary" employees managed to "'stay temporary' for the rest of their lives."[45] The U.S. Supreme Court, though, eventually delivered mortal blows to Chicago's and other big-city patronage systems. In its 1976 *Elrod v. Burns* and 1990 *Rutan* decisions, the Court placed sharp limitations on partisan-based hirings, firings, and promotions. In *Rutan,* the Court effectively ruled that politically based hiring and promotions deprived an individual of his or her First Amendment rights of freedom of speech, belief, and association.[46]

Restrictions on immigration, enacted by the federal government beginning in the 1920s, also drained the machine's basin of potential supporters. As earlier waves of immigrants climbed the social and economic ladder, the machine needed to find new voters. But with curbs placed on immigration, the machine lost its natural source of voters.

The latter-day political machines turned to other groups, African Americans and Hispanics, whose members still needed the benefits the machine could provide. But **racial polarizations** soon took their toll on the machine, especially as African Americans began to withdraw their support from white-ethnic-dominated political organizations unwilling to challenge residential and school segregation.

Rising levels of national **prosperity and education** also help to explain the machine's decline. More wealthy and educated voters proved to be increasingly independent; they were less willing to trade their votes for the machine's paltry favors. America's wealth also led to a new geographical mobility; the onset of the suburban boom further undercut the geographically rooted loyalties of the big-city machine. The Republican organization of Nassau County, Long Island, in suburban New York City, was an exception. The Nassau County organization may actually have been the last of the nation's strong political machines.[47]

The **growth of the welfare state,** beginning with Franklin Delano Roosevelt's New Deal, also undermined local machines as citizens were no longer dependent on the limited benefits the machine could provide. The local machine could not compete with the new federal programs. The fabled hod of coal offered by the machine could not match the cash, housing, and food relief now provided by government agencies.

In some cases, local bosses were able to use the federal largesse as an additional source of patronage.[48] In Detroit, Mayor Coleman Young used federal antipoverty programs as a new source of patronage, building a network of loyal neighborhood organizations that would canvass neighborhoods on election day.[49] In the long run, however, the dominant impact of the federal programs was to undercut the reliance of voters on machine-dispensed benefits.

Finally, **changes in the mass media and social activities** also weakened the machine. The classic machine provided highly valued social activities in the overcrowded, poverty-stricken tenement districts of the manufacturing city.

In the modern city, however, television, professional sports, and weekend family trips all superseded the political clubhouse picnics, dances, and sporting events of old. No block or precinct captain can hope to maintain a close personal relationship with local residents. Nowadays, a machine captain who tries to pay a family visit will be intruding on the family's television time or DVD viewing.

The rise of television has also led to a nation that is more media-oriented and independent. As a result, the patronage-based armies have been displaced by the modern mass-media campaign with its pollsters, computer experts, and direct-mail and advertising specialists. Even in Chicago, "the last bastion of party machine politics, the era of cash-based, candidate-centered electoral politics has arrived."[50]

AFRICAN AMERICANS AND THE POLITICAL MACHINE

Even where African-American voters were crucial to the machine's electoral success, black citizens seldom received a full and fair share of benefits in return for their support. In Chicago in the 1950s and 1960s, the local Democratic machine rolled up its largest margins of victory in the city's black wards. Richard J. Daley won the 1955 mayoral primary and emerged as the undisputed boss of Chicago only as a result of the backing he received from African-American voters and Congressman William Dawson, the head of the city's South Side "machine within a machine." In part, Dawson backed Daley to punish incumbent Mayor Martin Kennelly for having interfered with the "numbers" (or "policy") games from which Dawson profited. Blacks also rejected Kennelly for the attacks he made on Dawson in a blatantly racist effort to appeal to white voters.[51]

But how much did African Americans receive in return for their support? Not much beyond patronage appointments and limited welfare-style benefits.[52] Under Daley, the Chicago machine resisted demands for integrated schools and housing. Instead, the city built a "second ghetto" or "wall" of high-rise public housing apartment buildings, to keep the city's black population from spilling over into white ethnic neighborhoods.[53] The Dan Ryan Expressway "was shifted several blocks during the planning stage to make one of the ghetto walls."[54] In the wake of the 1966 summer riots, Daley spurned demands for workplace, housing, and school integration and instead responded by placing portable swimming pools in the troubled neighborhoods.[55] Portable swimming pools did not threaten the city's white neighborhoods.

Popular accounts have sometimes portrayed the urban political machine as a **rainbow coalition** that dispensed material benefits to a diverse coalition of racial and ethnic constituencies. But the machine was not always very responsive to the diversity of a city's ethnic groups, especially to African Americans. Instead of trying to appeal to all voters, machine leaders often sought to assemble a minimal winning coalition that would allow them to reserve benefits for members of their own core ethnic group.[56] In Chicago, "The Daley

Harold Washington's grassroots campaign for mayor, Chicago.

political machine functioned not as a ladder of political empowerment but as a lid blocking African-American political empowerment."[57]

By the 1980s, conditions were ripe for an African-American challenge to the "plantation politics" of the political machine. In 1983, Congressman Harold Washington, an African American, gained the Democratic nomination for mayor in a primary where competing factional leaders divided the white vote. Washington promised a fairer distribution of city services, new neighborhood programs, increased citizen participation, and a ban on municipal hiring and firing on political grounds. Washington sought more community-oriented industrial development policies to retain blue-collar jobs, which was a challenge to the development priorities of the machine and its downtown-oriented growth coalition.[58]

Harold Washington challenged the machine's mode of operations. Legendary ward committeeman Vito Marzullo and other white machine leaders did the unheard-of in Chicago: they abandoned the Democratic ticket, crossed party lines, and threw their support to Washington's little-known Republican opponent. Marzullo called Washington a "Buffalo Bill" and a "nitwit": "After he got the nomination, you'd think we elected Mussolini and Hitler put together. This man here he want to do away with the patronage office. Do away with the power of the ward committeeman. What is this?"[59]

Washington won a bitterly contested general election, gaining a narrow victory over a Republican opponent who had been considered a political nonentity—that is, until he unexpectedly became the only white electoral alternative to Washington. Washington's election revealed the three keys to the election of a black mayor in the city: The first was black unity and the **mobilization of black voters.** In just the five months between the gubernatorial election and the April 1983 mayoral election, over 92,000 new black voters registered to vote.[60] African Americans also turned out in record numbers: "No black ward turned out lower than 73 percent. Washington captured close to 97 percent of the black vote."[61] Second, Washington reached out and attracted over 50 percent of the Hispanic vote. Third, Washington also won the support of a narrow band of white liberals (in Chicago known as Lakefront liberals) whose votes, like those of Hispanics, made the difference in the election.

Harold Washington suffered a heart attack and died early in his second term in office. Since then, no black candidate in Chicago has been able to replicate Washington's difficult balancing act of mobilizing black voters while also winning support from the Hispanic community and Lakefront liberals. As a consequence, Richard M. Daley, the son of the legendary boss, emerged triumphant. (See "Chicago's New Daley: The Machine Adapts," below.)

CHICAGO'S NEW DALEY: THE MACHINE ADAPTS

Judicial rulings meant that Richard M. Daley could not rebuild the job patronage armies of his father, Mayor Richard J. Daley. Like his father, Richard M. Daley attempted to centralize power in city hall. But operating in a new age, Richard M. Daley could not rely on patronage alone. Instead, he produced a pliant city council by steering political donations to favored aldermanic candidates.

Richard M. Daley projected himself not simply as an old-style political boss but as a good-government reformer, a capable city executive who can effectively manage municipal government. In an effort to appeal to tax-conscious middle-class voters, Daley even privatized some municipal services for greater efficiency. Such privatization also afforded Daley new sources of "pin-stripe" or contract patronage; the mayor rewarded political supporters with no-bid consulting contracts, legal work, and various other city favors. He received millions of dollars in campaign donations from the financial services industry and local construction firms and labor unions.

Richard M. Daley also made substantial efforts to appeal to Chicago's black citizens. In his initial victorious mayoral campaign, Daley even made conspicuous stops in black neighborhoods where he had little hope of winning many votes. Such stops were essential as he sought to appeal to more moderate and liberal white voters who wanted to restore city unity. As mayor, Daley appointed a black woman, Avis LaVelle, as his first press secretary. He also appealed to the city's Hispanic community, winning the key endorsement of 26th Ward Alderman Luis Gutierrez, whom Daley would later endorse for Congress.

Daley's approach to governance proved popular and won him repeated reelection. Richard M. Daley's tenure in office represents no simple "restoration" of his father's political machine. Rather, Richard Daley's governing approach was "part machine/part reform;" it was "machine politics reform style."

Sources: Dick Simpson, *Rogues, Rebels, and Rubber Stamps: The Politics of the Chicago City Council from 1863 to the Present* (Boulder, CO: Westview Press, 2001), pp. 253–262, 269–272, 278–281, and 287–290; Melvin G. Holli, "The Daley Era: Richard J. to Richard M.," in *The Mayors: The Chicago Political Tradition*, rev. ed., eds. Paul M. Green and Melvin G. Holli (Carbondale and Edwardsville: Southern Illinois University Press, 1995), pp. 227–229; William J. Grimshaw, *Bitter Fruit: Black Politics and the Chicago Machine* (Chicago: University of Chicago Press, 1992) pp. 206–224. The quotations in the last paragraph are from Grimshaw, p. 206.

Critics attacked black mayors such as Chicago's Harold Washington and Detroit's Coleman Young for resorting to patronage and other machine-style practices that they had publicly scorned. But these black mayors saw themselves as reformers carrying the fight against established political machines that were "nefarious to black interests."[62] Black mayors such as Harold Washington and Philadelphia's Wilson Goode ran as reformers who appealed to white liberals.

Yet Newark and Philadelphia have in more recent years seen the election of black mayors who cannot be characterized as reformers. Newark's Sharpe James has manipulated machine-style rewards and sanctions. Philadelphia's John Street used pinstripe patronage (the award of important contracts and jobs to his political allies) to win the backing of the remnants of his city's regular Democratic organization. While Street, in his initial election, won the endorsement of the city's major newspapers and of outgoing Mayor Ed Rendell, he did not appeal to the voices of reform. Even "good-government African Americans opposed the machine politics, honest-graft style of John Street."[63] Whereas Chicago under Harold Washington represents a reform-oriented approach to black empowerment, Philadelphia under John Street provides a counterexample, a machine-politics model for the distribution of benefits to the city's black community.[64]

WOMEN, THE MACHINE, AND REFORM

Historically, the fight for women's rights has clearly been associated with political reform, not with machine politics. The political machine had a constricted view of participation and public policy. In old San Francisco, women gained patronage jobs as teachers in the public school system, but their jobs were dependent on the fate of male officeholders. Lacking merit protection, the teachers could be ousted with a change of administrations.[65]

With its emphases on hierarchy, unquestioned obedience, and loyalty, the machine resembled a patriarchal organization. The political machine also operated at a time when public life was seen as clearly distinct from home life. Women were part of the home sector, not the public sector; their concerns were politically invisible. Even when women entered the workplace, the machine, with its ties to local businesses and "sweatshops," did not fight to protect their rights, a fact that was tragically revealed in New York in the Triangle Shirtwaist factory fire of 1911; 146 people, mainly teenage immigrant girls, died when the factory's flammable materials caught fire and the exit door was locked.

At the turn of the twentieth century, machine leaders resisted the idea of giving women the vote for fear that women would challenge the corruption of party bosses and their ties to saloonkeepers and brewery and liquor interests.[66] The saloon was an important institution in ethnic neighborhoods that reflected European cultural norms and offered men an opportunity to drink together. Opening a saloon also represented a rare business opportunity for cash-starved immigrants. Saloonkeepers contributed to the political machine as they needed the machine's political protection against the threat of restricted hours and Sunday closing laws posed by puritanical reformers. As women and children were often the victims of alcohol-related violence, women occupied prominent leadership roles in the temperance movement.

Reformers attacked the political machine for protecting prostitution and "white slavery" rings in return for bribes and payoffs.[67] Women fought the machine on questions of temperance and women's suffrage.

Women were also prominent figures in the social reform movement, which sought to combat the disgraceful conditions of the tenement house slum districts that the political machine and its allies chose to ignore. In Chicago, Jane Addams set up **Hull House,** a settlement house designed as a woman's place, both to care for the poor and to instill immigrant women with middle-class values. In the 1890s, Addams organized two unsuccessful campaigns to oust the local boss, councilman Johnny Powers.[68]

As we shall see in the next chapter, social reform was only one branch of the larger reform movement. Women tended to occupy prominent positions in some social reform organizations. But in other reform organizations, especially those devoted to changing the rules and operation of city politics, traditional business interests and social elites dominated, and women were not key players.

CONCLUSIONS: MACHINE POLITICS EVALUATED

The urban political machines lasted as long as they did because they served important functions. The political machine offered social-welfare and job benefits to those in need, especially to immigrants who were not welcomed by more well-established Americans. The machine assured cooperative businesses that their important requests would receive expeditious city approval. The machine centralized power and helped abet city growth during a period of rapid industrialization and urbanization.

Yet there is danger of overglorifying the machine. In reviewing the literature on machine politics, Clarence Stone has concluded, "Today nostalgia is no longer in fashion . . . Present-day scholars question the 'good old days' scenario, showing that it is highly incomplete at best . . . Thus to view the old urban machine as vehicles for inclusion and massive upward mobility is a romantic misreading of the past."[69] Machine leaders sought to conserve limited rewards rather than freely dispense benefits to every new urban claimant. The machine also enjoyed a mutually profitable working relationship with tenement house and factory owners and with other important elements in a city's business community, a relationship it could ill afford to jeopardize.

Machine politicians were primarily concerned with their own power, not with aiding new immigrants or the urban poor. Many machine politicians were also grafters interested in payoffs and their own self-enrichment. The machine bought votes, punished its enemies, and otherwise manipulated and corrupted the electoral process. Machine practices were antithetical to democracy. Boss Richard Croker began his political career as a Tammany "strong arm" who led groups of "repeaters" to vote in one polling place after another. In 1874, in a fight on election day, he shot a member of a rival gang. His trial resulted in a hung jury, a jury that was likely influenced by bribery.

New York's Tweed Ring did spend some money in ways that helped the poor. Yet the Ring enriched its own members while draining the municipal coffers, leading the city to virtual bankruptcy. It would be facile "to praise the Tweed machine as a kind of rough-and-ready populist operation."[70]

Yet it is also undeniable that immigrants looked favorably on the machine. In Boston, James Michael Curley, who held public office throughout much of the first half of the twentieth century, was a populist hero, at least among Irish voters. Despite his obvious graft and corruption, he was beloved by the Irish for the hospitals and schools he built and for the favors he dispensed. In 1946, Boston voters reelected Curley as mayor even while he was serving time in jail. Thousands lined up at his coffin to mourn his death.[71]

The relationship between the political machine and a city's racial minority communities is particularly troublesome. In Memphis, Tampa, Chicago, and other cites, the regular party organization provided African Americans with important, but quite limited, favors. In return, the machine expected blacks to show fealty and accept subordinate status. The Chicago Democratic organization was typical of the white ethnic political organizations that retarded racial integration. The political machine was no fair broker of minority demands.

When viewed through a **class-based or Marxist perspective,** even the machine's distribution of patronage jobs and welfare-style benefits merits only limited praise. The urban machines acted as a conservatizing force that retarded the full political incorporation of immigrants and racial minorities. The ward politicians taught the immigrants how to play politics American-style; European-style class solidarity was lost in the process. By dispensing emergency relief, the machine bought off the anger that might have produced a demand for class-based policies and economic redistribution. By distributing its rewards through a specific exchange process, the machine individualized politics, undermining any sense of class identity and the prospects for collective action. By distributing its benefits, the political machine averted mass disorder, maintained social control, and diminished the demand for more extensive redistributional policies.

Yet this critique of machine politics is just as overstated as the view that exaggerates the machine's populist, public-serving attributes. The critique that the political machine killed a class-based social movement is valid only to the extent that socialist politics ever had any real chance of taking root in the United States. But the enactment of socialism never had that much prospect in the United States. Workers—especially skilled workers—sought advancement through job unionism, not through more radical political movements demanding "socialists' utopian fantasies."[72] Also, as American labor leader Samuel Gompers observed, those in power were not hesitant to use violence to suppress radical challenges to the existing order.[73]

In American cities, the election of socialist officials was a rare event. In Chicago, the German-dominated Socialist Labor Party reached the peak of its power in the 1870s, electing five aldermen, three state assemblymen, and a state senator.[74] Socialists also won office in Milwaukee. But there was no class unity among workers severely divided by ethnic antagonisms. Some German immigrants and Jewish intellectuals embraced socialism, but the ideology never found great support among other ethnic groups. Left-wing critics blame machine politicians for exacerbating ethnic antagonisms that undermined the unity of the working class. Yet ethnic antagonisms existed in cities that lacked strong political machines.

The political machine cannot be blamed for the failure of socialism to take root in the United States. The promise of socialism did not offer the urban poor realistic and immediate benefits. By comparison, the political machine *did* provide real and important benefits to people in need of jobs and emergency relief.

As Amy Bridges documents, the urban poor fared better in the political-machine cities in the Northeast than they did in the partyless cities of the Sunbelt. The party organizations helped direct benefits to the urban poor. Party workers contacted voters, worked the neighborhoods, and turned out the vote: "Machine politics must be judged a veritable school of politics for working-class and minority voters, compared to big-city reform."[75]

Machine politicians too often ran the city on the basis of votes and favoritism, not on technical expertise and fairness. As cities grew, municipal government would require the skills of professionally trained managers. The reform movement gave a new prominence to management, reducing the importance of party organizations. The reformers also sought to restructure the rules of municipal government in order to change just whose views were represented in city hall. This is the story of our next chapter.

NOTES

1. For a good description of machine politics in one southern city, see James Duane Bolin, *Bossism and Reform in a Southern City: Lexington, Kentucky, 1880–1940* (Lexington: University Press of Kentucky, 2000).
2. Clarence N. Stone, "Power and Governance in American Cities," in *Cities, Politics, and Policy: A Comparative Analysis*, ed. John P. Pelissero (Washington, DC: CQ Press, 2003), p. 136.
3. Timothy B. Krebs, "Fund-Raising Coalitions in Mayoral Campaigns," *Urban Affairs Review* 37 (September 2001): 67–84.
4. James Dao, "Philadelphia Trial's Focus Is 'Pay to Play' Corruption," *The New York Times*, February 23, 2005; Andrew Jacobs, "Newark Relives Day of Machine in Mayor's Race," *The New York Times*, April 9, 2002; Andrew Jacobs, "After Loss in Newark, Opponents Sense Sharpe James' Wrath," *The New York Times*, November 29, 2002.
5. Lincoln Mitchell, "What Makes Reform So Difficult: The Case of America's Cities and the Problems of Elites," in *Democracy's Moment: Reforming the American Political System for the 21st Century* (Lanham, MD: Rowman and Littlefield, 2002), pp. 199–211.
6. Alan Feuer, "2 Brooklyn Lawyers, Ex-Insiders, Outline a Court Patronage System," *The New York Times*, January 5, 2000; Leslie Eaton, "Behind a Troubled

Bench, an Arcane Way of Picking Judges," *The New York Times,* June 30, 2003; Clifford J. Levy, "Where Parties Select Judges, Donor List Is a Court Roll Call," *The New York Times,* August 18, 2003.

7. Edward C. Banfield, *Political Influence* (New York: Free Press, 1961).

8. Steven P. Erie, *Rainbow's End: Irish Americans and the Dilemmas of Urban Machine Politics,* 1840–1985 (Berkley: University of California Press, 1988).

9. Richard A. Keiser, *Subordination or Empowerment? African-American Leadership and the Struggle for Urban Political Power* (New York: Oxford University Press, 1997), pp. 34–35.

10. Adam Cohen and Elizabeth Taylor, *American Pharaoh: Mayor Richard J. Daley, His Battle for Chicago and the Nation* (Boston: Little, Brown, 2000), pp. 28, 42.

11. William L. Riordan, *Plunkitt of Tammany Hall,* edited by Terrence J. McDonald (Boston: Bedford Books of St. Martin's Press, 1994), p. 62.

12. Ibid.

13. Donald L. Miller, *City of the Century: The Epic of Chicago and the Making of America* (New York: Touchstone, 1996), p. 454.

14. Alan Ehrenhalt, *The Lost City: The Forgotten Virtues of Community in America* (New York: Basic Books, 1995), pp. 162–163.

15. Dayton David McKean, *The Boss: The Hague Machine in Action* (Boston: Houghton Mifflin, 1940), p. 271.

16. Dick Simpson, *Rogues, Rebels, and Rubber Stamps: The Politics of the Chicago City Council from 1863 to the Present* (Boulder, CO: Westview Press, 2001).

17. Martin Shefter, "The Emergence of the Political Machine: An Alternative View," in *Theoretical Perspectives on Urban Politics,* eds. Willis D. Hawley and Michael Lipsky (Englewood Cliffs, NJ: Prentice-Hall, 1976), chap. 2.

18. Robert K. Merton, "The Latent Functions of the Machine: A Sociologist's View," pp. 71–82 of his book *Social Theory and Social Structure* (New York: Free Press, 1957), reprinted in *The City Boss in America,* ed. Alexander B. Callow, Jr. (New York: Oxford University Press, 1976), pp. 23–33. The quotation appears on p. 26.

19. Shefter, "The Emergence of the Political Machine: An Alternative View," p. 22.

20. John M. Allswang, *Bosses, Machines, and Urban Voters* (Port Washington, NY: Kennikat Press, 1977), p. 52.

21. Tomasz Inglot and John P. Pelissero, "Ethnic Political Power in a Machine City: Chicago's Poles at Rainbow's End," *Urban Affairs Quarterly* 28, 4 (June 1993): 526–543. The contemporary Chicago machine may also fail in the dispensation of benefits to the city's numerous Asian groups, which may explain depressed voter participation in those wards where old-style machine organizations still prevail. See John P. Pelissero, Timothy B. Krebs, and Shannon Jenkins, "Asian-Americans, Political Organizations, and Participation in Chicago Electoral Precincts," *Urban Affairs Review* 35 (July 2000): 750–769.

22. Erie, *Rainbow's End.*

23. Paul Kantor, *The Dependent City Revisited* (Boulder, CO: Westview Press, 1995), pp. 59–60.

24. Shefter, "The Emergence of the Political Machine: An Alternative View," pp. 27–30.

25. Keiser, *Subordination or Empowerment?* pp. 35–38.

26. Martin Shefter, *Political Crisis/Fiscal Crisis: The Collapse and Revival of New York City* (New York: Basic Books, 1985), p. 17.

27. Edwin G. Burrows and Mike Wallace, *Gotham: A History of New York City to 1898* (New York: Oxford University Press, 1999), p. 935.

28. Merton, "The Latent Functions of the Machine," p. 27.

29. William J. Grimshaw, *Bitter Fruit: Black Politics and the Chicago Machine, 1931–91* (Chicago: University of Chicago Press, 1992), pp. 59 and 82–84.

30. Ira Katznelson, "The Crisis of the Capitalist City: Urban Politics and Social Control," pp. 214–229, in *Theoretical Perspectives on Urban Politics*, eds. Willis D. Hawley and Michael Lipsky (Englewood Cliffs, NJ: Prentice-Hall, 1976); and Kantor, *The Dependent City Revisited*, pp. 59–60 and 68–71.

31. Erie, *Rainbow's End*, p. 8.

32. Amy Bridges, *A City in the Republic* (Ithaca, NY: Cornell University Press, 1987), chap. 1.

33. Alan DiGaetano, "The Rise and Development of Urban Political Machines: An Alternative to Merton's Functional Analysis," *Urban Affairs Quarterly* 24 (December 1988): 250.

34. Elmer E. Cornwell, Jr., "Bosses, Machines and Ethnic Groups," *Annals* 353 (May 1964): 27–39.

35. Simpson, *Rogues, Rebels, and Rubber Stamps*, p. 90.

36. New York's Tammany Hall was initially hostile to the attempts by labor unions to organize the young women who worked in the cramped, unsanitary, and danger-ous sweatshops of the city's garment industry. Tammany's position changed markedly after 146 persons, predominantly young women, died in the Triangle Shirtwaist factory fire of 1911. The factory's exit doors were locked shut, and many of the teenage girls who worked in the factory jumped to their deaths. Only then did Tammany, under Boss Charles Murphy and his protégés Robert F. Wagner and Alfred E. Smith, begin to see the necessity and the political advantage of pushing workplace safety, health, and housing reforms. See Ric Burns and James Sanders, with Lisa Ades, *New York: An Illustrated History* (New York: Alfred Knopf, 1999), pp. 276–293.

37. V. O. Key, Jr., *Southern Politics* (New York: Alfred A. Knopf, 1949), p. 274; Robert A. Caro, *Means of Ascent: The Years of Lyndon Johnson* (New York: Knopf, 1990).

38. Robert A. Caro, *The Path to Power: The Years of Lyndon Johnson* (New York: Vintage, 1982), p. 721.

39. Key, *Southern Politics*, pp. 397–398.

40. Ibid., pp. 63–64.

41. Kenneth D. Wald, "The Electoral Base of Political Machines: A Deviant Case Analysis," *Urban Affairs Quarterly* 16 (September 1980): 19.

42. The Crump machine's relationship with the black community in Memphis is described by Marcus D. Pohlmann and Michael P. Kirby, *Racial Politics at the Crossroads: Memphis Elects Dr. W. W. Herenton* (Knoxville: University of Tennessee Press, 1996), pp. 62–63, and 100–104.

43. Gary R. Mormino, "Tampa: From Hell Hole to the Good Life," in *Sunbelt Cities*, pp. 144–145.

44. The quotations are from Riordan, *Plunkitt of Tammany Hall*, pp. 54 and 56–57.

45. Mike Royko, *Boss: Richard J. Daley of Chicago* (New York: Signet, 1977), p. 69. Also see Milton Rakove, *Don't Make No Waves. . . . Don't Back No Losers: An Insiders Analysis of the Daley Machine* (Bloomington: Indiana University Press, 1975), p. 112; Anne Freedman, *Patronage: An American Tradition* (Chicago: Nelson-Hall Publishers, 1994), pp. 39–45.

46. Freedman, *Patronage: An American Tradition*, p. 6. See pp. 1–8 and 109–111 for a review of the *Rutan* decision and of Justice Antonin Scalia's dissent defending patronage as an American political tradition.

47. Freedman, *Patronage: An American Tradition*, pp. 227–267; Michael Cooper, "As Gulotta Exits, Nassau Republicans Try to Retool Their Broken Machine," *The New York Times*, March 15, 2001; Bruce Lambert, "Party Machine A Ballot Issue for the G.O.P. in Nassau," *The New York Times*, November 3, 2001.

48. Michael Lewis, "No Relief From Politics: Machine Bosses and Civil Works, *Urban Affairs Quarterly* 30, 2 (December 1994): 212–223, 222–223; Erie, *Rainbow's End*, pp. 201–208, and 224.

49. Alan DiGaetano, "Machine Politics in the Post-Industrial Era" (paper presented at the annual meeting of the Urban Affairs Association, St. Louis, March 10–13, 1988); Wilbur C. Rich, *Black Mayors and School Politics: The Failure of Reform in Detroit, Gary, and Newark* (New York: Garland, 1996), p. 145.

50. Anthony Gierzynski, Paul Kleppner, and James Lewis, "Money or the Machine? Money and Votes in Chicago Aldermanic Elections," *American Politics Quarterly* 26, 2 (April 1998): 171.

51. Grimshaw, *Bitter Fruit*, pp. 42–44 and Chapters 5 and 6.

52. Keiser, *Subordination or Empowerment?*, p. 35. Also see p. 38.

53. The complicity of the Chicago machine in public housing segregation is described by Hirsch, *Making the Second Ghetto*, pp. 212–275.

54. Royko, *Boss: Richard J. Daley of Chicago*, p. 137.

55. Ibid., pp. 154–155. In 1968, Daley took an even more aggressive approach to the civil disorders that occurred in the wake of Martin Luther King's assassination. Daley asked President Lyndon Johnson to send federal troops to help patrol the streets. As the gunfire, burning, and looting continued, Daley also ordered the city police to "shoot to kill" arsonists and to "maim" looters. See Roger Biles, *Richard J. Daley: Politics, Race, and the Governing of Chicago* (DeKalb: Northern Illinois University Press, 1995), pp. 144–147.

56. Erie, *Rainbow's End*, pp. 9–10.

57. Richard A. Keiser, "Explaining African-American Political Empowerment: Windy City Politics from 1900 to 1983," *Urban Affairs Quarterly* 29 (September 1993): 112.

58. Pierre Clavel and Wim Wiewel, eds., *Harold Washington and the Neighborhoods* (New Brunswick, NJ: Rutgers University Press, 1991); Joel Rast, *Remaking Chicago: The Political Origins of Urban Industrial Change* (DeKalb, IL: Northern Illinois University Press, 1999), especially pp. 103–104.

59. "This Daley Ward Boss Won't Back a 'Nitwit,'" *Washington Post*, April 10, 1983.

60. Michael B. Preston, "The Resurgence of Black Voting in Chicago: 1955–83," in *The Making of the Mayor: Chicago* 1983, eds. Melvin G. Holli and Paul M. Green (Grand Rapids, MI: Wm. B. Eerdmans Publishing, 1984), p. 48.

61. Ibid., p. 49.

62. Rich, *Black Mayors and School Politics*, p. 145.

63. Richard A. Keiser, "Philadelphia's Evolving Biracial Coalition," in *Racial Politics in American Cities*, 3rd ed., eds. Rufus P. Browning, Dale Rogers Marshall, David H. Tabb (New York: Longman, 2003), p. 104. See Keiser, pp. 87–110, for a description of Philadelphia politics under mayors Wilson Goode and John Street.

64. Rufus P. Browning, Dale Rogers Marshall, and David H. Tabb, "Has Political Incorporation been Achieved? Is It Enough?" in *Racial Politics in American Cities*, eds. Browning, Marshall, and Tabb, pp. 362–363; Keiser, Philadelphia's Evolving Biracial Coalition," pp. 108–110.

65. Philip J. Ethington, *The Public City: The Political Construction of Urban Life in San Francisco, 1850–1900* (Berkeley, CA: University of California Press, 2001), pp. 332–335.

66. M. Margaret Conway, Gertrude A. Steurnagel, and David W. Ahern, *Women and Political Participation* (Washington, DC: CQ Press, 1997), p. 12; Miller, *City of the Century,* pp. 446–449, describes the relationship between saloonkeepers and the Chicago political machine.

67. Janet Staiger, *Bad Women* (Minneapolis: University of Minnesota Press, 1995), pp. 110–111.

68. Miller, *City of the Century,* pp. 452–455 and 464–465, describes the development of Hull House and the relationship between Jane Addams and Chicago alderman Johnny Powers. For a more complete description of Addams' philosophy, see Jean Bethke Elshtain, ed., *Jane Addams Reader* (New York: Basic Books, 2001), especially Addams' essays "Why the Ward Boss Rules" and "If Men Were Seeking the Franchise."

69. Clarence N. Stone, "Urban Political Machines: Taking Stock," *PS: Political Science and Politics* 29 (September 1996): 446–450.

70. The quotations are from Adam Gopnik, "The Man Who Invented Santa Claus: Thomas Nast's Eye for Who's Been Naughty and Who's Been Nice," *The New Yorker,* December 15, 1997: p. 94.

71. Jack Beatty, *The Rascal King: The Life and Times of James Michael Curley, 1874–1958* (Cambridge, MA: Da Capo Press, 2000). For a breezy television documentary that gives a balanced overview of Curley's actions, see *Scandalous Mayor* from PBS' *The American Experience* series.

72. Burrows and Wallace, *Gotham,* p. 1090.

73. Ibid., pp. 1089–1090.

74. Miller, *City of the Century,* p. 467. See pp. 468–482 for a description of how city elites used the Haymarket riot to discredit both anarchism and Chicago's growing labor radicalism of the late 1880s.

75. Amy Bridges, *Morning Glories: Municipal Reform in the Southwest* (Princeton, NJ: Princeton University Press, 1997), p. 216. Also see pp. 159–170.

REFORM POLITICS

The political reformers sought to rid the cities of partisanship, favoritism, and corruption. They wanted cities that would be well run and professionally managed. In undercutting the power of the old party machines, the reformers gave new decision-making power to municipal experts. In doing so, the reformers created entrenched bureaucracies that

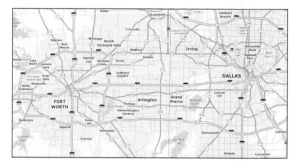

were not always very responsive to citizen concerns.

In this chapter, we look at the origins of the reform movement, the specific reforms that were enacted, how the reforms improved municipal operations, and the continuing impact that "reform" has had on the distribution of power in the modern city.

THE PRINCIPLES OF REFORM

Reform groups believed that government should pursue the "public interest," not parochial interests. In the eyes of the reformers, the machine's "ward heelers" (its local committeemen) pandered to the interests of narrow-based, geographical constituencies; the machine did not pursue the interest of the city as a whole. The reformers wanted government that would respect the values of economy and efficiency. "Good government" required that elected officials show great deference to the administrative decisions made by qualified technicians and professional managers.

The reformers believed that local government dealt with technical matters that could be placed in the hands of well-trained experts recruited on the basis of merit. Political parties were irrelevant to the running of local government. In the eyes of the reformers, there was no Democratic or Republican way to pave streets or pick up the garbage. Instead, the modern city was a large enterprise that needed to be run "like a business." Popularly elected mayors and their patronage appointees lacked the necessary accounting, planning, budgeting, personnel, and civil engineering skills to run a city efficiently.

The National Municipal League, founded in 1894, served as the intellectual center of the reform movement. Over the years, the League promoted a Model City Charter that emphasized such reform staples as the manager-council form of government, nonpartisan elections, and the short ballot.

The National Municipal League proved successful in gaining adoption of its suggested reforms in smaller and middle-sized cities. Larger cities adopted numerous reformed institutions but never accepted the League's total program. The populations of larger cities were just too heterogeneous for governing arrangements that assumed a common citywide interest.

THE CLASS AND RACIAL BIAS OF REFORM

The reformers saw themselves as principled and above politics. Yet, this view was more than just a bit self-serving. Their view of the public interest was, of course, colored by their class background, position, and self-interest.

A good deal of hard evidence points to a strong class bias of the reform movement. Historian Samuel Hays found that the reform movement was dominated by upper-class professionals and the owners and managers of large businesses, people who sought to redesign city government in order to minimize the impact of lower- and middle-class voters. The reformers "wished not simply to replace bad men with good; they proposed to change the occupational and class origins of decision makers."[1] In the Sunbelt, business-led reform coalitions acted to restrict the provision of services to African-American, Hispanic, and working-class communities.[2]

But the reform movement was actually more diverse than Hays' description admits. As the history of the reform movement in Cleveland demonstrates, there are two distinct branches of reform: one that is conservative and pro-business, and another that is progressive, even radical, in its pursuit of social justice. Progressive reformer Tom L. Johnson, elected mayor in 1901, sought to raise taxes and regulate private industries in order to provide better benefits for the working class. He fought to preserve the three-cent fare of the private streetcar company, he established a municipal light plant to lower utility fees, and he municipalized garbage collection and street cleaning. Johnson's progressive version of reform appealed more to immigrant and working-class voters than to the native-stock and upper-class groups usually associated with reform.[3]

Johnson, a self-made millionaire, "was considered a traitor to his class." Upper-class groups in Cleveland proposed a set of reforms—nonpartisan elections, at-large elections, and the introduction of the council-manager form of government—in "an effort to disenfranchise foreign-born votes, especially Roman Catholics." As Todd Swanstrom continues, "the radical roots of reform" in Cleveland "were killed off, leaving a spineless plant clinging congenially to big business." Reform in the post-Johnson era "was overwhelmingly financed and staffed by the business elite."[4]

Melvin G. Holli differentiates *social reform* from *structural reform*.[5] **Social reformers** such as Cleveland's Tom Johnson and Detroit Mayor Hazen S. Pingree (1890–97) placed their faith in the people and sought to reduce utility rates, extend government-provided relief and public services, and increase the tax bill borne by business to pay for city services.

In contrast, **structural reformers** sought to restructure municipal government so that cities would be run by educated, upper-class citizens and technical experts. Structural reformers sought business-like efficiency, not the provision of new services to working-class neighborhoods and the poor.

The structural reformers largely succeeded in their goal of insulating a city from the policy demands of lower-class citizens. One classic study of 200 cities found that reformed cities tend to spend less and tax less than did unreformed cities.[6] Yet other studies question the degree to which reformed institutions discriminate against lower-class citizens. One study, for instance, found that the impact of nonpartisan and at-large election systems on the policy views of council members "appears to be quite small."[7]

Yet the choice of voting rules—unreformed or reformed—can have a great impact on representation. In 1977, San Francisco's switch from at-large to district voting led to the election of the first black woman and the first avowedly gay supervisor, Harvey Milk. Milk, who had lost an earlier bid under the at-large system, gained his seat by mobilizing the gay population of San Francisco's Castro district.

In the greater Miami area, too, a change in voting rules produced a dramatic change in local representation. For many years, Metropolitan Miami-Dade County (popularly referred to as "Metro") was governed in accordance with reform principles. With a council-manager form of government and nonpartisan, at-large elections, Metro sought to reflect the county-wide interest and insulate decision makers from local political pressures: "Metro's structure dissuades candidates from running as strong advocates of minority political interests."[8]

CORBIS

Harvey Milk outside his camera store in the Castro district of San Francisco, 1977. The city's switch to district elections helped Milk to become the first avowedly gay member of the San Francisco Board of Supervisors, representing the Castro. A year after his election, both Milk and Mayor George Moscone were assassinated by a disgruntled former city supervisor who had recently resigned his office.

Advocates of increased minority representation brought judicial action that led Metro to institute a new system of district elections. The results were dramatic. Under the old at-large voting rules, the Metro Commission never had more than one black and one Hispanic among its nine members. The 1993 elections, the first conducted under the new district representational system, produced a sea change, resulting in the election of six Hispanics and four blacks to Metro's new 13-member body. The change in election rules clearly changed who exercised power in metropolitan Miami.[9]

Reformed urban institutions have also affected the prospects for Hispanic power in U.S. cities. Hispanics gained greater political incorporation and responsiveness in Denver, with its unreformed institutions, than in reformed Pueblo (Colorado) and reformed cities in northern California. In Denver's unreformed system, elected officials—a strong mayor and 11 of 13 council members elected by district—have the motivation to act in the interests of the city's growing African-American and Hispanic districts. In 1983, Federico Pena was the city's first Latino to be elected mayor. He was succeeded in office by Wellington Webb, the first African American to be elected mayor of Denver.[10]

WOMEN AND REFORM

Women's groups were actively involved in social reform. In the early American city, they served as "foot soldiers" in moral reform societies, fighting prostitution and providing assistance to exploited women.[11] During the industrial era, women's groups were involved in the work of settlement houses, charitable societies, education institutions, and other religious and social reform associations. These associations "provided women with acceptable vehicles for activity in the public sphere" at a time when women were denied the right to vote.[12]

In Chicago, the wives of prominent businessmen became social activists and real figures of importance. The Woman's Club in the late 1800s provided protective services to women and children, especially to those working in poorhouses or residing in asylums. The Woman's Club also provided legal advice to women in danger of losing their children, to battered women, and to shop girls and maids fighting to regain lost wages.[13]

The social reform activity of women's groups was often shaped by the moralism, piety, and sometimes even the nativism of women who, reflecting their more privileged backgrounds, were an "earnest, public-spirited class."[14] Jane Addams and others active in Chicago's Hull House admirably provided much-needed assistance to the poor. But their work was also shaped "by their own restricted social vision."[15] Hull House professed to respect the immigrant traditions of the women they served; yet the settlement house pursued the "moral uplift" of the immigrant,[16] seeking to Americanize the immigrant women, break down ethnic roots, and hasten assimilation. The women who worked in the settlement houses sought to teach young Italian and Greek working-class wives upper-class manners and the values of the idealized middle-class home.[17]

In San Francisco, women reformers fought for the nonpartisan administration of the public schools. An end to the political-party control of schools would allow teachers, who were predominantly women, the freedom to teach without having to devote time to party politics in order to protect their patronage-awarded jobs.[18]

While some reform leaders welcomed women's activism, others were just as patriarchal in their view of women's role in society as were the leaders of the urban political machines. San Francisco reform leader James Phelan, elected mayor in 1896, resisted the entrance of women into politics. He complained of women holding jobs outside the home. Phelan's vision of reform did not embrace giving women the right to vote. Women who wished "to right fancied wrongs," he argued, could simply "appeal to men for even greater consideration."[19]

THE REFORMS

In Chapter 5 we reviewed two important reform structures: the council-manager and commission systems of government. In this chapter we shall identify and evaluate the remaining reform innovations that have had a lasting influence on local politics and administration.

AT-LARGE ELECTIONS, DISTRICT ELECTIONS, AND THE QUESTION OF MINORITY REPRESENTATION

One of the most popular reforms is **at-large elections,** in which voters elect council members citywide instead of on a district basis. Approximately 60 percent of local governments use at-large voting systems; another 30 percent rely on a mixed or combination plan under which some council members are elected at-large while others are chosen by district. Only 10 or so percent of all local governments elect council members solely from districts or wards.[20]

The reformers argued that council members elected at-large would give greater attention to citywide policy concerns, not to the parochial demands of a district voting base. The reformers also believed that a greater number of high-quality candidates would be able to run for a city council elected at-large as the best qualified public servants were not scattered, one per district, throughout the city.

In more recent years, cities have begun to abandon pure at-large voting systems, which are charged with discriminating against a geographically concentrated or ghettoized ethnic or minority voting group. Under district elections, a ward or district dominated by African-American, Hispanic, Polish, or even gay and lesbian voters can elect "one of their own" to the city council. When council elections are conducted at-large, a minority group may be easily outvoted by the city's majority population. For decades, Boston had no African-American member on its school board, due in part to its at-large voting rules for school elections. Numerous studies demonstrate that at-large elections tend to dilute black voting strength.[21]

THE SOUTH: AT-LARGE ELECTIONS AND CIVIL RIGHTS. In the South, cities adopted at-large voting rules in an effort to assure the existence of white-dominated electoral constituencies, blocking the election of blacks to local office. Immediately following the Civil War, Mobile, Atlanta, Memphis, Chattanooga, and Nashville all switched to at-large elections in an attempt to keep newly enfranchised blacks from winning office.[22] Nearly a century later, during the Civil Rights era, another wave of southern cities enacted numerous measures, including a switch to at-large elections, in an effort to diminish the power of black voters. In Georgia, twenty county governments and boards of education switched from district to at-large elections. The State of Mississippi enacted a law requiring that all county boards of supervisors and county school boards be elected at-large.[23]

The federal **Voting Rights Act (VRA) of 1965** was enacted to protect blacks and other minorities against efforts to diminish their ballots. Section 5 of the Act required federal approval or "pre-clearance" before a city with a past history of discrimination can switch to at-large voting rules, given the potential that at-large rules have to dilute the power of minority voters.

In Mobile, Alabama, African Americans, who constituted 35 percent of the population, had no representation on the city council elected at-large. A federal judge ordered the city to institute a system of ward-based elections in order to more fairly represent the city's black minority, an order that was appealed to the U.S. Supreme Court.[24] Dallas and Montgomery (Alabama) both witnessed the election of black city councilors immediately upon their switch from district to at-large elections.

Proposals for annexation, where a city absorbs a neighboring area into its borders, have been used in conjunction with at-large elections in an attempt to minimize the prospects of minority electoral power. When elections are conducted at-large, annexation may enable a city's white population, swollen by the addition of former suburban voters, to outvote a city's growing black or Hispanic population. African-American leaders, in particular, view annexations accompanied by at-large voting rules as a continuing threat to black political power.

AT-LARGE ELECTIONS AND HISPANIC REPRESENTATION. Are at-large elections as biased against Hispanics as they are against African Americans? In the Southwest, at-large elections coupled with annexations have acted to dilute Latino voting power. In San Antonio, the city's business booster coalition pushed an aggressive program of annexation. The U.S. Department of Justice charged that 13 of the 23 annexations completed by the city during 1972–74 served to diminish the voting power of the city's Mexican-American community. Views as to the importance of district elections were clearly polarized. In San Antonio in 1977, over 80 percent of the vote in the city's Mexican-American areas approved of a plan to establish 10 voting districts; in contrast, over 70 percent of the vote in Anglo areas of the city opposed the move, preferring the city's at-large system of elections.[25]

Latinos generally fare better under district elections.[26] District elections have aided the election of Latinos to school boards.[27] Denver moved from an all at-large to a district-based system of school elections some twenty years after it had made the switch for city council elections. At the time of the change, Denver's school board did not have a single Hispanic member, despite the fact that 40 percent of the city's population was Hispanic.[28]

While Hispanics are clearly underrepresented on city councils relative to their population, the evidence is unclear as to what extent the process of at-large elections exacerbates this problem.[29] Latinos are not as segregated or ghettoized residentially as are blacks. As a consequence, a switch to district elections may not produce the same political gains for Latinos as for African Americans.

For a long period of time, Los Angeles County had districts that were so large that they had the same discriminatory effects as did at-large elections. In 1991, Gloria Molina became the first Hispanic in 115 years to be elected to the county's powerful five-member Board of Supervisors. This occurred only after a federal judge found that the existing five-member board system—which produced five white supervisors—enabled whites in each district to outvote the county's three million Hispanic residents. A court-ordered remap created a Hispanic-dominated district.

Because of the relative geographical dispersion of Hispanics, it is also generally more difficult to create politically safe Hispanic districts than to create African-American districts. In Dallas, Latinos objected to council redistricting plans that were not able to tie together sufficient concentrations of Latino population to create districts would assure the election of Latino council members. In Chicago in the 1990s, the city's first Hispanic congressional district was formed by creating it in the shape of a "C." Two separate areas of Hispanic concentration were joined together by having a narrow strip of the district line run along an interstate highway (see Figure 7-1).

A system of district elections may help to increase minority representation on a city council; but by itself, it does not guarantee the substantial redistribution of benefits in favor of a city's minority community. In San Antonio, Mexican Americans gained a council majority as a result of the switch to district elections, but the result was more an "illusion of inclusion." Residents of the wealthier, Anglo areas of the city still reported receiving better levels of service provision than did the residents of Latino and African-American neighborhoods.[30]

DO AT-LARGE ELECTIONS DISCRIMINATE AGAINST WOMEN, GAYS, AND LESBIANS? A system of at-large elections does not pose the same barrier to the election of women as it does to blacks or even Hispanics.[31] The reason for the difference is simple: At-large ballot rules diminish the voting clout of a geographically concentrated minority. Women are neither a minority, nor are they a spatially segregated population. In some cases, though, women may have difficulty in gaining access to the large financial contributions necessary to compete successfully on a citywide basis.

Does the form of a local election have a clear impact on the ability of gays and lesbians to win office? The evidence here is somewhat ambiguous. Where lesbians and gays are concentrated geographically, the impact of voting systems is similar to that experienced by African Americans; district elections help to facilitate their electoral success.[32]

But in cities where the gay and lesbian population is more geographically dispersed, the impact of voting systems is more analogous to that experienced

■ FIGURE 7–1

CHICAGO'S HISPANIC CONGRESSIONAL DISTRICT,
THE FOURTH CONGRESSIONAL DISTRICT, MID-1990s

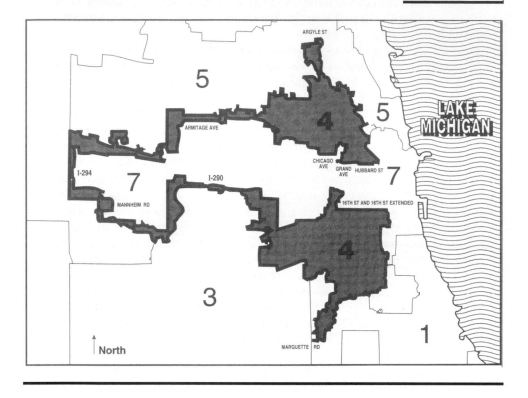

by women: district elections provide no clear advantage. In many cities, the identifiable "gay ghetto" is seldom large enough to guarantee the election of a gay or lesbian to office.[33] The Castro district in San Francisco and the North Halsted area of Chicago, of course, stand out as notable exceptions. Gay and lesbian candidates are often able to draw on citywide support from the homosexual community. San Francisco employed an at-large election system in 1996; three gays and lesbians still succeeded in gaining seats on the 11-member board of supervisors.[34]

In an interesting turn of events, white voters in minority-majority cities have complained that they are the newest "minority" whose fair representation is denied by at-large elections. In Birmingham, Alabama, whites challenged the city's at-large voting rules for diluting their representation on the city council. Under a federal court consent decree, the city agreed to a new system of district elections, one that would create three predominantly white council districts and six predominantly black districts.[35]

DISTRICT ELECTIONS AND "SECONDARY" MINORITY GROUPS: VOTING RIGHTS AND ASIAN AMERICANS, JEWS, AND GAYS AND LESBIANS. District lines that are drawn to enhance the representation of a protected minority under the Voting Rights Act may work against the election of "secondary" minority groups living in the community. As a result, the drawing of district lines often results in bitter intergroup arguments.

In numerous cities, African Americans and Latinos have often quarreled over the drawing of district lines. In New York, Los Angeles, San Francisco, and Seattle, Asian Americans argued that district boundaries drawn to ensure the election of African Americans undercut the possibilities of electing Asians to office. In New York, the drawing of district lines was particularly contentious. Hasidic Jews objected to a districting plan designed to abet African-American empowerment. In the Park Slope area of Brooklyn, gays and lesbians, too, objected when their population was dispersed among four newly created council districts as district lines were drawn to help ensure the election of African-American council members.[36]

AT-LARGE ELECTIONS, VOTER DISINTEREST, AND THE PROBLEM OF POLITICAL MONEY. Other criticisms of at-large elections go beyond matters of race and identity. At-large elections may compound voter disinterest. In district elections, localized campaign activity by council candidates can help to spur voter turnout. Council members elected by district also engage in those activities, including the performance of constituency service casework, that keep their names before district voters. The many candidates running citywide, in contrast, enjoy no similar ability to establish more personal and service relationships with voters in each district of the city. Nor can citywide candidates be expected to have intimate knowledge of the particular problems of each ward or neighborhood.

At-large and district election systems also reward different types of candidates. At-large elections will tend to draw candidates who have the contacts to raise the money for a citywide organization and media campaign. Candidates lacking substantial financial backing will have a difficult time making an at-large race. In contrast, a system of ward-based or district elections puts less of a premium on political money. Instead, neighborhood activists and other candidates with strong grassroots backing enjoy a reasonable chance of victory.

Can the switch from at-large to district elections reenergize the local political arena? On the one hand, the impact of such a switch is likely to be marginal; a switch to district elections does not produce a great increase in voter turnout.[37] Yet, in the Southwest, the reintroduction of ward-based representation helped to reshape local politics:

> Dramatic political changes appeared in the immediate aftermath of changes to district elections. More candidates ran for open seats; issues were more prominent in campaigns; portraits of districts, neighborhoods, and the concerns of their residents appeared in the news; candidates boasted their familiarity with neighborhoods they hoped to represent. Newly-elected city councils were more racially diverse than the councils of big-city reform.[38]

NONPARTISAN ELECTIONS

In **nonpartisan elections,** candidates run for office without party designations next to their names on the ballot. Nonpartisan elections force voters to focus on local issues and the quality of local candidates, not on national issues and partisan ties. Reformers argue that political parties introduce unnecessary conflict and parochial concerns that have no place in a city's affairs.

Nonpartisanship in local government is one of the lasting legacies of the reform movement. Approximately three-fourths of local governments in the United States use the nonpartisan ballot in municipal elections. In the West, virtually all local jurisdictions have nonpartisan elections. Only in the Mid-Atlantic region is there a general tendency toward partisan local elections.[39]

Nonpartisan election systems prevail in large as well as small cities. Boston, Cincinnati, Detroit, Los Angeles, Milwaukee, San Francisco, Seattle, and numerous Sunbelt cities all employ nonpartisan elections. Even in Chicago, with its history of machine politics, city council elections are nominally nonpartisan.

However, there are different variations of nonpartisanship. In truly nonpartisan cities, party organizations play little or no role in the election process. Such is the case in most small cities. In some nonpartisan cities, such as Dallas, parties effectively disguise themselves behind other local organizations.

In other nonpartisan cities, parties are absent from the ballot but still play a large role in slating candidates, raising support, and turning out the vote. Chicago and Cincinnati are examples of cities where extensive party activity lies barely beneath the surface of a nominally nonpartisan system. Houston is another. In Houston's nonpartisan 2001 mayoral election, Orlando Sanchez, a registered Republican, was supported by campaign commercials that featured former President George Herbert Walker Bush (a Houston resident) and post-9/11 hero Rudy Giuliani, the Republican Mayor of New York. The incumbent, Mayor Lee P. Brown, a registered Democrat, ran with the help of local Democratic organizations.[40] In Oakland, San Jose, Sacramento, Stockton, and other northern California cities, the growing population of racial minorities has altered the nature and culture of local governing systems, as Democrats have come to dominate the nominally nonpartisan council elections.[41]

There are strong criticisms of nonpartisan voting systems. The absence of party labels confuses voters. Party labels provide important cues or shortcuts that help voters find their preferred candidates in the absence of other meaningful pieces of information.[42] In low-visibility races such as those for city council, voters find that they must choose from among a group of candidates without even a party label to provide a hint as to what a candidate represents.

In the absence of party labels, voters will turn to whatever cue is available, including the ethnicity of a candidate's name. Nonpartisan systems encourage ethnic voting, as evident in the historic success in Boston of candidates with obviously Irish and Italian names. In nonpartisan elections, voters tend to focus on candidates' personal qualities, background characteristics, name recognition, and local activism—and not on issues.[43]

Nonpartisanship also aggravates the class bias in voting turnout. Better-educated middle- and upper-class citizens are self-starters when it comes to politics. They can sort through the various candidates' issue positions, select a favored candidate, and go out and vote. In contrast, in the absence of party labels, lesser-educated lower-class persons are more likely to be confused and stay home rather than vote. In truly nonpartisan systems, there are no organizations of local party workers to bring lower-class citizens to the polls on election day. As a result, a proposal to introduce a nonpartisan elections in a city can entail a fair amount of class and racial conflict. (See "New York Debates Nonpartisan Elections," on p. 208.)

Nonpartisan elections for school boards produce especially low turnouts when they are held on dates when there are no other offices on the ballot. Reformers argue that the separate or **off-time scheduling of elections for local office** allows voters to focus on the race at hand; candidates for offices such as a school board should not have to answer questions that arise from contests for other offices. Yet in such isolated elections, turnout can run as low as 10 or 15 percent—and sometimes even lower! Such low turnout rates give inordinate voting power to organized groups with a material stake in the election. A disproportionate portion of the ballots in school elections and bond referenda are cast by teachers and other employees of the school system and their immediate families.

Finally, nonpartisanship may also destroy an important resource for governance. Nonpartisan city councils lack the "glue" of party loyalty; there is no sense of party loyalty or discipline that might prove useful in helping to bring council members together on a difficult issue. The mayor of a nonpartisan city may find that leadership is impossible in cities where council members are individualistic and highly independent.[44]

Where reformers have not been able to eliminate partisan elections, they have attempted to ban the **party-column ballot,** a device that enables voters to cast a ballot for a party's candidates for all offices simply by marking the party box on top of the ballot. Reformers argue that elimination of the party box forces a voter to look at the individual candidates rather than mindlessly casting a ballot for a party's entire ticket of office seekers. Yet this reform has partisan and class-based effects. In Michigan in 2001, a Republican-controlled state government eliminated the party-column ballot over the objection of Democratic Party leaders. The partisan motivation underlying the Republican move was obvious; in the preceding election, over three-fourths of the voters in lower-class, Democratic Detroit had voted a straight-party ticket.[45]

VOTER REGISTRATION REQUIREMENTS

The more corrupt political machines relied on **repeaters,** voters who were paid to vote again and again in an election (hence, as the old machine slogan urged: "Vote Early and Vote Often"). The introduction of voter registration was necessary to eliminate such fraud. Requiring voters to register in advance of an

NEW YORK DEBATES NONPARTISAN ELECTIONS

Mayor Michael Bloomberg spent $7.5 million of his own money in an effort to get New York City to switch to a system of nonpartisan elections, a key element in his 2003 drive for charter reform. Bloomberg argued that many New Yorkers did not even bother to vote as the city was so overwhelmingly Democratic that whoever the Democrats nominated for office was almost certain to emerge victorious in the general election. Bloomberg argued that a switch to nonpartisan voting would give citizens an increased incentive to vote in the general election. The move would also give new voice to political independents who, under New York's long-standing partisan rules, were barred from voting in the city's Democratic primaries, the contests that for all intents and purposes chose the council victors in most districts. Bloomberg argued that the proposed changes would break the control that local party bosses exerted over council nominations.

Yet some of Bloomberg's claims were suspect. Academic studies seldom showed that nonpartisan elections led to increases in voter turnout. In fact, without the cues provided by party ties, some voters, confused, simply did not vote.

Critics saw Bloomberg's proposal as self-serving, especially as the mayor, a Democratic self-identifier who won office as a Republican, lacked deep roots in the Democratic party. In winning office, Bloomberg depended on the support of independent voters. Bloomberg also possessed the personal wealth to purchase extensive television advertising, a key advantage in races where the competing influence of political party ties is removed.

Harlem Congressman Charles Rangel and other Democratic Party leaders and spokespersons for racial minorities charged that Bloomberg's proposal threatened blacks, Latinos, and Asians. They argued that turnout among these groups would likely decline under a nonpartisan system. Community activists further charged that many Latino and African-American candidates lacked the money to compete in media-oriented nonpartisan campaigns.

Bloomberg said that his proposal would bring "good government" to New York. But New Yorkers did not want it, and the measure was handily defeated, 70% to 30%.

Sources: David R. Jones, "Nonpartisan Elections: Perfect for Billionaire Candidates," *The Amsterdam News*, February 28–March 5, 2003; Doug Muzzio, "Nonpartisan Elections and Charter Revision," *Gotham Gazette*, January 1, 2003: available at: www.gothamgazette.com/article/voting/20030122/17/196; Greg Sargent, "Lynch Defects From Mayor's Un-Party Plan," *New York Observer*, August 14, 2003.

election was a simple way to maintain a list of who was eligible to vote in each precinct.

But voter registration was not simply an attempt to clean up politics. It was also a weapon that was used selectively to reduce the number of votes in urban immigrant areas. Voter registration embodied "that old-stock nativist and corporate-minded hostility to the political machine, the polyglot city, and the immigrant which was so important a component of the progressive menta-lity."[46] In some cases, when initially enacted, voter registration was required in cities with their ethnic populations, but not in other parts of a state. The Pennsylvania state legislature required personal registration in cities, but not in small towns or rural areas.[47] In California in the 1800s, voter registration laws were used to limit the vote of the Irish, a Democratic Party voting bloc.[48]

In state and cities in the Southwest, so-called "good government" elites used voter registration laws to restrict mass participation. Phoenix required citizens to register anew for each municipal election; a citizen who failed to re-register was not allowed to vote. Coupled with poll taxes and literacy tests targeted against racial minorities, the registration laws served to restrict the franchise. From 1947 to 1975, voter turnout in Phoenix, Albuquerque, and Dallas averaged less than 20 percent. Such low turnouts paled when compared to the much higher voter participation rates of machine-style cities during the same era: 44 percent in New York, 54 percent in Chicago, and 57 percent in New Haven (Connecticut).[49]

The class bias of personal registration requirements is clear. Lesser-educated and lower-income citizens tend to get excited during the later days of an elec-tion campaign but find it impossible to vote if the registration deadline has already passed. Liberalizing registration laws "would have by far the greatest impact on the least educated."[50]

Over the years, court decisions and state legislative action have removed the most restrictive registration requirements. States have brought the registration cut-off date closer to the election, facilitating registration by younger and more mobile voters. Still, most states close voter registration about four weeks before election day, barring participation by last-minute enthusiasts.

SAME-DAY REGISTRATION AND "MOTOR VOTER." By the early 2000s, six states (Minnesota, Maine, Wisconsin, New Hampshire, Wyoming and Idaho) enacted **same-day (election day) voter registration,** enabling citizens to add their names to the voter rolls as they go to the polls to cast their ballots. These systems produced minor increases in voter turnout.

Voting advocates also enacted new procedures to allow voters to register when they renew their driver licenses. Yet the **Motor Voter Act of 1993** (the less formal name for the National Registration Act of 1993) "failed miser-ably" to increase voter turnout.[51] By itself, "Motor Voter" did not mobilize the urban poor or other voters who were not engaged in the political process.

Voter turnout in American cities would increase if states and municipali-ties were to follow the practice of many European nations, where it is the government's responsibility to maintain a current list of eligible voters. This would eliminate the burden on citizens themselves to register. But, as the motor-voter experience has demonstrated, the relaxation of registration bar-riers will not by itself redistribute power to the urban poor and racial minori-ties. Community organizing efforts and face-to-face voter registration drives must also be a part of any strategy designed to mobilize underrepresented urban constituencies.

MAIL-IN VOTING AND EXTENDED VOTER HOURS. Allowing voters to cast their ballots through the mail represents an alternative strategy for increasing voter turnout. Where it has been tried—San Diego, Berkeley, Modesto, and Napa (California), Rochester (New York), and the State of Oregon—mail balloting decreased the costs of administering elections while increasing voter turnout. In San Diego, the large-scale use of mail-in ballots led to a record turnout increase of over 60 percent. In other cities, the gain in turnout was less overwhelming but still substantial. With the use of bar-coded envelopes that pull up a voter's signature for instant verification, the possibility of voter fraud may even be less in a mail-in ballot election when compared to having citizens cast their ballots in polling booths.

Oregon has conducted its elections by mail-in ballots, reducing the costs of staffing polling sites, and gaining significant increases in voter turnout. Modesto and Napa (both in California) also conduct their entire voting process by mail, with both cities witnessing a dramatic increase in voter turnout.[52]

Other changes in voting laws can help to promote public participation. **Extended voting hours,** that is, keeping the polls open from dawn until 9 p.m., serves to increase the turnout of young adults.[53]

INSTANT RUNOFF VOTING. It is sometimes argued that American voters suffer from election fatigue, that turnouts in local elections are low as citizens tire of voting in so many different primaries and elections held on different dates. San Francisco was the first major U.S. city to institute **instant runoff voting (IRV)** in an effort to eliminate the need for a second-round or runoff election should no candidate receive a majority vote in the initial municipal election. Under IRV, each citizen ranks his or her top three choices for an office. Should no candidate gain the required percentage of votes for victory when each voter's top choice is counted, the votes for the less popular candidates are reallocated according to a voter's second-choice, and, if necessary, third-choice preferences. Vancouver (Washington), Santa Clara County (California) and the State of Vermont have also adopted instant runoffs. Cambridge (Massachusetts) uses a proportional representation variation of the instant runoff ballot.

Instant runoff voting helps to counter the problem of voter fatigue and saves a municipality the costs of having to hold a second round of elections. IRV also has the potential of increasing citizens' willingness to cast a ballot for a third-party candidate, as citizens know that they are not wasting their ballot when they vote for a preferred candidate who has little chance of winning an election outright; their marked second preference could still help to determine the outcome of a closely contested race.[54]

Instant runoff voting also eliminates the problem posed by plurality elections in which an extremist candidate, distasteful to a majority of voters, can win office by gaining only 30 or so percent of the vote in a crowded multicandidate field. The IRV system can reallocate votes until a majority winner emerges.

DIRECT PRIMARY

In the old days, political party leaders met in closed party conventions or caucuses to select their party's slate of candidates. The public was often shut out of the nominating process. To counter this, reformers instituted the **direct primary,** which allows the citizens themselves to choose who will be their party's candidates in the ensuing general election.

While quite laudable, this reform, too, has a middle- and upper-class bias. In nearly all elections in the United States, upper-status people participate at significantly higher rates than do lower-status people. However, this class differential in participation levels is greatest in elections, such as primaries, in which the overall voting turnouts are low and lower-class citizens are least involved. In party primaries, middle- and upper-class voters comprise an even greater share of the primary electorate than they do of the general-election-day electorate.

INITIATIVE, REFERENDUM, AND RECALL: THE TOOLS OF DIRECT DEMOCRACY

The Progressive Era reformers used three institutions of direct democracy—the *initiative, referendum,* and *recall*—in their attempt to weaken the grip of corrupt political parties and powerful private interests on the political process. While provisions for referenda can be found in cities across the United States, the initiative and recall are more commonplace in the Southwest and the West than in the East. About 90 percent of western cities allow for the initiative and recall; fewer than a third of Mid-Atlantic states permit these procedures.[55] Use of the initiative is especially popular—and controversial—in California.

As we shall see, the initiative, referendum, and recall have proven to be imperfect reforms. Clearly, at times, the public needs these tools to force an otherwise irresponsive government to address its needs. But in recent years, powerful groups have also learned to use these tools to advance their own interests.

THE INITIATIVE. Nearly half the states permit some form of voter initiative. The **initiative** process sets out the number of signatures that are required for a citizen's group to draft a piece of legislation or a charter amendment to be put before the voters in the next election. By using the initiative process, citizens themselves can directly enact new statutes, bypassing party-controlled and interest group-dominated legislatures that might have lost touch with the people.

Recent experience, however, has led critics to argue that the initiative process is fundamentally flawed. Written by citizen groups, initiatives are often poorly drafted and subject to legal challenge. More important, the initiative also bypasses the process of representative government that allows elected officials to consider and balance the competing concerns of many different groups of citizens and come up with a workable compromise. An initiative campaign, in contrast, allows for no such compromise; instead, voters simply vote "Yes" or "No" on the ballot measure before them. In the public debate over an initiative, passions may rule and the potential ill effects of the ballot proposal may not be fully discussed or taken into account.

The debate over the use of the initiative is illustrated in the case of the 1978 statewide vote for **Proposition 13** in California. Proposition 13 provided Californians with much-needed relief from soaring property taxes. Yet voters did not fully understand how the lion's share of tax breaks would be enjoyed by corporations and other large property holders; nor did they recognize how the initiative would lead to service reductions, cutbacks in education spending, and tax inequities in California's communities.[56] With local education in a state of disrepair, the State of California increased its aid to, and control over, local schools, a solution that prompted new voter objections.

California's much publicized fiscal problems in the early 2000s can also be attributed to the fondness of Californians for governing by the initiative process. A series of voter initiatives over the years made it nearly impossible for governments in California to increase taxes, but, at the same time, voter initiatives also mandated continued spending for schools and other identified purposes. These restrictions effectively impeded the state government's attempts to ward off the looming fiscal crisis.[57]

As initiative campaigns can be quite expensive to mount, well-organized and financially well-heeled interest groups have used the initiative process to fight for their policy goals. Affluent interest groups can hire professional firms to garner the signatures necessary to place a measure on the ballot. The increased reliance on paid professional signature gatherers marks a move away from the citizens' ideal, as signature gathering is no longer an indicator of public interest in a measure. When a single wealthy individual (or a few individuals) provides the financing for a ballot effort, even the ability to raise funds for an initiative is no longer indicative of the breadth of voter interest in a measure.[58]

Big-money groups also buy substantial media time to present their views on an issue. The gambling industry spent lavishly on behalf of ballot measures authorizing casino gambling in Atlantic City (New Jersey) and a state lottery in California. In the state of Washington, Microsoft cofounder and billionaire Paul Allen, owner of the Seattle Seahawks, spent over $10 million on an initiative drive to have state taxpayers help fund a new football stadium. Allen's spending appears to have made the difference, as the measure passed with only 51 percent of the vote.[59]

In a number of states, the initiative and referendum devices have been used in attempts to promote exclusionary, even discriminatory, policies. In California in the 1990s, voter initiatives were used in an effort to limit affirmative action programs, bilingual education, and state assistance to immigrants. In Arizona and Massachusetts, ballot measures similarly imposed sharp restrictions on bilingual instruction. A number of states nationwide have seen voter efforts to enact new legislation and constitutional provisions to limit same-sex marriage and gay and lesbian rights.

THE REFERENDUM.   The **referendum** is similar to the initiative except that the process typically begins when the legislature votes to put an item before the citizens for their approval or disapproval. The exact referendum process varies from city to city and from state to state. In some cases, citizens themselves can petition for a public vote on a bill that has already been passed by the council. Alternatively, the city council (or, at the state level, the state legislature) can vote to put a bill before the people. In New York City in 1998, City Council Speaker Peter Vallone proposed a binding referendum to allow the city's voters to decide the fate of Mayor Rudy Giuliani's plans to replace an aging Yankee Stadium with a costly new facility on the West Side of Manhattan.

In many Sunbelt cities—and in certain non-Sunbelt communities such as Cape Cod (Massachusetts) and Minneapolis—neighborhood and environmental groups have used the initiative and referendum processes to counter the power of local growth coalitions. In a process that Roger Caves has called **ballot-box planning** or **electoral land-use planning,** voters angered by classroom over-crowding, increased pollution, traffic congestion, and other threats to the environment have used the initiative and referendum processes to impose restrictions on new development.

San Diego voters in the mid-1980s passed Proposition A as antigrowth forces urged "No L.A.! Yes on A!" In the years that followed, San Diego residents voted on numerous other growth-control measures, some passing and some going down to defeat amid massive spending by the development industry. In San Francisco, Proposition M placed an annual cap on new construction and required developers to pay various linkage fees; at the time it was characterized as the toughest big-city growth limitation measure in the United States. In Seattle, citizen activists helped enact into law Initiative 31, the Citizens' Alternative Plan, which sought to limit the development of new downtown office space, capping the skyscraper development that had been transforming the character of the city. In 1997, Minneapolis citizens voted overwhelmingly to limit city financial assistance for any new professional sports facility.[60]

THE RECALL.   The **recall** threatens officials with removal from office, thereby leading elected office holders to pay greater heed to the wishes of the people. Under the recall procedure, voters sign petitions seeking the removal of an elected official from office before his or her term expires. If a sufficient number of valid signatures are gathered, the recall question is put on the ballot; citizens can then vote whether or not to oust the official from office.

Oregon, California, and Michigan are the states with the highest number of local recall elections. Recalls have also been a regular part of local politics in Washington, Alaska, Idaho, and Nebraska. A number of mayors have had to face the threat of a recall election. Atlantic City Mayor Michael Matthews, indicted on charges of corruption, was recalled from office by the voters in 1984. Omaha Mayor Mike Boyle was recalled in 1987 after having dismissed the local police chief. Cleveland's Dennis Kucinich and San Francisco's Dianne Feinstein were two big-city mayors who successfully won recall elections and were able to complete their terms in office.

Does the recall process always lead to good public policy? Like the other institutions of direct democracy, recalls have been criticized for intruding on responsible, representative government. Under the threat of a recall, an elected official is likely to prove increasingly responsive to the sentiments of recall activists, not to the policy needs of the general public. The intensity of their effort and their ability to mobilize votes in a low-turnout election gives the recall organizers influence beyond their numbers. In some communities, anti-tax activists begin recall efforts any time a local official votes for a raise in taxes—even when a revenue increase is needed to maintain services, keep schools open, or get a community out of a tight fiscal squeeze.

In suburban communities, activist citizens have also used the recall in an effort to maintain local exclusion. In wealthy Westport, Connecticut, a recall attempt was started against school board members who had voted to admit 25 inner-city students to the exclusive suburb's schools. In affluent Birmingham, Michigan, three city commissioners who voted to provide subsidized housing to the poor and the elderly were recalled.[61]

The debate over the desirability of the recall process gained national visibility when California citizens voted in 2004 to make popular actor Arnold Schwarzenegger, a Republican, their governor, removing Gray Davis, a Democrat, from office only a year after Davis had won reelection. Davis' supporters argued that the recall process had been politicized and abused, that the Governor had committed no crimes, and that California's economic problems were beyond his control. The recall campaign was also aided by Republican Congressman Darrell Issa, who poured $1.3 million of his own money into the recall effort. Issa had hoped to replace Davis as governor, before finally stepping aside after Schwarzenegger's entry into the race.

Advocates of the recall effort respond that the Davis recall was appropriate and that voter anger was genuine because Davis had hid the extent of the state's fiscal problems during his reelection campaign. Voters distrusted the government and thought that Sacramento under Davis was headed in the wrong direction. Organizers of the recall further point to the unusually large turnout of voters that resulted in Schwarzenegger's election. The recall was the only tool available to voters seeking to retake government from Sacramento politicians and their interest-group allies.[62]

CIVIL SERVICE AND MERIT SYSTEMS

The reformers established **civil service rules** for merit hiring, spelling out the necessary qualifications and testing requirements for each position in the municipal bureaucracy. Civil service rules greatly reduced patronage and partisan favoritism, increasing the expertise, efficiency, and fairness of local government.

Yet merit personnel systems had the unintended effects of creating new problems in terms of governmental performance, accountability, and bias. Insulated from the direct control of elected officials, the city bureaucracies became new power centers in urban politics. As we shall describe in Chapters 8 and 9, in more recent years, new measures—including citizen participation, service decentralization, and privatization efforts—have been introduced in an attempt to remedy some of the rigidities that result from civil-service–protected systems.

CITY PLANNING COMMISSIONS AND DEPARTMENTS

The political machine often allowed partisan favoritism to intrude on questions of city development. Planning and zoning approvals were often given in exchange for a developer's contributions to the party organization. The reformers wanted to cut the nexus between politics and urban development. They wanted a system whereby rational planning principles, including concerns for orderly development and civic beauty, would guide city growth.

The reformers placed development decisions in the hands of a group of non-political actors, the independent **city planning commission.** In other cities, reformers created a powerful **city planning department,** in which well-paid professional planners would use their expert training to guide the city on development matters.

In general, the planning commissions and departments represented an improvement over the partisan-ridden process they replaced. Yet the planning commissions and departments had biases of their own. Part-time, unpaid commission members were often ill-equipped to challenge the growth projects presented to them by municipal departments and the city's business elite. Large-scale citizen protests finally challenged new highway construction and downtown redevelopment and slum clearance projects that uprooted citizens and destroyed city neighborhoods and buildings of historic value. Citizens had begun to recognize that the "nonpartisan" boards and allegedly "objective" experts did not always recommend policies that were good for their neighborhoods.

Typically, however, neighborhood groups lack the expertise and staff resources to effectively challenge a city's plans. The reformed processes of city planning was now itself in need of reform. Some activist planners called for a new style of **advocacy planning,** whereby planners would work not for the city but for community groups, in effect becoming the "hired guns" of the community in its fight against city hall. Other professionals called for **equity planning,** whereby planners working for the city would show a concern for neighborhood needs and preservation and not just for economic growth and downtown development. As director of city planning in Cleveland in the 1970s, Norman Krumholz took a strong advocacy stance in favor of the poor, distancing his planning department from the reformed principles of neutrality and objectivity that characterized planning in most cities.[63]

REFORMED INSTITUTIONS AND THE SUNBELT

Sunbelt municipalities are generally characterized by such reformed institutions as the manager-council form of government, nonpartisan and at-large elections, and professionalized administrative systems. Reformed institutions allowed business-led growth coalitions in southwestern cities great latitude in pursuing economic development projects. In many Sunbelt cities, including San Antonio, San Diego, and San Jose (California), the city manager's office helped to facilitate the aggressive capital improvement, growth, and annexation strategies favored by growth-oriented elites. San Jose became a "paradise for developers."[64] Unlike the machine cities of the North and the Midwest, there was no mass-based party organization to counterbalance the will of the business community. In Phoenix, Albuquerque, and other southwestern cities, the cities' booster coalitions helped to dictate the direction of growth policies, oftentimes leaving poor, Hispanic, and African-American communities outside a city's boundaries with their residents not entitled to sewerage, water, and other basic municipal services.[65]

The pluralization of interests in the Sunbelt led to a new citizens' assault on the link between reformed institutions and local growth. San Jose, Long Beach, Sacramento, Stockton, Oakland, Watsonville (California), Tacoma, San Antonio, Dallas, Fort Worth, El Paso, Albuquerque, Richmond, Montgomery, Charlotte, and Raleigh were among the cities that reinstituted some form of district elections in order to increase the effective representation of racial minorities in city hall. San Diego and Oakland were the most notable cities that decreased the power of the city manager's office in order to give the mayor, the people's elected official, greater authority over development decisions.

If the manager-council plan and nonpartisan and at-large voting systems served historically to enhance the power of the growth coalition in Sunbelt cities, another set of reforms—the initiative, referendum, and recall—gave homeowner groups, environmentalists, and the region's growing Latino population the means to challenge local growth regimes. By 1990, the central political institutions of big-city reform in the Southwest were "dismantled."[66]

REFORM AND THE GROWTH OF BUREAUCRATIC POWER

Merit systems of municipal hiring produced a municipal bureaucracy that was not demographically representative of the city's polity. In the 1960s and 1970s, blacks, Hispanics, and women's groups demanded the introduction of affirmative action hiring and promotion policies in order to change the racial and gender composition of municipal agencies.

Civil-service–protected municipal officials and centralized bureaucratic structures were often impermeable to citizens' demands. Citizen dissatisfaction was not confined to minority communities. In white and minority neighborhoods alike, parents sought to get greater responsiveness from nonperforming teachers and school administrators.

Civil service and other reforms produced a city that, in the words of Theodore Lowi, was "well-run but ungoverned." Agency officials followed their own technical training and professional standards, resisting the demands of citizens and elected officials. Mayors lacked the power to dismiss civil-service–protected officials who refused to follow their policy directions. (See "Los Angeles: Can Anyone Fire Chief Gates," on p. 217.) The municipal bureaucracies were "'islands of functional power' before which the modern mayor stands denuded of authority."[67]

Their power in running the city is so great that Lowi labeled the civil-service–protected bureaucracies the **New Machines.** A mayor who wins election with political debts to municipal unions will find that he or she is in a perilously weak bargaining position relative to the municipal agencies.

LOS ANGELES: CAN ANYONE FIRE CHIEF GATES?

As a tense Los Angeles awaited the 1992 verdict in the trial of the four officers accused of beating Rodney King, police chief Daryl Gates decided to attend a political fundraising dinner rather than take direct charge of the potential riot situation. As the outbreak began, the police were withdrawn from the riot area for fear that their continuing presence would serve only to precipitate new incidents of violence. The withdrawal, however, allowed the violence to escalate.

One particularly dramatic piece of televised news footage showed a gang of violent thugs pulling a driver, Reginald Denny, from his truck, kicking him and dropping a cement block on his head. There were no police in sight. Denny survived the attack only because several black men and women in the community came to his assistance.

Mayor Tom Bradley and other critics of Chief Gates used the Rodney King beating and Gates' mishandling of the South Central riots to demand the chief's removal from office. But the mayor lacked the formal authority to fire his long-time political rival. Gates and Bradley did not get along. The chief had even refused to meet with the mayor to discuss preparations as a combustible Los Angeles awaited the Rodney King jury verdict. As Gates reported in his autobiography *Chief: My Life in the LAPD,* he and the mayor "were scarcely on speaking terms;" they had learned over time "to tolerate each other, barely—speaking only when we had to, mainly by telephone." Bradley, too, recalled that he had not spoken to the police chief in 13 months!*

In Los Angeles, as in a great number of other cities, the reform movement had essentially created a political system that assured professional administrators virtual independence from elected officials. Los Angeles' police department was notoriously independent. Willie Williams, Gates' successor, observed that as the city's top cop he was under no legal obligation to meet with the mayor or other high city officials to coordinate actions: "I don't have one operating superior." Williams continued, "The first six months I thought I was mayor!"**

Gates' insularity and his mishandling of the South Central disturbances finally led Los Angeles voters to change the city charter in order to limit a
continued

LOS ANGELES: CAN ANYONE FIRE CHIEF GATES? (CONT.)

police chief's tenure in office and to give public officials greater say in a chief's tenure and removal.

* Daryl F. Gates, *Chief: My Life in the LAPD* (New York: Bantam Books, 1992), as reported by Jane Fritsch, "Los Angeles Mayor Comes Under More Attacks in Police Chief's New Book," *The New York Times*, May 6, 1992. For details of the Bradley-Gates feud and Gates' handling of the 1992 riots, see: Raphael J. Sonenshein, *Politics in Black and White: Race and Power in Los Angeles* (Princeton, NJ: Princeton University Press, 1993), pp. 210–226; and Lou Cannon, *Official Negligence: How Rodney King and the Riots Changed the LAPD* (New York: Times Books/Random House, 1997), pp. 121–122.

** Los Angeles Police Chief Willie Williams, comments to the annual meeting of the National Civic League, Los Angeles, November 13, 1992.

The reformers' faith in independent agencies also led to the creation of autonomous **metropolitan and special service districts** to provide the efficient provision of services across city-suburban boundaries. But once again, there was no certainty that the administrators of these districts would respond to any directives other than their own narrowly defined determination of the public good. For much of its history, the Port Authority of New York and New Jersey kept its investment in commuter rail to a minimum, refusing to use its vast revenues from the region's bridges, airports, and tunnels to help upgrade the region's decaying rail system. The commissioners came from the business community and looked upon any investment in rail transit as a losing proposition. In a case of "bureaucratic egotism," the Port Authority built the World Trade Center with its 110-story twin towers, assuring that the bulk of the Authority's "excess revenues would be committed for many years to come, thus reducing pressure to divert these funds to mass transit."[68]

The reform ideology failed as it assumed that cities could best be run by **neutral specialists**,[69] highly educated experts who would make decisions according to professional criteria free from outside partisan influences. What the reformers failed to realize was that no matter how expert or well trained, the specialists could never be neutral. Even dedicated public servants make decisions that reflect biases of their own class and personal backgrounds and the narrow perspectives of their professional training.

DO BLACKS AND WHITES HAVE DIFFERENT VIEWS OF REFORM?

To traditional good-government reformers and a city's business elite, reform has historically meant increasing a city's managerial competence for greater economic efficiency. In African-American communities, however, the primary goal of reform politics often has *not* centered on economic efficiency. Instead, black reform groups, strongly rooted in black churches, have viewed politics as a moral enterprise for the pursuit of equity and fairness.[70] Reform organizations that emphasize only businesslike efficiency, not the achievement of a more just society, have only the most limited appeal in black neighborhoods.

In Chicago, white and black reformers even differed somewhat in their evaluations of the reform credentials of Harold Washington, the city's first African American to be elected mayor. Some white reformers objected that the mayor's Chicago First jobs program, which required city contractors to hire workers from a list approved by the Washington administration, was a return to machine-style patronage practices. Black reform forces, in contrast, applauded Mayor Washington's effort to distribute jobs and services more equitably by directing them to the city's underserved African-American neighborhoods. Black reformers dismissed the patronage charges against Mayor Washington as inconsequential, viewing Washington's actions as a means of ending the biased practices of the city's white ethnic machine.[71]

In Philadelphia, too, concerns for racial empowerment competed with more traditional good-government definitions of reform. Black voters in 2003 rallied behind Mayor John Street, an African American, after the city's police department found FBI listening devices planted in his office. Federal authorities had been looking into a number of allegations of municipal corruption, including the improper award of city contracts to political contributors and relatives. Black voters rallied to Street, a Democrat, who charged that the wiretaps were part of a national Republican effort to discredit black empowerment and help a Republican gain office.[72]

THE REFORM OF REFORM: THE RISE OF A NEW REFORM MOVEMENT

The reforms of the Progressive Era "cleaned up" city politics in important ways. But in doing so, the reforms created municipal governments that were not fully responsive to the demands of citizens, especially to the new voices of a city's growing minority population.

Hence, it should come as no surprise that one study of ten northern California communities has found that "minority incorporation" in municipal affairs was strengthened in those cities that threw off parts of the old reform theology. Oakland, San Jose, Sacramento, Stockton, and San Francisco all switched from at-large to district elections in an effort to increase minority representation and community responsiveness. Minority incorporation was also enhanced in cities (Berkeley, Oakland, San Jose, Sacramento, Stockton, and San Francisco) where the power of elected officials was increased at the expense of the city manager.[73]

Today, the concern over the irresponsiveness of bureaucratized municipal government cuts across racial lines. Minority groups, environmentalists, and community activists have all recognized the need to "reform the reforms" in order to enhance citizen participation and the responsiveness of service providers.

A new era of reform efforts has embraced district elections, citizen participation, decentralization, increased mayoral and council power, ethics laws,
campaign finance reform, and other cures to governmental insularity and distance. A new generation of reform leaders has come to recognize the need to
alter the old reform philosophy. In Cincinnati, proposals for increased neighborhood power were endorsed by such traditional reform constituencies as the
League of Women Voters and the city manager: "'Reform' was losing some of
its traditional meaning in Cincinnati."[74]

The reform movement has evolved over time: "Democracy is now the primary goal; achieving efficiency is now secondary."[75] Even the good-government
National Civic League (the modern-day name for the old National Municipal
League) revised its Model City Charter, recognizing that some cities will find it
necessary to adopt district or mixed elections in order to increase the representation of racial minorities.[76]

In a number of cities, the "reform of reform" entailed attempts to increase
the potential for urban leadership by strengthening the authority of the mayor's
office. Oakland (California) Mayor Jerry Brown pushed through a strong-
mayor form of government, arguing that centralized leadership authority was
necessary to turn around conditions in that poverty-plagued city. Using his new
authority, Brown ousted the city manager and proposed to downgrade the city
manager's position, giving the mayor the authority to hire and fire department
heads.[77] Kansas City Mayor Emanuel Cleaver similarly argued for a strengthened mayoral office, arguing that in the modern city, the mayor must be much
more than just the most prominent member of the city council:

> Kansas City is now a big-league city and when the mayor of the city sits around with
> the president and CEO of a major corporation trying to get them to relocate here,
> the mayor is at a disadvantage, because other mayors can cut the deal at the table.
> We are at a disadvantage in many instances when we are out competing.[78]

Even Cincinnati, a bastion of Progressive Era municipal reform, at long last
switched to a strong-mayor system. Before the change, Cincinnati had been
characterized as a leaderless city where the mayor did not even enjoy the leadership potential that comes from being chosen by voters citywide. Before its
change, the mayor of Cincinnati was merely the council member who received
the most votes in the general election.[79]

Los Angeles, too, in many ways the nation's most reformed city, began to modify the imposing bureaucratic structures that prior generations of reformers had
built. Los Angeles' 1925 City Charter embodied the faith that reformers had
placed in professional expertise. The city's 1937 charter amendments gave the
police chief civil-service protection, assuring the office's independence from partisan forces. Continuing revelations of police abuses and scandal, however, led voters in 1991 to give the mayor an opportunity to replace the police chief, who
would now be appointed only for a five-year term.[80] Soon thereafter, L.A. voters
also approved other measures that strengthened the mayor's office and established a new system of advisory neighborhood councils, all in an effort to increase
the responsiveness of L.A.'s government.

Yet some critics urged caution as cities began to increase the power of elected officials. These observers point to the continuing importance of maintaining professional competence in municipal decision making:

> Professional managers serving elected officials and the public bring distinctive values that enrich and elevate the governmental process in policy making and service delivery. These include the commitment to basing policy and service delivery on need rather than demand, stressing the long-term interests of the community as a whole . . . Something important is lost if there is no professional chief administrator to channel professional values into the governmental process at the highest and most general level . . .[81]

ETHICS LAWS AND CAMPAIGN FINANCE REFORM

The new reformers found it difficult to write precise and workable **ethics laws** that prohibit certain conduct and practices. Detailed **conflict-of-interest laws** and **requirements for financial disclosure** intrude on privacy and may deter qualified persons from assuming positions in public service. Such laws have also proven difficult to implement and enforce.

Cities and states have enacted **open-meeting or sunshine laws** that prohibit a city's business from being conducted in closed-door meetings and unofficial gatherings. The Los Angeles County Board of Supervisors still met in private, informal sessions to reach a consensus on solutions, which would then be ratified with little debate in official public sessions—despite state laws that seemingly barred such sessions.[82]

Cities have also begun to enact **campaign finance reform** measures, with at least 75 municipalities taking steps to reduce the influence of money in local elections. Albuquerque has experimented with locally imposed **limits on campaign spending.** San Francisco and Austin (Texas) are among the cities that have set **contribution limits.** Austin voters passed a charter amendment capping at $100 the amount any individual or political action committee can give to a campaign and limiting the total amount that council and mayoral candidates can receive from non-Austin residents. Critics argue that the contribution limits are too low and that they impede a candidate's ability to run a campaign that can get the attention of, and inform, voters. San Francisco's campaign finance law was successfully challenged in court on the basis that it interfered with the ability of candidates to communicate with voters.[83]

Twelve local communities (including Austin, Boulder [Colorado], Long Beach, Los Angeles, Miami-Dade County, New York, Oakland, Petaluma [California], San Francisco, and Tucson) provide for the **partial public funding** of elections in which contributions to candidates from the municipal treasury are given in an effort to reduce the reliance of candidates on special-interest money. These laws provide public monies to candidates who demonstrate a certain minimal level of public support and who in return, agree to limit their overall campaign spending. But these cities are exceptional, only a few cities are willing to incur the expense involved in helping to pay for local candidacies.

Even in those cities, the level of assistance provided to candidates is not always sufficient to induce candidates to sever their ties to special interest groups.[84]

U.S. Supreme Court rulings have undermined both national and local efforts to regulate campaign finance. In its 1976 *Buckley v. Valeo* decision, the Court essentially created an **independent expenditures** loophole in campaign finance laws, ruling that legislatures may not enact campaign laws that restrict the First Amendment free-speech rights of candidates and independent groups. Essentially, candidates and independent groups have a right to spend unlimited amounts of money in political races unless they voluntarily surrender those rights. In Los Angeles, the public funding of elections placed new spending limits on candidates for public office; but, as a review by the city's Ethics Commission showed, public funding in L.A. has not been able to control independent expenditures, which have risen to "unprecedented levels, as spending by businesses, political parties, [and] unions" have undercut the goals of campaign finance reform.[85]

The Supreme Court's ruling effectively limits the ability of a city to restrict expenditures made by independent organizations on behalf of a candidate. Even political parties are seen to have independent free-speech rights and have been able to raise and spend money beyond the reach of local campaign finance laws. In 1993, the New York State Democratic Party spent a half million dollars on radio and direct mail advertising in support of incumbent Mayor David Dinkins, money that was not counted against Dinkins' allowable spending ceiling.[86] The U.S. Supreme Court's ruling also apparently allows multi-millionaires and billionaires who refuse to accept public funds the ability to retain their "free speech" right to spend unlimited sums of their own personal money on their campaigns. (See "New York's Billionaire Mayor," below.)

NEW YORK'S BILLIONAIRE MAYOR

New York City has the nation's most generous system of public funding of municipal elections. In the 2001 mayoral race, the City offered candidates a $4 match in public funds for each $1 that the candidate raised in contributions of $250 or less.

This generous system of public funding has worked fairly well in encouraging and supporting candidacies for the city council. Yet, the system fell totally apart in the 2001 mayoral race when billionaire Michael Bloomberg spent over $73 million of his money to help ensure his election. Knowing that he could rely on his personal wealth, Bloomberg refused to accept public campaign funds. He thereby did not have to comply with any city legislation that sought to curtail campaign spending; he retained his free-speech right to spend as much money as he desired on his own election.

continued

New York's Billionaire Mayor (cont.)

His opponent, Mark Green, lacked Bloomberg's extensive wealth. By accepting public funds, Green agreed to the accompanying restrictions that limited his campaign's spending. Green, spent only $16 million on the race, less than a fourth of the amount spent by Bloomberg. Green even qualified for a more generous 5-to-1 "bonus" match in public funding as he faced a general election opponent who refused to abide by the rules of the public funding system. But the public funds really did very little to level out\t the critical spending differential that marred the mayoral race..

It was hardly a fair fight. Bloomberg spent over $90 for each vote he received. His campaign ran 6,500 television commercials compared to the 2,500 aired by Green. Bloomberg's wealth enabled him to flood the airwaves with political commercials in the closing days of the race, so much so that candidates for other offices had a difficult time getting their views across on radio and television.

But the money differential was not the only story of the 2001 mayoral race. As the election was held in the immediate wake of the 2001 terrorist attacks on the World Trade Center, and Bloomberg also enjoyed the considerable advantage of running with the endorsement of outgoing Mayor Rudy Giuliani, who was riding the crest of his enormous post-2001 popularity. But even here, money helped allow Bloomberg to shape his image. One Bloomberg commercial, shown repeatedly during the New York Yankees-Arizona Diamondbacks World Series despite the daunting costs of air time, featured Mayor Giuliani urging voters to elect Bloomberg.

Bloomberg won a 53-percent-to-47 percent victory. His personal wealth and virtually unlimited spending allowed Bloomberg, running as a Republican, to win the mayoralty in a city where Democrats outnumber Republicans five to one. As Green campaign strategist Richard Schraeder caustically observed of Bloomberg's victory, "He [Bloomberg] bought it fair and square."

As mayor, Bloomberg opposed changes that would increase the public matching funds given to candidates who chose to participate in the public funding system, especially candidates who faced millionaire (or billionaire), self-financed candidates like Bloomberg. Reformers argued that the changes were necessary to level the playing field. Bloomberg countered that such proposals were designed to benefit his 2005 political rivals.

Source: New York City Campaign Finance Board, *An Election Interrupted . . . The Campaign Finance Program and the 2001 New York City Elections*, Part I (New York: NYCCFB, 2002); the executive summary of the report is available at www.nyccfb.info/PDF/per/Exec_summary_2001. pdf; Michael Cooper, "At $92.60 a Vote, Bloomberg Shatters an Election Record," *The New York Times*, December 4, 2001; Susan Reefer, "New Campaign Financing Proposals—and Who They Benefit," GothamGazette.com, April 2003, available at www.gothamgazette.com/article/ voting/2003-12-15%2000:00:00/17/803.

Meaningful campaign finance reform is quite difficult to achieve. "Interested money" tends to find ways around legislative restrictions. Billionaire developer Donald J. Trump testified that he was able to circumvent a New York State law that limits corporate contributions to $5,000; he made contributions through 18 subsidiary corporations that had been established.[87]

TERM LIMITS

In the 1990s, an anti-incumbency mood led voters across the nation to place limitations on the reelection of elected officials. Although anti-incumbency sentiment was initially directed against members of Congress, citizens soon began to limit number of terms allowed to state and local officials.

In a number of states and cities, citizens used the initiative process to enact term-limitation measures. In other municipalities, city councils read the voters' mood and by referendum placed the issue on the ballot. Cincinnati, Houston, Jacksonville, Kansas City, Los Angeles, New Orleans, New York, San Antonio, San Francisco, San Jose, and Washington, DC are among the more populous cities that adopted term limits.

Term limits caught on by wildfire. In 1992, fewer than 300 municipalities had term limits. By 1998, a mere half dozen years later, the number swelled to nearly 3,000.[88] Typically, the measures permitted city and county legislators to serve only two two-year terms in office.

Advocates of term limitations point to the virtues of returning to the **Jeffersonian ideal** of the citizen-legislator. They argue that term limitation measures are needed to break the stranglehold that special interests have had over legislators dependent on their financial contributions for a career in politics. The arguments for term limitations are especially strong in those cities where officeholders gain repeated reelection and serve long tenures in office.

However, critics point to the numerous undesirable aspects of term limitations. They argue that city and county councils lose **institutional memory** when term restrictions force those few legislative members with substantial experience in municipal government to leave office. Critics further argue that by decreasing legislative competence and know-how, term limits serve to increase the power of the bureaucracy, legislative staff, and special-interest groups. Inexpert, novice legislators are reliant on the information and studies provided by outsiders.

Yet the initial wave of term limitations did not produce the massive shift in power to the bureaucracy that the foes of term limits had predicted. A study of term limits and officials' attitudes in Anaheim, Huntington Beach, Irvine, Santa Ana, and other Orange County, California communities indicated no perceived shift in power to the city manager or career bureaucrats.[89]

Critics further argue that local governments do not need the strong medicine of term limits. City councils, unlike Congress, are not fossilized with members from uncompetitive districts who serve long, extended careers in office. In contrast to the congressional pattern, each new city council, especially in small- and medium-sized cities and suburbs, brings substantial membership turnover and the infusion of "new blood" to the legislature. Data from 1991 reveals that 47 percent of all council members were serving their first term of office.[90] Rather than suffering from careerism, city councils have been generally populated by new arrivals unschooled in the technical workings of municipal affairs.

The initial impacts of term limitation measures appear to be more marginal than both advocates and critics had predicted. Term limits increase the number of open seats in an election. Term limitations also work to diminish legislative expertise and experience. However, they did not pose an insurmountable barrier to the ambitions of career politicians; nor did term limitations serve to create a true citizens' legislature. Instead, term limitation often resulted in a game of "musical chairs," in which elected officials facing a cap on their service in one office simply sought another office.[91] Term-limited power broker Willie Brown, Speaker of the California House of Representatives, simply refocused his ambitions and won election as mayor of San Francisco.

Smaller communities often have difficulty in finding capable persons willing to undertake the burden of public office. Smaller municipalities that adopted term limitation measures even had trouble finding a sufficient number of candidates willing to serve in public office. In Colorado, over 60 communities repealed or modified their term limitations measures, and dozens of others canceled elections, because of a shortage of candidates.[92]

CONCLUSIONS

In light of recent retreats from the reform model of government, it is easy to lose sight of the gains won by the reform movement. The movement's achievements were substantial; its institutions influence the structure and operations of municipal government and elections throughout the United States.

Cities and counties are indeed better run as a result of reform. The reformers generally cleaned up the election process, protected the integrity of the ballot, and introduced a standard of fairness in the allocation of city jobs and services. Jobs and services were no longer allocated on the basis of whom you knew or for whom you voted. The reformers reduced corruption and brought technical competence to city government.

The reformers brought a new concern for the background, training, and experience of municipal officials. The increased professionalism of city departments upgraded the quality of administration and raised performance standards. Wherever cities continue to suffer from the ills of exaggerated partisanship, corruption, and administrative incompetence, adoption of the first generation of reforms is still in order.

Yet all the achievements of reform came at a cost. The reforms created relatively uncontrollable bureaucratic bastions of power and diluted the power of lower-class and minority voting groups. Depersonalized administration created a new distance between citizens and their government, leading to demands for new reforms that would increase administrative responsiveness.

No one wants to return to the unmitigated partisanship and ills of the unre-formed city. Yet where reform has yielded underperforming, rigid municipal administrations insensitive to the demands of the diversity of a city's citizens, a second generation of reforms is in order. In a number of cities, the second wave of reform is already under way, with a new generation of reformers identifying innovative measures to increase citizen participation and provide for more flexible and effective service delivery.

Neighborhood activists fought for the rights of citizens and participation beyond voting. A new generation of city managers and administrators has been schooled in the importance of citizen participation, decentralization, commu-nity relations, and social equity. Across the country, mayors such as New York's Rudy Giuliani, Los Angeles' Richard Riordan, Philadelphia's Ed Rendell, Indianapolis' Stephen Goldsmith, Milwaukee's John Norquist, and Jersey City's Bret Schundler all made their reputations by pursuing a **New Public Management,** seeking the privatization of municipal services and adopting private-sector performance practices.[93] Decentralization, citizen participation, privatization, and other strategies to increase the effectiveness of service delivery and "consumer" satisfaction are the topics of our next chapters.

NOTES

1. Samuel P. Hays, "The Politics of Reform in Municipal Government in the Progressive Era," *Pacific Northwest Quarterly* 55 (1964): 157–169, reprinted in *Readings in Urban Politics: Past, Present, and Future,* eds. Charles H. Levine and Harlan Hahn (White Plains, NY: Longman, 1984), pp. 54–73.
2. Amy Bridges, *Morning Glories: Municipal Reform in the Southwest* (Princeton, NJ: Princeton University Press, 1997), especially pp. 151–174.
3. Kenneth Finegold, *Experts and Politicians: Reform Challenges to Machine Politics in New York, Cleveland and Chicago* (Princeton, NJ: Princeton University Press, 1995). The story of the changing nature of reform politics in Cleveland is told by Todd Swanstrom, *The Crisis of Growth Politics: Cleveland, Kucinich, and the Challenge of Urban Populism* (Philadelphia: Temple University Press, 1985), pp. 36–43.
4. The quotations in this paragraph are from Swanstrom, *The Crisis of Growth Politics,* pp. 47, 36 and 50, respectively.
5. Melvin G. Holli, *Reform in Detroit: Hazen S. Pingree and Urban Politics* (New York: Oxford University Press, 1969). Finegold, *Experts and Politicians,* sees three types of reform politics: *traditional reform,* emphasizing businesslike efficiency and appealing to native-stock, upper-class interests; *municipal populism,* where mayors such as Cleveland's Tom Johnson appealed to foreign-stock and working-class voters: and *progressive reform,* in which mayors such as New York's John Purroy Mitchel (elected in 1913) combined traditional reform and more populist appeals.
6. Robert L. Lineberry and Edmund P. Fowler, "Reformism and Public Policies in American Cities" *American Political Science Review* 61 (September 1967): 714–715.
7. Susan Welch and Timothy Bledsoe, *Urban Reform and Its Consequences* (Chicago: University of Chicago Press, 1988), p. 101. Also see David Morgan and John Pelissero, "Urban Policy: Does Political Structure Matter?" *American Political Science Review* 74 (December 1980): 999–1006.

8. Christopher L. Warren, John G. Corbett, and John F. Stack, Jr., "Hispanic Ascendancy and Tripartite Politics in Miami," in *Racial Politics in American Cities*, 2nd ed., eds. Rufus P. Browning, Dale Rogers Marshall, and David H. Tabb (New York: Longman, 1990), p. 158.

9. Christopher L. Warren and Dario V. Moreno, "Power Without a Program: Hispanic Incorporation in Miami," in *Racial Politics in American Cities*, 3rd ed., eds. Rufus P. Browning, Dale Rogers Marshall, and David H. Tabb (New York: Longman, 2003), pp. 290–291. The quotation appears on p. 291.

10. Rodney E. Hero, "Hispanics in Urban Government and Politics: Some Findings, Comparisons and Implications," *Western Political Quarterly* 43, 2 (June 1990): 403–414; Rodney E. Hero and Susan E. Clarke, "Latinos, Blacks, and Multiethnic Politics in Denver: Realigning Power and Influence in the Struggle for Equality," in *Racial Politics in American Cities*, 3rd ed., eds. Rufus P. Browning, Dale Rogers Marshall, and David H. Tabb (New York: Longman, 2003), pp. 312–320.

11. Paul Boyer, *Urban Masses and Moral Order in America, 1820–1920* (Cambridge, MA: Harvard University Press, 1978), p. 15 and 18–19.

12. David C. Hammack, *Power and Society: Greater New York at the Turn of the Century* (New York: Columbia University Press, 1982), p. 143.

13. Donald L. Miller, *City of the Century: The Epic of Chicago and the Making of America* (New York: Touchstone/Simon and Schuster, 1996), p. 355 and 416–417.

14. Hammack, *Power and Society*, p. 305. Also see Christine Stansell, *City of Women: Sex and Class in New York, 1789–1860* (Urbana: University of Illinois Press, 1986), pp. 63–75. Alan I. Marcus, *Plague of Strangers: Social Groups and the Origins of City Services in Cincinnati* (Columbus: Ohio State University Press, 1991) presents a detailed exploration of how social reform organizations sought to train "groups of strangers in the ways of American living" (p. 227).

15. Miller, *City of the Century*, p. 459.

16. Boyer, *Urban Masses and Moral Order in America*, pp. 153–158.

17. Miller, *City of the Century*, pp. 419–420 and 460.

18. Philip J. Ethington, *The Public City: The Political Construction of Urban Life in San Francisco, 1850–1900* (Berkeley: University of California Press, 1994), pp. 334–335.

19. Ibid., p. 385. Ethington, pp. 377–387, details the misogynist views of James Phelan, generally considered a San Francisco progressive reformer.

20. Tari Renner and Victor S. DeSantis, "Contemporary Patterns and Trends in Municipal Government Structures," *The Municipal Year Book* 1993 (Washington, DC: International City/County Management Association, 1993), pp. 67–68.

21. See, for instance, Albert K. Karnig, "Black Representation on City Councils: The Impact of District Elections and Socioeconomic Factors," *Urban Affairs Quarterly* 12 (December 1976), especially p. 229. Susan A. MacManus and Charles S. Bullock, "Minorities and Women Do Win at Large!" *National Civic Review* 77 (May/June 1988): 231–244, argue that Hispanics, blacks, and women have done quite well in at-large elections in Austin, Texas. These authors suggest that "the negativism attributed to reform structures may be waning" (pp 242–243) as increases in education have led to more color/gender-blind voting patterns in which whites have shown an increased willingness to support minority candidates.

22. J. Morgan Kousser, "The Undermining of the First Reconstruction: Lessons for the Second," in *Minority Vote Dilution*, ed. Chandler Davidson (Washington, DC: Howard University Press, 1989), pp. 32–33.

23. Chandler Davidson, "Minority Vote Dilution: An Overview," in *Minority Vote Dilution*, p. 11.

24. In *City of Mobile v. Bolden*, 446 U.S. 55, 100 S. Ct. 1490 (1980), the U.S. Supreme Court refused to impose district elections, reasoning that the plaintiffs had failed to prove that the discrimination was intentional. Congress responded to the Court's ruling by passing the Voting Rights Act Amendments of 1982, which eased the standards of evidence required in voting rights cases. With the new law on the books, the Supreme Court in *Thornburg v. Gingles*, 478 U.S. 30 (1986), eliminated the need for plaintiffs to prove discriminatory intent in minority vote dilution cases. See Bernard Grofman, Lisa Handley, and Richard G. Niemi, *Minority Representation and the Quest for Voting Equality* (New York: Cambridge University Press, 1992), chaps. 1 and 2; and Richard Scher, Jon L. Mills, and John J. Hotaling, *Voting Rights and Democracy: The Law and Politics of Districting* (Chicago: Nelson-Hall Publishers, 1997), pp. 60–93.

25. Arturo Vega and John G. Bretting, "The Hollow Promise of Single Member Districts for Mexican Americans? Representation in San Antonio Municipal Politics" (paper presented at the annual meeting of the American Political Science Association, Atlanta, Georgia, September 2–5, 1999). For a more extensive discussion of the importance of district elections to the election of Hispanic council and school board members, see J. L. Polinard, Robert D. Wrinkle, Tomas Longoria, and Norman E. Binder, *Electoral Structure and Urban Policy* (Armonk, NY: M. E. Sharpe, 1994).

26. Timothy B. Krebs and John P. Pelissero, "City Councils" in *Cities, Politics, and Policy*, ed. John P. Pelissero (Washington, DC: CQ Press, 2003), p. 174.

27. Kenneth Meier and Joseph Stewart, Jr., *The Politics of Hispanic Education* (Albany: State University of New York Press, 1991), cited by Hero, *Latinos and the U.S. Political System*, p. 141.

28. Susan Clarke and Rodney Hero, "The Politics of Education Reform in Denver" (paper presented to the annual meeting of the Urban Affairs Association, New Orleans, March 4, 1994).

29. Rodney E. Hero, *Latinos and the U.S. Political System: Two-tiered Pluralism* (Philadelphia: Temple University Press, 1992), pp. 141–142, summarizes the conflicting results of the studies attempting to research the impact of at-large systems on Latino representation.

30. Vega and Bretting, "The Hollow Promise of Single Member Districts for Mexican Americans?" Also see Rodolfo Rosales, *The Illusion of Inclusion: The Untold Political Story of San Antonio* (Austin: University of Texas Press, 1999).

31. Susan A. MacManus, "How to Get More Women in Office: The Perspectives of Local Elected Officials (Mayors and City Councilors)," *Urban Affairs Quarterly* 28 (September 1992); 164–165 and 167 (footnote 2); Susan A. MacManus and Charles S. Bullock III, "Women and Racial/Ethnic Minorities in Mayoral and Council Positions," *Municipal Year Book 1993* (Washington, DC: International City/County Management Association, 1993), p. 78.

32. James W. Button, Kenneth D. Wald, and Barbara A. Rienzo, "The Election of Openly Gay Public Officials in American Communities," *Urban Affairs Review* 35, 2 (November 1999): 188–209, especially 199–203.

33. Gary M. Segura, "Institutions Matter: Local Electoral Laws, Gay and Lesbian Representation, and Coalition Building Across Minority Communities," in *Gays and Lesbians in the Democratic Process*, eds. Ellen D.B. Riggle and Barry L. Tadlock (New York: Columbia University Press, 1999), p. 225.

34. Ibid., p. 230.

35. Steven H. Haeberle, "Exploring the Effects of Single-Member Districts on an Urban Political System: A Case Study of Birmingham, Alabama," *Urban Affairs Review* 33, 2 (November 1997): 287–297.

36. Robert W. Bailey, *Gay Politics, Urban Politics: Identity and Politics in the Urban Setting* (New York: Columbia University Press, 1999), pp. 215–248.

37. Michael V. Haselswerdt, "Voter and Candidate Reaction to District and At Large Elections: Buffalo, New York," *Urban Affairs Quarterly* 20 (September 1984): 31–45; Polinard et al., *Electoral Structure and Urban Policy*, p. 166; Haeberle, "Exploring the Effects of Single-Member Districts."

38. Bridges, *Morning Glories*, p. 200.

39. Renner and DeSantis, "Contemporary Patterns and Trends in Municipal Government Structures," pp. 67–68.

40. Jim Yardley, "In Houston, a 'Nonpartisan' Race Is Anything But," *The New York Times*, November 30, 2001.

41. Rufus P. Browning, Dale Rogers Marshall, and David H. Tabb, *Protest Is Not Enough: The Struggle of Blacks and Hispanics for Equality in Urban Politics* (Berkeley, CA: University of California Press, 1984), pp. 34–36, 201–202, and 241–242.

42. Anthony Downs, *An Economic Theory of Democracy* (New York: Harper & Row, 1957), p. 234. See pp. 207–238 for Downs' discussion as to the "costs" to citizens of becoming informed and how voters thereby delegate analysis and evaluation to interest groups and political parties.

43. Paul Raymond, "The American Voter in a Nonpartisan, Urban Election," *American Politics Quarterly* 20 (April 1992): 247–260.

44. For an overview of the effects of nonpartisan elections, see Susan Welch and Timothy Bledsoe, "The Partisan Consequences of Nonpartisan Elections," *American Journal of Political Science* 30 (February 1986): 128–139.

45. Chris Christoff, "State GOP Flexes the Muscles of Power," *Detroit Free Press*, December 15, 2001.

46. Walter Dean Burnham, *Critical Elections and the Mainsprings of American Politics* (New York: W. W. Norton, 1970), pp. 79–81. For further discussion of the impact of voter registration requirements, see Ronald Hayduk, "The Weight of History: Election Reform during the Progressive Era and Today," in *Democracy's Moment: Reforming America's Political System for the 21st Century*, eds. Ronald Hayduk and Kevin Mattson (Lanham, MD: Rowman and Littlefield, 2002), pp. 29–44.

47. Burnham, *Critical Elections and the Mainsprings of American Politics*, pp. 81–85.

48. Philip J. Ethington, *The Public City: The Political Construction of Urban Life in San Francisco, 1850–1900* (Berkeley: University of California Press, 1994), p. 226.

49. Bridges, "Textbook Municipal Reform," pp. 98–102.

50. Raymond E. Wolfinger and Steven J. Rosenstone, *Who Votes?* (New Haven, CT: Yale University Press, 1980), p. 79.

51. This section's discussion of the Motor Voter law and mail-in ballots relies greatly on Robert J. Waste, *Independent Cities: Rethinking U.S. Urban Policy* (New York: Oxford University Press, 1998), pp. 29–37.

52. Bob Pinzler, "What if they gave an election and nobody came?" (2001). Available at: www.easyreader.hermosawave.net/news2001/0405/localgovernment.asp.

53. Raymond E. Wolfinger, Benjamin Highton, and Megan Mullin, "Between Registering and Voting: How State Laws Affect the Turnout of Young Registrants" (paper presented at the annual meeting of the American Political Science Association, Boston, August 29–September 1, 2002).

54. Bob Richie, Caleb Kleppner, and Terrill Bouricius, "Instant Runoffs: A Cheaper, Fairer, Better Way to Conduct Elections," *National Civic Review,* 89 (Spring 2000): 95–110; Eric C. Olson and Steven Hill, "Big Wins for Democracy: San Francisco and Vermont Vote for Instant Runoff Voting," *National Civic Review* 91 (Summer 2002): 201–204.

55. Renner and DeSantis, "Contemporary Patterns and Trends in Municipal Government Structures," pp. 68–69.

56. David O. Sears and Jack Citrin, *Tax Revolt: Something for Nothing in California* (Cambridge, MA: Harvard University Press, 1982); and Terry Schwadron and Paul Richter, *California and the American Tax Revolt: Proposition 13 Five Years Later (Berkeley: University of California Press, 1984).*

57. Liz McNichol, "The State Fiscal Crisis: Extent, Causes, and Responses," Center on Budget and Policy Priorities, Washington, DC, April 24, 2003. Available at: www.cbpp.org/4-24-03sfp.htm.

58. Richard J. Ellis, *The Democratic Delusion: The Initiative Process in America* (Lawrence: University Press of Kansas, 2002), pp. 49–61. Peter Schrag, *Paradise Lost: California's Experience, America's Future* (New York: W. W. Norton, 1998), pp. 188–256, reviews many of the problems of the initiative processes and the unintended ills that have resulted from the "March of the Plebiscites" in California.

59. Galen Nelson, "Putting Democracy Back Into the Initiative and Referendum," in *Democracy's Moment: Reforming America's Political System for the 21ˢᵗ Century,* eds. Ronald Hayduk and Kevin Mattson (Lanham, MD: Rowman and Littlefield, 2002), p. 159. A balanced assessment of the initiative process is presented by Larry J. Sabato, Howard R. Ernst, and Bruce R. Larson, eds., *Dangerous Democracy? The Battle Over Ballot Initiatives in America* (Lanham, MD: Rowman and Littlefield, 2001).

60. Roger W. Caves, *Land Use Planning: The Ballot Box Revolution,* Sage Library of Social Research Volume 187 (Newbury Park, CA: Sage Publications, 1992), and Patrick Sweeney, "Minneapolis Residents Cap Stadium Spending," (St. Paul, MN) *Pioneer Press,* November 5, 1997. For a review of the various ballot measures limiting growth in San Francisco, see Richard Edward DeLeon, *Left Coast City: Progressive Politics in San Francisco, 1975–91* (Lawrence: University of Kansas Press, 1992).

61. Many of the details concerning local recall elections were obtained from Joseph F. Zimmerman, *The Recall: Tribunal of the People* (Westport, CT: Praeger, 1997), pp. 97–130.

62. Daniel Weintraub, "The Recall's a Democratic Revolt Against Ruling Elites," *The Sacramento Bee,* July 6, 2003; Mark Baldassare, "The Role of Public Opinion on the California Governor's Recall in 2003: Populism, Partisanship, and Direct Democracy," *American Politics Research* 22 (2005): 163–186; Brian K. Arbour and Danny Hayes, "Voter Turnout in the California Recall: Where Did the Increase Come From?" *American Politics Research* 22 (2005): 187–215.

63. Pierre Clavel, *The Progressive City: Planning and Participation 1969–84* (New Brunswick, NJ: Rutgers University Press, 1986); and Norman Krumholz and John Forester, *Making Equity Planning Work: Leadership in the Public Sector* (Philadelphia: Temple University Press, 1990).

64. Philip J. Trounstine and Terry Christensen, *Movers and Shakers: The Study of Community Power* (New York: St. Martin's Press, 1982). Also see Amy Bridges, "Winning the West to Municipal Reform," *Urban Affairs Quarterly* 27 (June 1992): 494–518; and Bridges, *Morning Glories.*

65. Bridges, "Textbook Municipal Reform," p. 110.

66. Bridges, *Morning Glories,* p. 29.

67. The quotations are from Theodore Lowi, "Machine Politics-Old and New," *Public Interest* 9 (Fall 1967): 86–87.

68. Michael N. Danielson and Jameson W. Doig, *New York: The Politics of Urban and Regional Development* (Berkeley: University of California Press, 1982), p. 316–321. Also see Eric Darton, *Divided We Stand: A Biography of New York City's World Trade Center* (New York: Basic Books, 2001).

69. Lowi, "Machine Politics-Old and New," p. 85.

70. This observation, and much of this chapter section, are based on William J. Grimshaw, "Race and Reform: Minority Empowerment and the White Liberal Question" (paper presented at the annual meeting of the American Political Science Association, Chicago, September 2–5, 1993).

71. William J. Grimshaw, *Bitter Fruit: Black Politics and the Chicago Machine,* 1931–91 (Chicago: University of Chicago Press, 1992), pp. 186–188.

72. Lynette Clemetson, "Mayor Turns U.S. Inquiry to Campaign Advantage," *The New York Times,* October 31, 2003.

73. Browning, Marshall, and Tabb, *Protest Is Not Enough,* pp. 201–202.

74. John Clayton Thomas, *Between Citizen and City: Neighborhood Organizations and Urban Politics in Cincinnati* (Lawrence: University of Kansas Press, 1986), p. 78.

75. Gerald Benjamin and Frank I. Mauro, "The Reemergence of Municipal Reform," in *Restructuring New York City Government: The Reemergence of Municipal Reform,* eds. Frank I. Mauro and Gerald Benjamin, *Proceedings of the Academy of Political Science* (1989): 11. Also see Douglas Muzzio and Tim Tompkins, "On the Size of the City Council," pp. 83–96 in the same volume.

76. James H. Svara, "The Model City and County Charters: Innovation and Tradition in the Reform Movement" *Public Administration Review* 50 (November/December 1990): 688–692.

77. Janine DeFao, "Oakland Studies Stronger Mayor Ballot Measure," *San Francisco Chronicle,* July 11, 2003.

78. Rob Gurwitt, "Nobody in Charge," *Governing* (September 1997). See Gurwitt for the details of the criticisms that were made of old-style reformed institutions in Kansas City, Cincinnati, and Dallas.

79. Gurwitt, "Nobody in Charge."

80. Raphael J. Sonenshein, "Memo to the Police Commission: Govern Now and Spin Later," *Los Angeles Times,* December 10, 2001.

81. James H. Svara, "Do We Still Need Model Charters? The Meaning and Relevance of Reform in the Twenty-First Century," *National Civic Review* 90 (Spring 2001): 19–33.

82. Evelyn Larrubia, "Supervisors' Decisions Made Mostly Behind Closed Doors," *Los Angeles Times,* March 26, 2002.

83. Carl Castillo and Mike McGrath, "Localism and Reform: The Benefits of Political Diversity," *National Civic Review* 90 (Summer 2001): 140–142.

84. For a more detailed discussion as to how these laws work, see Paul Ryan, "Beyond BCRA: Cutting-Edge Campaign Finance Reform at the Local Government Level," *National Civic Review* 92 (Spring 2003): 3–18.

85. Los Angeles City Ethics *Commission, Campaign Finance Reform in Los Angeles: Lessons from the 2001 City Elections,* Executive Summary, October 2001, p. 3. Available at: http://ethics.lacity.org/news.cfm.

86. "Campaign Finance Chicanery" (editorial), *The New York Times,* October 13, 1993.

87. Joyce Purnick, "Koch to Limit Contributions in Race," *The New York Times*, June 21, 1988.

88. U.S. Term Limits Organization, "U.S. Term Limits," Washington, DC (1998). Available at: www.free-market.net/partners/u/ustl.html.

89. Mark P. Petracca and Karen Moore O'Brien, "Municipal Term Limits in Orange County, California," *National Civic Review* (Spring-Summer 1994): 192–193.

90. Victor S. DeSantis and Tari Renner, "Term Limits and Turnover Among Local Officials," in *Municipal Year Book 1994* (Washington, DC: International City/County Management Association, 1994), pp. 36–42. Also see Alan Ehrenhalt, "If Term Limits Are the Answer, What's the Question? They Are Designed to Solve a Problem that May No Longer Exist." *Governing* (May 1994): 7–8.

91. Peter I. Haas, "Evaluating Term Limits for City Councils: Lessons from San Jose" (paper presented at the annual meeting of the American Political Science Association, San Francisco, August 28–September 1, 1996); John David Rausch, "Testing Legislative Term Limitations: The San Mateo Board of County Supervisors as Laboratory," *National Civic Review* 82 (Spring 1993): 149–156.

92. Peggy Lowe and Ellen Miller, "Term Limits Hurt Small Towns," *Rocky Mountain News*, December 2, 2002. Available at: www.msnbc.com/local/rmn/DRMN_1581934.asp?cp1=1.

93. See, for instance, Lynne A. Weikart, "The Giuliani Administration and the New Public Management in New York City," *Urban Affairs Review* 36 (January 2001): 359–381.

CITIZEN PARTICIPATION AND DECENTRALIZATION

The reform movement placed decision-making power in the hands of professionally trained administrators. These officials, however, did not always pursue policies that were responsive to all citizens and neighborhoods. In the middle of the twentieth century, racial minorities were especially vocal in charging that

their needs were being ignored by white middle-class–dominated police departments, public school systems, and welfare agencies. City officials pursued urban renewal projects and new highway connector projects that destroyed neighborhoods and displaced people from their homes.

Soon, other citizen groups joined the chorus, criticizing government for being overly bureaucratized, indifferent, and remote. Environmentalists protested new development projects that consumed green space and promoted sprawl. Suburbanites worried about the impact of growth on traffic congestion and school overcrowding. Middle-class parents sought to make school systems more responsive to their concerns. Homeowners fought to put a lid on rising taxes.[1]

A virtual citizen participation and bureaucratic decentralization revolution took place. Like private business firms, public sector agencies came to see the benefits of structuring more flexible organizations responsive to the wishes of the citizenry, their customers. Citizen participation and administrative decentralization became permanent institutionalized features of the urban political landscape. Yet as we shall see, participatory mechanisms face severe limitations when it comes to redistributing power in the metropolis.

CITIZEN PARTICIPATION: CLASSICAL THEORY AND TODAY

The idea of citizen participation is as old as democracy itself. The ancient Greek city-states emphasized the virtue of having all citizens participate in decision making. In the city of Corinth, when the senate met, any citizen of the city could come forward and propose a piece of legislation. If it passed that same day, the citizen who proposed the bill would be rewarded with a sumptuous banquet in his honor, including food, drink, and entertainment. However, as the story has it, if the proposed piece of legislation failed to pass the senate, the person proposing it was brought to the public square, where one of his hands was chopped off. Aside from its obvious cruelty, this unique system can also be seen as having two benefits: It markedly improved the quality of the legislation that was introduced, and it drastically reduced the amount of legislation the senate had to consider.

The United States is too large, in terms of both population and geography, to practice the classic, Greek-style form of **direct democracy** (also called **primary democracy** or **face-to-face democracy**). Instead, the United States has a **republican form of government,** in which elected representatives speak and vote for their constituents.

Primary or face-to-face democracy is practiced only in relatively small political jurisdictions, most notably in New England **town hall meetings,** at which the collective voice of the citizens can provide an alternative to representative processes that are too often dominated by well-organized interest groups.[2] In cities and suburbs of any substantial size, neighborhood organizations offer the best possibility for face-to-face citizen interaction.

In essence, **citizen participation** requires that citizens be given enough information so that they can participate in initial decisions on the allocation of resources that affect their lives.[3] Sherry Arnstein goes further, defining citizen participation as:

> a categorical term for citizen power. It is the redistribution of power that enables the have-not citizens, presently excluded from the political and economic processes, to be deliberately included in the future. It is the strategy by which the have-nots join in determining how information is shared, goals and policies are set, tax resources are allocated, programs are operated, and benefits like contract and patronage are parceled out. In short, it is the means by which they can induce significant societal reform which enables them to share in the benefits of the affluent society.[4]

Suburban residents, too, value participatory mechanisms and the opportunities they allow members of the community to shape the character of the local schools and to influence the direction of local taxing, growth, and development.

THE ROOTS OF CITIZEN PARTICIPATION PROGRAMS: THE WAR ON POVERTY AND THE FEDERAL ROLE

Urban renewal and a few other federal programs in the 1950s had perfunctory requirements for citizen participation and consultation. Yet the new emphasis on citizen participation did not really begin until the 1960s with Lyndon Johnson's War on Poverty and its goal of empowering poor people. The Economic Opportunity Act created the **Community Action Program (CAP),** which required the **maximum feasible participation** of the poor in locally guided antipoverty programs. The urban riots of the 1960s served to reinforce the urgency of involving the poor themselves in shaping the programs that affected their lives.

Disadvantaged urban residents saw citizen participation as a vehicle for redistributing power and authority in the city. But bureaucrats and elected officials, who often did not want to redistribute power, saw citizen participation programs as something that had to be undertaken only to the extent necessary to satisfy federal guidelines and appease local communities.

Chicago Mayor Richard J. Daley and mayors around the country objected that federal antipoverty programs were helping local activists challenge the decisions of duly elected municipal officials. Congress responded by passing the **Green Amendment** (named after Congresswoman Edith Green of Oregon), giving local government officials the option of taking control of community action agencies. In Chicago, Daley used the program as a new source of patronage to reward his allies. He undermined citizen participation, shutting out those community activists who were critical of the city's performance.[5]

Attempts to increase citizen participation often proved quite frustrating. The formal mechanisms for involving citizens did not meet even the most minimal expectations. The voting turnouts for elections to community action boards were dismal: Philadelphia (2.7 percent), Los Angeles (0.7 percent), Boston (2.4 percent), Cleveland (4.2 percent), and Kansas City (5.0 percent).[6] Community advocates argued that there was little reason for residents to participate in elections when city officials refused to devolve meaningful decision-making responsibility to neighborhood institutions.

The 1970s saw a virtual explosion of federal requirements for citizen participation. In program after program, federal aid legislation required state and local agencies to "hold hearings," "involve citizens," or "seek consultation with affected parties." Requirements for citizen participation were written into a wide range of federal legislation, including the Coastal Zone Management Act, the Federal Water Pollution Control Act, the Regional Development Act (1975), and the Resource Conservation and Recovery Act, to name only a few. By the late 1970s, 155 of the nearly 500 federal grant programs available to state and local governments required some form of citizen participation; these 155 programs accounted for over 80 percent of federal grant expenditures in fiscal year 1977.[7] The General Revenue Sharing Act required some 39,000 units of local government to inform citizens, hold open public meetings, or otherwise involve citizens in the decisions on how to spend the community's shared revenues.

By the latter part of the twentieth century, citizen participation had become more routinized, expected, and a less conflictual part of the governmental process. The Ronald Reagan administration, however, saw the federal regulations for citizen participation as unnecessary, expensive, and even undemocratic. Reagan sought to limit the burden that federal "red tape" imposed on local elected officials, the duly chosen representatives of local populations. Reagan believed that citizen participation requirements unfairly helped liberal activist groups challenge the decisions that were properly made by local elected officials.

Despite the Reagan assault, the citizen participation revolution continued. Citizen participation was just too valuable an idea. A Democratic-controlled Congress also kept in place most of the participatory requirements of federal aid programs.

As community organizations became regular participants in local politics, the style of local participation began to change. Grassroots and nonprofit groups adopted a negotiations approach in place of the conflict-oriented tactics of the 1960s.

In the 1990s, the Clinton Administration's goal of "reinventing government" served as a further impetus to the development of local—not just federal—strategies of participation and consumerism. In an effort to improve the performance of government, local executives sought to make citizen involvement part of agency performance measurement.[8] But their efforts were often met by the opposition of the police department, municipal labor unions, and other powerful constituencies.

THE LEVELS OF CITIZEN PARTICIPATION

The concept of citizen participation covers a wide range of activities, running along a continuum from voting to violence. Letter writing, neighborhood organizing, testifying before the city council, lobbying, picketing, nonviolent demonstrations, and sit-ins and obstructionist tactics are all variants of citizen participation.

Sherry Arnstein has attempted to sort out the various meanings of the concept according to an eight-rung **ladder of citizen participation** (see Figure 8-1). She categorizes the bottom two rungs of the ladder, *manipulation* and *therapy*,

■ FIGURE 8–1

EIGHT RUNGS ON A LADDER OF CITIZEN PARTICIPATION

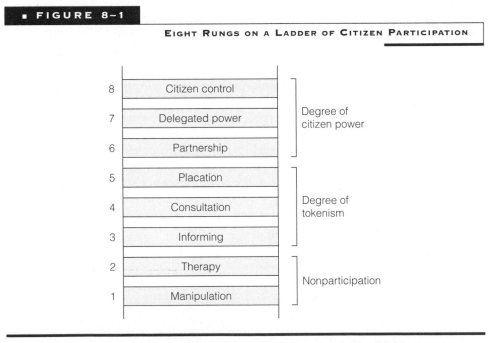

SOURCE: Sherry R. Arnstein, "A Ladder of Citizen Participation," *Journal of the American Institute of Planners* 35 (July 1969): 217. Reprinted with permission from the *Journal of the American Planning Association,* copyright July 1969 by the American Planning Association.

as **nonparticipation.** The middle three rungs indicate degrees of **tokenism,** which she labels *informing, consultation,* and *placation.* The top three rungs indicate various degrees of genuine citizen power, including *partnership, delegated power;* and *citizen control:*[9]

1. Under **manipulation,** citizens are appointed to advisory boards and committees where they are indoctrinated into accepting the rationale behind the local officials' plans of action. Oftentimes citizen participation mechanism are designed as instruments of cooptation, where citizens are brought into the decision-making process but are denied any real decision-making power; instead, they are given only the appearance or rituals of participation.

2. In **therapy,** powerlessness is seen to be synonymous with an illness. Citizens are brought together to discuss ways of altering their behavior instead of changing the behavior of public officials whose actions have helped to cause the problem at hand. Public-housing tenant meetings that focus solely on modifying tenants' behavior and attitudes are a good example of this quite limited conceptualization of citizen participation.

3. Under **informing,** citizens are made aware of program goals and recipients' rights, responsibilities, and options in a one-way flow of information from government officials to citizens. A governmental agency may merely inform the audience by holding a "dog and pony" show that allows little genuine audience participation. Oftentimes, the information is presented too late in the policy-making process to allow citizens an effective response; there is no real prospect for bargaining or compromise.

4. **Consultation** can be an important component of citizen participation. Citizen opinions are solicited through surveys, hearings, and neighborhood meetings. However, if no process is established for incorporating these views into policy decisions, consultation may prove superficial. Agencies may consult but not really listen to citizens' desires that conflict with an agency's priorities.

5. Under **placation,** a number of community residents are selected to sit on police, education, housing, health, and planning boards. However, these representatives are not necessarily accountable to their constituents. Few in number, these citizen representatives are likely to be outvoted by other board members on questions of substance.

6. Beginning with **partnership,** a city moves to the more significant forms of citizen participation. Under partnership, power is shared among citizens and local officials. Neither partner can act or alter arrangements without the other. In effect, both citizens and administrators possess a mutual veto over proposed actions. One form that a partnership can take is to give citizens and city officials equal representation on a decision-making board, allowing, for instance, school officials and

members of the community an equal say in the recruitment of a new school principal.

7. Under **delegated power,** citizen boards have the real authority to make certain decisions. They possess a degree of autonomy in certain specified program areas. Chicago's experiment with school decentralization was a short-lived attempt to give citizen boards specified budgetary and personnel powers. The experiment was ended when the citizen boards found themselves enmeshed in controversy and proved incapable of turning around the performance of Chicago's schools. The power that the government had delegated to the community boards was later withdrawn.

8. Finally, under **citizen control,** residents exercise final authority over a program, including making the ultimate decisions that affect how the program is to be run. In a number of cities, **neighborhood development corporations** can be seen as an important means of citizen control over funding decisions and neighborhood development projects.

The Arnstein typology shows that not all forms of participation entail real power sharing. Bureaucrats and city officials are generally more willing to utilize those forms of participation toward the bottom of the ladder. They are willing to give citizens only limited access and the illusion of decision-making power. Bureaucrats often see citizen participation mechanisms as a means of leading citizens to accept an agency's goals and plans. In many cities, the War on Poverty's community action agencies neutralized potential critics by giving activist citizens leadership positions on community boards or jobs with local action agencies. In other cities, however, neighborhood leaders chose to remain outside the government so that they would not be compromised in their efforts to represent the views of community residents.

Arnstein's ladder can be used to help evaluate the success of such innovations as community policing. **Community policing** seeks to forge a new partnership between neighborhoods and the police; citizens play a heightened role in helping to set police priorities. In Chicago, community policing entails monthly **beat meetings** at which the "cop on the beat" and neighborhood residents review problems and identify solutions. The goal, applying Arnstein's model, is to create a genuine police-community *partnership* with joint decision making. Too often, however, the beat meetings fell short of establishing a genuine partnership. In some instances, police officers used the meetings to build the public's support for traditional police practices, a form of participation that falls under the rubric of *cooptation* and *manipulation*. In other cases, officers were content with *informing* the public of police practices and had no real intent of making changes in response to audience concerns. In some instances, the beat officers could not even capably answer the public's questions, as cases had been handed off to detectives who were not responsible to district commanders.[10]

Arnstein's ladder is rooted in the experiences of the conflict-oriented 1960s; it portrays citizens and bureaucrats as engaged in a struggle over power. But might bureaucrats and citizens be willing to work cooperatively in an effort to improve service delivery? A new generation of community activists has come to emphasize joint problem solving and effective service provision rather than confrontation. In the contemporary city, citizen participation often emphasizes education, information, consultation, feedback, joint planning, and mediation.[11]

CITIZEN PARTICIPATION: WHO IS SERVED? WHO PARTICIPATES?

Dayton (Ohio), Indianapolis, Minneapolis, St. Paul, Richmond (Virginia), Birmingham (Alabama), San Antonio, Phoenix, Portland (Oregon), and Santa Clarita (California) are all cities that have been lauded for their extensive citizen participation efforts.[12] New York City similarly has an extensive structure for participatory involvement, including 59 community boards focused on local land use and service delivery.

But who really participates in such programs? Do citizen participation mechanisms give a voice to the average citizen and to the poor? Or do better-off citizens take advantage of the opportunities offered by the new participatory processes? A quick review of the evolution of participatory programs in New York, Minneapolis, and elsewhere will help answer these questions.

New York's community board system has evolved greatly over time. Overall, community boards possess advisory powers and can be seen as a moderate form of decentralization.[13] The community boards give citizens influence in decisions affecting land use, the city budget, and service delivery; board recommendations have been seriously considered by other city agencies. Activist community boards, for instance, have been able to insist that developers scale back a project's size, rehabilitate a local subway station, or include increased parking or other amenities in their plans in exchange for a positive board vote.

Yet participation in such boards can also be seen as limited and, to a great extent, conservative. In Minneapolis as well as New York, community groups were largely pragmatic actors focused on neighborhood improvements; they did not constitute a larger social movement that challenged the city's overall priorities.[14] One study of New York's community board system reveals that "Poor and minority community districts do not fare as well as middle-class, predominantly white communities in securing their local budget priorities."[15]

Cities with extensive citizen participation efforts also tend to be those cities that are making extensive efforts to attract or retain geographically mobile, middle-class and upscale residents. Participatory efforts have become part of municipal strategy designed to attract and retain citizens who contribute to a city's tax base.[16]

In Minneapolis, community participation mechanisms were often dominated by white, middle-income homeowners. In Minneapolis as well as New York, citizen participation has taken on a middle-class character; participatory efforts have been used to promote concerns for service provision and preserving a neighborhood's attractiveness.[17]

Middle-class groups have clearly seized the new opportunities for influence offered by participatory mechanisms. As a result, citizen participation efforts often suffer from a pattern of class bias. Yet at times, participatory mechanisms can increase decision-making opportunities for the poor.

In Chicago, the residents of middle-class and highly educated neighborhoods took advantage of the opportunity to attend regular beat meetings offered by community policing. Yet attendance rates at beat meetings were the highest in African-American neighborhoods; attendance was also marginally higher in the poorer areas of the city. The salience of the gang and crime problems led the residents of impoverished neighborhoods to seize the opportunity to demand action.[18]

THE CHANGING STYLE OF CITIZEN PARTICIPATION: FROM CONFLICT TO COOPERATION

As the citizen participation movement matured, citizen groups moved away from the confrontational politics of the 1960s to a more consensual approach designed to build broad coalitions for housing construction, new economic development, and the provision of community social services.[19] The earlier politics of conflict was typified by the organizing approach of social activist Saul Alinsky and the Industrial Areas Foundation (IAF). But, as we shall see, a great many Alinsky groups now give their attention to the management of community services, not just to political protest.

The **Alinsky-style/IAF community organizing model** is rooted in the view that conflict and confrontation are essential parts of democracy. According to Alinsky, ordinary citizens need to build their own power resources in order to have control of their own destinies. Alinsky saw society as divided into distinct classes, each pursuing its own self-interests. The "haves" of American society will not voluntarily cede their privileges to the "have-nots" and "have-little-want-mores." Nor can the have-nots depend on alliances with outsiders who do not feel a community's pain and who will too often abandon or "sell out" a community in the middle of an intense struggle.[20]

The organizer—the person who seeks to mobilize the political force inherent in a community—works with a community's indigenous or native leaders to identify a neighborhood's problems. Religious congregations with their "social connectedness" provide a base of Alinsky/IAF-style organizing. Faith-based congregations help to give a new organizer, oftentimes an outsider, legitimacy in the local community; they also help pay his or her salary. IAF organizing around churches has been especially important in Hispanic communities, with their strong Catholic faith tradition, in Texas and the American Southwest.[21]

The Alinsky-style organizer pursues change by uncovering the source of grievances in a community. After uncovering grievances, the organizer then seeks to rub wounds raw, mobilizing the community to attack the target of the protest action. The organizer polarizes and freezes the target of the protest action, allowing the target no excuses or ability to shift the blame for inaction to others. The organizer seeks a quick victory that will serve to mobilize followers on to greater struggle. The organizer skillfully chooses tactics that will protect the organization's members while disorienting and intimidating the target of the action.

The Woodlawn Organization (TWO) in Chicago is only one of the many notable community organizations that used Alinsky-style tactics in the 1960s to take on a number of targets. TWO dramatically publicized which merchants were shortchanging neighborhood residents, forcing change through targeted boycotts. TWO also transported ghetto residents downtown to browse in major department stores, threatening to scare off middle-class customers, ultimately convincing store managers to change hiring and promotion policies. TWO fought the expansion of the University of Chicago, an expansion that threatened to displace community residents.[22]

By the 1970s, TWO shifted its focus, as captured in its new slogan "From Protest to Programs." TWO, like numerous other IAF-style organizations, became less concerned with protest activities and more concerned with providing services that would make real and immediate improvements in the daily life of community residents, for example, by building low-income housing and by running day-care centers, dental clinics, and other neighborhood programs.[23] In the decades that followed, protest organizations across the nation gave way to a new style of **governing nonprofits,** community groups that adopted a more cooperative approach aimed at building working relationships with government, business, and other nonprofit groups in order to obtain the resources to run community-based programs.[24]

By the end of the twentieth century, even groups schooled in the Alinsky/IAF methods began to refine their approach, giving less emphasis to confrontation and new emphasis to running programs that could provide

CORBIS

African-American women of the Chicago Housing Authority (CHA) Tenant Patrol escort schoolchildren on the elevator at the Ida Wells Housing Project which is threatened by gangs.

better housing and community services. As community organizations gave a new emphasis toward the provision of housing, health care, and other services of concern to poor women and their children, women assumed an even greater role in community organizations. (See "Women and the Fight for Affordable Housing" below.) Community organizing lost some of the "macho" posturing that had characterized the style of an earlier generation of labor and community organizers trained in the Alinsky/IAF tradition.

WOMEN AND THE FIGHT FOR AFFORDABLE HOUSING

In Chicago and many other cities, women have played a prominent role as tenant organizers in low- and moderate-income buildings. Women were especially visible in the fight to preserve housing affordability.

Why have women been so prominent as housing organizers? First, as poverty in the United States is a female-related condition, female-headed households make up a large portion of the population in subsidized housing. Second, women's activity in housing issues is also rooted in the traditional domain that women have been accorded as managers of the family and household sphere.

In the ethnically diverse Uptown area of Chicago in the 1980s, landlords sought to take advantage of an early buyout provision of their HUD-subsidized mortgages. The buyout would have allowed landlords to evict large numbers of low- and moderate-income tenants from HUD-subsidized housing units, buildings that could then be renovated and leased to new tenants at much higher rents. Cynthia Reed, the president of Uptown's Sheridan-Gunnison Tenants' Association, explained her involvement as a matter of self-interest. Low-income, single mothers raising children have little real alternative in their search for quality housing. They must battle to preserve their subsidized homes, even if it means that they have less time for work and their children. Women played dominant roles on tenant governing boards and committees in the fight for affordable housing.

In the Carmine Marine building in Chicago's Uptown neighborhood, the fight was led by Kathy Osberger, who had previously been a community organizer in the Bronx for about 10 years. She organized her neighbors to fight announced rent increases. They also fought the sale of the building to a new landlord and forced their existing landlord to hire a new management company. The Carmine Marine Tenants' Association eventually succeeded in convincing HUD to allow the tenants themselves to purchase the building, the first such tenant purchase in the nation. The tenants not only succeeded in their protest; they made the transition to resident ownership and building management.

In Chicago, the role of gender in the fight for affordable housing seems to vary by nationality. In the African-American community, women played the dominant leadership role. Among Nigerians, Ethiopians, Pakistanis, and

continued

WOMEN AND THE FIGHT FOR AFFORDABLE HOUSING (CONT.)

Indians, in contrast, men were more likely to get involved. Women from the Middle East, too, played a more restrained role in the housing struggles.

Despite the variations by race and ethnicity, the larger pattern is still worth noting: women—especially poorer women—are often the foot soldiers and the leaders in grassroots organizations. Larry Bennett has observed that "women are important participants of every neighborhood organization. . . . And within the literature of women's studies, it is axiomatic that political work directed at neighborhood-, housing-, and school-related issues represents a field where women, for generations, have had a conspicuous impact." As Bennett concludes, "gender, far more than social class and race/ethnicity, structures grassroots activism."

Sources: Philip Nyden and Joan Adams, *Saving Our Homes: The Lessons of Community Struggles to Preserve Affordable Housing in Chicago's Uptown*, a report completed by researchers at Loyola University of Chicago in collaboration with Organization of the Northeast, Chicago, April 1996. The quotations are from Larry Bennett, *Neighborhood Politics: Chicago and Sheffield* (New York: Garland Publishing, 1997), p. 246.

In New York's South Bronx, the Banana Kelly Community Improvement Association (named for the curved block on Kelly Street) similarly assumed new management and service responsibilities when it acquired distressed properties and ran low-income housing cooperatives. Banana Kelly had earlier earned a reputation for railing against landlords. Beginning in the late 1970s, however, the association shifted its emphasis from protest to housing management, rehabbing hundreds of units of affordable housing and, in effect, becoming the landlord who must collect overdue rents and somehow find the money for necessary repairs.[25]

Baltimoreans United in Leadership Development (BUILD) is another community-based organization in the Alinsky tradition that has sought to balance protest activities with a new service orientation. With the core of its membership in 45 to 50 churches in Baltimore's African-American community, BUILD reinvigorated local black activism and empowered the poor. BUILD used Alinsky-style confrontation tactics to fight bank redlining and unfair auto insurance rates. BUILD also organized mass membership meetings to pressure mayoral and council candidates into making important policy commitments.

As BUILD matured, it shifted much of its attention to education and human resource programs. BUILD even fashioned a cooperative working relationship with the Greater Baltimore Committee, an association of 1,000 of the city's top business leaders. BUILD's leaders came to recognize the advantages of establishing partnerships with members of the business community who possessed the ability to fund job training programs and who could promise jobs to high-school graduates with good attendance records and good grades. BUILD worked with private sector actors, parents, and volunteers to establish a "Child First Authority" to provide extended-day programs, homework assistance, and a safe after-school environment. A 1,000-person BUILD membership meeting led Mayor Kurt Schmoke to promise that he would commit $1.5 million to the Child First Authority; Art Modell, the owner of the Baltimore Ravens football team, promised another $500,000. Another mass membership meeting led Maryland Governor Parris Glendening to make a similar commitment.[26]

The Alinsky/IAF organizing approach has been of invaluable assistance in enabling poor people to fight for meaningful improvements in their lives. Yet, while not abandoning protests, community organizations have moved beyond confrontation. Urban black churches, as typified by the First African Methodist Episcopal (FAME) Church in Los Angeles, have chosen to go beyond protest activities for the sake of partnering with government agencies in the delivery of services to the poor.[27]

In Dayton, Birmingham, Portland (Oregon), and St. Paul, citizen organizations have moved beyond the narrow neighborhood or localist focus that dominated much of Alinsky/IAF organizing. Neighborhood organizations in these cities have gotten involved in electoral politics and have entered city hall, while maintaining a cautious attitude from fear of being coopted by the city power structure.[28]

In an age of globalization, a new generation of activists sees the need for organizing efforts that transcend local borders. These critics see Alinsky's focus as too place-oriented, too rooted in neighborhood and individual self-interest to confront decisions made outside the community that help to produce gentrification, the disappearance of high-wage manufacturing jobs, and other urban inequalities. Organizing efforts, such as the 1999 demonstrations against the World Trade Organization meeting in Seattle, are an attempt to surmount self-interest and build a collective challenge to global decision makers across local boundaries.[29] Whether such protests against globalization produce more than "noise" and bring real benefits to the lives of the poor, as Alinsky-style organizing has done, remains to be seen.

COMMUNITY GROUPS IN A CHANGED SUNBELT AND PACIFIC NORTHWEST

Sunbelt politics was once relatively quiescent. More recent years, however, have seen the emergence of neighborhood organizations willing to challenge the priorities of traditional governing elites. In a number of cities, community groups have used the tools of direct democracy to check the growth initiatives of government officials.[30]

In Seattle and other communities in the Pacific northwest, grassroots activism has come to dominate local politics, with citizens pointing to the adverse impact of continued growth on quality-of-life and environmental-protection concerns. Critics, in turn, charge that **NIMBY** ("not in my backyard") activists overstate the harm brought by new growth, and that their fervent opposition can lead to paralysis in the vital arena of economic development.[31]

The Phoenix and Seattle examples point to the middle-class sources of citizen activism in many Sunbelt communities, where community groups have pressed for environmentalism, good government, and homeowner concerns. In Tucson, college-educated professionals formed a neighborhood network in an effort to ward off the "LosAngelization" of Tucson.[32]

The Southwest's growing minority population has also led to a new neighborhood activism. In El Paso, a city with a population that is two-thirds Hispanic, EPISO (the El Paso Interreligious Sponsoring Organization) adopted an activist, church-sponsored, grassroots, Alinsky-style approach to organizing.[33]

In San Antonio, the competing agendas of middle-class citizen groups and poorer minority (especially Latino) groups have at times clashed.[34] San Antonio is a divided city, with a relatively well-off, predominantly Anglo north side and a less prosperous, predominantly Hispanic west side. In 1974, flood runoff from the Anglo neighborhoods inundated large sections of the poor, flat, west side. Incensed, over twenty neighborhood groups formed a federation, **Communities Organized for Public Services (COPS),** to protest the underprovision of infrastructure and other services in the Mexican sections of town. Building on the organizational base provided by local churches, COPS relied on mass "accountability meetings" to pressure public officials. COPS used its organizing and electoral power to steer community development spending toward affordable housing, health clinics, and, in one case, away from the purchase of a golf course. COPS even clashed publicly with Mayor Henry Cisneros, a Mexican American, over his plans to build a 65,000-seat domed stadium and convention center. COPS argued that the project promised benefits to wealthy business executives while imposing new taxes on poorer San Antonians. The city, however, built the Alamodome despite COPS' opposition.[35]

On San Antonio's north side, middle-class and environmentalist groups mobilized in efforts to block new suburban development. The Aquifer Protection Association (APA) was organized to stop the construction of a new shopping mall over the recharge zone of the city's groundwater supply. Initially, COPS kept its distance from APA, as citizens in the wealthier parts of San Antonio had opposed increased public spending for improvements in the poorer sections of the city. Eventually, though, COPS decided to join the fight, hoping that limits imposed on suburban development would serve to channel investment and jobs back to the city's downtown.

COPS, too, has shifted its style over the years as the organization gained clout through voter registration drives and new acceptance at the bargaining table. Previously regarded as a protest group, the San Antonio city council has honored COPS for its years of public service.[36]

In Houston, The Metropolitan Organization (TMO) similarly used the pressure of a mass membership "accountability meeting" to convince Mayor Kathryn Whitmire to sign a compact with the organization. Whitmire agreed to meet with TMO's leadership once a month and to attend future TMO mass meetings. On the whole, though, TMO was less effective in Houston than COPS was in San Antonio. Minorities were a smaller part of Houston's population. Tensions among African Americans, Hispanics, and poor whites in Houston have also acted to impede the development of a strong grassroots coalition.

In recent years, TMO, COPS, EPISO, and other Alinsky-style organizations—including Austin Interfaith and the Allied Communities of Tarrant in Forth Worth)—have sought to increase parental involvement in school decision making. These groups have increasingly adopted such consensual tactics as organizing a "Walk for Success." Still, these groups are capable of organizing more confrontational actions as the situation requires.[37]

In the poor and gang-ridden neighborhood of East Los Angeles, a schism has developed between more explicitly political community groups and those community organizations that have chosen to gain a greater involvement in neighborhood service delivery. Neighborhood political activists formed the United Neighborhood Organization (UNO), a church-sponsored, Alinsky-style organization, in response to their sense that a more established group, The East Los Angeles Community Union (TELACU), had abandoned its citizen participation roots. TELACU, a community development corporation, depended on professional and technocratic skills in building contacts with funding agencies. Extensive citizen participation served to slow down and jeopardize the search for new program funds. As one TELACU official said, "Who cares about an organization that doesn't maximize citizen participation if in the end the job gets done?"[38]

UNO emerged after Bishop Juan Arzube visited San Antonio in 1975 to observe how COPS used mass meetings to pressure city council members into action. Ernesto Cortes, who had put together COPS, was hired as UNO's principal organizer. Cortes built his new Los Angeles group on the foundation of its citizens' Hispanic cultural heritage, including their attachments to the church. Home-to-home interviews by UNO organizers led the organization to discover the immense outrage over the exorbitant automobile insurance rates that East Los Angeles residents had been paying as a result of redlining by auto insurance companies. After UNO secured a 37-percent reduction in auto insurance rates, the organization turned its attention to the problems of education, housing, transportation, and gang violence.

What does a review of the activities of these community groups reveal? Primarily, it demonstrates the vitality of community groups in the Sunbelt and how the changing demographics of the region have begun to reshape the politics of many Sunbelt cities. Community organizations have relied on both conflict-oriented strategies and more consensual approaches to service provision and building alliances for change.

The new citizen voices, however, did not always succeed in stopping elite-led development projects. Neighborhood protests stopped numerous projects, only to see new ones soon emerge.

MAKING CITIZEN PARTICIPATION WORK

The citizen participation programs of the 1960s and 1970s were criticized for failing to promote widespread participation. The early programs were quite primitive as they provided citizens with little opportunity for face-to-face deliberation and no real control over government programs. As a result, local citizens saw no reason to participate.

Yet other cities—including Indianapolis, Birmingham, Portland, and St. Paul—have initiated more recent and more successful citizen participation programs. The experience of these cities shows that effective community participation programs can be built.[39]

What are the keys to building effective local participation programs? First, real powers must be turned over to the citizen bodies. These bodies cannot simply be planning or advisory boards. Only when neighborhood bodies possess authority to allocate significant goods and services will citizens see participation as worthwhile.

Second, the city must employ the necessary rewards and sanctions to make sure that administrators interact with neighborhood groups. Otherwise, administrators will resist the loss of their power.

Third, citizen participation must be initiated citywide. Participatory programs implemented in only a certain few neighborhoods are seen as unfair and discriminatory. They lack the widespread public support to sustain them against the assaults that will be made by officials and interests who are threatened by participation.

Fourth, cities and charitable foundations must provide neighborhood organizations with the staff and financial resources so that these associations can engage in substantial outreach to bring residents into the process. Participation often requires outside assistance. The City of Indianapolis created a Neighborhood Resource Center, a center designed to aid new neighborhood and homeowner associations and spur grassroots activism. A Neighborhood Power Initiative, funded by the Annie Casey Foundation, the Lilly Endowment, and the Ford Foundation, helped to fund full-time staff for community organizations in targeted neighborhoods.

Finally, neighborhood organizations must have the ability to communicate with every neighborhood resident on an ongoing basis. The geographical area that a community organization serves must be small enough to promote face-to-face contact. Yet community organizations must not be so narrow-focused that they have no potential for electoral power and lack an ability to influence decision making beyond the neighborhood's borders.

SUMMING UP: ASSESSING CITIZEN PARTICIPATION

The major arguments advanced for developing a meaningful program of citizen participation (CP) can be summarized as follows:

- CP is consistent with democratic theory. It increases the number of people in the decision-making process and helps assure that government officials are more aware of and responsive to citizen concerns.

- CP mechanisms help to nurture the development of community leaders who otherwise might not emerge.

- CP mechanisms help to create political and social networks essential to building a community. Citizen participation rooted in faith-based organizations can also build important bridges to community groups outside the community.

- CP acts to reduce feelings of powerlessness and create a sense of efficacy in a community. Government is perceived as more legitimate when city residents see that they have access to government and that public officials are listening to their point of view.

- By bringing citizen involvement in service production, CP also improves the efficiency of service delivery.

These arguments are impressive. Yet the expectations set for citizen participation must be realistic. Citizen participation efforts cannot, by themselves, correct serious resource deficiencies and overcome deep-seated community problems and resentments.

The major arguments against CP are:

- CP tends to heighten parochial concerns to the detriment of citywide concerns. At their worst, neighborhood actions can be narrow-minded and exclusionary.

- CP is never completely representative of the range of community interests. It can never be said with any certainty that citizen activists represent a community's point of view. Even in cities with noteworthy programs for citizen involvement, middle-class and professional citizens, not the poor, take the greatest advantage of participatory opportunities.

- CP is lengthy and time-consuming. It slows down the process of government, retarding service delivery and project completion. CP can be frustrating for government officials and citizens alike.

Community organizations are not always a force for progress. In neighborhoods across the United States, local associations have mobilized to bar the provision of shelters and assisted housing. Community organizations in gentrified sections of the city have also fought against low-income housing and other projects that they believe will introduce crime into their neighborhoods. Other grassroots organizations have opposed policy measures that will strain local services or raise local property taxes.[40]

Citizen participation derives its force from democratic values. Whatever the flaws and imperfections of participatory mechanisms, efforts to enhance citizen democracy will continue.

DECENTRALIZATION

Decentralization denotes efforts to devolve decision making closer to the people. The concept of decentralization is quite similar to that of citizen participation; both seek to increase the citizen's voice in municipal decision making.

Decentralization can be defined as an institutionalized arrangement that "involves the allocation of authority and responsibility to lower territorially based echelons of the established bureaucracy or to geopolitical levels lower than the large municipality or school district."[41] Decentralization occurs when a central office yields authority to agency field offices or to neighborhood organizations.

The decentralization movement grew from a recognition that decisions are too often made in a bureaucracy's central headquarters by officials who are not fully aware of, or responsive to, the concerns of residents in the neighborhoods. In an attempt to make government more accessible, the decentralization movement sought to establish new municipal offices in the neighborhoods and to give greater decision-making authority to officials who worked in the neighborhood.

Oftentimes, municipal officials resisted calls for decentralization in policing, fire protection, and education, observing that their services were already decentralized. Evidently, public officials viewed decentralization quite differently than did the neighborhood groups. Public officials saw decentralization simply as a matter of devolving certain responsibilities to field offices. Citizen groups, in contrast, wanted to restructure urban decision making to increase the voice of community groups.

TYPES OF DECENTRALIZATION

One way to better understand the large variety of decentralization mechanisms is to categorize decentralization according to how much power is actually devolved.[42]

GEOGRAPHICAL DECENTRALIZATION

Geographical decentralization occurs when local governmental officials decide to locate a branch or field office closer to the clients who are being served. Under geographical decentralization, an agency may lease a storefront where a few staff persons do the initial intake of applications for service and pass citizen complaints along to higher administrative levels. Members of the field office staff have no real discretion to exercise political or administrative power on their own.

Such neighborhood offices function as city grievance centers or complaint centers. Citizens entering the office fill out forms describing their complaints and are told that they will hear from the appropriate agency in the near future. If they receive a quick response and serious efforts are made to redress their grievances, word will quickly spread through the community and other clients will begin to use the office. If citizen complaints go unanswered, or if responses are less than satisfactory, community interest in the services provided by the field office will soon decline.

This model of decentralization seeks to take government to the people. The storefront and neighborhood offices provide citizens with relatively convenient sites at which they can apply for new services or register their complaints. Because complaints are merely fielded and then passed downtown, there is no real devolution of authority. Final decision-making power remains in the hands of central office bureaucrats who may be out of touch with local citizens and insensitive to neighborhood needs.

ADMINISTRATIVE DECENTRALIZATION

Administrative decentralization vests significant administrative discretion in the hands of the staff members situated in a field office. Under administrative decentralization, field employees do not merely forward complaints downtown; instead they possess some real discretionary power in program implementation and the allocation of benefits. Under administrative decentralization, for instance, a social services worker can make certain decisions on the spot about a client's eligibility for program benefits. Administrative decentralization is also evident when a parole officer is given the authority to decide if a parolee will be allowed to travel out of the state for a short period of time to attend a relative's funeral.

Community policing provides an important contemporary example of administrative decentralization. The community policing model seeks to abridge the traditional hierarchical organization of police departments in order to give beat officers who work with neighborhood residents a new ability to set neighborhood law enforcement priorities. Community policing uses a variety of mechanisms—small neighborhood substations, community surveys, neighborhood advisory boards, officers on bicycles and on foot patrol—in order to establish a two-way flow of communication between the police and the public. Community policing seeks to transform the culture of local police departments by building a new partnership between customer-oriented law enforcement officials and neighborhood residents.[43]

Little city halls and multiservice centers are two long-loved examples of administrative decentralization. **Little city halls** were first initiated in the 1960s and 1970s by Boston Mayor Kevin White and New York Mayor John Lindsay; the innovation was soon copied in other cities. Under the little city hall arrangement, agency branch offices are located in an easily identifiable neighborhood facility; the mayoral appointee in charge of the center is empowered to make a range of administrative decisions on the spot. The program not only seeks to improve service responsiveness; it also allows the mayor to build the support of neighborhood residents.

Multiservice centers usually occupy large facilities and provide a fairly large menu of in-house services in a neighborhood. Residents can easily identify where they must go to apply for services. With multiple agencies housed under the same roof, the referral of citizens and coordination of services are also improved.

Administrative decentralization provides a speedier approach to service delivery compared to the time delays that occur under the geographical approach where additional paperwork is processed and sent downtown. Administrative decentralization also assures that increased decision-making power is vested in the hands of people located in the community who are more likely to know and understand a community's needs.

Yet under the administrative approach, final authority is still retained by city officials who may not yield to neighborhood concerns. In cities such as Detroit, little city hall administrators were not given the sufficient authority or resources to make meaningful improvements in neighborhood services.[44]

Under the little city hall arrangement, it is the mayor's appointee who retains final authority; in the multiservice center, it is a decentralized bureaucratic employee. Similarly, while community policing seeks to push numerous law-enforcement decisions down to the neighborhood and street level, final decision-making authority remains with the police department and not with neighborhood residents.

POLITICAL DECENTRALIZATION

Political decentralization implies a shift in power and authority from city and county agencies to recognized community groups. Elected or appointed community representatives join public officials in the development and implementation of policy. Political decentralization implies parity between the community and the city; neither can impose its programs on the other. An example of such power sharing occurs when a community board screens the candidates seeking to become the local school principal, and the superintendent must choose from the list of top candidates recommended by the board.

COMMUNITY CONTROL

Community control entails a clear shift in power from the government agency to the community group. Under community control, a community-selected subunit of government is given the authority to make policy, allocate resources, and veto unwanted governmental intrusions. One early instance of community control occurred in the late 1960s when Washington, DC created an independent school in the Adams-Morgan area and endowed it with power to hire its own teachers, determine its own curriculum priorities, purchase its own supplies, and establish its own local school board.

The volatile politics surrounding the New York City Board of Education's 1968 decision to establish three experimental school districts shows the controversial nature of community control. The local community board in the impoverished Ocean Hill–Brownsville section of Brooklyn hired community residents who were not members of the United Federation of Teachers. The board also sought to transfer teachers it did not want to other schools. The teachers' union objected, and teachers citywide went on strike. Police officers were called in to quell disturbances and to maintain law and order. New York was rocked by repeated citywide teacher strikes as the union and the community board fought over one issue after another.

Ideally, under community control, a neighborhood board should control the flow of revenues, which it can then allocate in its service decisions. But few if any inner-city areas are given such authority; community control districts are still dependent on the funding allocations granted to them by city hall.

To a great extent, community control exists in middle- and upper-class suburban communities, not in the inner city. Suburbs exercise the financial and political autonomy that is sought, but rarely attained, by lower-income, inner-city minority communities.[45]

This typology provides a framework for understanding the continuing debate over decentralization. Governmental officials prefer to minimize any shift of power away from their agencies; they prefer the geographical and administrative forms of decentralization. Community groups, in contrast, insist on the more extensive devolution of power inherent in political decentralization and community control.

COMMUNITY DEVELOPMENT CORPORATIONS

One of the continuing bright spots on the urban scene is the emergence of neighborhood-based groups dedicated to the provision of housing and other important community services, organizations that work with political actors outside the inner city in order to increase corporate investment in lower-income communities. By the mid-1990s, over 2,000 **community development corporations (CDCs)** were established throughout the country. CDCs were particularly successful in constructing and rehabilitating housing in inner-city areas that had largely been ignored by private financial institutions.

Under the CDC approach, a corporate entity controlled by neighborhood residents is granted a charter from the state. The community corporation then assumes authority over designated economic development and physical rehabilitation activities. The CDC seeks to assist local entrepreneurs and stimulate neighborhood investment, especially in such areas as affordable housing and job creation. A CDC may also contract with governmental agencies to administer health clinics, day-care centers, and other social service programs.

CDCs stress cooperation more than confrontation. They seek to improve neighborhoods through **bridge-building activities** with banks, private investors, and nonprofit organizations. The actions of CDCs became especially vital to neighborhood health as the federal government decreased its own commitment to the provision of affordable housing.[46]

Bethel New Life in Chicago and the Nehemiah Project of the East Brooklyn section of New York are two nationally renowned examples of faith-based community development corporations committed both to the political empowerment of the poor and to the provision of affordable housing. Under the leadership of the Rev. Johnny Ray Youngblood, the more-than-50 religious congregations of United Congregations of East Brooklyn have come together to support Nehemiah Homes, building over 5,000 affordable, single-family, owner-occupied homes in a once largely abandoned part of the city. Ray's organization also brought a new health clinic and school to the community and established job-mentoring programs to encourage students to stay in school and pursue a career.[47]

The success of CDCs, especially in the field of housing, has been outstanding. The Banana Kelly Community Improvement Association in the Bronx revitalized over 25,000 housing units since 1978, weatherized an additional 8,000 units, and sponsored the construction of 500 houses. The Mid-Bronx

Desperadoes (MBD) built or renovated another 23,000 housing units. Similarly, in New York, the Abyssinian Development Corporation (ADC) created hundreds of units of housing and promoted the commercial revitalization of Harlem's famed 125th Street. All of these successes serve as testimony to the potential inherent in faith-based CDCs.[48]

While the CDC record of success is most notable in the area of housing (over 90 percent of all CDCs are engaged in housing projects), CDCs arc also active in a whole host of community-building activities, including youth and education programs, after-school programs, community organizing, neighborhood clean-ups, tenant counseling, home weatherization, food pantries, and job placement. CDCs operate in comprehensive terms; they provide a multitude of services to narrowly targeted areas in order to restore the health of neighborhoods. CDCs are **gap fillers;** they respond to the problems created by the gradual withdrawal of financial institutions and other entities from declining neighborhoods.[49]

CDCs tend to adopt a "consensus organizing" approach, spurning the confrontational tactics and polarizations of IAF/Alinsky-style organizations and activist groups such as ACORN (the Association for Community Organizations for Reform Now).[50] The CDC strategy emphasizes self-help, cooperation, and the building of new bridges between a community and outside institutions. CDCs seek to bring together various organizations—private investors, corporate managers, financial institutions, nonprofit associations, governmental agencies, and community groups—to support consensual solutions to problems. Private and institutional investors are more willing to invest in neighborhood projects in which CDC coordination and know-how reduce the risk of failure.[51]

Critics of CDCs argue that the devolution of power falls short of true neighborhood government and community control. Critics also question the degree to which CDC staff members are responsible to the larger community. As the TELACU case in East Los Angeles demonstrated, sometimes a CDC's responsiveness to neighborhood citizens may be diminished by its need to cultivate its government and nonprofit foundation funding sources. Many CDCs are reluctant to attack private, nonprofit, or governmental institutions when their funding and support are needed for future projects.

Other CDCs fail as they pursue their social goals too aggressively, with little regard for maintaining their political support both in the immediate community and in the larger city. The Whittier Alliance in Minneapolis closed its doors after encountering "vociferous community opposition" to its plans to introduce additional units of very low-income housing. Similarly, the Oak Cliff Development Corporation in Dallas lost city funding when its plans for a new subdivision of 122 units of affordable housing aroused intense community opposition.[52]

Indeed, CDCs, whatever their stated social mission, will have to pay careful attention not just to political considerations but also to financial, managerial, and accounting constraints in order to avoid collapse.[53] The sad tale of Banana Kelly's demise in the South Bronx points to the limitations of what can be expected from community organizations with poor managerial and planning skills. If CDCs are to do more, especially amid cutbacks in the federal commitment to subsidized housing, the public and nonprofit sectors must do more to train CDC board members and staff in such areas as property management, cost projections, and financial underwriting.[54]

CDCs must also be careful not to be overly reliant on HUD or any other single funding source. When the Reagan administration cut back its support of community organizations, the Mission Housing Development Corporation in San Francisco found that its ability to act was severely jeopardized, despite its award-winning record of building and managing safe and successful low-income housing.[55]

CDCs have also been criticized for adopting an "apolitical" approach that pays too much attention to bricks-and-mortar concerns—especially housing and real estate projects—and too little attention to political organizing and the development of more broad-scale attacks on social and economic inequities. The political involvement of CDCs is limited by the 501(c)(3) provisions of the tax laws, which allows them to accept tax-exempt grants from charitable foundations.

As CDCs have become service providers, developers, and landlords, their energies have been diverted away from more political organizing and protest activities.[56] As CDCs become more professionalized, with their directors by necessity giving greater attention to property management and financial planning concerns, the corporations risk losing their grassroots authenticity.

CDCs are also relatively weak as they pay low salaries that result in the loss of experienced executive directors.[57] Critics further question the representative nature of CDC staff and governing boards in those organizations in which nonresidents occupy key positions.

The presence of a CDC does not remove power from the hands of municipal agencies. The municipal bureaucracies ultimately determine just what services and responsibilities are delegated to a CDC in a management contract. The municipal bureaucracies can even abrogate management contracts in cases in which they feel a CDC has been grossly inefficient or incompetent.

Even when CDCs prove successful, traditional problems of organizational life sometimes reemerge and plague CDC actions. CDCs learn that bureaucratic organization is essential to any organization's existence; bureaucratic standards provide an accepted way of accomplishing tasks. In order to run programs successfully, CDCs and other community-based organizations must recruit staff, set pay scales, prepare job descriptions for employees, establish criteria for personnel evaluation and promotion, and maintain personnel and financial records. As the neighborhood organization grows and expands, it becomes more bureaucratic.[58]

Despite their imperfections, the overwhelming weight of the evidence is clear. In Boston, Cleveland, Indianapolis, Memphis, and other cities, community development corporations have pursued cooperative and comprehensive strategies in their efforts to provide affordable housing and services in working-class urban neighborhoods.[59] CDCs have become important actors in the urban arena.[60]

SUMMING UP: ASSESSING DECENTRALIZATION

Advocates of decentralization generally argue that:

- Decentralization brings government closer to the people, enhancing communication between citizens and government officials and making municipal service delivery more flexible and responsive to neighborhood needs and concerns.

- Decentralization increases the legitimacy of government, improving city-community relations by making people feel that government is closer to them and more willing to listen to their concerns.

- Decentralization fits in with notions of grassroots democracy. In decentralized service delivery, citizens enjoy a better chance of getting to know and gain access to local public officials.

Decentralization has proven to be an important tool in the efforts to combat both AIDS (Acquired Immune Deficiency Syndrome) and homelessness. Community-based care provides more humane treatment to people with AIDS at a lower cost than does institutionalized care. A decentralized approach to dealing with AIDS allows for wide-ranging experimentation in finding new ways to deal with this complex health and social problem.[61]

Similarly, a program of decentralized shelters permits homeless people to stay in the familiar and supportive confines of their communities as they deal with the problems that led to their homelessness, problems such as the loss of a job, substance abuse, marital tensions, and family breakup. Decentralized sites provide the homeless with a sense of normalcy as clients attempt to reestablish themselves.[62]

Yet despite these claims and stories, a number of empirical studies have drawn mixed conclusions about the success of decentralization. One early study, for instance, found little evidence that decentralization decreases feelings of powerlessness among community leaders.[63] Yet other studies found that similar efforts did build citizen trust and confidence in government.[64]

Critics of decentralization argue that:

- Decentralization is inefficient. The professional expertise of departmental experts can be overridden by lay citizens with their parochial concerns and lack of professional training. Economies of scale are lost when service decisions are made on a neighborhood, as opposed to a citywide, basis.

- Decentralization can exacerbate racial and ethnic tensions as a majority in a neighborhood may ignore the concerns of a minority. The polarizations surrounding New York City's Ocean Hill–Brownsville decentralization experiment serve as a notable case in point.

- Decentralization will result in lower standards of service. Decentralization allows for new opportunities for corruption as the vestiges of backroom ward politics reemerge.

The troubled histories of community school boards in New York City and Chicago attest to the mismanagement and corruption that can accompany decentralization. In New York, teachers discovered that political ties to elected school board members and their powerful political friends were often the key to promotion. Community board members dispensed jobs as patronage to loyal campaign workers and family members, with little concern for education. State elected officials finally decided to rein in the community boards, giving new appointment powers and administrative authority to both the chancellor of the city schools and the mayor.[65]

Similarly in Chicago, corruption, mismanagement, and the general ineffectiveness of community school councils in the face of declining test scores and staggeringly low graduation rates led to a near-complete reversal of policy direction. The State of Illinois pulled the rug out from under school decentralization and gave Mayor Richard M. Daley direct authority over school administrators and budgets.[66]

Advocates of decentralization respond that corruption, waste, fraud, and inefficiency characterize centralized as well as decentralized systems. Advocates of decentralization further argue that professional expertise does not always produce superior decision making, that on a great many issues neighborhood residents do not need sophisticated training in order to evaluate the program choices that affect their lives.

Also, economies of scale are not readily apparent in all service areas. Policing, social work, and education are some areas in which services can be provided better and more efficiently by small-scale neighborhood organizations than by large, remote, citywide bureaucracies.

Nor is decentralization at the root of racial polarizations in the city. Neighborhood service delivery may even serve to reduce neighborhood tensions by increasing the sense of legitimacy of local government.

CONCLUSIONS: CITIZEN PARTICIPATION AND DECENTRALIZATION TODAY

The nation has undergone a minor governmental revolution; cities and counties across the country have adopted new processes of citizen participation and organizational decentralization. A new generation of professional administrators has also been schooled as to the legitimacy of client participation. Bureaucrats have come to recognize that decentralization improves communications, reduces lead time in providing services, and increases responsiveness to citizens. Middle-class as well as lower-class residents have an interest in decentralization and citizen participation measures that will make city decision making more responsive to their needs.

Much of the acrimony that surrounded the citizen participation efforts and decentralization experiments of the 1960s and early 1970s has faded, and a new, more cooperative spirit has come to dominate community organizations. Neighborhood groups that have assumed new service-delivery responsibilities are less focused on protest and more focused on building partnerships for better education, housing, job training, and health care. Community groups redefined "empowerment." They no longer see their goal simply as "a struggle over contested issues (power over)"; instead, they increasingly see power as "the formation of relationships that provide a capacity to act (power to)."[67] Excessive conflict can eat away at a community's capacity to form problem-solving coalitions across racial and class lines.[68]

Neighborhood groups, including churches and faith-based organizations, help to form and shape a community's identity, including its desirability and marketability. Community organizations help promote network building. Local groups that have external ties serve as a bridge to resources outside the community—including potential contributors, investors, tutors, and other community partners.[69]

Los Angeles has turned to a system of neighborhood councils to diminish the distance between citizens and their government. Los Angeles officials hoped that the creation of neighborhood councils will diminish calls for secession by the residents of the San Fernando Valley and other outlying sections of the city. However, it remains to be seen if the new councils will be embraced by citizens and neighborhood activists. The financial dependence of the councils on the city also raises the prospect that activist voices will be coopted by the city.[70]

There are limits as to what citizen participation and decentralization can accomplish. Municipal bureaucrats and entrenched interests at city hall do not always warmly greet participatory efforts. Governmental bureaucrats and elected officials have generally been more willing to accept the lower rungs of citizen participation as opposed to genuine power sharing. They have been willing to accept administrative decentralization but not political decentralization.

Frustrated by the lack of responsiveness of large citywide housing authorities, tenants in a number of public housing projects in St. Louis, Chicago, Boston, Jersey City, Cleveland, New Orleans, and Washington, DC have turned to resident management of troubled public housing projects.[71] Under **resident management** (also called **tenant-run housing**), tenants in an individual building or group of buildings select their own management board. The tenant board then directs budgets and repairs to where they are most needed and ensures that service personnel complete repair and maintenance projects as directed. Resident management usually serves to increase citizen vigilance in keeping drug sales out of the projects and protecting public spaces against vandalism.

Yet the history of resident management also points to the limitations of participatory urban strategies. Resident management has not worked well in a great many public housing projects. The success of resident management is highly dependent upon the strength of tenant leaders as well as the technical assistance and level of funding given to the tenant groups.[72] The local housing authority is often reluctant to yield authority and budgetary power to tenant organizations. Nor have governments been willing to give tenant organizations the budgetary assistance necessary for structural repairs, building rehabilitation, and effective building security.

Citizen participation mechanisms are also essential for the representation of disadvantaged women. In cities such as Houston and Dallas, where corporate leaders and their city hall allies have dominated decision making, the needs of women in the urban core for assured physical safety, access to transportation, and adequate day care were largely ignored. In contrast, in Orlando and San Diego, participatory mechanisms allowed women a greater influence in urban planning decisions, with the result that redevelopment efforts also gave a heightened emphasis to transportation, crime prevention, affordable housing, and the preservation of residential neighborhoods.[73]

Women are also strongly represented on the boards and staffs of neighborhood development organizations. The inclusion of such organizations in decision-making processes will help to ensure that urban revitalization efforts are responsive to women's needs.[74] Women-led community development organizations take a broad, inclusive definition of community development. They do not see themselves as solely as economic entrepreneurs. Nor do they value legal, financial, and technological expertise over other community voices that are normally excluded from development deal making. In rebuilding their communities, the women who headed CDCs found that their conceptualizations of community development did not always meet the expectations of bankers, other financiers, and construction contractors.[75]

Community development corporations attest to the importance of community-based organizations for a balanced urban policy. CDCs helped to fill "the vacuum in U.S. housing policy innovation created by the federal withdrawal" since the 1980s.[76] CDCs have an enviable record in promoting the construction of affordable housing. Yet the collapse of a number of CDCs and the mergers of others in the face of difficult financial problems point to the limitations of the CDC approach: "CDCs, alone, however, cannot rebuild these central city neighborhoods."[77]

Citizen participation and decentralization have reshaped urban programs but are not a total solution to the urban problem. As a result, cities and suburbs have begun to experiment with still other innovative mechanisms to improve urban service delivery, including the professionalization of service personnel, privatized management strategies, vouchers, and state-chartered schools. These are the subjects of our next chapter.

NOTES

1. Jeffrey Berry, Kent Portney, and Ken Thomson, *The Rebirth of Urban Democracy* (Washington, DC: Brookings Institution, 1993), pp. 34–39; Hindy Lauer Schachter, *Reinventing Government or Reinventing Ourselves: The Role of Citizen Owners in Making a Better Government* (Albany: State University of New York Press, 1997).
2. Joseph F. Zimmerman, *The New England Town Meeting: Democracy in Action* (Praeger, 1999); Frank M. Bryan, *Real Democracy: The New England Town Meeting and How it Works* (Chicago: University of Chicago Press, 2003).
3. Edgar S. and Jean Camper Cahn, "Citizen Participation," in *Citizen Participation in Urban Development,* ed. Hans B. Spiegel (Washington, DC: NTL and National Education Association, 1968), pp. 218–222.

4. Sherry R. Arnstein, "A Ladder of Citizen Participation," *Journal of the American Institute of Planners* 35 (July 1969): 216. Also see: John Clayton Thomas, *Public Participation in Public Decisions: New Skills and Strategies for Public Managers* (San Francisco: Jossey-Bass Publishing, 1995), chap. 1.

5. In Chicago, the machine's control over the local community action agencies was quite substantial, yielding a situation that Greenstone and Peterson have labeled "minimum feasible participation." See J. David Greenstone and Paul E. Peterson, *Race and Authority in Urban Politics: Community Participation and the War on Poverty* (Chicago: University of Chicago Press, 1976), pp. 19–24.

6. Lillian Rubin, "Maximum Feasible Participation: The Origins, Implications and Present Status," *Poverty and Human Resources Abstracts* (November/December 1967).

7. Advisory Commission of Intergovernmental Relations, *Citizen Participation in the American Federal System* (Washington, DC: ACIR, 1979), chap. 4.

8. Richard C. Kearney, Barry M. Feldman, and Carmine P.F. Scavo, "Reinventing Government: City Manager Attitudes and Actions," *Public Administration Review*. 60, 6 (November 2000): 535; Richard C. Kearney and Carmine Scavo, "Reinventing Government in Reformed Municipalities: Manager, Mayor and Council Actions," *Urban Affairs Review* 37, 1 (2001): 43–66. Also see Alfred Tat-Kei-Ho, "Reinventing Local Governments and the E-Government Initiative," *Public Administration Review* 62, 4 (July–August 2002): 4–14.

9. Arnstein, "A Ladder of Citizen Participation," pp. 216–224. The following discussion relies heavily on Arnstein, pp. 218–223.

10. Wesley S. Skogan and Susan M. Hartnett, *Community Policing, Chicago Style* (New York: Oxford University Press, 1997), pp. 17, 55–56, and 113–137.

11. Desmond M. Connor, "A New Citizen Participation Ladder," *National Civic Review* 77 (May/June 1988): 250.

12. Berry, Portney, and Thomson, *The Rebirth of Urban Democracy;* Rob Gurwitt, "A Government That Runs on Citizen Power," *Governing* (December 1992), pp. 48–54; Robert B. Parks, Avra J. Johnson, David Robb, Lydia Amerson, Sue E. S. Crawford, and David Swindell, "Neighborhood Empowerment: Can It Happen? Does It Matter?" (paper presented at the annual meeting of the Urban Affairs Association, New York, March 13–16, 1996). Indianapolis Mayor Stephen Goldsmith describes his city's extensive efforts at citizen participation in his book, *The Twenty-First Century City* (Lanham, MD: Rowman and Littlefield, 1999), pp. 159–163.

13. Robert F. Pecorella, *Community Power in a Postreform City: Politics in New York City* (Armonk, NY: M.E. Sharpe, Inc., 1994), p. 170.

14. Susan S. Fainstein and Norman I. Fainstein, "The Changing Character of Community Politics in New York City: 1968–88," in *Dual City: Restructuring New York,* eds. John Hull Mollenkopf and Manuel Castells (New York: Russell Sage Foundation, 1991), pp. 315–332; Susan S. Fainstein and Clifford Hirst, "Neighborhood Organizations and Community Planning: The Minneapolis Neighborhood Revitalization Program," in *Revitalizing Urban Neighborhoods,* eds. W. Dennis Keating, Norman Krumholz, and Philip Star, (Lawrence, KS: University Press of Kansas, 1996), pp. 96–111.

15. Robert F. Pecorella, "Community Input and the City Budget: Geographically Based Budgeting in New York City," *Journal of Urban Affairs* 8 (Winter 1986): 58 59. Also see Pecorella, "Community Governance: A Decade of Experience," in *Restructuring the New York City Government: The Reemergence of Municipal*

Reform, eds. Frank J . Mauro and Gerald Benjamin, *Proceedings of the Academy of Political Science* 37, 3 (1989): 97–109.

16. Carmine Scavo, "The Use of Participatory Mechanisms By Large American Cities," *Journal of Urban Affairs* 15 (1993): 93–109, especially pp. 96 and 108.

17. Fainstein and Hirst, "Neighborhood Organizations and Community Planning."

18. Skogan and Hartnett, *Community Policing, Chicago Style,* pp. 117–119.

19. The transition from protest to a new emphasis on community economic development is described by Robert Fisher, "Neighborhood Organizing: The Importance of Historical Context," in *Revitalizing Urban Neighborhoods,* eds. W. Dennis Keating, Norman Krumholz, and Philip Star (Lawrence: University of Kansas Press, 1996), pp. 39–49.

20. Saul D. Alinsky gave the clearest description of his principles for organizing in his *Rules for Radicals* (New York: Vintage Books, 1971).

21. Mark R. Warren, *Dry Bones Rattling: Community Building to Revitalize America* (Princeton, NJ: Princeton University Press, 2001), especially pp. 20–22, 191–210, and 239–247.

22. Charles Silberman, *Crisis in Black and White* (New York: Vintage Books, 1964), pp. 308–355, provides a good description of many of TWO's actions.

23. Robert Bailey, Jr., *Radicals in Urban Politics: The Alinsky Approach* (Chicago: University of Chicago Press, 1974), pp. 61–62; James G. Cibulka, "Local School Reform: The Changing Shape of Educational Politics in Chicago," in *Research in Urban Policy, Volume* 4: *Politics of Policy Innovation in Chicago,* ed. Kenneth K. Wong (Greenwich, CT: JAI Press, 1992), p. 159; Clarence N. Stone, "The Dilemmas of Social Reform Revisited: Putting Civic Engagement in the Picture" (paper presented at the annual meeting of the American Political Science Association, Atlanta, September 2–5, 1999).

24. Richard C. Hula and Cynthia Jackson Elmoore, "Nonprofit Organizations, Minority Political Incorporation, and Local Governance," in *Nonprofits in Urban America,* eds. Richard C. Hula and Cynthia Jackson-Elmoore (Westport, CT: Quorum Books, 2000), pp. 121–150.

25. Despite its many celebrated successes, Banana Kelly also suffered huge problems resulting from poor planning, mismanagement, and mounting debt. As conditions of its buildings deteriorated (with some units lacking hot water or usable toilets), Banana Kelly was forced to surrender management responsibilities of its buildings. For an overview of the evolution of Banana Kelly, see: David Gonzalez, "In the South Bronx, the Grass Roots Grow Up and Are the Establishment," *The New York Times,* January 7, 1993; Jim Rooney, *Organizing the South Bronx* (Albany: State University of New York Press, 1995); Jill Grossman, "Banana Kelly Gets a New Bunch," *City Limits Weekly,* November 11, 2002, available at: www.citylimits.org/content/articles/weeklyView.cfm?articlenumber=873.

26. Marion Orr, "Urban Regimes and Human Capital Policies: A Study of Baltimore," *Journal of Urban Affairs* 14, 2 (1992): 173–187; Marion Orr, "BUILD: Governing Nonprofits and Relational Power," *Policy Studies Review* 18, 4 (Winter 2001): 71–90; and, Marion Orr, "Baltimoreans United in Leadership Development: Exploring the Role of Governing Nonprofits," in *Nonprofits in Urban America,* eds. Hula and Jackson-Elmoore, pp. 151–167.

27. Michael Leo Owens, "Politics by Other Means: Urban Black Churches, Community Development Corporations, and Public Policy" (paper presented at the annual meeting of the American Political Science Association, Philadelphia, August 28–31, 2003). Also see Owens, "Black Church-Affiliated Community Development

Corporations and the Coproduction of Affordable Housing in New York City," in *Nonprofits in Urban America*, eds. Hula and Jackson-Elmoore, pp. 169–198.

28. Ken Thomson, *From Neighborhood to Nation: The Democratic Foundations of Civil Society* (Hanover, NH: University Press of New England, 2001), especially pp. 74–76, 82–85, and 109–114.

29. David Ranney, *Global Decisions, Local Collisions. Urban Life in the New World Order* (Philadelphia: Temple University Press, 2003), especially pp. 224–234.

30. Michael N. Danielson, *Home Team: Professional Sports and the American Metropolis* (Princeton, NJ: Princeton University Press, 2001), pp. 268–271, describes how "voter skepticism" frustrated the development of a number of proposed stadium projects.

31. Margaret T. Gordon, Hubert G. Locke, Laurie McCutcheon, and William B. Stafford, "Seattle: Grassroots Politics Shaping the Environment," in *Big City Politics in Transition*, eds. H. V. Savitch and John Clayton Thomas (Beverly Hills, CA: Sage Publications, 1991), pp. 216–234.

32. Sallie A. Marston, "Urban Growth, Neighborhoods, and the Changing Dynamics of Political Arrangements" (paper presented at the annual meeting of the Urban Affairs Association, Baltimore, March 8–11, 1989).

33. Roberto E. Villareal, "EPISO and Political Participation: Public Policy in El Paso politics" (paper presented at the annual meeting of the Western Political Science Association, Anaheim, California, March 26–28, 1987). Also see Donald C. Reitzes and Dietrich C. Reitzes, *The Alinsky Legacy: Alive and Kicking* (Greenwich, CT: JAI Press, 1987), pp. 129–131. For a brief review of EPISO's evolution over the years, see Robert H. Wilson and Peter Menzies, "The Colonias Water Bill: Communities Demanding Change," in *Public Policy and Community: Activism and Governance in Texas,* ed. Robert H. Wilson (Austin: University of Texas Press, 1997), pp. 241–242 and 245–248.

34. For details on community organizing in San Antonio, see: Sidney Plotkin, *Keep Out: The Struggle for Land Use Control* (Berkeley: University of California Press, 1987), pp. 121–145; David R. Johnson, John A. Booth, and Richard J. Harris, eds., *The Politics of San Antonio: Community Progress and Power* (Lincoln: University of Nebraska Press, 1983), especially Joseph D. Sekul, "Communities Organized For Public Service: Citizen Power and Public Policy in San Antonio," pp. 175–190; and Reitzes and Reitzes, *The Alinsky Legacy,* pp. 117–126.

35. Heywood T. Sanders, "Communities Organized for Public Service and Neighborhood Revitalization in San Antonio," in *Public Policy and Community: Activism and Governance in Texas,* pp. 36–68; Warren, *Dry Bones Rattling,* pp. 47–71. Warren, pp. 61–65, also describes the problems that TMO faced in its organizing efforts in sprawling, diverse Houston.

36. Sanders, "Communities Organized for Public Service and Neighborhood Revitalization in San Antonio," pp. 62–65; Warren, *Dry Bones Rattling,* pp. 56–57. Like COPS, Fort Worth's Allied Communities of Tarrant is another Texas Alinsky-style group that gave a new emphasis to service provision (especially in the area of education) without abandoning its use of confrontation strategies.

37. Dennis Shirley, "Community Organizing for Parental Engagement: The Educational Collaboratives of the Texas Industrial Areas Foundation," in *Public Policy and Community: Activism and Governance in Texas,* pp. 166–228. Warren, *Dry Bones Rattling,* pp. 98–123, describes the problems that the Allied Communities of Tarrant faced in its efforts to build a multiracial coalition for school reform in Fort Worth.

38. Curtis Ventriss and Robert Pecorella, "Community Participation and Modernization: A Reexamination of Political Choices," *Public Administration Review* 44 (May/June 1984): 226. Also see Reitzes and Reitzes, *The Alinsky Legacy,* pp. 35–41.

39. Our discussion here relies greatly on Berry, Portney, and Thomson, *The Rebirth of Urban Democracy,* especially pp. 47–51, 61–63, and 295–299. Also see Thomson, *From Neighborhood to Nation,* especially pp. 110–114.

40. Gordana Rabrenovic, *Community Builders: A Tale of Neighborhood Mobilization in Two Cities* (Philadelphia: Temple University Press, 1996), pp. 53 and 195–196; J. Phillip Thompson, "The Failure of Liberal Homeless Policy in the Koch and Dinkins Administrations," *Political Science Quarterly* 111, 4 (1996–97): 639–660.

41. Henry J. Schmandt, "Decentralization: A Structural Imperative," in *Neighborhood Control in the 1970s,* ed. George Frederickson (New York: Chandler Publishing, 1973), p. 19.

42. For a more detailed discussion of the typology presented here, see Bernard H. Ross and Louise G. White, "Managing Urban Decentralization," *Urban Interest* 3 (Spring 1981): 82–89. Also see Henry J. Schmandt, "Municipal Decentralization: An Overview," *Public Administration Review* 32 (October 1972): 573.

43. Skogan and Hartnett, *Community Policing, Chicago Style,* especially pp. 5–9 and 61–62; Merry Morash and J. Kevin Ford, eds., *The Move to Community Policing: Making Change Happen* (Thousand Oaks, CA: Sage Publications, 2002); William M. Oliver, *Community-Oriented Policing: A Systemic Approach to Policing,* 3rd ed. (Englewood Cliffs, NJ: Prentice-Hall, 2003); Geoffrey P. Alpert and Alex R. Piquero, eds., *Community Policing: Contemporary Readings* (Waveland Press, 2000).

44. Darren A. Nichols, "Neighborhood City Halls Fail to Help," *The Detroit News,* October 29, 2001.

45. David C. Perry, "The Suburb as a Model for Neighborhood Control," in *Neighborhood Control in the 1970s,* pp. 85–89.

46. Ross Gittell and Avis Vidal, *Community Organizing: Building Social Capital as a Development Strategy* (Thousand Oaks, CA: Sage Publications, 1998), pp. 14–15, 33–35 and 52–54. For a discussion of CDC achievements, also see Avis C. Vidal, "CDCs as Agents of Neighborhood Change: The State of the Art," in *Revitalizing Urban Neighborhoods,* eds. Keating, Krumholz, and Star, pp. 149–163; and Paul S. Grogan and Tony Proscio, *Comeback Cities: A Blueprint for Urban Neighborhood Revival* (Boulder, CO: Westview, 2000), pp. 63–101.

47. Andrew Billingsley, *Mighty Like a River: The Black Church and Social Reform* (Oxford University Press, 2002), pp. 145–146; Diane Ravitch, *City Schools: Lessons from New York* (Baltimore: Johns Hopkins University Press, 2000), pp. 304–309.

48. David J. Wright, "Saving City Neighborhoods; New Findings, Trends and Policies," *Rockefeller Institute Bulletin 1999,* a publication of the Nelson A. Rockefeller Institute of Government, Albany, NY, pp. 93–95; and Meredith Ramsey, "Redeeming the City: Exploring the Relationship Between Church and Metropolis," *Urban Affairs Review* 33, 5 (May 1998): 610–611; Billingsley, *Mighty Like a River,* p. 149. Sean Zielenbach, *The Art of Revitalization: Improving Conditions in Distressed Inner-City Neighborhoods, Contemporary Urban Affairs,* vol. 12 (New York: Garland Publishing, 2000), pp. 234–238, also points to the importance of churches in the process of community revitalization.

49. Gittell and Vidal, *Community Organizing,* pp. 14–15 and 34–36; Sara E. Stoutland, "Community Development Corporations: Mission, Strategy, and Accomplishments," in *Urban Problems and Community Development,* eds. Ronald F. Ferguson and William T. Dickens (Washington, DC: Brookings Institution Press, 1999), pp. 193–240.

50. Gittell and Vidal, *Community Organizing,* pp. 51–54; Michael Eichler, "Consensus Organizing: Sharing Power to Gain Power," *National Civic Review* (Summer-Fall 1995): 256–261. For a balanced assessment of the accomplishments and weaknesses of CDCs, see William M. Rohe, "Do Community Development Corporations Live Up to Their Billing? A Review and Critique of the Research Findings," in *Shelter and Society: Theory, Research, and Policy for Nonprofit Housing,* ed. C. Theodore Koebel (Albany: State University of New York Press, 1998), pp. 177–199.

51. Zielenbach, *The Art of Revitalization,* pp. 230–234. Herbert J. Rubin, *Renewing Hope Within Neighborhoods of Despair* (Albany, NY: State University of New York Press, 2000), pp. 98–132 and 163–188, points to the key role played by community-based development organizations in piecing together the funds for new community investment. These organizations serve as a community's intermediaries with government agencies, private corporations, banks and other credit institutions, and nonprofit foundations.

52. Rachel G. Bratt and William M. Rohe, "Organizational Changes among CDCs: Assessing the Impacts and Navigating the Challenges," *Journal of Urban Affairs* 26, 2 (2004): 215–216.

53. David A. Reingold and Craig L. Johnson, "The Rise and Fall of Eastside Community Investments, Inc.: The Life of an Extraordinary Community Development Corporation," *Journal of Urban Affairs* 25, 5 (2003): 527–549.

54. Bratt and Rohe, "Organizational Changes among CDCs," pp. 211–212.

55. Ross Gittell and Margaret Wilder, "Community Development Corporations: Critical Factors that Influence Success," *Journal of Urban Affairs* 21, 3 (1999): 341–361.

56. Gittell and Vidal, *Community Organizing,* pp. 39–40 and 51; Margaret Weir, "Power, Money, and Politics in Community Development" and "Comment" by Peter Dreier, both in *Urban Problems and Community Development,* eds. Ferguson and Dickens, pp. 139–192. For a cautious yet positive assessment of the potential inherent in CDCs, see Thad Williamson, David Imbroscio, and Gar Alperovitz, *Making a Place for Community: Local Democracy in a Global Era* (New York: Routledge, 2003), pp. 212–222 and 226–235.

57. Spencer M. Cowan, William Rohe, and Esmail Baku, "Factors Influencing the Performance of Community Development Corporations," *Journal of Urban Affairs* 21, 3 (1999): 325–340.

58. For further discussion of how community organizations try to avoid taking on some of the characteristics of the "bureaucracy" that they once opposed, see Bernard H. Ross, "The Management of Neighborhood Organizations," *South Atlantic Urban Studies* 4 (1979): 32–42.

59. David J. Wright, *It Takes a Neighborhood: Strategies to Prevent Urban Decline* (Albany, NY: the Rockefeller Institute Press, 2001).

60. For a discussion of CDC efforts and successes in a vast variety of cities, see Robert J. Chaskin et al., *Building Community Capacity* (New York: Aldine de Gruyter, 2001).

61. Walter J. Jones and James A. Johnson, "AIDS: The Urban Policymaking Challenge," *Journal of Urban Affairs* 11 (1989): 95–96 and 98–99.

62. Michael J. Lang, "Urban Homelessness and Local Shelter Policy: A Case Study" (paper presented at the annual meeting of the Urban Affairs Association, Baltimore, March 8–11, 1989).

63. Douglas Yates, *Neighborhood Democracy* (Lexington, MA: Pegasus, 1970), pp. 102–107.

64. See, for instance, Richard Cole, *Citizen Participation and the Urban Policy Process* (Lexington, MA: D. C. Heath, 1974), pp. 106–111.

65. Lydia Segal, "The Pitfalls of Political Decentralization and Proposals for Reform: The Case of New York City Public Schools," *Public Administration Review* 57, 2 (March/April 1997): 141–142. Also see Joseph Berger, "School Board Ineptitude Gave Chancellor Power," and Somini Sengupta, "Crew to Use New Power Quickly in 27 Districts," both in *The New York Times,* December 18, 1996.

66. For an earlier review of Chicago's 1989 school decentralization program see: Marilyn Gittell, "School Reform in New York and Chicago: Revisiting the Ecology of Games," *Urban Affairs Quarterly* 30 (September 1994): 136–151. For a discussion of the turn from decentralization back to centralization, see Paul C. Bauman *Governing Education: Public Sector Reform or Privatization* (Boston: Allyn and Bacon, 1996), pp. 111–118.

67. Stone, "The Dilemmas of Social Reform Revisited: Putting Civic Engagement in the Picture."

68. Clarence N. Stone, Jeffrey Henig, Bryan Jones, and Carol Pierannunzi, *Building Civic Capacity: The Politics of Reforming Urban Schools* (Lawrence, KS: University Press of Kansas, 2001), p. 154.

69. Barbara Ferman and Patrick Kaylor, "The Role of Institutions in Community Building: The Case of West Mt. Airy, Philadelphia," in *Nonprofits in Urban America*, eds. Richard Hula and Cynthia Jackson-Elmoore (Westport, CT: Quorum Books, 2000), pp. 93–120; Warren, *Dry Bones Rattling,* pp. 98–123, shows how community groups in Texas were able to build understanding and trust across racial lines. Religious institutions are particularly important as a unifying force among diverse communities.

70. Juliet Musso and Alicia Kitsuse, "Urban Regimes, Social Movements, and the Politics of Neighborhood Councils in Los Angeles." (paper presented at the conference on "Reform, L.A. Style: the Theory and Practice of Urban Governance at Century's Turn," Los Angeles, September 19–20, 2002. Available at: www.haynesfoundation.org/WordDocs/Musso.doc.

71. Daniel J. Monti, "The Organizational Strengths and Weaknesses of Resident-Managed Public Housing Sites in the United States," *Journal of Urban Affairs* 11 (1989): 39–52; and William Peterman, "Options to Conventional Public Housing Management," *Journal of Urban Affairs* 11 (1989): 53–68.

72. Michael A. Stegman, *More Housing, More Fairly* (New York: Twentieth century Fund Press, 1991), pp. 81–89 and 120–122; William Peterman, "The Meanings of Resident Empowerment: Why Just About Everybody Thinks It's a Good Idea, and What It Has to Do with Resident Management," in *New Directions in Urban Public Housing,* eds. David P. Varady, Wolfgang F. E. Preiser, and Francis P. Russell (New Brunswick, NJ: Center for Urban Policy Research Press/Rutgers, The State University of New Jersey, 1998), pp. 47–60. For a good journalistic account of the difficulties of tenant management in Boston, where the Boston Housing Authority canceled its contract with the tenant management organization, see Pamela Ferdinand, "Tenant-Run Housing Takes a Hit in Boston," *Washington Post,* November 24, 1998.

73. Robyne S. Turner, "Concern for Gender in Central-City Development Policy," in *Gender in Urban Research, Urban Affairs Annual Review,* vol. 42, eds. Judith A. Garber and Robyne S. Turner (Thousand Oaks, CA: Sage Publications, 1995), pp. 271–289.

74. Marilyn Gittell, Jill Simone Gross, and Kathe Newman, "Women and Minorities in Neighborhood Development Organizations" (paper presented at the annual meeting of the Urban Affairs Association, New Orleans, March 1994).

75. Marilyn Gittell, Isolda Ortega-Bustamante, and Tracy Steffy, *Women Creating Social Capital and Social Change: A Study of Women-led Community Development Organizations* (New York: The Howard Samuels State Management and Policy Center, The City University of New York, 1999).

76. Edward G. Goetz, "The Community-Based Housing Movement and Progressive Local Politics," in *Revitalizing Urban Neighborhoods,* eds. Keating, Krumholz, and Star, p. 177.

77. W. Dennis Keating and Norman Krumholz, "Future Prospects for Distressed Urban Neighborhoods," in *Rebuilding Urban Neighborhoods: Achievements, Opportunities, and Limits,* eds. Keating and Krumholz (Thousand Oaks, CA: Sage Publications, 1999), p. 193.

THE URBAN BUREAUCRACY PROBLEM

The reformers undercut the political machine by placing decision-making authority in the hands of administrative experts. Insulated against political intrusion, the civil-service–protected bureaucracies became the new power centers of local government. As Theodore Lowi observed, "The legacy of reform is the bureaucratic city-state." Lowi even referred to the urban service bureaucracies as the "new machines" to underscore the power of these agencies to control action in their individual service areas.[1]

The reform movement changed the linkage between citizens and city government. Whatever its shortcomings, the party machine had an interest in making sure that bureaucrats were responsive to citizens who would then vote for the machine's slate of candidates. Civil service cut the electoral connection between citizens and government. Program administrators no longer had to bend to the requests of citizens and politicians.

The growth of bureaucratic power posed a new question of governmental accountability: Would the autonomous municipal agencies follow the public's wishes as opposed to their own agendas? As Lowi observed, "Bureaucratic agencies are not neutral; they are only independent."[2]

SOURCES OF BUREAUCRATIC POWER

A municipality's appointed administrators and career bureaucrats collectively wield immense power in the day-to-day running of the city. City councils have neither the time nor the expertise to pass legislation that spells out implementation steps in great detail. Much of the legislation passed by local elected bodies is skeletal in nature, requiring administrative agencies to develop detailed rules and regulations. In essence, municipal bureaucrats are given a great deal of **administrative discretion,** the leeway to decide just how a law's general goals and principles will be applied to specific situations. Citizens demand administrative flexibility, so that police officers, teachers, and other municipal servants will have the freedom to tailor their actions to the individual needs of clients.

Bureaucracies are also repositories of **expertise,** the specialized body of knowledge concerning the programs and policy problems assigned to their agencies. Administrators use their expert knowledge to help draft the legislation for a new program, formulate the program's administrative guidelines, implement the program, and monitor and evaluate the program in operation. Elected officials and top political appointees come and go; an agency's career bureaucrats provide program continuity. These bureaucrats are a source of **institutional memory;** they have the knowledge of past decisions and program rules and the practices necessary to keep governmental programs functioning smoothly.

Bureaucrats also are often effective in the **mobilization of client groups** to support an agency's activities. When a program is under attack, bureaucrats pass the word to supportive client groups. School teachers and administrators, for instance, are very effective in mobilizing parents in efforts to ward off school consolidation and other reorganization plans.

Bureaucrats have learned the art of **delay,** deflecting unwanted program changes by prolonging decision making and slowing things to a standstill. In a process that moves haltingly to begin with, delay can often prove fatal to efforts by outsiders to change or reform a program.

CHARACTERISTICS OF BUREAUCRACY

In his writings on bureaucracy, the German sociologist Max Weber developed a set of characteristics that help to describe these large-scale organizations. Weber believed that the "ideal type" bureaucratic organization possessed the following characteristics:

- Hierarchy
- Recruitment and promotion based on competence, not patronage
- The use of written rules and regulations
- Fixed areas of official jurisdictions
- Development of a career system
- Impersonal performance of one's duties[3]

Hierarchy connotes a pyramidal relationship among people that determines their role and influence in the organization (see Figure 9-1). A large number of officials work at the bottom of the organization; progressively fewer people work at each level as you go up the administrative hierarchy. Each level supervises the work of the people directly below; the few top administrators direct many subordinates by issuing directives and orders.

Hierarchy, then, is clearly established in an agency's **written rules,** which not only detail agency procedures but also set forth who reports to whom in the organization. Administrators are taught to "go by the book." In addition

■ FIGURE 9–1

THE PYRAMIDAL STRUCTURE OF A
MUNICIPAL BUREAUCRACY

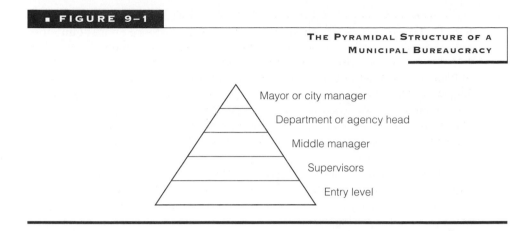

Mayor or city manager

Department or agency head

Middle manager

Supervisors

Entry level

to formal rules, organizations also have many **unwritten or informal rules and customs** that guide agency practices. In some cases, enshrined informal practices may contradict official agency practices. Quite often, though, the unwritten rules act to reinforce the hierarchical structure of bureaucratic agencies. It does not take a new employee long to determine which actions and practices will gain the approval of his or her supervisor or peer workers. Veterans in an organization help to instruct newcomers in the informal code of conduct that governs behavior. Newcomers, are socialized into the agency's culture even when the informal norms contradict official agency policy.[4]

Rules and regulations assure the even-handedness and fairness of agency operations. A strict application of rules and regulations assures that all clients are treated the same; there is no favoritism. When carried to extremes, however, rules and regulations become burdensome and pose obstacles to good service performance. Conformity to the rules can become a goal in and of itself.

Administrators also use rules as a protective shield. Bureaucrats can hide behind rules to deny an unusual or extraordinary request for service. A bureaucrat who sticks closely to the rules significantly reduces his or her chances of getting into trouble.

Another characteristic of bureaucratic organizations is **specialization;** each worker becomes expert at the tasks he or she is assigned. Each department has specialists in the different aspects of the department's work. A health department, for instance, has specialized units for mental health, prenatal care, disease control, and outpatient care.

One problem with this division of labor or specialization is that it can lead to parochialism. Each agency division or subunit will tend to see problems from its own narrow vantage point. A narrowness of perspective and training can preclude a service worker from dealing with the "total" client. Police officials, for instance, have historically tended to approach problems of domestic violence according to their own training in law enforcement. The efforts of women's advocacy groups and the passage of the Violence Against Women Act were instrumental in getting law enforcement officials to work more closely with health care providers, child welfare workers, substance abuse counselors, and members of the clergy in order to develop more comprehensive approaches to meeting the needs of abused women.[5]

The norm of **impersonal performance** demands that bureaucrats treat all clients equally; the political opinions and personal feelings of the bureaucrat do not enter into the process. A certain level of insensitivity to individual case concerns is also essential if the bureaucrats are to be able to process a large number of service requests without being overwhelmed by the sorrows and needs of their clients. But impartiality and fairness increase the distance between the service provider and the client. The norm of impersonality discourages bureaucrats from becoming overly involved with a client.

Citizens quite rightly complain of the impersonal, rigid responses of seemingly uncaring city officials. As a result, bureaucratic reformers have introduced a number of innovations, including community policing and other decentralization efforts in an effort to restore a bureaucracy's flexibility and responsiveness to community concerns. (See "Community Policing" below.) For other critics, however, bureaucratic action is hopelessly ineffective and rule-bound. These critics seek various privatization strategies that will remove as much authority as possible from the hands of municipal agencies.

COMMUNITY POLICING

Traditionally, police departments across the United States were structured in military-like hierarchy. Rigid adherence to the chain-of-command helps to assure the uniform application of the law and to prevent police misbehavior. But citizens, especially in the central city, complain that such centralized control precludes a more flexible approach to policing that would respond to the different needs of different neighborhoods.

Community policing is an innovation that seeks to restore public confidence by allowing neighborhood residents to play a role in setting police priorities. Community policing replaces the militaristic, hierarchical approach to law enforcement with a more decentralized approach based on two-way communication. Citizens work with the police to identify community problems and policing priorities. Beat meetings, neighborhood advisory boards, police substations, foot and bike patrols, and neighborhood watch groups are all employed to increase police responsiveness to citizens' concerns. Community policing attempts to get police officers out of the station house and back on the street.

New York, Chicago, Houston, San Diego, Portland, Tempe (Arizona), and St. Petersburg (Florida) are only a few of the great many cities that have begun to experiment with community policing. Community policing is a nationwide movement.

continued

COMMUNITY POLICING (CONT.)

More traditional officers, however, object that community policing is not real police work but "social work." They resent the demands on their time imposed by seemingly endless neighborhood meetings and youth-group activities. Traditional police officers further argue that community participation undermines professional policing standards.

Community policing can also be viewed through the lens of gender. Community policing emphasizes communication and a cooperative, compassionate orientation as opposed to the more militaristic, masculine style that prevailed when law enforcement was exclusively a man's profession.

Sources: Wesley G. Skogan and Susan M. Hartnett, *Community Policing, Chicago Style* (New York: Oxford University Press, 1997); Gerasimos A. Gianakis and G. John Davis, III, "Reinventing or Repackaging Public Services? The Case of Community-Oriented Policing," *Public Administration Review* 58, 6 (November/December 1998): 485–98; Susan L. Miller, *Gender and Community Policing: Walking the Talk* (Boston, MA: Northeastern University Press, 1999).

Weber had mixed feelings about bureaucracies. He found them to be a relatively efficient and capable way for society to organize action and assure reliable service provision. However, Weber also recognized that bureaucracies were protective of their power and secretive in their control of important information.

THE IMPORTANCE OF STREET-LEVEL BUREAUCRACY IN URBAN GOVERNMENT

Urban bureaucracies deliver public services to citizens. The success or failure of urban programs often rests with the bureaucrats who implement the program. The public's faith in local government is also dependent on the manner in which bureaucrats deliver services.

The phrase **street-level bureaucrat** refers to "those men and women who in their face-to-face encounters with citizens, 'represent' government to the people."[6] The "foot soldiers" of the local bureaucracy are often in daily contact with the clients they serve. These employees possess the ability to award or withhold important municipal services upon which clients depend.

The Weberian model of organizational hierarchy assumes that the top administrators make the important policy decisions and that low-level bureaucrats complete tasks as they are told. According to Michael Lipsky, quite the opposite is often true. The foot soldiers at the bottom of the bureaucratic pyramid effectively "make policy" when they decide how to dispense services and treat clients.

Street-level bureaucrats possess a high degree of **discretion** or independence in making decisions. In effect, they exercise power. Their actions in the field are not easily reviewed by superiors in the organization. Street-level workers need considerable discretion in dealing with such "wicked" problems as poverty, unemployment, homelessness, crime, drug abuse, and family decay.[7]

The ranks of street-level bureaucrats include police officers, teachers, housing inspectors, judges, welfare workers, and other service providers who regularly interact with clients or citizens. In addition to the high degree of administrative discretion that street-level bureaucrats possess, the work of these employees differs in other important ways from that of bureaucrats who work in offices further removed from the public.

Street-level bureaucrats often serve **nonvoluntary** clients who are dependent upon agency action for the provision of vital services. Poorer and working-class citizens, for instance, depend on the public schools as they cannot afford to pay private tuition. Court officials, the police, and building and health inspectors all have the authority to intrude directly on people's lives. Dissatisfied clients cannot "vote with their feet" by going to another provider of assistance. As a result, "Street bureaucrats usually have nothing to lose by failing to satisfy clients."[8]

Street-level bureaucrats often face difficult job conditions. Street-level bureaucracies seldom possess sufficient resources to do their required tasks well. Police forces are understaffed, welfare workers face caseloads that preclude individualized assistance, and teachers have classes that are too big with too wide a range of student ability levels and language skills to allow for effective teaching. Street-level workers often face physical and psychological threats and challenges to their authority. Police officers risk death. Social workers, housing inspectors, and public school teachers, too, face risks to their personal safety, especially when they work in crime-ridden neighborhoods. These street-level bureaucrats also fear losing control and being overwhelmed by the job.

To cope with these difficult work conditions, street-level bureaucrats often rely on **stereotypes** and other **shortcuts,** categorizing clients and reading cues. Police officers look for the "wrong" type of person walking down a residential street late at night. A teacher may give greater time to "deserving" students, after having first categorized students on the basis of their behavior, dress, or past academic records.

The street-level bureaucrat views such stereotypes and shortcuts as an application of expert judgment. To outsiders, such categorizations may appear to be an act of prejudice or discrimination. Police officers often argue that **racial profiling** is a valid means of identifying potential lawbreakers. African Americans stopped by the police in an affluent neighborhood for being the wrong age and color respond that their only "crime" is DWB—Driving While Black.

The decisions of street-level bureaucrats are particularly important in **slotting,** or determining just how citizens are categorized in their initial dealings with a public agency; these initial decisions oftentimes determine the future treatment that an individual will likely receive.[9] For instance, the law enforcement officer who responds to a call of domestic violence must decide whether or not a woman's complaint is serious enough so that she will gain entry to the criminal justice system and receive assistance from domestic abuse counselors and health care professionals. As a result, women's advocates have recognized the importance of developing screening protocols to ensure that law enforcement officials will refer abused women to supportive social service agencies.[10]

The limits of an agency's resources mean that its personnel will at times have to limit or **ration services,** making clients wait for intake interviews and even requiring clients to come back for a second visit. Low-income people have a poor track record of keeping second appointments; failing to return, they will lose service.

An agency may also couch its rules and decisions in a language that clients cannot understand; the **mystification of an agency's rules** and regulations means that citizens will have difficulty in challenging an administrative decision. An agency's virtual monopoly over information helps to insulate its decision from challenge. Parents, for instance, will often lack the information to fight a school system's decision to place their child in one program and not another. Citizens often require the assistance of advocacy groups and trained paraprofessionals to challenge an agency's action. In the area of domestic violence, victim advocates help ensure that battered women receive the full range of available services.[11]

Street-level personnel do work that is of societal importance. They are often the urban "heroes" who provide client-serving action beyond expectations. Programs that "mainstream" developmentally disabled children into regular classrooms work as well as they do only because dedicated teachers have been willing to develop individualized treatment plans and attend seemingly endless meetings with parents, administrators, legal staff, and special education and support personnel.[12]

Good pay, continued training, peer support, and public recognition of their efforts are all essential to keeping public service personnel client-oriented. Street-level servants will perform even better when they assume the role of "leaders" who initiate and build support for client-oriented actions.[13]

PROFESSIONALISM AND URBAN BUREAUCRACY

In contrast to the bureaucrat who follows an agency's rules, a *professional* is inner-guided and committed to a higher service ethic. **Professionalism** denotes more than the fact that an employee has advanced education and training; professionalism implies that the administrator will adhere to an accepted code of conduct recognized by the profession. That code of conduct mandates that the practitioner place service to the community above his or her own self-interest. A professional in the field can be trusted to use his or her discretion wisely even in the absence of direct supervision.

Education, engineering, and social work are among the urban service fields that have witnessed a high degree of professionalization over the years. Employment in these fields usually requires a college degree and state certification.

National and international professional associations also provide the local administrator with new program ideas and valuable continuing education and technical assistance.

In contrast, police officers and firefighters are **semi-professionals;** educational standards and in-service training in these fields have increased, but not to the extent apparent in the more established professions. On the bottom end of the status ladder are highway workers and municipal clerical help; in such jobs, low pay, high turnover, and the lack of advanced education hinder the development of a meaningful sense of professionalism.

Semi-professionals and nonprofessionals usually claim to be professionals even though they have not demonstrated all the attributes of the professional model. These workers correctly note that they are experts in their jobs, but they confuse narrow expertise with the larger perspectives and obligations of a professional. All workers desire the higher pay, respect, and greater freedom accorded to professionals.

EFFICIENCY, EFFECTIVENESS, AND EQUITY

How should we judge public service delivery? Three competing criteria are efficiency, effectiveness, and equity. **Efficiency** measures are concerned with costs. How can a unit of government maximize its output from a specific allocation of resources? Efficiency measures tell us how much it costs to collect one ton of garbage, keep a police officer on the beat, treat a drug overdose patient in an emergency room, and operate a city bus on a per-mile basis.

Efficiency measures do not reveal how effective these programs are in reaching important societal goals, only how much it costs to perform a service. Since the budgetary concerns are often so crucial in local government, it is not surprising that local officials often think in terms of efficiency criteria. But when services are assessed primarily according to efficiency, competing concerns for quality (effectiveness) and fairness (equity) are slighted.

Effectiveness measures are concerned with objectives, with how well problems are being solved. Effectiveness measures are goal-oriented and focus on analyzing outcomes as opposed to the costs of service delivery. Are health care services readily available? Have elementary school test scores improved? Has crime been reduced in the central business district? These are all questions of program effectiveness.

The third term, **equity,** denotes fairness. But as there are competing definitions of fairness, this concept presents difficult problems for guiding urban service delivery.[14]

Equity can mean **strict equality** (sometimes also referred to as **equal opportunity**) under which all citizens would receive the same level of service regardless of their level of need or the amount of taxes they paid.

Market equity, in contrast, views fairness as citizens receiving services roughly in approximation to the contribution or taxes they pay. The more taxes a citizen pays, the higher the level of service he or she should receive.

When citizens in well-to-do areas demand new street lighting or a higher standard of neighborhood policing as a result of the taxes they pay, they are voicing a demand for market equity. Metropolitan fragmentation can also be defended in terms of market equity. Residents who have bought houses in upper-middle-class suburbs feel that they have a right to better-quality schools and service levels than do the residents who live in other parts of the metropolis.

A third standard of equity is that of **equal results.** Under this type of equity, agencies allocate disproportional resources to people and neighborhoods with greater needs. Most social service, public welfare, and community development programs reflect a redistributional version of equity.

EQUITY IN URBAN SERVICES: DISCRIMINATION, BUREAUCRATIC DECISION RULES, AND POLITICAL POWER

What determines how services are allocated by municipal governments? Do people in power consciously discriminate against certain groups or geographical areas in the city? Or are there other explanations for the intra-city inequalities or variation in service levels?

One popular view, the **underclass hypothesis,** suggests that poor and minority neighborhoods suffer discrimination as a result of the racial and class biases of decision makers. Poor people also lack the political power to secure more equitable service provision.

But is there a consistent pattern of discrimination against the urban poor and minority neighborhoods as the underclass hypothesis assumes? Even when services are provided unequally throughout the city, there may not be any consistent bias against the poor. Instead, unpatterned inequalities in municipal service delivery may reflect a bureaucracy's internal **administrative decision rules,** the procedures that agencies formulate to routinize work and guide their daily actions.

In his classic study of San Antonio, Robert L. Lineberry found no consistent pattern of underservice based on race. Lineberry offered a less conspiratorial hypothesis for the variations in service levels in the city. According to Lineberry's **ecological** hypothesis, a neighborhood's age, population density, state of housing disrepair, and other relevant criteria all help to determine the level of services that are provided. Variation in service levels may not represent class and racial discrimination as much as a response to neighborhood need and demand.[15]

A number of studies have also pointed to the importance of a **bureaucracy's decision rules** in determining the allocation of services. A municipal sanitation department, for instance, might decide on the seemingly egalitarian rule of picking up refuse from each and every household once a week. In another city, the sanitation department may try to keep all neighborhoods equally clean, sending trucks more frequently to densely populated neighborhoods where garbage can be a greater public nuisance.[16] Neither department was acting from class or racial prejudice; yet one department's rules would lead to greater trash pick-up in the poorer, more crowded, minority sections of town.

Yet the evidence on this point is hotly debated. While some studies underscore the influence of an agency's internal decision rules, other studies nonetheless point to a continuing discrimination against poor and minority neighborhoods.[17]

PERFORMANCE MEASUREMENT

Beginning in the 1990s, more and more cities, counties, and states began to stress programs of performance measurement in order to provide greater accountability in public service provision. Performance measures give citizens the information to demand improved service quality. Performance measures also aid municipal officials in making more effective choices in allocating agency resources. (See "The Long Beach Police Department Measures Up" below.)

THE LONG BEACH POLICE DEPARTMENT MEASURES UP

In the early 1990s, the Long Beach (California) Police Department was in bad shape. Long Beach's citizens felt unsafe and expressed great dissatisfaction with the department's performance. The city spent more on law enforcement than did similar cities and yet was not achieving equivalent results.

The department began to turn things around by redefining its mission to that of winning citizens' trust and ensuring that residents felt safe in the community. The department then developed performance measures (also called **benchmarks**) in different service areas to gauge program effectiveness and guide future change. For instance, the department developed three specific measures of neighborhood security: the percent of citizens who reported in surveys that they frequently observed gang activity; hard statistics on property crimes in a neighborhood; and citizen survey data on how well the city responded to reported crimes. The department used the data it gathered to target resources strategically in those neighborhoods with the biggest crime problems.

As a result of the department's efforts, violent crime and gang-related activity in Long Beach fell nearly 40 percent, improvements that were much greater than national trends. Long Beach had begun to turn things around.

Source: Jonathan Walters, *Measuring Up: Governing's Guide to Performance Measurement for Geniuses and Other Public Managers* (Washington, DC; Governing Books, 1998), pp. 13–24.

The process of performance measurement entails a number of steps.[18] First, local officials must decide what objectives to measure. Keys can usually be found in departmental mission statements. Agencies also involve citizens and elected officials in identifying performance objectives.

Second, officials then develop performance measures in such areas as work-load, efficiency, effectiveness, service quality, and client satisfaction. Some measures of performance are easy to develop; others are more complex.

The third step entails the collection of data. Analysts compile data from available sources and present it in useful form. Many governmental agencies distribute citizen questionnaires and program evaluation cards as a means of assessing agency performance. Even crude and unscientific indicators of client satisfaction can help guide public officials. In addition to "customer surveys," some cities utilize **focus groups,** in which 8 to 12 "customers" are asked to discuss in depth what they do and do not like about a municipal service.

Other cities seek more extensive and reliable measures of performance. Municipal departments can hire **trained observers** to monitor the levels of trash on streets, the condition of roads, and the serviceability of playground equipment in local parks. Observers can take photographs to document the physical conditions they report. Other cities seek comparative data in an attempt to assess just how well a service in their city compares to that of similar cities.[19]

Fourth, the collected data must be analyzed and interpreted. This is fol-lowed by the reporting of results. A local government must decide how often and how widely to disseminate evaluation results. More sophisticated cities present reports in different formats to different targeted audiences.

Finally, local officials use performance data to develop short- and long-term strategies for improving agency performance. Performance data can be a vital part of the budget and strategic planning processes.[20]

One of the more successful programs of performance measurement was car-ried out in the New York City Police Department under the leadership of Chief William Bratton. Bratton initiated a system of assessing crime rates in the area of each district commander. High-crime areas were given extra resources and targeted for immediate action. District supervisors were threatened with demotion or transfer if they did not meet their goals. Despite the substantial publicity that he received as a result of the dramatic reductions in crime, Bratton was later dismissed by New York Mayor Rudy Giuliani after their working relationship broke down. But Bratton was soon hired by Los Angeles to see if he could bring similar reductions in crime to that city.

Not all cities take performance measurement seriously. Some local agencies lack the skills, resources, and time necessary to do a quality job of perform-ance measurement. Some municipal departments have to contract out the analysis. Other departments do their assessments with an eye to developing indicators that will justify budgetary demands for additional resources. Still other departments seek to document program success with the hope that good performance will justify the award of a bonus or a pay raise.

COPRODUCTION AND NEIGHBORHOOD-BASED
SERVICE DELIVERY

Coproduction (sometimes referred to as **self-service**) allows citizens to work jointly with governmental agencies in the provision of desired services. For example, residents fearful of crime can take part in citizen street patrols and neighborhood watch programs designed to monitor activity in their communities.

In the Park Slope section of Brooklyn, New York, residents decided to fight back against the rising tide of muggings, burglaries, and drug dealing. Led by long-time resident Terri Asch, the community instituted an informal block watch program. Asch founded the North Slope Alliance to mobilize and coordinate the resources of twelve block associations. Working closely with local police in its precinct, the Alliance put its first private patrol car on the street, keeping watch on the community. The cost was about $600 per week, paid for by the Alliance, which imposed an assessment of $1 per night on each of the area's brownstone homes. In a few months the Alliance raised enough money to fund three patrol cars, each working 16 hours a day, thwarting potential felonies and using their car radios to call the police to make an official arrest.[21]

Under the model of community policing, police officers and neighborhood residents come to recognize that they are "coproducers" of public safety. In the Rogers Park neighborhood of Chicago, Operation Beat Feet encouraged "positive loitering." Residents armed only with flashlights, cellular phones, and notepads walked nightly rounds, increasing surveillance levels and reporting suspicious activity to police officers. The increased "people presence" produced immediate success; in just six months, crime in five targeted areas was 33 percent lower when compared to a comparable period during the prior year.[22] In Detroit, parents and community activists walked the streets at night, bringing a virtual end to the rein of pre-Halloween "Devil's Night" arson that had plagued the city over the years.

Coproduction can also be seen in numerous small actions. Homeowners help make their areas safer by turning on outside lights at sunset. Neighborhood cleanliness is improved when residents organize community clean-up days. Neighborhood associations can "adopt" and take care of a local park, maintaining the working condition of playground equipment. Parents can volunteer to assist in remedial reading or math programs in the schools. Coproduction not only improves service levels but can also produce financial savings for local agencies.

Critics, however, charge that coproduction is a "rip-off" in which citizens supply the time and labor—in addition to their tax dollars—for services that the municipality should provide. Coproduction may also exacerbate class-based inequities in service provision, especially where only upper-status people have the time and motivation to volunteer as well as the money to donate to supplement public service provision.

Despite these criticisms, coproduction provides a valuable route toward improving service delivery. Coproduction is an important element in the community fight against AIDS. Patients in the later stages of the illness have difficulty in getting to outpatient clinics, and hospitals; extended institutional care can also be very expensive. San Francisco relies on volunteers and non-profit and community organizations in the gay community to help with public health education, risk-reduction strategies, home-based health care, psychological counseling, and long-term care. Such community-based efforts provide a caring alternative to hospitalization; they also add to the cost efficiency and effectiveness of service delivery: "Estimates are that the cost of care for an AIDS patient in San Francisco is only half that of care for a similar patient in New York City."[23]

Informal, neighborhood-based support organizations are also a key to convincing battered Latina women to take advantage of available government-provided services. In the absence of such neighborhood-based organizations, battered Latinas may be unaware of the existence of shelters and other services; they may also be reluctant to use facilities that are located outside of Latino neighborhoods. Lower-class Latina women tend to be mystified by the idea of counseling and intimidated as a result of language problems. Community-based organizations need to work hand-in-hand with service providers to win the trust of Latina women.[24]

Coproduction is closely related to another option designed to increase the involvement of local citizens, neighborhood-based service delivery. Under neighborhood-based service delivery, a local government devolves authority to neighborhood organizations, contracting for the provision of specified services to local residents.

There are limits as to what coproduction can accomplish. In low-income neighborhoods, citizen involvement is not always easy to bring about. In the public schools in poorer neighborhoods, coproduction efforts can falter when more involved parents move to the suburbs or decide to enroll their children in specialized schools and private academies.[25]

BUSINESS IMPROVEMENT DISTRICTS (BIDS)

One of the more popular innovations designed to improve urban service delivery in recent years is the **business improvement district (BID)**, a self-taxing, self-help, quasi-governmental organization in which property owners in an area vote to pay a supplemental tax in return for the provision of a higher level of services. BIDs allow public and private interests to work together for the revitalization of urban centers and commercial strips.[26]

The creation of a BID allows business owners to use the taxing powers of government for service improvements. The municipality collects an additional tax and returns it to the BID management association. While residential tenants and city officials also serve on a BID's district management association (DMA), property owners clearly dominate the board of a DMA. While the city retains some oversight power, essentially it is the business community that decides how a BID's funds will be spent. BIDs have paid for numerous activities designed to increase the attractiveness of commercial areas, including improved street and sanitation services, the steam cleaning of sidewalks, security and safety patrols, new street lighting, landscaping and beautification efforts, new street signs, and even community festivals and jazz concerts.

By the end of the 1990s, there were more than 1,200 BIDs at work in the United States. BIDs were especially popular in New York City (which had more than 40), Los Angeles (where 17 were created between 1995 and 1998 and another 27 were on the drawing board), and in the state of Maryland (with 18).[27] New York Mayor Michael Bloomberg was an enthusiastic booster of BIDs, especially of smaller BIDs, which he saw as vital to meeting the needs of small businesses.[28] Philadelphia, Boston, Baltimore, Milwaukee, San Diego, San Francisco, and Pasadena (California) are only a few of the prominent cities in which BIDs have been established.

The exact rules governing BID formation and governance differ from state to state. Generally speaking, business leaders desiring heightened service levels initiate the establishment of a BID, which requires a joint contractual agreement among property owners, merchants, and tenants located within the BID area. Votes are weighted by the value of property owned; it takes the owners of a majority of the value of the commercial property in an area to establish a BID.

A BID is not quite a voluntary association; it is a quasi-governmental entity. Once a BID is formed, it collects the additional tax (more properly a "surtax") from all businesses in the area, even from property owners who did not vote to form the BID. Business leaders in the district write the annual budget, hire staff, award contracts, and oversee the day-to-day operations of the new service entity. Municipal officials determine the boundaries of a BID, identify the services to be provided, and retain approval over the BID's contract and its annual budget and financial plan.

Ed Rogowsky and Jill Simone Gross have identified a typology of BIDs.[29] The largest are **corporate BIDs** dominated by large commercial property owners. Their budgets exceed $1 million. New York City has ten corporate BIDs, the largest of which is the Grand Central Partnership, which covers 54 square blocks and encompasses 71 million square feet of commercial, retail, and hotel space. Its annual budget in the late 1990s was $9 million. Other large corporate BIDs include New Orleans' Downtown Development District, with 200 blocks and a budget of $3.5 million, and Philadelphia's Center District BID, with an 80-block area and a $7 million budget.

A second type of BID, the **Main Street BID,** focuses on developing those downtown areas of central cities that have experienced an exodus of retail business to suburbia. Main Street BIDs have budgets that are in the $200,000 to $1 million range. They usually cover 5 to 20 square blocks and often focus on new immigrant communities. In Trenton, New Jersey, the Downtown Association has a budget of $350,000 and focuses on sanitation, marketing, and promotion of services. The Seattle Association has a budget of $575,000.

Finally, there are **community BIDs** found in poorer neighborhoods where resources are scarce. Many are but a few square blocks in size, and their budgets, around $200,000, are relatively small.

BIDs allow for the provision of services beyond what stretched municipal budgets could otherwise afford. The private sector is often willing to contribute for benefits that it needs. As one downtown spokeswoman observed: "These aren't like taxes that get lost in the general fund. . . . The money stays inside the business district . . . where businesses can see results."[30]

While BIDs provide heightened levels of service provision, they also raise important questions regarding power, democracy, and fairness. Corporate BIDs are often dominated by big business, with little assurance that residential and neighborhood voices will be adequately heard. The owners of small businesses, too, often protest that they are forced to pay additional taxes for services they do not really want.

In New York, Mayor Rudolph Giuliani fought hard to curb the autonomy of the city's largest BIDs, bodies that played an important role in taxing and spending decisions while enjoying considerable insulation from the direct control of city hall. Giuliani objected that one person, Dan Biederman, had become known as "the mayor of midtown" as a result of the fiefdom he carved out by gaining the directorship of three of the city's largest BIDs. Before he was ousted, Biederman controlled budgets worth tens of millions of dollars; he earned a combined salary of $335,000, over twice the salary paid to Mayor Giuliani.[31]

The proliferation of BIDs raises serious concerns for service inequity and urban dualism. Richer areas of the city that establish BIDs receive a higher level of service while poorer areas of the city must get by with less. (See "The Debate over BIDs in New York and California: Should Wall Street Get More Cops?" below.) Opponents have castigated the elitist nature of a BID on New York's luxurious Upper East Side. One critic charged that the creation of BIDs was breaking the city into a series of "mini city-states" in which rich neighborhoods could secure additional law enforcement and other important services.[32]

THE DEBATE OVER BIDs IN NEW YORK AND CALIFORNIA: SHOULD WALL STREET GET MORE COPS?

Business Improvement Districts have acted to reverse the decline of numerous troubled commercial areas. New York's Grand Central Partnership, the nation's oldest and largest BID, helped to finance the restoration of the city's glorious rail station, revitalizing the once "seedy" area that surrounded it. The Times Square BID changed the image of New York's entertainment center by funding improved trash pick up, graffiti removal, and new safety patrols. The Bryant Park Restoration Corporation reclaimed from drug dealers the park adjacent to the city's central public library (a setting familiar to non-New Yorkers as the library was featured in such movies as *Ghostbusters* and *Spiderman*), opening the park to tourists, shoppers, and office workers on their lunch breaks. *continued*

THE DEBATE OVER BIDs IN NEW YORK AND CALIFORNIA: SHOULD WALL STREET GET MORE COPS? (CONT.)

In California, BIDs helped to revitalize Old Pasadena, Santa Monica's Third Street Promenade, and San Francisco's Union Square. The Fashion District BID in Los Angeles emphasized trash removal, graffiti clean up, and crime control in an effort to alter customers' perception of an area that had suffered severe decline. In the Westwood section of Los Angeles, BID-funded security, jazz concerts, and street festivals have raised the area's profile, bringing back people and shoppers. BIDs also worked to improve the image of numerous shopping strips, including Ventura Boulevard in the San Fernando Valley and the automobile row along Van Nuys Boulevard. In California, business owners and municipalities also resorted to BIDs in their search for funds for local service provision, given the severe constraints imposed on municipal taxing by Propositions 13 and 218 and other tax limitation measures.

Yet BIDs have their critics. Los Angeles' first BID, the 1995 Miracle on Broadway, cleaned up overflowing trash cans and improved the atmosphere of a predominantly Latino shopping area. But the BID was dismantled after just one year when downtown merchants objected to paying extra for sidewalk sweeping and bicycle cops—services that they thought should be the city's responsibility to provide. In San Francisco, critics of a proposed Union Square district argued against the desirability of allowing private security forces into the street, fearing that these "ambassadors" would also hassle the homeless in an attempt to remove them from the shopping area.*

In New York, concerns for the homeless were at the center of the controversy surrounding the Grand Central Partnership. The Partnership's business-oriented directors sought to remove the homeless from the station and nearby streets; the Partnership ventured into outreach services and even offered shelter to the area's homeless people. When many of the homeless refused to avail themselves of the new services, the Partnership used its security guards and outreach workers to hassle panhandlers and oust the homeless. The Partnership was also sued for violating federal minimum wage laws; it paid homeless workers $1.16 an hour to remove other homeless persons from the ATM-machine vestibules they inhabited, as the Grand Central Partnership attempted to fulfill its contractual obligations to keep banking machine areas free from homeless people. In California, the Downtown Sacramento Partnership similarly employed "city guides" to patrol the area and call the police whenever they found anyone panhandling or sleeping on the streets.**

The Alliance for Downtown New York, a BID representing many Wall Street companies, pushed to have New York City place a new police substation in Lower Manhattan, despite the fact that the area's street crime rate was among the lowest in the city. The Alliance offered the city $5 million to set up and maintain a new substation with 200 officers, with the provision that 40, 50,

continued

THE DEBATE OVER BIDs IN NEW YORK AND CALIFORNIA:
SHOULD WALL STREET GET MORE COPS? (CONT.)

or more officers would be assigned to patrol the area. Other neighborhoods complained that the new substation would require the redeployment of officers from other areas of the city where crime rates were greater. Queens Councilman Sheldon Leffler objected that the affluent Wall Street area was buying a level of police protection that poorer neighborhoods were denied: "It raises very disturbing questions about whether city resources are going to be allocated where they're needed or auctioned off to the highest bidder."***

The Alliance for Downtown New York was a prominent actor in efforts to prettify Lower Manhattan, set up street concerts, and otherwise bring tourism and commercial activity back to the area devastated by the 9/11 attacks.

Sources: * Marla Dickerson, "Improvement Districts Spur Revival—and Division," *Los Angeles Times,* January 20, 1999; Jill Loevy, "Valleywide: 2 New Improvement Districts Approved," *Los Angeles Times,* July 2, 1998; and Edward Epstein, "Business Tax Zone Set Up to Neaten Union Square," *San Francisco Chronicle,* November 3, 1998.

** Heather Barr, "More Like Disneyland: State Action, 42 U.S.C. 1 1983, and Business Improvement Districts in New York," *Columbia Human Rights Law Review* 28 (Winter 1997); Evelyn Nieves, "Cities Try to Sweep Homeless Out of Sight," *The New York Times,* December 7, 1999. Heather Mac Donald, "BIDs Really Work," in *The Millennial City: A New Urban Paradigm for 21*ˢᵗ*-Century America,* ed. Myron Magnet (Chicago: Ivan R. Dee, 2000), pp. 388–403, presents a much more positive assessment of the actions of the Grand Central Partnership.

*** David Kocieniewski, "Wall St. to Pay to Add a Base for the Police," *The New York Times,* February 17, 1998. Also see Dan Barry, "Mayor Orders Review of Plan for Substation," *The New York Times,* February 19, 1998.

SERVICE CONTRACTING AND PRIVATIZATION

Privatization strategies seek to make public sector operations more like those of the private sector. Sometimes, privatization simply entails government borrowing of private sector techniques. Other variants of privatization enable citizens to secure privately provided services as an alternative to deficient municipal services.

One particularly important form of privatization is **service contracting,** in which a municipal government enters into a contractual relationship with a private firm or nonprofit agency to provide services that had previously been delivered by a municipal agency. Local governments have contracted with private and nonprofit sector organizations for the provision of such diverse services as trash collection, drug-abuse counseling, recreational activities, office maintenance, emergency ambulance service, jail administration, and the operation of shelters for the homeless. (See "The Privatization of Policing?" on p. 284.) As we shall see in our discussion of regional cooperation (Chapter 13), intergovernmental service contracts, in which a city purchases services from a county, are also quite common.

THE PRIVATIZATION OF POLICING?

Even a service as seemingly "public" as policing can be privatized, or at least partially privatized. There is no reason why protective service must be delivered only by police officers who are paid public salaries. In certain cases, private security guards can be hired in place of public officers. Community organizations can be given grants to encourage citizen observers and neighborhood watches to supplement municipal police efforts. Alternatively, community groups can be given city funds to secure their own protective services from private security firms.

Advocates argue that private policing may often prove more flexible and responsive to community needs. In an age of terrorism, where public resources are stretched thin, private action to safeguard corporate offices and sports arenas represents a valuable coping strategy.

Critics, however, worry about the loss of public control over private officers, who, in pursuing the protection of property, may infringe on individuals' civil rights and civil liberties. Privatization also raises important questions of equity as more affluent and better-organized sectors of the community are able to purchase superior protection.

Source: Brian Forst and Peter K. Manning, *The Privatization of Policing: Two Views* (Washington, DC: Georgetown University Press, 1999).

Conservatives and Republicans have traditionally called for privatization as part of their efforts to reduce the size of government. But increasingly, local managers have begun to view privatization in less ideological terms. They view contracting and privatization as tools that can make scarce public resources go further.[33]

Privatization is based on the distinction that can be made between the decision to *provide* a public service, and the decision as to who can best *produce* the desired service:

> [T]o provide a service is to decide that a service shall be made available and to arrange for its delivery. This is an integral part of a local government's policy-making process. To deliver a service is to actually produce the service. Although a local government may decide to provide a service, it does not necessarily have to be directly involved in its delivery.[34]

A service in the public interest does not necessarily have to be produced by a governmental agency. Where permitted by state law, a city or county can contract with a private firm or a nonprofit agency to deliver the service. The government can choose the service deliverer that offers the highest-quality, least-expensive alternative. Service contracts with nonprofit organizations allow local governments to draw on the expertise, experience, enthusiasm, and commitment of the staffs of voluntary and faith-based organizations. New York turned over the daily management of Central Park to the nonprofit

Central Park Conservancy in an effort to restore the park's appearance and prominence. As a private group, the Conservancy was even able to supplement city funds with additional monies secured through foundation and corporate fund-raising.[35]

ARGUMENTS FOR CONTRACTING AND PRIVATIZATION

There are numerous arguments for contracting out public services.[36] Proponents argue that:

- **Contracting encourages competition that reduces costs and improves efficiency.** Contractors must be efficient in the performance of their work; otherwise they will lose the city's business to a competing firm able to submit a lower bid. Former Indianapolis Mayor Stephen Goldsmith argues that competition is the key to innovation and efficiency brought by privatization. Public agencies will be led to improve their performance if they know they must fend off a possible competitive bid from an alternative service provider. A city does not gain any advantage if its privatization strategy fails to build a competitive environment and simply replaces a "public monopoly" with a "private monopoly."[37]

- **Contracting allows the government to circumvent the rigidities of civil service systems.** Protected by civil service regulations, public-sector workers do not always show concern for the quality performance of their jobs or their responsiveness to clients. In contrast, workers in private businesses must perform effectively and respond to clients' wishes, or else jeopardize their chances for promotions and perhaps even their jobs. Workers in voluntary and nonprofit agencies exhibit a commitment and a caring attitude that is too often absent among tenured government employees.

- **Contracting permits the introduction of cost-cutting measures that may not otherwise be available to government.** Private sector firms usually enjoy greater flexibility than civil-service constrained government agencies in assigning work tasks and even in transferring a worker from one division to another. Private sector firms also possess a greater flexibility in their workforce, being able to hire part-time and temporary employees as needed, rather than adding permanent positions. In addition, private firms may pay workers less than the prevailing wage in government.

- **Contracting permits government to borrow successful private-sector management systems.** Private firms can offer greater incentives to the top managers than would be permitted in government by civil service rules.

- **Contracting can reduce a city's need for large, initial capital outlays for infrastructure, equipment, and training.** A city does not have to buy new computers but may simply choose to hire a private firm to perform a certain record-keeping or data-entry task. Similarly, a city can contract out certain construction tasks that are only periodically performed rather than having to buy its own expensive heavy equipment.

- **Contracting allows government the flexibility to take on new responsi-bilities and expand services as needed without adding to the size of its permanent workforce.** A municipality does not need to expand its per-manent workforce to gain the capacity to complete a short-term task. A municipality can simply contract outside agencies to complete such tasks as modernizing government data and record-keeping systems. Once a task is completed, the government can let a contract expire.

The advocates of privatization further point out that businesses and upper-income residents have the ability to purchase private services that meet their needs. A private firm or gated community can hire its own security guards to deter crime; wealthier families can escape unsatisfactory public schools by paying tuition for their children to attend private schools. Privatization strategies seek to give more citizens the ability to secure services from private providers.

ARGUMENTS AGAINST CONTRACTING AND PRIVATIZATION

Opponents of contracting argue that:

- **Contracting is not always efficient.** Contracting can cost more when all of the hidden costs are calculated. Hidden costs involve monitoring the contract, evaluating the work to be performed, performance lost due to turnover, and the training and oversight of new contractors.

- **The bidding process for contracts often leads firms to underestimate or lowball costs.** To win a city contract, a private firm may submit an unre-alistically low bid. In subsequent years, when the city is dependent on the contractor, the costs billed to the city often rise dramatically as the contrac-tor seeks payments that cover the true cost of producing the service.

- **Contracting encourages contractors to cut corners and deliver inferior quality in an attempt to maximize profits.** Once a contractor wins the right to perform a service, it is difficult for the city to monitor and second-guess every decision. A contractor may seek to increase profits through cost-saving procedures that compromise the quality of service delivery.

- **Contracting lengthens the accountability cycle, thereby making evalua-tion more difficult and increasing the opportunities for corruption.** Con-tracting reduces the local government's ability to make changes rapidly in response to client demands. Contractors can cite the terms of the con-tract in refusing to cede to the changing demands of citizens and public officials.

- **Contracting reduces the expertise possessed by municipal government employees.** Should the contract be terminated, it would be difficult for local government to resume providing the service.

- **The public sector has the more successful record of affirmative action hiring.** This includes the employment of women as well as minorities.

- **Contracting is antiunion.** Under privatization arrangements, unionized municipal workforces can be displaced by non-union firms. Faced with the competition offered by lower-cost nonunion contractors, municipal workforces and unionized contractors will have to restrain their own salary demands.

New York mayors Rudy Giuliani and Michael Bloomberg used private contracting as a weapon against the fabled power of the school custodians' union. In the early 1990s, individual school custodians in the city received as much as $80,000 a year, worked second jobs, routinely put relatives on the payroll, and were highly unresponsive to the requests of principals, teachers, parents, and community activists to use school facilities after hours. In some cases, custodians were paid for the full year even when their work, such as air conditioning repair, was largely seasonal in nature. Giuliani and Bloomberg privatized about a third of the school custodial jobs, using the threat of further privatization as a means of pressuring the unionized custodians to reduce their job prerogatives.[38]

The advocates of privatization often base their arguments on a negative stereotype of public workers. Their critics respond that public employees are often highly qualified, energetic, and dedicated public servants. The privatization ideologues also unfairly contrast the worst of the public sector with a highly idealized portrait of the way private business works. The pressures of competition do not guarantee that private delivery systems will be lean and trim. Firing or transferring a worker, especially a senior worker, in the private business world is not as easy as privatization enthusiasts suggest. As national headlines of corporate scandals have revealed, the performance of private business firms, too, is often marred by waste, payoffs, skimming, and corruption.

PRIVATIZATION: WHAT THE EVIDENCE SHOWS

A number of studies have documented the cost savings and performance advantages inherent in privatization. E. S. Savas, a privatization enthusiast, has repeatedly found that private trash collection firms offer similar or better service at lower cost than do municipal agencies. Municipal pickup in New York costs more than private trash hauling for several reasons. Municipal sanitation workers are unionized and receive higher pay and more fringe benefits than do nonunion workers. Municipal unions make it difficult for the city to implement productivity measures and cost-cutting techniques that might reduce the size of its workforce. Finally, civil-service–protected workers and public monopolies do not have great incentives to be efficient or concerned with client satisfaction.

Savas and other researchers have examined other cities and found similar gains from privatization in additional service areas, including fire protection, licensing, and inspection services.[39] Rural Metro, an employee-owned, private fire-fighting company in Scottsdale, Arizona, enjoys the quickest response times in the metropolitan Phoenix area for a little more than half the estimated cost of protection by a municipal fire department.[40]

A Los Angeles metropolitan area study that compared service contracting with direct municipal service production found that the practices of private contractors led to cost savings. The private contractors:

- Require more work from their employees for equivalent salaries, but with less liberal vacation benefits.
- Guard against the over-qualification of personnel hired to perform a task.
- Use part-time employees whenever feasible.
- Allow first-line supervisors to hire and fire personnel.
- Use less labor-intensive approaches to produce each service.[41]

Critics of privatization respond that cost savings gained from privatization are often quite moderate and not nearly as large as the private-sector enthusiasts claim. The success of privatization is even less clear when it comes to increasing service quality. Privatization that is narrowly focused on cost efficiency can also jeopardize service equity.[42]

Bid-rigging and the manipulation of contracts by organized crime also can serve to diminish the promised benefits of private competition.[43] In New York City, commercial businesses, by law, must use commercial trash haulers. But private hauling resulted in an increased (not decreased) costs when "a Mafia-run cartel had rigged prices and denied customers any choice in selecting haulers or in negotiating contracts." When a crackdown on garbage industry abuses finally gave businesses a free choice of haulers and allowed new hauling companies to compete for business, one office tower on Fifth Avenue saw its monthly bill for garbage hauling dramatically drop from $10,000 to $950.[44]

The competitive pressures created by privatization can even lead municipal departments to "shape up" and adopt more efficient and effective forms of service delivery. In Phoenix, the public sanitation department reformed its practices and won back many of the contracts it had lost to private haulers. In Indianapolis, the city's public works department implemented new cost-savings practices as it sought to beat out private competitors in those districts of the city where trash collection was put out for bid.[45] Even Chicago, despite its legendary use of public jobs as patronage armies, has taken major steps toward privatization. (See "Service Contracting in Chicago" below.)

SERVICE CONTRACTING IN CHICAGO

Cities turn to service contracting in an effort to achieve cost savings. In Chicago, Mayor Richard M. Daley reduced the size of the city's workforce by privatizing services in areas such as automobile fleet maintenance, tree stump removal, window cleaning, parking garages, abandoned car removal, golf course management, and drug addiction treatment. Daley found that his city,

continued

SERVICE CONTRACTING IN CHICAGO (CONT.)

like other cities, had taken on services over the years that historically had been provided by the private sector.

Richard M. Daley's privatization initiatives are especially noteworthy as they represent a reversal of the political machine approach of his father. His father, the legendary boss Richard J. Daley, used a large municipal workforce as a source of job patronage. But court rulings over the years restricted the political dispensation of municipal jobs. Mayor Richard M. Daley could not rebuild the patronage armies of his father's days. Instead, he sought to win public support by showing voters that he could efficiently manage and run the city. Privatization was one of his tools.

Yet Richard M. Daley's critics take a less charitable view of the mayor's turn to contracting. They charge that Daley steered contracts to major financial contributors and political supporters—in effect, using the award of contracts as **pin-stripe patronage,** a modern variant of the way his father had dispensed municipal jobs as patronage.

Sources: Charles Mahtesian, "Taking Chicago Private," *Governing* (April 1994): pp. 26–31; Rowan A. Miranda, "Privatization in Chicago's City Government," in *Research in Urban Policy,* volume 4, ed. Kenneth K. Wong (Greenwich, CT: JAI Press, 1992).

Smaller communities, too, have come to see the advantages of using private firms for enhanced municipal service provision. In Sonoma County, California, Sheriff Mark Ihde turned to contracting when he found that he was spending increasing amounts of time on activities not directly related to law enforcement and corrections. Ihde oversaw 50 contracts that covered such services as inmate transportation, food services, helicopter services, and privatized medical service, privatization efforts that saved the county about $370,000 in its first year.[46]

The debate over privatization and contracting continues. But there is little doubt on one score: As cities search for more economical and effective ways of providing services, privatization efforts will continue. As one study of 66 cities across the United States concluded, "Privatization is now firmly entrenched as a viable, alternative service delivery option in most of America's largest cities, but it is clearly not viewed as a cure-all for urban fiscal difficulties."[47]

THE PRIVATE MANAGEMENT OF PUBLIC SCHOOLS

One very controversial privatization effort relates to the decision of some cities to turn over the day-to-day management of their schools to private-sector firms. Advocates argue that privately administered schools would give teachers and administrators new leeway to introduce innovative teaching tools. Public schools, by contrast, are too bound by union rules and bureaucratic procedures to introduce much-needed changes. Privately run schools would also be more able to apply private business expertise and managerial techniques, sharing the cost savings with the public.

Yet the record of the private management of public schools is much more clouded than its advocates would suggest. Miami was the first city to contract with a private firm, the Minneapolis-based Educational Alternatives, Inc. (EAI), to run a public school. Under the EAI approach, each student was given an individualized learning plan. Principals and other administrators were relieved from such chores as maintenance and repairs, which were contracted to EAI's partners. Teachers in Miami applied to work at what was promised to be a "dream school" outfitted with the latest in computers and math and reading programs. But 61 teachers soon filed a complaint for having to work a longer school day with no extra pay, a key part of EAI's new managerial approach.[48]

In 1992 Baltimore signed a five-year contract that allowed EAI to run nine of its schools. In 1994, Hartford, Connecticut turned over all 32 schools in its much-troubled system to EAI. But all three school systems—Baltimore, Hartford, and Dade County (Miami)—canceled or declined to renew EAI's contract, having had quite a tumultuous relationship with EAI.

Privatization efforts are motivated, at least in part, by an antiunion animus that sees public labor organizations as an obstacle to educational reform. Consequently, teacher unions almost uniformly oppose the introduction of private managerial firms. Union members charge that the private managers attempt to breach tenure and other job protections. In Baltimore, EAI hired nonunion custodians; it also hired $7-an-hour college students as teacher aides to replace $13-an-hour union members. The Baltimore Teachers' Union was the most notable opponent of the city's school privatization effort.[49]

In Hartford, teacher groups were outraged when EAI proposed a budget that sought to free up millions of dollars for technology and new initiatives by eliminating 300 teaching positions. Conflict also erupted when teachers loyal to Apple computers refused to accept the PCs that EAI had bought for school computer labs. According to EAI, the teachers were resistant to change and unwilling to give students the preparation and skills demanded in the business world. In turn, the teachers scorned the management company for being insensitive to their classroom needs.[50]

Neighborhood groups were mixed in their reaction to school privatization. Some welcomed private management as the first step to turning around failing local schools. But activist groups, such as Baltimore's BUILD, a local Alinsky-style organization, opposed privatization from fear that for-profit schools would ignore neighborhood needs and would reinforce capitalist, not community, values. Numerous members of the African-American community were also concerned that EAI was headed by a white businessman, a community outsider.[51] They also objected that EAI schools in Baltimore were given greater funding per student than other schools in the city and still were unable to demonstrate corresponding gains in student performance.

EAI's signed contracts did not allow the management company the leeway to dismiss problem teachers and to hire more responsive school personnel. EAI argued that big-city school boards denied the corporation the freedom to do its job.

As a result of its Miami, Baltimore, and Hartford problems, EAI decided that it would no longer focus on central-city schools; instead, the company would seek only to manage schools in "less political and less volatile" suburban districts[52] and in states friendly to charter schools and innovative school management. TesseracT (the new name assumed by EAI after its earlier controversies), however, faced continuing financial problems and was forced to lay off staff, file for bankruptcy, and even close a few of its schools in Arizona and New Jersey.[53]

The tale of EAI/TesseracT shows that private management is no "magic bullet" that will cure the ills of central-city school systems. Defenders of private management point to those EAI elementary schools that reported gains in reading and math scores.[54] Yet in Baltimore and other public school systems, private management produced no meaningful educational gains.

SCHOOL CHOICE: VOUCHERS, TAX CREDITS, MINISCHOOLS, AND CHARTER SCHOOLS

Critics of public education argue that the state of public schooling has declined to the point that radical restructuring is necessary. If public schools cannot be made more effective, parents can be given the option to send their children to private and religious schools. A variety of **school choice** plans seek to allow parents greater options in their children's education.[55]

The most radical proposals call for a system of **vouchers,** under which students receive a certificate that they can use to purchase education at the school of their choice. But the exact impact of vouchers on schools and children depends on the size of the voucher and the rules governing its use. Obviously, larger vouchers would allow many children to escape the public school system. In contrast, vouchers that cover only part of the costs of a private education are of only limited use to poor families. Vouchers that regulate school admissions in the name of fairness would work to avoid the unfairness and discrimination that might result in an unregulated voucher system in which each receiving school sets its own criteria for admission.[56] Voucher efforts targeted to the inner-city school populations, as was the case in Milwaukee and Cleveland, also differ greatly from more broad voucher plans that would enable middle-class students to flee troubled and racially mixed schools.

Choice advocates also embrace a system of **tax deductions and credits** that would use the tax code to subsidize a family's choice of a private school education. Critics, however, counter that such programs of tax incentives often contain a pernicious class bias and provide only the most limited assistance to the poor. For instance, the **education savings account (ESA) system,** established in 2001, allows parents to set aside up to $2,000 a year in interest-free accounts to help pay for a child's K–12 tuition. Middle- and upper income families enjoy the tax benefits offered by ESA, benefits which are not worth anything to low-income parents who have no tax liability. Also, as the tax benefits cover only part of the cost of private schooling, the program does not really enable choice by children in families that lack the resources to pay private tuition.[57]

Citizens clearly desire more choice in education. The defenders of the public school system argue that choice can be increased in public education without going to voucher plans and tax credits with their accompanying dangers. Public school systems can offer students a greater range of specialized schools or **minischools,** each with its own distinctive curriculum.

As we shall see, **charter schools** have become a popular means of offering greater choice within the public school system. Under a system of charter schools, innovative schools are established (or chartered) under the sponsorship of an authorized governing body. Governmental regulations are relaxed, and charter schools enjoy increased autonomy to offer innovative programs desired by teachers, parents, and schoolchildren. Yet charter schools do not possess the fuller freedoms of voucher-funded schools. A great many state rules and regulations are kept in place, and the state retains the authority to oversee and limit the operations of charter schools.[58]

Some states and cities have also begun experimenting with the use of **publicly and privately funded scholarships** in an effort to increase the school choices available to students from low-income families. In 1999, Florida became the first state in the nation to turn to a system of state-funded "opportunity" scholarships—in effect, a voucher that certain students can use to help pay tuition. Governor Jeb Bush argued that the scholarships would allow students to escape schools that receive a failing performance grade from the state year after year. However, Florida did not provide the funding that would allow a mass exodus from the public schools. Instead, the program sought to force failing public schools to improve their performance. Failing schools would have to take steps to improve schooling or else face the loss of funds if their students were to become eligible for the opportunity scholarships.[59]

THE ARGUMENTS FOR CHOICE PLANS

Advocates of privatization argue that vouchers, tax credits, and charter schools offer students a way out of public schools that too often settle for providing custodial care as opposed to genuine education. According to this argument, public school teachers are overly protected by tenure, unionization, and a promotion system based on seniority. Their creativity and spirit for innovation are further stifled by bureaucratic rules that mandate the uniform treatment of students. Public schools, in general, lack the flexibility that characterizes the operation of the nation's better private schools.[60]

Advocates of vouchers, charter schools, minischools, and tax credits argue that choice plans can promote racial integration by enabling students to attend schools outside local districts, overriding district attendance boundaries that reinforce racial separation. Choice programs also sustain voluntary integration by allowing students to attend school based on a common interest in science, the performing arts, or some other discipline. Appropriate controls over admissions can be used to avoid inappropriate selectivity and the possibility of segregation.

THE ARGUMENTS AGAINST CHOICE PLANS

Opponents argue that choice advocates lack the evidence to support their claims. A report of the prestigious Carnegie Foundation observed that the movement toward school choice has been guided more by ideology than by evidence, that "many of the claims for school choice have been based more on speculation than experience,"[61] and that choice plans did not necessarily result in improved student performance.

The Carnegie Foundation further warned that choice programs can also exacerbate urban dualism. In Massachusetts, a school choice program caused fiscal havoc in the financially troubled city of Brockton when 135 students chose to transfer to the tiny neighboring district of Avon. While the students who made the switch were pleased with their decision, "The picture is far grimmer for the 14,500 students left behind in Brockton."[62] The students who transferred took with them nearly $1 million in state aid, compounding the impact of state budget reductions, resulting in the layoff of 200 Brockton teachers.[63]

There is also no clear evidence that choice plans will promote racial integration and class mixing. A broad or universal program of school vouchers, charter schools, or tax credits could all act to facilitate "white flight" and thereby exacerbate class and racial stratification in education. Tax credits and voucher plans that allow for **add-ons** will likely worsen class stratification and racial segregation of schools. Middle- and upper-middle-income families will add money beyond the value of the tax credit or voucher; low-income families who lack the additional money to "add on" to the value of the voucher or tax credit will have no choice but to have their children continue to attend the schools that other students have chosen to leave. These schools will face an exodus of the most active students and parents. They will also suffer a reduction in state aid. The poor, in effect, will be consigned to the **dumping ground schools** of an increasingly segregated, lower-class, and underfunded public school system.

These deleterious effects, though, are not apparent in tightly targeted voucher programs, such as those in Milwaukee and Cleveland, where participation is restricted to the inner-city poor. The Milwaukee and Cleveland programs are so highly targeted on poor and minority students that they have not added to white flight; instead, the vouchers have enabled some minority students to move to less stratified schools.[64]

Critics also score the undesirability of vouchers and tax credits that aid parochial schools (that is, religious-related schools, especially Catholic schools in the inner city), violating the American tradition and constitutional requirements of the separation of church and state. Yet a sharply divided U.S. Supreme Court in 2002 ruled in *Zelman v. Simmons-Harris* [65] that Cleveland's program, which allowed the use of publicly funded vouchers for parochial school tuitions, did not violate the U.S. Constitution's First Amendment prohibition of the establishment of religion. The Court saw the Cleveland voucher program as "neutral" in terms of its respect toward religion. The Cleveland voucher program had a clear secular, not a religious, purpose; it sought to assist the education of poor children trapped in a failing public school system. Furthermore, the program provided no aid directly to the religious schools;

rather, any tax revenue flowing to parochial schools was the result of individual decisions freely made by parents, not by the state.

Dissenters responded that the Court was blind to the clear subsidy that vouchers provided religious schools, as secular private schools refused to participate in the program. In fact, 96 percent of the state-provided voucher funds were spent in Cleveland's parochial schools, schools that teach a religious doctrine.

The *Zelman* ruling meant that states and localities could establish voucher systems that included parochial schools, but were not required to do so. Even after *Zelman,* a Florida appeals court struck down the state's Opportunity Scholarship Program, which allowed students in failing public schools the freedom to use state-provided vouchers to attend parochial schools. The court saw the vouchers as an indirect aid to religion, a violation of Florida's constitutional provisions barring the use of public money to support religious organizations.[66]

Milwaukee's low-income school voucher experiment

In 1990, the state of Wisconsin enacted the first school voucher program in the nation, a program intended for Milwaukee public school students whose families had household incomes no greater than 1.75 times the poverty line. As the program was targeted only to students from low-income families, it was not a spur to suburban flight by better-off students. To avoid charges of selection bias and "creaming" (selecting the best students—the cream of the crop, so to speak), voucher schools were barred from admitting students on the basis of a student's prior educational or behavioral record.

Private schools that accepted a former Milwaukee public school student received state aid (initially set at $3,000 per student in 1993) in lieu of tuition. In its early years, only secular schools were eligible to participate in the program; later, the program was expanded to allow the participation of parochial schools. As the program proved popular, the size of the voucher and the "cap" limiting the number of students in the program were both expanded.[67]

Early evaluations of the Milwaukee program yielded mixed results. On the plus side, the program attracted students who had been performing poorly in terms of academic achievement. It enhanced the options of poor parents, especially poor African-American parents, who were dissatisfied with the Milwaukee public schools.

Yet participating students initially demonstrated little clear improvement on standardized tests.[68] There was also evidence of a self-selection class bias among the families who exercised choice; the public schools lost the children of more active and better-educated parents. Also, approximately half of the students in the program chose not to re-enroll for the second year, indicating a number of problems with the program.[69]

In an effort to liberate schools from onerous regulatory requirements, the Milwaukee plan provided little oversight of the voucher schools. The "dangers of this regulatory vacuum," however, quickly became apparent in the first year of the program, when the newly established Juanita Virgil Academy was shut down in the middle of the school year amid charges of mismanagement and the school's lack of textbooks, overcrowding, and poor cleanliness and discipline. In a similar situation in California, 6,000 students were left at the beginning of the school year to scramble and find new schools when an operator of 60 storefront charter academies suddenly closed the schools and filed for bankruptcy.[70]

Overall, the Milwaukee plan "failed to demonstrate that vouchers can, in and of themselves, spark school improvement."[71] While a number of students gained the freedom to pursue new education options, overall, there was no evidence that the students made significant academic gains.[72]

Yet choice enthusiasts counter that voucher students did show moderate gains by their fourth year of participation. The gains were especially apparent when voucher students were compared to a comparable group of students from low-income families attending the public schools.[73] The competitive environment created by the voucher plan also led Milwaukee's public school system to increase its own innovative school offerings, strengthen graduation requirements, and institute new efforts at school accountability. Yet competition brought only mild limited reforms, not a revolution in public school operations. The Milwaukee teachers' union blocked attempts to modify seniority rules, close schools, and strengthen the process for evaluating teachers. In Milwaukee, Cleveland, and the Edgewood Independent School District in San Antonio, school officials did not greatly fear that choice plans would cost them their jobs.[74]

The debate over school vouchers continues. But on one point, there can be little doubt: the Milwaukee and Cleveland efforts were not broadly based, universal programs. Instead, the Milwaukee and Cleveland approaches represent a relatively limited voucher program targeted toward racial-minority students and students from low-income families. Although the evidence on educational gains is mixed at best, the Milwaukee and Cleveland programs did serve to increase the choices available to disadvantaged students and their parents. African-American parents, in particular, voiced their support of a program that enabled their children to escape troubled public schools.[75] As limited programs, the Milwaukee and Cleveland efforts do not raise the equity issues or represent the threat to public schools that would be posed by an expanded, universal voucher program that offered choice to middle-class and non-minority students.

Minischools: The debate over East Harlem's school district 4

Vouchers have the potential to undermine the public schools. Yet choice can be increased within the public school system through the creation of minischools.

One much-publicized example of such a program is East Harlem's Community School District 4, a New York City school district that offered parents a choice of elementary and junior high schools that students could attend. The East Harlem plan gave teachers great autonomy to shape the educational program in each school, and by the late 1980s, 52 different schools had been created in 20 buildings. The District 4 experiment was credited with enabling teacher innovation, increasing school attendance, raising test scores, reducing instances of violence, and facilitating parental control. Advocates of school choice held out District 4 as a model for the nation.[76]

But critics argue that the gains reported by School District 4 have been over-sold. Test scores increased primarily due to the selective admission of students from outside the District who sought admission to the District's schools. While education in District 4 is undeniably better than what it was before, it may also be increased school spending, not choice, that made the difference. The administrators of District 4 aggressively pursued outside money; at one time the District received more federal funding per pupil than any other district in the country. When East Harlem began to face the same acute tight-money situation that confronted the rest of New York City's schools, the pace of innovation slowed, students received fewer enrichment activities, and the District lost good teachers to schools in suburban Nassau and Westchester counties.[77]

As the choice system in District 4 aged or "matured" over time, the district's array of schooling options became increasingly well known throughout Spanish Harlem. Choosing an appropriate minischool for one's child became part of the local culture. In an effort to reduce possible racial and class discrimination, the school district also established an extensive outreach program, informing parents in Spanish as well as English of the various alternatives that awaited their children.[78]

In sum, East Harlem's District 4 provided an improved education and a possible path out of the *barrio* for some students, but only at the cost of diverting resources, including good students and parents, from the more traditional public schools in neighboring districts. District 4 schools were in many ways successes. Yet School District 4 does not provide convincing evidence that choice, as opposed to selectivity in admissions and increases in school spending, made the difference in student learning.

A NEW WAVE: CHARTER SCHOOLS

As political opposition stood in the way of the widespread adoption of voucher programs, choice advocates turned to the creation of charter schools as an alternative. As we have already seen, a **charter school** is a state-authorized, state-funded school that is freed from many of the rules and regulations that normally govern public schools. In essence, charter schools are public schools that are given more flexibility for curriculum reform and educational innovation. Charter schools represent a moderate form of choice, a means of creating new alternatives to conventional public schooling while still preserving state authority over the schools. The educational establishment and the teacher unions have sought to place charter schools under the authority of local school boards and to forbid the operation of charter schools by profit-seeking companies.

As a state's laws permit, a group of parents, teachers, community activists, or even a private corporation may apply to a state chartering agency for permission to establish a charter school. Once established, the charter school receives a fixed sum of state money per pupil, in many states an amount roughly the equivalent of the aid that the state provides for a student attending a regular public school. Some states limit or cap the number of charter schools that can be created.

The number of charter schools has grown rapidly. There were 250 charter schools in 1995.[79] By the 2003–04 school year, 41 states and the District of Columbia authorized charter schools, and there were 2,996 charter schools nationwide. Arizona (464 charter schools in 2003), California (428), Florida (227), Texas (221), and Michigan (196) were the states with the most charter schools.[80]

Charter schools are popular because of their small classes, their emphasis on academics, and their focus on curriculum reform and specialization. Many charter schools make a concerted effort to involve families in the educational process.

Like a program of vouchers, charter schools also help to create a new competitive environment that can lead conventional public schools to reform their curriculum and practices. Yet more traditional public school officials resist change, arguing that the charter schools had nothing worth emulating.[81] In Arizona, competition from charter schools had only a very limited impact on pushing neighboring public schools to improve.[82]

Charter schools have had a solid record of admitting their fair share of inner-city, low-income, and racial minority students; about half of the students in charter schools come from minority backgrounds.[83] In a number of cities, charter schools have been created specifically for inner-city students with programs focused on college prep courses, industrial training, and the creative arts.

But in some states, charter schools are used by parents and children as an escape from more racially integrated public schools. In Michigan, in the city of Pontiac and in the inner-ring Detroit suburb of Ferndale, new charter schools helped undercut local compliance with federal school-desegregation orders.[84] In California, as of 2001, no school had ever had its charter revoked for failing to meet state-required ethnic diversity goals.[85]

In some instances, the charter school movement has a strong religious base. The schools run by National Heritage Associates, a charter school company founded by J. C. Huizenga, a wealthy businessman and conservative Christian, stress morals, values, and character development, albeit not an explicitly religious education.[86] In New York City, religious leaders, including African-American and Hispanic ministers, welcomed charter school legislation that gave them the ability to establish taxpayer-financed schools on church property.[87] A growing number of charter schools are "quasi-religious" schools, despite the requirement that they provide a nonsectarian education.[88]

Charter schools pose a number of other problems. Most troubling, there is no clear evidence that charter schools result in clear educational gains. The first national comparison of the reading and math scores of students in charter schools and conventional public schools actually showed the charter school students lagging behind. The proficiency rates of children in both types of schools was embarrassingly low. As the George W. Bush administration was committed to choice programs, the Department of Education released the data with little fanfare, seeking to bury it in a mountain of data.[89]

Because of their relative independence, charter schools are difficult to monitor and assess. While the vast majority of charter schools perform at satisfactory levels, others provide a less-than-quality educational experience for children. In most states, monitoring agencies provide little real program oversight. Arizona's monitoring agency spent most of its time processing applications for new charter school start-ups; it lacked the staff to evaluate individual school performance.[90]

While many choice advocates see charter schools as a compromise between a "true" system of choice and the status quo, Bryan Hassel argues that charter schools are actually preferable to vouchers.[91] Compared to a system of universal vouchers, charter schools run less risk of exacerbating class, race, and religious separatism. Charter schools are prohibited from charging tuition or asking families to add to the money provided to the schools by the state. Charter schools also enjoy only limited selectivity; schools that are oversubscribed usually are required to admit students by lottery, not on the basis of admission tests or other performance scores.

School choice in perspective: Public or private benefits?

Choice arrangements allow individual students to escape failing schools and seek out teachers and a curriculum more responsive to their needs. As the parent of a Cleveland voucher student explained: "After being in the Cleveland public schools, my daughter was listed as a behavior problem. She was a 'D' and 'F' student. . . . [Now my daughter's] behavior and grades are wonderful." The parent of a seventh-grade Milwaukee voucher student similarly pointed to the differences between her daughter's new school and the public schools: "As soon as I came here it was a big change. Here teachers care about you. . . . [In public schools] the teachers were too busy to help."[92]

Yet choice by itself provides no panacea or magic bullet that will remedy the ills of urban education. In many cases, increased funding, not just administrative restructuring, is needed to shape up troubled school districts.[93] School choice arrangements are only one weapon in a broader arsenal of educational reform strategies.[94]

School choice emphasizes only the *private* benefits of schooling, the preferences of the family. Choice plans help children and parents to achieve their personal goals. Yet market-based plans are not always appropriate for *public* education. Charter schools can be set up by evangelical parents, minority activists, and business entrepreneurs who possess a narrow vision of education and what constitutes an appropriate curriculum. Schools of like-minded families pursuing their own narrow-focused, distinctive curriculum and values do not bring the larger American community together. Choice arrangements threaten to undermine the historic success public schools have had instilling in children a sense of shared history, democratic tolerance, and inclusive community values.[95]

Nor do choice arrangements deliver on the promise of increasing racial integration and reducing class stratification. In Cleveland, state-funded scholarships for low-income students did little to increase school integration as suburban school districts refused to participate in the plan.[96]

Critics wonder if the poor are being used as "the poster children in a process that will gradually erode support for all public education."[97] Highly targeted efforts such as the Milwaukee and Cleveland voucher programs certainly can be seen as worthy efforts to bring a better education to inner-city, minority children. But the more enthusiastic advocates of choice are not likely to stop with such targeted programs. They argue that if choice is good for the poor, it is also good for the middle- and upper-middle classes. But expanded choice programs are likely to exacerbate white flight and drain resources from the public schools, undermining both the quality of education and racial integration in public schools.

"NO CHILD LEFT BEHIND"

As a candidate for president, George W. Bush emphasized testing so that administrators and parents could gauge a school's performance and hold schools accountable. The 2002 **No Child Left Behind (NCLB) Act** sought to develop "challenging" and "rigorous" academic standards, assuring that all students will be proficient in reading and math within 12 years. Schools are required to implement testing and then develop strategies for bringing students up to state standards. Each school's scores or "report card" are made public. Parents can then exert pressure for improved school performance; alternatively, they can decide to place their children in better schools.

Specifically, NCLB, as it was written, requires that:

- States annually test students in grades 3 through 8 in math and reading.
- States administer an additional test in high school.
- Schools must show "adequate yearly progress." Schools must develop strategies and show how they are making annual progress toward their educational goals, which must be reached within 12 years.
- Schools that fail to meet progress goals two years in a row are placed on a "Needs Improvement" list. In failing schools, low-income parents can request such services as free tutoring. They are also given the option of enrolling their child in another school within the district.
- Schools meet standards for the education of key subgroups, including students with special education needs, African Americans, Hispanics, American Indians, the poor, and those with limited English speaking ability. If one subgroup fails to pass the test, the entire school is labeled as failing.

Consistent with the decentralization philosophy of the Bush administration, the federal government did not dictate the exact testing instruments, nor did it set exact educational standards. Rather, NCLB left these responsibilities to the states: "So much has been left to state and local governments, the most important political battles are more likely to be waged at these levels than in Washington."[98]

The law was enacted with bipartisan support. But the testing requirements and penalties for failure, which were so easy to write into the law, proved troublesome in the field. Local schools complained that the federal government gave them insufficient resources to implement the testing and improvement strategies required by NCLB. The states argued that the NCLB was an **unfunded mandate** that placed costly new responsibilities on schools districts without providing sufficient funds to cover the associated expenses.[99]

Across the country, school administrators and teachers complained that the law was unduly tough in labeling an entire school as failing when one subgroup, such as special education students, was unable to meet federal standards. In 2004, 87 percent of Florida's schools failed to meet the federal standards. More than 1,400 schools met Florida's own state standards but were considered failing under NCLB.[100]

Educators worried that too much classroom time was being devoted to tests and re-tests and to "teaching to the test," with too little attention given to the social aspects of education. As the tests focused on math and reading, critics further argued that school systems gave inadequate attention to instruction in such fields as the social sciences and the arts. Other schools cut back on field trips and even time for recess in order to prepare students for the tests.[101]

The Bush administration was soon forced to accept numerous compromises in its application of the law as school districts across the nation just could not comply with the initial NCLB requirements. Even the promise that students would be able to transfer out of failing schools proved relatively meaningless in cities such as New York, Los Angeles, and Chicago, because there simply were few seats open in good schools.[102]

In the face of intense opposition from school administrators, teacher unions, and activist parent groups, NCLB was forced to turn away from its initial "hard" or "coercive" approach to promoting increased school accountability. In place of deadlines, penalties and sanctions, greater reliance was given to a "softer" approach in which school "report card" scores would serve to catalyze a process sufficient to bring about fundamental changes.[103]

CONCLUSIONS

A bureaucracy's guiding rules and the actions of individual bureaucrats are important determinants of local service provision. Street-level bureaucrats possess considerable discretionary power; they can decide how to respond to citizens' requests for services, and they may not respond in ways that are in the best interests of their clients. The distribution of public services in a city may often represent unpatterned inequalities, inequalities that result from an agency's internal decision rules; service discrimination is not simply a matter of class and racial bias.

Coproduction, neighborhood-based systems, privatization, contracting out, and the increased use of vouchers, tax credits, and other school-choice systems are all attempts to improve the efficiency and effectiveness of urban service delivery. Individual students have been able to use choice programs to escape unsatisfactory school systems. However, the impact of these programs on student achievement is much less clear. Critics also argue that these alternative service delivery techniques are implemented at the expense of equity concerns and concern for the public good.

In this chapter, we paid especially close attention to the politics of education reform. But our analysis of choice programs can also be applied to other policy areas. Voucher enthusiasts have argued for housing certificates to promote a competitive housing market and increased tenant voice and mobility. **Section 8 housing vouchers** have been around for decades and allow a limited number of families to find their own alternatives to public housing. But the program does not work for everyone. Vouchers offered tenants no real choice in tight housing markets with high rental prices. Vouchers are of the most limited value to the poorest of the poor, families that are the hardest to relocate, including large families, grandparent-led families, people with mental and physical health problems, drug abusers, and ex-offenders.[104] Under such conditions, the demolition of public housing and the "vouchering out" of housing programs often leads to the reconcentration and resegregation of the poor, not real choice and mobility.[105]

Privatization and choice strategies provide important routes to improved service delivery and increased citizen satisfaction. Service restructuring can provide for greater service efficiency and effectiveness. But it is quite difficult to assure that privatization and other service reform efforts will also respect equity values and respond to the demands of the diversity of urban citizens. It is to a further consideration of one aspect of diversity—gender—that we now turn.

NOTES

1. Theodore J. Lowi, "Machine Politics Old and New," *Public Interest* (Fall 1967): p. 86.
2. Ibid.
3. H. H. Gerth and C. Wright Mills, eds., *From Max Weber: Essays in Sociology* (New York: Oxford University Press, 1946), pp. 196–204.
4. Joseph Wambaugh has written several novels about how veteran police officers socialize new members of the force to the established ways of doing things. See, for instance, *The Blue Knight, The New Centurions,* and *The Black Marble.* James Ellroy's gritty *L.A. Confidential* and many other of police thrillers often center around the tensions between idealistic newcomers and veterans on the big-city police force. To date no exciting novel has been written about how senior sanitation workers instruct new coworkers in how to follow unwritten agency norms.

5. Sandra J. Clark, Martha R. Burt, Margaret M. Schulte, and Karen Maguire, "Coordinated Community Responses to Domestic Violence in Six Communities: Beyond the Justice System," Washington, DC: The Urban Institute (October 1996), available at: www.urban.org/crime/ccr96.htm.

6. Michael Lipsky, "Toward a Theory of Street-Level Bureaucracy," in *Theoretical Perspectives on Urban Politics*, eds. Willis Hawley et al. (Englewood Cliffs, NJ: Prentice-Hall, 1976), p. 196. Also see Michael Lipsky, "Standing the Study of Public Policy Administration on Its Head," in *American Politics and Public Policy*, eds. Walter Dean Burnham and Martha Wagner Weinberg (Cambridge, MA: MIT Press, 1978), p. 397.

7. Janet Coble Vinzant and Lane Crothers, *Street-Level Leadership: Discretion and Legitimacy in Front-Line Public Service* (Washington, DC: Georgetown University Press, 1998), pp. 43–44.

8. Michael Lipsky, *Street-Level Bureaucracy: Dilemma of the Individual in Public Services* (New York: Russell Sage Foundation, 1980), p. 55.

9. Jeffrey M. Prottas, "The Power of the Street-Level Bureaucrat in Public Service Bureaucracies," *Urban Affairs Quarterly* 13 (March 1978): 289.

10. Clark et al., "Coordinated Community Responses to Domestic Violence in Six Communities: Beyond the Justice System."

11. Ibid.

12. Richard Weatherly, *Reforming Special Education: Policy Implementation from State Level to Street Level* (Cambridge, MA: MIT Press, 1979).

13. Vinzant and Crothers, *Street-Level Leadership*, p. 146.

14. The discussion that follows is based on Frank Levy, Arnold Meltsner, and Aaron Wildavsky, *Urban Outcomes: Schools, Streets and Libraries* (Berkeley: University of California Press, 1974), pp. 16–17. Deborah Stone, *Policy Paradox: The Art of Political Decision Making*, revised ed. (New York: W.W. Norton, 2002), pp. 39–85, presents a detailed discussion of the competing definitions of the term *equity*. She challenges the belief that policies that advance equity goals always entail a reduction in economic efficiency.

15. Robert L. Lineberry, *Equality and Urban Policy: The Distribution of Municipal Services* (Beverly Hills, CA: Sage Publications, 1977), chap. 3. A study of service delivery in Oakland, California reported similar results; see Levy, Meltsner, and Wildavsky, *Urban Outcomes*, chap. 3.

16. Bryan D. Jones, Saadia R. Greenberg, Clifford Kaufman, and Joseph Drew, "Service Delivery Rules and the Distribution of Local Government Services: Three Detroit Bureaucracies," *Journal of Politics* (May 1978): 332–368.

17. Frederic N. Bolotin and David L. Cingranelli, "Equity and Urban Policy: The Underclass Hypothesis Revisited," *Journal of Politics* 45 (1983): 209–219.

18. Gregory Streib and Theodore H. Poister, "Performance Measurement in Municipal Governments," *Municipal Year Book* 1998 (Washington, DC: International City/County Management Association, 1998), pp. 9–15. Also see David Ammons, *Municipal Benchmarks: Assessing Local Performance and Establishing Community Standards* (Thousand Oaks, CA: Sage Publications, 1996).

19. Harry P. Hatry, *Performance Measurement: Getting Results* (Washington, DC: The Urban Institute, 1999), pp. 45–46 and 75–93.

20. For more details as to the processes, achievements, and limitations of performance management, see: David Ammons, "Overcoming the Inadequacies of Performance Measurement in Local Government: The Case of Libraries and Leisure Services," *Public Administration Review* (January/February 1995); Patricia Keehley et al.,

Benchmarking for Best Practices in the Public Sector: Achieving Performance Breakthroughs in Federal, State and Local Agencies (San Francisco: Jossey-Bass, 1997); Kathryn E. Newcomer, ed., *Using Performance Measurement to Improve Public and Non-Profit Programs* (San Francisco: Jossey-Bass, 1997).

21. Eric Pooley, "Fighting Back Against Crack," *New York Magazine*, January 23, 1989, pp. 38–39.

22. Wesley G. Skogan and Susan M. Hartnett, *Community Policing, Chicago Style* (New York: Oxford University Press, 1997), pp. 8 and 173.

23. Anne Elder and Ira Cohen, "Major Cities and Disease Crises: A Comparative Perspective" (paper presented at the annual meeting of the Midwest Political Science Association, Chicago, April 14–16, 1988). Also see P. Arno, "The Nonprofit Sector's Response to the AIDS Epidemic: Community-Based Services in San Francisco," *American Journal of Public Health* 76 (1986): 1325–1330.

24. Anna M. Santiago and Merry Morash, "Strategies for Serving Latina Battered Women," in *Gender in Urban Research, Urban Affairs Annual Review* 42, eds. Judith A. Garber and Robyne S. Turner (Thousand Oaks, CA; Sage Publications, 1995), pp. 228–233.

25. Jeffrey R. Henig, Richard C. Hula, Marion Orr, and Desiree S. Pedescleaux, *The Color of School Reform: Race, Politics, and the Challenge of Urban Education* (Princeton, NJ: Princeton University Press, 1999).

26. For analyses of the BID movement, see: Heather Mac Donald, "BIDs Really Work," in *The Millennial City: A New Urban Paradigm for 21st-Century America*, ed. Myron Magnet (Chicago: Ivan R. Dee, 2000), pp. 388–403; Jerry Mitchell, "BIDs and the New Revitalization of Downtown," *Economic Development Quarterly* 4 (2001): 115–123; Martin Symes and Mark Steel, "Lessons from America: The Role of Business Improvement Districts as an Agent of Regeneration," *Town Planning Review* 3 (2003): 301–314; and Lawrence O. Houston, *Business Improvement Districts* (Washington, DC: Urban Land Institute, 2003).

27. Marla Dickerson, "Improvement Districts Spur Revival—and Division," *Los Angeles Times*, January 20, 1999. New York City had 44 BIDs in 2002.

28. "Mayor Michael R. Bloomberg and DBS Commissioner Robert Walsh Announce Eight Initiatives Designed to Boost the Positive Impact of Business Improvement Districts," press release, New York City Office of the Mayor, May 14, 2002. Available at: www.nyc.gov.

29. Edward T. Rogowsky and Jill Simone Gross, "To BID or Not to BID?" *Metropolitics* 1, 4 (Spring 1998), 7–8.

30. Carol Schatz, president and chief executive of the Los Angeles Downtown Center BID, quoted in Dickerson, "Improvement Districts Spur Revival—and Division."

31. Peter Grant, "BID Execs Pressured Out: Giuliani Prevails in Grand Central Partnership Dispute," *The (New York) Daily News*, September 23, 1998; David Firestone, "An Admirer of Giuliani Feels His Wrath," *The New York Times*, July 31, 1998; Thomas J. Lueck, "The Mayor's Reach," *The New York Times*, April 5, 1998.

32. Heather Barr, "More Like Disneyland: State Action, 42 U.S.C. 1 1983, and Business Improvement Districts in New York," *Columbia Human Rights Law Review* 28 (Winter 1997).

33. Bruce W. McClendon, *Customer Service in Local Government* (Chicago: American Planning Association, 1992), p. 104. For a discussion of privatization efforts in the area of mass transportation, see Simin Hakim, Paul Seidenstat, and Gary W. Bowman, eds., *Privatizing Transportation Systems* (Westport, CT: Praeger Publishers, 1996).

34. Carl F. Valente and Lydia D. Manchester, *Rethinking Local Services: Examining Alternative Delivery Approaches* (Washington, DC: International City Management Association, 1984), p. xi. Also see Ted Kolderie, "The Two Different Concepts of Privatization," *Public Administration Review* 46 (July/August 1986): 285–291; and Donald F. Kettl, *Sharing Power: Public Governance and Private Markets* (Washington, DC: The Brookings Institution, 1993). For an easy-to-read overview of the distinction between *provision* and *production* as it affects urban service delivery, see Ronald J. Oakerson, *Governing Local Public Economies: Creating the Civic Metropolis* (Oakland, CA: Institute for Contemporary Studies Press, 1999), pp. 7–9.

35. Douglas Martin, "Management of Central Park Is Going Private," *The New York Times,* February 12, 1998.

36. For a review of the arguments for and against privatization, see: Steve H. Hanke, ed., *Prospects for Privatization* (New York: Academy of Political Science, 1987); E. S. Savas, *Privatization: The Key to Better Government* (Chatham, NJ: Chatham House, 1987); Joseph Cordes, Jeffrey R. Henig, and Eric Charles Twombly, "Nonprofit Human Service Providers in an Era of Privatization: Toward a Theory of Economic and Political Response," *Policy Studies Review* 18, 4 (Winter 2001): 91–111; and Timothy Chandler and Peter Feuille, "Cities, Unions and the Privatization of Sanitation Services" *Journal of Labor Research* 15 (Winter 1994), pp. 53–77.

37. Stephen Goldsmith, *The Twenty-First Century City: Resurrecting Urban America* (Lanham, MD: Rowman and Littlefield, 1999), especially pp. 18–19.

38. Alison Mitchell, "Giuliani Warns Custodians They May Lose School Jobs," *The New York Times,* May 13, 1994; and John C. Fager, "School Custodians' Dirty Tricks," *The New York Times,* December 18, 1992; Elissa Gootman, "Education Dept. Plans Nearly 500 Job Cuts," *The New York Times,* December 9, 2003.

39. See E. S. Savas, "Municipal Monopolies versus Competition in Delivering Urban Services," in *Improving the Quality of Urban Management,* p. 483; Werner Z. Hirsch, *Privatizing Government Services: An Economic Analysis of Contracting Out by Local Governments* (Los Angeles: Institute for Industrial Relations-UCLA, 1991). E. S. Savas, *Privatization and Public-Private Partnerships* (New York: Chatham House/Seven Bridges Press, 2000), pp. 147–173, examines privatization efforts in the United States and around the globe.

40. Jeffrey D. Greene, *Cities and Privatization: Prospects for the New Century* (Upper Saddle River, NJ: Prentice-Hall, 2002), pp. 42–43.

41. Barbara Stevens, ed., *Delivering Municipal Services Efficiently: A Comparison of Municipal and Private Service Delivery* (New York: Ecodata, 1984); Eileen Brettler Berenyi and Barbara J. Stevens, "Does Privatization Work? A Study of the Delivery of Eight Local Services," *State and Local Government Review* 20 (Winter 1988): 11–20. Stevens compared public and private provision in eight service areas: street cleaning, janitorial services, residential refuse collection, payroll preparation, traffic signal maintenance, asphalt overlay construction, turf maintenance, and street tree maintenance. For all services except payroll preparation, considerable cost savings were recognized.

42. Graeme A. Hodge, *Privatization: An International Review of Performance* (Boulder, CO: Westview Press, 2000), especially pp. 232–240.

43. Elliott Sclar, *The Privatization of Public Service: Lessons From Case Studies* (Washington, DC: Economic Policy Institute, 1997); Lawrence L. Martin, *Selecting Services for Public-Private Competition* (Washington, DC: ICMA MIS

Report, Mark, 1996); and Arnold H. Raphaelson, ed., *Restructuring State and Local Services: Ideas, Proposals and Experiments* (Westport, CT: Praeger Publishing, 1998).

44. Selwyn Raab, "Cheaper Trash Pickup With New York's Crackdown on Mob Control," *The New York Times,* May 11, 1998.

45. Greene, *Cities and Privatization,* pp. 96–99.

46. "Sonoma County Sheriff Finds Privatization a Better Deal," *Governing* (July 1994): p. 41.

47. Robert Jay Dilger, Randolph R. Moffett, and Linda Struyk, "Privatization of Municipal Services in America's Largest Cities," *Public Administration Review* 57, 1 (January/February 1997): 25.

48. Jodi Mailander, "Teachers Dislike Pay, Workload at 'Dream School,'" *The (Miami) Herald,* December 18, 1996.

49. For a description of how unions view the management of public schools by for-profit companies, see James G. Cibulka, "The NEA and School Choice," pp. 165–166, and William Lowe Boyd, David N. Plank, and Gary Sykes, "Teachers Unions in Hard Times," pp. 204–206, both in *Conflicting Mission? Teachers, Unions, and Educational Reform,* ed. Tom Loveless (Washington, DC: Brookings Institution, 2000).

50. William Celis 3d, "Hartford Seeking a Company to Run Its Public Schools," *The New York Times,* April 19, 1994; George Judson, "Hartford to End Private Management of Schools, Citing Struggles Over Finances," *The New York Times,* January 24, 1996; George Judson, "Private Business, Public Schools: Why Hartford Experiment Failed," *The New York Times,* March 11, 1996.

51. Marion Orr, "The Challenge of School Reform in Baltimore: Race, Jobs, and Politics," in *Changing Urban Education,* ed. Clarence N. Stone (Lawrence: University of Kansas Press, 1998), pp. 106–113.

52. Michael Mintrom and Sandra Vergari, "Education Reform and Accountability," *Publius: The Journal of Federalism* 27, 2 (Spring 1997): 161.

53. "TesseracT Assures Parents: Schools Will Stay Open," *School Reform News,* a publication of The Heartland Institute (April 1, 2000), available at: www.heartland.org/Article.cfm?artId=11047.

54. John E. Chubb, "The Performance of Privately Managed Schools: An Early Look at the Edison Project" in *Learning from School Choice,* eds. Paul E. Peterson and Bryan C. Hassel (Washington, DC: Brookings Institution Press, 1998), pp. 213–248, especially pp. 238–241. Also see Tamar Lewin, "Edison Schools Say Students Gain," *The New York Times,* April 7, 1999.

55. For an overview of the variety of school reform and choice proposals, see Diane Ravitch and Joseph P. Viteritti, eds., *New Schools for a New Century: The Redesign of Urban Education* (New Haven: Yale University Press, 1997); Stephen Sugarman and Frank R. Kemerer, eds., *School Choice and Social Controversy: Politics, Policy and Law* (Washington, DC: Brookings Institution Press, 1999); and Brian P. Gill, P. Michael Timpane, Karen E. Ross, and Dominic J. Brewer, *Rhetoric Versus Reality: What We Know and What We Need to Know About Vouchers and Charter Schools* (New York: RAND Education, 2001).

56. There is a vast body of literature that advocates school vouchers. In particular, see: William G. Howell and Paul E. Peterson, *The Education Gap: Vouchers and Urban Schools* (Washington, DC: Brookings Institution, 2002); and Terry M. Moe, *Schools, Vouchers, and the American Public* (Washington, DC; Brookings Institution, 2001). John E. Coons and Stephen D. Sugarman, *Education by*

Choice: The Case for Family Control (Berkeley: University of California Press, 1976), propose a tightly regulated voucher system that does not allow parents to use their own wealth to supplement the vouchers. This proposal is quite different from the more unregulated voucher proposals advanced by other advocates of privatized schooling.

57. Gill et al., *Rhetoric Versus Reality,* pp. 50–51 and 144–145.

58. For a discussion of the charter school concept and its implementation, see: Sandra Vergari, ed., *The Charter School Landscape* (Pittsburgh, PA: University of Pittsburgh Press, 2002); Bryan C. Hassel, *The Charter School Challenge* (Washington, DC: Brookings Institution, 1999); and Danny Weil, *Charter Schools: A Reference Handbook* (Santa Barbara, CA: ABC-CLIO, 2000).

59. Mark Silva, "Session Ends With OK of Vouchers," *The (Miami) Herald,* May 1, 1999; Gill et al., *Rhetoric Versus Reality,* pp. 53–54; Howell and Peterson, *The Education Gap,* pp. 205–206.

60. John E. Chubb and Terry M. Moe, *Politics, Markets, and America's Schools* (Washington, DC: Brookings Institution, 1990), p. 26. Other arguments for increased choice in public schools can be found in Kenneth R. Godwin, "Using Market-Based Incentives to Empower the Poor," in *Public Policy for Democracy,* eds. Helen Ingram and Steven Rathgeb Smith (Washington, DC: Brookings Institution, 1993), pp. 163–197. Also see Ravitch and Viteritti, *New Schools for a New Century.*

61. Ernest L. Boyer, "Foreword" to The Carnegie Foundation for the Advancement of Teaching, *School Choice: A Special Report* (Princeton, NJ: Carnegie Foundation, 1992), p. xv. For a detailed explication of the criticisms of school choice, see Kevin B. Smith and Kenneth I. Meier, *The Case Against School Choice: Politics, Markets, and Fools* (Armonk, NY: M. E. Sharpe, 1995).

62. Ibid. p. 58.

63. Ibid.

64. Gill et al., *Rhetoric Versus Reality,* pp.160–183, reviews the arguments and evidence on the impact of choice programs on racial integration.

65. *Zelman v. Simmons-Harris,* 536 U.S. 639 (2002).

66. *Holmes v. Bush,* Circuit Court of the Second Judicial Circuit, Leon County, Florida, Case No. CV 99-3370 (August 5, 2002).

67. John F. Witte, *The Market Approach to Education: An Analysis of America's First Voucher Program* (Princeton, NJ: Princeton University Press, 2000), p. 45.

68. Carnegie Foundation, *School Choice: A Special Report,* p. 70.

69. Witte, *the Market Approach to Education.*

70. Carnegie Foundation, *School Choice: A Special Report,* p. 67; Sam Dillon, "Collapse of 60 Charter Schools Leaves Californians Scrambling." *The New York Times,* September 17, 2004.

71. Ibid., p. 73.

72. Witte, *The Market Approach to Education,* pp. 119–143.

73. Greene, Peterson, and Du, "School Choice in Milwaukee: A Randomized Experiment," pp. 338 and 345. Also see Greene, Peterson, and Du, with Leesa Boeger and Curtis L. Frazier, "The Effectiveness of School Choice in Milwaukee: A Secondary Analysis of Data from the Program's Evaluation" (paper presented at the annual meeting of the American Political Science Association, San Francisco, August 30, 1996). Available at: www.harvard.edu/pepg/op/evaluate.htm. Critics of the Milwaukee plan respond that the apparent improvement in performance was merely the result of self-election bias, that the voucher children were more

advantaged, that their parents were better educated, and that they came from fewer broken homes than did low-income children in Milwaukee's regular class-rooms. See Richard Rothstein, "Vouchers: The Evidence," *The American Prospect* 11, 1 (November 23, 1999): 51.

74. Frederick M. Hess, "Hints of the Pick-Axe: Competition and Public Schooling in Milwaukee," in *Charters, Vouchers, and Public Education,* eds. Paul E. Peterson and David E. Campbell (Washington, DC: Brookings Institution, 2001), pp. 173–175; Frederick M. Hess, *Revolution at the Margins: The Impact of Competition on Urban School Systems* (Washington, DC: Brookings Institution, 2002), pp. 17–18 and 197–208.

75. Howell and Peterson, *The Education Gap*, pp. 168–184; Moe, Schools, Vouchers, and the American Public, pp. 210–216 and 221–222; Witte, *The Market Approach to Education*, pp. 117–118; Patrick J. McGuinn, "Race, School Vouchers, and Urban Politics: the Disconnect Between African-American Elite and Mass Opinion," (paper presented at the annual meeting of The American Political Science Association, San Francisco, August 30–September 2, 2001).

76. Seymour Fliegel with James MacGuire, *Miracle in East Harlem: The Fight for Choice in Public Education* (New York: Times Books, 1993). p. 92. Also see Chubb and Moe, *Politics, Markets, and America's Schools,* pp. 212–215.

77. For studies that question the evidence normally used to document the success of School District 4, see David L. Kirp, "What School Choice Really Means," *The Atlantic Monthly* (November 1992): pp. 119–132; Billy Tashman, "Hyping District 4," *The New Republic,* December 7, 1992: pp. 14–16; The Carnegie Foundation, *School Choice: A Special Report,* pp. 38–46; and Jeffrey R. Henig, *Rethinking School Choice: Limits of the Market Metaphor* (Princeton, NJ: Princeton University Press, 1994), pp. 131–132 and 142–144.

78. Melissa Marschall, "The Role of Information and Institutional Arrangements in Stemming the Stratifying Effects of School Choice," *Journal of Urban Affairs* 22, 3 (2000): 333–350.

79. Paul E. Peterson, "School Choice: A Report Card," in *Learning from School Choice,* ed. Peterson and Hassel, p. 7.

80. Center for Educational Reform, "Number of Operating Charter Schools Up 10 Percent," press release, February 11, 2004. Available at: http://edreform.com/index.cfm?fuseAction=document&documentID=1704&sectionID=55. The CER data on state charter school leaders can be found at the U.S. Charter Schools website at: www.uscharterschools.org/pub/uscs_docs/o/index.htm.

81. Paul Teske, Mark Schneider, Jack Buckley, and Sara Clark, "Can Charter Schools Change Traditional Public Schools?" in *Charters, Vouchers, and Public Education,* eds. Peterson and Campbell, pp. 188–238; Frederick Hess, Robert Maranto, and Scott Milliman. "Coping With Competition: How School Systems Respond to School Choice," a working paper of the A. Alfred Taubman Center for State and Local Government's Program on Education Policy and Governance, Harvard University, 1998.

82. Robert Maranto, Scott Milliman, Frederick Hess, and April Gresham, "Do Charter Schools Improve District Schools? Three Approaches to the Question," in *School Choice in the Real World: Lessons from Arizona Charter Schools,* eds. Robert Maranto, Scott Milliman, Frederick Hess, and April Gresham (Boulder, CO: Westview, 1999), pp. 129–141.

83. Peterson, "School Choice: A Report Card," pp. 10–11.

84. Tamara Audi, "Desegregation an Issue in Charter School Plan," *Detroit Free Press*, September 3, 1998.

85. Priscilla Wohlsetter, Noelle C. Griffin, and Derrick Chau, "Charter Schools in California: A Bruising Campaign for Public School Choice," in *the Charter School Landscape*, pp. 48–49.

86. Peggy Walsh-Sarnecki, "National Heritage-run Charter Schools Making Profits," *Manatee-Bradenton-Sarasota Herald Today*, Knight Ridder wire story, January 15, 2003.

87. Anemona Hartocollis, "Religious Leaders Map Plans to Use New Law for Publicly Financed Charter Schools," *The New York Times*, December 29, 1998.

88. Peter Schrag, "The Voucher Seduction," *The American Prospect* 11, 1 (November 23, 1999): 52.

89. Diana Jean Schemo, "Nation's Charter Schools Lagging Behind, U.S. Test Scores Reveal," *The New York Times*, August 17, 2004.

90. Gregg A. Garn and Robert T. Stout, "Closing Charters: How a Good Theory Failed in Practice," in *School Choice in the Real World*, eds. Maranto et al., pp. 129–141.

91. Bryan C. Hassel, "The Case for Charter Schools," in *Learning from School Choice*, eds. Peterson and Hassel, pp. 33–37. Joe Nathan, *Charter Schools* (San Francisco: Jossey-Bass, 1996), pp. 6–8, also discusses the advantages of charter schools.

92. The quotations are from Peterson, "School Choice: A Report Card," pp. 17 and 19.

93. Carol Ascher, Norm Fruchter, and Robert Berne, *Hard Lessons: Public Schools and Privatization* (Washington, DC: Brookings Institution/Twentieth Century Fund, 1997). Also see Paul C. Bauman, *Governing Education: Public Sector Reform or Privatization* (Boston: Allyn and Bacon, 1996).

94. Carnegie Foundation, *School Choice: A Special Report*, pp. 83–84.

95. Henig, *Rethinking School Choice*, chap. 9 and pp. 199–209; Bruce Fuller, ed., *Inside Charter Schools The Paradox of Radical Decentralization* (Cambridge, MA: Harvard University Press, 2000). For the rejoinder to the argument that charter schools balkanize American society, see Chester E. Finn, Jr., Bruno V. Manno, and Gregg Vanourek, *Charter Schools in Action: Renewing Public Education* (Princeton, NJ: Princeton University Press, 2000), pp. 156–160. Also see Peter W. Cookson, Jr., and Kristina Berger, *Expect Miracles: Charter Schools and the Politics of Hope and Despair* (Boulder, CO: Westview, 2002), especially pp. 139–144; and Gill et al., *Rhetoric Versus Reality*, pp. 20–24 and 191–193.

96. Joseph P. Viteritti, "School Choice and State Constitutional Law," in *Learning from School Choice*, eds. Peterson and Hassel, pp. 413–414.

97. Schrag, "The Voucher Seduction," p. 49.

98. Martin R. West and Paul E. Peterson, "The Politics and Practice of Accountability," in *No Child Left Behind? The Politics and Practice of School Accountability*, eds. Paul E. Peterson and Martin R. West (Washington. DC: Brookings Institution, 2003), p. 19. Our description of the NCLB Act relies greatly on West and Peterson, pp. 1–20, and Andrew Rudalevige, "No Child Left Behind: Forging Congressional Compliance," in *No Child Left Behind*, eds. Peterson and West, pp. 25–27.

99. Michael Dobbs, "More States Are Fighting 'No Child Left Behind,'" *Washington Post*, February 19, 2004.

100. Michael Winerip, "Making Leaps, but Still Labeled as Failing," *The New York Times,* April 28, 2004.

101. Jay Mathews, "Federal Education Law Squeezes out Recess," *Washington Post,* April 9, 2004.

102. Diana Jean Schemo, "Effort by Bush on Education Faces Obstacles in the States," *The New York Times,* August 18, 2004.

103. Frederick M. Hess, "Refining or Retreating? High-Stakes Accountability in the States," in *No Child Left Behind,* eds. Peterson and West, pp. 54–79; West and Peterson, "The Politics and Practice of Accountability," pp. 12–15.

104. Susan J. Popkin, Martha Burt, and Mary K. Cunningham, "Public Housing Transformation and the 'Hard to House'" (paper presented at the annual meeting of the Urban Affairs Association, Washington, DC, April 3, 2004).

105. John Goering and Judith D. Feins, eds., *Choosing a Better Life? Evaluating the Move to Opportunity Experiment* (Washington, DC: Urban Institute, 2003), especially pp. 59–60, 172–173 and 398–399; Edward G. Goetz, *Clearing the Way: Deconcentrating the Poor in Urban America* (Washington, DC: The Urban Institute, 2003), pp. 57–58, 73–74 and 239–243.

WOMEN AND THE GENDERED CITY

Robyne S. Turner

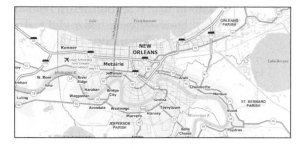

Throughout this book, we have seen examples of women participating in the urban arena. We have also begun to show how the urban situation has affected women's lives. This chapter focuses on how women's interactions with, and perceptions of, local government differ from those of men. Women experience the city differently than men and may approach politics with a different perspective than do men. These differences indicate that there is a *gendered* view of the city and urban policy making.

To see local politics through the eyes of women is to recognize that women often have a distinct point of view. Even when women share many opinions and political loyalties with men, they may arrive at their views based on different perspectives.

Most of our understanding about urban politics is shaped by men who have authored newspaper articles and textbooks. That perspective has become the dominant interpretation of local events, problems, and public policy. In this chapter, another vantage point is used that reflects how women see the city, how local government decisions affects women's lives, and how women wield influence and power in ways that are a bit different from the patterns demonstrated by men.

THE CITY AS A PLACE OF WOMEN

Women experience the issue of gender every day. **Gender,** defined as a social perspective (not as a person's biological sex), influences women's relationships both in the household and in the world of paid work and politics. Gender helps to shape the availability of important resources, including the payment of adequate salaries and the provision of government assistance in response to need. Gender factors, including the glass ceiling and gender-based perceptions of women's abilities, influence women's access to positions of leadership. Even when women hold the same jobs as men, including city manager and mayor, their background, experiences, and opportunities are different. As men do not experience the city in the same way as women, the women's perspective on important issues is not obvious to a male-directed power structure.

Women face unwritten rules as a result of their gender, rules that they do not always appreciate, desire, or even choose to follow. The family, the mass media, popular culture, and public policy all act to define women's roles. Women are expected to be mothers, caregivers, nurturers, supporters, and helpmates. This sometimes translates into subordination.

Women occupy many roles both in the home and in the public realm. While women assume such traditional "feminine" roles as homemaker, caregiver, and volunteer, they are also workers, business owners, breadwinners, elected representatives, civil servants, and heads of families. An increasing number of women have jobs that provide them with similar economic opportunities and resources as men. Yet despite these achievements, there is still a male-female difference when it comes to political power.

Pointed references in politics and society continue to underscore the continuing significance of gender. In contemporary elections, for instance, journalists and political strategists have pointed to "soccer moms" in order to underscore the pivotal importance of the suburban middle-class voters. Of course, there are also "soccer dads," but they do not receive the same media attention, nor are they portrayed in the same way as are women. The reference to moms in minivans sets a social-role expectation that may not be valid for all women. But that reference becomes the popular perception.

Of course, women's roles in the contemporary city are not as constricted as they were historically. It is not too much of an exaggeration to say that male architects, planners, politicians, and industrialists literally built the cities of the United States. Women's participation during earlier periods of urban development was sharply limited by the social conventions of the time and by laws that restricted women's financial and contractual independence. Women were even prohibited from voting before 1920.

However, women in the early twentieth century defied convention when it was obvious to them that a male-centered society was not responding to their needs. The most prominent example of such activism, as we discussed in Chapter 7, is provided by Jane Addams, who founded Hull House, the famous Chicago social service facility for immigrant women and their families.[1] Women were active in volunteer and **settlement house work**, aiding disease prevention and municipal sanitation (the domain of the home!), and providing schooling and playgrounds and other healthy recreation opportunities for immigrant women and their children. The Young Women's Christian Association (YWCA) and the National Association of Colored Women (NACW) were among the more prominent women's organizations that played key roles in providing important services to city dwellers, including safe havens for single women living in the city.[2]

Often overlooked in more conventional histories of the developing city is the relationship that municipal governments established with women. A movement called **municipal housekeeping** overtly connected the health, education, sanitation, and record-keeping functions of the city to the domestic activities of women in their homes and neighborhoods. Cities encouraged women's actions in assisting basic city health and disease prevention services, an extremely important policy area in developing cities too often ravaged by killer epidemics. Women were asked to keep their homes and streets clean, sanitize housewares, and keep their children healthy. Women, in effect, were used as an unrecognized volunteer corps of public servants.

Today, women have the vote and face no legal restrictions on their independence. They may work, volunteer, or contribute to society in whatever ways they see fit. But the social construction of gender in the urban arena continues. Women still must navigate the overt cultural and political expectations of their presence in the city, expectations that are different from those placed on men.

The popular television program *Sex and the City* provides an empowered cultural identity of women. Focused on life in New York City, the most urban of places, the show presents women as characters who are overtly sexual; yet the show's main characters are also portrayed as people who are able to direct both their personal lives and their careers, and take the city by storm.

Contrast *Sex and the City*'s portrayal of women's empowerment to the other popular references that structure a quite different urban environment that women must negotiate. Some urban rap songs, for instance, portray women in a sexual context using lyrics that are often deemed derogatory. The issue is not whether or not a woman should be called "hoes," but rather how the use of such language establishes an image that urban women of color must negotiate in their daily lives. An alternative, more empowering image of urban women is provided by the song "Keep Your Head Up" by Tupac:

> Girl keep your head up
> And when he tells you you ain't nuttin don't believe him
> And if he can't learn to love you you should leave him
> Cause sista you don't need him[3]

In exploring the gendered city, we must be careful of stereotyping. Women do not all face the same experience in the city; differences in income, race, and ethnicity create distinctive experiences. Mainstream feminist theory too often views women through the lens of middle-class white women. Inner-city women entered the urban labor force long before women's liberation. Even today, poor and working-class women do not have the economic luxury of choosing to work or be stay-at-home moms. For immigrant and minority women and their children, the city may provide inadequate economic opportunity, limited housing options, and a failing educational system. New York's Harlem is one neighborhood where community organizations have tried to take a comprehensive approach to providing services in response to the problems that low-income single mothers and their children face in the inner city on a daily basis. (See "The Harlem Children's Zone," p. 314.)

THE HARLEM CHILDREN'S ZONE

The Harlem Children's Zone (HCZ) Project describes itself as a comprehensive effort to provide "positive opportunities" for "all children" living within the 60-block area of central Harlem in New York's upper Manhattan. Despite the gentrification that continues to transform Harlem, central Harlem remains predominantly a low-income neighborhood, with 61 percent of its children below the poverty line and an unemployment rate of 18.5 percent. More than 40 percent of its children drop out of school *before* reaching high school.

The abundance of families in central Harlem are headed by single women. The Harlem Children's Projects seeks to re-shape the community for the healthy development of children. It seeks to assist parents, teachers and other stakeholders in creating "a safe learning environment for youth."

Unlike the more mainstream welfare reform efforts of the 1990s, the HCZ approach does not focus narrowly on getting poor women into the workplace. In contrast, the HCZ seeks to provide poor women and their children with a holistic program of help through the provision of parenting assistance and various after-school, educational, social, and medical programs. HCZ also seeks to establish a safer and better-functioning community and school environment. When children are prepared for school, do well at school, and are cared for after school, parents—especially young mothers—have a better chance to work on their own issues and succeed.

Founded in 1970 as the Rheedlen Centers for Children and Family, the agency initially had a small staff and focused on a single goal, truancy prevention. Reorganized by Geoffrey Canada in the early 1990s, the program changed its name to Harlem's Children Zone to reflect its expanded mission as an agency with 450 full- and part-time staffers providing comprehensive children and family services in the larger Harlem community.

In 2004, the HCZ served 8,400 children and 3,500 adults. Working in conjunction with doctors from Harlem Hospital, 3,000 children were screened for asthma, and 315 families were enrolled in its Asthma Institute, with the program reducing the need for emergency room visits.

The HCZ's "Baby College" seeks to provide low-income parents and grandparents with a "network of support" that will allow them to raise a healthy child who will enter school ready and able to learn. Saturday morning classes provide parents and grandparents child-bonding and disciplinary skills as well as information regarding child health. According to HCZ's 2004 report, 410 Baby College "graduates" enjoyed such benefits as parental reading, updated immunizations, and enhanced safety measures in the home.

The College practices aggressive outreach, using phone banks and door-to-door recruitment efforts, to enroll new participants. The program's recruiters even offer gift certificates, movie passes, and other prizes where necessary to get reluctant or disinterested parents to enroll in the Baby College and other HCZ programs. The HCZ also employs a West African graduate of the

continued

GENDERED REGIMES: DO WOMEN HAVE POLITICAL POWER IN THE CITY?

315

THE HARLEM CHILDREN'S ZONE (CONT.)

College to act as a specialist to reach out to other immigrants from West Africa and to keep in touch with them both during and after their enrollment in the cycle of classes.

Challenging the local environment, the Harlem Children's Zone has also set up its own charter school, much to the displeasure of the local teacher's union. The school is founded on the belief that children from educationally deprived backgrounds need a longer school day to catch up with students from more advantaged homes. The school day at Promise Academy School goes from 8 a.m. to 4 p.m., with after-school activities continuing until 6 p.m. for elementary students and even until 9 p.m. for teens.

While the primary focus of the HCZ is on education, Geoffrey Canada recognizes that marriage, too, can provide a key to success: "Children tend to do better when they have two parents in the house." Yet the HCZ does not seek to promote marriage, which is not even listed among the agency's goals. As Canada explained: "But what ability do we have to make an impact on that? None, right? If we tried to do that, we'd spend all our time just doing that."

Source: The Harlem Children's Zone web site, www.hcz.org. See, in particular, *Harlem's Children Zone: A Look Inside* newsletter (Summer/Fall 2002), available at www.hcz.org/downloads/lookinside3.pdf; "Profile: Harlem Children's Zone Promise Academy School," *Insideschools.org*, available at www.insideschools.org/fs/school_profile.php?id=1375&page=2; also see Paul Tough, "The Harlem Project," *The New York Times Magazine*, (June 20, 2004). The quotation from Geoffrey Canada is from the *Times* article.

GENDERED REGIMES: DO WOMEN HAVE POLITICAL POWER IN THE CITY?

As described in Chapter 4, "Who Has the Power? Decision Making and Urban Regimes," a *regime* denotes the alliances that emerge among city decision makers and key private groups as they attempt to accomplish a shared agenda. Typically, urban development is a dominant issue on the local political agenda. According to an urban political economy perspective, in many cities, a growth-oriented regime dominated by land-based interests drives local politics.

Are women and their interests well represented in local governing regimes? A gendered view of regimes would seek to identify the alternative sources of political power that women and their allies can use to affect local resource allocation and decision making. As women have become more engaged in the political process as community organizers, activists, and elected officials, their views can no longer be fully ignored by the local governing regime. But the extent of women's inclusion in the local regime varies from city to city. Even where women are elected to office and occupy positions in corporate boardrooms, their power is still shaped by gender. Women's influence is often distinct from men's and is channeled into sectors outside the male-dominated political and economic arenas.

Despite the changing shape of urban geography, workplaces are still largely separated from residential land uses. As a result, women in their roles as mothers and homemakers experience the city through different activities than do men who are freer to devote their energies to the workplace and to politics. The separation of home from work means that women and men are offered different opportunities to participate in politics and to shape local policy. The separation between suburban "bedroom" communities and the central business district means that men and women are often active in different geographic spaces with different priorities and expectations. We must remember that the urban form was defined primarily by the actions of men who saw the separation as natural, who believed that women should remain in the home while men played the dominant roles in business and politics. The division helps to produce a predisposition or a bias as to just what issues are seen as important and able to move up the policy agenda.[4]

Women find that they cannot so easily separate personal and "home" issues from their public interests. One helps drive the other. Women who take their children to day care or school in the morning before going to work have an interest in seeing that the city provides accessible child care and improved roads and mass transit. Such women have a perspective that they gain from their "multi-tripping" every work day. A businessman who does not make such daily school trips, in contrast, would likely be less concerned with the public provision of day care or of quality and safe transit. Such a businessman might even believe that the free market fairly determines the adequate provision of pre- and post-school child care. He would have a less "personal" view that sees transportation only in terms of the supportive infrastructure needed to get workers and goods to business.

This difference between the power of men and women is a reflection of the concept of *patriarchy*. In the study of urban politics, **patriarchy** refers to a systemized distribution of power, use of power, and appropriation of power that reflects how men see the city, how they use the city, and how their vision shapes what the city should be. Patriarchy does not recognize that women have different experiences in, and observations of, the city. Patriarchy leads to a skewed process that determines problems and produces public decisions, from zoning to transit to social services, only from a man's experience and perspective. Local government is especially important to the lives of women. (See "Gender and Local Government: A Global Perspective," on p. 317.) Women seek policies to increase the livability of cities, policies that will contribute to, rather than hinder, women's lives.[5] Men, in contrast, tend to take a more economic or competitive perspective in determining what they see to be the proper course of public policy.

The City of Denver struggled to find new designs for urban growth that would respond to the needs of working women.[6] The male-centered view of urban development had led to patterns of spatial segregation, with single-family structures built in residential areas located at some distance from corporate workplaces and supportive family services. This development approach discouraged the construction of family housing units in the downtown. Yet low-income women, single-heads of household, and single women do not necessarily want, nor can they afford, a traditional, single-family home in the suburbs. Women's groups pushed Denver for the construction of more

GENDER AND LOCAL GOVERNMENT: A GLOBAL PERSPECTIVE

"From a gender perspective, local government is the closest and most accessible level of government to women. Local governments traditionally provide services utilized by individual households such as electricity, waste disposal, public transport, water, schools, health clinics and other social services. The decisions of local governments therefore have a direct impact on the private lives of women, because they are traditionally responsible for providing for and caring for the family and the home in most countries. Women also have important and unique contributions to make to the development of these services. They must be fully part of the local democratic system and have full access to the decision making structure. Until the interests of women have been represented at the local level, the system is not fully democratic."

—International Union of Local Authorities (IULA)

Source: Diana Lee-Smith, "Women's Role in Urban Governance," *Habitat Debate* 6, 1 (1998). Available at: www.unhabitat.org/HD/hdv6n1/whd.html.

mixed-use developments in the central city, developments with retail stores on the ground floor and residential space on the upper floors. Women also argued for socially integrated urban neighborhoods with amenities for children, as well as stores and services that would shorten shopping trips. However, the City of Denver rejected the requests as too expensive. As land in the commercial core is highly priced, playgrounds and family amenities did not make economic sense; it did not represent using land at its highest value. The women's groups had wanted more housing options. But they ultimately were forced to accept the decision made by developers and city officials guided by the development concerns of a patriarchal power structure.

WOMEN ELECTED TO LOCAL OFFICE

One strategy for changing local policies relies on electing more women to office. Women are more likely to be elected at the local level of government than at the state or national level.[7] Yet women are still underrepresented at the municipal level. (See "Women Elected to Local Government" on p. 318.) Typically, women serve as mayors in about 20 percent of America's cities. For the nation's biggest cities, the figure is even less. Women are more likely to be elected mayor in cities where the position is part-time.[8] In 1998, nearly 100 mayors nationwide were African-American women.[9]

The structure of government can affect opportunity for women. Women are more likely to serve on larger sized councils and on councils where service is a part-time, not a full-time, job.[10]

Voting rules also influence just who gets elected to office. As we saw in Chapter 7, "Reform Politics," at-large voting rules dilute the voting power of spatially concentrated racial minorities. Numerous cities have adopted district

WOMEN ELECTED TO LOCAL GOVERNMENT

According to the 2000 Census, women make up 51 percent of the population. Yet:

- In 2004, women were mayors in only 14 of the largest 100 cities in the U.S.
- Of the 243 cities with a population of 100,000 or greater, women were mayors in only 37.
- Women were mayors in 17 percent or 188 of 1107 cities with a population over 30,000.
- In 2003, women won 17 percent, or 70 of the 411 mayoral elections. In the first half of the 2004 electoral cycle, women won 21 percent, or 39 of the 186 mayoral races.
- Women in 2001 made up 28 percent of the membership of city councils, the same figure as in 1979.
- Women held 24 percent of county offices and 44 percent of school board offices in 1998. The relatively high rate of service by women on school boards is easily explained. Schools and the caring of children have traditionally been considered as an "appropriate" domain for women's activism.

Sources: M. Margaret Conway, "Women's Political Participation at the State and Local Level in the United States," *PS Online* (January 2004): pp. 1–12; Center for American Women in Politics, "Fact Sheet: Women in Elective Office 2004," a publication of the Eagleton Institute for Politics, Rutgers University, New Brunswick, New Jersey, available at http://www.cawp.rutgers.edu/Facts/Officeholders/elective.pdf; Bill Woodwell, "Gender, Education Gaps Closing on City Councils," National League of Cities, (July 21, 2003), www.nlc.org.

and mixed voting systems in order to increase the representation of racial minorities.[11] But at-large voting systems have not had a similar discriminatory effect on the representation of women, as some women's advocacy groups initially thought. Women are not a spatially concentrated population; unlike racial minorities, they do not live in one part of the city. As a result, they are not necessarily disempowered by at-large voting systems. At-large voting systems, however, may work to diminish the numbers of African-American women elected to office.

The size of the city may also have a bearing on the electoral success of women. Women do somewhat less well in the race for mayor in the nation's largest cities than in smaller cities. In 2003, women were mayors in 14 percent of the nation's 100 largest cities, 15 percent of cities with a population over 100,000, and 17 percent in cities with populations over 30,000.[12]

The pattern is a bit different for city councils. Women held 36 percent of council seats in larger cities as compared to only 25 percent in small cities. As women are more likely to be elected to part-time or "volunteer" councils, suburban councils and boards offer a likely electoral location for women.

Incumbency also affects women's prospects for success in local elections. Because women are underrepresented in government, most incumbents who run for reelection are men; there are relatively few incumbent women who run for reelection in any given year.[13] As incumbency is a significant factor in elections, a system of term limits can reduce the advantages of incumbency and thereby aid women's electoral success. Term limits lead to more open-seat elections where women may be as competitive as men.[14]

Overall, the presence or absence of women candidates on the ballot continues to be the most significant factor in predicting whether women are elected to local office. Simply put, more women win when more women run for office. In some cases, political parties and the prevailing climate of social expectations act to discourage women from running for local office.

Could it also be that women simply choose not to engage in politics as much as men? Data from the American National Election Study in 2000 and 2002 indicate that even outside the electoral arena, men were significantly more likely than women to have participated in policy advocacy in local affairs.[15] One explanation for this difference is that women do not have as much discretionary time as do men. Women have responsibilities for caregiving, raising children, and running the household, in addition to holding paid jobs. These obligations limit how much time women can devote to public advocacy and political participation.[16]

In reviewing women's participation in local elections, it should also be noted that women are more likely than men to vote for women candidates.[17] Women vote for candidates who speak to the issues that resonate with their needs and experiences.

As just discussed, the type of electoral system (at-large or district-based) has no clear influence on the ability of women to win local office. Yet the form or structure of a city's government does appear to exert considerable influence on which issues are pursued by city hall. In the Sunbelt, as we discussed in Chapter 7, the business model of reformed city government flourished, and local developers and growth coalitions dominated city political regimes. This business-elite model of politics left women, who were not yet established in local businesses, on the outside with few routes to political influence.

But the Sunbelt and the city manager profession have both changed over the years. Women in Sunbelt communities have been leaders of a new entrepreneurial style of politics rooted in neighborhood activism that has challenged the dominant growth agenda. Greater levels of education and affluence have also led to a heightened awareness of women's issues and an increased willingness to elect women to office. A new breed of city managers, too, have shown a concern for women's and equity issues.

WOMEN'S LEADERSHIP IN LOCAL GOVERNMENT

CAREER PATTERNS

Women have begun to advance to the highest levels of elected public office. Yet the same advancement is not always evident in top administrative positions. Less than one-fifth of the top appointed positions are occupied by women. Women continue to dominate those positions that have traditionally been held by women. (See Tables 10-1 and 10-2.) Women are particularly underrepresented

■ TABLE 10–1

FEMALE MUNICIPAL OFFICIALS

Position	Total reporting (A)	Total females No. (B)	% of (A)
Chief elected official	4,311	613	14.2
Chief appointed administrative officer/ manager	3,403	379	11.1
Assistant manager/assistant CAO	1,102	377	34.2
City clerk/secretary	3,872	2,906	75.1
Chief financial officer	2,931	1,056	36.0
Director of economic development	1,031	197	19.1
Treasurer	2,824	1,366	48.4
Director of public works	3,621	46	1.3
Engineer	1,849	32	1.7
Police chief	4,068	27	0.7
Fire chief	3,446	5	0.1
Planning director	1,947	310	15.9
Personnel director	2,031	903	44.5
Risk manager	954	296	31.0
Director of parks and recreation	2,128	301	14.1
Superintendent of parks	1,362	61	4.5
Director of recreation	1,313	800	60.9
Librarian	1,729	1,165	67.4
Director of data processing/info. serv.	872	250	28.7
Purchasing director	1,356	793	58.5

SOURCE: *Municipal Year Book* 1995 (Washington, DC: International City/County Management Association, 1995), p. 188.

in posts that have been traditionally filled by men: the director of public works, city engineer, police chief, and fire chief. In remarkable contrast, 75 percent of all city clerks and 70 percent of county clerks are women, as are two-thirds of municipal librarians.

Women are not as likely to be city managers as they are to be mayors. Only 12 percent of all city managers in the U.S. are women, virtually the same percentage as in 1995.[18] In the cities of over 100,000 population, only 12 percent of the city managers were women in 2001.[19]

■ TABLE 10-2

FEMALE COUNTY OFFICIALS

Position	Total reporting (A)	Total females	
		No. (B)	% of (A)
Chief elected official	1,538	149	9.7
Chief appointed administrative officer	725	133	18.3
Clerk to the governing board	1,426	1,002	70.3
Chief financial officer	1,209	565	46.7
County health officer	937	337	36.0
Planning director	783	129	16.5
County engineer	806	13	1.6
Director welfare/human services	806	365	45.3
Chief law enforcement official	1,544	9	0.6
Purchasing director	626	249	39.8
Personnel director	754	350	46.4

SOURCE: *Municipal Year Book* 1995 (Washington, DC: International City/County Management Association, 1995), p. 268.

The career patterns of top women managers in large cities diverges from those of men. The women managers have a shorter average tenure in their current job than their male counterparts. Women managers in the largest cities are also more likely than men to have a Masters in Public Administration (MPA) degree. Also, 43 percent of women managers in large cities have been in only one city during their career. These figures suggest that while many of these women may be new to the job, others have risen through the ranks.

Conclusions drawn from these figures must be regarded as tentative as they represent findings based on the careers of the few women managers of large cities. A study of women managers in a variety of cities indicates that there may be greater similarity between their careers and those of their male counterparts. The greatest overall difference between men and women managers occurs as women city managers tend to be found in cities with larger average annual budgets; it may be that women are serving more affluent cities.[20]

Women in municipal administration often seek to advance only to the position of assistant city manager and no higher.[21] While men tend to seek greater professional advancement by moving to managerial positions in progressively larger cities, women tend to pursue their career path in only a single city. Women may simply be less willing than men to uproot their lives and the lives of their families to climb the career ladder in a new city.

GENDER AND LEADERSHIP STYLE

The most important differences between women and men city managers relate to their policy orientations and leadership styles. As one review of the attitudes of city managers concludes, "Women and men bring different voices to city management."[22] Women and men have qualitatively different priorities and different perspectives. Women managers tend to have a greater interest in issues that deal with workplace discrimination, homelessness, children's library services, day care, services for seniors, domestic violence, education, poverty, and after-school programs. Their male counterparts, in contrast, tend to focus more on concerns for economic development and revitalization, drugs and crime control, and taxes. When asked to identify the most important issues that their cities faced, women managers identified youth programs while men mentioned economic development.

Issue preferences are not entirely driven by gender. One other possible explanation for the observed differences in priorities is that women are more likely to work in liberal communities. The social liberalism of women as managers might simply reflect their community's larger political orientation.

Executive leadership style is another important area in which there is a difference by gender. (See "Leadership Style: 'Male Voice' and 'Female Voice,'" below.) Women mayors and managers are more likely to be consensus builders who give a high priority to communicating with other decision makers and members of the community. Men in top executive positions, in contrast, are less likely to seek consensual solutions to problems. Instead, their leadership styles are likely to reflect such male-centered norms as majority rule and individual self-reliance.[23]

LEADERSHIP STYLE: "MALE VOICE" AND "FEMALE VOICE"

The "female" voice in management style denotes a collegial rather than a top-down approach to leadership. This approach is referred to as a "female" style, as studies have observed that:

- Women city managers are more likely than men to define their role in terms of "community relations." Women give greater attention to communicating with council members, other governmental officials, and citizens. Women often seek to lead by helping to uncover a policy consensus. They seek to find solutions that are acceptable to a broad range of concerned stakeholders.

- Women managers tend to rely to a greater degree on citizen input to guide decision making than do men.

- Women tend to use their intuition about people, praise other employees, exhibit a sensitivity to subordinates, and demonstrate a willingness to get things done through compromise.

continued

LEADERSHIP STYLE: "MALE VOICE" AND "FEMALE VOICE" (CONT.)

Studies show that men, in contrast, tend to lead via a "male voice." They identify themselves as "entrepreneurs":

- Men tend to emphasize individual accomplishment. Men tend to define justice in terms of the marketplace—each individual gets what he or she works for—with less concern than women show for the disadvantaged.

- Men are more willing to engage in creative discovery and exploit new opportunities.

- Men are more willing than women to apply the standards of business to public life, emphasizing the need to promote efficiency and economic growth over competing social and equity values.

Of course, not all women lead with a "female" voice; nor do men possess only a "male" leadership orientation. Individuals are a mix of "male" and "female" leadership qualities. Still, on the whole, the approach that women take to leadership is quite a bit different than the style that has dominated the male world of politics over the years.

A recognition of the gendered nature of leadership styles means that, in certain localities, women may have difficulty in producing results as their approach to leadership does not quite fit the institutional norms that have developed over the years, norms that reflect "male" expectations of leadership. As more and more women assume public office, however, local political systems can be expected to show an increased acceptance of the alternative, more consensual leadership approach of women.

Source: Richard L. Fox and Robert A. Schuhmann, "Gender and the Role of the City Manager," *Social Science Quarterly* 81 (June 2000), 231.

WOMEN AS MAYORS AND CITY COUNCIL MEMBERS

Some women mayors have been able to discover their own leadership styles. (See "Women Mayors," p. 324.) Others have had to adapt to the dominant norms of the political arena.

In Houston, Mayor Kathy Whitmire served five terms, having entered office on a promise to challenge the influence of the "golden boys" growth machine at city hall. Most of her success as mayor, however, stemmed from her ability to improve the city budget, a traditionally "male" leadership realm. Whitmire had served as city comptroller before becoming mayor. She did not rein in developer interests to whom she was later beholden. Whitmire even joined with local development officials in actions that displaced low-income women from rental housing in historically black areas near Houston's central core.

Like Whitmire, Dallas' Annette Strauss (1987–91) campaigned to open decision-making in the city to a more diverse group of people. Strauss had an impact on race relations and moved Dallas out of its segregated past. She also

WOMEN MAYORS

Women have been elected as mayors of major cities throughout the latter half of the twentieth century. Pioneering women have in some cases broken racial and ethnic as well as gender barriers in their electoral victories. Here are some notable "firsts", U.S. cities and their first women mayors:

- **Chicago:** Jane Byrne, one term (1979–83)
- **Houston:** Katherine Whitmire, five terms (1982–91)
- **San Diego:** Maureen O'Connor, two terms (D, 1986–92), Susan Golding, two terms (R, 1992–2000)
- **Dallas:** Annette Strauss (1987–91)
- **Cleveland:** Jane Campbell (2002–06)
- **Pittsburgh:** Sophie Masloff (1988–93), finished her predecessor's term when he died, and then was elected and served one term
- **Atlanta:** Shirley Franklin, the first African-American woman to be mayor of a major southern city (2002–06)
- **Minneapolis:** Sharon Sayles Benton, two terms; first African-American mayor of Minneapolis (1993–2002)
- **Long Beach, CA:** Beverly O'Neill (1994–2006), won nearly 80 percent of the vote in her 1998 reelection and then won an unprecedented third term in 2002 as a write-in candidate
- **Kansas City, MO:** Kay Barnes, two terms, (1999–2007)
- **Portland, OR:** Vera Katz, three terms (1992–2004)
- **Orlando:** Glenda Hood, (1992–2003), left during her third term to become Florida's Secretary of State
- **Washington, DC:** Sharon Pratt Kelly, one term, first female African-American mayor of a major U.S. city (1991–95)
- **Sacramento:** Heather Fargo, two terms (2000–08)
- **Hollywood, FL:** Mara Giulianti (1986–2008, out of office from 1990–92). Mayor Giulianti's eighth term in office will end in 2008.

brought new arts and cultural development to Dallas. During her short tenure, however, she was unable to shift the city's agenda to a new concern for urban livability.

Other women mayors—notably San Diego's Susan Golding, Orlando's Glenda Hood, and Portland's Vera Katz—have had an impact on their cities that reflected gender-based concerns for community affairs. These mayors resisted the demands of the local growth coalition for unfettered development; instead, they sought to mitigate the problems associated with growth and to improve the quality of life in their cities. These mayors also sought inclusive programs of citizen participation, neighborhood empowerment, and afford-able housing. They worked from a broadened definition of civic life with agen-das that reflected the decision-making style and policy priorities of women.

In Kansas City, Mayor Kay Barnes made urban redevelopment her primary concern. Her emphasis on downtown-oriented strategies reflected a traditionally male concern for economic development. However, Barnes tempered traditional development concerns with her insistence on inner-city housing and plans that recognized the value of residential neighborhoods that ring the downtown.

Women's relational and caring experiences help to shape their decision-making styles in the public realm. A study of city councils in New Jersey underscores the difference that gender brings to decision making. When deal-ing with the issue of affordable housing, men on the city council emphasized management concerns, consistency in enforcing the law and housing regula-tions, and maintaining property values. Women council members shared many of these concerns but nonetheless gave higher priority to how housing decisions affected tenants' and families' lives. The women councilors paid attention to resident "need," not just the dictates of good "management." Male members of the councils criticized the women "for listening to the last sad story" and for approaching things "on a more emotional and personalized level."[24]

The deeply established, unwritten rules of local government act to limit the changes that can be brought by an individual woman. The dominant norms reflect the male emphasis on individualism and procedure rather than women's concern for community and equity. It will take the election of a critical mass of women in local government to reformulate the standards of government, to "rethink how politics operates."[25] As the New Jersey study underscores, the decision processes and policy actions of local government will change only as the representation of women increases.

THE GENDER GAP AND IDENTITY POLITICS

Women engage in local politics because it is a venue that affects the quality of life of both their community and their family. Men and women have some-what different policy priorities and preferences. Poll after poll reveals a **gender gap** in terms of the political attitudes. Women are more supportive than men when it comes to spending for social services; men, in contrast, are more sup-portive of increases in military spending and forceful foreign policy action that may even entail an increased risk of war.[26] The gender gap does *not* denote a lesser willingness of women to participate in politics; women are registered to vote and vote at a greater frequency than do men.[27]

For women, there can be no strict separation between the public arena and private life. Women's entrance into local politics "reflects a political strategy which is cognizant of the overlap between public and private spheres and which recognizes community politics as a useful arena for political change."[28]

So-called "women's issues" are too often accorded second-tier status and a lower priority than other issues. Do the concerns of women deserve lower status in the public arena? Or does the identity of women and their association with an issue act to reduce its status in the public arena?

Identity politics looks to a person's self-description as an indicator of his or her politics. In contrast to more orthodox interpretations of politics, economic status and social class are not seen to determine political attitudes. Instead, race, culture, ethnicity, sexuality, and gender are important identities that shape a person's understanding of issues and politics. (See "Identity Politics: Gay and Lesbian Politics," below.) For women, their identity as mothers, caregivers, and wives will have a bearing on how they feel about education, social services, and housing in ways that men do not feel. Men may even perceive the

---

IDENTITY POLITICS: GAY AND LESBIAN POLITICS

The cultural identity of women as women has had an influence on the formation of women's political attitudes that cuts across economic and social-class lines. A "postmodern" view of politics rejects simple "economism" or class-based explanation of political behavior. Instead, political attitudes and actions reflect important cultural or group identities.

Many of the "hottest" issues in the urban arena in recent years have dealt with group identity issues, noneconomic issues that entail a clash of competing cultural values. City and school administrators have been caught in the crossfire between the demand for bilingual education and outspoken criticism of opponents who insist on maintaining "English as the official language." School officials must also decide just whose religion, ethnicity, and holidays are to receive recognition in the multicultural classroom. School boards are further forced to deal with such controversial matters as the provision of sexual and birth control services to students and the degree to which alternative families are presented in classroom materials.

Gay men and lesbian women have a distinct social identity that has led to political attitudes that cannot be explained by reference to economic status. Highly educated gays and lesbians are among the economic "winners" who have found jobs in the transformed, postindustrial city. Nevertheless, despite their relative affluence, gay and lesbian voters are not necessarily the dependable allies of pro-growth elites. Even where more affluent gay and lesbian voters may approve of fiscally conservative management practices, they do not find themselves at home with conservatives on cultural and lifestyle issues.

For gays and lesbians—and other identity-based groups, as well—local politics is not simply about socioeconomic issues. Politics is also about symbols (such as the city's approval of a gay pride celebration or its recognition of a gay neighborhood with a "rainbow" on its streets) and the affirmation of a group's identity.

Source: Robert W. Bailey, *Urban Politics: Identity and Economics in the Urban Setting* (New York: Columbia University Press, 1999), especially pp. 3–14 and 327–330.

issues raised by women to be of less importance on the public agenda simply because they are associated with women. These dismissive associations are often very subtle and may not even be consciously acted upon, as contrasted with more overt prejudice and bigotry.

Women of color may have several identities that affect their issue positions, sense of the city, and approach to politics. To see one's self as a Latina is to be more than just a Spanish-speaking person of Hispanic origin. It is to be both a Hispanic and a woman with an identity separate and distinct from male counterparts. While women's liberation in the 1960s and 1970s generated a middle-class movement of women from the home to the office, other women had long been "liberated" and found few rights accorded to an identity dominated by their race and ethnicity.

WOMEN, POVERTY, AND COMMUNITY DEVELOPMENT

Poverty is not simply a matter of being poor. As the phenomenon known as the **feminization of poverty** clearly denotes, poverty is especially a women's issue. [29] Census data underscores that women suffer a greater risk of poverty than do men. [30] In 2001, 12.9 percent of the female population lived in poverty as contrasted to 10.4 percent of the male population. According to 2000 U.S. Census figures, women comprised 56 percent of the poverty population while men comprised only 44 percent.

Women are more prone to be in poverty than men, especially during their prime wage-earning years. Women who are single heads of households and who care for dependent children often find that their income is not commensurate with their family responsibilities. [31] There is also a significant wage gap between men and women: $27,313 for women in central cities in 2000 as compared to $34,586 for men.

Being poor is not simply a matter of economics; it is also a condition that is gender-, race-, and ethnicity-related. Poverty is highly concentrated within the urban African-American and Hispanic populations, especially among single-parent family households headed by women. [32]

Public welfare, social, and housing policies have not always reflected the barriers that poor women face. As a result, women, especially poor women, have had to utilize nontraditional routes of political participation in order to press local government to fashion policies more responsive to their needs: "Women's private concerns are made public at the level of the community." [33]

Community organizing in urban neighborhoods has long been an important political tool for urban women, especially for poor and minority women. Women's groups are active in a variety of issues that affect women's lives, from the fight for affordable housing to protests against immigration restrictions and the dumping of toxic wastes in poor communities. [34] Grassroots activity, especially around school issues, often provides women with an entry way into the urban political arena.

Women from different socioeconomic backgrounds have somewhat different approaches to community development issues: "Women leaders who are
not activists tend to emphasize expertise above participation and have a more
procedural style of leadership, while activist women tend to emphasize organizing and mobilization."[35]

Women have been highly active in community-based organizations and
community development corporations (CDCs) as local governments have not
been fully responsive to their needs. But because these organizations must
please the demands of financial lenders and investors, CDCs do not always
reflect a woman-centered view of progressive politics. Women community
activists find that their approach to leadership is structured not only by their
gender but also by the constraints they face as organization advocates.[36]

Women tend to adopt a more familial approach to political organizing.
Women leaders see neighborhood organizations as inclusive, community-
based operations; they resist the demands of financiers and other political
actors who live outside the neighborhood.[37] Women also participate in "gendered networks" that reflect their willingness to pursue a collective interest
based on family and friendship groups.[38]

In Detroit, over 70 percent of the executive directors and staffs of CDCs are
women.[39] A six-state study of neighborhood development organizations found
that women were well represented on both the staffs and boards of directors of
these organizations.[40] Women in leadership roles have steered community
organizations to a greater emphasis on issues such as child care and job training. In contrast, community organizations dominated by men give a greater
emphasis to more traditional economic and industrial development activities.

The Neighborhood Women's Renaissance in Brooklyn provides an example
of a community organization that has designed projects that reflect the interests
of low-income women.[41] In 1993, it was the only such female-run development
organization in New York City to partner with governmental, financial, and
nonprofit organizations in the pursuit of affordable housing. The group helped
convert a former hospital facility into a multiuse site for low-income housing, a
nursing home, and a medical clinic.

Not all such projects go as smoothly. The New York Asian Women's Center
attempted to establish a battered women's shelter in a residential brownstone
in the Brooklyn neighborhood of Carroll Gardens. But neighbors opposed it,
saying "not in our backyard." Some opponents even went so far as to publi-
cize the address of the shelter, endangering the safety of the women who
resided there. The opposition was rooted in fears derived from perceptions
based on gender and race, as the comments of one opponent revealed: "If in
fact these are individuals [battered women] who do not communicate in
English, how are they going to assimilate into our community?"[42]

Suburban communities, too, have at times resisted the opening of domestic-
violence shelters. In Rolling Meadows, outside Chicago, a two-year court battle finally ended when the city council at long last gave its approval to a zoning
change to allow Women in Need of Growing Stronger to locate a shelter in a
residential area.[43]

ENFORCING THE SEPARATION OF PUBLIC AND PRIVATE REALMS: ZONING, DEVELOPMENT, AND LAW ENFORCEMENT

The political and geographic space of urban places is divided into public and private realms. The *private realm* is represented by home and is typified by suburban residential areas. The *public realm,* in contrast, is the locus of commerce and government activity and decisions; it is typified by the urban downtown and the new corporate centers of edge cities.

Traditionally, women have been seen as homemakers, dwellers in the private realm with responsibility for children and domestic matters—even when they also worked in paid jobs outside the home. Men, in contrast, enter the public realm of work, investment, and politics, making decisions for the public at large. Of course this crude dualism does not capture the evolving reality of women's and men's lives. Today, women are increasingly in the workforce, and men may be stay-at-home dads.

Government policy has reinforced the patriarchal separation of public and private realms. In the past, women were restricted in their ability to sign a contract, own property, secure credit, and vote. Zoning, planning, and land-use decisions continue to encourage the separation of dual realms. At times, even crime control and surveillance decisions have made it difficult for women to sustain broadened activity outside the home.

Zoning and land-use decisions that perpetuate the segregation of residential from commercial property force the separation of home and work, perpetuating the distinction of gender roles.[44] Zoning contributes to an essentialist view of women that is unfounded.[45] Not all women want to live in the suburbs. Yet planning decisions that devote land use in central business districts to commercial towers, retail, and parking for commuters leave few realistic options for downtown housing suitable for families. According to the 2000 U.S. Census, 15 percent of all households were headed by women. Zoning and land-use decisions that restrict downtown living have the effect of isolating these women in suburban subdivisions. Fortunately, downtown housing options are becoming more diverse and abundant.

Suburban women often take jobs that are near the home due to "space-time constraints" of caring for children and aging parents.[46] Men, lacking similar responsibilities that tie them to the home, are freer to take jobs in corporate centers throughout the region. Women who confine their job search to the suburbs on average make less money than do men who search for employment in a regional job market.[47]

Cities establish zoning to protect property values, guarding residents against the intrusion of undesirable land uses. This is why activities such as heavy industry and adult bookstores and liquor stores are generally not permitted in the middle of residential neighborhoods. However, zoning may also determine which families are permitted in a neighborhood. Zoning regulations that limit the numbers of families or nonrelated persons living in a dwelling unit serve to restrict the housing options available to elderly women and to poor, single women with children. There are 2.3 million elderly women in poverty, according to the 2000 U.S. Census. For a long time, the prime-time television show *The Golden Girls* focused on the antics of four elderly women sharing a home. In some cities, the four golden girls would have been zoning scofflaws!

Fairfax, Virginia (outside Washington, DC) and the suburbs surrounding Philadelphia have begun to alter zoning restrictions as women faced soaring housing prices that were quickly climbing out of their reach. In the 1990s, Fairfax legislators began to revise local zoning ordinances in order to allow greater house-sharing by unrelated persons. Opponents, however, argued that the move would result in higher population densities and parking problems. Opponents also feared the move would lead to an increase in the number of minorities and latch-key kids in the community, leading to increased rates of delinquency and crime.[48]

San Jose, California is a city that has actually made land-use decisions with women in mind. The election of a woman as mayor helped to bring about a reexamination of the city's traditional development policies that gave top priority to downtown commercial development. Janet Gray Hayes' administration brought with it a new emphasis for housing and neighborhood concerns. The city began to examine how existing regulations, land use codes, and service patterns could be changed to enable the greater availability and operation of child-care facilities.[49]

Even decisions relating to the increased surveillance of public spaces, efforts aimed at curtailing crime and the possibilities of terrorism, have a gendered impact. In public spaces, men have the social license to observe.[50] The "male gaze" subjects a woman as the unwitting object of desire. Women consequently may avoid public spaces that are perceived as gendered space. Women are further warned to avoid locations that may make them the victims of unwelcome advances and criminal attacks.

Women face a new double-edged sword in the city where high-tech crime-fighting security cameras dot the landscape. Ostensibly, the cameras are there to protect women, yet "surveillance can be a way of reproducing and reinforcing male power."[51] Who is behind the camera and what are they observing? A study of women's attitudes regarding surveillance suggests that security cameras can act to make public space less welcoming for women.

The introduction of security cameras also introduces class, race, and ethnicity concerns: "Only certain women are being 'protected' from the supposed licentiousness of the urban jungle."[52] Women in low-income neighborhoods do not have security cameras for their protection. In many poor, inner-city areas, women have to traverse a landscape dotted with XXX-rated entertainment and adult bookstores, activities that make the public streets less comfortable for women.

WELFARE REFORM

National welfare reform legislation was implemented beginning in 1996. Welfare reform coupled with an expanding national economy acted to produce a dramatic decrease in welfare rolls. State welfare rolls fell from a high of 5.1 million families in March 1994 to 2.1 million in May 2001.[53]

While the drop in the welfare rolls was dramatic, there also was cause for concern in core cities and urban counties. Welfare reform prompted the easiest-to-employ recipients to find work, and a strong economy created new job opportunities. But some advocates of the poor questioned the quality of jobs that were created and the pay levels that were offered. The vast majority of welfare recipients continue to be women and children.

Welfare reform has not eliminated central-city welfare problems. Large urban counties harbored high concentrations of the nation's welfare caseload. The 30 largest urban counties in 1999 bore a greater share of the nation's welfare caseload in 1999 (39 percent of all cases) than in 1994 (33 percent of all cases).[54] Milwaukee County saw its share of Wisconsin's welfare caseload increase from 57 percent in 1994 to 86 percent in 1998. Urban counties moved welfare recipients off welfare at a slower pace than did other jurisdictions. Cities found themselves with the more intractable cases—recipients with multiple problems that served as a barrier to employment—at a time when national leaders were declaring the success of the fight for welfare reform.

The cutbacks in welfare also imposed new burdens on cities, including the need to cope with the potential for increased domestic violence. Consider the fact that 50 to 60 percent of women on welfare experience physical abuse by a partner, as compared to the 22 percent for the general population who suffer such abuse.[55] Urban women (and their children) who lose their eligibility for government support also lose a possible path out of a domestic violence situation.

By 2004, the George W. Bush administration and the Republican Congress cut the funding for both the TANF (Temporary Assistance for Needy Families) and the CCDBG (Child Care and Development Block Grant) programs targeted for low-income women. States responded to the reductions in federal aid by narrowing eligibility, reducing the number of children served by the programs.[56] Welfare reform that is responsive to women's needs requires continued funding for programs such as day care. Welfare reform that meets the needs of women and children requires supportive programs, not just deadlines, work requirements, and the threat of penalties. (See "Children and Welfare Reform," p. 332.)

Los Angeles has used a model welfare-to-work program called GAIN (Greater Avenues for Independence), which focused on giving women education and training before placing them in jobs. Women who went through the GAIN program earned higher wages than did welfare recipients who did not receive GAIN education and training.[57] GAIN's successes were formidable, but so were its limitations. Three-fourths of the GAIN participants still could not find jobs that paid an income that would allow them to maintain a family income above poverty.[58] A controversial 2003 study also indicates that the employment rate among GAIN participants was falling; nearly half of the GAIN recipients reported no earnings in 2001.[59]

Some women celebrated welfare reform because, with the proper training and support services, poor women could enter the workplace, take control of their lives, and reduce their dependency. Other feminists, however, criticized the general welfare-to-work approach, observing that it valued only "waged" work in the public sphere, not the "unwaged" caregiving work performed by women in the home.[60]

CHILDREN AND WELFARE REFORM

Senators Olympia Snowe (R, Maine) and Christopher Dodd (D, Connecticut) moved to amend welfare reform by significantly increasing the funding for child care assistance programs for low- and moderate-income families. According to the Center for American Progress, the investment in child care was important "to achieving two important goals—helping parents work and helping boost the quality of care to ensure that children enter school ready to succeed."

In endorsing the Snowe-Dodd proposal, the Center for American Progress went on to describe the importance of day-care assistance and the difficulties that low-income women face in attempting to find affordable day care:

> Evidence shows that child care assistance helps low-income parents work. Single mothers who receive child care assistance are 40 percent more likely to remain employed after two years than those who do not receive help in paying for child care. Former welfare recipients with young children are 82 percent more likely to be employed after two years if they receive help with child care expenses. In addition, child care assistance helps families afford higher quality care that promotes healthy child development. States also invest federal child care funds in statewide initiatives to bolster child care quality. Children in high quality care demonstrate greater mathematic ability, greater thinking and attention skills, and fewer behavioral problems.
>
> Finding quality child care is a daily challenge, especially for our lowest income families. Care for just one child can easily cost from $4,000 to $10,000 per year— more than tuition at a public university. Yet more than one-quarter of America's families with young children earn less than $25,000 per year. Two-thirds of poor working families headed by single mothers spent at least 40 percent of their income on child care. Women leaving welfare often enter low-wage jobs where they earn so little that they cannot possibly cover the cost of child care.
>
> Only one in seven children eligible for federal child care assistance now receives help. Many parents, working harder than ever to support their families, cannot expect any relief from state governments in the near future. In the past two years, because of limited funds, states have reduced the number of families eligible for child care assistance; raised parent fees; cut back rates for already low-paid child care providers; and slashed investments focused on improving the quality of care. Almost half the states now have long waiting lists for child care help and some must deny assistance to any family not on welfare.
>
> Studies and interviews with parents find that families without assistance face impossible choices between paying for child care and paying the rent, going into debt, or settling for what they clearly know is inadequate care because they have no other options. In some cases this might mean leaving children home alone or putting pre-teens in charge of younger siblings. Ultimately, many women in low-wage jobs that offer little flexibility are forced to quit their jobs and return to welfare.

Source: Helen Blank and Jennifer Mezey, "Working Families Can't Wait," Center for American Progress (March 30, 2004), available at www.americanprogress.org.

In the Bronx, New York, one organization tried to create a flexible approach to job training that also recognized the importance of women's caregiving work in the home: The mission of the Women's Housing and Economic Development Corporation (WHEDCO) is to "recognize women's often competing roles as sole breadwinners and primary caregivers of children; address the multiple barriers to women's access to, and success in, the employment mainstream; enable women to make [educated] choices about their lives and the lives of their families; include low-income women in program planning and public policy advocacy; and provide models for realistic and effective welfare-to-work and family-friendly workplace efforts."[61] WHEDCO helped find new economic opportunities for former welfare recipients in fields ranging from entrepreneurial microenterprise start-ups to the culinary arts.

HOUSING AND TRANSPORTATION

Welfare-to-work proponents often neglect the fact that women on welfare are single heads of households with responsibilities for child care and family transportation. In many cities, women also face substantial problems in finding quality affordable housing.

Single women compete for residential space with households that bring in two paychecks. Given the low salaries of clerical and service jobs, it is little wonder that single working women—not just women on welfare—face great difficulty in finding suitable housing in tight urban housing markets. Black and Hispanic women face additional problems of housing discrimination. Concerns for personal safety further act to narrow the areas of the city in which women choose to live.

Men face problems in finding housing too, but they are more likely to have a higher income than women. They also are less likely than women to face the problem of finding housing units big enough to accommodate children.

Single men made up 41 percent of the homeless population in 2002. Yet women who were the single head of a family faced a special risk of being homeless. While single women were only 13 percent of the homeless population, families with children accounted for 41 percent. The lack of affordable housing was the most frequently cited cause of homelessness. Domestic violence, too, led women to leave their homes.[62]

The provision of shelter does not by itself solve the problem of women and family homelessness. Women have used community organizations to design and manage housing projects responsive to their needs. In Los Angeles, the Casa Loma housing project in the Pico-Union neighborhood[63] and the Lincoln Place Tenants Association in the Venice neighborhood[64] both sought to meet the women's need for "community," providing child care and related services as well as housing.

Public transportation is another policy area that can be redesigned in response to women's needs. Traffic engineers, budgeters, and planners often design transit systems to facilitate the flow of morning and afternoon rush-hour traffic. Their designs seek the efficient use of resources in promoting home-to-work commutes, a typically male pattern. But women's use of transportation is different. Women do not simply go to work; they multitask. On their way to and from work, they run errands, pick up and drop off children, do the shopping, and carry packages. Mass transit routes often do not accommodate the needs of women to make multiple trips. Women need more flexible public transit. Public transportation would look different if redesigned to accommodate the needs of women.[65]

CONCLUSIONS

According to the gendered view of the metropolis, cities and suburbs replicate the social depiction of public and private spheres. Suburbs are assumed to be places where women raise children and work within the home. Today, more than ever, a great many suburban women work outside the home. Still, the basic premise inherent in the suburb/city dichotomy remains.

There is a spatial reality created for women that cordons their realm, whereas the public realm, still viewed as the location of men's activities, is accorded a preferred and seemingly more important status. The design of the urban area and the ability to traverse it are predicated on men's experiences and vision of urban life. This acts to produce local policy responses that are not always in tune with the reality of women's lives and experiences.

Looking at the city through the lens of gender provides an alternative understanding as to whose needs are and are not served in the contemporary metropolis. Housing, public transportation, and other public services are often designed from the perspective of male decision makers without adequate consideration for the different needs of women, especially women who assume the dual roles of worker and caregiver.

Traditional welfare reform measures, when conceived narrowly as workfare, reflect a male perspective. In contrast, more gender-aware welfare-to-work programs include the provision of child care, public transportation, education, job-training benefits, and even the continuation of certain income supports while a women works. Such programs even enable women to take jobs where wages are otherwise insufficient to support a family.

The election of an increased number of women to office can be expected to broaden the diversity of perspectives in decision making. Citizen participation mechanisms, community organizing, and the self-provision of services by neighborhood organizations all represent alternative empowerment strategies for women, including poor women and women of color.

Women are not a monolithic group. Women in different economic circumstances and who come from different racial and cultural backgrounds cannot be expected to have identical political outlooks, despite their common feminist experience.[66] As a result, strategies focused on community development and grassroots activism are not equally important to all women. We must not assume that the local community is the only, or always the most beneficial, place for women's civic activism.

Still, many of the decisions that affect women's lives are locally produced. Women are engaged in urban politics because such activism offers a means to advance their interests and to improve their quality of life. As Judith Garber observes, "The intimate connections between the daily lives of women and the life of the city suggest that political activity by coalitions of women aimed specifically at defining inclusive, 'good' communities might result in localities that are less marginalizing, hierarchical, and dangerous [to women]."[67]

As we have seen throughout this chapter, the division between city and suburb has reinforced the separation of the public and private spheres, a distinction that has helped to marginalize women's lives. In the next chapter, we take a more expansive look at the evolving nature of suburbia and its impact on metropolitan problems.

NOTES

1. For a biography that focuses on how Addams' personal life experiences as a young woman helped lead her to defy convention in a life of service and commitment to poor, immigrant women, see Gioia Diliberto, *A Useful Woman: The Early Life of Jane Addams* (New York: Scribner, 1999).
2. Daphne Spain, *How Women Saved the City* (Minneapolis: University of Minnesota Press, 2001).
3. Tupac Shakur, "Keep Ya Head Up," *Greatest Hits* (Interscope).
4. Lynn M. Appleton, "The Gender Regimes of American Cities," in *Gender in Urban Research,* eds. Judith A. Garber and Robyne S. Turner (Thousand Oaks, CA: Sage, 1995), pp. 44–59.
5. Susan E. Clarke, Lynn A. Staeheli, and Laura Brunell, "Women Redefining Local Politics," in *Theories of Urban Politics*, eds. David Judge, Gerry Stoker, and Harold Wolman (London: Sage, 1995), pp. 205–227.
6. Susan Saegert, "The Androgynous City: From Critique to Practice," in *Women, Housing and Community,* ed. Willem van Vliet (Aldershot, England: Avebury, 1988), pp. 23–37.
7. For a discussion of this literature, see Lisa DeLorenzo and Carol Kohfeld, "An Application of New Developments in Ecological Inference: Gender Based Voting in St. Louis City" (paper presented at the annual meeting of the Midwest Political Science Association, Chicago, April 1998).
8. M. Margaret Conway, "Women's Political Participation at the State and Local Level in the United States," *PS Online* (January 2004): 1–12.
9. Nicole Walker, "Women Mayors: African-American," *Ebony* (November 1998).
10. Conway, "Women's Political Participation."
11. Bill Woodwell, "City Councils Reflect Community Diversity," *National League of Cities,* July 14, 2003, available at: www.nlc.org/nlc_org/site/newsroom/nations_cities_weekly/display.cfm?id=5F198089-D366-41E8-A431BE64A14072EC.
12. Center for American Women in Politics, "Fact Sheet: Women in Elective Office 2004," a publication of the Eagleton Institute for Politics, Rutgers University,

New Brunswick, New Jersey, available at: http://www.cawp.rutgers.edu/Facts/Officeholders/elective.pdf.

13. Janet A. Flammang, *Women's Political Voice: How Women are Transforming the Practice and Study of Politics* (Philadelphia: Temple University Press, 1997), pp. 157–160.

14. See Charles M. Price, "The Guillotine Comes to California: Term-Limit Politics in the Golden State," p. 133, and Linda L. Fowler, "A Comment on Competition and Careers," p. 182, both in *Limiting Legislative Terms*, eds. Gerald Benjamin and Michael Malbin (Washington, DC: CQ Press, 1992); and Conway, Steuernagel, and Ahern, *Women and Political Participation*, p. 112.

15. M. Margaret Conway, "Women's Political Participation at the State and Local Level in the United States," *PS Online* (January 2004): 1–12, available at http://www.apsanet.org/PS/jan04/esymposium/conway.pdf.

16. Ibid.

17. DeLorenzo and Kohfeld, "An Application of New Developments in Ecological Inference," pp. 2–4.

18. Douglas J. Watson and Wendy L. Hassett, "Career Paths of City Managers in America's Largest Council-Manager Cities," *Public Administration Review* 64 (March/April 2004): 192–199.

19. Watson and Hassett, "Career Paths of City Managers."

20. Richard L. Fox and Robert A. Schuhmann, "Gender and the Role of the City Manager," *Social Science Quarterly* 81 (June 2000), p. 609. See their larger discussion, pp. 604–621.

21. Watson and Hewitt, "Career Paths of City Managers."

22. Fox and Schuhmann, "Gender and the Role of the City Manager," p. 618.

23. Of course, these differences are not confined to top executives and to local officials. Women who chair committees in state legislatures also tend to adopt a more inclusive, consensual, collaborative, caring, and integrative approach to leadership as opposed to their male counterparts whose leadership approach continues to reflect domination, that is, the right of those in power, backed by a majority votes, to rule. See Cindy Simon Rosenthal, *When Women Lead: Integrative Leadership in State Legislatures* (New York: Oxford University Press, 1998). Also see Gary N. Powell and Laura M. Graves, *Women and Men In Management*, 3rd ed. (Thousand Oaks, CA: Sage, 2003), especially Chapter 6.

24. Susan Abrams Beck, "Gender and the Politics of Affordable Housing," in *Gender in Urban Research*, eds. Garber and Turner, pp. 129–130 and 132–133. The quotations are from p. 130.

25. Beck, "Gender and the Politics of Affordable Housing," p. 121. Also see Virginia Sapiro, "Feminist Studies and Political Science–and Vice Versa," in *Feminism and Politics*, ed. Anne Phillips (Oxford, England: Oxford University Press, 1998), pp. 67–92.

26. M. Margaret Conway, David W. Ahern, and Gertrude A. Steuernagel, *Women and Political Participation: Cultural Change in the Political Arena* (Washington, DC: CQ Press, 1997), pp. 37–39.

27. Gender Gap in Government, "Local Government 2000," available at: www.gendergap.com.

28. Linda Trimble, "Politics Where We Live: Women and Cities," in *Canadian Metropolitics: Governing Our Cities*, ed. James Lightbody (Toronto: Copp Clark Ltd., 1995), p. 110.

29. Emily M. Northrop, "The Feminization of Poverty: The Demographic Factor and the Composition of Economic Growth," *Journal of Economic Issues* 24 (March 1990): 145–160.

30. U.S. Census Bureau, "Women and Men in the United States: March 2002," a Current Population Report, issued March 2003.

31. Northrop, "The Feminization of Poverty," pp. 146–147; John Paul Jones III and Jane E. Kodras, "Restructured Region and Families: The Feminization of Poverty in the U.S.," *Annals of the Association of American Geographers* 80 (1990): 163–183.

32. U.S. Census 2000, "Demographic Trends in the 20th century," pp. 160–161, available at: www.census.gov.

33. See Jacqueline Leavitt, "Where's the Gender in Community Development?" *SIGNS* 29, 1 (2003), 207–231. The quotation appears on p. 212.

34. Nancy A. Naples, ed., *Community Activism and Feminist Politics: Organizing Across Class, Race, and Gender* (New York: Routledge, 1998).

35. Marilyn Gittell, Isolda Ortega-Bustamente, and Tracy Steffy, *Women Creating Social Capital and Local Change: A Study of Women-Led Community Development Organizations* (Silver Spring, MD: McAuley Institute, 1999).

36. Robert Mark Silverman, "Progressive Reform, Gender and Institutional Structure: A Critical Analysis of Citizen Participation in Detroit's Community Development Corporations (CDCs)," *Urban Studies* 40, 13 (2003), 2731–2750.

37. These are the results found in the Hispanic communities of Boston. See Carol Hardy-Fanta, *Latina Politics-Latino Politics* (Philadelphia: Temple University Press, 1993).

38. Gordana Rabrenovic, *Community Builders* (Philadelphia: Temple University Press, 1996), pp. 23–30.

39. Silverman, "Progressive Reform, Gender and Institutional Structure," p. 2738.

40. Marilyn Gittell, Jill Gross, and Kathe Newman, "Race and Gender in Neighborhood Development Organizations" (report distributed by the Howard Samuels State Management and Policy Center, Graduate School and University Center, City University of New York, May 1994); Marilyn Gittell and Sally Covington, with Jill Gross, "The Difference Gender Makes: Women in Neighborhood Development Organizations" (report distributed by the Howard Samuels State Management and Policy Center, Graduate School and University Center, City University of New York, May 1994).

41. Lindsay McFarlane, "Women and Urban Planning," *The OECD Observer* No. 195 (August/September 1995): 37–41.

42. Tara Bahrampour, "Carroll Gardens: A Haven for Battered Women Ends Up in the Eye of a Storm," *The New York Times*, September 7, 2003, p. 8.

43. Erin Holmes, "WINGS Tells City Thanks for Being 'Shining Star'," *Chicago Daily Herald*, October 30, 2003, p. Local 1.

44. Trimble, "Politics Where We Live," p. 102. See the works of Gerda Wekerle as cited.

45. Robyn Dowling, "Suburban Stories, Gendered Lives: Thinking Through Difference," in *Cities of Difference*, eds. Fincher and Jacobs, pp. 1259–1260. Also, see the writings of Marsha Ritzdorf.

46. Mei-Po Kwan, "Gender and Individual Access to Urban Opportunities," *The Professional Geographer* 2 (1999), p. 210.

47. Virginia Carlson and Joseph Persky, "Gender and Suburban Wages," *Economic Geography* 75 3(1999): 237.

48. Lorraine Woellert, "Action Held on Law to Allow Home-sharing," *The Washington Times*, December 6, 1994, p. C7.

49. Flammang, *Women's Political Voice*, p. 249.

50. Kristen Day, "Introducing Gender to the Critique of Privatized Public Space," *Journal of Urban Design* 4, 2 (1999): 155–178.

51. Hille Koskela, "Video Surveillance, Gender, and the Safety of Public Urban Space," *Urban Geography* 23, 3 (2002): 257–278. Quote on p. 264.

52. Stephanie Lasker, "Sex and the City," *UCLA Law Review* 49 (April 2002): 1139.

53. U.S. House of Representatives, Committee on Education and the Workforce, Hearing on *Working Toward Independence: the Administration's Plan to Build upon the Successes of Welfare Reform,* "Building on the Success of the 1996 Welfare Reform Law" (April 9, 2002), available at: www.edworkforce.house.gov/hearings/107th/fc/welfare4902/wl4902.htm.

54. The Brookings Institution, Center on Urban & Metropolitan Policy, "The State of Welfare Caseloads in America's Cities: 1999," *Survey Series* (February 1999), pp. 1–8.

55. Family Violence Prevention Fund, "The Facts on Welfare and Domestic Violence," available at: www.endabuse.org/resources/facts/Welfare.pdf.

56. National Women's Law Center, "Progress Frozen: The Context for Child Care and Development Block Grant (CCDBG) Reauthorization in 2004" (January 2004), available at www.nwlc.org/pfd/CCDEBReauthorization2004.pdf.

57. Carla Rivera, "Work-First Approach Earns Critical Report Card: Welfare Study Says Value of Education is Overlooked in Push for Self-Sufficiency," *Los Angeles Times*, April 24, 1999.

58. Beth Barrett, "75 Percent of Los Angeles County Welfare Recipients in Poverty" *(Los Angeles) Daily News,* July 23, 2003.

59. Ibid.

60. Gwendolyn Mink, *Welfare's End* (Ithaca, NY: Cornell University Press, 1998), p. 32.

61. Karen Ceraso, "Urban Horizons: Fostering Economic Independence in the Face of Welfare Reform," *Shelterforce Online* 107 (September/October, 1999), a publication of the National Housing Institute, available at: www.nhi.org/online/issues/107/ceraso.html.

62. This paragraphs summarizes the findings of the U.S. Conference of Mayors, "A Status Report on Hunger and Homelessness in America's Cities 2002," Washington, DC (December 2002).

63. Stacy Harwood, "Gender and Planning: Towards a Feminist Theory and Practice" (paper presented at the American Collegiate Schools of Planning Annual Meeting, Ft. Lauderdale, Florida, September 1997).

64. Gail Sansbury, "Building Community Through Age and Gender Alliances," *Women & Environments* 14 (Spring 1995): 23–24.

65. Clarke, Staeheli, and Brunell, "Women Redefining Local Politics," pp. 213–220; Geraldine Pratt, "Grids of Difference: Place and Identity Formation," in *Cities of Difference,* eds. Fincher and Jacobs, pp. 26–49.

66. Liz Bondi, "Sexing the City," in *Cities of Difference,* eds. Fincher and Jacobs, p. 178.

67. Judith Garber, "Defining Feminist Community: Place, Choice, and the Urban Politics of Difference," in *Gender in Urban Research,* eds. Garber and Turner, p. 41.

The United States is a suburban nation. Since the 1970s, the population of suburbia has exceeded that of central cities. The 2000 Census reported that 62 percent of the metropolitan population resides in suburbs. During the 1990s, central cities reversed previous decades of decline and showed some minimal growth;

but they could not compete with the continuing growth of suburbia.

Yet we must be cautious not to stereotype suburbs. Not all suburbs are growing, and not all are prospering. The 2000 Census revealed that more than one-third of suburbs either enjoyed no significant population growth or actually lost residents over the previous decade. Inner-ring suburbs, predominantly in the Northeast and the Midwest (and especially in the Cleveland, Detroit, Buffalo, St. Louis, Pittsburgh, and Philadelphia areas), face city-like problems of decline.[1] The stereotype of suburban growth and affluence masks a great variation among rim communities.

On the whole, the residents of suburbia express great satisfaction with their communities. Employment, cultural, education, and entertainment facilities have grown in the suburbs; in many important ways, life in the suburbs can no longer be considered to be "sub" to life in the central city. Still, social commentators continue to point to the class and racial imbalances of the metropolis and the environmental costs of unabated suburban sprawl.

In this chapter, we examine the evolution of suburbia, paying particular attention to questions of gender, class, and race. We also look at three issue areas—schools, taxes, and land use—that have a special prominence in suburban affairs. We finish by pointing to two fairly new movements, "smart growth" and "new urbanism," that attempt to counter urban sprawl and build better suburbs.

HETEROGENEITY OF SUBURBS

Suburbia first entered the American consciousness during the post–World War II era. The 1950s stereotype, evident in such books and movies as *Peyton Place* and *The Man in the Gray Flannel Suit*, portrayed suburbia as a string of homogeneous, white, middle- and upper-class **bedroom or dormitory communities.** This stereotype did not recognize the existence of blue-collar and industrial suburbs.[2]

Today, "the myth of the suburban monolith"[3] is dead. Modern-day suburbia encompasses a broad diversity: affluent dormitory communities; mushrooming **technoburbs** with their research-and-development complexes and office parks; fast-growing **bedroom-developing suburbs**[4] that lack sufficient resources to build much-needed schools and other infrastructure; older working-class communities; minority-dominated suburbs; industrial enclaves; declining inner-ring suburbs;[5] **disaster suburbs** that differ little from the troubled central cities they border; the **privatopias** of common-interest developments and gated communities;[6] and more far-flung **exurbs** that have sprouted at some distance from the metropolitan center.

Globalization and a new immigration have helped to make suburbia multiclass, multiethnic, and multiracial.[7] While certain suburbs remain highly stratified by class and race, others are culturally and ethnically diverse. The 2000 Census reports that a growing number of African Americans, Asians, and Hispanics have found suburban homes, even though minority populations still tend to be overly concentrated in central cities. A majority of Latinos (54 percent) live in suburbs.[8] High-tech Cupertino, California, in the Silicon Valley, is half Asian-American.[9] Once the archetype of suburbia, Orange County, south of Los Angeles, has experienced a growing racial and ethnic diversity accompanied by heightened cultural antagonisms.[10]

Certain suburbs have grown so fast that they can be called **boomburgs.** Places of over 100,000 residents that have experienced double-digit rates of population growth include: Anaheim, Riverside, Santa Ana, San Bernardino, Chula Vista, and Fremont (California); Mesa, Glendale, Scottsdale, and Tempe (Arizona); Arlington (Texas), Naperville (Illinois), and Aurora (Colorado), just outside of Denver. While boomburgs are not the primary center of a region, the largest boomburgs are comparable to cities. Mesa has a larger population than Minneapolis, Miami, or St. Louis. Arlington has approximately the same population as Pittsburgh. Boomburgs are especially likely to be found in the Southwest where the limited availability of water serves to concentrate new development.[11]

Dynamic **edge cities,**[12] concentrations of office towers, research parks, college campuses, shopping galleries, and entertainment complexes, have emerged across the country, notably in Valley Forge and King of Prussia (both outside of Philadelphia), Monroeville (Pittsburgh), Towson (Baltimore), Bloomington (between Minneapolis and St. Paul), La Jolla (San Diego), Bellevue (Seattle), Tempe/Scottsdale (Phoenix), North Atlanta, North Dallas, and the Houston Galleria. The New York region can be seen to have four edge cities, centered around Morristown (New Jersey); the Route 1 corridor by Princeton (New Jersey); Huntington, Long Island; and White Plains (New York)/Stamford (Connecticut). These **new cities**[13] (as they are sometimes called) of office parks, the best shops, and residential privilege also suffer from traffic gridlock, inadequate mass transit, and a lack of affordable housing.

Yet even the concept of edge cities does not fully capture the continuing march of suburban development. Suburban office sprawl continues beyond the edge city in small clusters of offices along highways and interchanges. **Edgeless cities** lack the densities, mixed uses, and bounded nature of edge cities, yet in total contain double the office space of edge cities. Edgeless development is typified by the Margate/North Lauderdale area of Florida, where unglamorous offices have sprouted with no identifiable center and without even a shopping galleria. Edgeless cities can spill over hundreds of square miles, as is the case with the chaotic sprawl of offices in central New Jersey. Such sprawl development is particularly pernicious in its effects on the environment, gobbling up greenspace, wetlands, and agricultural land, while necessitating increased reliance on the automobile and greater commuting distances.[14]

The continuing development of the urban periphery also leads to **job sprawl.** In the nation's 100 largest metropolitan areas, on average, less than a quarter (22 percent) of the population worked within three miles of the city center. Over a third of a region's jobs are located 10 miles or more outside the city center.[15]

Suburbs as a whole are better off economically than central cities. The overall poverty rate of suburbia (8.3 percent in the year 2000) is less than half of that of central cities (18.4 percent).[16] Yet the general affluence of suburbia and the continued growth of technoburbs, suburban shopping galleries, and edge cities has helped to mask increases in suburban poverty. Half of all persons below the poverty line live in the suburbs. The 1990s was generally a decade of national economic prosperity, but the rate of poverty in suburbia increased.

A brief look at the Detroit metropolitan area underscores the diversity of suburbia. Birmingham, Bloomfield Hills, the Grosse Pointes and other well-to-do communities use their land-use and zoning powers to bar all except the most "pricey" and attractive residential and retail development. Southfield and Troy are "satellite downtowns" with tall office buildings and more office space than the city of Detroit. In the northern part of the metropolitan area, Auburn Hills has aggressively pursued growth and high-technology jobs, rezoning land for development and creating an industrial park and a tax increment financing district—all projects pushed by local and state officials and growth coalition elites. Professional basketball's Detroit Pistons play in the Palace in Auburn Hills, about 20 miles from their old arena in the city of Detroit.[17] The opening of the Great Lakes Crossing supermall, north of the Palace, exacerbated traffic congestion and threatened to stimulate new development even further up-county despite the objections of both environmentalists and the representatives of inner-ring suburbs. The opening of the I-696 rim road also brought substantial edgeless office development to Farmington Hills, Novi, Northville, Plymouth, and the highway leading to Ann Arbor.

A GENDERED VIEW OF THE SUBURBS

In the 1950s, suburbia was seen as a good place to raise children. It offered backyards, good schools, and relative physical safety.

But as the demographics of America changed, so did suburbia. Nowadays, couples tend to delay marriage, divorce is more prevalent, and people live longer.

As a result, the number of suburban elderly widows, singles, and divorcees now surpasses the number the of two-parent suburban families with children.[18] Suburbia is no longer an exclusive fortress of "familism."[19] Opinion surveys show that a majority of all age groups tend to prefer suburban living to the central city.[20]

Longer life spans have also led to the "graying of the suburbs." As the post–World War II baby boom generation approaches its retirement years, a growing number of retirees and near-retirees are expected to "age in place" in the suburbs.[21]

Feminist scholars criticize suburbs for the reinforcement of a private patriarchy that is not always supportive of the lifestyles of gays and independent women. Despite suburbia's increasing diversity, the more stereotypical communities assume the norm of heterosexual marriage and women's dependence on male breadwinners. Such suburbs provide little social space for female independence or a gay subculture.[22] Especially during the earlier years of suburban development, suburban life was criticized for the isolation suffered by women who stayed at home. Men would go to work, and women would be stuck in households outside the economic, social, and political mainstream. (See "Urban Films: Hollywood's Suburbia," below.)

URBAN FILMS: HOLLYWOOD'S SUBURBIA

Over the years, such classic television programs like *Father Knows Best, Leave It to Beaver, The Dick Van Dyke Show*, and *Happy Days* presented a fabled, fairy-tale image of suburbia, where cheerful, well-dressed, at-home mothers tended to the family, waiting for their husbands to return from work. These half-hour situation comedies "celebrated the goodness, wholesomeness, and fun of the idealized suburb."* Even Matt Groening's more sardonic *The Simpsons* still draws an affectionate view of America's most-beloved, dysfunctional, blue-collar suburban family.

Movies such as *Miracle on 34th Street* (1947, remade in 1994) also glorified the suburbs. The movie reaches its happy, emotional climax, when a little girl finally admits her belief in Santa Claus; she is rewarded when her mother remarries and the family buys an enormous home in suburbia.

Both television and Hollywood have largely portrayed suburbia in terms of the bedroom-community stereotype and have failed to capture the diversity of modern-day suburbia. Yet Hollywood's portrayal of life in the suburbs is infinitely darker; its social commentary is more critical. Even as early as the 1950s, such serious films as *The Man in the Gray Flannel Suit* (1956) and *Peyton Place* (1957) sought to strip away the apparent normalcy of the suburbs to reveal the hypocrisy, desperation, and family violence that lay beneath the surface. Suburban life was attacked for its artificiality, sterility, conformity, and dysfunction. In Hollywood's suburbs, bored housewives and frustrated executives-on-the-make both took refuge in the bottle and in illicit sexual affairs.

continued

URBAN FILMS: HOLLYWOOD'S SUBURBIA (CONT.)

In the 1960s and 1970s, the anti-suburban critique continued with such films as *The Graduate* (1967). Benjamin (played by Dustin Hoffman), the anti-hero, is so alienated with the plastic phoniness of the life before him that he drifts into a meaningless affair with the wife of a family friend. He finally asserts his individuality by falling in love with her daughter. They defy authority, breaking suburbia's conformity and unwritten rules. *The Stepford Wives* (1975, remade in 2004) is a satiric fable that presents the idealized suburban woman as literally a robot, a man-pleasing automaton with no mind of her own.

Contemporary films continue to reflect Hollywood's intellectual assault on suburbia. In *Edward Scissorhands* (1990), Tim Burton's charming take on the Frankenstein tale, the artificially created boy/monster (Johnny Depp) can never fit into the suburban world. He stands for everyone who has ever felt out of place with the enforced conformity of suburbia. In *Pleasantville* (1998), life in the suburbs is so vapid and colorless that portions of the film were shot in black and white. In *The Truman Show* (1998), suburban life is presented as so strictly ordered and antiseptic as to be totally controlled. Truman Burbank (Jim Carrey) does not realize that he has spent his entire life residing on what is essentially a huge, fabricated set as the unknowing star of a nationally popular television reality show.

American Beauty (1999) depicts suburban life as devoid of love and authentic feeling. Lester Burnham (Kevin Spacey) says that he is "already dead," and that the high point of his day is when he masturbates in the shower. His careerist wife, Carolyn (Annette Bening), enters into a loveless affair with the head of her real estate firm. Lester quits his job to break his routine and to bring some sense of feeling back to his life. *American Beauty* departs from the traditional stereotype by admitting the presence of drugs and gay couples in a changing suburbia. Nonetheless, *American Beauty* continues Hollywood's nightmarish view of suburban consumerism, careerism, and enforced conformity. In *American Beauty,* the suburbs are even depicted as a place where plastic covers are still on the furniture.

Do Americans share Hollywood's intellectual distaste for the suburbs? Not really. Polls show that Americans for the most part are satisfied with life in the suburbs. As a result, it should come as no great surprise that some of the most popular films in history, such as Steven Spielberg's *E.T.—The Extraterrestrial* (1981), have presented a more positive and joyful image of the suburbs. As seen in *E.T.,* life in the suburbs is busy and chaotic; yet suburban communities also offer the love and security of home, allowing children to grow up with a brimming self-confidence.

The films of director and producer John Hughes—including *Ferris Bueller's Day Off* (1986), *Uncle Buck* (1989), and *Home Alone* (1990)—all present an affectionate view of life in the upscale, north shore suburbs of Chicago.

continued

URBAN FILMS: HOLLYWOOD'S SUBURBIA (CONT.)

The portrayal of suburbia in *Ferris Bueller* is only a bit ambiguous. Ferris Bueller (Matthew Broderick) skips school to taste the vitality of life. Where can he experience life with its excitement and diversity? Not in the suburbs, but in the big city, of course! His parents, while genuinely caring, are so preoccupied with the business of their own lives that they do not even realize that he is gone. Whatever the shortcomings of suburban life, Bueller nonetheless enjoys comfort, love, and wealth—the American dream—all in the suburbs! The remake of *Miracle on 34th Street*, with its final scene that equates happiness with life in a suburban dream home, not surprisingly, was another feature film written and produced by John Hughes.

* Douglas Muzzio and Thomas Halper, "Pleasantville? The Suburb and Its Representation in American Movies, *Urban Affairs Review* 37, 4 (March 2002): 548. Muzzio and Halper, pp. 542–574, nicely develop the juxtaposition of television and Hollywood's picture of suburban life.

Over the years, women have entered the workplace, and the decentralization of jobs increased the opportunities available to suburban women. Yet, as we discussed in Chapter 10, "Women in the Gendered City," suburban jobs do not fully meet the needs of working women and single mothers. Mothers in suburbia often look for jobs convenient to schools and home, not the better-paying opportunities that may be available in the government and corporate offices of the central city.[23] The growth of jobs on the urban rim also adversely affects the employment prospects of poorer women and African-American and other minority women concentrated in the central city.[24]

Suburban large-lot zoning and restrictive land-use ordinances also add to the difficulty of daily life for working women who find that they do not live in close proximity to schools, shops, and supermarkets. The lack of public transportation and the distances involved put further burdens on "Mom's taxi" as "Mom" shuttles the children to various activities. Divorced women with children face the additional difficulty of have having to find suitable housing where local zoning ordinances limit the construction of apartments and affordable housing.[25] Local zoning ordinances also often restrict the availability of child care run out of a private home.[26]

However, suburbia continues to evolve. Over the years, suburban communities have begun to offer an increased variety of housing types that are more responsive to the needs of the changing American family. Homeowners rent out rooms under the pressure of mortgage and tax payments. Other homeowners have partitioned large houses in order to make room for grown children (including divorcees returning home), widowed patents, and nonrelated adults. Sympathetic local officials tend to overlook cases where such actions violate local ordinances.[27]

Planned suburban **new towns**, notably Columbia (Maryland), Reston (Virginia), and Irvine (California), contain design features, including the close proximity of homes to jobs, cultural facilities, and neighborhood schools, that liberate women from some of the tedium and isolation that have often characterized suburban living. Women in these communities have also fought for the provision of day-care facilities that enable them to return to careers outside the home. *Working Woman* magazine once rated Irvine as one of the top five cities nationwide for its child-care and preschool facilities. Women in these communities have also used their involvement in village boards and councils as springboards to other positions of political power.[28]

Suburbia today is also increasingly tolerant on the issue of gay rights,[29] reflecting, perhaps, the affluence and education of suburban populations. Larger suburbs allow a degree of anonymity and tolerance of lifestyle diversity unimaginable in smaller communities. Certain suburbs, including Oak Park (Illinois), Royal Oak (Michigan), and West Hollywood (California), have become havens for gay and lesbian residents. The 2000 Census revealed that lesbian couples, who are likely to have children, increasingly seek suburban homes. Gay men, in contrast, still tend to prefer central-city living.[30]

MINORITY SUBURBANIZATION AND THE DANGERS OF RESEGREGATION

MINORITY SUBURBANIZATION: HOW EXTENSIVE?

Suburbia is not equally open to all Americans. For many years, relatively few African Americans lived in suburbia, and those who did were concentrated in very few communities. Such inner-ring suburbs as East Chicago Heights (Illinois) and Yonkers (New York) had high percentages of minority population as a result of spillover from the central city.

However, minority suburbanization has increased markedly in recent years. The 2000 Census shows that racial and ethnic minorities constitute 27 percent of the population of suburbia, up from 19 percent just ten years previous.[31]

Still, the racial and ethnic mix of suburbia varies greatly from one community and metropolitan area to the next. In Milwaukee, Detroit, Gary (Indiana), Buffalo, Rochester, Syracuse (New York), Baltimore, Memphis, and Birmingham, African Americans remain quite concentrated in the central city. In Los Angeles–Long Beach and Fort Lauderdale, minorities are equally likely to be found in the suburban portion of the metropolis as in the central city.[32] Hispanic suburbs are especially prevalent in Florida, the southwestern United States, and southern California. Asians are more likely to live in suburbs than in central cities.[33]

The increased access of racial and ethnic minorities to the suburbs is significant. But relative to whites, Hispanics and African Americans continue to be underrepresented in suburbia. One piece of unmitigated good news, though, has been the virtual disappearance of the all-white suburb. Even by 1980, the number of Chicago suburbs without a single black household dropped to just 4, down from 23 just 10 years before.[34]

MINORITY CONCENTRATION, AND RESEGREGATION

While the entrance of racial minorities into the suburbs has increased, the integration of the suburbs is still very uneven. African Americans and Hispanics tend to be concentrated in a relatively small number of suburban communities. Washington, DC; Los Angeles; St. Louis; and Atlanta all have substantial black suburbanization. In other metropolitan areas, black suburbanization is more limited.

As Figure 11-1 underscores, the degree of metropolitan racial integration varies greatly from one region to another. Detroit in 1990 had a city population that was two-thirds black but a suburban population that was less than 5 percent black. New York and Atlanta were also marked by a severe city-suburban racial imbalance, although not of the magnitude found in greater Detroit. In general, Northeastern and Midwestern metropolitan areas exhibit severe racial imbalances.

Where African Americans and Hispanics have gained access to suburbia, it is often a far different suburbia from that enjoyed by whites. Whites have

■ FIGURE 11–1

RACE/ETHNIC PERCENT COMPOSITIONS OF CENTRAL CITY AND SUBURBAN POPULATIONS, 1990

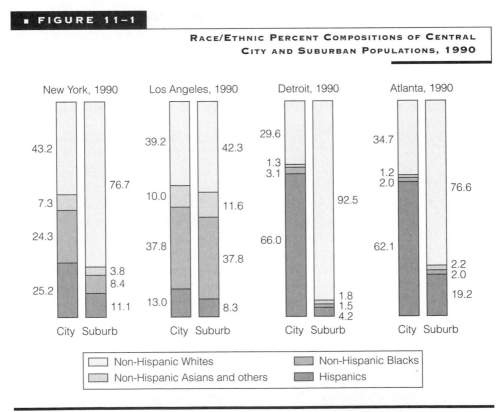

SOURCE: William H. Frey, "The New Geography of Population Shift: Trends Toward Balkanization," in *State of the Union: America in the 1990s,* Volume Two: *Social Trends,* edited by Reynolds Farley. © 1995 Russell Sage Foundation. Used by permission of the Russell Sage Foundation.

increasingly fled to the fringes of the metropolis, to places where services are better and where the population of African Americans is quite small. Black and multiethnic suburbs tend to be poorer than predominantly white communities. Suburbs with high-minority populations also suffer higher tax rates and debt loads and are more dependent on intergovernmental assistance.[35] Such distressed **disaster suburbs** as East St. Louis (Illinois), Camden (New Jersey—just across the river from Philadelphia), and Compton (California) each have a population over 95 percent black and Hispanic. African Americans and other ethnic and racial minorities gain very little from residence in declining, inner-ring suburbs at a time when job growth has shifted to more distant technoburbs and exurbs.

IS IT RACE OR INCOME THAT DETERMINES WHERE PEOPLE LIVE? THE CONTINUED IMPACT OF RACIAL STEERING AND DISCRIMINATION

What accounts for the racial imbalance of suburbia? Contrary to the widely held belief, differences in buying power do not explain why blacks and whites largely live in different communities.[36] If family income was the only factor that determined where people lived, America's cities and suburbs would be much more racially integrated than they are today: "The 'nature of the beast' is race, not class."[37]

CORBIS

Onlookers gather, after a week of disturbances and protests, as the first African-American family moves into Levittown, 1957. Levittown, which at the time had 15,000 homes, was notable for its tract housing that made suburbia affordable to the working class. Less celebrated, however, were policies that kept the community racially exclusive.

"In general, where people can afford to live has very little to do with the continuing separation of African Americans and whites in the St. Louis metropolitan area."[38] In Kansas City and Detroit, blacks and whites of equal income, education, and professional status live in different areas.[39] If economic factors alone explained residential location, each of Chicago's suburban counties would contain three to eight times the number of black families already living there.[40]

Nor does voluntary choice fully explain why black and white Americans live in different communities. Survey after survey shows that most African Americans prefer to live in mixed, as opposed to all-black, neighborhoods. African Americans and whites both value neighborhoods with high-quality, single-family, detached homes:

Federal fair housing laws have greatly reduced the most blatant discriminatory real estate and rental actions. Yet there are difficulties in gaining compliance with the law. The more subtle processes by which real estate agents and housing finance lenders steer people of different races and ethnicities to different neighborhoods continue.

These more subtle forms of racial steering and housing discrimination are not easily detected. Real estate agents may show racial minorities fewer homes in predominantly white neighborhoods than they show prospective buyers who are Caucasian. Real estate agents and institutional lenders may present minorities with less information about how the financing for a home in a desirable area can be creatively arranged. Yet how is the victim to know what information is being provided to other prospective home buyers?[41] As the victim seldom knows for sure that he or she has suffered an act of discrimination, effective fair housing enforcement cannot rely on victim-initiated lawsuits. Individuals also seldom have the money to pursue court action.

As a result, corrective action against discrimination necessitates a **housing audit** of the real estate and lending practices in a community. Such audits usually entail **paired testing,** in which closely matched white and minority individuals pose as home seekers in order to compare the treatment they receive from real estate agents and landlords. The evidence from housing audits reveals that black and white home buyers still continue to receive differential treatment despite the provisions of federal fair housing laws.[42] A 1992–97 audit of 1,484 pairs of testers in metropolitan Chicago found that real estate agents discriminated against African Americans and Hispanics 32.6 percent of the time.[43]

Few local governments vigilantly monitor and enforce fair housing laws. Nor has the federal government devoted the resources necessary to combat housing discrimination. The Reagan administration greatly cut the funding of federal fair housing efforts. The Clinton administration gave a renewed emphasis to fair housing but committed only a minuscule portion of the resources required to combat housing discrimination across the nation. Critics charged the Department of Housing and Urban Development (HUD) under Clinton with "producing more spin than substance" when it came to processing fair housing complaints.[44]

George W. Bush announced his intention to pay greater attention to fair housing enforcement. His HUD highlighted a Clinton-era study that documented the continuing rental market discrimination suffered by Native Americans.[45]

Mel Martinez, Bush's first Secretary of HUD, launched a new campaign, with the cooperation of the Ad Council and others, to inform Americans of their housing rights. Yet Bush's 2006 budget request proposed a reduction of over 20 percent in the funds devoted to fair housing enforcement.[46]

PROMOTING STABLE INTEGRATION: SHAKER HEIGHTS, CLEVELAND HEIGHTS, AND OAK PARK

Communities can quickly change their "color" when white residents flee a community that has become too "black." But when racial minorities enter a community, at what point do whites flee, causing resegregation to occur?

There is much scholarly debate over the exact **tipping point,** the point at which whites, observing an influx of racial minorities, quickly leave. Conventional wisdom says that when a community's population becomes 20 to 30 percent black, white flight ensues and resegregation takes place. Andrew Hacker argues that the tipping point is reached much sooner, when a community's population reaches only 9 or 10 percent black.[47]

The racial transition and resegregation of a suburb can be particularly rapid and dramatic. East Cleveland was once a premier suburb of Cleveland, with a population that was overwhelmingly white and affluent. In the 1960s whites began to flee in the face of an "invasion" of African Americans from the central city's east side. By the 1980s East Cleveland's population was over 90 percent black; over 40 percent were below the poverty line.[48]

Only a handful of suburbs have been willing to make the commitment to calm white fears and to promote stably integrated schools and neighborhoods. The rapid resegregation and decline of East Cleveland spurred two of its more progressive neighbors, Shaker Heights and Cleveland Heights, to act in order to avert a similar fate.

The city council of Shaker Heights banned "For Sale" signs on property in an attempt to prevent the sort of **blockbusting** tactics that real estate agents had used to promote fear and **panic selling** in East Cleveland.[49] Integration-minded community associations sought to assure that the suburb would continue to be attractive to white home buyers. The Shaker Heights Housing Office even provided some small financial assistance to white buyers who were willing to move into parts of the city that were becoming increasingly African American. Initially criticized for focusing its efforts on white prospects, the Housing Office since 1969 has sought to assist both black and white home buyers to move into Shaker Heights neighborhoods where they are underrepresented.

The Shaker Heights Board of Education also took strong steps, including a voluntary busing and magnet school plan, so that the racial makeup of a school's population would not be a factor in a home buyer's choice of a Shaker Heights neighborhood. In Shaker Heights, there is only one city school for fifth and sixth graders, one middle school, and one high school. The city's reputation for quality schools has been a continuing factor in the community's ability to attract both white and black residents. Evidence from Cincinnati and Wilmington (Delaware) confirms the importance of maintaining quality schools in any effort designed to retain middle-class homeowners.[50]

Overall, Shaker Heights' proactive approach helped to contain white flight. The city's nonwhite population, which stood at only 1 percent in 1960, reached just over 30 percent in 1990. The city actions have helped to maintain diversity and avoided rapid resegregation.

Yet similar efforts by neighboring Cleveland Heights raise the question as to just how long a pro-integration policy can be expected to produce such desirable effects. Cleveland Heights has upgraded the local housing stock and initiated legal action against real estate agents who engaged in racial steering. A Heights Fund rewards home buyers of all races for pro-integration moves. In 1990, the suburb's population was 37 percent black. However, parts of the community have become predominantly black. The African-American enrollment in the city's schools surpassed 60 percent, with some schools having a student body that is 80 percent or more nonwhite.

Two Chicago suburbs, Park Forest on the city's south side and Oak Park immediately to the city's west, have integration maintenance programs similar to those of Shaker Heights and Cleveland Heights. In Oak Park, local activists initiated positive steps in support of racial diversity after they saw the quick racial transition of Chicago's Austin community just across the suburb's border. The community even ran its own testing program to uncover discriminatory practices.[51] To head off panic selling, the village also banned "For Sale" signs and prohibited real estate agents from making uninvited solicitations of homeowners. The local housing office assists the integration-positive moves of new home buyers. The federal courts have upheld the constitutionality of such affirmative marketing practices and even the ban on "For Sale" signs, just as long as real estate agents have other outlets through which they can advertise homes for sale.

Civil rights groups generally applaud Oak Park's efforts to avoid the resegregation. Yet, like Shaker Heights and Cleveland Heights, Oak Park's policies have had only mixed success; African Americans are concentrated in the suburb's eastern housing tracts that border Chicago. Like Cleveland Heights, Oak Park's actions may be serving more to retard, not to halt, the process of resegregation.[52] Activists in the African-American community have also sharply criticized what they regard as an attempt by a suburb to limit the size of its black population.

However limited the success of these suburbs in promoting stable integration, what is even more noteworthy is how these suburbs stand out nationally. Very, very few suburbs have been willing to undertake the strong steps necessary to maintain racial diversity.

THE POLITICAL ATTITUDES OF SUBURBIA: THE ANTI-CITY IMPULSE AND THE GRASSROOTS IDEAL

It is perilous to generalize about the attitudes of the people living in diverse suburban communities. Still, certain political attitudes have historically been associated with suburbia, even though they are not found in equal force in every community and among every racial and ethnic group.

Suburbanites believe in the inherent superiority of the suburban way of life. They see their communities as the modern-day embodiment of small-town virtues, the **Jeffersonian agrarian ideal,** an alternative to the alleged venality, corruption, and welfarism of central cities.[53]

Residents see suburbia as the realization of "the American dream," a hard-earned reward for their work and efforts. They are generally pleased with suburban life and feel little responsibility for the problems of the central city. Suburbanites assert the value of individualism and they insist on maintaining the political autonomy of their communities.[54]

Suburbanites claim to value small-scale, participatory government. They believe that government closest to the people governs best. In smaller communities, council members are friends and neighbors who reflect community values. Small-scale government allows for greater responsiveness; a citizen with a problem does not need to navigate through an impersonal bureaucracy. Some developers of new suburban communities have even marketed their communities as offering a restoration of the grassroots ideal. (See "Is There Grassroots Democracy in Planned Communities? Irvine, California" below.)

IS THERE GRASSROOTS DEMOCRACY IN PLANNED COMMUNITIES? IRVINE CALIFORNIA

South of Los Angeles, the developers of the planned suburb of Irvine sought to re-create small-town-style democracy in relatively small, distinct residential villages within a city that was targeted to have a population of over 400,000:

> To further re-create the village atmosphere of the ideal traditional suburb, the company also organized homeowner associations charged with maintaining the neighborhood park and recreation facilities as well as enforcing architectural controls. Homeowners elected the association's governing board, which supposedly would speak for the neighborhood and enhance the sense of grassroots rule. Thus the Irvine Company sought to fashion a city of villages with the intimacy of the small town and the participatory government of friends and neighbors so intrinsic to traditional suburban ideology.

But Irvine does not totally live up to the grassroots democratic ideal. In Irvine, as in planned communities elsewhere, the community's developer sets numerous rules that locally elected officials are not free to contradict. Elected representatives have no ability to make decisions that will violate the integrity of the developer's guiding community plan.

Over the years, liberal activists have been able to increase the city's commitment to social policy and affordable housing. These activists object to the continuing influence exerted by the developer, the Irvine Company, over local affairs.

Source: Jon C. Teaford, *Post-Suburbia: Government and Politics in the Edge Cities* (Baltimore: Johns Hopkins University Press, 1997); the quotation is from p. 94; and Nicholas Dagen Bloom, *Suburban Alchemy: 1960s New Towns and the Transformation of the American Dream* (Columbus, OH: Ohio State University Press, 2001), pp. 109–116.

Suburban communities, however, seldom live up to the grassroots ideal. Many suburbs are so large that elected officials no longer have a close personal relationship with the citizens they serve: "The image of the country village where every voter knew the mayor and council members personally and volunteered to extinguish fires was increasingly incongruous in a suburbia of corporate headquarters and 100-store malls."[55] In larger suburbs, the picture of a citizens' democracy is further diminished as candidates for local office turn to big donors in order to fund media-centered campaigns.

Voter turnout in local suburban elections is also typically low. Nonpartisan electoral systems and the scheduling of elections during off years, features typical of suburban electoral systems, both serve to diminish turnout. The nonpartisanship ideal also leads suburbanites to entrust local affairs to elite-led civic associations and trained city managers. In more homogeneous suburbs, officials seek to avoid conflict, and citizens tend to defer to the decisions of professional managers and local elites.[56]

When it comes to school-related issues, however, suburbanites do generally show high interest and engagement. Across the nation, citizen groups have battled school boards and professional school administrators. Montgomery County (Maryland), Fairfax County (Virginia), and Marin and San Mateo Counties (California) are only a few of the places where the new local activism has extended beyond school matters as citizens have challenged plans for subsidized housing, highway construction, and the development of new metro rail systems.

The developers of one of the fastest growing forms of housing in suburbia, the private **common interest development (CID)**, more commonly referred to as a **gated community**, also see their developments as the modern-day reincarnation of the grassroots ideal. In the typical CID, the residents serve as the unpaid directors of the local homeowner association, the effective decision-making body in a number of policy areas. In reality, however, few residents actively participate, and substantial decision-making power is often assumed by the few active directors of the association.[57] As one critic of these **privatopias** has further observed, CIDs place decision-making authority "in the hands of untrained, uncompensated amateurs; establishing no qualifications for their participation; creating no public institutional support for on-the-job training; and leaving the directors essentially free of public regulation, increasingly with immunity from private regulation through lawsuit."[58] The "private governance" of gated communities is largely undemocratic and unaccountable.[59]

While the residents of gated communities value neighborliness, they often show little obligation to the larger community beyond the gates of their high-amenity developments. The residents of gated communities often vote against bond issues that would raise funds to support projects needed elsewhere in a county.[60]

KEY SUBURBAN ISSUES: SCHOOLS AND TAXES

THE POLITICS OF SCHOOL FINANCE REFORM

Over the past few decades, state aid has increased dramatically and has come to exceed local-based funding for schools. Yet the money that a school district has available is still greatly dependent on local property wealth and taxes.

Many suburban jurisdictions are in an enviable position when it comes to school finance. Districts rich in property valuation can generate significant money for schools even with relatively low property tax rates. Poorer districts, in contrast, cannot produce equivalent revenues for their schools even when they tax their citizens at much higher rates. As a consequence, it comes as little surprise that the residents of property-rich suburbs (that is, suburbs with highly valued homes and commercial property) generally oppose school finance reform efforts. They are satisfied with a system that allows them to outspend other school districts while keeping their tax rates low.

A California state Supreme Court case sparked a nationwide campaign for more equitable school spending. In the early 1970s, Baldwin Park, a low-income community near Los Angeles, taxed itself at double the rate of exclusive Beverly Hills; yet Baldwin Hills was able to spend less than half the amount that Beverly Hills spent per pupil. In *Serrano v. Priest* (1971), the Court ruled that such extreme disparities in the tax base available for education denied residents of poorer districts the equal protections guaranteed by both the federal and state constitutions.[61] In California and other states, parents initiated legal action that led states to increase the aid given to local schools.

Nationally, the school finance reform movement suffered a major blow when a divided United States Supreme Court ruled 5–4 in *Rodriguez v. San Antonio* (1973) that the use of local property taxes to fund schools was not a violation of a citizen's equal protection rights guaranteed by the Fourteenth Amendment of the United States Constitution.[62] According to the Court, education is not a "fundamental right," as it is not explicitly mentioned in the U.S. Constitution. When it comes to education, the Fourteenth Amendment's equal protection clause does not require full equality, only that schools provide students with the minimal skills necessary to participate in the political process. The Court was also unwilling to order the equalization of school monies because experts disagreed as to just how important levels of spending were in determining a child's learning and future life chances. Some experts argued that parents and peers, not levels of spending, were the critical factors in learning.

In the wake of the *Rodriguez* decision, citizens aggrieved by inequalities in school funding had to shift tactics and bring suit in state courts on the basis of state law and the provisions of state constitutions. In California, Texas, New Jersey, and a whole host of other states, courts found state constitutional provisions that made the effective provision of education a state responsibility; in these states, the courts ordered the legislature to reform school finances.

Over a quarter century of battles in the states led to increases in state aid that alleviated some of the inequality among districts. By the early 1990s, state efforts in California brought all but 5 percent of local school districts to within $300 of each other in terms of per-student spending. However, much of this parity was achieved by an "equalizing down" process that constrained increases in local school spending in wealthier districts. Still, inequalities persisted. The poorest districts in the state spent less than $3,000 per pupil while the richest spent over $7,000. Similarly, in Texas, despite repeated judicial intervention, district school spending in 1996 ranged from $3,643 to $20,849 per student.[63]

In Texas, New Jersey, and elsewhere, more far-reaching school finance measures often stalled in suburban-dominated state legislatures where members were unwilling to incur the wrath of voters by raising taxes. Voters in wealthier communities are unwilling to pay for increased spending in other districts. The New Jersey Supreme Court even shut down the schools in the state for a brief period of time in order to force the legislature to enact an income tax necessary to fund a state school aid package.

Suburban opposition to school finance reform persists. In New Jersey, a program that redistributed hundreds of millions of dollars in state aid to poorer school districts was a factor in Governor Jim Florio's reelection defeat at the hands of Christine Todd Whitman. New Jersey's courts, however, soon forced Whitman, too, to turn her attention to mitigating school finance disparities.

In Texas, citizen opposition to school finance reform helped lead to the election of George W. Bush as governor. The state supreme court had threatened to impose its own plan or to shut down Texas' schools if the state legislature continued to drag its feet in coming up with the revenues to fund a suitable school finance plan. Despite the judicial threat, voters in 1993 rejected by almost a 2-to-1 margin a constitutional amendment to create larger school districts, merging richer and poorer communities together. Governor Ann Richards endorsed the amendment and other school finance reform measures, unpopular stances that helped lead to her narrow 1994 reelection defeat at the hands of George W. Bush. Eventually, the Texas legislature did pass a plan that recaptured some of the tax base of the richest 10 percent of Texas school districts in order to aid the state's poorer districts.[64]

In Michigan, Republican Governor John Engler followed an alternative strategy in enacting a mildly equalizing school reform measure that gave some new money to poorer urban and rural districts. The measure also constrained increases in spending by property-rich districts. Part of Engler's genius was to combine a politically popular tax relief plan with a school aid reform so complex that it was not easy for voters to discern just who won and who lost under the plan.

THE TAXPAYER REVOLT AND SCHOOL FINANCE: CALIFORNIA AND THE NATION

The movement to reform school finance also stumbled in the face of a nationwide taxpayers' rebellion that began in 1978 with California's **Proposition 13.** Californians had suffered a huge rise in taxes that accompanied soaring property values. In some southern California suburbs, property reassessments doubled a homeowner's tax obligation in just three or four years. Voters demanded tax relief. Their outrage was further fueled by the revelation of a substantial state budget surplus. At a time when local property taxes were rising through the roof, the state government had been sitting on money that it could have used to fund property tax relief.

Proposition 13 rolled back property taxes to their prior levels and sharply limited any annual increase that could be levied on a property owner.

Proposition 13 and the other tax and spending limitation measures that followed were a "revolt of the haves" that gained greatest support among the well-to-do and middle-aged taxpayers.[65]

The taxpayers' revolt quickly spread from California to other parts of the country. In Massachusetts, voters enacted **Proposition 2½**, only one of the many voter-imposed measures across the nation that limited taxing and spending. Local taxpayer revolts, such as TRIM in Prince George's County, Maryland, further curtailed the ability of elected officials to pay for local services. Certain local communities also exhibited **recall fever,** with community groups using petition drives to remove from office any public official who voted for a tax increase.

In California, the new taxing and spending limitations made it difficult to pass school funding measures. Once the national leader in per pupil spending, California fell to twenty-sixth place just eight years after Proposition 13. By the early 1990s, California sank further, falling to forty-sixth. In terms of class size, California ranked dead last, with the largest class sizes in the nation.[66] The state's economic downturn at the end of the Cold War only compounded state and school fiscal problems.

Faced with the new tax limitation measures, California's cities and suburbs searched desperately to find additional funds for schools. Many schools turned to **user fees,** including student fees for participation in sports and extracurricular activities. Unable to get voter approval for bonds to build new classrooms, California communities turned to **developer fees** and **access charges,** where developers and new homeowners were forced to pay fees in addition to their normal tax obligations. Such **impact fees** levy one-time charges on new development for services that have traditionally been paid for by property taxes. In essence, new residents are asked to pay for the extra burden they are imposing on a community's water, sewer, roads, and school systems. Given local resistance to property taxes, impact fees often provide the only means for a local community to pay for the expenses associated with new development.[67]

Impact fees have been popular in California, Florida, Oregon, and other states where communities sought to find some way to cope with the expenses brought about by rapid growth. The fees, however, added substantially to the cost of buying a home, decreasing housing affordability. A 1991 survey of housing in California, Florida, Oregon, and Washington revealed that impact fees added about $12,000 to the cost of a 2,000-square-foot house.[68]

In 1988, with the state's economy recovering, Californians took a step in an effort to halt the continued decline of the state's schools. **Proposition 98** was a voter-imposed constitutional initiative that required the state to maintain specified levels of school funding in order to reduce class sizes. The proposition, however, made it difficult for the state to balance its budget. After his victory in California's special 2003 recall election, new Governor Arnold Schwarzenegger even suggested that that legislature consider suspending Proposition 98 to allow California to deal with its budget crisis. Schools essentially were being asked to forgo part of their normal funding to help the state deal with its budget shortfall.[69]

School integration: Whatever happened to school busing?

Suburbs generally are not required to participate in plans to enhance racial integration in a region's schools. In the important 1974 *Millikin v. Bradley* decision, the Supreme Court ruled that Detroit's suburbs did not have to join in a metropolitan desegregation plan even if interdistrict city-to-suburban school busing was the only available means of bringing a racially integrated education to Detroit's school children.[70]

In its rulings, the Court has laid out an **intent to discriminate** doctrine: a suburb can be forced to participate in a desegregation plan only if it can first be proved that the suburb, by its own actions, purposely acted to maintain racial segregation. Advocates of racial integration measures can easily demonstrate the continuing racial imbalance between city and suburban schools; however, they cannot easily prove that a racial intent underlies that imbalance. Suburban officials argue that such imbalances are the products of residential patterns and district borders, not purposeful discrimination. Suburbanites argue that they simply desire to maintain the advantages of local control and neighborhood schools.

Since the 1990s, the Supreme Court has given local school districts greater leeway to narrow or abandon unpopular busing efforts. According to the Court's *Oklahoma City v. Dowell* ruling, even school districts found guilty of past discrimination were free to terminate desegregation measures if the districts, for a "reasonable" period of time, had attempted to remove the "vestiges" of *de jure* discrimination "to the extent practicable."[71]

The Court allowed localities to terminate metropolitan desegregation plans even in areas where "white flight" to the suburbs had undermined court-ordered efforts to integrate central-city schools. In a case involving DeKalb County, Georgia, the Court ruled that districts need not take action to remedy those patterns of school segregation resulting from residential patterns and private choice.[72] Seattle, Denver, Kansas City, Minneapolis, Indianapolis, Cleveland, Pittsburgh, Buffalo, Dallas, Austin, Savannah, Nashville, Norfolk, and Wilmington (Delaware) are among the cities that have diminished their metropolitan school desegregation efforts in favor of a new emphasis on neighborhood schools.[73] In Charlotte-Mecklenburg, North Carolina, where a federal judge ruled that busing for racial integration was no longer required, black community leaders accepted the prospects of heightened resegregation and instead focused their efforts on securing additional resources for central-city schools.[74]

As the Civil Rights Project at Harvard University has concluded, "suburban school districts remain segregated." A new **resegregation** of public school systems has led to the decreased exposure of African-American, Latino, and Caucasian students to one another.[75]

SUBURBAN LAND USE AND EXCLUSION

ZONING AND THE ROOTS OF SUBURBAN EXCLUSION

Suburban jurisdictions use zoning ordinances and land-use restrictions to determine just which types of housing and economic activities, and, in essence, which types of people will gain access to their communities. Suburban communities can be described as **exclusionary** if they use their zoning and related powers to "build invisible walls" that restrict entry by people who are less well-off and may be of a different race than existing community residents. Exclusionary zoning denies suburban opportunities to low- and moderate-income people. Suburbs such as Darien and New Canaan, Connecticut developed as elite bastions of wealth and privilege as a result of their history of restrictive zoning ordinances, a rejection of public housing, and discriminatory real estate and lending policies.[76]

Zoning ordinances are not necessarily exclusionary in intent. Planning and zoning offer important protections, promoting community livability and protecting property values by separating industrial from residential activities. Land-use plans can also safeguard a community from overdevelopment. Suburban communities across the nation have attempted to set limits on the height and floor area of a house in order to restrict the construction of "McMansions" (also called "bigfoots"), giant-sized single-family homes that are out of character with other homes in established neighborhoods.

Zoning ordinances also promote safety. An absence of strong land-use regulations contributed to the deadliness of wildfires in the Oakland Hills in the San Francisco Bay Area region. Residential developments were built in hazardous woodland and hillside areas, and narrow roads barred easy access by fire trucks.[77]

Politicians in "free-market" Houston like to brag that theirs is the only major city in the United States to have no zoning regulations whatsoever. Yet even Houston does not allow totally unfettered development. Houston regulates land use through rules for street design and parking as well as through the municipal enforcement of private deed restrictions. The city also guides development through a capital investment program, a comprehensive planning process, and subdivision regulations that apply to newly developing areas. The majority of the other 33 cities in surrounding Harris County do utilize zoning.[78]

While zoning serves important purposes, many affluent suburbs also use zoning as an exclusionary tool. The motivations behind exclusion are varied. Some suburbanites want to ward off traffic congestion, crime, and other ills that accompany the continued growth and "citification" of their communities. Other suburbanites seek to protect property values by preserving the attractive character of their communities. Suburban residents often have substantial equity invested in their homes, and they fear that the changing social composition of a community may adversely affect the price when they decide to sell.

Fiscal considerations also underlie exclusionary measures. Better-off residents object to paying increased taxes to subsidize costly services, especially schools, for low- and moderate-income newcomers who occupy rental units and low-valued homes that generate little in the way of tax revenue.

Still, suburban exclusion can also reflect racist, nativist, and classist sentiments. Zoning and land-use controls allow suburbs to enforce a narrow sense of **fraternity** with "overtones of exclusiveness, narrowness, provinciality and clannishness."[79] Reinforced by zoning and land-use controls, socially segmented suburbs can become narrow **lifestyle enclaves** for people of similar backgrounds and preferences.[80]

THE TECHNIQUES OF SUBURBAN EXCLUSION

Suburbs use a variety of means to limit the housing opportunities available to poor, working-class, and, in many cases, even middle-class families. A community can **refuse to accept subsidized housing** within its borders. A community can also bar or **restrict the construction of multifamily housing.** One study of the greater New York area found that over 99 percent of the undeveloped land zoned for residential use was zoned for single-family dwellings, effectively excluding people who can afford only rental apartments.[81] Even where the construction of multifamily apartments is permitted, a community can keep large, poor families out by sharply restricting the number of units that are built with more than two bedrooms.

Most commonly, suburbs use **large-lot zoning,** requiring that homes be built on no less than a half acre, one acre, or even two acres of land. Such a requirement greatly drives up the price of a home, making it unaffordable to low- and even moderate-income families. **Minimum room space requirements,** above those demanded by reasons of health and safety, can similarly be used to drive up home prices. Similarly, suburbs can require **the use of more expensive construction technologies and materials** that further serve to increase home prices. Some suburbs bar modular homes and components, which pose a cheaper alternative to on-site construction. Suburban municipalities can also add thousands of dollars in **developer fees** and **access charges** to the price of new homes, with owners being made to pay the full cost of new street, sewer, and school construction in addition to the taxes they pay that help support community-wide services.

Exclusionary communities limit the land available for new construction through **sewer and water line moratoria** that ban the extension of service to developable areas. The designation of certain areas as **agricultural preserves** or protected **greenspace areas** can also limit new home construction, raising the market price for existing as well as for new homes.

Suburban jurisdictions can also defeat development projects by **constantly shifting development standards** and using a strategy of **delay.** When a developer meets one set of conditions, a city council can try to impose new and even more expensive ones. Once a developer fails to meet conditions, building permits are withdrawn. Of course, a developer may challenge the local government's actions in court; but judicial action often takes quite a bit of time and can be very expensive. As delay itself, often combined with inflation, drives up the costs of construction, developers will tend to avoid communities where the likely imposition of costly delays makes development a bad gamble.[82]

Suburban homeowners and politicians seldom admit to exclusionary motives. Classism is regarded as elitist; overtly racist sentiment has even less public support today. As a result, suburbanites often justify their exclusionist concerns by turning to the more socially respectable arguments of environmentalism. (See "Should Environmentalists Oppose Suburban Housing Development: Is There an Environmental Protection Hustle?" on pp. 359–360.)

SHOULD ENVIRONMENTALISTS OPPOSE SUBURBAN HOUSING DEVELOPMENT: IS THERE AN ENVIRONMENTAL PROTECTION HUSTLE?

In *The Environmental Protection Hustle,* Bernard Frieden looks at case studies of development in the San Francisco Bay area to make the provocative argument that environmentalists have become the unwitting allies of suburban exclusionists. Suburbanites have learned to use the respectable language of environmentalism to argue, for instance, that growth in their communities must be limited in order to protect valuable green space and unique natural areas.

Frieden reveals the contradictions that result when environmentalists and suburbanites rally against new fringe growth. In one case, environmentalists opposed the construction of 2,200 affordable town home and condominium apartment units in the foothills outside Oakland. They accepted a compromise plan for the building of 300 expensive estate homes. But the new plan resulted in more sprawl. The original plan for compact development had devoted 480 acres of open space to public use; the revised plan dedicated no public recreational space.

Similarly, in neighboring Marin County, residents blocked new home building, declaring the need to protect access to the beautiful Pacific coastline. Once the construction was barred, exclusion was maintained when they insisted on access restrictions that made it all but impossible for outsiders to visit the preserve.*

Land-use overregulation drives up the costs of development, decreasing housing affordability and making it harder for racial minorities and newly married couples to gain access to the suburbs. By one estimate, local land-use controls, excessive subdivision improvement requirements, unnecessary delays, and developer fees have added between 18 and 34 percent to the price of a new home in the Bay Area.** In Wisconsin, one report estimated that relaxing minimum lot-size requirements and other zoning and development restrictions would reduce the costs of new suburban housing by about 50 percent.†

Frieden's critics charge that he has not given sufficient weight to such important environmental considerations as the protection of the Bay Area's foothills and Marin County's beautiful coastline. They further point out that the Bay Area's housing costs, among the highest in the nation, are due more to market factors than to locally enacted zoning and growth restrictions.

Environmentalists also warn of the dangerous power shift that can result if arguments, such as those presented by Frieden, are used to undermine the legitimacy of environmental forces in the continuing debate over development. Property developers and their growth coalition allies already possess substantial influence in the local political arena. Without a vigilant environmentalist community, they will continue to push sprawl and unwise development. In southern California, for instance, Baldwin Builders Inc. contributed money to the campaign of a Los Angeles County supervisor and later received permission

continued

SHOULD ENVIRONMENTALISTS OPPOSE SUBURBAN HOUSING DEVELOPMENT: IS THERE AN ENVIRONMENTAL PROTECTION HUSTLE? (CONT.)

to build 1,500 homes that infringed on open space in an environmentally sensitive tract of the Santa Monica Mountains.‡

* Bernard J. Frieden, *The Environmental Protection Hustle* (Cambridge, MA: MIT Press, 1979), pp. 23–24, 38–41, and 52–59.

** David E. Dowall, *The Suburban Squeeze: Land Conversion and Regulation in the San Francisco Bay Area* (Berkeley, CA: University of California Press, 1984), pp. 133–134.

† Mary K. Schuetz and Sammis White, *Identifying and Mitigating Regulatory Barriers to Affordable Housing in Waukesha County, Wisconsin* (Milwaukee: University of Wisconsin-Milwaukee Urban Research Center, 1992), Table 2, cited by Mark Edward Braun, "Subdivision Sprawl in Southeastern Wisconsin: Planning, Politics, and the Lack of Affordable Housing," in *Suburban Sprawl: Culture, Theory, and Politics*, eds. Mathew J. Lindstrom and Hugh Bartling (Lanham, MD: Rowman and Littlefield, 2003), p. 263.

‡ T. Christian Miller, "Sunday Report: Developer Money Pours Into Campaign Coffer of Officials," *Los Angeles Times*, December 27, 1998; T. Christian Miller, "A Growth Plan Runs Amok," *Los Angeles Times*, December 27, 1998.

BEYOND ZONING: LIMITED GROWTH AND NO GROWTH

Suburbs can also enact limited-growth and no-growth ordinances that strictly regulate the number of new residential units that can be constructed in a community. Ramapo, a town in Rockland County about 35 miles outside New York City, gained fame, beginning in 1969, for its early use of slow-growth zoning. The municipality decided that it would issue a special permit for new residential development only when the required municipal services were already available and a particular proposal was judged by the city to be meritorious. Ramapo retreated from its slow-growth position only after its growth control measures appeared to be working too well, stunting the community's economic development by driving desirable projects to neighboring jurisdictions.[83]

Petaluma, California, a Sonoma Valley community north of San Francisco, similarly took steps to slow the community's runaway growth. Petaluma imposed an explicit annual quota that initially allowed only a mere 500 dwelling units to be built each year. Each year, the city chose the winners in an annual competition among housing claimants.[84] Boulder (Colorado) and Livermore (California) are among other cities that adopted growth limitation strategies.

Growth limitations have also been the result of a trend called **ballot-box planning,** in which citizen groups have utilized the tools of direct democracy in order to slow growth. In San Francisco and in numerous California communities, citizens have used the initiative and referendum processes to limit building permits and otherwise restrict new construction.[85] The initiative and referendum have also been used by voters in other parts of the country to impose growth controls. In Portland, Maine, voters approved a measure to preserve the city's waterfront for marine uses, limiting new residential development and the threat of "creeping condominiumism."[86]

The wisdom of planning decisions made through the ballot box, however, is open to question. Voters may ignore the reports of professional planners and the subtleties and trade-offs entailed in any land use decision when they are asked, quite simplistically, to vote "No L.A.—Yes on [Proposition] A," the slogan of one San Diego anti-growth campaign.

THE LEGAL STATUS OF EXCLUSIONARY ZONING AND GROWTH MANAGEMENT

Some Americans think that zoning and other land-use restrictions violate an individual's right to use property anyway that he or she sees fit. However, the Supreme Court, as far back as *Village of Euclid, Ohio v. Ambler Realty Co.* (1926), has upheld the constitutionality of zoning.[87] According to *Euclid,* zoning represents a legitimate use of the state's **police powers** to protect the public welfare against such nuisances as increased noise, congestion, and a general change in a community's character.

Advocacy groups for the poor and racial minorities contend that suburban zoning is often exclusionary and discriminatory, a violation of the "equal protection" rights guaranteed by the Fourteenth Amendment. Yet the U.S. Constitution does not bar discrimination on the basis of income or buying power. For a court to strike down a community's zoning ordinance, it must find that the intent to discriminate was racial, not economic, in nature.

The Supreme Court's 1977 **Arlington Heights decision** upheld the exclusionary zoning practices of an affluent, overwhelmingly white suburb northwest of Chicago.[88] A church group sought to build subsidized housing units in Arlington Heights despite local zoning laws that largely prohibited multifamily housing. The Supreme Court upheld the constitutionality of the restrictions, observing that zoning serves such reasonable purposes as preventing overcrowding, promoting orderly land development, and safeguarding local property values. The plaintiffs could not prove that a racial intent underlay the suburb's zoning and land-use laws. The plaintiffs could easily demonstrate the discriminatory *effect* of the restrictions in excluding minorities, but they could not prove that the regulations were enacted with a racially discriminatory *intent.*

The importance of the *Arlington Heights* decision is clear: A suburb's legal counsel can always argue that zoning serves respectable purposes. A community is under no obligation to modify its in-place zoning and land-use practices in order to increase class and racial integration.

When it comes to local actions that seek to preserve the environment, though, the Supreme Court has been willing to impose some outside limits on a government's zoning and land-use powers. The Court will not allow governments to enact restrictions that effectively deprive an owner of *all* economic value from a piece of property. Communities can continue to zone land in ways that limit development. But regulations that deny an owner all economic value of a piece of land are an unconstitutional **taking** of property, effectively a seizure of private property by the government.[89]

OPENING UP THE SUBURBS: THE *MOUNT LAUREL* CHALLENGE TO SUBURBAN EXCLUSION

Suburban-dominated state legislatures are not inclined to tackle local exclusion. As a result of the *Arlington Heights* case, a successful challenge is not likely to be mounted on the basis of the federal Constitution. As a consequence, activists who seek to "open" the suburbs have had to turn to state courts in efforts that seek to portray exclusionary practices as violations of state constitutions and state law.

Beginning in 1975, the New Jersey Supreme Court, in a series of controversial rulings that have come to be known as **the *Mount Laurel* decisions,** struck down the exclusionary practices of a broad range of communities throughout the state. In *Mount Laurel I,* a unanimous court ruled that developing communities must allow the building of variety of types housing within their borders. The court ruled that the New Jersey state constitution's "due process," "equal protection" and "general welfare" clauses meant that growing communities throughout the state had an obligation to allow the construction of their "fair share" of a region's low- and moderate-income housing units.[90]

The initial court ruling had little immediate impact. Suburban communities dragged their feet and rezoned as few parcels of land as possible. In Mount Laurel Township, not a single new affordable home was built to comply with the court's decision.

Eight years later, in *Mount Laurel II,* the court went much further, imposing on all communities in the state an affirmative obligation to provide affordable housing.[91] The court even authorized developers to sue communities where local ordinances continued to obstruct the building of affordable housing. Developers who won their case in court would be rewarded by being allowed to build at even higher densities than local regulations otherwise specified. The New Jersey Supreme Court also created special housing courts to expedite the cases brought by developers.

Suburbanites were outraged at the threat to their communities posed by *Mount Laurel II.* New Jersey's governor and legislature acted to weaken the open-housing thrust of *Mt. Laurel II.* In *Mount Laurel III* (1986), the court accepted the new state approach, where a politically appointed Council on Affordable Housing replaced the housing courts in determining just how many affordable housing units were to be built in a community.[92] Not unexpectedly, the new body reduced the required number of subsidized housing units. The new law also allowed suburbs to reserve a greater share of the new units for established residents (as opposed to newcomers) and the elderly.

The new state law even allowed a municipality to meet half of its fair-share obligation not by building housing within its borders but by helping to pay for subsidized housing elsewhere in the state. A significant number of suburbs exercised this option, transferring up to 50 percent of their fair-share obligation by helping older cities such as Newark, Paterson, and Jersey City pay for low-income housing. Wayne Township in 1993 paid over $8 million to low-income Paterson in order to escape from having to build nearly 500 units of affordable housing within its own borders.[93]

Mount Laurel led to an increase in the production of affordable housing. Suburban communities such as Mount Laurel eventually altered the composition of their housing stock in order to accommodate more than a token number of poorer people. The system of intermunicipal agreements also provided much needed assistance to fiscally strapped central cities as they built low-income housing. Between 1987 and 1996, 54 *Mount Laurel*-inspired intermunicipal agreements involved more than $92 million and the construction of 4,700 units of affordable housing.[94]

Yet overall, the *Mount Laurel* decisions underscore the limited ability of judicial action to bring about top-down change in this controversial policy area.[95] While the *Mount Laurel* decisions led to the construction of thousands of new affordable housing units, they did little to open the suburbs in terms of class and race. Suburbs rezoned as little land as possible and gave little assistance to the developers of low-income housing. As the state relaxed its definition of "affordable housing," communities turned to the construction of condominiums, town houses, and garden apartments, alternative housing that seldom went to central-city residents, to the poor, or to people of color. Eighty percent of the units that were built as a result of *Mount Laurel* were sold, not rented. These so-called "affordable" units were not made available to low-income households; instead, they went to the grown children of suburbanites, blue-collar workers, divorced mothers, and young couples who could draw on their parents for assistance.[96] Units were also given to police officers, nurses, and other public service workers and "young people whose life-time income profile is middle class but whose current wealth does not allow homeownership."[97]

Mount Laurel represents the most aggressive approach in the nation to opening the suburbs. Yet, while intermunicipal agreements helped finance the production of new subsidized housing in central cities, overall, the decisions did relatively little to integrate suburbs either economically or racially. In Parma, Ohio, Cleveland's largest suburb, a quarter of a century of judicial intervention similarly resulted in only the most marginal increase in the city's minority population.[98]

OTHER INCLUSIONARY EFFORTS

Montgomery County (Maryland) and Orange County (California) are among the national leaders in terms of **inclusionary programs,** relaxing zoning ordinances, modifying building codes, and providing financial assistance to developers in an effort to encourage the construction of affordable dwelling units.[99] **Density bonuses** permit a developer of low- and moderately priced units to build a greater number of units than local ordinances normally permit.

Under Massachusetts' Chapter 40B **Anti-Snob Zoning** law, the state can invalidate local land-use controls that unreasonably interfere with the construction of low- and moderate-income housing. Offending municipalities can also be denied development-related assistance. But the requirements of the Massachusetts law have not been aggressively enforced. Suburbanites bitterly complain that the Massachusetts law overrides local governance and gives powerful developers the ability to bypass local zoning restrictions. Responding to these criticisms, Governor Jane Swift in 2001 approved several modifications to the law, allowing localities to refuse large projects that are out of character with their communities.[100]

Rhode Island and Connecticut have statutes that are similar to some of Massachusetts' laws. In Connecticut, a special housing judge can overturn the decisions where local zoning officials cannot show that health and safety concerns outweigh the need for affordable housing.[101]

In Oregon, local zoning must gain state approval. The state requires that municipalities permit manufactured housing, ease subdivision requirements, and grant density bonuses to promote the development of lower-income housing.

California's housing laws merely require localities to prepare plans for affordable housing, not actually to build the units. Even so, four-fifths of California cities failed to comply fully with the requirement that they adopt a housing plan. Approximately 30 percent of cities in California have either quite dated plans or no housing plan at all.[102]

SUBURBAN AUTONOMY AND THE FRAGMENTED METROPOLIS

The concept of a metropolitan area denotes economic and social interdependence. Central cities provide warehousing, distribution, manufacturing, and other economic and systems-maintenance functions beneficial to the entire metropolis. They also provide housing for a region's low-wage workers. Despite the suburbanization of activities, central cities continue to be centers of art, culture, entertainment, and education.

Suburbs are not free-standing, socioeconomically balanced communities. Rather, they are only "slices of the metropolitan complex."[103] Yet no suburb is required to look out for the interests of neighboring communities or of the metropolis as a whole.

Metropolitan fragmentation denotes the lack of a powerful metropolitan-wide authority, that a metropolitan area is divided into numerous, smaller, self-interested jurisdictions. The Greater New York metropolitan area provides an archetypal example of metropolitan fragmentation. The 20-million-person metropolitan New York area sprawls into three states and contains a confusing array of 2,179 separate units of government, including cities, villages, towns, townships, and boroughs; 31 counties, 742 special districts (each responsible for providing a single service such as water or parks), and numerous authorities and regional and multistate agencies.[104] Allegheny County, Pennsylvania contains 130 separate municipalities including the City of Pittsburgh, and Allegheny is just one of the five counties that comprise the Pittsburgh metropolitan area.

THE COSTS OF METROPOLITAN FRAGMENTATION AND SUBURBAN SPRAWL

The consequences of suburban autonomy and metropolitan fragmentation are numerous:

- **Racial imbalance in the metropolis.** Suburban sprawl contributes to residential and school segregation. Despite increases in minority suburbanization, racial minorities, especially African Americans, remain concentrated in central cities. Patterns of racial imbalance are also being replicated in the suburbs. In metropolitan Detroit, there are "115 separate school districts empowered to erect walls around themselves"; there is no prospect of meaningful racial integration.[105] Schooling in the metropolis can be characterized as a system of "separate but unequal."[106]

- **Income and resource imbalance in the metropolis.** Zoning and land-use restrictions allow suburbs a fair degree of selectivity of residents and commercial activity. The central city and a region's more distressed suburbs become the repositories for low-income people and residents who need costly housing, schools, health care, income support, and social services. At the same time, these jurisdictions are denied the tax base needed to provide adequate services, as high-value housing and new commercial activities are increasingly located in a region's more attractive "favored quarter" suburbs.[107] Quickly growing working-class communities, too, often lack the property tax base necessary for new schools and quality local services.

- **The protection of privilege.** Suburbanites use land-use controls to maintain the relatively uncrowded, comfortable nature of their communities. These tools also protect fiscal privilege. Compared to central-city residents, suburbanites, especially in the "favored quarter" suburbs, pay lower tax rates for better-quality schools and public services.

- **Increased business power.** Metropolitan fragmentation affords considerable advantages to business owners and corporations. Owners seek business locations in low-tax communities. They can also threaten to move their facilities from one jurisdiction to another in an effort to coerce tax concessions and other favors from municipal officials.

- **The impact of suburbs on central cities.** Central cities are burdened by having to pay for services that benefit suburbanites. According to the **exploitation hypothesis,** commuters from the suburbs benefit from central-city fire and police protection and street repaving without paying their fair share of property and income taxes to support such services. Suburbanites also benefit from city-run parks, zoos, and museums where costs of operation are not fully covered by admission charges and user fees. Automobile commuting imposes still other costs on central-city residents in terms of environmental harm and neighborhood destruction. Even where states allow cities to levy income taxes on commuters, such tax rates by law are kept quite low. As one comparative study of city spending concluded, "[T]he suburban population, by its daily use of central city facilities, substantially raised the costs of municipal services."[108]

- **Exacerbated problems of housing affordability.** Suburban land-use restrictions inflate housing prices in a region by decreasing housing supply and adding to the costs of new home construction. In many metropolitan areas, housing affordability has become a concern of the middle class, not just of the poor.

- **Environmental consequences.** Each suburban jurisdiction pursues development in its self-interest with no respect for environmental values. A rim community can choose to expand its tax base with a new shopping mall, even if such a development reduces green space and lengthens automobile trips, increasing air pollution in the region. Other suburbs institute zoning and land-use plans that restrict growth, exacerbating sprawl by driving new development to the region's rim. The greater Los Angeles region suffers from a severe **spatial mismatch** in terms of residences and jobs, as high housing prices have pushed people farther away from areas of good-job growth, exacerbating traffic congestion and air pollution problems.[109]

  The runoff from roadways, parking lots, and other paved surfaces adds to water pollution with oil, road salts, and other contaminants that flow into lakes and streams. Sprawl also eats up open space, greenfields, and wetlands, destroying animal habitats and diminishing biodiversity. In southeast Wisconsin, new subdivisions on the edge of the greater Milwaukee area have driven up land prices, prompting the sale of farmland for nonfarm uses.[110]

- **Added costs and problems in service provision.** Suburban sprawl adds to service costs. It is estimated, for instance, that Salt Lake City could save $4.5 billion in transportation, water, sewer, and utility investments if it could simply contain growth.[111]

  Metropolitan fragmentation produces a problem of service coordination across the local political borders. Effective mass transit, for instance, is impossible where bus and rail service stops at the borders of a community where residents are unwilling to pay to support the service. Even the efficient provision of emergency medical services may be thwarted by metropolitan fragmentation; a community's ambulance drivers may not be permitted to respond to a call for help that requires them to cross a local political boundary.

  Metropolitan fragmentation can also lead to an expensive overlap and duplication of services when each community insists, for instance, on having its own fire station, hospital, or CT-scan equipment. Studies of local spending show that the higher levels of fragmentation in metropolitan areas are associated with the higher costs of government.[112] Services can be provided more cheaply if communities plan and share facilities. Metropolitan fragmentation denies citizens the advantages of **economies of scale,** in which cost savings can be realized by the larger-scale provision of a service. Instead, in the fragmented metropolis, citizens are left to pay the costs posed by empty hospital beds and high-technology equipment not used to full capacity.

Compared to Los Angeles and most other metropolitan areas, metropolitan Phoenix has developed as a relatively compact area with jobs remaining concentrated in the urban core. The limited availability of water and the region's late start in highway building have helped to constrain the geographic spread of the nation's most quickly growing metropolitan area. Yet recent years has seen an explosion of residential development on the region's rim, adding to traffic congestion and threatening agricultural and desert land. New highway construction is also threatening to alter Phoenix's shape. In Phoenix, there is the potential that water policy can be used to manage future growth.[113]

GROWTH MANAGEMENT AND "SMART GROWTH"

Can urban sprawl be contained? Some environmentalists argue for placing strict limits on new growth. But such proposals are politically contentious and often unrealistic. Metropolitan areas need to accommodate growing populations. Programs that adversely affect job development in a region are especially unpopular.

Rather than curb growth entirely, an increasing number of states over the years have sought **sustainable development** or **smart growth.** Sustainable development permits only growth that does not jeopardize natural resources for future generations. Growth management strategies focus on more compact and transit-oriented development patterns as an alternative to ever-spreading sprawl. Smart growth strategies seek to minimize highway congestion, automobile pollution, and the loss of agricultural land and greenspace, while minimizing the public's investment in roads, water mains, sewers and other public infrastructure.

States in the Sunbelt, especially in the Southwest and the West, face the prospects of explosive growth. In the absence of strategies to manage that growth, western states can expect to suffer continued sprawl, water shortages, and infrastructure problems. By the early 2000s, twelve states—Delaware, Florida, Georgia, Maryland, New Jersey, Oregon, Pennsylvania, Rhode Island, Tennessee, Vermont, Washington, and Wisconsin—had enacted statewide comprehensive planning reforms. Notably, Nevada and Arizona, had not.[114]

Certain states stood out as leaders in the smart growth movement:

Florida. In an effort to protect the Everglades and environmentally fragile coastal areas, Florida in 1985 became the largest state in the nation to adopt comprehensive growth management. Florida's Growth Management Act sought to encourage more compact development by requiring communities to identify the costs of new infrastructure. The state required localities to develop comprehensive development plans; localities were to permit new development only where the supporting infrastructure was available.

But Florida's act has not proven to be very effective in guiding new development. Localities, convinced of the benefits of new development, have not fully abided by growth management. In numerous cities, the local growth machine fought for the provision of new infrastructure in order to accommodate new growth. The Florida statutes also allowed new rim development where highway capacity was available. In Orlando, growth restrictions did not work as developers simply leapt over the county line and located developments in counties that were eager to accept new growth. In the pursuit of economic growth, Governor Jeb Bush also cut back Florida's "Eastward Ho!" effort, a policy that had attempted to steer new growth away from the ecologically fragile Everglades."[115]

Maryland and New Jersey. A small state, Maryland adopted smart growth legislation in the face of the prospect of further losses of farmland and greenspace with the expected arrival of more than a million new residents by the year 2020. Another half million residents were expected to leave cities for the suburbs, further adding to the pressures underlying sprawl. Governor Parris N. Glendening objected that such development would necessitate a huge public investment in sewers, roads, and other new public infrastructure on the urban rim.

Maryland's 1997 Smart Growth Areas Act used state investment as a carrot to guide growth. State subsidies for highways, sewage treatment, housing, and other infrastructure were directed to existing municipalities, communities in need of redevelopment, and other already-developed areas. Large-lot-housing subdivisions and greenfield areas did not qualify for priority funding. Other Maryland programs sought rural preservation and the reclamation of once-industrial brownfields.[116] Similarly in New Jersey, Governor Christine Todd Whitman gave preference to funding projects in areas that already had infrastructure in place.[117]

The Maryland and New Jersey approaches are noteworthy as they rely on incentives rather than strict prohibitions or regulations on growth. Yet incentives have only a limited reach. Despite Maryland's clear priorities, local officials and developers continued to build thousands of new housing units outside of designated growth areas.

Oregon. Compared to Maryland and New Jersey, Oregon has taken a more regulatory approach to growth management. Beginning in the 1970s, Oregon adopted a series of strong planning laws, including the requirement that cities formulate growth boundaries. Portland's **Urban Growth Boundary (UGB)** helped to protect farmland in the Willamette Valley from encroachment by new residential subdivisions. The UGB has also directed growth inwards, placing a new premium on **infill development** in established area. As a result, the economy and property

AP/WWP

Portland's Urban Growth Boundary (UGB)
sharply confines development, preserving
farmland and greenspace.

values boomed not just in Portland but in the region's older suburbs
as well.[118]

One downside of such regulated development, however, is that
people are able to buy less home for their money. Inside the growth
boundary, homes are built at higher densities, on relatively small
plots of land with small backyards. Critics also charge that the UGB
increases the costs of housing; by limiting the supply of developable
land, regulation acts to increase the prices of land on which housing
can be built.

But as Denver and Salt Lake City, cities without a growth boundary,
have experienced a similar rapid escalation in home prices, it is unclear to
what extent the UGB deserves the blame for home-price inflation in
Portland. Developers and home builders often exaggerate the claimed
impact of Portland's UGB on home prices. The market forces created by
rapid job and wage growth have a much greater effect than the UGB on
housing prices. Well-designed growth management policies can even
increase the supply of affordable housing in a region through inclusionary
provisions that require a mix of housing types and increased housing

densities. Oregon's local housing targets further help to ensure continued new home production.[119]

Georgia. Georgia was once a laggard when it came to growth management. But as extreme traffic congestion and pollution problems threatened to strangle Atlanta's economy, the state intervened with more aggressive action.[120] In 1998 the federal government even cut off aid for road building in the region in order to force state and local officials to formulate a regional transportation plan to reduce the area's severe air pollution.

Georgia Governor Roy Barnes responded by convincing the state legislature to create the **Georgia Regional Transportation Agency (GRTA),** a "superagency" with a 15-member board of directors. The GRTA supervises a 13-county area and has the power to approve a regional transportation plan. With influence over new roads, public transit lines, and associated land-use planning, the GRTA has the power to guide new development in greater Atlanta. The GRTA can even threaten to withhold federal and state transportation money from localities that refuse to support public transit or that refuse to steer high-density residential and commercial development to transit corridors.

Still, environmentalists have criticized GRTA for its early actions that were supportive of the automobile and automobile-related development. It is still too early to see just how effective the GRTA will be in curbing sprawl development in metropolitan Atlanta.[121]

The state of Washington. In Seattle, the city's growth machine used the ideology of smart growth as a cover to win public approval for new development efforts in this environmentally conscious city. City planners sought to direct growth inwards as an alternative to the continuing meteoric growth of the city's periphery. West Seattle neighborhoods were targeted for the development of new "urban villages." Neighborhood activists in West Seattle, however, charged that the plan would undermine the quality of life and their neighborhoods and would only further the "Manhattanization" of Seattle.[122]

CAN WE BUILD BETTER SUBURBS? THE NEW URBANISM MOVEMENT

The **New Urbanism** "is arguably the most influential movement in city design in the last half-century."[123] The movement seeks to provide an alternative to both sprawl and the isolation and anomie of life in faceless, homogenous suburban developments. The New Urbanism seeks to provide Americans with a restored sense of community and a better quality of life. New Urbanism emphasizes compact development, walkable communities, identifiable town centers, and the integration of suburban communities in regional mass transit

New Urbanism: White picket fences line a walkway in Seaside,
Florida, an award-winning planned community designed to evoke
America's small-town past.

systems. New Urbanism seeks the more efficient use of land through development design that reduces the vast acreage in conventional suburbia that is lost
to wide roadways, access ramps, and a sea of parking lots that surround shopping centers, malls, and office galleries.

THE GUIDING PRINCIPLES OF THE NEW URBANISM

New Urbanists seek to get Americans out of their cars and back on the street
and in touch with their neighbors. Conventional suburbs, designed for the
convenience of the automobile, place nearly insurmountable barriers in the
way of walking. Homes are located far from commercial destinations. High
schools and office centers are situated on virtual islands surrounded by acres
of parking that are almost untraversable on foot. Fast highways and access
ramps are nearly impossible for pedestrians to cross; they serve as moats separating one office and retail development from another. The workers in a suburban office tower cannot simply walk to a café or convenience store; they
have no safe and convenient alternative but to get into their car and drive
across one parking lot into another. With no visual attractions, the highway-
and parking-lot-dominated landscape makes suburbia "an incredibly boring
place to walk."[124]

New Urbanists seek to design communities with features that promote
short walking or bicycle trips. An attractive, old-style town center with cafés
and interesting shops will attract pedestrian traffic. Garages in the new town
center are pushed to the rear in order to promote a pedestrian friendly shopping and civic environment.

To further encourage walking, homes can be built close to sidewalks and located within a five-minute walk to schools, convenience stores, and other key facilities that serve as neighborhood focal points. Town homes and apartments are necessary to achieve the population densities needed to support such stores. Front porches can restore the "eyes" that watch over streets, helping to make streets safe and free of crime. Narrow and tree-lined streets, slowed automobile speeds, and the preservation of on-street parallel parking to protect pedestrians from the flow of traffic all promote pedestrian traffic. A conventional street grid, as opposed to dead-end suburban cul-de-sacs, further allows residents to choose from a variety of paths, adding to the interest of walking from one destination to another. Walkways and bike paths provide pleasant alternatives to the automobile.

New Urbanists emphasize diversity as an alternative to the isolation and insularity of the zoning-enforced homogeneity of conventional suburbs. New Urbanism seeks neighborhoods that have a mix of visually attractive apartments, town homes, and single-family homes. Affordable housing that contains elements of architectural expression can be made to blend in harmoniously with a community.

The New Urbanism recognizes the interdependence of communities in a metropolis. Hence, New Urbanists also seek to tie their communities to the central city and the larger region. Ideally, they propose more dense construction around a rail station, allowing the emergence of a transit-oriented village with shopping and other conveniences.[125] In Portland, Oregon, transit stations have become nodes for new development and pedestrian-friendly activity.

New Urbanism is not a movement that is concerned only with suburbs. New Urbanism principles have also been applied to city shopping districts, with mixed-use developments attempting to bring 24-hour-a-day life back to a city's downtown. New Urbanist principles have even been used to create more habitable public housing environments. In Chicago, Atlanta, Baltimore, Charlotte, and elsewhere, the Department of Housing and Urban Development (HUD) has demolished some of the nation's worst high-rise public housing and built a number of new low-rise, mixed-income replacement units according to New Urban principles. Subsidized units are blended in with market-rate units; the two are not distinguishable from the outside. HUD's HOPE VI program seeks to give public housing residents who are lucky enough to get the New Urbanism–style units a chance to reestablish connections with the larger community.[126]

LIMITATIONS AND CRITICISMS OF THE NEW URBANISM

But does the New Urbanism provide a viable alternative to conventional suburban development? The New Urbanism cannot greatly change patterns of land use and communities that have taken root over time. New Urbanist developers and planners have been most successful where they have had the freedom to design new developments according to their community-oriented principles.

The New Urbanism lacks the power to change the way most Americans live. Most homeowners in conventional suburbs express a great deal of satisfaction with their lives. Simply put, Americans have used their buying power to purchase big homes, with spacious backyards and a sense a privacy; they are satisfied with the escape that affluence and the automobile has put within their grasp. Constrained by market factors, New Urban developments often fail to attract the population densities needed to support the neighborhood facilities and vital town centers that are critical features of New Urban design. (See "The New Urbanism, Ideal and Reality," below.)

THE NEW URBANISM, IDEAL AND REALITY

With its small-town appearance, white picket fences, front porches, gabled roofs, narrow streets, walkways to the beach, homes of architectural distinction, and public spaces and beach pavilions, Seaside, Florida, in the state's panhandle, emerged in the 1980s as the first prominent community of the New Urbanism. Pleasant and attractive, Seaside even provided the setting for the motion picture *The Truman Show,* starring Jim Carrey.

Whatever its successes, Seaside does not represent a revival of small-town life. Rather, Seaside is little more than a fashionable, aesthetically pleasing beachfront community. Its housing sells at high prices and mainly caters to short-term vacationers, not permanent town residents.

Compared to other New Urban developments, Celebration, Florida, created by the Disney Corporation just outside of Walt Disney World, is noteworthy for its success in having maintained an attractive town center with a town hall, bank, post office, upscale grocery store, theater, trendy cafés, and a lakeshore path. Yet residents in Celebration, as in other New Urban communities, must routinely shop for groceries and clothing in the malls and suburban shopping strips beyond Celebration's borders. Celebration, like other New Urbanism communities, lacks the population density to support major stores. For years, Celebration maintained its attractive town center only as a result of the subsidized store leases offered by the Disney Corporation. Disney also aggressively advertised and marketed Celebration as a must-see tourist destination in the Orlando region, bringing in patrons who would not otherwise frequent the town's stores.*

In Kentlands, Maryland (located within Gaithersburg, a suburb of Washington, DC), there was no deep-pockets Disney corporation to subsidize store leases and to pay up-front for the development of an attractive town center. In Kentlands, market forces led developers to modify their original designs, compromising New Urbanism ideals. The Kentlands Square shopping center was even marred by vacant storefronts as Kentlands residents chose to drive to shops elsewhere. Indeed, Kentlands Square was rather like any other strip mall, only a bit more aesthetically pleasing. Shoppers still arrived by car and refused to frequent stores that were not easily accessible from the parking lot.**

continued

THE NEW URBANISM, IDEAL AND REALITY (CONT.)

New Urbanist planners express their commitment to diversity. But the developers of new communities lack the government subsidies to build extensive affordable housing. Developers are also constrained by the preferences of home-buyers who seek exclusivity and distance from lower classes. As a consequence, New Urbanism communities offer relatively few lower-income units, units that are usually separated from the more high-end parts of the community.

In Celebration, Disney did not want the construction of affordable housing within the community. Instead, the developer met its obligations under state law by contributing to a fund that assisted people with rents and down payments outside of Celebration's borders. As one critic observed: "It's true that Celebration does have some mix of housing, but it's a mixing of the upper class."[†]

For its critics, however, New Urbanism developments like Celebration are not all that noteworthy or different: "Celebration is a conventional suburban subdivision pretending to be a small town."[‡] Yet, the residents of these New Urbanism communities often express great satisfaction with their lives. They like the biking and hiking trails, the sense of freedom that comes with the ability of children to walk to schools and recreation, and the sense of neighborliness that they find. As two residents observed of life in Celebration: "You *can* be isolated in Celebration, but unlike in traditional suburbs, you have to work at it."[§]

---

* Alex Marshall, *How Cities Work: Suburbs, Sprawl, and the Roads Not Taken* (Austin, TX: University of Texas Press, 2000), pp. 8–14.

** Alexander Garvin, *The American City: What Works, What Doesn't*, 2nd ed. (New York: McGraw-Hill, 2002), pp. 415–416.

† Marshall, p. 27. This paragraph also relies on Douglas Frantz and Catherine Collins, *Celebration, U.S.A.: Living in Disney's Brave New Town* (New York: Owl Books/Henry Holt, 2000), pp. 74–77 and 219–225.

‡ Frantz and Collins, *Celebration, U.S.A.*, p. 313; also see pp. 255–256.

§ Marshall, *How Cities Work*, p. xviii.

New Urbanism offers a better alternative to the conventional suburb. However, the planners of New Urbanism have not been able to counter Americans' automobile-oriented lifestyles and preferences for stratified communities.[127] New Urbanists tried to construct an ideal community, but generally succeeded only in building an "automobile-oriented subdivision dressed up to look like a small pre-car-centered town."[128]

CONCLUSIONS: TOWARD WORKABLE REGIONALISM

The rise of growth management and the New Urbanism are only two indicators of the pressing nature of suburban problems and the need to take aggressive steps to counter the ill effects of suburban sprawl. Still, suburban communities jealously guard their autonomy; the interests of the region as a whole—in terms of environmental protection, the creation of socially and economically balanced communities, school integration, and rebuilding a lost sense of community—are ignored. Suburban autonomy protects privilege. Its residents generally pay lower tax rates and enjoy high-quality services. Businesses take advantage of fragmentation by playing one community off against the other in the search of tax abatements and other privileges.

Anthony Downs has observed that "the long-run welfare of suburban residents is still closely linked to how well central cities and their residents perform significant social and economic functions in each metropolitan area. The belief among suburbanites that they are independent of central cities is a delusion."[129] Urban commentator Neal Peirce has similarly called upon residents and decision makers to recognize their interdependence as citizens of metropolitan **citistates** that cross local political boundaries.[130] Yet there is no guarantee that the fragmented metropolis, with local communities jealously guarding their interests and prerogatives, will be able to undertake the joint action necessary to meet the challenges brought about by heightened interregional and global competition.

Just what are the prospects for effective regional action? This is the subject of our next chapter.

NOTES

1. William H. Lucy and David L. Phillips, "Suburbs and the Census: Patterns of Growth and Decline," a report of The Brookings Institution Center on Urban and Metropolitan Policy, Washington, DC, 2001.
2. For three good examples of the 1950s literature on suburbia, see: William H. Whyte, Jr., *The Organization Man* (New York: Simon & Schuster, 1956); David Riesman, *The Lonely Crowd* (Garden City, NY: Doubleday, 1957); and J. Seeley, R. Sim, and E. Loosley, *Crestwood Heights* (New York: Basic Books, 1956). There were, however, notable exceptions in which observers did recognize the existence of suburbs that did not conform to the bedroom community stereotype. See Bennett M. Berger, *Working-Class Suburb* (Berkeley: University of California Press, 1960); and Frederick M. Wirt et al., *On the City's Rim: Politics and Policy in Suburbia* (Lexington, MA: D. C. Heath, 1972), pp. 35–48.
3. Myron Orfield, *American Metropolitics: The New Suburban Reality* (Washington, DC: Brookings Institution, 2002), p. 28.
4. Ibid., pp. 2–3.
5. Robert Puentes and Myron Orfield, "Valuing America's First Suburbs: A Policy Agenda for Older Suburbs in the Midwest," a report of The Brookings Institution Center on Urban and Metropolitan Policy, Washington, DC, 2002.
6. Evan McKenzie, *Privatopia: Homeowner Associations and the Rise of Residential Private Government* (New Haven, CT: Yale University Press, 1994).
7. Rosalynn Baxandall and Elizabeth Ewen, *Picture Windows: How the Suburbs Happened* (New York: Basic Books, 2000), pp. 239–250.
8. Roberto Suro and Audrey Singer, "Latino Growth in Metropolitan America: Changing Patterns, New Locations," a report of The Brookings Institution Center on Urban and Metropolitan Policy, Washington, DC, 2002.

9. Patricia Leigh Brown, "In One Suburb, Local Politics With Asian Roots," *The Washington Post,* January 3, 2004.

10. For a provocative description of racial conflict in Orange County, California, see Mike Davis, "Behind the Orange Curtain," *The Nation,* October 31, 1994, pp. 485–490.

11. Robert E. Lang and Patrick A. Simmons, "'Boomburgs': The Emergence of Large, Fast-Growing Suburban Cities in the United States," Fannie Mae Foundation Note 06 (Washington, DC: June 2001). Available at: www.fanniemaefoundation. org/census_notes_6.shtml.

12. Joel Garreau, *Edge City: Life on the New Frontier* (New York: Doubleday, 1991).

13. Jonathan Barnett, *The Fractured Metropolis: Improving the New City, Restoring the Old City, Reshaping the Region* (New York: HarperCollins, 1995), especially pp. 1–13.

14. Robert E. Lang, *Edgeless Cities: Exploring the Elusive Metropolis* (Washington, DC: Brookings Institution, 2003).

15. Edward L. Glaeser, Matthew Kahn, and Chenghuan Chu, "Job Sprawl: Employment Location in U.S. Metropolitan Areas," a report of The Brookings Institution Center on Urban and Metropolitan Policy, Washington, DC, 2001.

16. Alan Berube and William H. Frey, "A Decade of Mixed Blessings: Urban and Suburban Poverty in Census 2000," a report of The Brookings Institution Center on Urban and Metropolitan Policy, Washington, DC, 2002.

17. Alan DiGaetano and John S. Klemanski, "Restructuring the Suburbs: Political Economy of Economic Development in Auburn Hills, Michigan," *Journal of Urban Affairs* 13, 2 (1991): 137–158.

18. William H. Frey and Alan Berube, "City Families and Suburban Singles: An Emerging Household Story from Census 2000," a report of The Brookings Institution Center on Urban and Metropolitan Policy, Washington, DC, 2002.

19. Hugh A. Wilson, "The Family in Suburbia: From Tradition to Pluralism," in *Suburbia Re-examined,* pp. 85–93.

20. Martha Farnsworth Riche, "The Implications of Changing U.S. Demographics for Housing Choice and Location in Cities," a discussion paper prepared for The Brookings Institution Center on Urban and Metropolitan Policy, Washington, DC, 2001.

21. William H. Frey, "The New Urban Demographics: Race, Space, and Boomer Aging," *Brookings Review* 18, 3 (Summer 2000): 18–21.

22. Lynn M. Appleton, "The Gender Regimes of American Cities," in *Gender in Urban Research, Urban Affairs Annual Review,* vol. 42, eds. Judith A. Garber and Robyne S. Turner (Thousand Oaks, CA: Sage Publications, 1995), pp. 44–59, especially p. 47.

23. Ibid., p. 54.

24. Ibipo Johnston-Anumonwo, Sara McLafferty, and Valerie Preston, "Gender, Race, and the Spatial Context of Women's Employment," in *Gender in Urban Research,* eds. Garber and Turner, pp. 249–250.

25. Appleton, "The Gender Regimes of American Cities," pp. 53–55.

26. Marsha Ritzdorf, "Land Use, Local Control, and Social Responsibility: The Child Care Example," *Journal of Urban Affairs* 15, 1 (1993): 79–91.

27. Baxandall and Ewen, *Picture Windows,* pp. 220–222.

28. Nicholas Dagen Bloom, *Suburban Alchemy: 1960s New Towns and the Transformation of the American Dream* (Columbus, OH: Ohio State University Press, 2001), pp. 208–222.

29. G. Scott Thomas, *The United States of Suburbia: How the Suburbs Took Control of America and What They Plan to Do With It* (Amherst, NY: Prometheus Books, 1998), p.165, presents brief polling evidence showing suburbia's relatively liberal views on gay rights.

30. U.S. Census Bureau, "Census 2000 Special Reports" (February 2003), available at: www.census.gov/prod/2003pubs/ccnsr-5.pdf.

31. William H. Frey, "Melting Pot Suburbs: A Census 2000 Study of Suburban Diversity," a report of The Brookings Institution Center on Urban and Metropolitan Policy, Washington, DC, 2001.

32. Frey, "Melting Pot Suburbs," pp. 4 and 10.

33. Ibid., p. 8.

34. John F. Kain, "Housing Market Discrimination and Black Suburbanization in the 1980s," in *Divided Neighborhoods: Changing Patterns of Racial Segregation, Urban Affairs Annual Review,* vol. 32, ed. Gary A. Tobin (Newbury Park, CA: Sage, 1987), p. 87.

35. Thomas J. Phelan and Mark Schneider, "Race, Ethnicity, and Class in American Suburbs," *Urban Affairs Review* 31, 5 (May 1996): 659–680; Robert M. Adelman, "Neighborhood Opportunities, Race, and Class: The Black Middle Class and Residential Segregation," *City and Community* 3, 1 (2004): 43–63.

36. Elizabeth D. Huttman and Terry Jones, "American Suburbs: Desegregation and Resegregation," in *Urban Housing Segregation of Minorities in Western Europe and the United States,* ed. Elizabeth D. Huttman (Durham, NC: Duke University Press, 1991), pp. 343–343.

37. Joe T. Darden, "Choosing Neighbors and Neighborhoods," p. 17. Also see Darden, Harriet Orcutt Duleep, and George C. Galster, "Civil Rights in Metropolitan America," *Journal of Urban Affairs* 14, 3 (1992): 470.

38. John E. Farley, "Race Still Matters: The Minimal Role of Income and Housing Cost as Causes of Housing Segregation in St. Louis, 1990." *Urban Affairs Review* 31, 2 (November 1995): 244–254.

39. Darden, "Choosing Neighbors and Neighborhoods: The Role of Race in Preference," in *Divided Neighborhoods,* pp. 16–20; Darden, "African-American Residential Segregation: An Examination of Race and Class in Metropolitan Detroit," in *Residential Apartheid: The American Legacy,* eds. Bullard, Grisby, and Lee, pp. 82–94.

40. John F. Kain, "The Extent and Causes of Racial Residential Segregation" (paper prepared for a conference on "Civil Rights in the Eighties," Chicago Urban League, June 15, 1984, Tables 1 and 2). This paper is cited by Gary Orfield, "Ghettoization and Its Alternatives," in *The New Urban Reality* (Washington, DC: Brookings Institution, 1985), p. 168.

41. George Galster, "Racial Discrimination in Housing Markets During the 1980s: A Review of the Audit Evidence," *Journal of Planning Education and Research* 9 (Summer 1990): 165–175; John Yinger, "Access Denied, Access Constrained: Results and Implications of the 1989 Housing Discrimination Study," in *Clear and Convincing Evidence: Measurement of Discrimination in America,* eds. Michael Fix and Raymond J. Struyk (Washington, DC: Urban Institute Press, 1993), pp. 69–102; and Joe R. Feagin, "A House Is Not a Home: White Racism and U.S. Housing Practices," in *Residential Apartheid: The American Legacy,* eds. Bullard, Grisby, and Lee, pp. 17–48, especially pp. 28–37.

42. Margery Austin Turner, "Limits on Neighborhood Choice: Evidence of Racial and Ethnic Steering in Urban Housing Markets," in *Clear and Convincing Evidence:*

Measurement of Housing Discrimination in America, eds. Fix and Struyk, pp. 117–152; John Yinger, *Closed Doors, Opportunities Lost:* The *Continuing Cost of Housing Discrimination* (New York: Russell Sage Foundation, 1995), pp. 51–86; Mary J. Fischer and Douglas S. Massey, "The Ecology of Racial Discrimination," *City and Community* 3, 3 (2004): 221–241; for a discussion of the debate over the methodology and ethics of housing audits, see Michael Fix, George C. Galster, and Raymond Struyk, "An Overview of Auditing for Discrimination," in *Clear and Convincing Evidence: Measurement of Discrimination in America,* eds. Fix and Struyk, pp. 1–49.

43. Michael Leachman and Philip Nyden, "Housing Discrimination and Economic Opportunity in the Chicago Region: A Report to the Human Relations Foundation of Chicago," prepared by the Center for Urban Research and Learning, Loyola University of Chicago, January 2000, p. 13.

44. John Relman, "Federal Fair Housing Enforcement at a Crossroads: The Clinton Legacy and the Challenge Ahead," in *Rights at Risk: Equality in an Age of Terrorism,* a report of the Citizens' Commission for Civil Rights (Washington, DC: 2002), pp 99–112; the quotations are from p. 99. Available at www.cccr.org/ Chapter8.pdf.

45. U.S. Department of Housing and Urban Development, *Discrimination in Metropolitan Housing Markets* (Washington, DC: HUD, 2000), as cited in the HUD press release, "HUD Study Shows More Than One in Four Native American Renters Face Discrimination," www.hud.gov/news/release.cfm?content=pr03-126.cfm.

46. The Campaign for Mental Health Reform, "The President's Budget At a Glance," February 8, 2005, available at www.mhreform.org/policy/fy206budget.htm.

47. W. Dennis Keating, *The Suburban Racial Dilemma: Housing and Neighborhoods* (Philadelphia: Temple University Press, 1994), pp. 11–13; and Andrew Hacker, *Two Nations: Black and White, Separate, Hostile, Unequal* (New York: Ballantine, 1992), pp. 35–38.

48. Mittie Olion Chandler, "Homogeneity and Conflict: A Case of Political Conflict in a Black Suburb" (paper presented at the annual meeting of the Midwest Political Science Association, Chicago, April 15, 1989); and Keating, *The Suburban Racial Dilemma,* Chap. 5.

49. Our description of the integration-maintenance efforts of Shaker Heights and Cleveland Heights draws heavily on Keating, *The Suburban Dilemma,* Chaps. 6 and 7; Donald L. DeMarco and George C. Galster, "Prointegrative Policy: Theory and Practice," *Journal of Urban Affairs* 15, 2 (1993): 141–160.

50. David P. Varady and Jeffrey A. Raffel, *Selling Cities: Attracting Home Buyers Through Schools and Housing Programs* (Albany: State University of New York Press, 1995), especially pp. 5 and 277–279.

51. Yinger, *Closed Doors, Opportunities Lost,* p. 127; Keating, *The Suburban Racial Dilemma,* pp. 211–217; William Peterman, "Twenty Years of Racial Diversity in Oak Park, Illinois" (unpublished); and Evan McKenzie, "Reconsidering the Oak Park Strategy: An Assessment of Integration Maintenance Policies in a Chicago Suburb" (paper presented at the annual meeting of the Midwest Political Science Association, Chicago, April 25–28, 2002).

52. Richard A. Smith, "Creating Stable Racially Integrated Communities: A Review," *Journal of Urban Affairs* 15, 2 (1993): 129–131.

53. Robert Wood, *Suburbia: Its People and Its Politics* (Boston: Houghton Mifflin, 1958), pp. 53 and 153.

54. Thomas, *The United States of Suburbia*, pp. 145–156. Also see Tom Martinson, *American Dreamscape: The Pursuit of Happiness in Postwar Suburbia* (Carroll & Graf, 2000).

55. Jon C. Teaford, *Post-Suburbia: Government and Politics in Edge Cities* (Baltimore: Johns Hopkins University Press, 1997), p. 86.

56. J. Eric Oliver, *Democracy in Suburbia* (Princeton, NJ: Princeton University Press, 2001).

57. Edward Blakely and Mary Gail Snyder, *Fortress America: Gated Communities in the United States* (Washington, DC: Brookings Institution, 1997), pp. 34–35.

58. McKenzie, *Privatopia*, p. 184.

59. Setha Low, *Behind the Gates: Life, Security, and the Pursuit of Happiness in Fortress America* (Taylor & Francis, 2003), Chap. 9.

60. Blakely and Snyder, *Fortress America*, especially pp. 22, 31–35, 59–62, 71–73 and 154–156. The quotations appear, respectively, on pp. 34 and 154.

61. *Serrano v. Priest*, 5 Cal. 3d 584, 487 (1971). Also see Jonathan Kozol, *Savage Inequalities* (New York: Crown, 1991), pp. 214 and 220.

62. *Rodriguez v. San Antonio Independent School District* 411 U.S. l (1973). Also see Kozol, *Savage Inequalities*, pp. 214–219.

63. Center for Public Policy Priorities press release, "New Report Highlights Texas School Financing Disparities," October 22, 1998, available at www.cppp.org/kidscount/press/finance.html.

64. The story of the judiciary's role in school finance reform in Texas and other states is told by Matthew H. Bosworth, *Courts as Catalysts: State Supreme Courts and Public School Finance Equity* (Albany, NY: State University of New York Press, 2001).

65. David O. Sears and Jack Citrin, *Tax Revolt: Something for Nothing in California* (Cambridge, MA: Harvard University Press, 1982), pp. 220–221.

66. Peter Schrag, "California Screamin'," *New Republic*, June 23,1986, 14–16; Peter Schrag, *Paradise Lost: California's Experience, Americas Future* (New York: W. W. Norton, 1998); Jon Sonstelie, Eric Brunner, and Kenneth Ardon, *For Better or For Worse? School Finance Reform in California* (San Francisco: Public Policy Institute of California, 2000).

67. Arthur C. Nelson and Mitch Moody, "Paying for Prosperity: Impact Fees and Jobs Growth," a report of The Brookings Institution Center for Policy Studies, Washington, DC, June 2003, available at www.brookings.edu/es/urban/publications/nelsonimpactfees.htm.

68. Alan A. Altshuler and Jose A. Gomez-lbanez, with Arnold M. Howitt, *Regulation for Revenue: The Political Economy of Land Use Exactions* (Washington, DC: Brookings Institution, 1993), pp. 124–125.

69. Dogen Hannah, "Schwarzenegger Suggests Suspending Proposition 98," *Contra Costa Times*, December 11, 2003; Jim Sanders, "Governor to Announce $2 Billion School Deal," *Sacramento Bee*, January 8, 2004.

70. *Millikin v. Bradley*, 418 U.S. 717 (1974).

71. *Board of Education of Oklahoma City v. Dowell*, 498 U.S. 237 (1991). For details regarding the resegregation of Oklahoma City schools and how neighborhood schools failed to boost achievement scores and racial integration, see Jennifer Jellison and Gary Orfield, *Resegregation and Equity in Oklahoma City*, a report of the Harvard Project on School Desegregation, Cambridge, MA (1996). A summary of the report is available at: www.gse.harvard.edu/news/features/oklahomacity09161996.html.

72. *Freeman v. Pitts*, 498 U.S. 1081 (1992).
73. Sue Anne Presley, "Charlotte Schools Scramble as Busing Ends," *The Washington Post*, November 18, 1999; Laurent Belsie, "School Busing: An Era in Decline," *Christian Science Monitor*, February 2, 1999. Also see Gary Orfield, Susan E. Eaton, and Elaine R. Jones, *Dismantling Desegregation: The Quiet Reversal of Brown v. Board of Education* (New York: New Press, 1997).
74. Stephen Samuel Smith, "Hugh Governs? Regime and Education Policy in Charlotte, North Carolina," *Journal of Urban Affairs* 19, 3 (1997); Megan Twohey, "Desegregation Is Dead," *National Journal*, September 18, 1999, pp. 2614–2620.
75. The quotation is from Gary Orfield, "Schools More Separate: Consequences of a Decade of Resegregation," a report of the Civil Rights Project of Harvard University, July 17, 2001. Available at: www.civilrightsproject.harvard.edu/research/deseg/separate_schools01.php. Also see Erika Frankenberg and Chungmei Lee, "Race in American Public Schools: Rapidly Resegregating School Districts," a report of the Civil Rights Project of Harvard University, August 8, 2002. Available at: www.civilrightsproject.harvard.edu/research/deseg/reseg_schools02.php.
76. Kenneth T. Jackson, "Gentleman's Agreement: Discrimination in Metropolitan America," in *Reflections on Regionalism*, ed. Bruce Katz (Washington, DC: Brookings Institution, 2000), pp. 191–197. Both quotations appear on p. 191.
77. Jane Gross, "Politicians, Amid Ruins, Talk of Laws," *The New York Times*, October 23, 1991; and Robert Reinhold, "Building on Sand: Pain Repays Reckless California," *The New York Times*, October 28, 1991.
78. J. Barry Cullingworth, *The Political Culture of Planning: American Land Use Planning in Comparative Perspective* (New York: Routledge, 1993), p. 229.
79. Wood, *Suburbia: Its People and Its Politics*, p. 275.
80. Robert N. Bellah, Richard Madsen, William M. Sullivan, Anne Swindler, and Steven M. Tipton, *Habits of the Heart: Individualism and Commitment in American Life* (New York: Perennial Library/Harper & Row, 1985), pp. 72–74.
81. Michael N. Danielson, *The Politics of Exclusion* (New York: Columbia University Press, 1976), p. 53.
82. For more on how exclusionary forces use delays to create paralysis and drive up housing costs, see: Bernard J. Frieden, *The Environmental Protection Hustle* (Cambridge, MA: MIT Press, 1979), pp. 60–71; and David E. Dowall, *The Suburban Squeeze: Land Conversion and Regulation in the San Francisco Bay Area* (Berkeley: University of California Press, 1984), pp. 122–129.
83. Alexander Garvin, *The American City: What Works, What Doesn't*, 2nd ed. (New York: McGraw-Hill, 2002), p. 454.
84. Ibid., pp. 454–456; Frieden, *The Environmental Protection Hustle*, pp. 32–36.
85. Roger W. Caves, *Land Use Planning: The Ballot Box Revolution* (Newbury Park, CA: Sage Publications, 1992); and Richard Edward DeLeon, *Left Coast City: Progressive Politics in San Francisco, 1975–91* (Lawrence: University of Kansas Press, 1992).
86. Caves, *Land Use Planning: The Ballot Box Revolution*, pp. 72–134. The "creeping condominiumism" remark appears on p. 133.
87. *Village of Euclid, Ohio*, v. *Ambler Realty Co.*, 272 U.S. 365 (1926). For an assessment of the impact of *Euclid* and zoning on communities in the United States, see Charles M. Haar and Jerold S. Kayden, eds., *Zoning and the American Dream: Promises Stilt to Keep* (Chicago: APA Planners Press, 1989).

88. *Arlington Heights v. Metropolitan Housing Development Corporation,* 429 U.S. 252 (1977).

89. Two important Supreme Court rulings in this area are: *First English Evangelical Lutheran Church of Glendale v. County of Los Angeles,* 107 S.Ct. 2378 (1987); and *Nollan v. California Coastal Commission,* 107 S.Ct. 3141,97 L. Ed, 677 (1987). Also see Lee P. Symons, "Property Rights and Local Land-Use Regulation: The Implications of *First English* and *Nollan,*" *Publius: The Journal of Federalism* 18 (Summer 1988), esp. p. 85.

90. *Southern Burlington County NAACP v. Township of Mount Laurel* 67 N.J. 151, 336 A. 2d 713 (1975). Charles M. Haar, *Suburbs Under Siege: Race, Space, and Audacious Judges* (Princeton, NJ: Princeton University Press, 1996) presents an in-depth discussion of the *Mount Laurel* decisions and offers the Mount Laurel approach as a model for the judicial attack on exclusionary practices.

91. *Burlington County NAACP v. Township of Mount Laurel,* 92N.J. 158, 336A. 2d 390 (1983).

92. *Hills Development Co. v. Township of Bernard,* 103 N.J. 1,510 A. 2d 621 (1986).

93. Patrick Field, Jennifer Gilbert, and Michael Wheeler, "Trading the Poor: Intermunicipal Housing Negotiation in New Jersey," *Harvard Negotiation Law Review* (Spring 1997) pp. 1–33.

94. David L. Kirp, John P. Dwyer, and Larry A. Rosenthal, *Our Town: Race, Housing, and the Soul of Suburbia* (New Brunswick, NJ: Rutgers University Press, 1995), p. 175. Kirp et al. present a detailed discussion of the *Mount Laurel* decisions and their impact.

95. Gerald Benjamin and Richard P. Nathan, *Regionalism and Realism: A Study of Governments in the New York Metropolitan Area* (Washington, DC: Brookings Institution, 2001), pp. 193–201.

96. Allan Mallach, "The Rise and Fall of Inclusionary Housing in New Jersey: Social Policy, Judicial Mandates, and the Realities of the Real Estate Marketplace" (paper presented at the annual meeting of the Urban Affairs Association, March 16, 1996).

97. Mark Alan Hughes and Peter M. VanDoren, "Social Policy Through Land Reform: New Jersey's Mount Laurel Controversy," *Political Science Quarterly* 105 (Spring 1990): 111; Benjamin and Nathan, *Regionalism and Realism,* p. 199.

98. W. Dennis Keating, "The *Parma* Housing Racial Discrimination Remedy Revisited," 45 *Cleveland State Law Review* (1997): 93.

99. For a good overview of Montgomery County's Moderately Priced Dwelling Unit Ordinance, see David Rusk, *Inside Game, Outside Game: Winning Strategies for Saving Urban America* (Washington, DC: Brookings Institution Press, 1999), pp. 178–200.

100. Gretchen Weismann, "More than Shelter: Housing the People of Greater Boston," in *Governing Greater Boston: The Policy and Politics of Place,* ed. Charles C. Euchner (Cambridge, MA: Harvard University's Rappaport Institute for Greater Boston, 2002), pp. 143–145.

101. George Judson, "Housing Law Disputes Zoning Boards' Power," *The New York Times,* November 5, 1991; Benjamin and Nathan, *Regionalism and Realism,* pp. 200–201.

102. Morris Newman, "The Struggle to Provide Affordable Homes: In Santa Monica, Neighborhood Politics Prevails," *The New York Times,* March 8, 1992.

103. Wood, *Suburbia*, p. 71. For more contemporary statements of the inter-
dependency of cities and suburbs, see Anthony Downs, New *Visions for
Metropolitan America* (Washington, DC: Brookings Institution, 1994),
and Larry C. Ledebur and William R. Barnes, *"All In It Together": Cities,
Suburbs and Local Economic Regions* (Washington, DC: National League
of Cities, 1993).

104. Benjamin and Nathan, *Regionalism and Realism,* pp. 3–26.

105. David Rusk, "Growth Management: The Core Regional Issue," in *Reflections
on Regionalism,* ed. Bruce Katz (Washington, DC: Brookings Institution, 2000), p. 88.

106. Kozol, *Savage Inequalities.*

107. Myron Orfield, *Metropolitics: A Regional Agenda for Community and Stability*
(Washington, DC, and Cambridge, MA: Brookings Institution Press and Lincoln
Institute of Land Policy, 1997), pp. 5–10.

108. John D. Kasarda, "The Impact of Suburban Population Growth on Central City
Service Functions," *American Journal of Sociology* 77 (May 1972): 1123. Also
see Bennett Harrison, *Urban Economic Development: Suburbanization, Minority Opportunity, and the Condition of the Central City* (Washington, DC: Urban
Institute, 1974), pp. 114–117.

109. These consequences are spelled out in *Sprawl Hits the Wall: Confronting the
Realities of Metropolitan Los Angeles*, a report of the University of Southern
California's Southern California Studies Center, Los Angeles, 2000. Available
at: www.usc.edu/schools/sppd/ced/Sprawl_hits_Wall.html.

110. Mark Edward Brown, "Subdivision Sprawl in Southeastern Wisconsin: Planning,
Politics, and the Lack of Affordable Housing," in *Suburban Sprawl: Culture,
Theory, and Politics,* eds. Matthew J. Lindstrom and Hugh Bartling (Lanham,
MD: Rowman and Littlefield, 2003), p. 263. For a general overview of the
environmental costs of urban sprawl, see David J. Cieslewicz, "The
Environmental Impacts of Sprawl," in *Urban Sprawl: Causes, Consequences,
and Policy Responses,* ed. Gregory D. Squires (Washington, DC: Urban
Institute Press, 2002), pp. 23–38.

111. American Planning Association, *Planning for Smart Growth: 2002 State of
the States* (Washington, DC; APA, 2002), as cited in Bruce Katz, *Smart Growth:
Future of the American Metropolis?* Report of the Centre for Analysis of Social
Exclusion, London School of Economics, © Bruce Katz, 2002, p. 17. Available
from The Brookings Institution Center on Urban and Metropolitan Policy,
Washington, DC at www.brookings.edu/dybdocroot/es/urban/publications/
20021104katzlse2.htm.

112. Drew A. Dolan, "Local Government Fragmentation: Does It Drive Up
the Cost of Government?" *Urban Affairs Quarterly* 26 (September 1990): 42;
Kathryn A. Foster, *The Political Economy of Special-Purpose Government*
(Washington, DC: Georgetown University Press, 1997), pp. 28–35 and 148–188.

113. *Hits and Misses: Fast Growth in Metropolitan Phoenix*, a report of
the Morrison Institute for Public Policy, Arizona State University, Tempe,
Arizona, 2000. Available at www.asu.edu/copp/morrison/growth.htm.

114. Arthur C. Nelson, "Toward a New Metropolis: The Opportunity to Rebuild
America," a discussion paper prepared for The Brookings Institution
Metropolitan Policy Program, Washington, DC, 2004, available at:
www.brookings.edu/dybdocroot/metro/pubs/20041213_RebuildAmerica.pdf;
Katz, *Smart Growth: Future of the American Metropolis?,* p. 17.

115. Our description of Florida's growth management efforts relies on Peter Calthorpe and William Fulton, *The Regional City: Planning for the End of Sprawl* (Washington, DC: Island Press, 2001). Also see Robyne S. Turner, "New Rules for the Growth Game: The Use of Rational State Standards in Land Use Policy," *Journal of Urban Affairs* 12, 1 (1990): 35–47.

116. Richard Moe and Carter Wilkie, *Changing Places: Rebuilding Community in the Age of Sprawl* (New York: Owl Books/Henry Holt, 1997), p. 253; Calthorpe and Fulton, *The Regional City*, pp. 188–190; James R. Cohen, "Maryland's 'Smart Growth': Using Incentives to Combat Sprawl," in *Urban Sprawl: Causes, Consequences, and Policy Responses*, ed. Gregory D. Squires (Washington, DC: Urban Institute Press, 2002), pp. 293–324.

117. Katz, *Smart Growth: Future of the American Metropolis?*, p. 18.

118. Our review of Portland UGB and its impact relies on Calthorpe and Fulton, *The Regional City*, pp. 105–125; and Carl Abbott, "Planning a Sustainable City: The Promise and Performance of Portland's Growth Boundary," in *Urban Sprawl: Causes, Consequences, and Policy Responses*, ed. Gregory D. Squires (Washington, DC: Urban Institute Press, 2002), pp. 207–235.

119. Arthur C. Nelson, Rolf Pendall, Casey J. Dawkins, and Gerritt J. Knapp, "The Link Between Growth Management and Housing Affordability: The Academic Evidence," in *Growth Management and Affordable Housing: Do They Conflict?* ed. Anthony Downs (Washington, DC: Brookings Institution Press, 2004), pp. 117–158. The various articles in the *Growth Management and Affordable Housing* volume present conflicting evidence and interpretations. While it does seem that growth management adds to housing prices in a region, there is no consensus on that point.

120. The problems resulting from Atlanta's "unbalanced" growth are described in detail in "Moving Beyond Sprawl: The Challenge for Metropolitan Atlanta," a report of The Brookings Institution Center on Urban and Metropolitan Policy, Washington, DC, 2000. Available at www.brookings.edu/dybdocroot/es/urban/ atlanta/toc.htm

121. Charles Jaret, "Suburban Expansion in Atlanta: 'The City without Limits' Faces Some," in *Urban Sprawl: Causes, Consequences, and Policy Responses,* ed. Gregory D. Squires (Washington, DC: Urban Institute Press, 2002), pp. 207–235.

122. Tom Hogen-Esch, "Washington's Growth Management Act and the Neighborhood Movement in West Seattle" (paper presented at the annual meeting of the American Political Science Association, San Francisco, August 30–September 5, 2001).

123. Alex Marshall, *How Cities Work: Suburbs, Sprawl, and the Roads Not Taken* (Austin, TX; University of Texas Press, 2000), p. xix. For a good review of the guiding principles of the New Urbanism, see Andres Duany, Elizabeth Plater-Zyberk, and Jeff Speck, *Suburban Nation: The Rise of Sprawl and the Decline of the American Dream* (New York: North Point Press, 2000); Peter Katz, *The New Urbanism: Toward an Architecture of Community* (New York: McGraw-Hill, 1994); Congress for the New Urbanism, *Charter of the New Urbanism* (New York: McGraw-Hill, 2000); Calthorpe and Fulton, *The Regional City*.

124. Duany et al., *Suburban Nation*, p. 30.

125. Michael Bernick and Robert Cervero, *Transit Villages in the 21st Century* (New York: McGraw-Hill, 1997).

126. Calthorpe and Fulton, *The Regional City*, pp. 253–265; Janet L. Smith, "HOPE VI and the New Urbanism: Eliminating Low-Income Housing to Make Mixed-income Communities," *Planner's Network* 151 (Spring 2002): 22–25.

127. Garvin, *The American City: What Works, What Doesn't*, pp. 336–337.

128. Marshall, *How Cities Work*, pp. xx and 6. Also see Alex Krieger, "Arguing the 'Against' Position: New Urbanism as a Means of Building and Rebuilding Our Cities," in *The Seaside Debates: A Critique of The New Urbanism*, ed. Todd W. Bressi (Rizzoli, 2002), pp. 51–58. For a defense of the New Urbanism that rebuts many of the critiques, see Cliff Ellis, "The New Urbanism: Critiques and Rebuttals," *Journal of Urban Design* 7, 3 (2002): 261–291.

129. Anthony Downs, *New Visions for Metropolitan America* (Washington. DC: Brookings Institution, 1994), p. 52.

130. Neal R. Peirce, with Curtis W. Johnson and John Stuart Hall, *Citistates: How Urban America Can Prosper in a Competitive World* (Washington, DC: Seven Locks Press, 1993).

The **fragmentation** of metropolitan areas impedes effective urban action. The governing authority in metropolitan areas is divided among a fairly large number of overlapping governmental units: municipalities, counties, towns, special authorities, and narrow special-purpose districts including school districts, community-college districts, water and sewer districts, and park districts.

The existence of so many independent governmental units undermines the prospects for effective, coordinated regional action. Cities and suburbs work cooperatively only when all partners realize mutual benefits.

In the greater San Francisco area, a number of localities initially decided not to participate in the construction of the Bay Area Rapid Transit (BART) system, with the result that BART trains still do not serve the entire region. It took decades of contentious bargaining over funding and routes to extend BART south, along the East Bay, to Milpitas, San Jose, and Santa Clara. In the Dallas-Fort Worth metroplex, the construction of a light-rail commuter system was similarly impeded by the refusal of certain municipalities to contribute to the venture.

For a long time, reformers proposed a cure-all: the creation of **metropolitan government**, a single centralized authority with the ability to legislate for the region, overriding local parochialism. The three major variants of the metropolitan government idea—*city-county consolidation, the two-tier* or *federation model,* and *the three-tier system* of Portland (Oregon) and the Twin Cities (Minnesota)—all share the same basic goal: to create a regional governmental body capable of acting in the interest of the metropolis as a whole.

In recent decades, the metropolitan government movement has clearly faltered. Suburbanites adamantly oppose centralization plans that abridge local autonomy. Local elected officials and racial minorities, too, resist ceding power to new regional bodies. As a result, general-purpose, metropolitan governing bodies have been established in only a few urban areas in the United States, notably in Jacksonville, Nashville, Baton Rouge, Lexington, Louisville, Indianapolis, Miami, Portland (Oregon), and the Minneapolis–St. Paul Twin Cities area. The powers of these metropolitan bodies fall far short of the metropolitan government ideal.

As we shall see, *public choice* theorists have even questioned the value of creating a strong metropolitan government. These theorists point to the virtues of small-scale, grassroots suburban government as opposed to the facelessness and irresponsiveness of large metropolitan institutions.

In this chapter, we will review the various efforts at metropolitan reform. We shall see that entrenched political factors impede the creation of powerful metropolitan governing bodies. Yet, as we continue our discussion in Chapter 13, "The Politics of Regional Cooperation," more realistic options for regional cooperation do exist and are quite commonplace.

METROPOLITAN GOVERNMENT

What can metropolitanism hope to achieve? When are metropolitan governments created? Why do metropolitan government plans almost always fall short of the expectations of their backers? To answer these questions, we review the three major variants of strong metropolitan government: city-county consolidation (as embodied in Indianapolis' Unigov and in Louisville and other cities), the two-tier or federation plan (with Miami-Dade County as the most notable example), and the three-tier systems of greater Minneapolis and Portland, Oregon.

CITY-COUNTY CONSOLIDATION

Under **city-county consolidation,** a county and its municipalities merge to form a single governmental unit. Where the consolidation is total, the county becomes the sole general-purpose local government for the entire area; all other local governments are eliminated. Yet city-county consolidations are seldom that complete. Instead, consolidations often merge the core city with the county while allowing other local bodies continue to exist post consolidation.

City-county consolidation is not a new phenomenon (see Table 12-1). Philadelphia, Boston, and New Orleans achieved city-county consolidation in the nineteenth century. In 1898, the five local counties (referred to as *boroughs* in New York) were merged to form a single city, Greater New York. The city's merchants, bankers, and realtors sought the consolidation to abet the city's growth and expansion. By extending its boundaries, Greater New York was able to develop a coherent transportation system and build new housing in what were then predominantly undeveloped areas. The consolidation of 1898 allowed New York to grow and become the nation's paramount urban hub.[1]

In more recent decades, city-county consolidations have been relatively infrequent and, with a few notable exceptions, have occurred primarily in smaller urban areas. Consolidation is quite difficult to achieve, as it usually requires voter approval in both the central-city and the noncentral-city parts of the county. As a brief review of important city-county mergers reveals, exceptional local circumstances often helped to drive successful consolidation efforts.

■ TABLE 12-1

CITY-COUNTY CONSOLIDATIONS

Year	City-County	State
1805	New Orleans–Orleans Parish	Louisiana
1821	Boston–Suffolk County	Massachusetts
1821	Nantucket–Nantucket County	Massachusetts
1854	Philadelphia–Philadelphia County	Pennsylvania
1856	San Francisco–San Francisco County	California
1874	New York (Manhattan)–New York County	New York
1894	New York–Bronx and Staten Island	New York
1898	New York–Brooklyn and Queens Boroughs and Richmond County	New York
1904	Denver–Arapahoe County	Colorado
1907	Honolulu–Honolulu County	Hawaii
1947	Baton Rouge–East Baton Rouge Parish	Louisiana
1952	Hamilton and Phoebus–Elizabeth City County	Virginia
1957	Newport News–Warwick City County	Virginia
1962	Nashville–Davidson County	Tennessee
1962	Chesapeake–South Norfolk–Norfolk County	Virginia
1962	Virginia Beach–Princess Anne County	Virginia
1967	Jacksonville–Duval County	Florida
1969	Indianapolis–Marion County	Indiana
1969	Carson City–Ormsby County	Nevada
1969	Juneau and Douglas–Greater Juneau Borough	Alaska
1970	Columbus–Muscogee County	Georgia
1971	Holland and Whaleyville–Nansemond County	Virginia
1971	Sitka–Greater Sitka Borough	Alaska
1972	Lexington–Fayette County	Kentucky
1972	Suffolk–Nansemond County	Virginia
1975	Anchorage, Glen Alps, and Girdwood–Greater Anchorage Borough	Alaska
1976	Anaconda–Deer Lodge County	Montana
1976	Butte–Silver Bow County	Montana
1984	Houma–Terrebonne County	Louisiana
1988	Lynchburg–Moore County	Tennessee
1992	Athens–Clarke County	Georgia

(Continued)

■ **TABLE 12–1**

CITY-COUNTY CONSOLIDATIONS (CONT.)

Year	City-County	State
1992	Lafayette–Lafayette Parish	Louisiana
1995	Augusta–Richmond County	Georgia
1997	Kansas City–Wyandotte County	Kansas
2001	Hartsville–Trousdale County	Tennessee
2001	Louisville–Jefferson County	Kentucky

SOURCE: National Association of Counties, Research Division. A slightly truncated version of this list can be found at www.naco.org/Content/ContentGroups/Publications1/County_News1/20035/6-2-03/Successful_City-County_Consolidations.htm.

NASHVILLE. In the 1960s, the residents of Nashville's underdeveloped new suburban areas saw consolidation as a means for gaining important municipal services. The residents of Nashville's suburbs resented paying higher taxes for water and other municipal services than did central-city residents. Suburban residents also detested having to pay for a green sticker to park on Nashville's streets.

The consolidation in Nashville–Davidson County led to the upgrading, professionalization, and greater equalization of service delivery throughout the county. The much-hated green-sticker fee was repealed, and water rates were equalized. The residents of Nashville's growing suburbs were the immediate beneficiaries of metropolitan reform.[2]

JACKSONVILLE. In Jacksonville, Florida, the criminal indictment of a number of public officials galvanized the demand for metropolitan reform. The city's school system was so poorly run that it faced a possible loss of accreditation. The consolidation of Jacksonville–Duval County in 1968 was viewed as a means of professionalizing local government and rooting out waste, inefficiency, and fraud. As was the case in Nashville, Jacksonville's rapidly growing suburbs also saw consolidation as a means of gaining much-needed public service improvements, especially upgraded sewage treatment and storm water drainage.

Consolidation in Jacksonville did not deliver much of what the metropolitan reformers had promised. There is no evidence that the merger produced greater efficiency and equity in urban service delivery. Taxes were kept relatively low, but service inequities persist. Service equity was undermined from the very beginning when three affluent beach towns and a logging community were left out of the consolidation plan.[3] In the years since the merger,

Jacksonville has suffered from suburban flight and core-city decline; it is one of the most segregated metropolitan areas in the country.

Political reform in Jacksonville was never only about efficiency and equity; it was also an exercise of self-interest and power. A corporate "growth machine" used the rhetoric of anti-corruption, good-government reform to wrest control from the "good ol' boys" local elite, which, reluctant to commit to public expenditures, had done little to revitalize the city.

Downtown business interests also saw consolidation as a means of diluting the power of Jacksonville's growing black community. In the consolidated government, white voters in the suburbs would help to offset the ballot-box strength of central-city African Americans, thereby averting the prospects of black electoral rule in the old city of Jacksonville. At the time of the merger, African Americans were 40 percent of the population of the central city but only one-fourth of the county. Although a system of district elections was instituted to ensure some black representation in the new countywide council, African Americans were still not the majority.

INDIANAPOLIS (UNIGOV).   Indiana lacks a strong home-rule tradition. A long history of direct state intervention in municipal affairs allowed the state legislature in 1969 to create Unigov (the "unified" government of Indianapolis–Marion County) without even seeking the approval of local voters in a referendum.

The creation of Unigov vividly illustrates how considerations of power and partisan advantage often underlie metropolitan reform initiatives. In Indianapolis, Republican party officials were the driving force behind consolidation. (See "Indianapolis: Unigov or Unigrab?" below.) Bond attorneys also were very active in the creation of Unigov, as the incorporation would enable Indianapolis to borrow more money for redevelopment projects. Local corporate elites saw metropolitan reform as a means to alter the city's "Indiana-no-place" image, creating in its place a government committed to economic growth and downtown revitalization.[4]

INDIANAPOLIS: UNIGOV OR UNIGRAB?

To a great extent, the creation of Unigov represents a power grab by state and local Republicans—a move so blatant that Democrats referred to it as **Unigrab**. Indianapolis Mayor Richard Lugar, a Republican, sold the state's Republican legislature and governor on the political gains that the party would enjoy by creating Unigov. Demographic trends indicated that if nothing were done, the Democrats would soon gain control of Indianapolis' city government. In a new consolidated government, however, the mayor would likely be a Republican with Republican voters in the suburbs providing the margin of victory.

continued

INDIANAPOLIS: UNIGOV OR UNIGRAB? (CONT.)

Subsequent election results underscored the success of the Republican ger-rymandering effort. In 1975, Republican William Hudnut lost in the old central city by 17,500 votes but was still able to win Unigov's mayoralty with the help of suburban votes. In 1991, Republican Stephen Goldsmith similarly gained the mayoralty despite having lost the old city by 15,000 votes. It was not until 1999, 30 years after the creation of Unigov, that a Democrat, Bart Peterson, was at long last elected mayor.

Source: The voting tallies are from William Blomquist, "Metropolitan Organization and Local Politics: The Indianapolis-Marion County Experience" (paper presented at the annual meeting of the Midwest Political Science Association, Chicago, April 9–11, 1992).

To assuage the fears of suburbanites, the Indiana state legislature left subur-ban school districts out of the merger plan so that consolidation would pose no threat of public school integration. A number of other local governments—municipalities, townships, and special districts and boards—were similarly allowed to continue to exist after consolidation. The name "Unigov" is actu-ally a misnomer, as it did not produce a truly unified system of government; there remain over 100 separate taxing units in the greater Indianapolis area.[5]

Unigov did succeed in establishing a system of strong, regional leadership for economic growth. Unigov's elected mayor serves as the voice of the county and, with the county council, controls what is arguably the strongest regional planning and economic development department in the entire country.[6] The mayor and the Department of Metropolitan Development have the authority to steer investment to Indianapolis' downtown; unlike officials in other metro-politan areas, they do not have to worry that independent suburbs will beseech corporations with competing subsidies and offers. Unigov officials persuaded the developers of Market Square Arena to locate the new sports facility in the center of the city rather than on the interstate highway. Unigov officials also convinced American United Life (AUL) to abandon plans for a suburban head-quarters facility and instead build a 38-story downtown office tower (the largest in the state!) for an anticipated 1,500 employees. Unigov's ability to speak for the region also helped Indianapolis win the 93-city competition for an $800 million United Airlines maintenance facility and its promise of 7,000 jobs over 10 years.[7]

Unigov has done less well when it comes to human services and equity con-cerns. The continued existence of numerous independent local governments and districts prevents service equalization throughout the county. With its sep-arate taxing and service districts, Unigov has not been able to provide relief for the old central city with its concentration of poor and minority populations.[8] The costs of Unigov's generous award of tax concessions to businesses have largely been borne by central-city homeowners and small businesses.[9]

LOUISVILLE. During the 30 years following the creation of Unigov, there was no other notable city-county consolidation. Hence, it was a newsworthy event when Louisville in 2001 merged with surrounding Jefferson County, allowing Louisville to climb immediately from the 64th to the 16th largest city in the nation, in terms of population.[10] Civic pride was part of the motivation behind the consolidation; without the merger, Louisville faced the prospect of being eclipsed by Lexington-Fayette as the largest city in Kentucky.

Advocates argued that consolidation would help to counter the decay of the city core, as the new regional government could tap suburban resources for revitalization projects. The merger of city and county offices also resulted in some immediate budget savings, especially as 700 city jobs were eliminated.[11] Whether the consolidation will result in long-term savings, however, remains to be seen.

As was the case with other city-county consolidation efforts, the consolidation in Louisville–Jefferson County was incomplete. The new Metro regional government was placed atop of the region's existing municipalities that maintained their own identities, their own city councils, their own taxing powers, and even their own police and fire forces. Only the old city of Louisville lost its existence as a result of the merger. In important aspects of numerous service areas, the citizens of Louisville's suburbs continue to control their own affairs; only the citizens of old Louisville had their influence diluted by the merger.

The consolidation also diminished black electoral power. While African Americans were 34 percent of the old city's population, they won only 23 percent (6 of 26) of the seats on the new Metro Louisville council.

Pointing to the loss of local and minority power, critics further argue that the consolidation was unnecessary. Even before the merger, Louisville and its suburbs had commenced cooperative efforts. The 1986 Louisville–Jefferson County compact reduced interlocal competition for new economic development. The compact provided for tax sharing, redistributing over $5 million a year in fiscal assistance to the city.[12] Louisville's suburbs had agreed to the compact as a means of warding off annexation by the city. The regional compact proved successful in initiating joint efforts that helped to attract thousands of new jobs to the region, including a new UPS facility and new investment in Louisville's downtown.

Over the years, growth coalition elites, including the city's newspaper, continued to push the merger, despite its earlier rejections at the hands of Louisville voters. In a consolidated Louisville, racial minorities and inner-city activists found themselves at a disadvantage in challenging a growth agenda. Metropolitan reform had altered power relations in Louisville.[13]

CITY-COUNTY CONSOLIDATION: AN OVERALL ASSESSMENT. The creation of Metro Louisville is the single important consolidation in over 30 years. Why is city-county consolidation so rare? Existing local officeholders, suburbanites, and central-city minorities all fear that consolidation will diminish their power. A half century ago, the residents of new suburbs may have seen advantages in consolidation. In the 1950s and 1960s, the residents of Nashville's and Jacksonville's still-growing suburbs saw consolidation as a means of tapping into the higher quality services provided by the central city. Today, however, the situation is quite different. Suburbanites generally resist consolidation for fear that it will break down the barriers that protect them from the impoverished central city.

Contemporary city-county consolidations are also quite incomplete. Numerous local governments, including independent school and service districts, continue to exist amid the consolidated governments of Jacksonville, Nashville, Baton Rouge, Indianapolis, Carson City, Lexington, and Louisville metropolitan areas. Consequently, city-county consolidation efforts seldom provide the full efficiency and equity benefits promised by metropolitan reformers. Nor has city-county consolidation led to school integration.

City-county consolidation also cannot provide an answer for problems that spill over the borders of a single county. In such areas, city-county consolidation may be considered, at best, only a plan for *subregional* government.

In city after city, consolidation enhanced the power of regional growth-oriented elites while seriously diluting the power of central-city minority groups. As a result of city-county consolidation, troubled inner-city neighborhoods "become poor and minority neighborhoods of a larger jurisdiction, and thereby find their voice weakened."[14]

Does city-county consolidation bring a region certain advantages in attracting new economic development and new jobs? The experience of Unigov would seem to say that the answer is yes. Yet the evidence is far from clear. The creation of Jacksonville–Duval did not produce increases in manufacturing, retail, or service sector growth.[15] Yet consolidated areas have fared better economically, enjoying better municipal bond ratings and slightly better job growth than comparable communities in nonconsolidated counties.[16]

Whatever the economic benefits of mergers, the future prospects for major city-county consolidation are quite dim. As Vincent Marando observes, "Metropolitan reorganization via consolidation is not a dead issue, but it is certainly not very healthy."[17]

THE TWO-TIER PLAN: MIAMI-DADE

Under **two-tier restructuring,** a new regional level of government is created to take care of problems while existing municipal governments continue to handle local service provision. Ideally, the two-tier plan allows for greater metropolitan planning and efficiency without sacrificing local political identity, participation, and flexibility.

Yet the two-tier plan suffers from notable problems. There is continuing debate over which service responsibilities should be handled by which level of government. Municipal voters and officials are particularly reluctant to abandon local control over such important policy areas as land use, zoning, taxation, and schools.

In Canada, the greater Toronto area experimented with a variation of the two-tiered system called the *federation plan.* (See "Toronto's Experiment with Federation," p. 393.) In the United States, Miami–Dade County (known more simply as Metro Dade or just Metro) is the only important example of a two-tier system. Established in 1957, a Metro regional (county) governing body coexists, side by side, with local governments. In effect, the residents of 27 incorporated cities in Dade County receive municipal services from both the county and city levels of government. Residents of the unincorporated portions of the county receive their services only from Metro.

Metro's creation was a response to the area's extraordinary population growth and the pressing need for planning and expanded municipal services. A number of special circumstances also facilitated the creation of Metro.[18] At the time of Metro's formation, many of the residents of Dade County's suburbs were émigrés from the North who had not yet developed strong attachments

---

TORONTO'S EXPERIMENT WITH FEDERATION

Under the **federation plan,** local governments retain their existence but are part of a regional federation that has responsibility for area-wide concerns. Metropolitan Toronto was governed by the federation plan until 1997. The regionalism inherent in the plan helped contribute to Toronto's livability; the regional government and the province (the Canadian equivalent of an American state) acted to aid mass transit, build affordable housing, and promote center-city development. Yet suburban economic concerns generally took precedence over central-city needs. As was the case in Nashville and Jacksonville, the creation of Metro Toronto in the 1950s was largely driven by the desire to use the capacity of the central city to provide the necessary infrastructure for the growth of outlying suburban communities. In more recent years, the federation's spending on highways helped to contribute to suburban growth, overriding the central-city orientation that had characterized Metro's earlier emphasis on mass transit.

In 1997, the Conservative Party–controlled provincial government replaced the federation plan with the even stronger, unified, **megacity** arrangement. The federation council, the city of Toronto, and five suburbs were all merged into a single political entity. In effect, in Toronto, a new unitary government replaced the old federal or two-tier system. Yet political factors once more intruded and limited attempts at metropolitan unification. Toronto's outer suburbs, bastions of Conservative Party support, were allowed to maintain their existence and were not made part of the new megacity arrangement.

Sources: Frances Frisken, "The Contributions of Metropolitan Government to the Success of Toronto's Public Transit System: An Empirical Dissent from the Public Choice Paradigm," *Urban Affairs Quarterly* 27 (December 1991): 268–292; Frances Frisken, "The Toronto Story: Sober Reflections on Fifty Years of Experiments with Regional Governance," *Journal of Urban Affairs* 23, 5 (2001): 513–541; David Rusk, *Inside Game/Outside Game* (Washington, DC: Brookings Institution Press, 1999), p. 149; Roger Keil, "Governance Restructuring in Los Angeles and Toronto: Amalgamation or Secession?" *International Journal of Urban and Regional Research* 24, 4 (2000): 764–769 and 775–778.

to their local communities or a strong antipathy against the City of Miami and its political leaders. The *Miami Herald,* the League of Women Voters, and other "good government" organizations all pushed for metropolitan reform as a vehicle that would displace local corruption with the county's administrative professionalism. Miami also lacked strong political parties and labor unions, organizations likely to oppose governmental restructuring. In the 1950s, Miami had no politically active minority fearful that metropolitan reorganization would bring vote dilution. African Americans were only 6.8 percent of the registered voters in Miami, and the great waves of Latin migration had yet to arrive at Florida's shores.

Wealthier communities in Dade County opposed the plan from the beginning. Over the years, a number of well-off communities—including Miami Beach, Surfside, Golden Beach, Bal Harbour, and North Bay Village—have attempted, without success, to secede from the county.

The exact division of powers between the two tiers of government has also proven to be a long, drawn-out, and complicated affair. By 1961, some 600 lawsuits challenging Metro's authority had already been filed with the courts.[19]

Demographic changes in the region led to new criticisms of Metro. African Americans (and, to a great extent, Hispanics as well) complained that Metro Miami's at-large system of electing members of the Metro Commission served to diminish their representation. Leaders in the predominantly poor, black Liberty City section of Miami in the 1980s even sought to incorporate their area as "New City," an independent municipal government that would have its own police force and other governing powers. The Metro Commission's lack of responsiveness to minority concerns was also evident in its 1981 decision to bow to the protests of white homeowners and reverse an earlier decision to build 20 units of low-income housing in the more affluent West Kendall section of southwest Dade County.[20] In 1992, a federal district court ordered Metro to switch to district elections, dramatically increasing the power of racial minorities, especially Hispanics, on a reconstituted county commission.[21]

Metro Dade brought improvements in such areas as mass transit, highway construction, countywide land-use planning, social services, voter registration, and countywide tax assessment and administration. Overall, the formation of Metro Dade led to the professionalization of government, a professionalism that was especially apparent when contrasted to the seemingly ceaseless episodes of corruption, maladministration, and patronage politics in the city of Miami. In the 1990s, Dade voters strengthened Metro by creating a more powerful county chief executive who would be directly elected by the people. Alex Penelas, a prominent Cuban American, became Metro Dade's first elected mayor.

Yet despite its successes, Metro Dade falls short of the idealized vision of two-tier reform. For the half of the county's population that lives in unincorporated areas, there is no two-tier system but one-tier governance by the county. Residents of these areas complain of their lack of local control over municipal service provision. Metro Dade has also been unable to impose order on the chaotic development of a sprawling south Florida megalopolis that extends beyond Dade County into Broward County (Fort Lauderdale), Palm Beach County, and even northern Monroe County (the Florida Keys). Other metropolitan planning efforts—the South Florida Regional Planning Council, the South Florida Water Management District, and state-ordered actions in growth management and the protection of the Everglades—have emerged in an effort to bring about effective regional action beyond Dade County's borders.[22]

THREE-TIER PLAN: PORTLAND AND THE TWIN CITIES

The three-tier reform is a rarely used approach to metropolitanism that, in multicounty areas, adds a third or regional level of government atop the already existing municipal and county levels. The plan does not eliminate existing local governmental units but, instead, creates an area-wide coordinating agency with some real powers. The two most prominent examples of the three-tier approach are the Greater Portland (Oregon) Metropolitan Service District and the Twin Cities (Minneapolis–St. Paul) Metropolitan Council.

PORTLAND   In the 1970s, the Oregon state legislature established the Portland Metropolitan Service District. In a 1978 referendum, voters in a three-county area gave the district (commonly referred to as Metro) responsibilities for waste disposal, zoo administration, and designated other services. In 1992, voters gave Metro new planning powers to manage the area's growth. Over time, the district's responsibilities have been expanded to include recycling, transportation planning, regional air and water quality programs, and the construction and operation of the Oregon Convention Center.

Portland's Metro is unique; it is the only directly elected multicounty regional government in the United States.[23] Metro cuts across the boundaries of 24 cities and three counties. It is a true multipurpose regional government.

Yet Portland's Metro "is at once pathbreaking as a mode of regional governance yet benign in its functions."[24] Metro is limited in its powers. It "operates within a sea of other governance structures, and its budget is piddling by comparison to many other governmental units."[25] In a great many policy areas, Metro has no real ability to control local action; the existing municipalities, not Metro, retain responsibility for most municipal service provision.

The Portland District's most notable achievements have been in the areas of land-use control, environmental protection, and transportation planning. Under state law, local land-use and zoning regulations must comply with the framework set by Metro. As we saw in Chapter 11, "Suburban Politics and Metropolitan America," Metro determines the region's **urban growth boundary,** a power that allows Metro to constrain the pace of urban sprawl and promote in-fill development. Portland's planners have also channeled new development to planned growth nodes in existing cities and near light-rail stations. Metro has sought to "build up" as opposed to "build out." Metro's planning efforts have helped to contribute to the vitality of Portland's downtown. The Portland area is also marred by less suburban sprawl and less disparity between city and suburbs than is typical of other metropolitan areas.[26]

Portland's Metro District is also charged with developing an affordable housing plan under which each of the region's 24 cities and towns must accept a proportionate share of low- and moderate-income housing. As a result, Portland suburbs often contain a greater presence of apartment buildings and small-lot housing than is typical of other suburban areas around the nation.

Metro's success is most apparent in those areas where there is a consensus as to the need for strong regional action. Metro has primarily addressed physical infrastructure problems and environmental and other quality-of-life concerns, not questions of social policy and racial equity. In a great many policy areas, local governments continue to operate untouched by Metro.[27]

Portland is often held out as a model of regional planning, and it has had notable successes in establishing a mass transit system, curbing sprawl, preserving open space and farmland, and maintaining the vitality of the region's core city.[28] However, it is no planner's paradise. Metro has had great difficulty in gaining increases in the supply of truly affordable housing. Urban sprawl, rush-hour traffic jams, and pollution also continue. In the face of continued population pressures, Metro has extended the urban growth boundary outward. The existence of the growth boundary has even spurred a flood of long-distance commuting. Metro also has not had great success in its efforts to work across state borders with the city of Vancouver, Washington to establish a regionwide mass transit system.

THE TWIN CITIES   The Minnesota state legislature created the Twin Cities Metropolitan Council in 1969 to deal with the problems brought by the capital area's rapid growth.[29] The Twin Cities Met Council is the regional planning organization for a seven-county area. In differs from Portland's Metro in one important area: Portland's Metro is popularly elected; the Met Council, in contrast, enjoys much less political legitimacy as its members are not elected but are appointed by Minnesota's governor.

The Twin Cities Metropolitan Council possesses real powers that normally are denied to other regional planning agencies around the country. The Metropolitan Council can levy property taxes, issue bonds, and pursue federal grants to support its activities. The Metropolitan Council develops long-term plans for the metropolitan area and oversees the actions of municipal and regional bodies in such areas as sewers, wastewater management, the protection of open space, and the development of sports facilities. It also serves as the region's housing authority. In 1974, the Metropolitan Council gained a virtual veto over transit and airport construction projects as the Metropolitan Transit Commission and the Metropolitan Airport Commission were placed under the Council's direction. Unlike other regional planning agencies, the Met Council is not reliant on the voluntary participation and contributions of local governments.

Of particular importance is the Metropolitan Council's power to formulate a **metropolitan development guide** (also called a **blueprint**). This is a "binding plan," in which the Council designates certain areas for concentrated development, reducing the prospects of unmitigated sprawl by protecting rural and agricultural acreage in the region.

As the review agency of federal sewer, water, and road-building dollars, the Council possesses a "carrot" that it can offer to communities that accept subsidized housing.[30] For a while, the Council was fairly successful in promoting the dispersion of subsidized housing, spending more Section 8 funds for the construction of subsidized housing in the suburbs than in the region's two core cities.[31] Yet the more affluent communities of the "fertile crescent" south and west of Minneapolis were still able to use exclusionary measures to preclude the development of low-income housing within their borders.[32]

As the political support for "fair share" housing diminished, the Met Council shifted to a policy of noninterference with local development patterns; suburban housing plans no longer included low- and moderate-income housing components. The Council defined houses costing $120,000 (in 1986) as affordable, allowing virtually all communities to meet their housing goals without undertaking much new action.[33] Even in implementing a court-related desegregation decision, the Council indicated that it would build public housing only in those communities willing to accept new units.[34] The Met Council also approved a new sewage interceptor and an extension of the local growth boundary as requested by affluent Maple Grove, despite the suburb's refusal to modify its exclusionary land-use practices. Lacking an electoral base, the Met Council has sought to avoid confrontation; it has never initiated a lawsuit against localities that failed to comply with its planning measures.[35]

Minnesota's regionalism extends beyond the creation of the Twin Cities Metropolitan Council. The state legislature also instituted **regional tax-base sharing**, a tax distribution plan that assures each municipality in the region a share of the tax revenue generated by new development, no matter where in the Twin Cities area the development is located. Under the state's **fiscal disparities law,** 40 percent of the net value of all new construction is placed in a pool for redistribution to localities based on population and need. Under tax-base sharing, all 186 communities in the greater Twin Cities area gain a portion of the tax revenues generated by the Mall of America, the region's featured attraction and the nation's largest indoor shopping mall, located in suburban Bloomington.

The fiscal disparities law has aided the region's poorer communities, reducing tax base disparities among communities in the Twin Cities area from a ratio of about 20:1 to about 4:1.[36] While tax-base sharing generally helps the region's declining communities, especially its older, blue-collar suburbs, it has not always worked to the advantage of the region's two major cities. In the 1980s and 1990s, Minneapolis was the site of new downtown development and, as a result, a net "loser" or "contributor" to the assessed value pool from which property tax revenues are redistributed to other communities.[37] While local tax-base sharing has not eliminated local fiscal disparities, it has worked at the margins to redistribute monies from wealthier to poorer communities.[38]

Much to the disappointment of its backers, local tax-base sharing has not greatly reduced the interlocal competition for business in the region. The 60-percent tax share that a jurisdiction retains is still a sizeable enough reward for local officials to pursue big-box and other new commercial development.[39]

Tax-base sharing is very controversial, and the region's better-off suburbs—and, at times, even the city of Minneapolis—have bitterly attacked the plan. (See "Jesse 'The Body' Ventura Views Regional Government" below.) The state legislature continually hears calls for the mechanism's repeal. The legislature even gave high-tax-base suburbs the right to opt out of a regional arrangement for the funding regional transit.[40]

JESSE "THE BODY" VENTURA VIEWS REGIONAL GOVERNMENT

In 1998, much to the surprise of political observers outside the state, Minnesotans elected former professional wrestler Jesse "The Body" Ventura as governor. Running under the banner of H. Ross Perot's Reform Party, Ventura emerged the plurality winner in a three-candidate field.

News reports that focused on Ventura's colorful career in wrestling and talk radio missed the fact that Ventura was also a veteran of local government. Ventura had served as mayor of Brooklyn Park, a Twin Cities suburb, rising to power as an antitax populist critical of big government. Brooklyn Park's so-called "Legion of Doom" vigorously opposed both taxes and low-income housing.

How did Ventura view regional tax-base sharing, the Twin Cities Met Council, and other regional initiatives? It appears that his views evolved considerably over time, sometimes depending on the position he occupied at the moment.

During his early political career, Ventura was disinclined to support regional tax-base sharing and other efforts at metropolitanism. However, as mayor of Brooklyn Park, Ventura came around to support tax sharing, which gave considerable revenues to his inner-ring, suburban municipality.

When Ventura moved to more affluent Maple Grove, he once again voiced a caustic view of regionalism. In his radio program, he sarcastically expressed his profound criticisms of a local tax-base sharing bill and its sponsor, state legislator Myron Orfield:

> Representative Myron "the Communist" Orfield, his latest wealth-sharing strategy, I mean this guy really needs to go to China. I mean I think he'd be most happy there. Oh Myron, Myron, Myron. You never realized the communists folded for a reason. You didn't figure it out, did you Myron?*

At times, Ventura called for the elimination of the Met Council. But, as governor, Ventura was a smart growth advocate who came to see the value of using the Council's planning powers to avert Los Angeles–style sprawl, to "protect what we love about Minnesota."** He elevated the Met Council chair to a state cabinet-level post and made the Met Council the lead agency in implementing state smart growth and multimodal transportation plans. Still, Ventura wanted a Met Council that would be less bureaucratic and didactic, one that would work in partnership with suburban communities and give them new room to initiate collaborative approaches of their own.†

continued

Ventura's successor, Governor Tim Pawlenty, a Republican, argued that the Met Council over the years had grown "too big for its britches." Like Ventura, he wanted the Met Council to give greater respect to local autonomy. But Pawlenty, too, came to recognize the value of Met Council guidance in steering new growth along rail corridors, ensuring the preservation of agricultural land in a region expected to absorb a million new residents by the year 2030.[‡]

* Myron Orfield. *Metropolitics: A Regional Agenda for Community and Stability* (Washington, DC: Brookings Institution Press, 1997), pp. 109–110 and 149. The quotation appears on p. 149.

** Governor Jesse Ventura, address to the "Growing Smart in Minnesota Conference," June 11, 1999. Available at www.legal-ledger.com/archive/629prim.htm.

[†] Ted Mondale and William Fulton, "Managing Metropolitan Growth: Reflections on the Twin Cities Experience," a case study prepared for The Brookings Institution Center on Urban and Metropolitan Policy, Washington, DC, September 2003.

[‡] Mara H. Gottfried, "Rift Near for Met Council, Governor," (St. Paul) *Pioneer Press*, October 17, 2002; Mara H. Gottfried, "Metropolitan Council: Growth Plan Narrows Its Focus," (St. Paul) *Pioneer Press*, October 15, 2003; David Peterson, "Pawlenty Appoints 16 Members to Met Council," (Minneapolis–St. Paul) *Star Tribune*, March 4, 2003.

At its weakest point, the Council was bypassed on a number of major development decisions, including the building of the Metrodome sports stadium, a new basketball arena, a World Trade Center skyscraper, and a new racetrack.[41] The Council also gave its approval to the construction of the suburban Mall of America, despite possible adverse effects that the giant new development could have on central-city retailing, older suburban shopping centers, and beltway traffic congestion. Minnesota's governor endorsed the project, and members of the Met Council were dependent on the governor for reappointment.[42]

Despite its formidable planning tools, the Met Council has largely been unable to limit suburban development. The bulk of job growth continues to take place in the suburbs, not in the region's two core cities.[43] The Council has been able to steer development to close-in suburbs; yet land-use restrictions have also driven new growth to exurban communities beyond the reach of the regional authority.[44]

In the early 1990s, the state legislature strengthened the Twin Cities Metropolitan Council, giving the body new responsibilities in the areas of metropolitan transit, sewers, waste control, and land-use planning. These changes transformed the Met Council from a $40-million-a-year planning agency to a $600-million-a-year regional government.[45] However, the state government responded to the concerns of suburbanites and refused to provide for the direct election of the council, a move that would have enhanced the Met Council's leadership potential.[46]

In summary, the creation of the Twin Cities Metropolitan Council, enacted without public referendum, was the product of the good-government orientation of Minnesota's citizens and its state legislature. Twin Cities regionalism has served as a model for the nation. Milwaukee, Sacramento, and a number of communities have begun to debate tax-base sharing plans of their own. Yet, despite their successes, the Met Council and metropolitan tax-base sharing arrangements represent highly controversial models of reform. Were they not already enshrined as law, it is highly unlikely that the Met Council and the fiscal disparities law would gain legislative passage in Minnesota today.[47]

IS METROPOLITAN GOVERNMENT DESIRABLE?

As we have already seen, the more comprehensive forms of metropolitan reorganization are quite difficult to realize. Some urban observers have even begun to question whether strong metropolitan government is even an ideal worth pursuing.

PUBLIC CHOICE THEORY: DEFENDING THE POLYCENTRIC METROPOLIS

There exists a sharp debate between two schools of thought regarding the desirability of metropolitan reform. **Metropologists** argue that a regional government can cure the problems of metropolitan fragmentation by providing services more uniformly, equitably, and efficiently across the metropolis. Metropologists point to possible **economies of scale,** the cost savings that can be gained by providing services on a large-scale basis. Planning done on a regional basis, for instance, can save money by allowing the closing of unnecessary police and fire stations and other local facilities. Metropolitan reformers further argue that a strong metropolitan government is essential for both equitable service provision and environmental protection.[48]

Polycentrists reject the school of metropology. In contrast, they contend that a multicentered or polycentric metropolis—not a centralized metropolitan government—better serves citizens. The polycentrists draw on the theory of *public choice,* which values both efficiency and the freedom of citizens to exercise individual choice. They argue that a strong metropolitan government would help to even out the local taxing and service levels in communities throughout a region, in effect diminishing the real choice of residences available to citizens.

Public choice theory applies market economic theories to metropolitan development and service delivery.[49] Public choice theorists observe that no single government can satisfy the diversity of citizens' tastes for different levels of services and taxation. Citizen satisfaction is maximized when each individual can make a choice of residence from a metropolitan market that offers many different and distinctive communities. Citizens willing to pay for a high level of educational, mass transit, and recreational services can choose to live in one community; citizens who prefer lower rates of taxation can choose another community.

Public choice theorists reject the metropolitanists' contention that large-scale, regional governments often achieve economies of scale. Instead, polycentrists argue that centralized governing structures are highly bureaucratized, bloated, irresponsive, and inefficient. Polycentrists argue that metropolitan government will result in numerous **diseconomies of scale,** where large, bureaucratized regional agencies will undermine efficiency in service delivery.

Public choice theorists further argue that the creation of metropolitan government is inadvisable as different types of services are best administered on different scales of production. Some services—for example, air pollution control or the processing of wastewater and sewage—are best administered by a regional agency. Cooperative arrangements enable intercommunity action when desirable. Yet in service areas that have a more human dimension—such as the more personal social services, education, law enforcement, and recreation—citizens prefer smaller units of government that can tailor service provision to local traditions and citizens' preferences.

Public choice theorists further argue that metropolitan fragmentation produces a **competition** among municipalities that is a spur to service efficiency. Municipalities that provide high-quality services while constraining tax increases will continue to attract high-value residences and new businesses. In more inefficient communities, municipal bureaucrats will be under pressure to upgrade service performance and keep taxes low in order to attract new corporate and residential investment.

The polycentric metropolis also serves to promote **innovation** in service delivery. In the fragmented metropolis, numerous communities are able to experiment with new ways of delivering services. Communities quickly copy the successful new practices of their neighbors.

CRITICISMS OF PUBLIC CHOICE THEORY

Public choice theory has constructed a highly articulate defense of the fragmented metropolis, pointing to the value of grassroots government and the problems posed by diseconomies of scale in service delivery. Yet the public choice interpretation of metropolitan development also suffers from serious shortcomings.

Critics of public choice theory argue that metropolitan fragmentation acts to preserve the residential choice exercised by more privileged residents only by denying an equivalent choice of communities to the poor. In the absence of a metropolitan government that can dictate land-use regulations, the residents of better-off communities adopt exclusionary zoning and restrictive land-use practices that diminish—not expand—the choice of communities available to racial minorities, the poor, and even younger workers and newly marrieds.

There is also little evidence to support the proposition that the competition among communities in a fragmented metropolis leads lagging communities to upgrade service and performance. Competition may even result in lowered qualities of service in poorer communities: "Indeed, competition feeds upon itself and makes the competitive more competitive, and the non-competitive more non-competitive."[50] More distressed communities lack the ability to invest in public recreation, senior citizen services, state-of-the art libraries, and other quality-of-life areas that make a community attractive to new residents.

Polycentrism also exacerbates the problem of parochialism. In the fragmented metropolis, each jurisdiction can pursue its own good to the detriment of its neighbors. If an already thriving suburb can gain new commercial development, it will do so, despite the jobs and businesses that such development will likely draw away from its more impoverished neighbors. In the fragmented metropolis, each jurisdiction need not be concerned with **externalities** or **spillovers**—the effects of its actions on neighboring communities.

Polycentrists recognize the need for governmental actions that extend beyond a municipality's borders. They argue that extensive intergovernmental cooperation already exists in the fragmented metropolis. Local governments can and do cooperate when economies of scale are apparent.

Yet as critics point out, voluntary intergovernmental action is also quite limited. Jurisdictions work together only when it is to their mutual advantage. Wealthier communities seldom join central cities and troubled older suburbs in cooperative efforts against such serious urban problems as poverty and the fiscal and racial imbalance of local schools.

CONCLUSION: TOWARD METROPOLITAN *GOVERNANCE*, NOT METROPOLITAN *GOVERNMENT*

In greater Indianapolis, Unigov has provided a new measure of executive leadership, especially in the field of economic development. Metro Dade has upgraded standards of service delivery and professionalism in the greater Miami area. The three-tier Portland and Twin Cities arrangements have sought to direct growth and maintain a respect for important housing, planning, and environmental goals.

Yet despite these achievements, the future prospects for comprehensive metropolitan reform are not very good. Too many powerful interests oppose the creation of new levels of metropolitan government. Suburbanites fear that a new metropolitan government will alter the social composition of their local communities and increase their taxes. Suburban business interests enjoy the tax advantages that result from interlocal competition for business in the polycentric metropolis. Racial minorities in central cities tend to oppose new metropolitan arrangements as a dilution of their political power. Elected officials and local bureaucrats, in both the central city and suburbs alike, fear that a consolidated metropolitan government might result in a dilution of their power and may even cost them their jobs.

Public choice theorists argue that the more comprehensive metropolitan reform plans are neither wanted nor desirable. Suburban residents express satisfaction with their communities and place no great value on consolidation and metropolitan reform. Even the movement for school district consolidation—that is, the joining of smaller school districts into a larger district capable of offering students more educational choices—has slowed to a virtual halt in New York and other states as citizens have placed a revived emphasis on community identity.[51] Big, bureaucratized governmental structures also often result in governmental irresponsiveness and waste, not enhanced efficiency.

In more recent years, metropolitan reformers have begun to focus on more incremental alternatives rather than comprehensive metropolitan restructuring. As public choice theorists have pointed out, a wide variety of interlocal cooperative arrangements do presently exist in the metropolis even in the absence of a comprehensive metropolitan government. Economic development and environmental protection are two important arenas in which local governments have begun to see the necessity of working cooperatively together. Even without a centralized, overarching metropolitan *government,* substantial regional cooperation or *governance* still takes place. That is the subject of our next chapter.

NOTES

1. David C. Hammack, *Power and Society: Greater New York at the Turn of the Century* (New York: Columbia University Press, 1982), pp. 187–229.
2. Daniel R. Grant, "A Comparison of Predictions and Experience with Nashville 'Metro,'" *Urban Affairs Quarterly* (September 1965): 35–54.
3. Tom Fiedler, "Salvation By Consolidation: '60s Jacksonville Mirrors '90s Miami," *The Miami Herald*, December 29, 1996. Our analysis of metropolitan reform in Jacksonville draws on Bert Swanson, "Jacksonville: Consolidation and Regional Governance," in *Regional Politics: America in a Post-City Age, Urban Affairs Annual Review*, vol. 45, eds. H. V. Savitch and Ronald K. Vogel (Thousand Oaks, CA: Sage publications, 1996), pp. 239–240; and Bert E. Swanson, "Quandaries of Pragmatic Reform: A Reassessment of the Jacksonville Experience," *State and Local Government Review* 32, 3 (Fall 2000): 227–238.
4. Mark Rosentraub, "City-County Consolidation and the Rebuilding of Image: The Fiscal Lessons from Indianapolis' UniGov Program," *State and Local Government Review* 32, 3 (Fall 2000): 180–191.
5. Ibid. The establishment of a variety of taxing and service zones was a notable feature of consolidation in Baton Rouge–East Baton Rouge. See G. Ross Stephens and Nelson Wikstrom, *Metropolitan Government and Governance* (New York: Oxford University Press, 2000), p. 69.
6. C. James Owen and York Willbern, *Governing Metropolitan Indianapolis: The Politics of Unigov* (Berkeley: University of California Press, 1985), pp. 1–2. Owen and Willbern provide an excellent overview of the creation of Unigov and the operation of the new government in its early years.
7. C. James Owen, "Indianapolis Unigov: A Focus on Restructured Executive Authority" (paper presented at the annual meeting of the Urban Affairs Association, Indianapolis, April 22–24, 1993). Indianapolis Mayor Stephen Goldsmith describes his success in building regional cooperation for economic development in *The Twenty-First Century City: Resurrecting Urban America*

(Lanham, MD: Rowman and Littlefield, 1999), pp. 75–94. The figures on the airport jobs are from Goldsmith, p. 36. Unigov's dynamic pro-growth orientation was strong; critics would argue too strong. By 2003, United Airlines walked away from its new aircraft maintenance center, built with the help of $320 million in taxpayer subsidies. See Louis Uchitelle, "State Pays for Jobs, but It Doesn't Always Pay Off," *The New York Times,* November 10, 2003.

8. john a. powell, "Addressing Regional Dilemmas for Minority Communities," in *Reflections on Regionalism,* ed. Bruce Katz (Washington, DC: Brookings Institution, 2000), pp. 236–237.

9. Rosentraub, "City-County Consolidation and the Rebuilding of Image," pp. 185–190.

10. *Beyond Merger: A Competitive Vision for the Regional City of Louisville,* a report of The Brookings Institution Center for Urban and Metropolitan Policy, Washington, DC, July 2002.

11. Bill Toland, "Louisville Becomes Lean, Less Mean After City/County Merger," *Pittsburgh Post-Gazette,* September 7, 2003.

12. H. V. Savitch and Ronald K. Vogel, "Metropolitan Consolidation versus Metropolitan Governance in Louisville," *State and Local Government Review* 32, 3 (Fall 2000): 201. This paragraph relies on Savitch and Vogel, pp. 198–212, and their argument for a "new regionalism" based on innovative interlocal cooperation rather than formal consolidation.

13. Joseph Gerth, "Merger: One Year Later," *The (Louisville) Courier-Journal* (December 22, 2003); H. V. Savitch and Ronald K. Vogel, "Suburbs without a City: Power and City-County Consolidation," *Urban Affairs Review* 39, 6 (July 2004): 758–790.

14. Roger B. Parks and Ronald J. Oakerson, "Regionalism, Localism, and Metropolitan Governance: Suggestions from the Research Program on Local Public Economies," *State and Local Government Review* 32, 3 (Fall 2000): 174.

15. Richard C. Feiock and Jered B. Carr, "A Reassessment of City/County Consolidation: Economic Development Impacts," *State and Local Government Review* 29, 3 (Fall 1997): 170.

16. Jered B. Carr and Richard C. Feiock, "Metropolitan Government and Urban Development," *Urban Affairs Review* 34 (January 1999): 476–488; David Rusk, "Consolidating Wheeling and Ohio County: A Review of the City-County Consolidation ("Unigov") Experiences Regarding Central City Health and Regional Economic Growth," paper prepared December 11, 2004, available at www.gamaliel.org/DavidRusk/Unigov%20report%20II.pdf.

17. Vincent L. Marando, "City-County Consolidation: Reform, Regionalism, Referenda and Requiem," *Western Political Quarterly* 32 (December 1979): 420.

18. Edward Sofen, *The Miami Metropolitan Experiment* (Bloomington: University of Indiana Press, 1963).

19. Raymond A. Mohl, "Miami: The Ethnic Cauldron," in *Sunbelt Cities: Politics and Growth Since World War II,* eds. Richard M. Bernard and Bradley R. Rice (Austin: University of Texas Press, 1983), pp. 82–83.

20. Raymond A. Mohl, "Miami's Metropolitan Government: Retrospect and Prospect," *Florida Historical Quarterly* 63 (July 1984): 48.

21. Larry Rohter, "Miami Court Decision Shifts Political Power to Minorities," *The New York Times,* December 25, 1992. The federal judge ruled that Metro Dade's at-large system of elections was an impermissible violation of the Voting Rights Act. At the time of the court's ruling, Anglo whites held

seven of the nine seats on the old at-large commission. The switch to district elections and an increase in the number of seats wound up changing the balance of power in the county. Hispanics were a majority of the population in seven of the new districts; blacks and Anglo whites were the majority in three districts each.

22. Genie Stowers, "Miami: Experiences in Regional Government," in *Regional Politics: America in a Post-City Age*, pp. 185–205.

23. These and other details of the evolution of Portland's Metro are taken from David Rusk, *Cities Without Suburbs* (Washington, DC: Woodrow Wilson Center Press, 1993); J. Linn Allen, "Dividing Line: Portland, Ore.'s Unique Approach to Growth Management Sets It Apart," *Chicago Tribune*, October 9, 1994. A good, readable overview of the Portland experience is provided by David Rusk, *Inside Game/Outside Game* (Washington, DC: Brookings Institution Press, 1999), pp. 153–177. For a good collection of articles assessing the Portland experience, see Carl Abbott, Deborah Howe, and S. Adler, *Planning the Oregon Way: A Twenty Year Evaluation* (Corvallis: Oregon State University Press, 1994).

24. Arthur C. Nelson, "Portland: The Metropolitan Umbrella," in *Regional Politics: America in a Post-City Age*, p. 253.

25. Ibid., p. 263.

26. Paul G. Lewis, *Shaping Suburbia: How Political Institutions Organize Urban Development* (Pittsburgh; University of Pittsburgh Press, 1996), pp. 162–207.

27. Ibid. pp. 263–264 and 268–270.

28. Christopher Leo, "Regional Growth Management Regime: The Case of Portland, Oregon," *Journal of Urban Affairs* 20, 4 (1998): 363–394, especially pp. 366–367 and 370.

29. The early history and evolution of the Twin Cities Metropolitan Council is described by Robert E. Einsweiler, "Metropolitan Government and Planning: Lessons in Shared Power," in *The Metropolitan Midwest: Policy Problems and Prospects for Change,* eds. B. Checkoway and C. V. Patton (Urbana: University of Illinois Press, 1985), pp. 285–301; John M. Levy, *Contemporary Urban Planning* (Englewood Cliffs, NJ: Prentice-Hall, 1988), pp. 261 272; and John J. Harrigan and William C. Johnson, *Governing the Twin Cities Region: The Metropolitan Council in Comparative Perspectives* (Minneapolis: University of Minnesota Press, 1978).

30. Judith A. Martin, "In Fits and Starts: The Twin Cities Metropolitan Framework," in *Metropolitan Governance: American/Canadian Intergovernmental Perspectives,* eds. Donald N. Rothblatt and Andrew Sancton (Berkeley, CA: Institute of Governmental Studies Press), pp. 229–230.

31. Joanne Vail and Rosanne Zimbro, *1986 Subsidized Housing in the Twin Cities Metropolitan Area* (Minneapolis: Metropolitan Council, 1986), quoted in Martin, "In Fits and Starts: The Twin Cities Metropolitan Framework," p. 230.

32. John J. Harrigan, "Governance in Transition: Regime Under Pressure in the Twin Cities" (paper presented at the annual meeting of the American Political Science Association, New York, September 2, 1994).

33. Edward G. Goetz, "Fair Share or Status Quo? The Twin Cities Livable Communities Act," *Journal of Planning Education and Research* 20 (2000): 37–51.

34. Edward G. Goetz, *Clearing the Way: Deconcentrating the Poor in Urban America* (Washington, DC: Urban Institute Press, 2003), pp. 98–99 and 189–190.

35. Orfield, *Metropolitics*, pp. 102–103, 152–154, 184–184, and 194–196; Goetz, *Clearing the Way,* p. 102–104.

36. Remarks of James L. Hetland, Jr., former chairperson of the Metropolitan Council, to the annual conference of the National Civic League, Denver, Colorado, October 27, 1989.

37. Martin, "In Fits and Starts: The Twin Cities Metropolitan Framework," p. 228; Myron Orfield, *Metropolitics: A Regional Approach for Community and Stability* (Washington, DC: Brookings Institution Press, 1997), pp. 109–111.

38. Wim Wiewel, Joseph Persky, and Kimberly Schaffer, "Less Sprawl, Greater Equity? The Potential for Revenue Sharing in the Chicago Region," in *Urban Sprawl: Causes, Consequences, and Policy Responses*, ed. Gregory D. Squires (Washington, DC: Urban Institute Press, 2002), pp. 267–271. Across the United States, there are a few other notable experiments with local tax-base sharing. Montgomery County, Ohio (the greater Dayton area), has a regional revenue sharing plan that is similar to the Twin Cities area tax-base sharing. The program seeks to promote countywide cooperation in efforts to pursue and retain jobs in the region. Unlike the Twin Cities, communities in Montgomery County are not required to participate in the revenue sharing arrangement but nonetheless gain rewards for being part of the plan. Wealthier communities are also offered financial protection as provisions of the law safeguard a community against a great loss of funds suffered under revenue sharing. One economically booming Vandalia, located adjacent to Dayton International Airport, has refused to join the plan.

In New Jersey, the Hackensack Meadowlands also has adopted a form of regional tax-base sharing in an attempt to get towns to spare valuable tidal wetlands from development. In the Pittsburgh area, the Allegheny Regional Asset District uses a regional sales tax to assist communities that shift reliance away from the property tax; the program effectively shifts aid to the county's less affluent communities.

For a greater description of how fiscal regionalism has worked in these communities, see Rusk, *Inside Game/Outside Game*, pp. 201–221, and David Y. Miller, *The Regional Governing of Metropolitan America* (Boulder, CO: Westview, 2002), pp. 110–117.

39. Miller, *The Regional Governing of Metropolitan America,* pp., 113–113; Edward G. Goetz and Terrence Kayser, "Competition and Cooperation in Economic Development: A Study of the Twin Cities Metropolitan Area," in *Approaches to Economic Development: Readings from Economic Development Quarterly*, eds. John P. Blair and Laura A. Reese (Thousand Oaks, CA: SAGE Publications, 1999), p. 203.

40. Myron Orfield, "Politics and Regionalism," in *Urban Sprawl: Causes, Consequences, and Policy Responses*, ed. Gregory D. Squires (Washington, DC: Urban Institute Press, 2002), pp. 245–248.

41. John J. Harrigan, "Minneapolis-St. Paul: Structuring Metropolitan Government," in *Regional Politics: America in a Post-City Age*, pp. 213–227; and Amy Klobuchar, *Uncovering the Dome* (Prospect Heights, IL: Waveland Press, 1986).

42. Martin, "In Fits and Starts: The Twin Cities Metropolitan Framework," pp. 233–236; Harrigan, "Governance in Transition: Regime Under Pressure in the Twin Cities;" Orfield, *Metropolitics*, pp. 101–103; Martin, "In Fits and Starts: The Twin Cities Metropolitan Framework."

43. Harrigan, "Governance in Transition: Regime Under Pressure in the Twin Cities."

44. Anthony Downs, "The Big Picture: How America's Cities Are Growing," *The Brookings Review* 16, 4 (Fall 1998): 11.

45. Orfield, *Metropolitics*, p. 13; Harrigan, "Minneapolis-St. Paul: Structuring Metropolitan Government," pp. 223–226.

46. Rusk, *Inside Game/Outside Game*, pp. 245–246.

47. Remarks of George Latimer, former mayor of St. Paul, Minnesota, to the annual conference of the National Civic League, Denver, Colorado, October 27, 1989.

48. For an interesting discussion of the evolving nature of metropolitan reform ideology and the metropolitan reform coalition, see Jeffrey R. Henig, "Equity and the Future Politics of Growth," in *Urban Sprawl: Causes, Consequences, and Policy Responses*, ed. Gregory D. Squires (Washington, DC: Urban Institute Press, 2002), pp. 325–350.

49. The most important statement of the public choice model as applied to urban political life is presented by Vincent Ostrom, Charles Tiebout, and Robert Warren, "The Organization of Government in Metropolitan Areas," *American Political Science Review* 55 (December 1961): 831–842. Other classic works include Robert L. Bish, *The Public Economy of Metropolitan Areas* (Chicago: Markham, 1971); Robert L. Bish and Vincent Ostrom, *Understanding Urban Government: Metropolitan Reform Reconsidered* (Washington, DC: American Enterprise Institute, 1973); and Vincent Ostrom and Elinor Ostrom, "Public Choice: A Different Approach to the Study of Public Administration," *Public Administration Review* 31 (March/April 1971): 203–216. For easy-to-understand overviews of the public choice debate, see Stephens and Wikstrom, *Metropolitan Government and Governance*, pp. 105–121, and Kathryn A. Foster, *The Political Economy of Special-Purpose Governments* (Washington, DC: Georgetown University Press, 1997), pp. 35–41.

50. Miller, *The Regional Governing of Metropolitan America*, pp. 137–143. The quotation appears on p. 143.

51. Gerald Benjamin and Richard P. Nathan, *Regionalism and Realism: A Study of Governments in the New York Metropolitan Area* (Washington, DC: Brookings Institution, 2001), pp. 168–175.

Cities and suburbs work with one another when they find it in their mutual interest to do so. A wide variety of cooperative arrangements (see Figure 13-1) permits regional *governance* even in the absence of a metropolitan or regional *government*. In this chapter, we shall review some of

the more commonplace means of regional cooperation, noting both their potential and their limits.

■ **FIGURE 13–1**

DAVID WALKER'S 17 REGIONAL APPROACHES TO SERVICE DELIVERY

Easiest

1. Informal cooperation
2. Interlocal service contracts
3. Joint powers agreements
4. Extraterritorial powers
5. Regional councils/councils of governments
6. Federally encouraged single-purpose regional bodies
7. State planning and development districts
8. Contracting (private)

Middling

9. Local special districts
10. Transfer of functions
11. Annexation
12. Regional special districts and authorities
13. Metro multipurpose district
14. Reformed urban county

Hardest

15. One-tier consolidations
16. Two-tier restructuring
17. Three-tier reforms

SOURCE: David B. Walker. "Snow White and the 17 Dwarfs: From Metro Cooperation to Governance," *National Civic Review* 76 (January/February 1987): 16.

THE "EASIEST" MEANS OF METROPOLITAN COOPERATION

INFORMAL COOPERATION

Informal cooperation occurs when two or more localities work together without a binding agreement set forth in writing. Informal cooperation might entail nothing more than exchanging information or sharing equipment. Communities quite frequently collaborate with one another on an informal basis; however, such cooperation "only rarely involves matters of regional or even subregional significance."[1] When projects require extensive fiscal support, more formal means of joint action are required.

Communities even cooperate informally across state and even international borders where the intricacies of interstate and international diplomacy may preclude the signing of formalized bi-state and binational agreements. Municipal officials in El Paso, Texas, a city of a half million people, clearly recognize that the health of their city is intricately tied to that of Ciudad Juarez, its million-person Mexican neighbor. Each working day, a county truck from the American side crosses the international bridge and sprays an 18-mile-long open sewage ditch that would otherwise provide a fertile breeding ground for disease-carrying mosquitoes. Under another informal understanding, Mexican children who break the law in El Paso are sent home to Mexico, where a social worker hired by the Texas Youth Commission makes sure that they go to school. This program saves Texas taxpayers the costs of housing offenders in juvenile facilities in Texas. Such cooperative agreements are often extragovernmental: "There are no treaties involved in the low-level diplomacy, and little Federal input. Only some of the joint programs are officially written down. Many are based on handshakes between local officials [in El Paso] . . . and their counterparts in Juarez."[2]

However, effective regional action almost always requires more than informal cooperation. El Paso and Ciudad Juarez needed to enter into a formalized interlocal agreement to establish cross-border municipal bus service between the two cities. Effective cross-border pollution control similarly required the negotiation of international pacts. Despite these common efforts, joint planning in El Paso–Ciudad Juarez is, on the whole, quite limited. The two cities are not functionally integrated and continue to view each other as competitors for new economic development.[3] San Diego and Tijuana are another pair of border cities where mutual dependency has led to joint action beyond informal understandings. (See "San Diego-Tijuana: A Cross-Border Metropolis," below.)

SAN DIEGO-TIJUANA: A CROSS-BORDER METROPOLIS

Cooperation between San Diego and Tijuana, Mexico, once unknown, is now increasingly routine. Officials from the two cities have met to coordinate disaster response plans, regulate traffic flow, increase cooperation between their police departments through ride-along exchanges and shared intelligence on

continued

SAN DIEGO-TIJUANA: A CROSS-BORDER METROPOLIS (CONT.)

street gangs, and promote economic development and tourism in the region. The two cities have exchanged environmental enforcement personnel and even offer a common Web page that lists recycling efforts on both sides of the border.

The mutual dependence of San Diego and Tijuana requires actions that go beyond the informal understandings. The two cities signed an Agreement on Binational Cooperation to formalize a number of the joint efforts that had been undertaken over the years. Joint action led to the building of a light-rail system to connect the two downtowns. Local officials also proposed the construction of a new international airport that would straddle the border. Officials have also sought to establish a transnational border authority to promote infrastructure investment, economic development, and other matters of joint benefit. San Diego residents also pushed for the construction of new sewage facilities to cope with the untreated effluent from Tijuana that washes up on California beaches.

Yet despite these occasional far-reaching projects, joint action between Tijuana and San Diego is still largely limited to informal understandings. The United States Constitution bars state and local governments from negotiating their own formal agreements with foreign nations; and San Diego has found it quite difficult to convince federal officials of the importance of negotiating new formal accords with Mexico.

Sources: Glen Sparrow and Dana Brown, "Black Water, Red Tape: Anatomy of a Border Problem," *National Civic Review* 75 (July/August 1986): 214–218; Sandra Dibble, "San Diego, Tijuana Mayors Set to Link Up in Cyberspace: It'll Be High-Tech Leap Across the Border," *The San Diego Union-Tribune,* February 28, 1997; Gregory Gross, "Cross-Border Cooperation Is Examined At Conference," *The San Diego Union-Tribune,* January 12, 1999; Zeferino Sanchez, Director of Public Works and Services, Tijuana, Mexico, "Tijuana and San Diego—Progress and Partnerships," remarks presented at the Mayors' Asia Pacific Environmental Partnership, Honolulu, Hawaii, January 31–February 3, 1999. Available at www.csis.org/e4e/MayorToC.html.

INTERGOVERNMENTAL AND PRIVATE SERVICE CONTRACTING

Intergovernmental service contracts are legally binding agreements under which one government purchases a service provided by another. For instance, a municipality can enter into a service agreement with a county for police protection, specifying the exact level of patrol service (such as the frequency of patrols and the number of officers in each patrol car) that the county will provide and the price that the city will pay for the service. Intergovernmental service contracting allows municipalities to take advantage of the **economies of scale** that may be realized when a service is provided beyond the borders of any single locality. A municipality that contracts with the county for police and fire protection no longer has to bear the costs of building and maintaining its own police and fire stations; instead, municipalities can share the costs of maintaining a relatively small number of centrally located police and fire stations. Contracting allows a smaller jurisdiction to obtain a service at a reasonable price, often a service it could provide for itself only at a very high cost.

Local jurisdictions often enter into service agreements with neighboring municipalities. Suburbs often purchase water from central-city municipal water systems. More common, still, municipalities purchase services from the county. Among the most popular contracted services are jail and detention home services, sewage disposal, fire prevention, tax assessing, computer and data processing, police training, libraries, and animal control.

Contracting further enhances efficiency by creating a **competitive market.** Where a municipality maintains the ability to purchase a service from the county, from another municipality, or even from a private provider, a competitive environment is created that helps to ensure that the best possible quality of service is offered at the lowest price. One notable variant of intergovernmental service contracting is the **Lakewood Plan,** in which Los Angeles County offers such a large menu of services that a participating local jurisdiction can purchase nearly all of its services from the county and have only a token municipal workforce of its own. (See "The Lakewood Plan: Cure or Contributor to Metropolitan Fragmentation?" below.)

THE LAKEWOOD PLAN: CURE OR CONTRIBUTOR TO METROPOLITAN FRAGMENTATION?

The Lakewood Plan takes its name from the City of Lakewood, the first suburban community in the region to incorporate once Los Angeles County offered its extensive menu of contract services. While the Lakewood Plan helps communities to realize cost savings, it also exacerbates some of the problems of metropolitan fragmentation. The plan led to a rash of municipal incorporations in the mid-1950s, including the formation of **minimal cities,** as suburbs with relatively small populations were able to incorporate as new municipalities and secure most of their services from the county. By establishing themselves as municipalities, these suburban areas gained the power to ward off annexation by neighboring municipalities. The City of Lakewood, itself, incorporated to escape the prospect of being annexed by the city of Long Beach.

The new incorporations provided attractive sites for exclusion and "white flight." The incorporation of very exclusive Rancho Palos Verdes, just outside of Long Beach, allowed wealthy homeowners to pass land-use laws to block new development, preserving the community's estate-like character and effectively barring entry by less affluent residents. Incorporated as municipalities, such wealthy tax islands were shielded from annexation, a factor that helped to undermine the long-term fiscal base of the region's more troubled cities such as Compton.

Major industries, too, took advantage of Lakewood Plan incorporations to escape the higher levels of taxation they would have to pay if larger cities were to annex their property. Even the names of some of the new communi-

continued

THE LAKEWOOD PLAN: CURE OR CONTRIBUTOR
TO METROPOLITAN FRAGMENTATION? (CONT.)

ties reflected their industrial and commercial roots. The city of Industry, California was created as a tax shelter for the railroad yards, factories, and warehouses within its borders; it is a city with no local industrial or residential property taxes. When incorporated, the town had only 624 residents. To meet the minimum population of 500 required for incorporation, the city had to count the 169 patients and 31 employees of a local psychiatric sanitarium. By the year 2000, the City of Industry still had a population of only 777.

Similarly, the City of Commerce was created to shield railroad and industrial property from the higher rates of taxation that would have resulted were the area annexed by a neighboring municipality. Local business leaders intentionally created Commerce as a predominantly industrial, not a residential, city, a hazardous and toxic waste area largely insulated from outside control.

Santa Fe Springs was created to shield the local industry from control by citizens in neighboring Whittier and South Whittier. The City of Dairy Valley was created as a tax island of agricultural land holdings, including the area's more than 400 dairies. In 1967 the community changed its name to Cerritos only after continued residential development changed the character of the community as local dairy operators and farmers sold their acreage to developers for high profits.

Sources: Gary J. Miller, *Cities by Contract: The Politics of Municipal Incorporation* (Cambridge, MA: MIT Press, 1981); Charles Hoch, "Municipal Contracting in California: Privatizing with Class," *Urban Affairs Quarterly* 20 (March 1985): 303–323; Mike Davis, *City of Quartz: Excavating the Future of Los Angeles* (New York: Vintage Books, 1992), pp. 165–169; Christopher G. Boone and Ali Modarres, "Creating a Toxic Neighborhood in Los Angeles County: A Historical Examination of Environmental Inequity," *Urban Affairs Review* 35, 2 (November 1999): 163–187.

Under **private and nonprofit contracting**, a municipal government purchases a service from a nongovernmental provider who may offer the service to a number of municipalities. In Indiana, Allen County and the City of Fort Wayne essentially merged their data processing staffs under the auspices of a contract that turned data processing over to a private company.[4] Pittsburgh contracts with nonprofit groups for the provision of cultural and arts programs.

Only half of the states permit their cities to enter into contracts with private and nonprofit agencies for the provision of services. Public sector unions oppose private sector contracting for fear that municipalities will use private service provision to circumvent union protections and undermine municipal workforce wage structures.

JOINT POWERS AGREEMENTS

Under **joint powers agreements,** two or more local governments formally agree to work together in the provision of a service. A joint powers agreement is typified by the agreement of Santa Rosa, Healdsburg, Petaluma, and Sonoma (California) to merge their libraries to form a consolidated library system. A variation of the joint powers agreement is **parallel action,** whereby two or more governments pursue their agreed-upon commitments separately, even though the results are designed to benefit both communities.

Interlocal agreements may be quite short and as "bare bones" as the two-page agreement that enables Wichita County and the City of Electra, Texas to cooperate in the provision of street repair, drainage, and waste disposal. On the other end of the spectrum, the agreement between Dallas and Fort Worth that spells out the financing and operations of the region's international airport runs well over 100 pages.[5]

As governments tend to cooperate only when it is in their interest to do so, joint powers agreements can be quite difficult to set up. In San Mateo County, just south of San Francisco, the representatives of 11 different localities sought to establish a joint powers authority to provide improved library service. However, wealthy Woodside objected that it would be contributing more money to the new countywide system than it cost to run its own library. Further down the peninsula, officials in Santa Clara, Sunnyvale, San Jose, and other South Bay communities attempted to create a joint powers arrangement that would build a new Santa Clara ballpark in their effort to lure the San Francisco Giants baseball team to the San Jose area. But the team's management rejected the resulting bureaucratic governing structure as complicated and unworkable.[6]

Mutual aid agreements, where localities agree to help one another in times of emergency, are quite common. The agreement between Thornton and Westminster, Colorado, to back up each other's computer system in the event of a disaster, is quite typical.[7] Yet communities are not always willing to enter into mutual assistance agreements with their neighbors. Each of the 19 suburbs that surround Detroit has mutual aid agreements with one another in case of fires and other disasters, but none has a similar arrangement with Detroit. Detroit's suburban neighbors fear the city's size, poverty, and "social distance."[8]

Before the 9/11 attacks, the New York Fire Department (FDNY) had no mutual aid agreements with surrounding jurisdictions; other municipalities were reluctant to enter into agreements with a city agency of such enormous size. Consequently, on 9/11, with half of its own force at the World Trade Center, the FDNY had no clear procedures for how to use reinforcements provided by neighboring Nassau and Westchester counties. There were gaps in joint training that would have enabled the firefighters and other first responders from various communities to work more smoothly together. The actions of regional first responders in New York on the morning of 9/11 suffered from poor coordination.[9] In contrast, at the site of the Pentagon attack, cooperation between the

Arlington Country Fire Department and its neighbors went more smoothly, as emergency departments in the region had learned their roles through 20 years of practice drills.

EXTRATERRITORIAL POWERS

Approximately 35 states grant their cities **extraterritorial power,** the authority to control some of the actions of contiguous unincorporated areas that lie outside a city's boundaries. Texas law is particularly noteworthy for the authority it grants to a city to regulate subdivisions in unincorporated areas adjacent to the city. Major cities in Texas can even prevent the incorporation of new suburban municipalities in the cities' extraterritorial jurisdiction. Major Texas cities can also bar competing cities from annexing surrounding land. Houston has an extraterritorial jurisdiction that extends five miles from the city's corporate limits and covers 1,900 square miles, including all of Harris County. Houston's extraterritorial jurisdiction effectively extends the geographic area under the influence of the city's growth-oriented business elite.

Houston, San Antonio, and other Texas cities have used their extraterritorial powers to prevent the incorporation of new suburbs, preserving areas of suburban development for annexation. Such "elastic cities" can later extend their borders, capturing new areas of population and economic growth.[10] In the 1970s, Houston captured nearly 90 percent of the region's population growth within its borders and its extraterritorial jurisdiction.[11]

COUNCILS OF GOVERNMENTS (COGs) AND REGIONAL PLANNING COUNCILS

A **council of governments** (COG) brings together, on a voluntary basis, the top elected officials of the municipalities in a region. In many ways, a COG can be viewed as a United Nations of the cities and suburbs in a region. The council provides a forum for study, discussion, and debate of common problems, but seldom, if ever, does the COG possess any real power to enforce action on uncooperative members.

Quite similar to a COG is the more staff-dominated **regional planning council (RPC).** An RPC is a metropolitan planning agency staffed by professional officials, lacking the round-table-of-elected-officials-on-top characteristic of a COG.

Early COG-like structures in the 1950s included the New York Metropolitan Regional Council; the Washington Metropolitan Conference (since replaced by the Metropolitan Washington Council of Governments); the Puget Sound Government Conference in Seattle; the Mid-Willamette Valley Intergovernmental Cooperation Council in Salem (Oregon); the Association of Bay Area Governments (ABAG) in greater San Francisco; and the forerunner of the present-day Southeast Michigan Council of Governments (SEMCOG) in the greater Detroit area.

In the 1960s, federal grants provided money for regional planning studies and the staffing of regional organizations. In over 100 programs, the application process for federal grants required comments by regional organizations as to how the desired project would affect the regional balance.

Urged on by federal regulations and nourished by federal funds, the growth of COGs and RPCs was rapid. By the mid-1970s, the number of regional planning agencies increased to over 650. However, the Reagan administration reduced the assistance for regional planning and weakened the federal regulations requiring the regional review of grant applications. As a result, by 1988, the end of the Reagan years, the number of COGs shrunk to fewer than 528. Many COGs survived the Reagan-era assault by finding new roles for themselves, providing managerial and technical assistance to member governments and aiding localities in the pursuit of new grants.[12]

COGs and regional planning councils are extremely weak regional organizations. First and foremost, COGs are only advisory and possess no legislative power and no authority to force local governments to respect regional needs. Member governments can ignore COG recommendations and can even withdraw from the organization. In both the Cleveland and Washington, DC metropolitan areas, member governments, upset at the regional council's action, seceded from the organization in protest and rejoined the COG only when the offending action was withdrawn.

COGs are dependent on the financial contributions of their member governments. As a result, COGs such as the Houston-Galveston Area Council (HGAC) seek to avoid antagonizing member governments. The HGAC focuses only on actions that can garner consensual support.[13] In the greater Chicago area, the Northeastern Illinois Planning Commission, greatly reliant on the voluntary contributions of local governments, has been unable to impose any serious constraints on the growth actions of suburban communities.[14] COGs also shy away from controversial social issues such as regional school and housing integration. Many COGs typically assume a posture of local boosterism, uncritically supporting members' applications for federal aid.

Typically, COGs are quite understaffed. The Metropolitan Washington Council of Governments (MWCOG), possibly the most activist and successful COG in the nation, is in many ways the exception. Serving 19 local governments in the nation's capital area, it is one of the few COGs with the budget and a large professional staff necessary for a substantial array of physical and transportation planning, environmental protection, public safety, homeland protection, disaster response, and social planning activities. Yet even this relatively strong COG has carefully sidestepped such controversial proposals as regional gun control or the imposition of a District of Columbia commuter tax.[15] MWCOG has also taken only the gentlest steps in its efforts to persuade Washington's suburbs to increase the supply of housing available to the region's more disadvantaged citizens.

Despite these serious shortcomings, in many metropolitan areas COGs and RPCs represent the only broad forum for the discussion of regional concerns. In the Detroit metropolitan area, the Southeast Michigan Council of Governments

(SEMCOG) played a vital role in formulating a clean-up plan for the Rouge River. SEMCOG also helped develop air-quality data analysis and related strategies to help achieve the goals of the Clean Air Act.[16]

The federal **Intermodal Surface Transportation and Efficiency Act,** or **ISTEA** (commonly pronounced "Ice Tea"), has given many COGs and RPCs new-found authority and funding in planning transportation projects for a better environment. In 1998, Congress updated the Act, calling it **TEA-21,** the Transportation Equity Act for the 21st Century. ISTEA/TEA-21 has become the federal government's main program in support of metropolitan planning.[17]

Under ISTEA/TEA-21, each metropolitan area designates a **Metropolitan Planning Organization (MPO).** MPOs serve as "a voice for metropolitan areas"[18] in planning more integrated and balanced transportation systems. Under ISTEA/TEA-21, MPOs can even shift funds that had been reserved for highways to commuter rail projects and the extension of bus routes.

The Southern California Association of Governments (SCAG) used its MPO authority to increase the funding of regional transportation projects. The Denver Council of Governments (known informally as "Dr. COG") used its control over transportation funds as a tool to promote its "Metro Vision 2000" planning principles for an eight-county region.[19] In other regions, however, weak and understaffed COGs were unable to fight state highway planners and change traditional patterns of highway-oriented spending.[20]

In large metropolitan areas, COGs that serve only a portion of the metropolis can provide an important forum for subregional action. The Barrington Area Council of Governments (BACOG), a council composed of seven upper-income, northwestern Chicago suburbs, has attempted to improve transportation and other services in response to the needs of the area's rapidly growing population.[21]

FEDERALLY AND STATE ENCOURAGED PLANNING BODIES

Federal and state aid requirements have encouraged single-purpose regional bodies in such areas as economic development, job training, metropolitan transportation, and the provision of assistance to Appalachia. As already noted, the federal ISTEA/TEA-21 legislation requires the establishment of MPOs. Yet fewer than half of the 340 MPOs across the country are filled by COGs and broad-based RPCs. In many regions, MPO responsibilities are lodged in bureaucratic departments and single-purpose bodies that possess only the responsibilities given to them under federal transportation laws.[22]

The ISTEA/TEA-21 process has allowed MPOs to increase the funding of light-rail systems in Salt Lake City, Denver, Dallas, Charlotte, Las Vegas, San Jose, and San Diego, expanding public rail transit outside the Northeast and the Midwest.[23] Yet single-purpose MPOs have often faced considerable opposition from state highway departments and other interests committed to highway spending.

The requirements of the federal Clean Air Act spurred California to create the Air Quality Management District. The AQMD has more than 1,000 employees, an annual budget of over $100 million, and authority over the greater Los Angeles air basin, a four-county region with more than 10 million residents.[24]

THE "MIDDLING" MEANS OF COOPERATION

There is a middle level of regional governance mechanisms that provide for a stable restructuring of service responsibilities in the metropolis without seeking the establishment of a comprehensive metropolitan government.

SPECIAL DISTRICTS

There are nearly 88,000 units of local government in the United States. Most of these, however, are not cities, counties, and townships, the general-purpose units that we generally think about when we popularly discuss local government (see Table 13-1). Instead, over half of the units of local government are **special districts,** autonomous, narrow units of government that provide a single service (such as drainage and flood control, solid waste management, fire protection, water supply, community college administration, or housing) or a set of related services. In 2002, there were over 35,000 special districts, of which 91 percent performed a single function.[25] In addition, there were another 13,500 special or independent local school districts.

Special districts set their own budgets. The majority of special districts, including independent school districts, have the authority to levy taxes. Others rely on user fees or charges.

The special district represents a flexible approach to regional cooperation, as the boundaries of a special district can cut across city, county, and even state lines. The size of special districts varies greatly. The Metropolitan Sanitary District of Greater Chicago, the Forest Preserve District of Cook County, and the Suburban Cook County Tuberculosis Sanitarium District each serve a geographical area larger than the city of Chicago. In contrast, special districts for libraries, fire protection, and parks and recreation typically have much smaller service areas.[26]

■ TABLE 13-1

NUMBER OF LOCAL GOVERNMENTAL UNITS IN THE UNITED STATES, BY TYPE: 1952–2002

Type of Government	1952	1962	1972	1982	1992	2002
Total Number of Local governments	116,756	91,185	78,218	81,780	86,692	87,849
County	3,052	3,043	3,044	3,041	3,043	3,034
Municipal	16,807	17,997	18,517	19,076	19,296	19,431
Town/Township	17,202	17,144	16,991	16,734	16,666	16,506
School district	67,355	34,678	15,781	14,851	14,556	13,522
Special district	12,340	18,323	23,885	28,078	33,131	35,356

SOURCE: U.S. Department of Commerce, Bureau of the Census, *2002 Census of Governments,* GC02-1(P), (July 2002).

Special districts are often subcounty; in a great many areas, they help bring better service provision to unincorporated communities on the suburban fringe. However, there are also special districts that are formed within a city or village boundaries to provide residents of the district with an enhanced level of services. Critics argue that such districts lead to service inequity as they enable the residents of more advantaged areas to secure higher quality services while ignoring the needs of inner-city residents.

In some cases, however, special districts help address service equity concerns. Districts that stretch beyond the borders of the central city in effect tax suburbanites to help pay for services used by city residents. Suburban residents, for instance, help fund the Milwaukee Sewerage District and the Milwaukee Technical College, special districts that provide disproportionate benefits to city residents.[27]

Table 13-1 underscores the rapid growth in the number of special districts. Still, over 30 percent of the non-school special districts are found in just five states: Illinois, New York, California, Pennsylvania, and Washington. In contrast, Connecticut, Ohio, Massachusetts, and Michigan have very few non-school special districts. The Houston, Seattle, Denver, Oakland, Sacramento, Portland, Hartford, and Atlantic City metropolitan areas all exhibit heavy utilization of special districts—as does the suburban Nassau-Suffolk County (New York) and Riverside–San Bernardino and Anaheim–Santa Ana (California). The Detroit, Dallas, Atlanta, New Orleans, Charlotte, Orlando, and Baltimore areas, in contrast, show low reliance on special districts.[28] State rules appear to be the critical factor in special-district creation.

Special districts offer efficiency and flexibility. However, their creation also compounds certain problems of urban governance, adding to metropolitan fragmentation and the problems of service coordination and confusion. It is a near-insurmountable task to bring direction to the greater New York City region with its 2,179 separate units of local government, including 742 special districts and authorities plus another 600 school districts.[29]

Special districts are also relatively invisible and unaccountable governments. The print and electronic news media give little coverage to district boards, and most citizens are probably only marginally aware of the existence of community college districts, sewer and water districts, and other such governmental bodies.

Land development interests are often the prime movers behind the creation of **urban fringe districts,** special districts that provide sewerage, water, and other important services on the growing edge of a metropolis. In California, **community service districts** provide water, sewage disposal, garbage collection, police and fire protection, street construction and lighting, library service, and recreation. In Texas, **municipal utility districts** provide water, drainage, sewage systems, garbage collection, fire fighting, and parks and recreational services. In the Southwest, such districts provide such a range of municipal services that they effectively serve as **junior cities.**[30]

Private land developers frequently serve on the boards of urban fringe districts, dominating their decision making during the early years when the population of a newly created district is small. These private interests also enjoy the advantages offered by the low visibility of special district decision making. Special districts possess the ability to finance new growth projects that might upset other local constituencies. The Disney Corporation sought the protection of a special district when it developed Disney World. The State of Florida responded by creating a new local special district that effectively insulated Disney's development plans from review by neighboring public officials.[31] (See "Is Disney World Its Own Government?" below.)

In the greater Houston area, private development interests used newly created water districts to their advantage. Under Texas law, water districts possess unlimited taxing and borrowing authority, powers that cities and counties lack. Consequently, water districts do much more than provide water; they underwrite much of the cost of providing new infrastructure to areas ripe for residential and commercial development. When the growing area is later annexed by Houston, it is the city and its taxpayers who pick up the debt that the annexed area has piled up. Real estate developers profit from this form of publicly subsidized land development. Local democracy, however, is diminished, as the developer-dominated water district governing boards operate with very little accountability to residents.[32]

IS WALT DISNEY WORLD ITS OWN GOVERNMENT?

One of the Disney Corporation's first steps in building Walt Disney World in Florida was to get the state legislature in 1967 to create a new 40-square mile special district, the Reedy Creek Improvement District. The establishment of the district meant that Disney would not have to go to Orlando, Kissimmee, or any other neighboring local government for various development permissions. Within its 40 square-mile zone, Disney possessed the power to decide such matters as land use, building codes, police and fire service, drainage, sewer line extensions, other infrastructure investment, and even the issuance of bonds without having to answer to a wider body of local voters. With its own unit of local government, the Disney Corporation was able to pursue corporate development plans without having to fear the local imposition of growth controls, taxes, impact fees, subsidized housing requirements, and environmental safeguards.

Disney officials dominate the voting in the Reedy Creek district with its small residential population; the board's representatives almost all have a family member who works for Disney. When the Disney-developed new town of Celebration, Florida gained population, it was de-annexed from the Reedy Creek district to ensure that its voters would have no say over Disney's affairs.

Sources: Richard Fogelsong, "When Disney Comes to Town," in *The Politics of Urban America: A Reader*, eds. Dennis R. Judd and Paul P. Kantor (Boston: Allyn and Bacon, 1998), pp. 238–241; Richard E. Foglesong, *Married to the Mouse: Walt Disney World and Orlando* (New Haven, CT: Yale University Press, 2003).

In sum, special districts have proven to be important vehicles for the effective provision of public services across normal local boundary lines. In recent years, spending by special districts has also enabled greater local service provision in the face of state-imposed taxing and borrowing restrictions on general-purpose municipal governments. However, their invisibility and elite-dominated character raise important questions as to the lack of democracy and accountability of governance by special district.

TRANSFER OF FUNCTIONS

A **transfer of functions** entails a permanent shift in service responsibility from one jurisdiction to another that is better able to handle the service. Cities most commonly transfer service responsibilities to the county; on occasion, they also transfer service responsibilities to COGs and special districts. However, not all states allow such a reassignment of functions. A number of states require voter approval before any transfer is finalized.

Advocates usually argue that a transfer of functions will improve service effectiveness and efficiency. Yet concerns for institutional and group interests also influence decisions regarding service transfers. In 1997, voters in West Covina, California overwhelmingly rejected a measure for the Los Angeles County Fire Protection District to absorb the little West Covina Fire Department. Reformers had argued that the more professional county unit could provide faster response times. Yet voters in West Covina suspected that the local firefighters' union had pushed the transfer as a route to gain the county's higher pay levels.[33] In Pima County, Arizona, a proposed reassignment of sewer functions was delayed and a virtual "sewer war" was fought as city and county residents debated effluent rights—a valuable resource in arid Arizona.[34]

ANNEXATION

Under **annexation,** a municipality extends its boundaries outward, absorbing neighboring territory. The laws of each state determine just when an annexation is permitted and what procedures must be followed. In the contemporary urban arena, annexations almost always entail the absorption of unincorporated areas, as most states protect the sovereignty of incorporated municipalities, making the annexation of already-established municipalities exceedingly difficult.

Over half the states require the approval of the area to be annexed before an annexation can proceed.[35] State laws often require **dual referenda;** citizens in both the larger municipality and the area to be annexed are given the right to vote yes or no on a proposed unification, a requirement that makes the annexation of an already-incorporated entity very unlikely. In some special instances, though, special state legislative action, judicial determination, and the rulings of state boundary commissions can produce annexations without dual referenda. Some states also grant municipalities the authority to annex very small land parcels without having to obtain the consent of the residents in the area to be annexed.

Los Angeles, San Francisco, Chicago, Detroit, St. Louis, Milwaukee, Pittsburgh, Cleveland, Boston, and Baltimore are among the nation's **land-locked cities**—cities that are completely surrounded by already incorporated suburban municipalities. Landlocked cities no longer have any real chance to grow through annexation.

Many of America's largest cities grew through annexations carried out toward the end of the nineteenth century. In 1854, Philadelphia used an aggressive annexation approach to expand its land area from two square miles to 136 square miles.[36] A half century later, Los Angeles vigorously pursued annexation, expanding from 108 square miles in 1915 to 415 square miles in 1925. Los Angeles relied on a strategy of **water imperialism;** L.A. refused to supply water to outlying communities unless they accepted incorporation into the city. L.A.'s civic leaders expanded the city's borders "by forcing other communities to accept annexation or die of thirst."[37] (See "Urban Films: *Chinatown* and Los Angeles Water Imperialism," below.)

State laws governing annexation in the Sunbelt have generally been quite permissive. In the 1960s and 1970s, cities in Texas, North Carolina, and California were able to use annexation as a tool for dynamic expansion. In the 1970s, Houston added over 200,000 additional residents through annexations. During the 1980s, the greatest annexations involved Sunbelt and Pacific Rim cities: San Antonio (73,000 persons annexed); Portland, Oregon (54,000);

URBAN FILMS: *CHINATOWN* AND LOS ANGELES WATER IMPERIALISM

Municipal officials in Los Angeles used their control over water as a weapon to annex new territory. The power play of water politics provided the backdrop for Roman Polanski's 1974 *cinema noir* classic, *Chinatown*. The film is based very loosely on the actions taken by Los Angeles water chief William Mulholland in constructing the Owens Valley aqueduct in 1913, a project that brought water from over 200 miles away, fueling the city's growth. San Fernando Valley orchard growers and ranchers charged that Mulholland had stolen their water from the Owens River. During the 1920s, ranchers dynamited sections of the aqueduct in their attempts to obstruct the project.

In Polanski's film, private detective Jake Gittes (Jack Nicholson) is shot at by Valley farmers and nearly has his nose cut off by private goons as he explores the mystery of why Los Angeles is dumping water in the midst of a water shortage. The fruit orchards in the surrounding Valley area are dying for water; their owners are suspicious of the city's machinations. Gittes uncovers a cesspool of power and personal corruption, much of it resulting from a scheme orchestrated by the "city fathers" to force the annexation of Valley land to facilitate the rapid growth and expansion of Los Angeles.

Houston (50,900); and Charlotte (37,700). Phoenix, too, was a national annexation leader, as were other North Carolina cities: Durham, Greensboro, Raleigh, and Winston-Salem.[38]

Local growth regimes pushed annexation. Where a city lacked a sufficient supply of developable land within its borders, developers and their construction and finance industry allies sought the annexation of land for new building sites. Albuquerque in the 1950s and early 1960s annexed sparsely populated acreage at the request of developers who hoped that the provision of city services would add to the marketability of new subdivisions.[39] Houston and Denver each used annexation to acquire the land necessary to build a new international airport.

Oklahoma laws are so permissive that a city can annex any piece of land it surrounds on three sides, even without the permission of the owners of the property in question. Acting under the prompting of the local chamber of commerce, Oklahoma City swallowed up as many land parcels as possible. Neighboring Edmond and other suburbs pursued defensive annexations of their own to block further expansion by Oklahoma City. As a result, Oklahoma City today is landlocked and has little room for new expansion.[40] In Texas, the residents of previously unincorporated suburban areas similarly rushed to incorporate their own municipalities in an effort to stave off annexation efforts by the central city.[41]

Annexation can be a key to a city's good fiscal health. David Rusk, the former mayor of Albuquerque, uses the phrase **elastic cities** to refer to Albuquerque, Charlotte, Houston, San Antonio, Columbus, and other cities that used their annexation powers to capture new suburban development, adding to the local tax base. Nashville and Indianapolis (as we described in Chapter 11, "Suburban Politics and Metropolitan America") can also be considered elastic cities as city-county consolidation afforded them expanded borders, at least for planning and economic development purposes. In contrast, **inelastic cities** such as Hartford, Cleveland, and Detroit are hemmed in by already-incorporated suburbs and cannot absorb the new economic growth taking place outside the city's borders.[42] Elastic cities are largely found in the Sunbelt, especially in the Southwest. Columbus, Ohio is the rare example of an elastic city in the north that successfully used a policy of aggressive annexation to maintain its sound fiscal health.[43]

In recent years, the wave of annexations has receded. Charlotte, Oklahoma City, and other erstwhile annexation leaders have already swallowed up all the easily annexable surrounding territory.[44] As suburban opposition intensified, new protective state legislation made it easier for opponents to fend off possible annexations. (See "Has the Age of Annexation Come to an End in Texas? on p. 424.) The maturation of county governments as service providers also means that unincorporated communities no longer look to a merger with the central city as a means of improving service provision. Only in the West have cities continued to grow via an aggressive strategy of annexations.[45]

HAS THE AGE OF ANNEXATION COME TO AN END IN TEXAS?

A bitter controversy over the largest annexation in the history of Texas led to new state laws that may mark an end to (or, at least, mark the decline of) the age of annexation in Texas. The roots of the controversy go more than two decades back when the City of Houston agreed to provide sewer and water extensions to the newly developed Kingwood subdivision. In return, Kingwood's developer agreed to the area's future annexation by the city whenever Houston's borders reached the subdivision. In 1996, Houston annexed upscale Kingwood, with its 55,000 residents and large homes.

Kingwood's mostly white residents showed up by the busloads at the state capitol. In the years that followed, the "Mother of All Annexation Battles" ensued as they were joined by residents from other parts of the state opposed to annexation efforts by Fort Worth, San Antonio, Austin, and other Texas cities. Leaders of Houston's African-American community, too, were critical of the Kingwood annexation, which they argued would have the effect of diluting black voting power in Houston. The Texas state legislature responded by enacting new laws that made future unilateral annexations more difficult and time consuming.

Sources: Scott N. Houston, "Municipal Annexation in Texas: 'Is It Really All that Complicated?'" (paper presented to the Texas Municipal League Annexation Workshop, Plano, Texas, September 26, 2003). Available at www.tml.org/legal_pdf/AnnexationUT2003.pdf. Also see Myron Orfield, *American Metropolitics: The New Suburban Reality* (Washington, DC: The Brookings Institution Press, 2002), p. 135; and Juliet F. Gainsborough, "Bridging the City-Suburb Divide; States and the Politics of Regional Cooperation," *Journal of Urban Affairs* 23, 5 (2001): 503–504.

REGIONAL DISTRICTS AND AUTHORITIES

Regional districts and authorities are usually established by state law; they can be viewed as metropolitanwide versions of the special district. The Bay Area Rapid Transit District, the Southern California Metropolitan Water District, the Massachusetts Bay Transit Authority, the Chicago Metropolitan Sanitary District, and the Seattle Port District each provide a single service for the region. In southern California, the Orange County Transit Authority and the (Los Angeles County) Metropolitan Transit Authority are virtual subregional governments.[46]

By interstate agreement, the Port Authority of New York and New Jersey has the ability to reach across state lines. In contrast to more narrow-purpose authorities, the Port Authority possesses broad powers in a number of service areas. The Port Authority maintains the New York-New Jersey region's freight terminals and port facilities; it is also involved in regional planning, highway construction, commuter rail and airport operations, and the maintenance of a giant bus terminal. As we saw in Chapter 1, the Port Authority built the original Lower Manhattan World Trade Center and was a major player in the post-9/11 rebuilding at Ground Zero.

Special authorities represent relatively unaccountable islands of power. Just whom do these governing bodies, with their considerable professional talent and financial resources, serve? Regional authorities may represent the interests of financial and development elites; they "are frequently as accountable to bond buyers as to the localities and the citizen consumers."[47]

As we began to describe in Chapter 1, "The Urban Situation and 9/11," during the 1970s, the Port Authority refused to accede to the demands of New York and New Jersey officials that the agency use some of its enormous revenues, garnered from tolls on the region's bridges and tunnels, to help rebuild the region's ailing commuter rail system. The Port Authority was dominated by conservative business executives who refused to commit money to such a "losing" proposition as mass transit, a system that by necessity operated at a deficit. The Port Authority was finally coerced into assuming greater responsibility for a bankrupt New Jersey–New York commuter rail line, but only after New York and New Jersey state officials agreed, in return, to the Authority's demand that it not be saddled with responsibility for other rail problems in the region. The Port Authority also chose to use much of its surplus funds to construct the original World Trade Center, thereby drying up funds that could have been made available for regional rail projects.

In more recent years, the Port Authority has been reined in by New York and New Jersey governors who used their appointment powers to gain greater control over the agency and its financial riches.[48] Each governor appoints half of the Authority's board of commissioners.

Much to the chagrin of New York, New Jersey officials have even sought to assure that New Jersey cities would get their "fair" share of Port Authority-financed building projects. New York Mayor Rudy Giuliani attacked the Port Authority for its policy of subsidizing the PATH (Port Authority-Trans Hudson) commuter rail system while failing to invest in the city's subway lines that serve the region's poorer citizens.[49] After 9/11, the Authority rebuilt the PATH tube station destroyed in the attack and sought to establish a bus link to John F. Kennedy International Airport. It did not seek to formulate a more aggressive or balanced transportation plan in response to the region's needs.[50] Giuliani had also accused the Port Authority of favoring extensive new development of Newark Liberty International Airport in New Jersey (including the opening of an Newark Air Train to speed passengers from Manhattan to the Newark jetport) to the disadvantage of New York's LaGuardia and Kennedy airports.

To a great degree, the Port Authority is "the only planning game in town" that seeks to address the broad development needs of the greater New York–New Jersey–Connecticut region.[51] But the Authority has been a relatively weak force of regionalism. It was unable to get localities to join in a common economic development strategy. Nor could the Authority get state and local actors to respect the regional "nonaggression pact" that the executives of the three states and New York City signed in 1991. The signatories of the Authority-authored agreement promised not to offer incentives to lure businesses away from neighboring communities. But the agreement had little real impact. In the "jobs war" that soon ensued, various jurisdictions offered new tax incentives and a variety of other subsidies in their efforts to entice corporations away from other jurisdictions in the region. New York officials were outraged when the State of New Jersey offered to subsidize the move of over 1,000 First Chicago Trust jobs from the corporation's offices in Lower Manhattan.[52] New York Governor George Pataki blocked expanded operations at the Elizabeth Marine Terminal in New Jersey until New Jersey's governor and appointees to the Authority granted new development concessions to New York City.

METROPOLITAN MULTIPURPOSE DISTRICTS

The Metropolitan Seattle District (known more informally as Metro) was the nation's most prominent example of a **metropolitan multipurpose district,** a regional district that was initially set up to provide a variety of services—including such important functions as sewage treatment and mass transit—until its absorption in the mid-1990s by King County. Metro's successes were so important that in 1960 it became the first "noncity" to win the National Civic League's "All-American City" award. Metro even possessed the ability to veto proposed developments that violated the region's urban growth boundary.

But in 1990, a U.S. District Court found that Metro, run by 45 members appointed by the participating local jurisdictions, violated the equal protection of citizens' voting rights. The Court ruled that Metro was a general-purpose local government with a governing body that must meet one-person-one-vote standards. As a result of the ruling, Metro, with its nonelected governing structure, could not longer continue to exist. In 1994, King County absorbed Metro. Metro died, but King County became the nation's most preeminent example of strengthened county government.[53]

STRENGTHENED COUNTY GOVERNMENT

Counties were once America's "forgotten governments"[54]—backward, rural oriented, understaffed, dominated by part-time elected representatives, and generally ill-structured for effective action. In more recent years, however, growing suburban populations, especially in the unincorporated parts of the metropolis, have demanded that urban counties modernize and provide improved, more professional services. As a result, urban and suburban counties assumed new service responsibilities in such areas as health and hospitals, public welfare, education, corrections, and environmental protection. Los Angeles County's role in service provision is so well established and so strong that the City of Compton dissolved its own police force in favor of contracting with the county for sheriff's services. Pomona similarly decided to have fire protection provided by the county.[55]

Counties found new revenue streams to finance heightened levels of service.[56] Counties have also initiated new economic development strategies, including efforts to market the entire county area to outside investors, including investors from overseas.[57]

Urban and suburban counties have also modernized their structures of government, turning away from the traditional **county commission** arrangement under which part-time elected officials directed the daily operations of county departments. Such part-time, amateur government lacked the expertise necessary to combat more serious urban problems.

The modernized **reformed urban and suburban county** has three variations. The **county administrator plan** gives the part-time legislature a full-time chief administrative officer (CAO) to assist in staff work, budget preparation, and the administration of its policies. More far-reaching is the **county manager plan,** which places even greater power in the hands of a professional executive who is authorized to coordinate a city's administrative affairs. The county manager plan is analogous to the city manager plan discussed in Chapter 5, "Formal Structure and Leadership Style."

The final reform plan, **the county executive plan,** is analogous to the strong-mayor system also described in Chapter 5. Under this plan, the voters directly elect an executive who is the political, administrative, and symbolic leader of the county. St. Louis County (Missouri); Nassau and Westchester Counties (New York); Bergen County (New Jersey); Wayne County (Michigan); Allegheny County (Pennsylvania); and Baltimore, Montgomery, and Prince George's Counties (Maryland) are all prominent examples of suburban counties that use the elected executive form of government. In contrast, as of 2001 none of California's 58 counties adopted the elected executive plan—that is, none except San Francisco, which is simultaneously a city and a county and has an elected mayor.[58]

In Florida, growing counties that switched to a "reformed" or "modernized" form of county government increased their spending for public services.[59] Yet counties are not important service providers in every state. Maryland counties possess important governing powers. In New England, in contrast, tradition vests powers in towns, and counties are not especially important units of local government. County governments in Massachusetts are weak; in a cost-saving move, the state legislature even abolished the governments of Middlesex, Worcester, and Hampden counties. Connecticut and Rhode Island have no meaningful county government.

Counties are no longer the forgotten governments. But even the modernized urban county cannot provide for regional vision and leadership beyond a county's lines. In the more than 150 metropolitan areas that spill over into two or more counties, enhanced county government represents, at best, only a subregional approach to metropolitan problems.

TOWARD A NEW REGIONALISM?

In recent years, cities and suburbs have begun to explore a new style of regional cooperation, especially in developing joint strategies and proposals for the pursuit of economic growth. Cooperative efforts can even extend well beyond the borders of a Metropolitan Statistical Area. Officials in Buffalo, New York, for instance, have established economic links with Rochester and

Toronto in developing a strategy to attract biomedical and other high-tech jobs to the entire region.[60]

A **new regionalism** emphasizes the formation of *ad hoc* metropolitan partnerships, attempts to find a joint solution to a particular problem, especially in the pursuit of economic development. Under the new regionalism, there is no effort to build a new system of metropolitan government; nor do communities attempt to enter into the more formalized intergovernmental arrangements that we described previously in this chapter.[61] Instead, private and nonprofit associations take the lead in arranging cooperative efforts that cross political borders.

The San Diego Regional Biology Initiative is typical of the new regionalism with its flexible and pragmatic patterns of cooperation. In San Diego, the vehicle of cooperation has largely been nongovernmental. The San Diego Regional Economic Development Corporation, the San Diego Association of Governments, BIOCOM (an industry association), and local universities all came together in an effort to help defense-related industries convert to other projects and to bring new biotechnology and biomedical jobs to the region.[62] South of San Francisco, the Silicon Valley Manufacturers Group (SVMG) has similarly worked to promote regional efforts to combat traffic congestion and sprawl, which have lengthened the time of workers' commutes and hurt Santa Clara County's competitive economic position.[63]

Environmentalists have looked to regional collaborations as a means of building regional transportation systems and initiating steps to contain urban sprawl. Antipoverty activists, too, have sought regional action to reduce the social isolation of the residents of the inner city and inner-ring suburbs. Still, despite these efforts, it is the concern for economic development that dominates the new regionalism: "Today's regional proponents spend little effort arguing the need to avoid waste and duplication . . . or calling on suburban America to accept their moral responsibility to care for the nation's cities. Instead, they argue that regional cooperation makes for optimal economic growth."[64]

Regional economic cooperation represents the most recent wave of metropolitanism.[65] The marketplace values an integrated, total labor market.[66] When it comes to attracting new businesses, communities in a metropolis find virtues in working together as they compete with communities in other regions.[67] Indeed, the United States can be viewed as a nation of competing local economic regions where the "economic fates and fortunes of cities and suburbs are inextricably interwoven."[68]

A high-tech firm may look favorably on the prospects of locating new facilities in a well-to-do technoburb; yet the firm's officers may be reluctant to build new facilities in a community where housing prices are so prohibitively high that the company will face great difficulty in recruiting workers who may have to reside 50 or more miles from work. A community's attractiveness to the corporation will increase if a regional planning team can assure corporate officials that a sufficient supply of attractive, affordable housing will be built in nearby jurisdictions.

Regional cooperation is a response to the economic interdependence of cities and suburbs in a global economy. Standing alone, no city or suburb can provide the airports, universities, land, transportation, material resources, and trained labor force demanded by businesses in a high-tech age.[69]

In an age of globalism, the "real city," according to urban journalist Neal Peirce, is in fact a **citistate** that is regional in scope and recognizes the economic interconnections of communities with a shared workforce and a shared economic and social future. Peirce argues that citistates must work together to marshal their internal strengths and "find a profitable niche in the new world economy."[70]

BUSINESS POWER AND THE NEW REGIONALISM

Local chambers of commerce, other business groups, governmental officials, nonprofit organizations, and citizen associations have been key players in various new regional partnerships. In Charlotte, for instance, the local university was asked to play a leading role in developing a regional marketing plan and in forging other efforts at regional cooperation. The university was seen to be a neutral third party with no turf of its own to protect.[71]

Regional business leaders, though, are most frequently the driving force behind the new regionalism. The Allegheny Conference on Community Development, Cleveland Tomorrow, and the Greater Houston Partnership are only a few of the business-led economic development partnerships that transcend local boundaries.[72] In the Allegheny Conference, private, nonprofit, and public institutions all worked together to "re-vision" a niche for the greater Pittsburgh region in a globalized, post-industrial economy. Private-sector groups helped to underwrite a planning process to overcome the severe political fragmentation of the region (with over 300 units of government in Allegheny County alone). The result was a plan for greater Pittsburgh to diversify its economy, making the switch from steel manufacturing to a high-tech and office headquarters economy.[73] In 1996, the Greater Pittsburgh Chamber of Commerce and five other industrial development councils formed a second public-private umbrella organization, the Pittsburgh Regional Alliance, to enhance coordination and collaboration on economic development projects in the region.[74]

In the greater Denver area, 40 local chambers of commerce pulled together to form the Denver Metropolitan Network to market the region to national corporations. When the city of Denver found that it could not gain the location of a new federal engraving and printing plant, it assisted neighboring Aurora in its efforts to win the competition for the new facility. Similarly, when Sears, Roebuck & Co. announced its intention to move its offices out of its namesake landmark skyscraper tower in downtown Chicago, numerous communities in the greater Chicago area and the State of Illinois joined together in an effort to keep as many of the company's jobs as possible in the region. Sears finally settled on a new suburban campus in Hoffman Estates, in the region's northwestern suburbs. Concerns for global competitiveness have also led the Commercial Club of Chicago, "a long-standing blue ribbon organization of Chicago's corporate elite," to initiate Metropolitan 2020, a call for increased regional cooperation in transit, housing, and other important matters.[75]

Miami's Beacon Council, the Greater Denver Corporation, and Cleveland Tomorrow are three business-led coalitions that have helped to determine the local regional agenda. These and similar associations assume the status of **shadow**

governments capable of making decisions regarding planning and investment in the region, with no clear accountability to the public.[76] An elite-dominated regional growth machine (or, to be more precise, a "smart-growth machine"[77]) pushed for the creation of the Greater Regional Transportation Authority, a state body with new powers to curb the traffic problems that were threatening the future economic vitality of the greater Atlanta region. (See "Atlanta Begins to Confront Sprawl: The Greater Regional Transportation Authority," below.)

ATLANTA BEGINS TO CONFRONT SPRAWL: THE GREATER REGIONAL TRANSPORTATION AUTHORITY

Atlanta has been the poster child for urban sprawl. During the 1980s and 1990s, the population of the region doubled, and new growth consumed an additional 500 additional acres a week. Atlantans suffered the longest traffic commutes and some of the worst air pollution in the nation.

Regional business advocates, civic leaders, and state lawmakers feared that unabated traffic congestion and highly polluted air would pose a substantial barrier to future economic growth. When Hewlett-Packard abandoned its plans for a second office tower for 1,700 workers on one of the region's traffic-clogged perimeter roads, state officials acted. The state in 1999 created a new "superagency," the Georgia Regional Transportation Authority (GRTA), a 15-member board appointed by the governor, with the ability to curb sprawl and promote smart growth, even by overriding local land-use and transportation decisions, if necessary.

The GRTA has authority over a 13-county region. Yet whether the GRTA proves to be effective in promoting regionalism and curbing sprawl remains to be seen. The GRTA was initially quite cautious in its actions, seeking to avoid the resentment of local governments and automobile commuters. Environmentalists criticized GRTA for approving the Northern Arc highway project in the outlying northeastern and northwestern portions of the region.

Still, the GRTA has the power to extend bus and rail lines. It has also threatened to withhold assistance from counties that refused to allow higher density residential and commercial development in designated transportation corridors. The GRTA can also withhold its approval of large development projects that will compound traffic and pollution problems. A locality, however, by a three-fourths vote, can override the GRTA's veto.

Grassroots representation on the authority is weak. Reflecting GRTA's business roots, 12 of the initial 15 appointments came from the business community, including a prominent developer of suburban apartment complexes.

Sources: Neal Peirce and Curtis Johnson, "Atlanta: Fame and Fall," excerpt from *Part 2 of The Peirce Report*, September 26, 1999, available at www.citistates.com/Tnatlant.htm; Charles Jaret, "Suburban Expansion in Atlanta: 'The City Without Limits' Faces Some," in *Urban Sprawl: Causes, Consequences and Policy Responses* (Washington, DC: Urban Institute Press, 2002), pp. 165–205; Ulf Zimmermann, Goktug Morcol, and Bethany Stich, "From Sprawl to Smart Growth: The Case of Atlanta," in *Suburban Sprawl: Culture, Theory, and Politics* (Lanham, MD: Rowman and Littlefield, 2003), pp. 275–287.

The new corporate-led regionalism is real. Yet the promise of shared benefits is not always sufficient to override local self interest. As previously observed in this chapter, the Port Authority of New York and New Jersey could not get state and local jurisdictions to abide by an economic nonaggression pact. Especially in older metropolitan areas, interlocal inequalities and a history of suspicions continue to undercut the prospects of regional cooperation.

Detroit's economically troubled "downriver" communities pulled together in a successful joint effort to get Mazda to build a new automobile assembly plant in Flat Rock, the site of a closed Ford plant. But the partnership soon dissolved as each community sought to undercut its neighbors in an effort to attract Mazda's suppliers.[78] Similarly in St. Louis, business leaders faced great difficulty in building a new regional airport; the social distance between communities and entrenched parochialism blocked regional unity even on a project crucial to the region's future economic development.[79]

Interregional and global competition will lead to new-style metropolitan cooperation, but it will not usher in a golden age of regionalism. The evidence of the economic benefits that each community realizes from cooperation is weaker than is often supposed.[80] A survey of local officials clearly reveals that cities and suburbs continue to see communities in their immediate metropolitan area and in their state and neighboring states—not communities in other regions or in foreign nations—as their primary competitors.[81]

BEYOND THE BUSINESS COMMUNITY:
THE CREATIVE POLITICS OF REGIONAL ALLIANCES

New-style regional alliances can be built beyond the economic development arena only if regional leaders act creatively to find solutions around which win-win partnerships can be structured. Myron Orfield, a member of the Minnesota House of Representatives, argues that if historical city-suburban suspicions can be overcome, an effective coalition of central cities and lesser advantaged suburbs can be built around such issues as regional "fair share" housing and the redirection of infrastructure subsidies and future economic growth to more needy communities. Central cities, declining suburbs, and low-tax-base-but-quickly-growing communities all can benefit from redirecting subsidies and economic investment away from a region's more prosperous or "favored quarter" suburbs.[82] If more affluent communities "don't start to build affordable housing," as the mayor of one older suburb explained, "we'll be swimming in this stuff."[83]

The issues of environmentalism, "smart" land use, and farmland preservation offer opportunities for central city-suburban cooperation—and even the possible formation of a city-farm alliance. In Portland, Oregon, environmentalists, farmers, business interests, and urbanists all came together to support growth-management measures to maintain the region's long-term attractiveness and economic competitiveness.[84] In Ohio, the First Suburbs Consortium organized a statewide coalition behind the Agricultural Preservation Act. Older suburbs and central cities saw themselves as losers when productive farmland was converted to sites for new sprawl development.[85]

Church groups and nonprofit associations add a moral dimension to the call for increased regional cooperation. In the mid-1990s, hundreds of church congregations and religious associations pushed the Minnesota state legislature for regional fair-housing and social justice legislation.[86] In northwest Indiana, an interfaith federation cut across racial and jurisdictional lines to block a planned move of the county juvenile courts from troubled City of Gary to Crown Point.[87] In the Chicago region, United Power, a 240-member coalition of church groups, labor unions, and nonprofit organizations, sought to build city-suburban connections to provide better health care and improved homeownership opportunities for low- and middle-income families.[88] Nonprofit grant givers such as the Washington Regional Association of Grantmakers, the Association of Baltimore Area Grantmakers, and the Southern California Association for Philanthropy have also encouraged community building across local borders.[89]

In Chicago, Mayor Richard M. Daley reached out to the suburbs and formed the Metropolitan Mayors Caucus to discuss common problems and pursue solutions of mutual benefit. The Caucus does not attempt to handle such divisive matters as the expansion of O'Hare International Airport or the development of a third airport for the region. The Mayors Caucus focused its early efforts on clean air, regional economic development, and even Daley's proposed gun control initiative—areas in which the city and suburbs have mutual concerns.[90]

CONCLUSIONS: POLITICAL POWER AND THE FUTURE OF METROPOLITAN REFORM

Even in the absence of full-fledged, metropolitan *governments,* extensive interlocal cooperation is possible. Regional cooperation or *governance* produces shared benefits and economies of scale. Especially promising are the prospects for new-style public-private partnerships that extend across local jurisdictional borders in the search for new economic development. In the bidding war that ensued after the Boeing Corporation's announcement to move its headquarters from Seattle, the Chicago, Denver, and Seattle metropolitan areas each submitted a regional proposal, as Boeing had required. The promise of Boeing's investments and jobs was just too much for communities to pass up.[91]

Environmentalists, too, have come to recognize the value of regional action in promoting smart growth and curbing sprawl. Faith-based and nonprofit groups have similarly worked across jurisdictional lines in an effort to attack housing and equity problems. Metropolitan reformers often pursue a "foot in the door" strategy to regionalism, building from more modest steps and expanding to more innovative win-win solutions.[92]

But new-style regional cooperation lacks public visibility; such efforts are seldom headed by elected officials.[93] Regional action is less likely in subsidized housing and other policy areas in which questions of redistribution and racial integration are at stake.[94] Critics argue that voluntary or lowest-common-denominator cooperation should not be mistaken for true regional governance.[95]

Business associations and business-led coalitions are frequently the dominant actors in regional efforts, raising important questions as to a **democratic deficit** in the new regionalism.[96] Business-led efforts, quite naturally, shift the regional agenda toward business concerns. Citizen and neighborhood groups often find it more difficult to pressure such regional bodies and private-led associations than to pressure city hall. The involvement of nonprofit and community-based leaders is essential to moderate the pro-business orientation of the new regionalism. In Minneapolis and St. Paul, church groups have been particularly important in providing the pressure for regional fair share housing action.

State and federal actions are key influences on regionalism. State rules can facilitate or impede local annexations. The states can redraw jurisdictional lines, create new regional authorities and districts, redefine service boundaries, require growth management and open land preservation, and provide subsidies for interlocal collaboration. New Jersey offers local communities grants and loans to develop new shared service strategies. New Jersey's Regional Efficiency Aid Program (REAP) even offers tax credits to taxpayers who live in communities that enter into shared service agreements.[97]

The federal government, at times, has also promoted regional action. ISTEA and TEA-21 forced regional action in transportation and environmental planning. The threat of federal clean air penalties also helped prompt Georgia officials to create the GRTA and exert greater control over the direction of development in Atlanta, which suffers some of the worst ozone levels in the country. Similarly, in greater Chicago, the region's continuing status as a "severe nonattainment" zone under the federal Clean Air Act prompted civic and business leaders to launch the Regional Dialogue on Clean Air and Redevelopment.[98]

In our next chapter, we provide a more full description of the impact of state and federal policy on cities and suburbs.

NOTES

1. David Walker, "Snow White and the 17 Dwarfs: From Metro Cooperation to Governance," *National Civil Review* 76 (January/February 1987): 16–17. Walker's typology builds on the earlier work of Roscoe C. Martin, *Metropolis in Transition* (Washington, DC: Housing and Home Financing Agency, 1963). David B. Walker, *The Rebirth of Federalism: Slouching Toward Washington* (Chatham, NJ: Chatham House, 1995), Chap. 9.
2. Lisa Belkin, "Separated by Border, 2 Cities Are United by Needs," *The New York Times,* December 17, 1988.
3. Samuel Schmidt, "Planning a U.S.-Mexican Bi-National Metropolis: El Paso, Texas-Ciudad Juarez, Chihuahua," in *North American Cities and the Global Economy: Challenges and Opportunities, Urban Affairs Annual Review* 44, eds. Peter Karl Kresl and Gary Gappert (Thousand Oaks, CA: Sage Publications, 1995): 201–203 and 216 (footnote 24).
4. Patricia S. Atkins, "Local Intergovernmental Agreements: Strategies for Cooperation," *MIS (Management Information Service) Report,* a publication of the International City Management Association, 29, 7 (July 1997): 5–6.

5. Atkins, "Local Intergovernmental Agreements: Strategies for Cooperation," pp. 2–3. Also see David W. Tees, Richard L. Cole, and Seth S. Searcy, *Durable Partnerships: The Interlocal Contract at Mid-Decade* (Arlington, TX: University of Texas at Arlington Institute for Urban Studies, 1995) for a review of the variety and reach of interlocal agreements in Texas.

6. Michaela Jarvis, "Joint Library Plan Splits Cities: 4 Cities Approve So Far-Tax Rich Woodside Balks," *San Francisco Chronicle*, July 4, 1998; Richard Edward DeLeon, *Left Coast City: Progressive Politics in San Francisco, 1975–91* (Lawrence: University of Kansas Press, 1992), p. 111.

7. Atkins, "Local Intergovernmental Agreements: Strategies for Cooperation," p. 5.

8. Lyke Thompson, "The Interlaced Metropolis: Cities in Layered Networks and Confederations in the Detroit Metropolitan Area" (paper presented at the annual meeting of the Urban Affairs Association, Fort Worth, Texas, April 1998).

9. Donald F. Kettl, *System under Stress: Homeland Security and American Politics* (Washington, DC: CQ Press, 2003), pp. 30–31 and 63–66.

10. David Rusk, *Cities Without Suburbs* (Washington, DC: Woodrow Wilson Center Press, 1993).

11. Robert E. Parker and Joe R. Feagin, "Houston: Administration by Economic Elites," in *Big City Politics in Transition,* eds. H. V. Savitch and John Clayton Thomas (Newbury Park, CA: Sage Publications, 1991), pp. 185–187.

12. Walker, "Snow White and the 17 Dwarfs," p. 18; James H. Svara, "Setting a Regional Agenda for Councils of Government in North Carolina" (paper presented at the annual meeting of the Urban Affairs Association, Cleveland, April 1992); Donald F. Norris, "Killing a COG: The Death and Reincarnation of the Baltimore Regional Council of Governments," *Journal of Urban Affairs* 16 (1994): 157–158.

13. Juliet F. Gainsborough, "Bridging the City-Suburb Divide: States and the Politics of Regional Cooperation," *Journal of Urban Affairs* 23, 5 (2001): 506.

14. Wim Wiewel and Kimberly Schaffer, "Learning to Think as a Region: Connecting Suburban Sprawl and City Poverty," *European Planning Studies* 9, 5 (2001): 608.

15. Jeffrey Henig, David Brunori, and Mark Ebert, "Washington, DC: Cautious and Constrained Cooperation," in *Regional Politics: America in a Post-City Age, Urban Affairs Annual Review,* vol. 45, eds. H. V. Savitch and Ronald K. Vogel (Thousand Oaks, CA: Sage Publications, 1996), pp. 101–129).

16. James P. Lester and Emmett N. Lombard, "Environmental Regulation and State-Local Relations," in *Governing Partners: State-Local Relations in the United States,* ed. Russell L. Hanson (Boulder, CO: Westview Press, 1998), pp. 155–158.

17. Sheldon Edner, community planner for the Federal Highway Administration, cited by James H. Andrews, "Metro Power: With ISTEA, MPO's Have Found There's No Such Thing as Politics as Usual," *Planning* 62, 6 (June 1996): 8ff. Also see U.S. General Accounting Office, *Urban Transportation: Metropolitan Planning Organizations' Efforts to Meet Federal Planning Requirements,* GAO/RCED-96-200 (Washington, DC: USGPO, September 1996).

18. Bruce Katz, Robert Puentes, and Scott Bernstein, "TEA-21 Reauthorization: Getting Transportation Right for Metropolitan America," a paper prepared for The Brookings Institution Center on Urban and Metropolitan Policy, Washington, DC, March 2003, p. 4. Available at www.brookings.edu/es/urban/publications/tea21.htm.

19. Marina O'Neill, "Utah Searches for Way to Slow Urban Sprawl," *Standard-Examiner,* September 21, 1997.

20. Katz, Puentes, and Bernstein, "TEA-21 Reauthorization," pp. 6–7.

21. Bonnie Lindstrom, "Regional Cooperation and Sustainable Growth: Nine Councils of Government in Northeastern Illinois," *Journal of Urban Affairs* 20, 3 (1998): 327–342.

22. Robert W. Gage, "ISTEA and the Role of MPOs in the New Transportation Environment: A Midterm Assessment," *Publius: The Journal of Federalism* 25, 3 (Summer 1995): 135; and Andrews, "Metro Power: With ISTEA, MPO's Have Found There's No Such Thing as Politics as Usual," p. 8.

23. Katz, Puentes, and Bernstein, "TEA-21 Reauthorization," p. 4.

24. Anthony Downs, *New Visions for Metropolitan America* (Washington, DC: Brookings Institution, 1994), pp. 174–175; Neal R. Peirce, with Curtis W. Johnson and Stuart Hall, *Citistates: How Urban America Can Prosper in a Competitive World* (Seven Locks Press, 1994), pp. 6 and 32; and Alan L. Saltzstein, "Los Angeles: Politics Without Governance," in *Regional Politics in a Post-City Age, Urban Affairs Annual Review,* vol. 45, eds. H. V. Savitch and Ronald K. Vogel (Thousand Oaks, CA: Sage Publications, 1996), pp. 59–65.

25. U. S. Census Bureau, "2002 Census of Governments," GC02-1(P), July 2002. www.census.gov/govs/cog/2002COGprelim_report.pdf.

26. Kathryn A. Foster, "Specialization in Government: The Uneven Use of Special Districts in Metropolitan Areas," *Urban Affairs Review* 31, 3 (January 1996): 289, observes that two special districts can differ quite considerably in terms of their size and "their reasons for being." For her review of the variety of special district governments, see Foster, *The Political Economy of Special-Purpose Governments* (Washington, DC: Georgetown University Press, 1999).

27. Brett W. Hawkins and Rebecca M. Hendrick, "Do Metropolitan Special Districts Reinforce Sociospatial Inequalities? A Study of Sewerage and Technical Education in Milwaukee County," *Publius: The Journal of Federalism* 27, 1 (Winter 1997): 135–143.

28. Samuel Nunn and Carl Schoedel, "Special Districts, City Governments, and Infrastructure: Spending in 105 Metropolitan Areas," *Journal of Urban Affairs* 19, 1 (1997): 66–67.

29. Gerald Benjamin and Richard P. Nathan, *Regionalism and Realism: A Study of Governments in the New York Metropolitan Area* (Washington, DC; Brookings Institution Press, 2001), pp. 22–23 and 27. Michael N. Danielson and Jameson W. Doig, *New York: The Politics of Urban Regional Development* (Berkeley: University of California Press, 1982), p. 4, report that there are 661 independent school districts in the New York Metropolitan area.

30. Virginia Marion Perrenod, *Special Districts, Special Purposes: Fringe Governments and Urban Problems in the Houston Area* (College Station: Texas A&M University Press, 1984). The reference to junior cities is from John C. Bollens, *Special District Government in the United States* (Westport, CT: Greenwood Press, 1957), p. 114, and is cited by Perrenod, p. 3. For the classic statement as to the visibility and accountability problems that special districts pose, see Stanley Scott and John Corzine, "Special Districts in the Bay Area," in *Metropolitan Politics: A Reader,* 2nd ed., ed. Michael N. Danielson (Boston: Little, Brown, 1971), pp. 201–213.

31. Foster, *The Political Economy of Special-Purpose Government,* pp. 103–104; Nancy Burns, *The Formation of American Local Governments: Private Values in*

Public Institutions (New York: Oxford University Press, 1994), pp. 4–6, 14–15, 25–32, and 114–117.

32. Perrenod, *Special Districts, Special Purposes.*

33. "West Covina: Voters Reject Fire Dept. Merger with L.A. County," *Los Angeles Times,* December 11, 1997.

34. Keith J. Mueller, "The Politics of Functional Realignment: Consolidating Wastewater Management in an Urban County," *Journal of Urban Affairs* 4 (Winter 1982): 67–79.

35. Jamie L. Palmer and Greg Lindsey, "Classifying State Approaches to Annexation," *State and Local Government Review* 33, 1 (Winter 2001): 68–69.

36. Joel C. Miller, "Municipal Annexation and Boundary Change," *Municipal Year Book 1986* (Washington, DC: International City Management Association, 1986), p. 77.

37. David L. Clark, "Improbable Los Angeles," in *Sunbelt Cities: Politics and Growth Since World War II,* eds. Richard M. Bernard and Bradley R. Rice (Austin: University of Texas Press, 1983), p. 274. Details of Los Angeles' annexation policy during this period are provided by Robert M. Fogelson, *The Fragmented Metropolis: Los Angeles, 1850–1930* (Cambridge, MA: Harvard University Press, 1967), pp. 223–228.

38. Miller, "Municipal Annexation and Boundary Change," *Municipal Year Book 1986,* p. 77; Joel Miller, "Annexations and Boundary Changes in the 1980s and 1990–91," *Municipal Year Book 1993* (Washington, DC: International City/County Management Association, 1993), p. 104.

39. Howard N. Rabinowitz, "Albuquerque: City at a Crossroads," in *Sunbelt Cities: Politics and Growth Since World War II,* eds. Richard M. Bernard and Bradley R. Rice (Austin: University of Texas Press, 1983), pp. 258–259.

40. Richard M. Bernard, "Oklahoma City: Booming Sooner," in *Sunbelt Cities: Politics and Growth Since World War II,* eds. Richard M. Bernard and Bradley R. Rice, p. 222.

41. Platon N. Rigos and Charles J. Spindler, "Municipal Incorporation as a Defense against Annexation: The Case of Texas" (paper presented at the annual meeting of the Urban Affairs Association, Vancouver, BC, April 1991).

42. Rusk, *Cities Without Suburbs,* pp. 9–12, 17–23, 29–38, and 41–44; Rusk, *Inside Game/Outside Game: Winning Strategies for Saving Urban America* (Washington, DC: Brookings Institution Press, 1999), pp. 3–10 and 126–145.

43. Ziona Austrian and Thomas Bier, "Importance of Land Assembly to Central Urban Counties in the Great Lakes" (paper presented at the annual meeting of the Urban Affairs Association, New York City, March 14, 1996).

44. Timothy D. Mead, "Governing Charlotte-Mecklenburg," *State and Local Government Review* 32, 3 (Fall 2000): 194.

45. David Y. Miller, *The Regional Governing of Metropolitan Areas* (Boulder, CO; Westview, 2002), pp. 120–122.

46. Saltzstein, "Los Angeles: Politics Without Governance," p. 66.

47. Walker, "Snow White and the 17 Dwarfs," p. 22.

48. Jameson Doig, *Empire on the Hudson: Entrepreneurial Vision and Political Power at the Port of New York Authority* (New York; Columbia University Press, 2002), pp. 379–386 and 397–402; Benjamin and Nathan, *Regionalism and Realism,* pp. 126–134.

49. Benjamin and Nathan, *Regionalism and Realism,* p. 125.

50. Susan Fainstein, "The Port Authority of New York and New Jersey and the Rebuilding of the World Trade Center" (paper presented at the annual meeting of the Urban Affairs Association, Washington, DC, April 1, 2004).

51. Bruce Berg and Paul Kantor, "New York: The Politics of Conflict and Avoidance," in *Regional Politics in a Post-City Age,* eds. Savitch and Vogel, p. 39. Their reference to "the only game in town" refers to Annmarie Walsh and James Leigland, "The Only Planning Game in Town," *Empire State Report* (May 1983): 6–12.

52. Berg and Kantor, "New York: The Politics of Conflict and Avoidance," pp. 39–50.

53. Allan D. Wallis, "Inventing Regionalism: The First Two Waves," *National Civic Review* (Spring-Summer 1994): 170–171; David Rusk, *Baltimore Unbound: A Strategy for Regional Renewal* (Baltimore, MD: Abell Foundation, 1996), pp. 45–46.

54. Vincent L. Marando and Robert D. Thomas, *The Forgotten Governments: County Commissioners as Policy Makers* (Gainesville, FL: Florida Atlantic University/University Presses of Florida, 1977).

55. For a description of Los Angeles County's heightened role in municipal service provision, see Christopher Hoene, Mark Baldassare, and Michael Shires, "The Development of Counties as Municipal Governments: A Case Study of Los Angeles County in the Twenty-First Century," *Urban Affairs Review* 37, 4 (March 2002): 575–592.

56. Victor S. DeSantis, "County Government: A Century of Change," *Municipal Year Book 1989* (Washington, DC: International City Management Association, 1989), p. 63. Also see Kee Ok Park, "Determinants of County Growth," pp. 34–36, and Beverly A. Cigler, "Revenue Diversification Among American Counties," pp. 166–183, both in *The American County: Frontiers of Knowledge,* eds. Donald C. Menzel and John P. Thomas (Tuscaloosa, AL: University of Alabama Press, 1996).

57. William J. Pammer, Jr., "Economic Development Strategies among Counties," in *The American County,* pp. 184–199.

58. Raphael J. Sonenshein, "The Prospects for County Charter Reform in California," a report of the California State University Faculty Research Fellows Program, March 2001. Available at www.csus.edu/calst/government_affairs/reports/countyreform.pdf.

59. J. Edwin Benton, "The Impact of Structural Reform on County Government Service Provision," *Social Science Quarterly,* 84, 4 (December 2003): 858.

60. David Perry, remarks at the "Colloquy on Regional Economic Governance" (panel presentation to the annual meeting of the Urban Affairs Association, Louisville, Kentucky, April 16, 1999).

61. Peirce, with Johnson and Hall, *Citistates,* pp. 322–323.

62. Barry Bluestone, Joan Fitzgerald, David Perry, and Martin Jaffe, "The New Metropolitan Alliances: Regional Collaboration for Economic Development," a report prepared for CEOs for Cities, Boston, 2002. Available at www.ceosforcities.org/research/2002/regional_alliances/Metro%20Report.pdf.

63. Henry R. Richmond, "Metropolitan Land-Use Reform: The Promise and Challenge of Majority Consensus," in *Reflections on Regionalism,* ed. Bruce Katz (Washington, DC: Brookings Institution Press, 2000), pp. 24–25

64. Norman Krumholz, "Regionalism Redux," *Public Administration Review* 57, 1 (January/February 1997): 84.

65. Wallis, "Inventing Regionalism: The First Two Waves," pp. 159–175; Allan D. Wallis, "The Third Wave: Current Trends in Regional Governance," *National Civic Review* 83 (Summer-Fall 1994): 290–310; and Allan D. Wallis, "Inventing Regionalism: A Two-Phase Approach," *National Civic Review* 83 (Fall-Winter 1994): 447–468.

66. Rusk, *Cities Without Suburbs*, p. 86.

67. William R. Dodge, "Strengthening Intercommunity/Regional Governance: New Strategies for Intercommunity Problem Solving and Service Delivery" (paper presented at the annual meeting of the National Civic League, Minneapolis, September 19–21, 1991); and John J. Kirlin, "Citistates and Regional Governance," *National Civic Review* 82 (Fall 1993): 371–379.

68. William R. Barnes and Larry C. Ledebur, *Local Economies: The U.S. Common Market of Local Economic Regions* (Washington, DC: National League of Cities, 1994), p. 11.

69. Hank V. Savitch and Ron Vogel, "Regional Patterns in a Post-City Age" (paper presented at the annual meeting of the American Political Science Association, New York, September 1994). A revised version of this paper appears in their book *Regional Patterns in a Post-City Age.*

70. Peirce, with Johnson and Hall, *Citistates*, p. 292. Also see pp. 6 and 33–34.

71. William J. McCoy and Michael Gallis, "Regional Approaches: The Charlotte Region" (paper presented at the annual meeting of the Urban Affairs Association, Indianapolis, April 21–24, 1993). Also see Peirce, with Johnson and Hall, *Citistates*, pp. 322–323.

72. Krumholz, "Regionalism Redux," p. 88.

73. Louise Jezierski, "Pittsburgh: Partnerships in a Regional City," in *Regional Politics in a Post-City Age,* eds. Savitch and Vogel, pp. 159–181; H. V. Savitch and Ronald K. Vogel, "Perspectives for the Present and Lessons for the Future," in *Regional Politics in a Post-City Age,* eds. Savitch and Vogel, p. 292.

74. Bill Barnes, "Broad Cooperation among Organizations Aids Pittsburgh's Development Scene," *Nation's Cities Weekly,* February 15, 1999.

75. Wiewel and Schaffer, "Learning to Think as a Region," pp. 608–609; David K. Hamilton, "Regionalism in Metropolitan Chicago: A Work in Progress," *National Civic Review* 91, 1 (Spring 2002): 63–81.

76. This paragraph is based on Rosabeth Moss Kanter, "Business Coalitions as a Force for Regionalism," in *Reflections on Regionalism*, pp. 154–181.

77. Ulf Zimmermann, Goktug Morcol, and Bethany Stich, "From Sprawl to Smart Growth: The Case of Atlanta," in *Suburban Sprawl: Culture, Theory, and Politics* (Lanham, MD: Rowman and Littlefield, 2003), pp. 276–277.

78. Michael Indergaard, "Beyond the Region: The Rise and Fall of Economic Regionalism in Downriver Detroit," *Urban Affairs Review* 34, 2 (November 1998): 241–262.

79. Alan V. Tucker, "The Politics of Airport Expansion in Denver and St. Louis" (paper presented at the annual meeting of the American Political Science Association, New York, September 1–4, 1994).

80. Todd Swanstrom, "What We Argue About When We Argue About Regionalism," *Journal of Urban Affairs* 23, 5 (2001): 479–496.

81. John Kincaid, *American Cities in the Global Economy: A Survey of Municipalities on Activities and Attitudes* (Washington, DC: National League of Cities, 1997), especially p. 30.

82. Myron Orfield, *Metropolitics: A Regional Agenda for Community and Stability* (Washington, DC: The Brookings Institution, 1997, 1998), pp. 104–172.

83. Myron Orfield, "Conflict or Consensus? Forty Years of Minnesota Metropolitan Politics," *The Brookings Review* 16, 4 (Fall 1998): 34.

84. Christopher Leo, "Regional Growth Management Regime: The Case of Portland, Oregon," *Journal of Urban Affairs* 20, 4 (1998): 376–382.

85. David Rusk, "The Exploding Metropolis: Why Growth Management Makes Sense," *The Brookings Review* 16, 4 (Fall 1998): 13–16. Also see Robert Puentes and Myron Orfield, *Valuing America's First Suburbs: A Policy Agenda for Older Suburbs in the Midwest,* a report of The Brookings Institution Center for Urban Affairs, Washington, DC, April 2002, available at www.brookings.edu/dybdocroot/es/urban/firstsuburbs/firstsuburbsexsum.htm.

86. Orfield, *Metropolitics,* pp. 129–131, 140–141, and 169–170.

87. Rusk, *Inside Game/Outside Game,* p. 278.

88. Wiewel and Schaffer, "Learning to Think as a Region," p. 605.

89. Alison Wiley, "Community Building and Philanthropy: The Regional Community," *National Civic Review* 86, 4 (Winter 1997): 315–324. Also see Anne F. Peterson, "Examining the Impact of the Peirce Reports on Metropolitan Development" (paper presented at the annual meeting of the American Political Science Association, Boston, September 3–6, 1998).

90. Bonnie Lindstrom, "Regional Institutions and Social Capital Governance Structures in the Chicago Region" (paper presented to the annual meeting of the Urban Affairs Association, Louisville, Kentucky, April 15, 1999).

91. Joel Rast and Virginia Cohen, "When Boeing Landed in Chicago: Lessons for Regional Economic Development" (paper presented at the annual meeting of the Urban Affairs Association, Washington, DC, April 2, 2004).

92. Margaret Weir, "Coalition Building for Regionalism," in *Reflections on Regionalism,*" p. 149.

93. Anja Kurki, "Democratic Regionalism: A Way to Improve Individuals' Life-Chances?" (paper presented at the annual meeting of the Urban Affairs Association, Detroit, April 25–28, 2003).

94. Victoria Basolo and Dorian Hastings, "Obstacles to Regional Housing Solutions: A Comparison of Four Metropolitan Areas," *Journal of Urban Affairs* 25, 4 (2003): 449–472.

95. Donald F. Norris, "Prospects for Regional Governance under the New Regionalism: Economic Imperatives Versus Political Impediments," *Journal of Urban Affairs* 23, 5 (2001): 557–571.

96. Comments by Susan E. Clarke at the "Colloquium on the New Regionalism in the United States and Canada," at the annual meeting of the Urban Affairs Association, Detroit, April 27, 2001.

97. Miller, *The Regional Governing of Metropolitan Areas,* pp. 108–109.

98. Wiewel and Schaffer, "Learning to Think as a Region," p. 606.

Cities and suburbs exist in a federal system, and are greatly affected by the decisions made in state capitals and in Washington, DC. Yet cities and suburbs do not simply occupy the bottom rung of the ladder with little choice but to follow the dictates imposed on them from above. While national and state policies impose constraints

on local actions, local governments nonetheless possess considerable discretion in program implementation.

National housing policy, for instance, is marked by the "illusion of federal control."[1] To meet housing objectives, federal housing officials find that they must be respectful of the points of view of local governments and developers. Federal housing administrators are further constrained as developers and other housing industry officials are often big contributors to congressional and presidential campaigns.

The national government provides fiscal assistance to help states and localities reach important domestic policy objectives. Despite the accompanying rules and regulations, the daily management of intergovernmentalized programs is largely left in the hands of state, county, and local officials who decide just how to apply the federal rules and guidelines.[2]

In this chapter, we describe the changing nature of the American federal system and the impact of federal and state policy on cities. In the 1960s and 1970s, Democratic administrations in Washington launched a "War on Poverty" and attempted the formulation of a national urban policy. Republican administrations, however, produced a powerful response, a **New Federalism** policy that sought to limit federal power, returning policy-making responsibility to the states and cities. The Republican doctrine of **devolution** seeks to cut federal budgetary commitments while returning policy responsibilities to the cities and the states.

THE GROWTH OF NATIONAL POWER: FROM DUAL TO COOPERATIVE FEDERALISM

The power of the national government has clearly grown since the early years of the Republic. The once-prominent constitutional view of *dual federalism* has been superseded by a more modern notion of *cooperative federalism*.

Dual federalism is a reading of the U.S. Constitution that stresses states' rights and gives only the most limited authority to the federal government. Dual federalism gives great weight to the **reserved powers** allocated to the states under the **Tenth Amendment,** which reads:

> The powers not delegated to the United States by the Constitution, nor prohibited by it to the States, are reserved to the States respectively, or to the people.

Under the doctrine of dual federalism, the national government possesses only the few **expressed powers** (also called **delegated powers** or **enumerated powers**) spelled out by Article I, Section 8, of the Constitution. These include the power to tax, coin money, regulate interstate commerce, raise an army, declare war, enter into treaties with other nations, and establish post offices. All other powers, under the doctrine of dual federalism, are reserved to the states by the Tenth Amendment.

Dual federalism is often described as **layer cake federalism:** each level of government is given its own separate areas of responsibility under the Constitution.[3] The federal government is restricted to its few expressed or enumerated functions, and the Constitution (the layer of cream in the cake) keeps the federal government from encroaching on the policy prerogatives properly belonging to the states.

Dual federalism was a fairly accurate description of the distribution of power in the American federal system into the early 1900s. However, it does not describe the more dynamic and intricate relationship that has evolved as national and subnational governments jointly work together to combat modern problems. Since the Great Depression and Franklin Roosevelt's New Deal in the 1930s, the federal program reach has grown as Americans expect their government to play an active role, and not stand idly by, in the face of domestic ills.

Political scientists Michael Reagan and John Sanzone have observed: "Federalism—old style—is dead. Yet federalism—new style—is alive and well and living in the United States. Its name is intergovernmental relations."[4] **Intergovernmental relations,** also called **cooperative federalism,** implies a strong sharing of responsibilities by the state, local, and national governments, even though intergovernmental programs are at times marked by conflict as well as cooperation.[5] In contrast to dual federalism, there are no distinctly separate spheres or levels of state and national authority. Cooperative relationship is often described as **marble cake federalism.** In a marble cake, the chocolate is swirled and blended into the yellow cake. Under cooperative federalism, the different levels of government similarly mix and interact as they undertake joint action to combat policy problems.

Adherents of dual federalism charge that the federal government has taken on responsibilities beyond those that the Constitution and the Tenth Amendment allow. But advocates of dual federalism ignore other portions of the Constitution that provide the basis for enhanced federal action. Article VI, also called the **supremacy clause,** for instance, provides that the laws passed by Congress shall be the supreme law of the land and that judges throughout the country shall be bound by these laws.

Possibly of even greater significance, the Supreme Court has given a broad reading of the Constitution's **necessary and proper clause** (also called the **elastic clause**), paving the way for the more expansive program reach of the national government. After the list of the federal government's enumerated powers in Article I, Section 8, the Constitution states that the national government has the right "to make all laws which shall be necessary and proper for carrying into execution the foregoing powers." This clause provides the basis for the **doctrine of implied powers;** the national government is not limited to the few powers expressly listed for it in the Constitution but has the authority to undertake a whole host of actions, implied by the words *necessary and proper,* related to those powers. As early as 1819, in one of the earliest and most famous Supreme Court cases, *McCulloch v. Maryland,* Chief Justice John Marshall ruled that the national government possessed all those powers that could reasonably be implied from the delegated powers.

McCulloch provided the constitutional framework for the expansion of federal authority that would occur over 100 years later during the Great Depression and Franklin Delano Roosevelt's New Deal. The Supreme Court initially threw out major elements in Roosevelt's initial recovery program; but soon the Court responded to the public's cry that the federal government be allowed to step in and provide relief. The Court took a very expansive view of the Constitution's **interstate commerce clause,** seeing an extremely wide range of economic, regulatory, and domestic policy activities as having effects on interstate commerce that justified federal government action.

By the late New Deal period, the Tenth Amendment no longer imposed any significant restraint on the power of the federal government. By 1941, the Supreme Court saw "the Tenth Amendment as simply stating a truism, 'that all is retained which has not yet been surrendered.'"[6] During the decades that followed, neither the Tenth Amendment nor the system of federalism was seen to impose any serious restraints on the domestic actions of the national government.

THE REHNQUIST COURT AND THE REDISCOVERY OF AN OUTER LIMIT TO NATIONAL GOVERNMENT ACTION

Beginning in the mid-1970s, a Court dominated by the appointees of Republican presidents began to exhibit an interest in resurrecting a doctrine of federalism that recognized some limitations on the national government's powers. Yet there was no return to dual federalism; the Court did not greatly roll back the national government's role in domestic policy.

In *National League of Cities v. Usery* (1976), a sharply divided Court ruled that the Congress could not compel states and localities to observe federal minimum wage and maximum hour laws for their own state and municipal employees.[7] The federal wage and hour laws were seen as interfering with the structure of state and local governments. The Court had at long last found a case in which federal overreaching had violated the authority of the states.

The rejoicing at the state and local level, however, was short-lived, as the Court in 1985 reversed itself in *Garcia v. San Antonio Metropolitan Transit*

Authority.[8] The Court would not use the Tenth Amendment to protect states and cities against federal intrusion.

Three years later, the Court reaffirmed its *Garcia* precedent, again ruling against the states in *South Carolina v. Baker*.[9] The case dealt with the narrow issue of whether the national government could mandate the exact form that state and local bonds must take to earn federal tax-exempt status. The larger question was whether the national government could impose rules on state and local financing, a matter crucial to subnational authority. The Supreme Court ruled that the national government did possess such authority, and that the Constitution posed no such limits to the actions of the national government. Justice Sandra Day O'Connor led the dissenters in the case, arguing that the federal rules were a threat to state and local autonomy.

Justices Antonin Scalia and Clarence Thomas also voiced the view that there are boundaries to the national government's power in a constitutionally arbitrated federal system. The O'Connor-Scalia-Thomas point of view prevailed in a set of Rehnquist court rulings that recognized an outside limit to the reach of the national government's powers.

In *United States v. Lopez* (1995),[10] the Court invalidated the Gun Free School Zones Act because Congress had made no attempt whatsoever to show how the prohibition of firearms in school zones was related to interstate commerce. For the first time since 1936, the Supreme Court struck down an act of Congress for having fallen outside the scope of the Congress' power to regulate interstate commerce.[11]

Two years later, in *Printz v. United States*,[12] the Supreme Court referred to the doctrine of federalism when it stuck down a provision of the Brady Handgun Prevention Act. A local sheriff had objected to the Act's requirement that law-enforcement officials conduct background checks on prospective handgun buyers. The Court ruled that, under their "retained authority," the states "remain independent and autonomous within their proper sphere of authority." State and local officers simply cannot be "dragooned" or commandeered into administering federal law.[13]

In *U.S. v. Morrison* (2000),[14] the Supreme Court again recognized the existence of a boundary that separates national and state action. In striking down a provision of the federal Violence Against Women Act that had allowed victims of rape to sue their attackers in federal court, Chief Justice William Rehnquist explained that such a provision did not properly fall under Congress' interstate commerce powers.

This brief review of important constitutional cases reveals that the Supreme Court has been an inconsistent arbiter of federalism. It has not consistently ruled either in defense of, or against, the extended reach of the national government. Overall, the Court has accepted, and has not challenged, the wide scope of central authority that has grown up since the New Deal.[15] Still, in its more recent rulings, the Court has moved away from the expansive view of federal power that it took in *Garcia*. In its *Lopez, Printz,* and *Morrison* rulings, the Court has revived the concept of federalism as imposing some outer limit on the federal government's claim of powers.[16]

FISCAL FEDERALISM: THE GRANT-IN-AID SYSTEM

Federal assistance to subnational governments largely takes the form of grants-in-aid. A **grant-in-aid** is a transfer of money from one level of government to another for specific purposes, subject to rules and guidelines established by law and by administrative regulations. Grants-in-aid are the lifeblood of fiscal federalism.

The use of grants-in-aid expanded markedly beginning with Franklin Roosevelt's New Deal. It further mushroomed in the 1960s and has continued to expand over time. In 1932, only about $10 million in federal grants was dispensed to cities. By 1960, federal and state aid to local governments reached $7 billion. As the United States entered the twenty-first century, the number of federal grant programs had increased to over 600 at an annual cost of more than $300 billion.

Federal assistance increases the ability of states and cities to fight deep-seated and complex problems. Federal assistance has also helped establish more uniform service standards across the nation, alleviating the gross geographical inequalities of an earlier era. Federal grants have led to an upgrading of local services, providing incentives for localities to act in a number of program areas they otherwise might have ignored. Numerous federal programs—including, just to name a few, Head Start, special education, child nutrition and health protection, and the provision of assistance for the construction of hospitals, mass transit, and solid waste disposal facilities—have made remarkable headway in achieving their goals.

Associations of state and local governments in Washington, often referred to as **PIGs** (short for **public interest groups**), have also actively pushed for increases in federal program assistance. In their attempts to shape critical legislation, cities and counties rely heavily on such national associations as the U.S. Conference of Mayors, the National League of Cities (NLC), and the National Association of Counties (NACO).[17] The nation's mayors, too, are frequent visitors to Washington as they lobby for policies and aid awards that affect their cities. A number of states and big cities maintain their own offices in Washington to help them in their efforts to secure federal program dollars.

TYPES OF GRANTS

There are two major types of grants: *categorical grants* and *block grants*. **Categorical grants** are designed for very narrow and specific objectives. A recipient government has limited discretion in the use of categorical grant funds. A local government that receives a categorical grant to upgrade its police communications equipment cannot use that grant for any other police or nonpolice purposes. Categorical grants have been enacted for a broad variety of purposes, including, to name only a few, vocational education, child nutrition, reading programs in poverty-impacted school districts, public libraries, and urban parks and sewage plant development.

Categorical grants take one of two forms: *formula grants* and *project grants*. **Formula grants** are distributed to all states or eligible local governments in accordance with statistical criteria written into the law. How much a state or locality receives depends upon the factors written into the aid formula. The level of assistance may vary with such factors as a jurisdiction's population, per capita income, poverty rate, tax effort, age of housing stock, number of senior citizens, or the daily attendance of children in schools. Recipient governments are entitled to the grants by law; they do not have to submit elaborate proposals and compete for available funds.

Project grants are more competitive as they are not dispensed to all jurisdictions. Instead, eligible jurisdictions must take the initiative in submitting a proposal to apply for the grant; jurisdictions compete for the money.

Block grants, by comparison, allow recipient communities increased discretion in using federal assistance within a relatively broad functional or service area. For instance, under the Comprehensive Employment Training Act (CETA), a very well-known block grant of the 1970s, local governments were given quite a bit of flexibility to design their own local job-training efforts; they could not, however, divert the money to housing, streets, or other areas of need.

While the first two block grants were initiated by Democratic President Lyndon Johnson, the block grant idea gained momentum as a result of the New Federalism policies of the Richard Nixon and Ronald Reagan presidencies, Republican administrations that sought to increase state authority and diminish the power of spending-oriented Washington bureaucracies. Block grants were also a key component of the late-1990s welfare reform effort, allowing states and localities new flexibility in designing welfare-to-work transition programs. George W. Bush also proposed block grants to allow states greater program freedom in such policy areas as Head Start, Medicaid, subsidized housing, and child protective services.[18]

PROBLEMS WITH THE GRANT SYSTEM

Most federal aid programs continue to take the form of narrowly focused categorical grants. Congress relies on categorical grants, with their accompanying strings, to ensure that subnational governments use the grant money to pursue designated program goals.

Critics of categorical grants complain that they result in a **loss of subnational program flexibility.** States and localities also complain that categorical grants produce **skewed or distorted subnational program priorities,** as state legislatures and city councils are virtually forced to spend their precious funds not in their areas of greatest need but in program areas that will generate generous federal **matching grants.** Critics further complain of **grantsmanship,** as project grants are not always given to the neediest or most deserving communities but to those communities that have hired professional staffs most expert in the game of applying for federal funds.

One other criticism of a categorical grant-dominated system relates to the drift of authority from state and local elected officials to program bureaucrats, a concept often referred to as **picket fence federalism (PFF)**[19] (see Figure 14-1). PFF underscores the power possessed by an interlevel alliance of program

■ **FIGURE 14–1**

PICKET FENCE FEDERALISM: A SCHEMATIC
REPRESENTATION

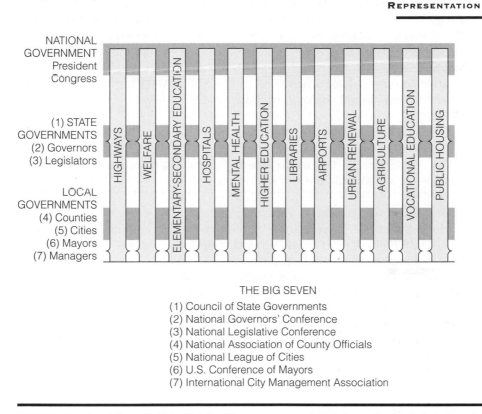

NATIONAL
GOVERNMENT
President
Congress

(1) STATE
GOVERNMENTS
(2) Governors
(3) Legislators

LOCAL
GOVERNMENTS
(4) Counties
(5) Cities
(6) Mayors
(7) Managers

HIGHWAYS
WELFARE
ELEMENTARY-SECONDARY EDUCATION
HOSPITALS
MENTAL HEALTH
HIGHER EDUCATION
LIBRARIES
AIRPORTS
UREAN RENEWAL
AGRICULTURE
VOCATIONAL EDUCATION
PUBLIC HOUSING

THE BIG SEVEN
(1) Council of State Governments
(2) National Governors' Conference
(3) National Legislative Conference
(4) National Association of County Officials
(5) National League of Cities
(6) U.S. Conference of Mayors
(7) International City Management Association

SOURCE: Reprinted from Deil S. Wright, "Intergovernmental Relations: An Analytical Overview,"
Annals of the American Academy of Political and Social Science (November 1974): 15.

specialists and managers to join together to write program rules and administer and evaluate programs.

The vertical slats in the picket fence point to the alliances of program specialists who often dominate the administration of programs in each different service
area. These program administrators do not willingly cede control of their
cherished programs to elected officials. When a local program gets funding
largely from an intergovernmental grant, program administrators are protected
against the efforts of state and local elected officials to gain program control.
Subnational executives and legislators cannot turn off the spigot of intergovernmental grant money going to a program that they disapprove. Program specialists further argue that federal rules require them to continue to administer a
program in a certain manner despite the displeasure of state and local elected
officials.

The various criticisms of a categorical grant–dominated system led to the increased use of block grants in an effort to enhance subnational program flexibility and place greater choice in the hands of local elected officials. Block grants are very popular. Yet the history of programs such the Community Development Block Grant, which was formed by the consolidation of older antipoverty and urban renewal categorical grants, would indicate that subnational governments do not always use their discretion wisely when they are freed from strict federal program review. (See "Can the Cities Be Trusted? The Case of Community Development Block Grants" below.)

CAN THE CITIES BE TRUSTED? THE CASE OF COMMUNITY DEVELOPMENT BLOCK GRANTS

Do state and local governments always act more capably, efficiently, and fairly than does the federal government? The history of the Community Development Block Grant (CDBG) program raises important concerns about devolving program responsibility to local governments.

Enacted in 1974, the CDBG program combined a number of urban renewal, urban parks, and Model Cities social service programs into a single block grant. The consolidation gave local governments new program flexibility. Still, the national legislation listed certain priorities: eliminating slums and blight, aiding low- and moderate-income families, and meeting urgent community needs.

Bridgeport, Connecticut officials essentially ignored the priorities set under the law. Bridgeport devoted a sizeable chunk of community development money to parks development, with most of the spending going to the better-off side of town. The city council earmarked funds to build new tennis courts on the city's more affluent north side.

In the second year of the program, the city spread CDBG monies around for parks development in all neighborhoods to "give everybody a piece of something." Each city council member sought to use CDBG monies for district projects that would enhance his or her electoral support. Bridgeport made little attempt to target community development spending on the areas of the city most in need. City planners slighted low- and moderate-income housing and instead tried to use CDBG funds to build a new pier and marina project. Officials from the national Department of Housing and Urban Development finally ruled the marina project ineligible.

Was Bridgeport's experience unique? Unfortunately not. While many localities used their program monies well, the misuse of local discretion in the CDBG program was a nationwide phenomenon. Cities spent CDBG funds on programs that were popular with the local electorate, not on programs for poor people. Cities also emphasized physical development, including parks

continued

> ## CAN THE CITIES BE TRUSTED? THE CASE OF COMMUNITY DEVELOPMENT BLOCK GRANTS (CONT.)
>
> and recreational facilities, as opposed to social services. It took a tightening of federal rules, regulations, and oversight to eliminate much of the abuse of discretion and goal diversion that marred the early days of the CDBG program. Federal rules for citizen participation also forced city councils to pay attention to concerns of neighborhood groups that otherwise would have been ignored.
>
> Sources: Donald F. Kettl, *Government By Proxy: (Mis?)Managing Federal Programs* (Washington, DC: CQ Press, 1988), pp. 54–66. For good overviews of the history of the CDBG program, see Benjamin Kleinberg, *Urban America in Transformation* (Thousand Oaks, CA: Sage Publications, 1995), pp. 196–209, and R. Allen Hays, *The Federal Government and Urban Housing*, 2nd ed. (Albany: State University of New York Press, 1995), pp. 187–232.

THE ISSUE OF UNFUNDED MANDATES

Unfunded federal mandates refer to the many instances in which the central government requires, but does not provide the financial assistance to pay for, state and local action. State and local governments complain of the huge costs imposed by such mandates. A National Association of Counties survey in 1993 indicated that 120 counties paid a total of $4.8 billion to comply with just 12 federal laws. Counties estimated that the costs of mandate compliance accounted for 12.3 percent of locally based revenues.[20] In fiscal 1995, the states complained of having to find an estimated $34 billion of their own monies to meet federal program requirements.[21]

In 1995, the Republican-controlled Congress passed the **Unfunded Mandates Relief Act,** requiring that the government provide specific funding sources and fully pay for any new mandate with a cost in excess of $50 million annually. While the legislation deterred a number of new mandates from being proposed, overall, the law was weak and tolerated numerous exceptions.[22] The mandate problem persists despite the relief promised by the 1995 law.

State and local education officials objected that George W. Bush's **No Child Left Behind (NCLB) Act** constitutes a mandate that burdens school districts with the costs of testing, remediation, and school choice programs far in excess of the federal aid provided. Yet Congress' rules limiting mandates do not apply to NCLB. The Individuals With Disabilities Education Act (IWDEA) provides another case in which the national government has not fully reimbursed subnational governments for required actions. Technically, neither NCLB nor the IWDEA is considered a mandate, as participation by the states is seen as voluntary; the Mandate Relief Act views the new costs imposed on the states as permissible grant conditions.[23] In another important area, the federal government has failed to fully reimburse localities for the training, protection, and coordination expenses incurred as part of homeland defense.

While the states complain about the costs of federal mandates, the states themselves often impose costly new service responsibilities on local governments. State-imposed mandates on local governments even occur in states that have legislation that attempts to bar or limit such impositions.[24]

NATIONAL POLICY TOWARD CITIES

The nation's cities have rarely been a focal point of national policy. Indeed, it is not really accurate to speak of a national urban policy in the United States. The United States has never developed and implemented a policy designed to guide the growth and development of cities and suburbs. While the central government has on numerous occasions undertaken strong actions against specific urban ills, it has never developed a holistic policy designed to address the broader roots of the urban situation.

A review of the evolution of federal urban policy underscores the extreme difficulties that policymakers face when trying to fashion and implement strong and effective national policies toward cities. Members of Congress tend to look out for their constituencies and are not enthusiastic about programs that promise benefits outside their districts. The shift of population and voting power to the suburbs and the Sunbelt serves to weaken even further the constituency for strong policies focused on the nation's most distressed and declining communities.

WHATEVER HAPPENED TO MODEL CITIES?

The failure to fashion a strong national urban policy was even apparent in President Lyndon Johnson's **Great Society** and **War on Poverty** programs of the 1960s. Johnson's advisers saw the roots of urban ills as deep and complex. As a result, they argued that effective antipoverty action would require simultaneous measures taken on a whole host of fronts, including education, job training, housing, child care, and social work. Great Society planners conceived of a **Model Cities** program to demonstrate what could be accomplished by a broad, multiagency, coordinated attack on poverty in riot-torn Detroit and a handful of other demonstration or model cities.

However, the presidential advisory task force charged with developing the Model Cities legislation soon realized that Congress was not likely to enact a program that targeted a vast array of benefits on such a small handful of cities. As a result, the task force broadened the original proposal and urged the creation of 66 model cities across the nation. Congress went even further, spreading the program to nearly 140 model cities. To appease powerful members of Congress, model cities were set up in such unlikely states as Maine, Tennessee, Kentucky, and Montana.[25]

The dispersion of program assets meant that, in fact, no real model city was created anywhere in the nation. Spread so thinly, the effects of Model Cities' spending were diluted; there was no critical mass of resources for a sustained, multipronged attack on poverty in any city. Congress' parochialism and constituent orientation had undermined the entire Model Cities concept.

NIXON'S NEW FEDERALISM

President Richard M. Nixon relied on two innovative tools—general revenue sharing and block grants—in his new federalism efforts to give greater decision-making power to states and localities.

REVENUE SHARING. **Revenue sharing** provided all 50 states and nearly every general-purpose local government in the nation with no-strings-attached grant money that the recipient government could spend in almost any way it desired. Advocates argued that no-strings-attached aid would provide much-needed subnational flexibility in a grant-in-aid system overwhelmingly dominated by categorical grants. Advocates also argued that shared revenues would encourage the states and localities to undertake more creative and innovative program actions. Mayors of the nation's most distressed communities, however, complained of the inequity of a program that provided funds that well-off communities used for tennis courts while financially troubled communities were having difficulty providing basic services.

As federal budget deficits began to climb, fiscal conservatives began to question the wisdom of a federal program that provided shared revenues to states, most of which enjoyed budget surpluses. Congress in 1980 terminated the state portion of revenue sharing.

Six years later, President Ronald Reagan terminated local revenue sharing, which he saw as unnecessary and wasteful. Reagan believed that shared revenues only encouraged overspending on projects that local communities, left to their own, would not normally choose to fund.

In one important aspect, revenue sharing did not live up to the expectations of the program's originators. States and localities did not use their new program monies to innovate and take on new program responsibilities. Instead, local officials used shared revenues primarily to maintain existing services, fund police activities, supplement capital expenditures, and stabilize taxes.[26] State and local officials did what was popular; in spending shared revenues, they responded to the desires of powerful middle-class and upper-strata voters.

BLOCK GRANTS. Nixon's second grant-in-aid innovation, the increased use of block grants, would prove to have a more long-lasting impact on the intergovernmental system. Succeeding administrations would pursue the creation of new block grants.

Before Nixon came to office, virtually all intergovernmental aid was in the form of categorical grants that greatly constrained state and local action. Nixon sought to merge numerous small, narrow categorical grants into larger block grants that permitted subnational officials new discretion in spending federal funds within broad program areas.

The Democratic Congress, however, objected that Nixon's proposal allowed state and local officials too great an ability to ignore the needs of less powerful poor and minority communities. The result was a compromise; new block grants were created, but Congress added "strings" requiring citizen participation and requiring that state and local officials spend a portion of program monies to benefit low- and moderate-income communities. Democratic presidential administrations tended to enforce such participation and spending requirements; Republican administrations tended to defer to the spending plans of local elected officials.[27]

JIMMY CARTER: THE FIRST AND LAST ATTEMPT AT A NATIONAL URBAN POLICY

When he ran for president in 1976, Democrat Jimmy Carter promised the nation's mayors that he would be the first president to formulate an explicit national urban policy. Once he gained office, the mayors pressured Carter to deliver on his promise. Carter announced a *New Partnership to Preserve America's Communities* that embraced three guiding principles:

- **Targeting.** Federal spending would be focused on troubled urban communities, not spread thinly across the country to satisfy political interests.

- **Economic development.** In contrast to the focus on social services during the Kennedy and Johnson years, the Carter urban policy emphasized local economic development and job creation. Carter proposed the creation of a **National Development Bank** (originally called an **Urban Bank**) to offer grants, loan guarantees, and other incentives to businesses that chose to locate or expand in distressed communities.

- **Partnership.** As the federal government did not possess the full resources needed to turn around troubled communities, it would work hand in hand with private investors, subnational governments, and voluntary and community groups.

For all the publicity it received, the Carter urban policy went virtually nowhere. Congress defeated the National Development Bank and the administration's major proposals for labor-intensive public works and special fiscal assistance targeted on the nation's most distressed communities. In an era of mounting budgetary deficits, Congress would not commit monies to major new urban initiatives. Representatives from the suburbs and the Sunbelt would not vote for programs that channeled aid to the declining cities of America's rustbelt. Congressional committee and subcommittee chairs from the South blocked the passage of programs that focused aid on the high-unemployment, declining population centers of the Northeast and the Midwest.

When Carter attempted to increase the targeting of the revitalization assistance provided by the Department of Commerce's Economic Development Administration (EDA), Congress moved in the exact opposite direction, defining "distress" so broadly that 90 percent of the nation's population lived in areas eligible to apply for EDA assistance.

A Democratic Congress failed to pass the national urban policy of a Democratic president. In succeeding years, the prospects to the enactment of a national urban policy would dim still further as Republicans gained increasing power in Washington and population shifts gave additional representation to suburban and Sunbelt constituencies. No president since Carter has attempted to make cities the explicit focus of national policy.

REAGAN-BUSH: "WASHINGTON ABANDONS CITIES"

Unlike Carter, Ronald Reagan did not seek to stimulate *local* economic revitalization. Reagan would not use federal resources in an attempt to lure business back to sites that, he believed, business had rightly deserted as inefficient and unprofitable.[28] Nor would Reagan support costly urban and social programs that he believed sapped the nation's economic competitiveness. Reagan's concern was exclusively with *national* economic growth.

Under Reagan, the government would reinforce, not contradict, the choices made by investors and the market. The government would not give special aid in an attempt to halt or ameliorate the conditions of urban decline. An early 1982 draft of the *President's National Urban Policy Report* bluntly stated, "Cities are not guaranteed eternal life." Instead of responding with increased urban aid, Reagan wanted cities to adjust to the needs of business—by reducing taxes and regulations and reversing pro-union policies.

Reagan saw New Federalism decentralization as a means of reducing federal spending and regulation. Reagan offered extensive regulatory relief, reducing the paperwork and bureaucratic burdens imposed on state and local governments. To cite one example, his administration reduced from 52 to just 2 the number of pages of rules governing local spending of CDBG funds.[29] However, Reagan preferred subnational action only when he believed subnational governments would act to limit governmental intrusion in the economy. His administration did not approve of the use of discretion by local governments to raise environmental standards or increase public housing spending beyond what the administration favored.[30]

Reagan's devolution efforts went beyond those of Richard Nixon. Nixon had sought to increase state and local control over the use of federal funds. Reagan wanted to cut federal spending and reduce the intrusion into the economy of all levels of government: "In short, Reagan did not aim simply at decategorizing the system; he ultimately sought to defund it."[31] For Reagan, block grants were only a "transitional device," a "halfway house" on the road to withdrawing federal support from affected policy areas."[32] While Republicans Richard Nixon and Gerald Ford sought to increase the government's use of block grants, Reagan cut block grant spending levels.

Year after year, Reagan proposed reducing or "zeroing out" the funding for numerous urban and social programs. The Democratic Congress saved the CDBG program, the revitalization programs of the Economic Development Administration (EDA), and the Small Business Administration from termination by placing them in megabills that included programs that Reagan could not afford to veto.

Still, Reagan forced drastic reductions in numerous urban programs, cutting, in real-dollar terms, one-third of CDBG money, half of mass-transit money, two-thirds of the monies available for employment and training, and 70 percent of the funding for the EDA.[33]

Annual public housing appropriations under Reagan were reduced by three-fourths; the President brought a halt to the construction of new subsidized housing. In his last year in office, he terminated the Urban Development Action Grant (UDAG) program, a tool that had been used for downtown revitalization.

Under George H. W. Bush (the first President Bush), federal aid to state and local governments once again began to increase.[34] However, the gigantic size of the budget deficits of the Reagan years acted to crowd out the money available for new urban programs. More stringent rules governing congressional budgeting and spending, too, acted to restrain federal spending on behalf of cities.

Demetrios Caraley succinctly summarized the Reagan-Bush urban policy as "Washington Abandons Cities."[35] During the first 10 Reagan-Bush years, cities lost nearly 46 percent ($26 billion) in aid. Much-troubled Detroit lost over half its federal funds.[36] It was "fend-for-yourself federalism."[37] Reagan's view was that if a city "cannot pay for a service at the level where it is provided, then do without it."[38]

Growing communities that were not highly dependent on federal funds, especially in the Sunbelt, survived the Reagan-era budget onslaught in fairly good shape. However, declining cities, especially in the Northeast and Midwest, were forced to cut back such critical services as job training and subsidized day care for the poor.[39] Cities also postponed street repaving, sewer upgrading, and bridge repair projects. The states, scissored by their own growing budgetary problems and a tax revolt among voters, did not come forward with additional spending to compensate cities for the federal cutbacks.

BILL CLINTON: THE "REFRIGERATOR LIST" AND "STEALTH" APPROACHES TO URBAN POLICY

Bill Clinton was more committed to urban programs than were his Republican predecessors. Immediately upon coming to office, Clinton increased urban aid, doubling annual expenditures for the homeless and launching a new, but small, Community Reinvestment Fund to assist community development corporations and minority-owned banks.

Yet Clinton did not attempt to undo the Reagan program terminations; nor could he bring about a return to the funding levels of the pre-Reagan era.[40] As a New Democrat, Clinton had won office by rejecting the big-government spending approaches of the past. Early in office, Clinton suffered the disastrous defeat of his proposed system of national health care, a defeat that served to reinforce his sense of political caution and his reluctance in advancing new policy initiatives. The Republican takeover of Congress in the 1994 mid-term congressional elections further served to convince Clinton of the political wisdom of fashioning numerous small policy initiatives that could win the support of middle-class voters (the so-called "soccer moms" of the 1996 presidential election).[41]

Clinton pursued a strategy that political scientist Robert Waste labeled the **refrigerator list presidency;**[42] the President pushed a series of small, discrete, and politically popular urban-related programs, not the major urban policy initiatives that would galvanize his conservative opponents. The Clinton crime bill contained a popular ban on assault weapons. It also appealed to public sentiment for stiffer sentences for certain felonies ("three strikes and you're out"). Clinton provided money for prisons and the hiring of 100,000 new police officers. Sold as crime and drug prevention programs, the legislation funded social programs aimed at youth, including after-school and summer programs, midnight basketball leagues, and creative arts programs. Under Clinton's Officer Next Door program, the Department of Housing and Urban Development offered police officers financial assistance to buy homes in urban neighborhoods.[43] His brownfields revitalization program drew the support of environmentalists; it promised to clean up contaminated sites to make new land available for private investment, bringing new jobs to inner-city neighborhoods.

Clinton also played to voters' antigovernment sentiment by **reinventing government,** his program to make government perform better with less.[44] Clinton placed Vice President Al Gore in charge of a reinvention effort that sought to eliminate waste and make government more entrepreneurial.

States and localities were seen as **laboratories of democracy** and given new latitude, including waivers of federal regulations in such areas as welfare, to experiment with new policy approaches of their own.[45]

After the disastrous losses suffered to the Republicans in the 1994 mid-term elections, Clinton sought to take a dramatic step to convince voters that he was not part of the Washington problem. The President considered eliminating the Department of Housing and Urban Development (HUD), divvying its program responsibilities among other agencies. Often criticized by cities for being bureaucratic and aloof, HUD responded by reinventing itself to avoid the prospects of termination. HUD eliminated thousands of positions and initiated a series of reforms designed to make the agency more streamlined, decentralized, and consumer friendly. HUD developed new performance-based grants, similar to block grants, reducing federal oversight, requiring recipient communities only to establish plans and performance indicators.

Clinton succeeded in helping cities by advancing programs that were not explicitly urban in nature. Clinton largely followed the path of a **stealth urban policy** of pursuing urban goals through "nonurban" means, through programs that were not perceived to be focused on cities.[46]

The President did not talk about the state of cities but about the need for heightened law enforcement, education assistance, and brownfields reclamation. Clinton sought targets of opportunity, tapping Congress' willingness to fund popular programs, including an expanded Head Start program, child nutrition programs, a violence-against-women initiative, and assisted housing for the homeless. He secured additional assistance for housing vouchers, job training, and day care, all in the name of welfare reform, of moving people from welfare to work.

Possibly Clinton's greatest achievement in his stealth urban policy was the expansion of the **Earned Income Tax Credit (EITC)** program. The EITC provides millions of dollars annually in income assistance to the working poor.

Low-income workers get a refundable tax credit, that is, additional money in their paychecks. Clinton expanded EITC eligibility and benefits, so that a working mother with two children could receive up to $3,370 annually in income assistance. Families earning as high as $27,000 received small income supplements.

As a credit offered through the tax code, the EITC enjoyed a number of political advantages. Seen as a tax policy, the EITC changes were not readily understood by, or even visible to, the American public. Given only to workers, the additional assistance was not seen as "welfare," an encouragement to indolence.

The expanded EITC program helped cities. Workers in big cities were most likely to receive EITC benefits, closely followed by workers who live in rural areas.[47]

In 1998 alone, EITC assistance to working families pumped $737 million into the Chicago region, boosting the region's economy; nearly 60 percent went to families living in the city of Chicago.[48] EITC was also a great boon to neighborhoods with large number of immigrants. Its benefits can also be seen as a hidden housing subsidy, salary supplements that ease the costs of housing on low-income families.[49]

Clinton pursued politically pragmatic, small, doable, urban *policy pieces*, not a Carter-like, articulated, national urban *policy*. Clinton also focused primarily on programs that sought to aid *people*, not *places*. Only the Clinton empowerment zone program, a major place-based initiative with a focus on distressed communities, transcended the refrigerator list approach of the Clinton presidency. (See "Empowerment Zones and Enterprise Communities" below.)

EMPOWERMENT ZONES AND ENTERPRISE COMMUNITIES

The Clinton **empowerment zone** program offered wage credits and other benefits to firms that hired the residents of specified troubled geographical areas. Big cities competed for empowerment zone designation, desiring both the tax provisions and the promise of $100 million in cash assistance offered under the program. Smaller communities could win designation as **enterprise communities** and be allowed the expanded use of tax-exempt state and local bonds for new development.

The Clinton approach emphasized local partnerships. To win a zone designation, city officials, business leaders, and community groups had to demonstrate that they had worked together to develop a plan that would increase private investment and offer benefits to community residents. The program sought to mobilize the involvement of grassroots groups and that had not always been at the table when local economic development decisions were made.

In the first year of competition, over 500 cities submitted plans in their efforts to win empowerment zone and enterprise community designation. New

continued

York, Chicago, Detroit, Baltimore, Atlanta, and Philadelphia/Camden were the initial big-city winners. The second round saw the naming of 20 additional empowerment zones, including zones in Boston, Los Angeles, and St. Louis. The government also named numerous enterprise communities.

Despite the hullabaloo that surrounded the creation of empowerment zones, there is great doubt as to how much they actually accomplished. In a number of cities, mayors intervened to steer the zone toward more traditional economic development activities. Chicago Mayor Richard Daley violated the grassroots, bottom-up spirit of the program when he acted to draw zone boundaries to facilitate the revitalization of the city's manufacturing corridors and urban brownfields. In New York, Mayor Rudy Giuliani took steps to ensure that zone boundaries included Yankee Stadium, so that the city could use zone financial incentives as part of its efforts to keep the baseball team in the city.

Overall, empowerment zones did not live up to the high expectations that accompanied their creation. Detroit was generally recognized as being among the leaders in terms of empowerment zone performance. The city gained the cooperation of local banks and created a zone that aided investment by the city's auto industry. Yet empowerment zone progress was slow and did little to alter the nature of Detroit's urban crisis. In Camden, New Jersey, zone performance was so poor and plagued by corruption and political infighting that the Clinton administration threatened to drop the city from the program.

Sources: Marilyn Gittell, Kathe Newman, Janice Bockmeyer, and Robert Lindsay, "Expanding Civic Opportunity: Urban Empowerment Zones," *Urban Affairs Review* 33, 4 (March 1998): 530–558; Robert W. Bailey, "The Challenges to Community Empowerment: Experiences from the Philadelphia/Camden Empowerment Zone Program," *Metropolitics* 1, 4 (Spring 1998); Robin Boyle and Peter Eisinger, "The U.S. Empowerment Zone Program: The Evolution of a National Urban Program and the Failure of Local Implementation in Detroit, Michigan" (paper presented at the European Urban Research Association, Copenhagen, Denmark, May 17, 2001).

GEORGE W. BUSH: "COMPASSIONATE CONSERVATISM"
DOES NOT AN URBAN POLICY MAKE

George W. Bush came to the White House in 2001 committed to faith-based initiatives and education reform. A self-professed "compassionate conservative," he sought to provide educational and social services in ways that were consistent with more traditional, conservative values. He also used vouchers and block grants in an attempt to make government perform better with less.

Bush was no free-market conservative, ideologically intent on reducing the role of government in domestic policy. Conservative groups even attacked the President for tolerating increases in discretionary domestic spending. The Cato Institute, a conservative think-tank, decried that "Bush Is No Reagan."[50]

Yet Bush pushed for major cuts in urban programs. While community development block grants and the Low-Income Housing Tax Credit continued, other programs suffered as Bush stressed tax reductions. The Bush administration's record-breaking deficits also put the squeeze on domestic spending. Bush opposed particular urban and social programs, especially HOPE VI subsidized housing, as wasteful. As his administration's involvement in the war on terror and the war in Iraq intensified, his support for urban and social programs—including job training and Section 8 housing vouchers[51]—decreased.

NO CHILD LEFT BEHIND.   Bush's **No Child Left Behind** program sought to push public schools toward increased accountability through testing. Bush argued for transparency; test scores would allow students and parents to see how their schools were performing so they could make a more informed choice of schools and pressure the schools to improve performance. Students in failing schools would also be provided with vouchers that would allow them to seek supplemental services and alternative schooling.

School administrators complained that they were not given the resources to do the new tasks assigned their schools. The Bush administration provided increased funding for schools, but not all the money necessary to implement the reforms demanded by NCLB. Teachers and administrators also argued that test scores did not reflect the reality of education in their schools. Teachers further complained that "teaching to the test" took up too much of the school day, taking time away from more interesting and substantial class activities. NCLB standards were relaxed when so many local districts could not meet the Act's "passing" standards and lacked the resources to comply with the remedial parts of the program.

FAITH-BASED INITIATIVES.   In his **faith-based initiatives**, Bush sought a "level playing field" to end what he saw to be government discrimination against church-related organizations in awarding contracts for the delivery of social services.[52] Bush saw that faith-based organizations often did the hard work in communities. In such areas as substance abuse, job training, and the administration of homeless shelters and affordable housing programs, the President believed that people of faith often had the passion and motivation to do a better job in administering publicly funded programs than did government agencies and secular organizations.

Bush further recognized the importance of aiding smaller community groups, groups that were often faith-related, to enhance their problem-solving capabilities. These groups build "social capital" by bringing people together; they are the backbone of their communities. Bush also believed in the transformational power of faith-based organizations, their ability to build community and to provide people with the spark and inspiration to reform themselves and pull their lives together.[53]

Yet there are serious concerns regarding the performance of faith-based organizations, including questions regarding proselytizing and the separation of church and state. There is no evidence that demonstrates that faith-based organizations systematically perform more effectively than do secular organizations.[54] Even where faith-based organizations have performed well, they may lack the number of committed personnel and technical capacity to expand their mission. There is also the delicate matter of funding religious-based groups outside the American mainstream.

Support for faith-based organizations is extensive in the African-American and Latino communities, with their strong church traditions. Church-related groups are especially important in new immigrant neighborhoods. In a Mexican-American neighborhood of Chicago, the local Catholic parishes pulled together to help form a number of community-based advocacy and development organizations, including the Pilsen Resurrection Development Corporation, the Pilsen Housing Coalition, and other affordable housing efforts. Yet Hispanic neighborhood activists were not always well represented in Chicago as a church hierarchy dominated by members of older ethnic groups effectively made many of the decisions for the community. Questions of power need to be asked when faith-based organizations are given a greater role in urban problem solving: "We need to better understand who controls religious institutions, how decisions are made within them, and how these decisions affect poor communities of color."[55]

BLOCK GRANTS, ONCE AGAIN.   As with other Republican presidents, George W. Bush turned to block grants in an effort to put a cap on federal expenditures, forcing states and localities to effect new economies in an effort to control program costs. Welfare reform during the Clinton years allowed the states increased policy discretion under **Temporary Assistance to Needy Families (TANF)** block grants. Bush proposed to go even further, endorsing a system of **superwaivers** to give the states still additional room to undertake innovative policy action in such areas as welfare reform, child care, health services, job training, and housing.[56]

The Bush administration also proposed the block granting of public housing assistance[57] in a **Flexible Voucher Program.** Under the proposed block grant, the overall level of federal assistance would be reduced. No longer would the level of federal assistance be tied to the costs of maintaining the current number of housing vouchers in a local market. Local public housing authorities, with no prospect of additional federal aid, were likely to raise the rents charged to low-income families (which were no longer limited by federal regulations to 30 percent of a family's income) and make cuts in program services. Faced with a cap on their spending, local housing authorities could also be expected to reduce the number of families assisted through vouchers.[58]

THE FATE OF THE LOW-INCOME HOUSING TAX CREDIT.   The **Low-Income Housing Tax Credit (LIHTC)** allows individuals and corporations who invest in properties with a specified portion of their units set aside for low- and moderate-income families to take, over a 10-year period, a dollar-for-dollar credit against their other tax obligations. It is a nonentitlement program run similarly to a block grant. The federal government gives each state the authority to issue a certain amount of credits; the states award the credits to developers in a competitive fashion.[59]

Simply put, the LIHTC provides a considerable spur to private investment in low-income housing as it offers investors substantial tax advantages. The tax credit is the nation's most important program for the production of low-income housing, having built more than 1.5 million housing units since its inception 1987.[60] The benefits provided by the LIHTC also helped lead corporate and financial institutions to enter into working agreements with community development corporations (CDCs); without the substantial tax advantages provided by the LIHTC, many of these institutions would not have committed their monies to the construction and rehabilitation of affordable housing units.

The LIHTC also does a relatively good job of promoting the construction of affordable housing in the suburbs. When compared to other project-based federally assisted housing, a greater percentage of LIHTC units are found in the suburbs.[61]

A complex program that is part of the tax code and not easily understood, the LIHTC has often been shielded from attack. Yet conservatives targeted the program for cuts as a result of the considerable **tax expenditures** entailed, the cost to the public treasury in terms of foregone public revenue. The LIHTC cost the government an estimated $19.6 billion in lost revenues over the five-year 1998–2002 period.[62] Fiscal conservatives also charged that the program gave excess benefits to housing developers and their lawyers and accountants, money that is siphoned off and does not really go to house the poor.

Unlike the program's free-market conservative critics, President George W. Bush continued to support the LIHTC. He even proposed the creation of a similar single-family affordable housing tax credit to promote home ownership.

However, Bush's tax cuts threatened the usefulness of the LIHTC approach. Bush's proposed elimination of the tax on dividends especially had the potential of canceling out much of the value of the LIHTC. When investors have little or no tax liability to offset, the LIHTC loses its ability to promote low-income housing construction.[63]

IGNORING RENTAL HOUSING STOCK: TARGETING HOPE VI FOR ELIMINATION. One of Bush's most controversial urban-related moves concerned his attempt to terminate the HOPE VI housing program. The **HOPE VI (Housing Opportunities for People Everywhere VI)** program, begun by Congress in 1992, was designed to transform public housing and its surrounding neighborhoods. HOPE VI provided assistance for local public housing authorities to tear down the "islands of hopelessness," the most distressed public housing projects. In their place, HOPE VI money helped finance the construction of low-rise townhouses and garden apartments in mixed-income developments built according to New Urbanism principles.[64] Built with design elements of a traditional small town, the new units provided a more humane living environment than the high-rises they replaced.

The new developments were also intended to foster community. By mixing housing units for low- and moderate-income tenants with those of homeowners paying market rates, the new income-integrated development sought to reinforce expectations of work and success.

Critics pointed to the flaws and limitations of the HOPE VI approach. To assure the success of the new mixed-income communities, tenant applicants were screened; problem families from public housing were not allowed in the new developments.

To facilitate the construction of mixed-income housing, the federal government relaxed its old rule that had required the **one-for-one replacement** of low-income units that are torn down, a rule that often made it too expensive for localities to demolish even the worst public housing buildings that had many unoccupied units. Under HOPE VI, local authorities built many fewer units for the poor than the number of apartments torn down. In city after city, only a lucky few of the former public housing residents were reaccommodated in the new HOPE VI mixed-income developments.

What about the residents of public housing who were not fortunate enough to win places in the new HOPE VI developments? In many cases, public housing displacees were given vouchers that allowed them to move to housing in better physical condition in better neighborhoods with somewhat lower poverty rates than the areas they left. The moves, however, seldom produced greater racial integration. In other cities, the vouchers were inadequate to assuring real tenant choice; the high price of rental housing in a tight local housing market, coupled with the reluctance of private landlords to rent units to former public housing residents, restricted tenant mobility. In cities that gave inadequate attention to relocation assistance and counseling, public housing displacees often wound up living in other parts of the ghetto.[65] A concentration of housing vouchers led to a resegregated living environment.

CORBIS

The Cabrini-Green public housing project in Chicago, 1995. The John Hancock building on the city's Magnificent Mile is clearly seen in the background. The close proximity to the shops and offices of Chicago's world-class downtown made the Cabrini area attractive to the developers of higher-income housing.

HOPE VI new construction was also very expensive. In cities where substantial subsidies were given to attract homebuyers to the new developments, much of the program's benefits went to fairly well-off homeowners and not to low- and moderate-income families. In cities such as Chicago, HOPE VI was attacked as a land grab, an effort by developers and their political allies to tear down high-rise public housing in an effort to make the surrounding area, situated near the center of the city, more attractive to high-end housing and commercial projects.

Despite these criticisms, HOPE VI was a program that worked reasonably well. HOPE VI built new public housing and improved the conditions of surrounding neighborhoods. In Atlanta and other cities, it turned around conditions in distressed projects such as Techwood Homes, making them more vibrant communities.[66] In Chicago, well-designed low rises bordering the old Cabrini-Green housing towers (some of which were torn down) became showcases that helped catalyze the revalorization of land and new housing and commercial development in the surrounding area. HOPE VI also allowed the former tenants of public housing to move to better quality and safer housing.

Yet President Bush called for the termination of HOPE VI, arguing that the program had outlived its usefulness and had already succeeded in its mission of tearing down the most severely distressed public housing units. Bush administration officials pointed out that public housing authorities in Chicago and

A complex of mixed-income townhomes and apartments is built by the Cabrini-Green public housing complex in Chicago, 2003. The housing was built in accordance with New Urbanism design principles. But fewer housing units were built than were torn down, and relatively few of the new units were set aside for the residents of public housing.

CORBIS

other cities were not even able to spend their full allocations of HOPE VI money. Bush proposed canceling the program in fiscal 2004; Congress barely kept it alive, cutting its funding by three-fourths (from $570 million to $150 million per year). In fiscal 2005, Bush once again proposed terminating the program.

Housing advocates called for the reform of, not the elimination of, HOPE VI. They argued that Bush's proposed termination of HOPE VI represented the federal government's abandonment of subsidized housing production. The federal government had shifted its focus to housing vouchers; it was no longer concerned, especially in tight housing markets, with the construction of much-needed new rental units for the poor.[67]

CONCLUSION: SHRINKING FEDERALISM AND THE NEW EMPHASIS ON THE STATES

The New Federalism left a permanent mark on the structure of intergovernmental relations. A number of major urban aid programs have been eliminated or have had their funding levels reduced. Even where federal spending for domestic programs continued, virtually all presidents since Richard Nixon have stressed the limits of federal action in urban affairs. The sense of national stewardship for the condition of America's communities has diminished considerably.

Since the New Deal, an expanded federal grant system accomplished a number of important objectives. Federal grants prompted states, counties, and cities to act on some of their more pressing urban and social problems. By encouraging state and local action, federal programs brought a new equity to service provision, helping to remediate the gross interstate and interlocal service inequalities of old. Federal aid and requirements also brought to the forefront new concerns for civil rights, citizen participation, and environmental protection.

However, as federal aid grew, more and more citizens and local governments objected to the waste, inefficiencies, intrusiveness, and lost accountability of a system that had grown too complex, bureaucratized, and distant. Anti-Washington sentiment prevailed as voters demanded more state and local control.

A suburban, parochial Congress has only the most limited tolerance for programs targeted to distressed communities. Senators and members of Congress tend to support programs that provide benefits to their states and districts for which they can then claim political credit. The result is a spread of program benefits nationwide, not a rational effort to target the government's limited resources to the neediest jurisdictions.

Even the war on terrorism has suffered from this spread effect as Congress acted to ensure that each state receives a minimum portion of homeland security assistance. In essence, three-fourths of homeland security funds were allocated without regard to threat. In fiscal 2004, New York City received only 3 percent of the $2.9 billion spent in the three largest homeland security programs. New York received much less per capita than did small states such as Wyoming.[68] By a 237 to 131 vote, rural, suburban, and Republican members of the House of Representatives rejected a proposal to redirect security spending away from rural areas to provide greater assistance to first responders in cities that are most likely to be the targets of terrorist attacks.[69]

In recent years, federal **place-based aid programs** for local economic revitalization (including Urban Development Action Grants and the programs of the Economic Development Administration) and housing (including HOPE VI) have either been terminated or greatly reduced. Instead, Congress and the presidency have turned to **people-based aid,** programs such as EITC and school and housing vouchers that provide assistance directly to persons in need and do not attempt to rebuild troubled localities.[70] Programs such as EITC have at times provided an infusion of disproportionate funds to distressed urban communities. Yet there is no guarantee that people-based aid will provide the concentration of resources that will allow the rebuilding of inner-city urban economies, schools, and assisted housing. School and housing vouchers that enable individual choice act to drain the resources available for central-city schools and public housing renovation. The shift of aid from places to individuals has also increased the assistance dispensed in suburban communities with their growing populations.

The federal government by itself cannot reverse urban decline. The national government simply lacks the resources and capacity to solve major urban problems. Over the years, the national government has come to see the wisdom and the necessity of forging **partnerships,** working with subnational governments, community-based and nonprofit organizations, and private businesses—all institutions that control critical resources in urban rebuilding.

Partnerships increase subnational flexibility in problem solving. But as a review of contemporary federal aid programs has revealed, the devolution of program authority should be attended with great caution, as local governments, too, tend to do what is popular and are not always willing to promote participatory and equity-oriented programs.

Federal devolution has also altered the environment for community-based organizations, producing a **contest federalism** in which nonprofit groups must compete for money; the more professional groups emerge triumphant while smaller groups often fail to survive. Where devolution has led to the disappearance of smaller groups, the New Federalism has worked to decrease, not increase, grassroots democracy.[71]

Devolution has also allowed cities to pursue development in tune with the demands of private interests. Chicago used HOPE VI funds to demolish public housing projects that impeded the gentrification of Bronzeville, the city's African-American heritage area, while ignoring the revitalization of more isolated public housing units located in the less desirable fringe areas of the city. In Chicago and elsewhere, local officials used HOPE VI funds to promote new commercial development, subordinating the interests of tenants to the demands of more powerful growth-oriented elites.[72]

By the end of the twentieth century, the federal government was no longer playing the active role in urban affairs that had characterized its urban renewal approach of the 1950s and 1960s: "The bottom line, however, is that the federal government was less significant in redevelopment and renewal in the last quarter of the 20th century than during the 25 years of federal urban renewal . . . The age of large-scale, federally funded clearance projects is over."[73]

Between 2003 and 2004, George W. Bush's faith-based initiatives led to a doubling of the money given to religious-based organizations. But at the same time, Bush slashed the funds available for more traditional urban programs in such areas as public housing, social services, community development, food stamps, and energy assistance.[74] Bush further attempted to shift empowerment zones, brownfields development programs, and numerous other economic development programs from the Department of Housing and Urban Development, with its ties to activist neighborhood groups and the poor, to the Department of Commerce, with its greater receptivity to the demands of local businesses.[75]

The federal government's increased reliance on housing vouchers also represents a shrinking of long-term federal urban responsibility. Congress, through its budgetary and appropriations processes, can decide in any year to reduce spending for vouchers. Federal contracts for the construction of subsidized housing, in contrast, represent a long-term commitment of funds that cannot so easily be cut back.

The limited reach of the federal government has led to the rediscovery of the important role played by the states in urban affairs. Over the years, state aid to cities has increased,[76] and states across the nation have shown a new activism in welfare-to-work, environmental protection, economic development, and a number of other important policy areas. A number of states have also initiated smart growth measures in an effort to contain sprawl.[77] In reforming urban education, states such as Massachusetts, New Jersey, Connecticut, Illinois, and Michigan took the unprecedented step of taking over troubled school districts and giving mayors new authority to shake up failing schools. The state of New Jersey provided over $100 million of state funds and loans—twice the total raised by corporate, foundation, and philanthropic giving—to build a performing arts center as part of an arts-based strategy intended to bring about the revitalization of Newark, the state's biggest city and one of the nation's most troubled urban centers.[78]

While the new state activism is a cause for celebration, the devolution of power to subnational governments should not be celebrated uncritically. State officials, too, answer to suburban and rural constituencies that demand their own share of aid and development projects. A greater reliance on block grants would also allow states and localities to shift housing programs toward middle-income tenants and homebuyers and away from very low-income renters.[79] State officials also tend to stress economic development goals—job and tax-base promotion—over competing social policy goals. In New Orleans, the governor's involvement in local affairs served to produce a pro-growth agenda; the needs of the Crescent City's poorer residents were ignored.[80] Federal rules continue to be an important guarantor of citizen participation, nondiscrimination, and environmental protection.

The federal aid cutbacks and program terminations of the New Federalism have served to change the "moral tenor" of city politics. Mayors and other local actors have had to pay greater attention to public investment, manage-ment, and efficiency, turning away from the social agendas of an earlier urban era: "[C]ity hall is far less likely to be used these days as the bully pulpit from which mayors once sought to exercise leadership on major social, racial, and economic issues."[81]

New Federalism aid cutbacks also forced cities to become increasingly reliant on property taxes and other own-source revenues. Cities have had to be creative in discovering new revenue-producing and development-finance strategies. Municipalities have had to give greater attention to budgeting and strategic planning. These are the subjects of our next chapter.

NOTES

1. Charles J. Orlebeke, "The Evolution of Low-Income Housing Policy, 1949 to 1989," *Housing Policy Debate* 11, 2 (2000): 505–506.
2. Bernard H. Ross, Cornelius Kerwin, and A. Lee Fritschler, *How Washington Works: The Executive's Guide to Government* (Sun Lakes, AZ: Thomas Horton Publishers, 1996), Chaps. 5–6.
3. The classic bakery metaphors for the changing federal system are usually associated with the writings of federalism scholar Morton Grodzins. The marble cake metaphor was first presented by Joseph E. McLean, *Politics Is What you Make It*, Public Affairs Pamphlet no. 181 (Washington, DC: Public Affairs Press, 1952), p. 5.
4. Michael D. Reagan and John G Sanzone, *The New Federalism*, 2nd ed. (New York: Oxford University Press, 1981), p. 3.
5. William T. Gormley, Jr., "An Evolutionary Approach to Federalism in the U.S." (paper presented at the annual meeting of the American Political Science Association, San Francisco, August 30–September 2, 2001).
6. Reagan and Sanzone, *The New Federalism*, p. 10. The quotation is from *U.S. v. Darby*, 312 U.S. 100, 1941.
7. *National League of Cities v. Usery*, 426 U.S. 833 (1976).
8. *Garcia v. San Antonio Metropolitan Transportation Authority*, 464 U.S. 546 (1985).
9. *South Carolina v. Baker*, 108 S. Ct. 1935 (1988).
10. *United States v. Lopez*, 514 U.S. 549 (1995).
11. Charles Wise, "Judicial Federalism: The Resurgence of the Supreme Court's Role in the Protection of State Sovereignty," *Public Administration Review* 58, 2 (March/April 1998): 96.
12. *Printz v. United States* 117 S. Ct. 2365 (1997).
13. Wise, "Judicial Federalism," p. 97. For a view critical of the Court's decision in *Printz*, see Matthew D. Adler, "State Sovereignty and the Anti-Commandeering Cases," *Annals of the American Academy of Political and Social Science* 574 (March 2001): 158–172.
14. *U.S. v. Morrison* 120 S. Ct. 1740 (2000).
15. Edward L. Rubin, "Puppy Federalism and the Blessings of America," *Annals of the American Academy of Political and Social Science* 574 (March 2001): 37–51, observes that the United States enjoys a sense of national unity with little real public sentiment for a return to dual federalism. As a result, the federalism rulings of the Rehnquist Court have not really done much to challenge the existence of

the modern, centralized, administrative state. Robert F. Nagel, "Judicial Power and the Restoration of Federalism," pp. 62–65 in the same issue of the *Annals,* similarly sees little public support for a return to dual federalist decentralization.

16. Michael S. Greve, *Real Federalism* (Washington DC: American Enterprise Institute Press, 1999), pp. 79–86; Wise, "Judicial Federalism," pp. 95 and 98. For further analysis of the court's evolving federalism doctrine, see David H. Rosenbloom and Bernard H. Ross, "Toward a New Jurisprudence of Constitutional Federalism: The Supreme Court in the 1990's and Public Administration," *American Review of Public Administration* 28 (June 1998), pp. 107–125; Richard A. Brisbin, Jr., "The Reconstruction of American Federalism? The Rehnquist Court and Federal-State Relations, 1991–97," *Publius: The Journal of Federalism* (Winter 1998): 189–215; and Timothy J. Conlan and Francois Vergniolle De Chantal, "The Rehnquist Court and Contemporary American Federalism," *Political Science Quarterly* 116, 2 (Summer 2001): 253–275.

17. In addition to the three organizations mentioned in the paragraph, the ranks of the public interest groups (PIGs) also include the International City/Council Management Association (ICMA), the National Governors Association (NGA), the National Conference of State Legislatures (NCSL), and the Council of State Governments (CSG).

18. See The Brookings Institution Public Forum on "Block Grants; Past, Present, and Prospects," Washington, DC, October 13, 2003. Transcript available at www.brookings.edu/comm/events/20031015.htm.

19. David Walker, *The Rebirth of Federalism* (Chatham, NJ: Chatham House, 1995), pp. 11–13.

20. *The Burden of the Unfunded Federal Mandates: A Survey of the Impact of Unfunded Mandates on America's Counties* (Washington, DC: National Association of Counties, October, 1993).

21. Molly Stauffer and Carl Tubbesing, "The Mandate Monster: Unfunded Federal Mandates Are Back, and They Are Costing States Millions," *State Legislatures* (May 2004): 22.

22. Paul L. Posner, "Unfunded Mandate Reform Act: 1996 and Beyond," *Publius: The Journal of Federalism* 27 (Spring 1997): 53–71; Theresa Gullo and Janet Kelley, "Federal Unfunded Mandate Reform: A First Year Retrospective," *Public Administration Review* (October 1998): 379–387; Paul L. Posner, *The Politics of Unfunded Mandates* (Washington, DC: Georgetown University Press, 1998); Donald F. Kettl, "Mandates Forever," *Governing* (August 2003): 12; Janet M. Kelly, "The Unfunded Mandate Reform Act: Working Well For No Good Reason," *Government Finance Review* 19, 1 (February 2003): 28–30.

23. Stauffer and Tubbesing, "The Mandate Monster," p. 23; David S. Broder, "President's Unfunded Mandates Criticized," *Washington Post,* March 11, 2004.

24. Joseph Zimmerman, "State Mandate Relief: A Quick Look," *Intergovernmental Perspective* (Spring 1994): 28–30. Also see Janet M. Kelly, *Anti-Mandate Strategies: Reimbursement Requirements in the States* (Washington, DC: National League of Cities, 1994); and Janet Kelly, "Institutional Solutions to Political Problems: The Federal and State Mandate Cost Estimation Process," *State and Local Government Review* (Spring 1997): 90–97.

25. Bernard Frieden and Marshall Kaplan, *The Politics of Neglect* (Cambridge, MA: MIT Press, 1975); Marshall Kaplan and Franklin James, eds., *The Future of National Urban Policy* (Durham, NC: Duke University Press, 1990). For a brief

overview of the Model Cities experience, see Benjamin Kleinberg, *Urban America in Transformation: Perspectives on Urban Policy and Development* (Thousand Oaks, CA: Sage Publications, 1995), pp. 175–184.

26. Bruce A. Wallin, *From Revenue Sharing to Deficit Sharing* (Washington, DC: Georgetown University Press, 1998), pp. 137–139 and 56–95; David A. Caputo and Richard L. Cole, "General Revenue Spending Expenditure Decisions in Cities over 50,000," *Public Administration Review* 35 (March/April 1975): 136–142; and Richard P. Nathan and Charles F. Adams, Jr., *Revenue Sharing: The Second Round* (Washington, DC: Brookings Institution, 1977): pp. 27–32.

27. Richard P. Nathan and Paul R. Dommel, "Federal-Local Relations under Block Grants," *Political Science Quarterly* 93 (Fall 1978): 421–442; and Paul R. Dommel, "Social Targeting for Community Development," *Political Science Quarterly* 95 (Fall 1980): 465–478.

28. Myron A. Levine, "The Reagan Urban Policy: Efficient National Economic Growth and Public Sector Minimization," *Journal of Urban Affairs* 5 (Winter 1983): 17–28.

29. *National Journal* (October 3, 1981), p. 1785.

30. Conlan, *New Federalism*, p. 212; Howard E. McCurdy, "Environmental Protection and the New Federalism: The Sagebrush Rebellion and Beyond," in *Controversies in Environmental Policy*, eds. Sheldon Kamieniecki, Robert O'Brien, and Michael Clarke (Albany: State University of New York Press, 1986), pp. 85–107; and Harry Spence, director of the Boston Public Housing Authority. Testimony before the House Subcommittee on Housing, U.S. Senate Committee on Banking, Housing and Urban Affairs, March 20, 1982.

31. Kleinberg, *Urban America in Transformation*, p. 229.

32. Conlan, *New Federalism*, p. 160.

33. U.S. Conference of Mayors, figures cited by Peter Eisinger, "City Politics in an Era of Federal Devolution," *Urban Affairs Review* 33, 3 (January 1998): 311.

34. Timothy J. Conlan, *From New Federalism to Devolution* (Washington, DC: Brookings Institution Press, 1998), pp. 218–219.

35. Demetrios Caraley, "Washington Abandons Cities," *Political Science Quarterly* 107, 1 (1992): 1–30.

36. Carol F. Steinbach, "Shelter-skelter," *National Journal* (April 8, 1989), pp. 851–855.

37. John Shannon, "The Return to Fend-For-Yourself Federalism: The Reagan Mark," *Intergovernmental Perspective* 13, no. 3/4 (Summer-Fall 1987), cited in John D. Donahue, *Disunited States* (New York: Basic Books, 1997), p. 29.

38. Thomas R. Swartz and John E. Peck, "The Changing Faces of Fiscal Federalism," *Challenge* 33, 6 (November–December 1990): 41, cited in Donahue, *Disunited States*, p. 29.

39. George E. Peterson and Carol W. Lewis, eds. *Reagan and the Cities* (Washington, DC: Urban Institute Press, 1986).

40. Eisinger, "City Politics in an Era of Federal Devolution," pp. 310–314.

41. Dick Morris, *Behind the Oval Office* (New York: Random House, 1997).

42. Robert J. Waste, *Independent Cities: Rethinking U.S. Urban Policy* (New York: Oxford University Press, 1998), p. 90.

43. Department of Housing and Urban Development, *The State of the Cities 1999* (Washington, DC: DHUD, 1999).

44. The theoretical underpinnings of reinventing government are presented by David Osborne and Ted Gaebler, *Reinventing Government: How the Entrepreneurial*

Spirit Is Transforming the Public Sector from Schoolhouse to State House, City Hall to Pentagon (Reading, MA: Addison-Wesley, 1992). For an overview of the attitudes of local executives toward the reinventing government paradigm, see Richard C. Kearney, Barry M. Feldman, and Carmine P. F. Scavo, "Reinventing Government: City Manager Attitudes and Actions," *Public Administration Review* 60, 6 (December 2000): 535–548.

45. William A. Galston and Geoffrey L. Tibbetts, "Reinventing Federalism: The Clinton/Gore Program for a New Partnership Among Federal, State, and Tribal Governments," *Publius: The Journal of Federalism* 24 (Summer 1994); 25; David Osborne, *Laboratories of Democracy* (Boston: Harvard Business School Press, 1990).

46. Myron A. Levine, "Urban Policy in America: The Clinton Approach," *Local Economy* 9 (November 1994): 278–281. Kaplan and James, *The Future of National Urban Policy*, also argue the political necessity of pursuing national urban policy goals by "nonurban" policy tools.

47. Alan Berube and Thacher Tiffany, "The 'State' of Low-Wage Workers: How the EITC Benefits Urban and Rural Communities in the 50 States," a study of The Brookings Institution, Washington, DC, February 2004. Available at www.brookings.edu/es/urban/publications/eitc/20040203_berube.htm.

48. Alan Berube and Benjamin Forman, "Rewarding Work: the Impact of the Earned Income Tax Credit in Greater Chicago," a study of The Brookings Institution Center on Urban and Metropolitan Policy, Washington, DC, November 2001. Available at www.brookings.edu/es/urban/eitc/chicago.pdf.

49. Alan Berube, "¿Tienes EITC? A Study of the Earned Income Tax Credit in Immigrant Communities," a study of The Brookings Institution Metropolitan Policy Program, Washington, DC , May 2005, available at www.brookings.edu/dybdocroot/metro/pubs/20050412_tieneseitc.pdf; Michael Stegman, Walter Davis, and Roberto Quercio, "Tax Policy as Housing Policy: The EITC's Potential to Make Housing More Affordable for Working Families," a study of The Brookings Institution Center on Urban and Metropolitan Policy, Washington, DC, October 2003, available at www.brookings.edu/es/urban/publications/200310_stegman.htm.

50. Veronique de Rugy and Tad DeHaven, *Cato Institute Tax & Budget Bulletin*, No. 16, August 2003.

51. Bush's proposed Fiscal 2005 budget called for a reduction of $1.66 billion in housing vouchers, a move that would cut off assistance to an estimated 250,000 families. See the National Low Income Housing Coalition, "Bush Proposal Will Dismantle Housing Program for Lowest Income People," press release, February 2, 2004. Available at www.nlihc.org/press/pr020204.html.

52. The White House, Office of Faith-Based and Community Initiatives, *Unlevel Playing Field: Barriers to Participation by Faith-Based and Community Organizations in Federal Social Service Programs* (Washington, DC: WHOFBCI, 2001). Available at www.whitehouse.gov/news/releases/2001/08/unlevelfield.html.

53. For the competing arguments regarding Bush's faith-based initiatives, see: Amy E. Black, Douglas L. Koopman, and David K. Ryden, *Of Little Faith: The Politics of George W. Bush's Faith-Based Initiatives* (Washington, DC: Georgetown University Press, 2004), pp. 15–19, 66–69, and 264–265; and Jo Renee Formicola, Mary C. Segers, and Paul Weber, *Faith-Based Initiatives and the Bush Administration: The Good, the Bad, and the Ugly* (Lanham, MD: Rowman and Littlefield, 2003).

54. Formicola, Segers, and Weber, *Faith-Based Initiatives and the Bush Administration*, p. 172; Partha Deb and Dana Jones, "Does Faith Work? A Comparison of Labor Market Outcomes of Religious and Secular Job Training Programs," paper prepared for the Charitable Choice Research Project, the Center for Urban Policy and the Environment, Indiana University-Purdue University Indianapolis, October 2003, available at http://ccr.urbancenter.iupui.edu/PDFs/DC%20Conference/ faithjobtraining-10031.pdf. Various studies of the Charitable Choice Research Project are critical of the claims made by enthusiasts of faith-based initiatives. These studies can be found at http://ccr.urbancenter.iupui.edu/.

55. Kathe Newman, "Faith Based Institutions—Possibilities and Limitations: The Catholic Church in Chicago" (paper presented at the annual meeting of the Urban Affairs Association, Detroit, April 25–28, 2001).

56. For an analysis that points to both the benefits and risks of the superwaiver idea, see Pietro S. Nivola, Jennifer L. Noyes, and Isabel V. Sawhill, "Waive of the Future? Federalism and the Next Phase of Welfare Reform," *Brookings Institution Policy Brief* #29, Washington, DC, 2004, available at www.brookings.edu/es/research/projects/wrb/publications/pb/pb29.htm.

57. Jill Khadduri, "Should the Housing Voucher Program Become a State-Administered Block Grant?" *Housing Policy Debate* 14, 3 (2003): 235–269, points to the favorable results that can be expected from the block granting of housing assistance, as long as certain safeguards are kept in place. Her analysis is available at www.fanniemaefoundation.org/programs/hpd/pdf/ hpd_1403_khadduri.pdf. For a more critical view that cautions against converting housing vouchers into a state-administered block grant, see Margery Austin Turner and Susan Popkin, "Comment on Jill Khadduri's 'Should the Housing Voucher Program Become a State-Administered Block Grant?' A Housing Block Grant Is a Bad Idea," pp. 271–281 in the same volume, available at www.fanniemaefoundation.org/programs/hpd/pdf/ hpd_1403_turner.pdf.

58. Barbara Sard and Will Fischer, "Administration Seeks Deep Cuts in Housing Vouchers and Conversion of Program to a Block Grant," a report of the Center on Budget and Policy Priorities, March 24, 2004; Sard and Fischer, "Passing the Buck: The Administration's Flexible Voucher Program Would Compel Housing Agencies to Impose Deep Cuts in 2005 and Subsequent Years," a report of the Center on Budget and Policy Priorities, March 16, 2004.

59. For a description of the exact workings of the LIHTC, see: Orlebeke, "The Evaluation of Low-Income Housing Policy," pp. 511–515; Kirk McClure, "The Low-Income Housing Tax Credit as an Aid to Housing Finance: How Well Has It Worked?" *Housing Policy Debate* 11, 1 (2000): 91–114.

60. Department of Housing and Urban Development, "Data Sets: Low-Income Housing Tax Credit," Washington, DC June 8, 2004, available at www.huduser.org/datasets/lihtc.html; Remarks by Stockton Williams, senior director of public policy for The Enterprise Foundation, Washington, DC, February 21, 2003, available at www.nlihc.org/press/threattolihtc.pdf.

61. Lance Freeman, "Siting Affordable Housing: Location and Neighborhood Trends of Low Income Housing Tax Credit Developments in the 1990s," a report of The Brookings Institution Center on Urban and Metropolitan Policy, Washington, DC, April 2004. Available at www.brookings.edu/urban/publications/ 20040405_freeman.htm.

62. Morton J. Schussheim, *Housing the Poor: Federal Housing Program for Low-income Families* (Washington, DC: Congressional Research Service, 1998), as cited by Orlebeke, "The Evaluation of Low-Income Housing Policy," pp. 513–514.

63. "NLIHC President Sheila Crowley's Statement on HUD FY2004 Budget," Low-Income Housing Coalition, Washington, DC, February 4, 2003, available at www.nlihc.org/press/pr020403.html; Anne Kim, "Dividend Proposal Would Hit Affordable Housing," Progressive Policy Institute, Washington, DC, March 19, 2003, available at www.ppionline.org/ndol/print.cfm?contentid=251406.

64. See Charles C. Bohl, "New Urbanism and the City: Potential Applications and Implications for Distressed Inner-City Neighborhoods," *Housing Policy Debate* 11, 4 (2000): 761–801, and the "Comments" in the same volume by Michael Pyatok, pp. 803–812, and Shelley R. Poticha, pp. 815–819. In Chapter 11, we reviewed New Urbanism principles as applied to suburban development.

65. G. Thomas Kingsley, Jennifer Johnson, and Kathryn L. S. Petit, "Patterns of Section 8 Relocation in the HOPE VI Program," *Journal of Urban Affairs* 25, 4 (2003): 427–447; Janet L. Smith, comments during the colloquy on "The Racial Segregation of Public Housing" at the annual meeting of the Urban Affairs Association, Detroit, April 27, 2001; Susan J. Popkin, *The HOPE VI Program: What About the Residents?* a policy brief of The Urban Institute, Washington DC, December 2002, available at www.urban.org/url.cfm?ID=310593; Susan J. Popkin, Mary K. Cunningham, Erin B. Godfrey, Beata A. Bedna, Janet L. Smith, Anne Knepler, and Doug Schenkleberg, *CHA Relocation Counseling Assessment: Final Report,* a report of The Urban Institute, Washington, DC, July 1, 2002, available at www.urban.org/url.cfm?ID=410549. Also see David P. Varady and Carole C. Walker, "Vouchering Out Distressed Subsidized Developments: Does Moving Lead to Improvements in Housing and Neighborhood Conditions?" *Housing Policy Debate* 11, 1 (2000): 115–162.

66. Henry Cisneros and Bruce Katz, "Keep HOPE (VI) Alive," *MetroView* (May 17, 2004), available at www.brookings.edu/urban/20040517_metroview.htm.

67. Susan J. Popkin, Bruce Katz, Mary K. Cunningham, Karen D. Brown, Jeremy Gustafson, and Margery A. Turner, *A Decade of HOPE VI: Research Findings and Challenges* (Washington, DC: The Urban Institute and The Brookings Institution, 2004), available at www.urban.org/urlprint.cfm?ID=8864. *A Decade of HOPE VI* provides an excellent over of the history of HOPE VI, its accomplishments, limitations, and call for continuation and reform.

68. Hillary Rodham Clinton, "Give New York Its Fair Share of Homeland Money," *The New York Times,* August 22, 2004.

69. "House Rejects Effort to Shift Anti-Terror Fund for Cities," Associated Press wire report appearing in online version of *The New York Times,* June 18, 2004. Available at www.nytimes.com/aponline/national/AP-Security-Spending.html?hp.

70. John Kincaid, "*De Facto* Devolution and Urban Defunding: The Priority of Persons Over Places," *Journal of Urban Affairs* 21, 2 (1999): 135–167.

71. Janice L. Bockmeyer, "Devolution and the Transformation of Community Housing Activism," *Social Science Journal* 40 (2003): 175–188.

72. Alexander J. Reichl, "Public Housing and the Urban Landscape in Chicago and New Orleans" (paper presented at the annual meeting of the Urban Affairs Association, Cleveland, March 26, 2003); Reichl, "The Place of Public Housing in 21st-Century Cities" (paper presented at the annual

meeting of the American Political Science Association, Washington, DC, August 31–September 3, 2000).

73. Jon C. Teaford, "Urban Renewal and Its Aftermath," *Housing Policy Debate* 11, 2 (2000): 460–461.

74. Michael A. Fletcher, "Two Fronts in the War on Poverty: Bush Seeks More Aid for Church Groups, Others Face Uncertainty," *The Washington Post,* May 17, 2005.

75. Jonathan Weisman, "Bush Plans Sharp Cuts in HUD Community Efforts," *The Washington Post,* January 14, 2005.

76. Advisory Commission on Intergovernmental Relations, *Significant Features of Fiscal Federalism 1994* (Washington, DC: ACIR, 1994), p. 35, Table 45.

77. Jerry Anthony, "Do State Growth Management Regulations Reduce Sprawl?" *Urban Affairs Review* 39, 3 (2004): 376–397.

78. Elizabeth Strom, "Let's Put on a Show! Performing Arts and Urban Revitalization in Newark, New Jersey," *Journal of Urban Affairs* 21, 4 (1999): 423–435.

79. Edward G. Goetz, "Potential Effects of Federal Policy Devolution on Local Housing Expenditures," *Publius: The Journal of Federalism* 25, 3 (Summer 1995): 99–116.

80. Peter Burns and Matthew O. Thomas, "Governors and the Development Regime in New Orleans," *Urban Affairs Review* 39, 6 (2004): 791–812.

81. Eisinger, "City Politics in an Era of Federal Devolution," p. 309.

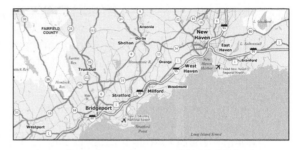

This chapter explores how cities obtain revenues, borrow money, and budget expenditures. Local governments operate amid a federal system of rules that tightly constrains their revenue-raising abilities. The anti-tax sentiment of voters further limits the ability of cities and suburbs to raise the necessary revenues to pay for municipal services. As the mid-1990s bankruptcy of Orange County, California demonstrated, even relatively affluent communities face constraints when attempting to fund local services.

According to accounting practice, *revenue* is a narrower term than *income*. The concept of **revenue** excludes funds that are borrowed through the issuance of notes and bonds.[1] In this chapter, we will discuss **income,** the more inclusive concept that encompasses borrowing as well as taxation and other sources of municipal revenue. We start by describing some of the more important sources of local revenue and the potential and limitations of each revenue source.

THE STRUCTURE OF LOCAL REVENUE SYSTEMS

Local governments rely on a complex variety of income sources. Quite obviously, local governments levy taxes—property taxes and, where states allow, sales and income taxes. Local governments also impose a large number of license fees, user fees, and "nuisance" taxes that generate smaller but still important sums of revenues. The exact taxes and fees that a locality is permitted to levy vary from state to state.

The vast majority of cities are greatly reliant on local property taxes, which account for 73 percent of local tax collections.[2] In 2002, 28 states also permitted local sales taxes. Only 16 permitted their local governments to levy an individual income tax. Put another way, nearly all municipalities in the United States levy a property tax. But only a bit more than half (58 percent) of the 555 cities with a population greater than 50,000 have some capacity to impose a sales tax. Very few, only 1 in 12 (or 8 percent), can impose a local income tax.[3]

The national figures hide important city-to-city variations in the taxing patterns that are largely the result of state law. Milwaukee, Portland, Buffalo, and Boston are greatly reliant on the property tax. Oklahoma City, Shreveport, and

Dallas, in contrast, show a greater reliance on the sales tax. Oklahoma state law virtually forces local governments to rely on the sales tax for local tax revenues. New York, Philadelphia, Baltimore, Cleveland, Columbus, Cincinnati, and Louisville collect substantial revenues from local income taxes.[4]

Local governments, however, do not depend on taxes alone for the money they need. As we discussed in Chapter 1, "The Urban Situation and 9/11," and Chapter 14, "National and State Policy toward Cities," localities receive large sums in the form of intergovernmental grants. Local jurisdictions also finance local projects by borrowing money from creditors by issuing short-term tax anticipation notes and long-term bonds.

The composition of local revenue systems has changed over time as a result of changes in state law and new trends in intergovernmental assistance.[5] Yet, as Figure 15-1 documents, the property tax remains the single most important component of local financing, providing a little over a quarter of local revenues. Sales and income tax receipts combined come close to matching the property tax, providing 21 percent of local tax revenues. Figure 15-1 also points to the importance of special charges and fees (11 percent) and state aid (13 percent). Federal funds account for a mere 2 percent of local general fund resources. This analysis, however, understates the real importance of federal aid to the health of urban communities. Federal assistance also supports local actions administered by specialized agencies, assistance that falls outside the scope of the general-fund figures reported in Figure 15-1.

STATE-IMPOSED LIMITS AND EXCLUSIONS

A **tax** is a compulsory contribution for the support of government, exacted without regard for individual benefit. A citizen cannot refuse to pay a tax simply because he or she receives no particular benefit from it.

■ FIGURE 15–1

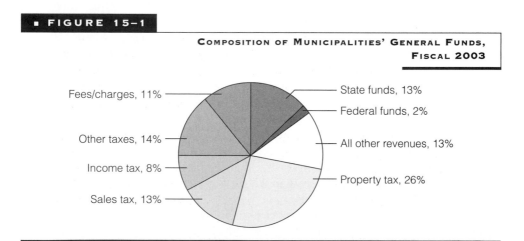

COMPOSITION OF MUNICIPALITIES' GENERAL FUNDS, FISCAL 2003

Fees/charges, 11%
State funds, 13%
Federal funds, 2%
Other taxes, 14%
All other revenues, 13%
Income tax, 8%
Property tax, 26%
Sales tax, 13%

SOURCE: Michael A. Pagano, *City Fiscal Conditions in 2004* (Washington, DC: National League of Cities, 2004), p. 4.

Local governments may impose only those taxes the states permit them to levy. A state's constitution and legislative statutes impose restrictions and limitations upon the taxing abilities of a state's municipal corporations.

Local revenues are diminished by state provisions that exempt certain classes of property from taxation. Local governments may not tax property owned by the federal and state governments. Property used for educational, religious, or charitable purposes, too, is commonly exempted from taxation. Most states also provide exemptions of one sort or another for veterans and for certain kinds of industrial and agricultural properties. Over 30 states seek to cushion the impact of property taxes on lower income or elderly residents with a **circuit breaker or homestead exemption** that makes their homes either wholly or partially nontaxable. As a result of these numerous exemptions, a very substantial proportion of real estate does not appear on local tax rolls, greatly reducing the property tax revenues that cities can collect.

Local property taxes are also subject to state-imposed **levy limits or millage limitations.*** States limit the rates that local governments may impose for such specific purposes as school construction, street repair, or recreation. As an illustration, a municipality may be authorized to levy up to five mills on each dollar of assessed valuation for street purposes, three mills for parks, two mills for health care, and so on.

States can also set an overall limitation on property taxes where the combined levies on a single piece of property may not exceed a designated maximum. States may also require that local voters approve increases in millage, making it difficult for localities to raise the property tax even when there are no specific state-imposed limits. In California and other states, municipal leaders have attempted to circumvent such limitations by having services provided by special districts that are not subject to the tax limitations placed on general-purpose local governments.

PROPERTY TAXES

The property tax has been at the heart of urban finance for 200 years. As we have observed, over one-fourth of municipal general revenue comes from property taxes (see Figure 15-1). While most cities rely heavily on property taxes, Oklahoma cities are an exception. Enid, Oklahoma does not levy a property tax for general municipal services; Enid residents, nonetheless, still pay property taxes levied by the school district and the county.

Despite their near-universal use, property taxes are politically unpopular. In a **property tax revolt,** voters in state after state have used the initiative device to curb property tax increases. State legislators also responded to the voters' anti-tax sentiment by placing other limits on local property taxation. As a result, as Tables 15-1 and 15-2 document, property taxes have been declining

---

* **Millage** is a tax rate expressed in mills per dollar that is normally used in property taxation. A mill equals one-thousandth of a dollar. A 10-mill rate is the equivalent of a 1-percent tax. Usually, property tax rates are expressed per hundred or per thousand of assessed value.

■ TABLE 15–1

PROPERTY TAXES AS A PERCENTAGE OF GENERAL
REVENUE, BY LEVEL OF GOVERNMENT, VARIOUS YEARS

		Local Governments					
Year	States	All	Counties	Municipalities	Townships	School Districts	Special Districts
1962	2.1	48.0	45.7	44.2	65.3	51.0	25.0
1967	1.7	43.2	42.1	38.1	61.8	46.9	21.5
1972	1.3	39.5	36.5	31.3	64.9	47.3	17.3
1977	1.3	33.7	31.0	25.8	56.8	42.1	14.0
1982	1.1	28.1	26.6	21.4	52.1	35.8	9.5
1986	1.1	28.2	27.3	20.5	52.1	36.2	10.4
1991	1.1	29.9	28.1	22.9	55.8	37.2	11.3
1992	1.1	29.3	27.9	23.1	56.9	37.4	11.0

SOURCE: U.S. Department of Commerce (1962, 1967, 1972, 1977, 1982), table entitled "General Revenue by Type of Government." For 1986 and 1991 data, see the Bureau of the Census, *Governmental Finance*, 1986 and 1991. 1992 data provided by the Bureau of the Census.

■ TABLE 15–2

PROPERTY TAXES AS A PERCENTAGE OF TAXES,
BY LEVEL OF GOVERNMENT, VARIOUS YEARS

		Local Governments					
Year	States	All	Counties	Municipalities	Townships	School Districts	Special Districts
1962	3.1	87.7	93.5	93.5	99.3	98.6	100.0
1967	2.7	88.6	92.1	70.0	92.8	98.4	100.0
1972	2.1	83.7	85.6	64.3	93.5	98.1	94.9
1977	2.2	80.5	81.2	60.9	91.7	97.5	91.2
1982	1.9	76.1	77.2	52.6	93.7	96.8	79.6
1986	1.9	74.0	74.5	49.3	92.7	97.4	79.8
1992	2.0	75.6	74.3	52.6	93.0	97.4	67.6

SOURCE: U.S. Department of Commerce (1962, 1967, 1972, 1977, 1982), table entitled "General Revenue by Type of Government." For 1986 and 1991 data, see the Bureau of the Census, *Governmental Finance*, 1986 and 1991. 1992 data provided by the Bureau of the Census.

in relative importance in local revenue and tax systems. In 1962, the property tax provided about half of municipal own-source revenues; by 2001, the figure had dropped to 26.5 percent,[6] greatly affecting the ability of local governments to provide services.

Property taxes also remain of critical importance in school finance. While state aid to public schools has increased and now provides over half of local school budgets, the property tax accounts for nearly all locally raised revenues by school districts (Table 15-2).

As we have already noted, localities cannot impose taxes on state and federal property. The property of churches, colleges, and nonprofit [501(c)(3)] organizations is similarly exempt from taxation. In communities with many public facilities, these exemptions pose serious problems for the ability of local governments to raise needed revenues. In some cases, large nonprofit institutions have agreed to make voluntary **payments in lieu of taxes;** however, such payments seldom match the figure that localities would have collected through the application of the property tax.

Ideally, property taxes should be **universal;** that is, they should be levied on all forms of property. Property taxes should also be **uniform** (levied at the same rate on all forms of property). Unfortunately, in the real world, neither of these ideals has been achieved.

As the different types of property multiplied, the concept of universality became unattainable. Governments find it much easier to tax **real property** (land and improvements) as opposed to **personal property** (furnishings, appliances, automobiles, and inventories and equipment at work). The government cannot easily assess the value of personal property for tax purposes. Owners can hide much of the value of personal property that has a low degree of visibility or is easily mobile. As a result, governments often levy taxes on tangible personal property items that are required to be registered with the state, including cars, boats, mobile homes, and RVs.

Today, real and tangible personal property no longer represents a citizen's true wealth. Wealth also takes the form of cash, stocks, and bonds, all of which are classified as **intangible personal property.** However, intangible personal property often escapes taxation, as such taxes are difficult to enforce. For a long time, Ohio counties imposed an intangibles tax, but many residents simply evaded the tax.

Over the years, state and local governments have retreated from the goal of universality and have given up the effort to tax intangibles and hard-to-locate household personal property. Consequently, a significant portion of the wealth of the members of any community lies beyond the reach of local property taxes.

Uniformity, too, has come into question. Most states began by requiring that all property be taxed at the same rate. Yet legislators soon began to levy higher taxes on industrial and commercial than on residential property, arguing that the owners of industry and commerce had a greater ability to bear the burden of such taxation. Today, legislators further compromise the ideal of uniformity when they give tax concessions as part of a package to lure or keep important business development, tax advantages that are denied other property owners in the city.

The property tax also suffers from being a **regressive tax;** the tax paid by a low- or moderate-income homeowner often represents a greater percentage of that family's annual income than does the property tax paid by an upper-income household. In Northern Virginia and other rapidly growing areas with soaring home values, a doubling (and sometimes even a tripling) of property tax bills has made it difficult for Habitat for Humanity homeowners and other low-income owners to be able to stay in their homes.[7]

It is often charged that renters pay no property taxes. This is not exactly true. A good portion of property taxes is passed on to tenants through higher rents, except where rents cannot be raised for market reasons or where rent controls, such as in New York City and a few other cities, prohibit immediate rent hikes. Renters do not escape property taxation, for in the long run they do bear the burden of property taxes. Yet tenants often fail to turn out to vote in as strong numbers as homeowners on referenda dealing with local spending and property tax levels.

A central administrative problem in property taxation concerns *assessment*. A **tax assessor** has the responsibility of determining the assessment or the value of property for tax purposes.

It is not a simple task to assess the value of property for tax purposes. Some local governments value residential property at lower rates than commercial property. Also, in a number of states, different local jurisdictions can assign two equivalent pieces of property quite different values for the purpose of levying taxes. This is largely a legacy of past practices when municipal governments attempted to shield local property against state taxation by assessing their land at only a fraction of full market value.[8] Where fractional assessments still persist, equalization procedures must adjust for the difference in local assessment practices so that property owners are not financially punished for living in jurisdictions that assess at full market value.

As a result of further problems with assessment practices, two comparable parcels of land may still wind up being assessed at different values. Despite computerization, local assessors still often have difficulty in bringing assessments up to date with changes in the market value of real estate in a neighborhood. No jurisdiction has the capacity to assess or reassess all the property within its borders each year. As a result, property that has been assessed more recently often bears a higher tax burden than does older property in the same area, undermining the concept of uniformity in taxation.

In other cases, undeveloped land is seriously underassessed as the result of pressure applied by land owners, developers, and real estate interests. These groups insist that tracts waiting for development be assessed as agricultural land and not at the higher valuations placed on land that it is demand for residential, commercial, or industrial property.

To remedy this problem, local governments have increasingly adopted the policy of assessing all land at its highest usage level. But this practice creates new problems. The owners of older, single-family homes face the unhappy prospect of paying whopping tax increases when they find that their values of their property areas have soared as the areas have become "hot" sites of new development.

When land is assessed at its highest usage value, the tax burden imposed on farms in growing suburban and exurban areas may serve to take land out of agricultural use. Incredible as it may seem, citrus groves in southern California suburbs have been assessed as potential residential developments in recognition of the huge profits that will be realized when the property is converted to such use. Faced with the prospect of such taxes, farmers sooner or later sell their land to developers, in a process that exacerbates urban sprawl. Some states have tried to cope with this problem by providing special taxing categories and lower assessments that protect agricultural land. Other states allow agreements with owners that require them to keep land in agricultural use or as wetlands in return for lower property tax assessments.

Property tax reform is difficult to achieve because any change will wind up raising taxes on some people while cutting the taxes on others. In many communities, especially in "property poor" jurisdictions, the property tax base does not provide adequate revenue to support much-needed city services. In recent years, much of the thrust for reforming the property tax has come from people interested in providing more equitable local school finance.[9]

SALES TAXES

Just about half of the states allow municipalities to levy a sales tax. Over the past 30 years, the use of municipal and county sales taxes has been on the upswing (see Table 15-3). Most states permit municipalities to **piggyback** the local levy onto the state sales tax, retaining the collection and administration at the state level. This reduces the costs of collection to local governments while producing maximum revenue for municipalities.

Sales taxes, though, have major faults. Most significantly, they are regressive; sales taxes impose a greater burden proportionally on lower-income groups than on the wealthy, since the poor spend a greater proportion of their incomes on purchases subject to taxation. Sales taxes applied to groceries, medicine, and other necessities of life are particularly distressing. Many states exempt the purchase of such items from taxation; some exempt clothing as well. These exemptions make the tax burden less regressive and nearly "flat" in some cases.

Sales taxes also have not provided a dependable stream of income for localities. The receipts from the sales tax (and from the income tax, as well) are highly dependent on national as well as local economic conditions. Local revenues grew considerably in the economic boom period that followed the end of the national recession in 1993. However, the post-9/11 economic slump resulted in falling sales that diminished income tax revenues. In 2001, sales taxes provided only 4.6 percent of local general revenues.[10]

The rise of e-commerce, phone sales, and Internet transactions poses a significant vehicle for evading the sales tax, especially for transactions across state lines. Jurisdictions lose considerable money, as a state or city cannot easily

■ TABLE 15–3

GENERAL AND SELECTIVE SALES TAXES
AS A PERCENTAGE OF GENERAL REVENUE,
BY LEVEL OF GOVERNMENT

		Local Governments				
Year	States	All	Counties	Municipalities	Townships	School Districts	Special Districts
1962							
General	16.4	2.5	1.1	6.6	*	*	*
All	38.6	3.8	1.5	9.9	1.5	*	*
1967							
General	17.1	2.1	1.6	5.1	0.1	0.1	*
All	35.7	3.4	2.1	8.5	1.5	0.1	*
1972							
General	17.9	2.6	3.2	5.4	*	0.2	0.8
All	33.7	4.1	3.8	9.1	1.6	0.2	0.9
1977							
General	18.3	3.1	3.9	5.8	*	0.3	1.2
All	31.0	4.6	4.7	9.6	2.1	0.3	1.2
1982							
General	18.3	3.6	4.4	6.9	*	0.4	2.2
All	28.6	5.3	5.5	11.1	0.1	0.4	2.2
1986							
General	19.0	4.2	5.6	7.4	*	0.3	3.9
All	28.6	5.9	6.7	12.0	*	0.4	3.9
1991							
General	18.7	4.1	5.8	7.1	*	*	4.3
All	12.9	5.9	7.1	11.9	*	0.3	4.4

* Less than 0.1 percent.
General: includes state and local government general sales and gross receipt taxes.
All: includes state and local government selective excise taxes, general sales, and gross receipt taxes.
SOURCE: U.S. Department of Commerce (1962, 1967, 1972, 1977, 1982), table entitled "General Revenue by Type of Government." For 1986 and 1991 data, see the Bureau of the Census, *Governmental Finance,* 1986 and 1991.

enforce the collection of the sales tax unless a seller is physically located in the jurisdiction. Congress further constricted the possible yield of subnational taxes on the Internet when it passed a moratorium that exempted Internet access from state and local taxes. Internet advocates argue that the federal law is critical to avoiding the constraints on broadband growth that would result from a confusing array of state and local tax laws. State and local officials, however, respond that the legislation creates loopholes that undermine subnational revenue systems. They have urged Congress to pass new legislation that would allow for uniform and simplified state and local taxes applied to the Internet.[11]

INCOME TAXES

The income tax, which is so productive at the national level, is a growing but still relatively small feature of local revenue systems (see Table 15-4). While 16 states allow some or all of their cities, counties, and school districts to levy income taxes, the importance of local income taxes varies greatly from city to city. In Louisville, Columbus (Ohio), and Philadelphia, the income tax provides a quite substantial portion of local tax collections

Local income taxes are generally seen to be fair as they are less regressive than sales and property taxes. In some states, municipal income taxes are characterized by **flat tax rates;** the same rate of taxation is imposed on all citizens and does not vary with a taxpayer's wealth. In other cities, the local income tax is a **progressive tax** in which wealthier residents are taxed at higher rates than are poorer citizens.

In some states, local income tax is a **piggyback tax** that the state collects for a community when the state collects its own tax revenues. Piggyback taxation reduces the local costs of administering and collecting the tax.

Local income taxes face serious shortcomings. In areas in which localities must collect and administer the tax, these costs run particularly high. Moreover, the imposition of local income taxes on nonresidents has led to controversies in virtually every city that has adopted the income tax. Municipalities seek to tax nonresidents who work within their boundaries, arguing that commuters should help pay for police and fire protection and other services that

■ TABLE 15-4

INDIVIDUAL INCOME TAXES AS A PERCENTAGE OF
GENERAL REVENUE, BY LEVEL OF GOVERNMENT,
VARIOUS YEARS

		Local Governments			
Year	States	Counties	Municipalities	Townships	School Districts
1962	8.8	0.1	2.0	0.2	0.3
1967	9.4	0.1	4.2	0.4	0.3
1972	13.2	0.8	5.4	0.7	0.3
1977	15.1	0.9	5.1	1.1	0.3
1982	16.6	1.0	4.3	1.4	0.3
1986	17.1	1.0	4.5	1.3	0.3
1991	17.9	1.1	4.7	1.4	0.3

SOURCE: U.S. Department of Commerce (1962, 1967, 1972, 1977, 1982), table entitled "General Revenue by Type of Government." For 1986 and 1991 data, see the Bureau of the Census, *Governmental Finance,* 1986 and 1991.

the central city provides. Nonresidents, however, vociferously object to paying an income tax to a jurisdiction in which they do not live or vote. State legislatures have responded to suburban voting power by denying localities the rights to impose an income tax or, in other cases, by requiring that the tax on nonresidents be set at a lower rate than the tax paid by residents. In Michigan municipalities that have a local income tax, city residents pay 1 percent, while commuters are taxed at only half that rate. Nonresident taxes are also imposed only on the portion of income that a commuter earned in the city, not on the taxpayer's total income.

States have greatly limited the local use of income taxes. As a result of the continuing growth of suburban populations and voting power, the income tax does not appear to be a politically feasible, long-term solution to the revenue problems of most cities. In 2001, the personal income tax provided less than 2 percent of local general revenues.[12]

MINOR TAXES, LICENSING FEES, AND USER CHARGES

Most cities impose minor taxes and licensing fees (often referred to as **nuisance taxes**) to supplement their revenues. Many localities have a **wheel tax** levied on residents (and, in some cities, commuters) who park in the city. Cities also tax amusements, the occupancy of hotel rooms, and the sale of cigarettes and alcoholic beverages. Many areas also require paid licenses for the sale of alcoholic beverages, the operation of taxicabs, and other services. These licensing requirements serve a dual purpose: They regulate activities while producing new revenue for the city. Such taxes and fees, however, seldom provide a significant portion of local revenues.

An increasingly popular form of taxation is the imposition of **charges or user fees** for services rendered; only those people who use a service pay for it. Urban transit systems are partially funded through the fare box. Public utilities providing water, power, and sewage disposal also are financed, at least in part, by charges to customers. Other improvements (streets, sidewalks, and street lighting, for example) are often financed by special assessments against property owners in the affected area. Even the construction of new sports stadiums can be financed, at least in part, by user fees or the creation of a special user tax district. (See "Who Should Pay for a City's New Sports Stadium?" on p. 483.)

User fees are popular, as they are seen by many citizens to be a fair way of raising revenue. User fees are also paid by nonresidents who use a city's services. Taxpayers by a wide margin prefer user fees to raising the level of other taxes.[13] In a tight revenue situation, local governments have become increasingly reliant on user fees. Special districts are especially reliant on user fees, gaining approximately 60 percent of their revenues from current charges and various other fees.[14]

Conservatives also argue that user fees can be employed to help stem the growth of government. If citizens are made to pay the full costs every time they use a service, they will no longer regard municipal services as "free." Citizens

WHO SHOULD PAY FOR A CITY'S NEW SPORTS STADIUM?

In city after city, the owners of professional sports teams have asked governments to foot the costs of building new arenas with luxury boxes and state-of-the-art technology and amenities. Team owners, as well as sports boosters and other members of a city's growth coalition, justify taxpayer subsidies by pointing to economic and intangible benefits that such development brings to a city. Much debate, however, continues over just which taxes are most appropriate in subsidizing the construction of such facilities, where costs can exceed $500 million.

David Swindell and Mark S. Rosentraub argue that the economic and intangible benefits promised by the backers of the news sports stadiums and arenas are often grossly overstated. Fans, players, owners, and concession operators are the real beneficiaries of a new sports facility. New stadiums generally do little to bring economic prosperity to neighborhoods and residents outside of the immediate area of the new facility. It is a sports team's fans who feel the greatest sense of pride when a new facility is built.

Consequently, Swindell and Rosentraub argue that it is inappropriate to use broad-based general taxes (such as sales and property taxes) and broad-based special taxes (such as increases in the taxes imposed on hotel rooms, car rentals, or the sale of alcohol and tobacco) that have large numbers of citizens pay for a new sports facility that concentrates benefits on a relatively narrow portion of a city's population. Swindell and Rosentraub argue for the sense of fairness inherent in a "benefit principle": Those who enjoy the benefits of the new stadium should pay the most to support the new facility.

The authors urge the creation of a "special user tax district" in the area immediately adjacent to the facility; the new stadium could be financed through income taxes on players and taxes imposed on tickets, souvenirs, and food and beverage consumption. Citizens who do not attend events at a stadium would not have to pay to support its construction.

Sources: David Swindell and Mark S. Rosentraub, "Who Benefits from the Presence of Professional Sports Teams? The Implications for Public Funding of Stadiums and Arenas," *Public Administration Review* 58, 1 (January/February 1998): 11–20. Also see Roger G. Noll and Andrew Zimbalist, "Sports, Jobs, and Taxes: Are New Stadiums Worth the Cost?" *The Brookings Review* (Summer 1997): 35–39.

who pay the full cost of using a service will demand a higher quality of service; alternatively, they may seek the elimination of those services that are not worth the charge. For this to happen, though, user fees must be set at the true price of the service provided; user fees that are set too low represent only token charges that encourage the overutilization of services—even services of poor quality.[15]

User fees can pose great equity and access problems if people in need of a service cannot afford the required fee. Public transportation presents a good example of the problems that result when user fees are relied upon to finance a service; people who need public transportation the most are the ones least able to pay for it, especially if fares are increased to reflect the true costs of service. Raising the fare-box price only discourages ridership, leading people back to pollution-causing automobiles. Consequently, fare-box revenues and user fees must be supplemented with general tax revenues to provide for the necessary funds for the expansion and equitable provision of public transportation and similar services.[16]

GAMBLING

States and cities have turned to government-sponsored gambling as a way to augment their resources. Faced with budgetary shortfalls and reductions in intergovernmental aid, gambling has become an increasingly attractive alternative source of revenues.

LOTTERIES. In 2002, 38 states and the District of Columbia had state lotteries. Eighteen states **earmarked funds,** requiring by state law that a portion of the profits from the lottery be used to finance education; 13 states required that the entire proceeds of the lottery be used solely for education. Ten states earmarked a portion of lottery funds for such urban-oriented purposes as senior citizen programs, transportation, economic development, and property tax relief.[17]

Critics charge that the advocates of lotteries and other forms of government-sponsored gambling often overstate the benefits and understate the costs of introducing gambling to a community. Lottery revenue, for instance, has not been the cure to the public schools' financial problems. Even in states that earmark lottery revenue for education, the reality is that the proceeds from the lottery are used to help support other services, not just education. Even when lottery receipts are dedicated to help fund education, state legislators gain the ability to divert other revenues to nonschool purposes. The impact of lottery proceeds on schools is diminished by this spending diversion.

Critics also point out that lotteries are a regressive means of financing public services that extract a disproportionate burden from poorer, less educated residents who do not realize that the state odds are stacked against the buyers of lottery tickets and casino players. Mathematician Roger Jones has referred to state lotteries as "a tax on the mathematically challenged."[18]

CASINOS. Over the years, more and more cities have turned to casino and riverboat gambling in an effort to find new revenues. Advocates of casino gambling argue that the fees and tax revenues associated with casino gambling represent an important and almost voluntary stream of revenues for state and local governments. Casinos attract patrons from out of state, generating taxable proceeds that diminish the burden a state must place on its own taxpayers. The promise of revenue inherent in casinos is so great that state and local governments have sought out Native-American tribes to sponsor casino gambling and other forms of gaming that would otherwise be prohibited by state law.

The benefits of casino gambling are often overstated, as casino gambling brings new costs as well as revenues to a community. Cities must increase police activities and are often asked to build new convention centers and make other necessary infrastructure improvements to support the casino and convention trade. High-paying casino jobs also attract talented workers away from a city's school and public health systems.

As is also the case with lotteries, revenues from casinos often fall short of expected projections as states and cities compete with one another for gambling dollars. Casinos have spread nationwide to an ever-growing number of cities, Indian reservations, riverboats, and **racinos** (racetracks permitted to install slot machines and other casino-style devices). A city that permits casinos no longer monopolizes the gaming industry as Las Vegas and Atlantic City once did. No person needs to travel a great distance to gamble; people have numerous opportunities closer to home. The market for gambling is so competitive and fragmented that a number of casinos, even in Atlantic City, have gone bankrupt. New York governor George Pataki's plans for casinos in the Catskills mountains area outside of New York City was seen by Connecticut and New Jersey as a raid to lure gambling dollars away from casinos in New York's neighboring states. Massachusetts and Rhode Island similarly began to consider additional gaming activities of their own rather than continue to see the outflow of gambling dollars to neighboring states.[19]

Not all cities have the potential to capture the financial benefits associated with casino gambling. Cities gain the greatest benefits when gambling attracts conventioneers and tourists who stay for a couple of nights or more, spending money outside the casinos. In such cases, casinos can act as a spur to economic development elsewhere in the city. Cities benefit much less when casinos attract only **day trippers** who come to gamble and then leave for home before the day is over. Casino operators also seek to provide entertainment, shopping, and restaurants (including free or discounted meals) that keep gamblers inside a casino, close to the betting tables and slot machines. Such casino design features internalize activity, minimizing the extent to which gamblers will spur the revitalization of city neighborhoods by patronizing outside restaurants and stores.

Las Vegas has the climate and attractions to draw major conventions and tourism. But can casinos in Detroit and Gary (Indiana) be similarly attractive to national gatherings? Even though casinos in Atlantic City failed to generate a tourist trade of the magnitude enjoyed by Las Vegas, Atlantic City nonetheless still draws large numbers of day trippers from the New York metropolitan area. But can casinos in Detroit and Gary attract a similar flow of customers when there are so many alternative gambling sites in Canada and on Indian reservations and riverboats throughout Michigan, the Chicagoland area, and the entire Midwest? Even where casinos fail to generate the revenues for cities that their backers envisioned, they still produce the social ills that often accompany legalized gaming.

The Atlantic City experience shows that, despite the claims of a city's growth coalition, casinos are a poor tool for urban redevelopment. By the late-1990s, one of every three jobs in Atlantic County, New Jersey were casino-related; however, the city still suffered double-digit unemployment. City residents employed by the casinos were concentrated in low-wage hotel jobs that offer little opportunity for investment. As of 1997, the Casino Redevelopment Authority (CRDA) committed over $670 million to redevelopment projects in Atlantic City; but much of the money subsidized an expanded convention center, a visitor's welcome center, a new baseball stadium, and other casino-related and tourism projects, not neighborhood renewal. The CRDA's investment of more than $185 million in low- and moderate-income housing primarily aided moderate-income families, not the city's poor. Casino development has even exacerbated the housing-problems for low-income residents by generating a process of land speculation that raised rents and displaced residents from the low-income areas surrounding casino projects.[20]

The expectations that riverboat gambling can revive troubled local economies are especially misplaced. Riverboats tend to attract day trippers, not vacationers and tourists. Where riverboats are required by state law to travel a river, patrons have no opportunity to leave and patronize local shops and restaurants. Except for a case such as Joliet, Illinois, located an hour away from Chicago, riverboat gambling seldom attracts a large number of visitors to a city.[21]

In cities in which the gambling industry fails to flourish as predicted, casino operators and their growth coalition allies demand new subsidies and concessions from the city—including such expensive public projects as a new convention center or a modernized airport or road system—in order to increase their customer base and profitability. In Atlantic City, the state of New Jersey relaxed its ban on 24-hour gambling and other regulations in response to the "growing pains" being felt by the casino industry. When Philadelphia Mayor Ed Rendell announced plans to launch riverboat gambling in his Pennsylvania city just across the river from New Jersey, the State of New Jersey responded with new measures to establish an atmosphere friendly to casinos. The state gave new tax credits for hotel construction in Atlantic City. New Jersey Governor Christine Todd Whitman pushed for the deregulation of casinos and announced a plan of major road and tunnel construction to aid the development of new gambling sites. Atlantic City mayor James Whelan also declared his willingness to use the city's power of eminent domain to abet casino expansion—a reversal of his previous vow to preserve neighborhoods: "We cannot rebuild a city and allow a handful of home owners to hold us hostage."[22]

Attempts to regulate the industry to control the ill effects of gambling do not always work well. Missouri sought to limit casino gambling to riverboats. But developers dug a "boat moat" just outside St. Louis, allowing a huge floating casino to remain connected to the Mississippi River while lying permanently at anchor; the casino did not resemble a boat at all. In city after city, casino operators pressed for the relaxation of regulations, arguing that local casinos can be economically viable only if they are accorded the flexibility to compete with other gambling venues. In Missouri, Nevada, New Jersey, Iowa, and other states, there is continuing suspicion that the enforcement of regulations on casinos is further compromised as the result of a "revolving door" career pattern in which government regulators seek lucrative jobs in the casino industry.

The extent to which gambling is good for a state or city is greatly dependent on how the proceeds of gambling are distributed. Just what percentages go to the city and to the state? What percentages go to the gambling industry and, where appropriate, to the sponsoring Native-American tribes? In addition, what percentage of gambling proceeds is dedicated to making improvements in the casino district, as the casino operators demand, as opposed to being placed in the municipal treasury to help pay for more general public services? The exact terms of a gambling agreement determine the extent to which gambling helps a city and its people and not just the state and the gambling industry.

Casinos sponsored by Native Americans that are developed outside of reservation land can pose a challenge to local authorities. In Sonoma County, California, a casino-hotel development project on 2,000 rural acres initiated by Native Americans was met with the outcry of local officials who claimed that they were not adequately consulted on the project. U.S. senator Dianne Feinstein argued for the need to give local governments a greater voice in such developments: "This presents serious problems for local governments, because the local government has absolutely no control over zoning, police, fire, roads, or any other local ordinance."[23]

Over the years, the chorus of opposition to casino gambling has diminished considerably as more and more states and cities have realized substantial revenue gains from gambling. City after city has turned to casinos from the fear of losing revenues to gaming in neighboring jurisdictions. In Detroit, a public vote in support of casinos finally passed after a number of similar measures had gone down in defeat in previous years. The opening of casinos in Windsor, Ontario (just across the river from Detroit), the spread of casinos to Native-American reservations in Michigan, and the likely adoption of casino gambling by other cities in the Midwest all acted to change public opinion in the city. Voters in Detroit were jumping on the bandwagon of casino gambling. As more and more cities were permitting citizens to gamble, their city, too, might as well share in the economic and fiscal benefits.

Government and gambling interests have come to a new accommodation. In California in 2004, Native-American tribes and governor Arnold Schwarzenegger reached an agreement to raise the number of gaming machines allowed on reservations. In his gubernatorial campaign, Schwarzenegger had promised to increase the state's proceeds from tribal gaming. Given the state's huge budgetary deficit, California desperately needed the agreed-to payments. Opponents countered that California would not receive nearly the full revenues that Schwarzenegger predicted.

INTERGOVERNMENTAL REVENUES

Intergovernmental assistance to cities takes various forms. In shared tax revenues, for instance, states return to local governments a portion of some taxes collected within the local jurisdiction. States give local jurisdictions a percentage of the motor fuel tax to maintain and improve local streets and highways.

As we described in Chapter 14, the federal and state governments provide localities with grants-in-aid, as local taxes, charges, and fees are often not sufficient to support an adequate level of important services. Grant assistance is provided especially in policy areas in which the consequences of local inaction are deemed most serious. However, as we have seen, the narrowness of aid categories and the accompanying program rules or strings also lead to program inflexibility that impedes the performance of local government.

Federal and state officials are willing to provide assistance, but they are seldom willing to pay the whole costs of solving a local problem. Donor officials usually require local **matching funds,** the commitment of local money to help fight the problem at hand. Critics charge that such requirements effectively allow higher levels of government to gain too great an influence on local resource allocation.

Intergovernmental assistance is an important but unreliable source of program funds to cities. The new federalism brought cutbacks to intergovernmental aid in numerous program areas. A growing national economy yields increases in state revenues that allow for the provision of greater assistance for urban services; however, such assistance is cut back during economic downturns, at times when cities need the aid the most. In the early 2000s, with the huge tax cuts, war spending, and large budgetary deficits of the George W. Bush administration, the prospects of increases in federal urban aid vanished.

MUNICIPAL BONDS AND URBAN DEBT

As costs have increased and funds have become harder to find, urban governments have turned to borrowing to support their programs and pay for the growth of new facilities. Cities engage in both short-term and long-term borrowing.[24]

Short-term obligations are called **tax anticipation notes (TANs)** and are usually repaid in 30 to 120 days from a city's normal revenues. Cities borrow money for short periods of time to smooth out irregularities in revenue and expenditure cycles. Cities need money to pay workers, contractors, and suppliers today, yet property taxes may not be due for another month or so. Hence, municipalities borrow against expected revenues.

Most municipal loans, however, are for long-term, not short-term, purposes. **Long-term borrowing** is used to finance capital expenditures such as the purchase of new road-building equipment or the construction of schools or a municipal auditorium. The payment cycle for these long-term bonds is usually over the "useful life" of the equipment purchased or the facility constructed. As a result, the financial burden of constructing new facilities is not placed solely on the shoulders of present-day taxpayers; future residents of a city will help pay for facilities they, too, will enjoy. This principle is often referred to as **intergenerational equity.**[25]

There is a variety of long-term borrowing instruments that a city can use to raise money. The most traditional are **general obligation bonds,** also called **full faith and credit bonds,** which impose a legal obligation on the city to appropriate funds in the future to repay the money borrowed. General obligation bonds are only one type of city indebtedness; yet, they are often the only type of debt that is sharply restricted by the state.

State law often requires voter approval through a public referendum before a city can issue general obligation bonds. Such referenda are not easily won. The referendum requirement impairs local borrowing power; many citizens vote "No," as they do not want to pay the taxes associated with bond repayment.

Cities that need to borrow greater sums of money than can be secured through general obligation bonds have increasingly turned to revenue bonds and other alternative long-term borrowing instruments. **Revenue bonds** are issued to help finance the construction of a particular project such as a bridge, parking garage, or civic auditorium. The holders of revenue bonds are repaid not from the general treasury but from revenues—tolls, user fees, or admission charges—derived from the project. In contrast to general obligation bonds, a city is under no legal obligation to commit future tax money to pay off this debt; rather, the tolls, user fees, and other revenues from the completed project are used to repay the bondholders. As this form of debt is not backed by the full faith and credit of a city, revenue bonds incur a greater risk for lenders than do general obligation bonds. Consequently, cities usually pay greater rates of interest on revenue bonds than on general obligation bonds. In many cases, it is not the municipality itself, but an independent authority (that is, a bridge or tunnel authority) that issues revenue bonds.[26]

Cities have developed still more creative ways to borrow money. With **moral obligation bonds** a city declares its moral obligation to repay borrowed funds; in contrast to general obligation bonds, there is no legal obligation for the city to commit revenues for the repayment. Unlike revenue bonds, moral obligation bonds do not dedicate the monies derived from a project for bond repayment. Cities have turned to the issuance of moral obligation bonds when they have reached the limits set by state law on the local indebtedness that can be incurred through the issuance of general obligation bonds.

Cities have also been able to skirt state-imposed borrowing restrictions through **lease-purchase** or **lease-back agreements** under which a city agrees to the long-term lease of a facility that is built by the private sector, often with the funding assistance of a revenue bond. As the arrangement is not technically seen as "borrowing," cities can use leasing arrangements to circumvent state-imposed debt ceilings and requirements for public votes that limit new borrowing.

Under a typical agreement, the city enters into a contract in which a private contractor builds a new parking facility or auditorium that the city leases for a period, say 10 years. Lease-back arrangements reduce the cash outlays that a city needs up front—and the amounts that a city must often borrow—for expensive new projects. The payments made during the lease also reduce the price that the city will pay when it buys the facility at the end of the lease period. Leasing arrangements also allow cities to avoid the liability problems that accompany municipal ownership. As a result of these advantages, public sector leasing is a rapidly growing tool of local government finance.

Cities are able to issue municipal bonds and thereby borrow money at relatively low rates of interest only because federal tax law creates incentives for investors to purchase municipal bonds. The interest that an investor earns on municipal bonds is tax-exempt under federal law. In 1988, the Supreme Court in *South Carolina v. Baker* ruled that there is no constitutional requirement that municipal bonds be tax-free. Congress, should it choose to do so, could attempt to reduce the federal budget deficit by eliminating the tax exemption on municipal bonds. Such a move would force local governments to pay much higher rates of interest, rates that would impede the ability of cities, counties, and school districts to undertake new projects.

Faced with a tight fiscal situation, localities have sought investments that earn a high rate of return. In some cases, municipalities have engaged in the high-risk strategy of borrowing money to invest in what they hope will be high-yield opportunities. If successful, the strategy allows a city to pay for service provision without having to raise taxes. Should the value of an investment unexpectedly decline, however, the municipality will find itself in a situation of extreme financial distress, unable to repay creditors. (See "Borrowing for Investment: Orange County and the High-Wire Act of Creative Financing," below.)

BORROWING FOR INVESTMENT: ORANGE COUNTY AND THE HIGH-WIRE ACT OF CREATIVE FINANCING

In December 1994, Orange County, California, the fifth most populous county in the country, became the largest local entity in the history of the United States to declare bankruptcy. As a result of an aggressive investment strategy that turned sour, Orange County lost nearly $2 billion from its investment pool and faced a severe financial crisis.

The situation in Orange County was quite different from that of New York, Philadelphia, Cleveland, Washington, Miami, and Bridgeport (Connecticut), cities that had faced difficult fiscal situations as a result of deindustrialization and a deterioration of their economic positions. Economic restructuring and decline did not produce the fiscal crisis in affluent Orange County; instead, the crisis was the result of choices the county had made in borrowing money for investment.

Orange County had procured $12 billion in loans that it hoped to convert into profitable investments, averting the need to raise taxes. In the face of state-imposed tax limitations and a constituency unwilling to support new taxes, county managers looked upon investment as the only route that would maintain service levels. However, when the bottom dropped out of the financial market, the county faced a projected $2 billion loss.

continued

BORROWING FOR INVESTMENT: ORANGE COUNTY
AND THE HIGH-WIRE ACT OF CREATIVE FINANCING (CONT.)

Across the continent, Cuyahoga County (metropolitan Cleveland), Ohio lost a reported $114 million when expected rates of interest fell sharply. The State of Texas and San Diego County similarly reported sharp drops in the market value of their portfolios.

Unable to repay its debts, Orange County filed for bankruptcy, closed library branches, cut school programs, reduced social programs and policing, and stopped testing for fecal coliform bacteria on its beaches. County voters, however, rejected a half-cent increase in the local sales tax to help put the county's fiscal house in order.

Orange County eventually agreed to a moderate reform plan, issuing new bonds that would be repaid over 30 years by diverting revenues from public transportation, harbors, beaches, parks, and flood control. Reductions in the "safety net" public services provided the poor were not fully restored.

Orange County's bankruptcy was not inevitable. Citizens in Orange County had the ability to pay for public services, but they did not want to do so. Proposition 13 and various other state-imposed taxing and revenue restrictions also acted to impede the ability of local officials to find necessary revenues, both before and during the crisis. Indeed, state-imposed limitations helped to lead Orange County officials on their aggressive search for alternative, nontax sources of revenue.

Orange County actually declared bankruptcy, where other cities—New York, Philadelphia, Washington, and Cleveland—all undertook difficult reform steps to avoid a formal filing of bankruptcy. Unlike New York and Cleveland, Orange County did not increase taxes to repay the money it owed. Instead, Orange County used its declaration of bankruptcy as a negotiating weapon in an attempt to strike a deal under which creditors would agree to accept less than the full amount owed. Orange County's voters and officials acted with little sense of public responsibility, seeming to care little about how their actions would raise borrowing costs for all municipalities and school districts by showing investors that a municipality may not deliver on its moral obligation to repay debts in full.

The county treasurer and other county officials do not by themselves bear the full blame for Orange County's fiscal misdoings. Orange County's voters had demanded high-quality public services, but were unwilling to pay increased taxes, expectations that led county officials to their high-risk borrowing strategy. Private securities companies, too, willingly supported Orange County's high-risk investments from which they earned considerable fees and profits. After the crisis, in the summer of 1998, Merrill Lynch and Company agreed to pay the Securities and Exchange Commission (SEC) a $2 million civil penalty as a result of its role in the Orange County fiasco. Merrill Lynch also reached a settlement with Orange County, paying Orange County $437 million while denying any wrongdoing.

Sources: Mark Baldassare, *When Government Fails: The Orange County Bankruptcy* (Berkeley: University of California Press, 1998); "Merrill to Pay SEC $2 Million: Penalty Stems from '94 Bankruptcy of Orange County," *The Washington Post*, August 25, 1998.

OUTSIDE ACTORS IN CITY FINANCE: A LOOK AT BIG CITIES IN CRISIS

As cities routinely borrow money to finance the construction of capital facilities and to maintain services despite fluctuations in the flow of revenues, the buyers and sellers of municipal bonds and related financial institutions are influential actors whose decisions can affect a city's fiscal health.[27] Nonmunicipal actors play an especially important role in determining how big-city fiscal crises are resolved.

A look at the fiscal crises in Orange County, New York City, Philadelphia, Washington, DC, and Miami helps to underscore that when it comes to borrowing and capital investment, cities are not "closed" political systems; instead, cities are greatly affected by the "rules" set down by private actors and the state and national governments.[28] Local officials lead within the confines imposed by state, national, and private sector actors.

PRIVATE SECTOR ACTORS

Financial institutions, such as Moody's and Standard and Poor's, assess the creditworthiness of cities to rate bond quality, determining the interest that a municipality will pay to lenders. The bond ratings issued by Moody's and Standard and Poor's, nongovernmental institutions, help to determine investors' willingness to buy municipal bonds.

In the early 2000s, Moody's awarded an excellent "Aaa" rating to the general obligation bond issues of Dallas, Austin, Minneapolis, and Columbus, allowing these cities to borrow money at advantageous rates of interest. In contrast, Moody's gave a disastrously low Baa3 rating to the bond issue of Washington, DC as a result of that city's severe fiscal problems and its history of mismanagement problems and past difficulties in repaying debt. Washington's bond ratings in the 1990s were so low that they virtually precluded the city from borrowing, precipitating a fiscal crisis that resulted in federal intervention. Philadelphia, New Orleans, and Detroit received similarly low Baa2 and Baa1 bond ratings.[29] In essence, the nation's poorest and most troubled cities were forced to pay substantially more in interest costs to borrow money than did better-off communities.

In Philadelphia, mayor Ed Rendell took office in 1991 confronting a $200 million annual budget deficit and a projected cumulative deficit of $1.4 billion. Low bond ratings precipitated a crisis, forcing Rendell to respond. The year before Rendell assumed office, national rating agencies reduced the city's bonds to junk grade; the city could not get the loans it needed for services, as investors were not willing to buy the city's bonds. In various fiscal crises, including New York, Cleveland, and Orange County, Moody's and other fiscal houses helped to determine the terms on which the city would be allowed to reenter the bond market. The city's creditors, too, demanded certain fiscal reforms before they would once again buy the city's securities.

Moody's and Standard and Poor's are not the only nongovernmental institutions to play key roles in city fiscal crises. New York City's flirtation with bankruptcy in the 1970s reveals the role of Wall Street financial houses that were willing partners in extending new loans to a city that had already reached its borrowing limits.[30] New York City faced a population in need of services at a time when the city saw its industrial tax base shrinking. City and state actors sought to circumvent the limits on the city's general obligation debt by issuing moral obligation bonds to pay for housing, medical, and higher education facilities. Private bonding houses and investors willingly cooperated with this circumvention, seeing the promise of high commissions and high rates of return.

The decision of Chase Manhattan Bank to "dump" its New York bond portfolio signaled other investors not to buy New York City bonds, precipitating the actual crisis. Chase Manhattan had earned considerable money by investing in New York City bonds but soon came to see its holding of New York City debt as excessively risky, especially when more lucrative investment opportunities existed elsewhere.

As the crisis continued, New York's business leaders pushed for measures that restructured the city more to the liking of the business community. The municipal workforce was cut, with 13- to 20-percent reductions in the police, sanitation, and social service departments. New York's municipal labor unions also agreed to certain salary deferrals.

In Orange County, private lending institutions, blinded by the county's wealth, conservative reputation, and high Standard and Poor's credit rating, continued to encourage new lending to the county. Wall Street financial firms also helped to create complicated "reverse repurchase agreements" to allow the county to use its limited investment funds to borrow still greater amounts of money for additional risky investments. Merrill Lynch and Company initially warned the county of the risky nature of its investment strategy, but then turned around and encouraged new investment, even after market conditions had begun to sour.[31]

INTERGOVERNMENTAL ACTORS

State and federal intervention is often necessary to help near-bankrupt cities regain access to the credit market. State and national officials, however, are often reluctant to act; if they aid one city, other cities may ask for similar assistance. As a result, state and federal assistance is not provided cost-free to a city in trouble. Accompanying regulations, financial controls, and fees deter other cities from seeking similar help.

Faced with the prospects of default, New York City began to lay off civil servants and cut standards of municipal services. However, the city still could not meet its payroll or pay off its debts. The day before D (for Default) Day, the state imposed a temporary solution on New York City in the form of the Municipal Assistance Corporation (MAC). "Big Mac" was set up to transform

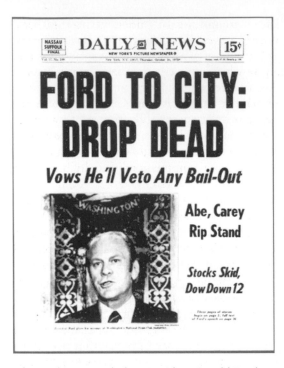

The Daily News rebukes President Gerald Ford for his reluctance to help New York City in the midst of its 1975 fiscal crisis. Ford blamed city officials for overspending. The risk to the national economy, though, eventually led the President to approve of federal loan guarantees—not new grants—so that private investors would continue to lend the city money while it restructured its debt. These loan guarantees were no outright gift; New York City not only repaid its debt but also paid a fee to the federal government for its services.

$3 billion in city short-term debt into state long-term debt. In effect, the state of New York was using its financial reputation to help get New York back into the bond market.

However, these actions were insufficient to solve the crisis, and the state found that its actions had put its own credit rating at risk. Eventually, the national government stepped in and offered loan guarantees so that New York would be able to reenter the bond market; the city would borrow new money, repay its creditors, and pay a fee to the federal government for its guarantees. New York State then set up the Emergency Financial Control Board (EFCB) to oversee the city's finances and reform the city's financial practices.[32] Private business had demanded the creation of Big Mac and the EFCB to force the city to "clean up its act" and introduce new businesslike, efficiency-minded fiscal practices. New York received the help it needed to survive the crisis; however, the city also lost some of its political autonomy as intergovernmental and private sector actors gained new powers to review municipal revenue and spending decisions.

In Pennsylvania, as in New York, the state government, faced with the possible bankruptcy of its largest city, had no real choice but to step in. The Pennsylvania legislature allowed the city to levy a special penny sales tax. The state also created the Pennsylvania Intergovernmental Cooperation Agency (PICA) to issue bonds to provide Philadelphia with the immediate influx of cash it needed. The PICA also oversaw the city's finances. In return for this help, however, the state demanded a five-year plan of tough fiscal reform by the city. Mayor Ed Rendell immediately set out to clean house, cut costs, and raise revenues. Rendell had his share of difficulties in changing city work rules and in convincing city workers to buy into his plan. Municipal workers walked off their jobs but returned to work when Rendell revealed a plan to unilaterally implement contract cuts. Rendell's contracting, privatization, and competitive bidding reforms emphasized the principles of "reinventing government."[33]

In Washington, DC, too, the severity of the fiscal and social problems led to the intervention of powerful outside actors. In the midst of its fiscal crisis, the District was placed under a federally appointed control board that was given authority over every aspect of the city's financial affairs. Congress in 1995 created the District of Columbia Financial Responsibility and Management and Assistance Authority to ensure that the city undertook the necessary changes to balance its budget within a four-year period.

The District had always complained about its lack of autonomy, that it was in effect the last American federal colony. In the wake of the fiscal crisis, the federal government became an even more important player than ever in the city's affairs. The new fiscal control board was arguably the strongest of its type ever created. It was given much greater powers than those possessed by the control boards in New York in the 1970s and Philadelphia in the early 1990s. The new financial board in the District was given final say over all city budgets, contracts (including all labor contracts), and loans; it even possessed supervisory authority in such areas as the city jails and Medicaid system. The control board dismissed members of the mayor's cabinet and installed a new chief fiscal officer in each city agency. Mayor Marion Barry, scorned for both his managerial ineptitude and his record of drug use, was effectively stripped of much of his power over most of the city's government.

The influence of the Republican congressional majority and the business community assured that the focus of efforts would be on reducing the city's payroll, curtailing spending, and putting the city's fiscal house in order. There was little effort to expand federal assistance or allow the city to tap the wealth of middle-class homeowners and businesses that had migrated to the city's suburbs.

A similar pattern of intervention was also witnessed when Miami, in the mid-1990s, faced the prospect of bankruptcy as the result of an annual budget of $275 million. As was the case in Washington, Miami's fiscal problems were, at least in part, self-inflicted, resulting from the mismanagement and corruption of Miami's personalized, machine-style political system. At the time, Miami's city manager was not professionally trained and had turned a blind eye to the shenanigans.

To resolve the crisis, Florida's governor eventually appointed a financial emergency oversight board while the state advanced the city $22 million in sales tax revenues. The oversight board was given immense authority. Once again, the state and private sector actors gained a new ability to shape local priorities and force the city to adopt new economies and reforms.

School districts, too, have been the subject of state "takeovers" in the midst of a fiscal crisis. In 2003, Oakland, California schools could not meet their payroll, necessitating a $100 million state bailout loan. A state-appointed administrator was given the power to run the schools, and the locally elected school board lost much of its authority.[34]

The next year, the nearby Vallejo City Unified School District was made to submit to new state oversight of its finances and spending as a condition for receiving a $60 million state bailout loan. Caught between a tight revenue situation and the continued demands of outspoken parents and a strong teacher's union, the local school district was unable to impose fiscal discipline and implement necessary spending cutbacks. Local officials were also reluctant to cut education services to the Vallejo's schoolchildren, many of whom were poor and did not speak English as their first language. Instead, the school district overpredicted state aid and underestimated salary costs. Vallejo was the seventh district to be placed under supervision by the State of California since 1991.[35]

EXPENDITURE PATTERNS

How do local governments spend money? Education is the number-one local spending priority (see Figure 15-2). Highways, street maintenance and construction, and police and fire protection are all traditional areas of local service responsibility. Depending on state law, localities also have various social welfare responsibilities. In recent years, spending for health and hospitals has constituted an increasingly important area in local budgets.

Direct general expenditures by state and local governments have steadily increased. The combined totals, which stood at $51.9 billion in 1960, rose to over $1 trillion dollars in 1992. The number of state and local government employees also rose sharply, from 6.4 million in 1960 to over 16 million in 1994.[36]

Municipal expenditures have grown way beyond the increases required by population growth and inflation. Planners and program administrators push for program expansion. But pressure for expanded public services also comes from the private sector. In recent years, technological changes have led to demands for new public services, as businesses have sought improved transportation and telecommunications infrastructure and the public has demanded

■ FIGURE 15–2

GENERAL EXPENDITURES OF LOCAL GOVERNMENTS,
2002

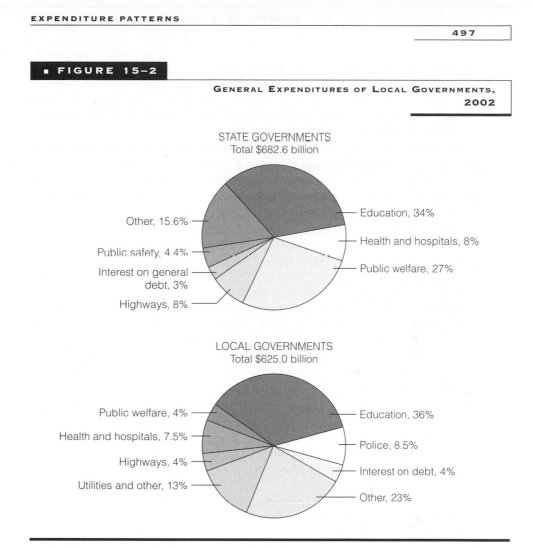

STATE GOVERNMENTS
Total $682.6 billion

Education, 34%

Health and hospitals, 8%

Public welfare, 27%

Other, 15.6%

Public safety, 4.4%

Interest on general debt, 3%

Highways, 8%

LOCAL GOVERNMENTS
Total $625.0 billion

Public welfare, 4%

Health and hospitals, 7.5%

Highways, 4%

Utilities and other, 13%

Education, 36%

Police, 8.5%

Interest on debt, 4%

Other, 23%

SOURCES: Prepared from figures presented by The Tax Foundation, *Facts and Figures on Government Finance.* 36th ed. (Washington DC, 2004), pp. 262–263, Table F5, "Local Government Expenditures By Function, Percentages," pp. 262–263, available at www.taxfoundation.org/files/7ca0eadb3813bc30417c0a3533491263.pdf

more effective air and water pollution control. Citizens also demand better schools and other quality-of-life services.

Do central cities spend more than suburbs? Comparisons of expenditures among municipalities must be treated with great caution, as the figures can be very misleading as a result of variations in governmental structure and state law. In some cases, education is a city or county function with expenses reported in local budgets; in other cases, the schools are run by an independent district with its own separate budgetary authority.

Suburban governments tend to spend less per capita (that is, per citizen) than do central cities. However, that does not necessarily mean that suburbs are inherently more efficient than central-city governments; the budgets of central-city governments often include the costs of services that are not a part of suburban budgets. Suburban budgets do not reflect the costs of providing education, which, in suburbia, is usually provided by independent school districts. In many central cities, the huge costs of running schools may appear in the local budget. Central cities also provide services to persons more in need of governmental assistance. As a result, central cities may be saddled with costs of certain services, such as public transit or specialized health care, not reflected by many suburbs. The stereotypical picture of high-cost central cities and efficient suburbs is often based on misleading information and oversimplification.

THE BUDGETARY PROCESS

Taxing and spending decisions lie at the heart of urban politics. The **municipal budget,** also called the **operating budget,** provides an overall statement of taxing and spending priorities, and a guide for departmental programs and day-to-day service decisions.

The responsibility for preparing the budget varies from community to community. In most cases, the executive, usually the mayor or the city manager, is responsible. In larger cities, the chief executive has the assistance of a budget (or finance) director, who supervises the collection of data and actual formulation of the budget within the guidelines set by the chief executive. However, in some municipalities, the responsibility for budget preparation still lies with the city council or a legislative committee, depriving the mayor of a valuable leadership tool. In still other cities, the executive formulates the budget in conjunction with a legislative committee.

Budgets determine just how much money will be allocated to different programs. This process of setting program priorities is probably the most crucial part of the entire budgetary process. Budget makers do not operate in a political vacuum but respond to pressures and perceived opportunities. St. Paul (Minnesota) and Portland (Oregon) have made great strides in attempting to include citizen groups and neighborhood organizations in budget formulation.

When it comes to spending, appropriations may be lump sum or itemized. With **lump-sum appropriations,** each agency is granted all its funds as a single amount, and the department director determines exactly how the money will be spent. This approach allows departmental discretion and flexibility.

In contrast, **itemized appropriations** detail exactly how money is to be spent by an agency, item by item. This form of budgeting furthers administrative planning and control, but may result in undue rigidity. Fiscal experts generally look upon itemized or highly segregated appropriations with disfavor, as fixed line items do not allow administrators the flexibility to use funds as needed. While line-item budgeting continues in a great many localities, it is not generally seen as a modern, progressive administrative practice. A mere listing of line items does not lead an administrator to consider alternative programs, the alternative ways that resources can be used to achieve agency goals.

An **allotment system** maintains centralized fiscal responsibility while allowing a good deal of flexibility. Under this approach, each department's appropriations for a year are dispensed in 4 or 12 portions, depending upon whether the allotments are made quarterly or monthly. Overall expenditure controls are established, as the city's accounting officer will not approve expenditures during a particular quarter or month in excess of the allotment. Of course, the pattern of monthly or quarterly allotments may have to be revised from time to time if a department finds that it must respond to a crisis or an unexpected situation.

How do cities set their priorities and decide on the amount of funds to allocate to each service each year? Most cities follow an approach that can be called **incremental budgeting,** in which each municipal department or agency assumes that it will receive at least as much funding in the upcoming fiscal year as it did in the current one. In preparing its budget request, an agency focuses on explaining the reasons for any proposed budget increases.

Incrementalism is a pervasive characteristic of budgeting for a number of reasons. First, incrementalism reduces the amount of information and time needed to prepare a budget. The existing programs, or **base** of a budget, are for the most part accepted as a given; critical attention can then be focused on examining the proposed additions or **increments** contained in the budget. Second, incremental budgeting tends to minimize the amount of conflict inherent in the budgetary process. Existing programs are embedded in the budgetary base; arguments favorable and critical of these programs are not rehashed every time a budget is presented to the city council. Third, incrementalism encourages compromise and mutual adjustment among competing interest groups, departments, and city agencies. Each group acts to safeguard the programs that it feels are most important.

The obvious criticism of incremental budgeting is that existing programs embedded in the base of the budget are not critically scrutinized. Programs that have outlived their usefulness continue to receive funding, and opportunities are lost to shift funds to meet new and more important priorities.

Tight fiscal times force local governments to resort to **decremental budgeting.** In times of economic recession, cost inflation, declining federal grant dollars, and citizen resistance to tax increases, municipal departments cannot assume that they will have sufficient funds to maintain their agency's budgetary base. Instead, localities have had to find new ways to economize or, failing that, to impose program cutbacks. As an alternative to steep cutbacks, cities and departments can develop sophisticated accountability systems designed to assess and enhance program and departmental performance.

CAPITAL BUDGETS

The **capital budget** details proposed capital expenditures and the means for financing them. A **capital expenditure** pays for the construction or purchase of a facility (such as the replacement of streets, the building of a new school, or the reconstruction of a bridge) that provides benefits over a considerable period of time. Rather than using taxes to pay for infrastructure improvements and other projects with a long life, a local government can sell bonds to finance a capital project. The process is similar to the way a family purchases a home by taking out a mortgage and making monthly payments instead of paying the full amount at the time of purchase.

The capital budget is an important financial planning tool that complements the regular budgeting process. How does a municipality determine a plan for capital investment? Demographic studies help planners determine a city's future needs for schools, streets, parks, and highways. A capital budget program is founded on economic base studies, land-use reports, and population and migration studies. Data on existing industries, the city's economic history, and an analysis of economic development trends are contained in economic base studies. Land-use reports reveal population densities and present inventories of property developments. Other reports assess migration trends and the characteristics, income, and talents of the local population.

Capital budgeting makes possible some measure of long-range planning for expensive public improvements. A capital budget also sets forth a plan for big-expenditure items that city officials might otherwise choose to postpone. As capital projects are sporadic, their tendency to be concentrated in short periods can be counteracted through the leveling effects of a planned schedule of bond offerings.

Capital and operating budgets may be distinct parts of the same budget document, or they may take the form of separate documents. The distinction between capital and operating expenditures is a commonplace feature of the financial practices of large corporations for many decades. Local governments often tend to imitate corporate fiscal practices.[37]

CURRENT TRENDS AND PROBLEMS

COPING WITH TAX LIMITATIONS

As we observed in previous chapters, in numerous cities and states, citizens' anti-tax movements have compounded conditions of local fiscal stress. The nationwide movement to limit taxes shot to national prominence with California's passage of **Proposition 13** in 1978. This constitutional ballot measure, spurred on by a grassroots movement led by anti-tax crusaders Howard Jarvis and Paul Gann, essentially rolled back property taxes to 1975 levels and limited any annual increase to just 2 percent. It passed by a 2-to-1 margin. The next year saw a 3-to-1 victory for Proposition 4 (called the Gann limit), which placed a constitutional spending ceiling on all levels of government in California.

The tax revolt spread like wildfire. As early as the early 1980s, 19 states passed some form of tax limitation. **Proposition 2½** in Massachusetts probably had the most drastic effect. This amendment reduced property taxes from 10 percent of fair market value to 2½ percent. The measure led the city of Boston to plan for a 25-percent cut in funds for the police and fire departments, a 60-percent cut for the parks department, and a 30-percent reduction in public works.

How have local governments responded to voter- and state-imposed tax limitations? As the Boston case shows, sometimes the result has been severe local service cutbacks. In California, the impact of Proposition 13 was not immediately seen, as the state used its surplus to provide increased aid for schools and other key local services. The real constraints that Proposition 13 imposed on local service delivery were delayed and were not fully felt until California cities suffered the economic recession and state revenue take-aways of the early 1990s.

In Los Angeles, the impact of the new revenue limitation measures was particularly extreme. Los Angeles County was forced to increase its debt and mortgage and sell its assets to balance its budget and provide mandated services. In important ways, Los Angeles County became "little more than a financially dependent 'service delivery arm' of the state."[38]

In other California communities, the impact of Proposition 13 and succeeding state-imposed limitations was less extreme. Some communities held votes, as allowed under the Gann resolution, to authorize increases beyond the state-imposed ceilings.

Many California localities imposed user charges for services.[39] To pay for new classrooms in fast-growing school districts, local governments levied special **developer fees** on new subdivisions, often adding thousands of dollars to the costs of home ownership.[40] Developers and new homeowners alike complained about the inequitable nature of such charges levied in addition to normal school and property taxes.

In some states, tax limitation measures roll back the assessments faced by established homeowners in a community, but not the assessments imposed on newcomers. Proposition 13 rolled back property assessments to 1975 levels; but once a home was sold, it was reassessed at current market value. Consequently, a newcomer to a community pays a higher tax rate on an equivalent piece of property than does an existing homeowner.

Such **"welcome stranger" taxes** levied on new homeowners have been challenged in the courts. The U.S. Supreme Court in 1989 struck down a Webster County, West Virginia ordinance that systematically assessed newly sold property at higher rates than neighboring properties. The Court held Webster County's practices to be in violation of the Equal Protection Clause to the Fourteenth Amendment.[41] However, in California, the courts have upheld the differential taxing of resident and newcomer property.

Localities throughout the nation have had to find ways to cope with the new fiscal constraints imposed by the property tax revolt. Florida cities and counties, faced with the limits on property taxes imposed by Amendment 10 (the "Save Our Homes" Amendment), turned to the imposition of a number of special assessments.[42] As was the case in California, the state's courts ultimately decide just which special local assessments and charges are still allowed, and which are prohibited, by various tax-limitation measures. Localities impose special charges for a variety of local services, including solid waste disposal, street improvements, and fire protection. While local officials see these charges as an important way to cope with revenue shortfalls and maintaining services, anti-government voters complain that the charges undermine the tax relief promised in the tax-limitation initiatives.

Voter-imposed tax limitations are expressions of direct democracy that enable a state's anti-tax majority to dictate the course of public policy. Yet certain provisions of the anti-tax movement run contrary to the spirit of majoritarian democracy. In California, a majority of local voters no longer possess the power to increase taxes for a new service; it takes a supermajority to do so. In states such as California and Nevada, protracted fights over school aid bills are the result of requirements that any spending plan be approved by two-thirds of the state legislature. A one-third legislative minority stridently against tax increases can thwart efforts at new school construction, class-size reduction, special education, and any other school spending plan desired by the popular majority.[43]

California legislators are caught in a difficult bind; voter-imposed tax limitations impede revenue raising while court orders and other voter initiatives mandate the provision of a high level of school and other services. In such a difficult situation, the two-thirds requirement makes effective leadership all but impossible. In 2003, governor Arnold Schwarzenegger won office in a special recall election, but he still had great difficulty in gathering the support of two-thirds of the state legislature behind a spending plan that included numerous urban aid cutbacks.

THE NEW POPULARITY OF TAX INCREMENT FINANCING

Faced with voter-imposed limitations on local taxing and borrowing, cities in California turned to **tax increment financing (TIF)** as an innovative tool for promoting redevelopment.[44] TIFs were sweeping the nation, not just California.

A TIF program promotes new development in a targeted district, usually a distressed area, by setting aside the gains in property taxes resulting from the new investment to help pay for further improvements in the district. To be more specific, tax increment financing "freezes the assessed valuation of all property parcels in a designated area (the TIF district) for a specified period of years . . . [T]axes derived from the increases in assessed values (the tax increment) resulting from new development are used to pay for the infrastructure needs and development expenditures in the TIF district."[45] If designed carefully, the debt a TIF incurs does not even count against state-imposed ceilings on local borrowing through general obligation bonds.[46]

A TIF enables spending on improvements related to economic development that a municipality might otherwise not be able to afford. A TIF authority can borrow the money to pay for the street, sewer, road, and other infrastructure improvements demanded by a business intent on expansion; the property tax gains from the highly valued new development are used to pay off the debt. TIFs are often a self-financing tool that allows a city to pursue new economic development without increasing the burdens on taxpayers.[47] In an era of constricted intergovernmental aid, TIFs are one of the few development tools that cities possess.

TIFs are exceedingly popular with private industry and state and local officials. Nearly all states authorize the creation of TIF districts; as of 1997, only Delaware and North Carolina did not.[48] TIFs are an important tool that localities use in the pursuit of business. Local officials can combine a TIF with other incentives in an effort to lure new business development to a targeted area. TIFs help to create public-private partnerships.

However, critics argue that the TIF approach is highly wasteful and inefficient. When a TIF is created, a city may even lose revenues for general public services that it might otherwise have gained from new development. In the competition for business, cities often create TIFs (and sacrifice general fund revenues) when there is no need to do so, when there is no evidence that the TIF is the decisive factor in a business' choice of locations.

In Missouri and other states, high-tax-base suburbs created TIFs in areas that were already attractive to investment. Wealthier communities used TIFs to win the competition for still more development. However, such TIFs, especially those in outlying greenfield sites, reinforced sprawl development and diverted investment away from inner-ring communities.[49]

Education officials argue that the creation of a TIF effectively drains money away from public schools. In the absence of a TIF, the tax revenues from new development would help support schools and social services; a TIF, however, diverts those revenues to development projects in the TIF district. It is uncertain that voters would continue to support the program if they knew that TIFs effectively took resources away from education to help pay for new economic development.[50]

Mayor Richard M. Daley's Chicago has been so aggressive in using TIFs in the pursuit of jobs and the construction of new upscale housing that it has been called "The Town that Loves to TIF." Under Daley, the number of TIFs in Chicago grew to over 100. Daley argued that the TIFs help to jump-start neighborhood renewal and generate new commercial development.[51] Neighborhood activists countered that the TIFs spurred gentrification and displacement while draining revenues away from schools, parks, and neighborhood services. Addison, Illinois, a suburb of Chicago, used the creation of two TIF districts to catalyze new development, forcing the displacement of sizeable pockets of the city's low-income Hispanic population.[52]

TRENDS IN MUNICIPAL DEBT

A major trend in urban borrowing is the increased reliance on nonguaranteed debt. In the 1960s and 1970s, general obligation bonds accounted for about 60 percent of long-term municipal borrowing. Twelve years later, nonguaranteed debt climbed to virtually the same figure, reaching 59 percent of the total.[53] Cities resorted to nonguaranteed debt as a way to escape debt limitation ceilings and requirements of voter approval for the issuance of new general obligation bonds. **Industrial revenue bonds,** in which the revenues derived from a project are used to repay creditors, were also used to finance various economic development activities.

Unlike traditional bonds backed by local property taxes and a city's full faith and credit, nonguaranteed bonds are often referred to as **junk bonds** because repayment is not assured but is dependent upon revenue derived from the successful completion of a project. Investors purchase these bonds for their relatively high returns that are tax free when it comes to federal income tax. Yet the purchase of these bonds can entail great risk. In the greater Houston area, Northwest Harris County Municipal Utility District No. 19 issued $2.6 million in bonds in 1982 to finance the water and sewer lines for a new housing development. The bonds were to be repaid from the tax revenues derived from the new homeowners. Five years later, "the utility district went bust, leaving investors holding the defaulted bonds."[54]

In some localities, semiautonomous authorities have their own borrowing capacity. They can issue bonds to build schools, hospitals, an airport, or a new stadium, thereby circumventing state-imposed debt limitations placed on general-purpose governments. The issuance of bonds by independent authorities often does not even require voter approval in a public referendum. Such practices raise great questions of public accountability, as important borrowing and project decisions are made by actors who are not fully visible to the public and who do not answer directly to voters in elections.[55]

CUTBACK MANAGEMENT

Limits on taxation coupled with reductions in federal aid have forced local officials to make hard decisions. **Cutback management** is more than just service reduction; it also entails a heightened concern for productivity improvement, including efforts to "reinvent government" through increased citizen participation, neighborhood coprovision, performance benchmarking and measurement, customer choice, service contracting, and privatization.[56]

Local officials have two alternative strategies for making cutbacks. Under the **equity approach,** each department is asked to take the same percentage cut. This approach has an element of justice in it. It is easy to defend before client groups, and it requires little or no in-depth analysis to discriminate among programs.

The **efficiency approach** to cutbacks, in contrast, is more rational but also more difficult; it targets or concentrates the greatest reductions in those programs that, after analysis, appear to be most inefficient or expendable. This approach requires a much greater commitment of staff time to assess each program's contribution to the overall mission of the department. The process of evaluating and ranking programs often leads to bitter infighting, as client groups and municipal administrators fight to save their cherished programs.

PUBLIC RISK MANAGEMENT

Risk management is one of the fastest growing fields in local government. Over the past quarter of a century, cities have been forced to pay great attention to risk management to reduce their insurance and liability costs. Local risk managers look at public safety, insurance and claims management, workers' compensation, employee training, employee benefits, litigation management, and emergency preparedness. In any operation where there is a potential for human or financial loss, risk managers are involved.[57]

What caused this new concern for risk management? Cities were facing a "liability crisis" that seriously threatened to impair the ability of local governments to provide residents with necessary and desired services. Legal changes at the state and federal levels had left municipalities vulnerable to civil suits for large monetary damages. The increased liability led to escalating insurance costs, jeopardizing certain municipal undertakings.

For a long portion of the United States' history, it was difficult to sue local governments. Municipalities enjoyed sovereign immunity under the Anglo-American theory that the king or sovereign could do no wrong; consequently, civil suit against the government was largely pointless. However, the states and federal government have increasingly waived their sovereign immunity and are at times punishable for the negligence and mistakes of their policy makers and their agents.

Local governments have become a soft target for litigation. Local government and their personnel have a great deal of daily contact with the public; mistakes and even injuries are inevitable. Injured citizens and lawyers assume that cities with their "deep pockets" can be made to pay. When cities face lawsuits, taxpayers' dollars are diverted to pay excessive premiums or large damage awards.

In addition to their state tort liability, local governments are subject to civil suits for money damages under the Civil Rights Act of 1871, an act that was initially passed to counter the Ku Klux Klan. Section 1983, as the law is now called, has a broad sweep. It changes federalism by subjecting state and local officials to suits in federal court for alleged violations of individuals' federally protected constitutional or statutory rights.

For almost 90 years after the passage of the Civil Rights Act, Section 1983 was hardly used. Approximately 20 suits were brought in the first 50 years, and from 1920 to 1960, most of the suits were for violations of voting rights, not for acts of municipal liability.[58]

Today, the picture is drastically different. Most state and local governmental officials can be sued personally for compensatory and punitive damages. When these officials exercise discretion, they have a qualified immunity from suit and can be held liable only for violations of "clearly established constitutional or statutory rights of which a responsible person would have known" *(Harlow v. Fitzgerald)*.[59] In essence, "the state of the law" must provide public employees with "fair warning" that their actions are unconstitutional.[60] If such violations occur, damages may be assessed regardless of whether the official or employee acted in good faith. As a general rule, public officials and employees retain absolute immunity when engaging in a judicial or legislative function. Private individuals engaged in governmental action, such as prison guards in privatized prisons, are potentially liable for their misdoings and enjoy no immunities.

Since the Supreme Court's decision in **Monell v. Department of Social Services of the City of New York** (1978),[61] municipalities and their agencies are considered "persons" within the meaning of Section 1983 who can be sued in federal court for their constitutional torts and for violations of federally protected statutory rights. Municipalities are liable only for compensatory damages; no punitive damages can be assessed against them under Section 1983.[62]

Monell established that municipalities or their agencies are liable when their official policies violate an individual's constitutional rights. In *Owen v. City of Independence,* the Supreme Court removed the possibility of a municipality raising a "good faith defense"; the Court ruled that a government "will be liable for all of its injurious conduct, whether committed in good faith or not."[63]

A city may be sued not only for its actions but even for its inaction. A court may treat deliberate indifference to an obviously necessary policy as if the city had deliberately decided not to act. In *City of Canton v. Harris,* the Supreme Court held that a municipality's failure to provide training may incur liability when the need for training is "so obvious, and the inadequacy so likely to result in the violation of constitutional rights, that the city can reasonably be said to have been deliberately indifferent to the need." [64]

Faced with the potential of liability, urban managers have had to show increased concern for directing subordinates and controlling the exercise of their discretion. But, as we discussed in Chapter 9, "Urban Bureaucracy and Service Delivery," it is impossible for a city to establish and monitor a specific set of procedures to be carried out by all departmental employees. In policing, health care, social welfare, education, and numerous other service areas, discretion is an integral part of fieldwork.

To reduce a municipality's potential liability, urban risk managers catalog potential dangers and develop contingency plans for the unknown ones. Contractors hired by the city are checked for liability insurance, past safety performance, the nondiscrimination of their hiring practices, and the quality of their workforces. All of these activities represent new challenges for urban management.

Finally, there is the rapidly expanding role of the risk manager in the urban arena. As the municipal liability crisis heightened, more and more cities and counties hired risk managers to assess the jurisdiction's potential risk and to provide a mix of risk control and risk financing to ensure the preservation of the city's fiscal assets. Risk managers are called upon to make major decisions about municipal liability activities across a broad spectrum of agencies and service areas.

CONCLUSIONS

Cities are faced with many problems that are, at the core, financial in nature. State law, in particular, limits cities in the taxes they can levy and the money they are allowed to borrow. State-, federal-, and court-imposed mandates also act to force cities and school systems to spend money on designated services. In California and a large number of states across the nation, voters have used the popular initiative and referendum to limit tax increases while requiring continued spending in important areas such as education. Local governments wind up caught in the squeeze between voters' conflicting demands for both high-quality services and tax reductions.

Cities borrow money both to finance long-term capital projects and to pay for short-term operations that need to continue while a municipality awaits the receipt of projected intergovernmental aid and local taxes. Many cities have turned to borrowing and creative revenue-raising instruments in an effort to circumvent state-imposed tax limitation measures. Cities have increasingly resorted to issuing nonguaranteed forms of urban debt, borrowing instruments that are not as strictly regulated or limited as is the city's issuance of general obligation bonds. Revenue bonds and the creation of tax increment financing districts are enormously popular vehicles that have allowed cities to finance projects demanded by business.

The tale of the Orange County fiscal crisis reveals local government's "scramble for nontax resources" as tax limitations have put the fiscal squeeze on suburban jurisdictions, not just on declining central cities.[65] Local officials face serious political constraints when it comes to raising taxes and finding the money to support necessary levels of service. Poorer cities, of course, face the greatest fiscal pressures. But even the governing officials of well-off cities have had to show a new concern for fiscal limitations, cutback management, and reinventing government for enhanced performance.

The fiscal crisis reflects a reordering of power in American cities. On the one hand, voters themselves, primarily middle- and upper-class voters, have been able to seize power through tax-cutting voter initiatives. In California, the Proposition 13 tax revolt has provided middle-class citizens with genuine tax relief. However, it is the wealthiest taxpayers and property owners (including the corporate owners of large tracts of industrial property) who often emerge as the biggest winners when tax reductions, especially reductions in the property tax, are enacted. A community's new immigrants, poor, and racial minorities—especially minority children—find that, as a result of tax limitations, they must get by with reduced levels of public services.

City finance is not a "closed" political system; nonmunicipal actors play a role in city fiscal policy. Private investors and bond rating firms such as Moody's help to determine the costs of borrowing to a city, costs that affect a broad range of city spending decisions. Cutback management policies, too, have acted to redistribute power within the urban political system.[66] State fiscal control boards have been established in times of financial emergency to impose new fiscal discipline on troubled cities and school systems. Local control is compromised by the powers of a new fiscal control regime.

Cities continue to experience tough fiscal times. During periods of national economic growth, local economic problems and service costs are reduced, and the pressures constraining state aid are eased. But even a growing economy does seem to be able to provide an answer to all urban fiscal problems. Growth is uneven nationwide; even during good economic times, some cities will lag behind in terms of their economic dynamism and tax revenues. In California and other states, local economic problems are compounded by the need to provide services for a large and diverse immigrant population. The challenge is all the more difficult when populist measures and court rulings limit the ability of local officials to raise taxes and impose developer and user fees.

What, then, is the future of cities as the United States enters the twenty-first century? The answer to this question is the subject of our concluding chapter.

NOTES

1. John W. Smith and John S. Klemanski, *The Urban Politics Dictionary* (Santa Barbara, CA: ABC CLIO, 1990), pp. 269–270.
2. The Tax Foundation, "State and Local Property Taxes, Special Report No. 106, Washington, DC, August 2001, available at www.taxfoundation.org/sr106.pdf.
3. Michael A. Pagano, *City Fiscal Conditions in 2002* (Washington, DC: National League of Cities, 2002), pp. 3–4.
4. Pagano, *City Fiscal Conditions in 2002*, p. 4.
5. For a review of the trends in fiscal federalism and local revenues and expenditures, see Wallace E. Oates, "Fiscal Structure in the Federal System," pp. 39–60, and Roy W. Bahl, Jr., "Local Government Revenues and Expenditures," pp. 79–101, both in *Management Policies in Local Government Finance*, 5th ed., eds. J. Richard Aronson and Eli Schwartz (Washington, DC: International City/County Management Association, 2004).
6. The 2001 figure is reported by Robert Tannenwald, *Are State and Local Revenue Systems Becoming Obsolete?* (Washington, DC: National League of Cities, 2004), p. 2. Also see Chris Hoene, "History, Voters Not Kind to Property Tax," *Nation's Cities Weekly*, May 14, 2001.
7. Annie Gowen, "Burned By the Boom in N.Va. Real Estate: Soaring Property Taxes Overwhelm Habitat for Humanity Homeowners," *The Washington Post*, February 14, 2005.
8. Irene S. Rubin, *Class, Tax, and Power: Municipal Budgeting in the United States* (Chatham, NJ: Chatham House, 1998), pp. 5–6.
9. For a more complete discussion of the property tax, see: Richard Netzer, "Property Taxes: Their Past, Present and Future Place in Government Finance," in *Urban Finance Under Siege*, eds. Thomas R. Swartz and Frank J. Bonello (Armonk, NY: M. E. Sharpe, Inc., 1993), pp. 51–78; and Arnold H. Raphaelson, "The Property Tax," in *Management Policies in Local Government Finance*, eds. Aronson and Schwartz, pp. 257–288.
10. The 2001 figure is reported by Tannenwald, *Are State and Local Revenue Systems Becoming Obsolete?*, p. 2. For a discussion of sales taxes, see Ronald K. Snell, "Our Outmoded Tax Systems," *State Legislatures* (August 1994), pp. 17–18; Irene Rubin, *The Politics of Public Budgeting*, 2nd ed. (Chatham, NJ: Chatham House, 1993), Chap. 2; and John L. Mikesell, "General Sales, Income, and Other Nonproperty Taxes," in *Management Policies in Local Government Finance*, eds. J. Richard Aronson and Eli Schwartz, pp. 293–303.
11. Deborah Rigsby, "Legislation Would Simplify Use, Sales Taxes," *Nation's Cities Weekly*, September 29, 2003; "Senator Seeks Solution in Internet Tax Debate," *Nation's Cities Weekly*, September 20, 2004.
12. In 2001, the property tax provided only 1.9 percent of local revenues, a figure reported in Tannenwald, *Are State and Local Revenue Systems Becoming*

Obsolete? (Washington, DC: National League of Cities, 2004), p. 2. For an overview of local income tax trends and issues, see Mikesell, "General Sales, Income, and Other Nonproperty Taxes," pp. 303–309.

13. Advisory Commission on Intergovernmental Relations, *Changing Public Attitudes on Government and Taxes* (Washington, DC: ACIR, 1986), p. 52.

14. Tannenwald, *Are State and Local Revenue Systems Becoming Obsolete?*, reports on p. 2 that in 2001 special districts received 40 percent of their revenues from current charges, 21 percent from "other," 15 percent from federal aid, and 24 percent from property, state, and sales taxes.

15. E. S. Savas, *Privatization: The Key to Better Government* (Chatham, NJ: Chatham House, 1987), pp. 248–250. Savas updates his argument in *Privatization and Public-Private Partnerships* (Chatham, NJ: Chatham House, 2000).

16. For a greater discussion of user fees, see C. Kurt Zorn, "User Charges and Fees," in *Local Government Finance,* eds. John Peterson and Dennis Strachota (Chicago: Government Finance Officers Association, 1991), Chap. 8; and Paul B. Downing, "The Revenue Potential of User Charges in Municipal Finance," *Public Finance Quarterly* 20 (October 1992), pp. 512–527; and, Edward J. Bierhanzl and Paul B. Downing, "User Charges and Special Districts," in *Management Policies in Local Government Finance,* eds. Aronson and Schwartz, pp. 315–344.

17. Neva Kerbeshian Novarro, "Does Earmarking Matter? The Case of State Lottery Profits and Educational Spending," Stanford Institute for Economic Policy Research Discussion Paper 02–19, December 2002, available at www.terry.uga.edu/hope/hope.lottery.pdf.

18. Quoted in "N.C. Center's Research Answers 13 Questions About State Lotteries," a press release of the North Carolina Center for Public Policy Research (undated). Available at www.nccppr.org/Lottery%20release.pdf.

19. Iver Peterson, "And They're Off, as States Across Northeast Race to Add Gambling Sites," *The New York Times,* November 18, 2002.

20. Marla K. Nelson, "Casino Gambling in Atlantic City: A Sure Bet for Whom?" (paper presented at the 1999 American Planning Association National Planning Conference, Seattle), available at www.asu.edu/caed/proceedings99/NELSON/NELSON.htm. For an older but still important review of the effects of casino gambling in Atlantic City, see George Sternlieb and James W. Hughes, *The Great Atlantic City Gamble* (Cambridge, MA: Harvard University Press, 1985).

21. Sabina Deitrick, Robert A. Beauregard, and Cheryl Zarlenga Kerchis, "Riverboat Gambling: Tourism and Economic Development," in *The Tourist City,"* eds. Dennis R. Judd and Susan S. Fainstein (New Haven, CT: Yale University Press, 1999), pp. 233–244.

22. Amy S. Rosenberg "New Jersey Is Now Betting that Atlantic City Can Be a Winner," *Philadelphia Inquirer,* June 23, 1996. John D. Donahue, *Disunited States* (New York: Basic Books, 1997), pp. 71–74, explains the thought-calculus that has led cities and states to rush to casinos and lotteries despite the severe costs that often accompany state-sponsored gambling.

23. Mark Simon, "Indian Casinos Facing Scrutiny: Feinstein Wants to Rein in Projects," *San Francisco Chronicle,* July 21, 2003.

24. For an overview of the various types of municipal bonds, the determinations of credit quality, and municipal bond defaults, see Paul A. Leonard, "Debt Management," in *Management Policies in Local Government Finance,* ed. Aronson and Schwartz, pp. 391–420.

25. See Ronald C. Fisher, *State and Local Public Finance* (Glenview, IL: Scott, Foresman, 1988), Chap. 12; J. Richard Aronson and John L. Hilley, *Financing State and Local Government*, 4th ed. (Washington, DC. Brookings Institution, 1986), Chap. 9.

26. Elaine B. Sharp, *Urban Politics and Administration: From Service Delivery to Economic Development* (New York: Longman, 1990), pp. 177 and 198–199; and Alberta M. Sbragia, *Debt Wish: Entrepreneurial Cities, U.S. Federalism and Economic Development* (Pittsburgh: University of Pittsburgh Press, 1990), pp. 159–162.

27. Two interesting studies of the key actors in urban finance are Esther R. Fuchs, *Mayors and Money: Fiscal Policy in New York and Chicago* (Chicago: University of Chicago Press, 1992); and Charles Brecher and Raymond Horton, *Power Failure: New York City Politics and Policy Since 1960* (New York: Oxford University Press, 1993).

28. Sbragia, *Debt Wish*, op. cit.

29. "How the 35 Cities Stack Up," *Governing* (February 2000): 40–41.

30. Robert W. Bailey, *The Crisis Regime: The MAC, the EFCB, and the Political Impact of the New York City Fiscal Crisis* (Albany: State University of New York Press, 1984), p. 151. Also see Martin Shefter, *Political Crisis/Fiscal Crisis: The Collapse and Revival of New York City* (New York: Basic Books, 1985); William K. Tabb, *The Long Default: New York City and the Urban Fiscal Crisis* (New York: Monthly Review Press, 1982).

31. Mark Baldassare, *When Government Fails: The Orange County Bankruptcy* (Berkeley: University of California Press, 1998), pp. 8, 90, 219, and 226.

32. The authors are grateful to Wilbur C. Rich for his assistance in identifying the exact sequence of events as the state and federal governments intervened in New York's fiscal crisis.

33. Heywood T. Sanders, "A Plethora of Disneylands: The Promise of Politics of Conventions and Tourism" (paper presented at the annual meeting of the Urban Affairs Association, Fort Worth, Texas, April 1998). Rendell's success is described by Scott Quehl, "The Bottom Line—And Beyond: Financial Plans Guided Philadelphia and New Haven to Recovery," *The Brookings Review* 18, 3 (Summer 2000): 31–33; and Ben Yagoda, "Mayor on a Roll: Ed Rendell," *The New York Times Magazine*, May 22, 1994: 26–29.

34. Matthew Leising, "State OKs Oakland Schools Takeover, *Contra Costa Times*, April 25, 2003.

35. Carrie Sturrock, "How Vallejo School District Got Itself $60 Million in Red," *San Francisco Chronicle*, June 29, 2004.

36. Advisory Commission on Intergovernmental Relations, *Significant Features of Fiscal Federalism* (Washington, DC: ACIR, 1995).

37. For a review of the various local government budgeting techniques and the difference between capital budgets and operating budgets, see Paul L. Salano, "Budgeting," in *Management Policies in Local Government Finance*, eds. Aronson and Schwartz, pp. 155–206. Also see J. Richard Aronson and Eli Schwartz, "Cost-Benefit Analysis and the Capital Budget," pp. 133–154 in the same volume.

38. Steven P. Erie, Christopher Hoene, and Gregory Saxton, "Assessing the Local Impacts of California's Post-Proposition 13 Regime: The Case of Metropolitan Los Angeles" (paper presented at the annual meeting of the American Political Science Association, Boston, September 3–6, 1998).

39. Terry Schwadron, ed., *California and the American Tax Revolt: Proposition 13 Five Years Later* (Berkeley: University of California Press, 1984), pp. 104–112.

40. Peter Schrag, *Paradise Lost: California's Experience, America's Future* (Berkeley: University of California Press, 1999), pp. 171–172 and 185.

41. *Allegheny Pittsburgh Coal Co. v. County Commission of Webster County, West Virginia*, 87 U.S. 1303 (1989). Also see Lee Ruck, "Supreme Court Requires Fairness in Assessments," *County News* (a publication of the National Association of Counties, Washington, DC), April 10, 1989.

42. Theodore J. Stumm and Pamela Pearson Mann, "Special Assessments in Florida Cities and Counties: Dodging Amendment 10?" (paper presented at the annual meeting of the Urban Affairs Association, Detroit, April 26–28, 2001).

43. Christian Berthelsen, Lynda Gledhill, and John Wildermuth, "Schools Chief Enters Fray Over Budget," *San Francisco Chronicle*, July 18, 2003.

44. Erie, Hoene, and Saxton, "Assessing the Local Impacts of California's Post-Proposition 13 Regime;" Jeff Chapman, "Tax Increment Financing and Fiscal Stress: The California Genesis," in *Tax Increment Financing and Economic Development: Uses, Structure, and Impact,*" eds. Craig L. Johnson and Joyce Y. Man (Albany, NY: State University of New York Press, 2001), pp. 113–135.

45. Joyce Y. Man, "Introduction," in *Tax Increment Financing and Economic Development*, p. 1.

46. J. Drew Klacik and Samuel Nunn, "A Primer on Tax Increment Financing," in *Tax Increment Financing and Economic Development*, p. 16.

47. Joyce Y. Man, "Introduction," pp. 2–6, presents a succinct summary of the various perceived benefits and criticisms of TIF.

48. Craig L. Johnson and Kenneth A. Kriz, "A Review of State Tax Increment Financing Laws," in *Tax Increment Financing and Economic Development*, p. 31.

49. Tom Luce, *Tax Increment Financing in the Kansas City and St. Louis Metropolitan Areas*, a discussion paper prepared for The Brookings Institution Center on Urban and Metropolitan Policy, Washington, DC, April 2003. Available at www.brookings.edu/es/urban/publications/lucetif.htm.

50. Robert G. Lehnen and Carlyn E. Johnson, "The Impact of Tax Increment Financing on School Districts: An Indiana Case Study," in *Tax Increment Financing and Economic Development*, p. 153. Also see Rachel Weber, "Equity and Entrepreneurialism: The Impact of Tax Increment Financing on School Finance," *Urban Affairs Review* 38, 5 (May 2003): 619–644.

51. Eli Lehrer, "The Town that Loves to TIF," *Governing* (September 1999): 44–46; Gary Washburn, "Study Criticizes Chicago TIFs," *Chicago Tribune*, March 12, 2002.

52. David A. Reingold, "Are TIFs Being Misused to Alter Patterns of Residential Segregation? The Case of Addison and Chicago, Illinois," in *Tax Increment Financing and Economic Development*, pp. 223–239.

53. Sharp, *Urban Politics and Administration*, p. 158.

54. Ibid., p. 9.

55. Alberta Sbragia, *Debt Wish*, Chaps. 7 and 8; Sharp, *Urban Politics and Administration*, pp. 176–177 and 201–208; Dennis Zimmerman, *The Private Use of Tax Exempt Bonds: Controlling Public Subsidy of Private Activity* (Washington, DC: The Urban Institute Press, 1991), Chaps. 2 and 4.

56. David Osborne and Ted Gaebler, *Reinventing Government: How the Entrepreneurial Spirit Is Transforming the Public Sector from Schoolhouse to Statehouse, City Hall to the Pentagon* (Reading, MA: Addison-Wesley, 1992); David Osborne

and Peter Plastrik, *The Reinventor's Fieldbook: Tools for Transforming Your Government* (San Francisco: Jossey-Bass, 2000).

57. For an overview of risk management in local government, see: Lauren Cragg and H. Felix Kloman, "Risk Management: A Developed Discipline," in *Risk Management Today,* eds. Natalie Wasserman and Dean G. Phelus (Washington, DC: International City Management Association, 1985); R. Bradley Johnson and Bernard H. Ross, "Risk Management in the Public Sector," *Municipal Yearbook 1989* (Washington, DC: International City Management Association, 1989), pp. 1–11; and Peter C. Young and Claire Lee Reiss, "Risk Management," in *Management Policies in Local Government Finance,* eds. Aronson and Schwartz, pp. 479–500.

58. Kenneth S. Geller, "Municipal Liability Under Section 1983: A Thumbnail Sketch," *Public Management* 68 (November 1986), pp. 9–12.

59. *Harlow v. Fitzgerald,* 457 U.S. 800,818 (1982).

60. *Hope v. Pelzer,* U.S.SCt, 01–309 (2002), majority opinion, p. 10.

61. *Monell v. Department of Social Services United States,* 436 US 658 (1978).

62. *Newport v. Fact Concerts, Inc.,* 453 US 247 (1981).

63. *Owen v. City of Independence,* 445 U.S. 622 (1980).

64. *City of Canton v. Harris,* 489 U.S. 378 (1989).

65. Baldassare, *When Government Fails,* pp. 210 and 217.

66. Terry Nichols Clark and Lorna Crowley Ferguson, *City Money: Political Processes, Fiscal Strain and Retrenchment* (New York: Columbia University Press, 1983).

In the conclusion of the previous edition of *Urban Politics,* we pointed to the newfound prominence that economic development policy had gained in the urban arena. Cities and suburbs focused their attention on local jobs and tax-base development, often slighting housing and social policy needs.

Economic development will continue to dominate local policy agendas in the near future. However, in the post-9/11 world, protective and anti-terrorism concerns will also lay claim on urban budgets.

In this chapter, we discuss the trends that are likely to shape the future politics of United States cities and suburbs. We close by outlining a possible basis for future national and state urban policy.

CONTINUING EMPHASIS ON ECONOMIC DEVELOPMENT

In the 1990s, urban politics became increasingly synonymous with the politics of local economic growth and development. Of course, big cities in the United States have always been concerned with growth and development. Even the old political party machines were part of a growth coalition; they built streets, extended sewer and streetcar lines, granted businesses valuable franchises and permits, and, in the process, received financial contributions and the control over jobs that were dispensed as patronage.

Yet questions of local economic development have not always dominated city politics. During the 1960s and 1970s, the "urban crisis" was defined by poverty concerns and social issues. Urban riots, community action programs, demands for law and order, racial identity politics, and calls for minority empowerment, school busing, and community control—not economic development—all caught the headlines in local news. Beginning with New York City's flirtation with bankruptcy in 1975, the urban crisis took a new turn, with questions of fiscal solvency and "cutback management" gaining a new prominence in city hall.

Technological change and post-industrial restructuring continued to undermine the stability of local economies. In the 1980s, federal aid cutbacks and

New Federalism devolution left local governments little alternative but to fend for themselves. As a result, by the 1990s, concerns for jobs and economic development had come to occupy a near-hegemonic position in the local arena. Cities and suburbs devoted their energies to efforts designed to increase local employment and the local tax base. Only the nation's most affluent cities could afford to be selective when it came to new local economic growth.

Today, economic development has become a normal function of government, as normal, say, as providing police services or picking up the garbage. Even in Texas, the bastion of free-enterprise culture, big and small cities alike offer various incentives and create industrial parks and tax increment financing districts in their efforts to attract "clean businesses." Small- and medium-sized cities even levy special sales taxes to finance economic development activities.[1] The intensified competition for economic development has put business—particularly big business—in "the driver's seat" in its continued quest for tax advantages, infrastructure improvements, and other favorable considerations from local policymakers.

Economists and other urban specialists argue that tax abatements and other development subsidies are often a waste of valuable municipal resources. Local tax rates tend to be only a relatively small factor in a firm's decision as to where to locate a new facility. The quality of the local labor force, the geographical proximity of suppliers and markets, and the availability of adequate transportation are all considerations that play a much greater role than tax levels in determining where a business will site a facility.

The evidence on this point, however, is not as clear as the critics of development subsidies contend. Local taxes may have an impact on a corporation's choice of locales *within* a metropolitan area, inasmuch as the corporation's access to suppliers, a qualified labor force, and markets is relatively the same throughout much of the metropolis.[2]

Whatever the exact evidence, local officials continue to offer subsidies and tax abatements as they *believe* that such incentives influence business decisions. Local officials believe that they must match the offers made by other cities in order to be competitive. Also, municipal officers can never be sure if a particular subsidy will or will not be the decisive factor in a development decision. Faced with uncertainty, elected officials take the safe route of offering the subsidy. Few elected officeholders want to risk being blamed for the loss of a prominent local business.

Fewer still want to be blamed for the loss of a popular local baseball or football team. As a result, municipal officials provide grand arenas and stadiums for professional sports teams; they allow team owners to garner generous shares of revenues from concessions, parking fees, and licenses for season seating. In doing so, the city and its taxpayers provide "welfare" for multimillionaire team owners and players.[3] Only when a growth project imposes an immediate threat to a specific community does intense neighborhood opposition mobilize.

Economic consultants also help drive the politics of local economic development as their studies often overstate the expected gains from a new arena and convention center. These development experts join with local growth elites to push a city to become a "player" in the competitive national and global environment by subsidizing new development. Such strategizing has produced a local policy orientation that Heywood Sanders has called **hotel socialism.** In their efforts to attract new conventions, municipal officials in Sacramento, Austin, Houston, Denver, St. Louis, and other cities have used taxpayer money to finance the building of hotels that Hyatt and other private investors have deemed to be too risky and unwise.[4]

Who are the losers when local governments are increasingly preoccupied with economic development? Who pays for the concessions and tax abatements that are given businesses?

Local economic development officials and other members of the local growth coalition contend that no one pays—that growth attracts new businesses that contribute to the city tax base and help to pay for other services. At times, this proves to be the case.

But in a great many cases, the revenues generated by a new business venture do not cover the costs of the services that the city provides, especially when a city's revenue gains are reduced by tax abatements and the costs of new infrastructure improvements. In such cases, the burden of supporting new megagrowth projects falls on a city's residents and small businesses.

Local school systems, too, suffer when revenue is foregone as the result of tax abatements given to industrial and commercial property. In Indiana and elsewhere, the creation of tax increment financing districts has had a detrimental impact on school financing.[5] With the creation of a TIF district, new gains in property tax revenues are dedicated to the improvement of facilities in the designated district; these funds cannot be used for public schools.

Chicago's reliance on TIFs to spur manufacturing has proven especially controversial, with the city's more than 110 TIF districts producing a long-term diversion of substantial monies away from the city's troubled school system. Only in more recent years has the city attempted to use some unspent TIF proceeds for new school construction.[6]

Tax abatements and other "sweetheart deals" with particular companies cost a city considerable money that could have been used to finance other important services. Cities often cave in too easily to business threats, forgoing potential revenues. In 1993, New York City gave the broadcasting giant CBS $15 million in tax subsidies to stay in Manhattan for 15 years. Just six years later the city granted the corporation an additional $10 million in tax breaks and electrical subsidies. Critics argued that the city gave away more money than was necessary, that the corporation may well have been bluffing in its threat to move to Jersey City.[7]

The intercity competition is severe. To succeed, city officials must do more than merely offer tax abatements. City leaders have deployed a variety of strategies in their attempts to lure business. Many cities have set up **business incubators,** facilities that offer new businesses low-cost spaces and shared office services, technological support, and managerial advice. Cities have used local universities to extend managerial and technical assistance to business.

San Diego and other cities have pursued marketing programs to promote the sale of locally produced goods in the global market.

Many cities have also engaged in "future-oriented public policies regarding infrastructure development," investing in "computer-age infrastructures that will provide them with comparative advantages for processing and transmitting information."[8] Municipal officials *wire* a city to provide the infrastructure needed by business. In an information age, cities provide fiber optics, cellular, and satellite connections. Larger cities and suburbs may even offer municipal supercomputer facilities that can be leased to information processing businesses on a cost-sharing basis. Cities have also begun to offer increased broadband access, creating wireless *hotspots* in an effort to attract smaller, more creative and entrepreneurial firms.

Soft factors, too, help determine a city's global competitive success. A city can invest in education and training programs that improve the skills, productivity, and flexibility of the local workforce. Cities can also improve the quality of parks and amenities and address other quality-of-life concerns in order to provide an environment that is attractive to business and upscale workers.[9]

Yet a city pursues such economic development strategies at the risk of exacerbating uneven development within the city. Municipal resources are limited. Cities that spend money to create a local environment attractive to major corporations and their technologically competent workforces may have less to spend on affordable housing and services that respond to the needs of less fortunate residents and neighborhoods.

The transformation of New York City provides an example of the lack of balanced development that can occur even in a city with a reputation for liberal social policies. In New York, corporate office development, upscale retail stores, fashionable hotels, and new restaurants have virtually driven out all but luxury housing south of 96th Street. Former manufacturing areas have been designated as sites for future commercial expansion; their use for affordable housing has been ruled out. The construction of a convention center and other large-scale economic development projects served to drive up housing prices in surrounding neighborhoods. In New York's tight housing market, private developers built for the well-off. In the absence of strong municipal action, the housing needs of the poor, displaced manufacturing workers, and newly arrived immigrants were ignored.[10]

The tourism industry is an important part of the economies of post-industrial cities, and cities increasingly cater to affluent visitors and conventioneers.[11] New York mayor Michael Bloomberg promoted the construction of a new convention corridor, including an expanded convention center, on Manhattan's West Side, promising an even more intensive development of New York City as a tourist city. His proposal to build a new West Side stadium for the football Jets, despite the objections of neighboring residential areas, only further exemplified Bloomberg's conceptualization of New York as a tourist city.

Active citizen groups—homeowner associations, environmentalist organizations, small business owners opposed to new taxes, and inner-city racial minority and neighborhood groups—have at times served as a counterweight to growth plans and corporate power. In the Sunbelt, citizen activism has helped to add a degree of balance to local political systems once dominated by downtown business elites.

At times, citizen groups have succeeded in forcing balanced growth policies and social and housing programs onto the local agenda. But the influence of civic and corporate elites remains substantial. In many metropolitan areas, quasi-independent authorities and special districts have been created to insulate public-private growth partnerships from direct accountability to citizen action. Special districts and authorities, with their low public visibility, limited public access, and independent sources of financing—and, in some cases, eminent domain powers, as well—allow "experts" to approve controversial development decisions with the advice of citizen "input."[12]

Can the stranglehold of economic development policy on the urban arena be broken? Federal revenue sharing, metropolitan tax-base sharing, plant-closing laws, strict land-use regulation, and state assumption of a greater share of local school expenditures are all strategies that would have *some* impact, leaving cities less reliant on having to win the cutthroat competition for economic development.[13] But there is little will in the United States to enact such solutions on a widespread basis. The federal government is not considering a return to revenue sharing. Suburbanites oppose tax-base sharing with poorer jurisdictions. Free-market economists object to plant-closing laws and strong land-use controls; states and communities that enact such laws risk gaining a reputation of being "bad for business." Nor is there any evidence that local tax-base sharing has had any great effect on reducing the interlocal competition for business.

Despite the priority given to economic development, city officials do have choices and do not have to cede to businesses' demands for tax abatements and other subsidies. Businesses are not just drawn to low-tax cities; they are also drawn to desirable areas with reputable schools, high amenities, and strong communities. Recent studies point to the importance of **quality-of-life concerns,** including the provision of good schools, convenient transportation, plentiful parks and recreational facilities, interesting arts and cultural programs, and other amenities, in attracting business. As the Seattle and Portland experiences attest, a good quality of life helps an area to attract quality employees.[14] Low taxes are not the only way to attract business. Often, the promise of low taxes alone will not do the job.

RISE OF THE SECURITY CITY

In the post-9/11 world, cities are saddled with the high costs of security. Cities must help protect airports, harbors, important public buildings, stadiums, subways, train stations, reservoirs, water filtration plants, and numerous other potential targets of a terrorist attack. Every time the nation raises a Code Alert (that is, when the Department of Homeland Security moves to an Orange level), it costs big cities millions of dollars in extended overtime and related expenses. Such demands have been a drain on city treasuries.

Cities across the nation are not equally saddled with the burden of providing enhanced security. Still, while the nation's more global cities are the prime targets for attack and bear the greatest costs of maintaining security, even small and medium-sized cities have responsibilities in helping to protect nearby defense industries, chemical plants, port facilities, and military bases.

Intergovernmental aid helps cities meet their new security responsibilities. Federal grants have helped cities pay for first responders and new security technology. Such aid can be justified because national security is a national government responsibility. Yet the level of federal assistance has not compensated localities for the full range of security burdens they must assume. In many ways the nation's homeland security program approximates another unfunded (or, rather, poorly funded) mandate, a requirement placed on cities from above without the financial assistance to allow full compliance.[15]

In the terrorist age, the social fabric of the city is also being reshaped. In the new and jittery security city, public space is diminished. Access to buildings is restricted as government and corporate offices seek secure environments and gate-controlled entrances. Immigrants and people of the "wrong" ethnicity or complexion face the prospect of increased police surveillance. Cities may also find that the new concern for security is intruding on important links to the global community; extensive passport checks and security screening obstructs easy air travel, impairing the transnational flow of corporate personnel and the ability of cities to function fully as global meeting places. In Jerusalem, Israel, a wave of terrorist assaults shrunk the notion of public space; life in cafes and other public places all but dried up as people sought the relative safety of private, defended spaces.[16]

As we saw in Chapter 1, "The Urban Situation and 9/11," New York City suffered enormous costs as a result of the 9/11 attacks. The attack came at a time when the city's economy was also reeling as a result of a national economic recession. Yet in many ways, the city astonishingly came back. By the spring of 2004, rents for retails stores in midtown Manhattan surpassed pre-9/11 levels; ticket sales for Broadway also rebounded, reaching new record levels.[17] Many fewer businesses relocated to sites outside the city than had been initially feared. Cities enjoy a great resiliency as they provide important, valuable functions.

Yet as terrible as it was, 9/11 represents only a one-day terrorist assault. What would be the impact on cities of a wave of terrorist attacks? What would be the consequences if a terrorist were to use a "suitcase bomb" to spread deadly radioactivity to a busy part of the central business district? What would happen if terrorists were to attack such "soft targets" as shopping centers and entertainment facilities, no longer confining their attacks to major buildings in a city's downtown? There is no guarantee that New York or any city will remain unaffected by such a series of attacks.

A series of assaults could lead businesses to seek the safety and stability of locations in the suburbs. A wave of assaults would likely traumatize big-city economies, with people quite fearful of working in tall skyscrapers and of gathering in public places. In New York City, the construction of the 1,776-foot-tall Freedom Tower was delayed as the project had to be redesigned in response to the concerns raised by security experts. Critics feared that the redesign would turn the building into an "armored bunker."[18] Goldman, Sachs & Company cast a pall over the entire Ground Zero rebuilding project when it cited security concerns as the reason why the company would not follow through on plans to build a 40-story headquarters building across the street from the Freedom Tower.

INCREASED SALIENCE OF WOMEN'S ISSUES

The global age has exaggerated the dual-city nature of American cities. For skilled and technologically competent workers, the city offers attractive new housing, job, and entertainment opportunities. People lacking the skills demanded by the information economy, however, find that the city has few good-paying jobs to offer and that the supply of affordable housing has shrunk.

Too often, conflict in the urban arena is viewed only through the lens of social class and race, with the result that gender inequalities have not always been observed. In the global, post-industrial city, however, gender divisions are highlighted as new attention is focused on the access of women to good wages, housing, transportation, child care, and income support.

Women comprise much of the *underside* of the dual workforce of America's global cities. Women dominate the poorly paid domestic, assembly, janitorial, and clerical job classifications, jobs that seldom receive union protection and health and other benefits. Immigrant women dominate the low-wage, low-skill "sweatshop" jobs of Los Angeles and other port-of-entry cities. Women are often the breadwinners in the underside of the new urban economy; single mothers provide for their children, and immigrant women often take low-wage employment where their husbands cannot.

Post-industrial society has paradoxically both created new opportunities for women and imposed severe constraints on women's advancement. The largest occupational group in the United States today is clerical workers, and women account for 80 percent of the nation's private and public clerical workforce. The new clerical positions of the transformed urban economy offer women, especially African-American women and Latinas, new opportunities to escape the low-wage drudgery of domestic and agricultural work. While some women have made their way into professional jobs (at times with the opportunities created by affirmative action programs), other women, especially minority women, are stuck in the "clerical ghetto."[19]

Advances in communications have changed the nature of work, leading to the creation of jobs demanding higher skills. Today, even clerical work requires data- and word-processing capabilities unheard of before the computer age. Yet in numerous other job categories, computerization and other technological advances have led to a "de-skilling" (or the "dumbing down") of jobs. Where computers do the more complex calculations and workers merely just enter data, pay levels are correspondingly low. The automation of data processing and record-keeping has also eliminated many jobs that once paid mid-range salaries.

When it comes to hiring and promoting women and minorities, government has a better record of achievement than does the private sector. Yet even in the public sector, minority women are still concentrated in lower-level jobs lacking significant opportunity for advancement. In New York and other tight housing markets, women in low-wage clerical jobs have difficulty affording housing. The problem of housing affordability is especially acute for minority women, who are more likely to be single mothers.[20]

In the post-industrial city, a gender-aware urban policy will be concerned with more than the feminization of poverty; it will also seek to protect women in the workplace, assure women adequate pay and benefits, assist with child care, provide safe and convenient transportation, and assure women's physical safety. The unionization of pink-collar (the low-wage service work usually performed by women) and white-collar jobs may also be crucial to the protection and advancement of women in the restructured urban workforce. The nation will continue to debate the merits of affirmative action in enabling both white and minority women to escape the clerical ghetto.

Yet it will not always be easy to design policies that meet the needs of women, especially of poor women. For instance, it is often argued that enhanced public transportation will help poor urban women, especially immigrant women who often work in domestic jobs in the suburbs. Without a car, these women may ride one bus and then another; on Sundays and in areas lacking mass transit, these low-paid workers may even find that they have no alternative to an expensive cab ride. But as the job sites where these women work are so geographically spread, even improved mass transit will not serve these women well: "The dirty little secret is that the mass transit solution is an illusion."[21] Recognizing this problem, some state welfare-to-work programs have begun to experiment with helping the "carless" poor buy and maintain automobiles.

DOWNTOWNS COME BACK, BUT THE SUBURBS STILL DOMINATE

The age of suburbanization continues unabated. Suburban populations and power dominate urban America.[22] The pro-city effects of gentrification pale when compared to the continuing tide of suburbanization. Edge cities, technoburbs, exurbs, and edgeless cities all represent evolving forms of suburban population growth, wealth, and power.

Many of the functions once filled by the central city are now being replicated in the new suburban downtowns. Advances in computerization and mass communications have even allowed the legal and financial communities, once the core of downtown functions even in the 1950s and 1960s, to decentralize. Large corporations find it increasingly convenient to have their headquarters and the regional offices in the suburbs. The growth of airports outside the central core has also spurred new technology-related development in the suburbs.[23]

World-class cities such as New York and Los Angeles still enjoy competitive advantages as they are the sites of large concentrations or nodes of corporate headquarters and financial and legal institutions. These cities, however, need to continually improve and update their technological and communications infrastructures and support services in order to maintain their competitive edge.

Over the last two decades, central cities have shown that they can rebuild and revitalize their downtowns. Downtown is clearly back![24] Cities have built sports stadiums, casinos, and a whole host of convention- and tourism-related facilities. Cities as diverse as Newark, San Jose, San Francisco, Anchorage, Fort Lauderdale, Miami, West Palm Beach, Escondido (California), Fort Worth, and Charleston (West Virginia) have pursued an arts-based approach to urban redevelopment, hoping that a new performing arts center, a museum district, or refurbished theaters will provide the catalyst for a downtown resurgence.[25] In the 1990s, continued immigration from overseas even led to the growth of central-city populations. Gentrification has brought new activity to the city. There is a life in central cities that Americans value. Suburban growth continues unabated; but central cities are far from dead.

In a suburban age, cities have no political alternative but to discover "common ground" with a growing suburbia. As we discussed in Chapter 13, "The Politics of Regional Cooperation," some core cities have already formed pragmatic alliances with declining older suburbs and too-quickly-growing-and-overburdened communities in an effort to identify equitable regional growth strategies. Central cities, older suburbs, and rural areas can find common ground with environmentalists in efforts to contain sprawl and preserve farmland and open space. In New Jersey, just such a coalition helped push Republican governor Christine Todd Whitman to propose an increase in the gasoline tax to fund open-space preservation. Policies that protect open space, farmland, and environmentally sensitive areas serve to guide new development to central cities and older suburbs.

Suburbia is no monolith. Instead, there is a growing diversity of suburbs and suburban populations. With the necessary imagination, will, and leadership, creative, politically pragmatic alliances between central cities and suburban communities can be struck.[26]

THE FUTURE OF MINORITY EMPOWERMENT

In recent years, African Americans and Hispanics have gained increased electoral power in major cities. The more militant rhetoric of an earlier generation has ceded way to the more pragmatic concerns of effective city governance as blacks and Latinos use their control over community resources and city hall for job promotion, economic development, more effective education, and the provision of affordable housing. Increasingly, minority leaders have sought to build effective electoral and governing coalitions across class and racial lines. As Roberto Villarreal, Norma Hernandez, and Howard Neighbor have observed in their review of Latino politics, the radicalism of the previous era has been replaced by "the policies of accommodation and recognition."[27]

In Los Angeles, the 2005 election of mayor Antonio Villaraigosa served as testimony to the potential inherent in the new style of Latino politics. Villaraigosa won easily, defeating incumbent Jim Hahn by a landslide 17-point margin in a city where Latinos were half of the city's population but only one-fourth of the electorate (as many were noncitizens or new citizens who did not vote). Villaraigosa was a coalition builder who ran on the theme of unity. He won by picking up 84 percent of the Latino vote, half of the white vote, and nearly half of the African-American and Asian-American vote. In part, he attracted the votes of African Americans whom his predecessor had alienated by refusing to reappoint Bernard Parks, an African American, as the city's chief of police. Villaraigosa gained the endorsement of Congresswoman Maxine Waters and other African-American leaders who had endorsed Hahn when he beat Villaraigosa four years earlier. The extent that Villaraigosa in office would be able to keep the fragile coalition together, muting the competition between the city's African-American and Mexican-American communities, remained to be seen.[28]

Not all voices in the minority community, however, are happy with the new style of pragmatic minority politics. Critics argue that such a pragmatic approach to governance is essentially conservative in nature, that community leaders and elected officials narrowly concerned with coalition maintenance and program management will fail to organize challenges to the prevailing power structure and the status quo. As one observer of Mexican-American politics concluded, the gain of power "seems to be more an achievement of the conservative middle class than of the masses."[29]

THE GROWTH OF LATINO POWER AND IDENTITY

Rapid Hispanic population growth is reshaping the politics of major U.S. cities, especially in Texas and the Southwest. The 2000 census documented the fact that Hispanics constituted nearly a quarter of the population of the nation's 100 largest cities, reaching virtual parity with the black population in those cities. The Hispanic urban population had increased 46 percent since 1990, primarily as a result of immigration. Most cities continued to suffer white flight to the suburbs. Hispanic population growth combined with the city's African-American population to produce a nonwhite majority in half of the cities.[30]

The growing Latino population has also begun to reshape America's suburbs, particularly in California and the Southwest. Anaheim, California, the home of Disneyland and once the iconic symbol of white middle-class suburbia, has become predominantly Hispanic. Even Disneyland has become a hangout for the area's Hispanic youth who buy relatively cheap season passes to the theme park.[31]

The growth in the Hispanic population, however, has not resulted in a proportional increase in Hispanic voting power. Hispanic voting power has been diminished by low voter registration and turnout; Hispanic voting turnouts are far below those of whites and even below those of African Americans.[32] The Voting Rights Act substantially reduced the structural barriers to Mexican-American voting, even providing bilingual voting materials. But it did not overcome the citizenship and economic barriers that still limit Latino electoral participation.[33] In cities such as Chicago, Latino voting was also diminished by a low sense of political efficacy, a sense among Latino citizens that their votes just do not make a difference.[34] Evidence from Los Angeles shows, however, that Latinos will turn out at rates equal to that of whites when a viable Latino candidate has the chance of winning an important office.[35]

As immigration continues, Hispanic numbers and political power will increase. Even where voting turnouts are low, Latino parents have been active in school affairs. In Orange County, California and many other communities, the Latino vote is a "sleeping giant" just beginning to awaken to its political power.[36] Agenda items rooted in the Hispanic community will increasingly define local affairs.

Often, the tensions between blacks and Hispanics emerge. Blacks and Latinos generally do not live in the same areas of the city. Nor do they share a common identity. Latinos are also arriving in a post-industrial city with a changed opportunity structure, one where low-wage assembly and service jobs do not pay enough for decent housing and the support of a family—or, in some cases, even the purchase of a car to commute to a job in the suburbs.[37]

In cities lacking a clear Hispanic majority, there will be calls for African Americans and Latinos to forge an effective coalition in the quest for power. In Miami, Los Angeles, and other cites, however, voting patterns often reveal a polarization between Latino and African-American voters who see one another as competitors for the same slices of a shrinking urban political and economic pie.[38] Public opinion polls reveal that African Americans perceive a greater sense of commonality with Latinos than Latinos perceive with blacks. Whether Latinos and African Americans (and Asian Americans, as well) can discover sufficient commonality to overcome their differences and sustain a mutually beneficial political alliance remains to be seen.[39]

Globalization and changing technology have also acted to alter the process of assimilation in the new immigrant communities in U.S. cities. Unlike the prior waves of immigrants who came from Europe, the new immigrants of "Mexican New York" make frequent return visits to their home county, maintaining links to their home community and forging a transnational identity.[40]

COURT DECISIONS AND MINORITY REPRESENTATION

The effective representation of racial minorities in national, state, and local legislatures is often contingent on districting plans designed to maximize the election of underrepresented groups. The active vigilance of minority groups is especially necessary during legislative redistricting to ensure that legislatures and courts draw district lines that maximize, rather than dilute, minority voting power. In 1990, pressure from both citizen groups and the federal district court finally forced the Los Angeles County Board of Supervisors to adopt a redistricting plan that at long last created a Hispanic-majority district.[41]

The Supreme Court, however, has put limits on the use of gerrymandering plans to maximize minority representation. In *Shaw v. Reno* (1993), the Supreme Court struck down a plan that strung together pockets of African-American population across North Carolina in order to create a black-majority congressional district. The Court observed that there is a limit as to how irregularly a district can be drawn even for the purposes of maximizing minority representation. In 1995, the Court went still further, ruling in *Miller v. Johnson* that race could not be "the overriding or predominant" factor in districting.

In *Holder v. Hall* (1994), a sharply divided Court refused to order a district plan that would give African Americans representation in Bleckley, Georgia. African Americans were one-fifth of the county's population but were effectively denied any representation in a county government governed by a single commissioner. The plaintiffs argued that the southern community used the single-commissioner plan to deny African Americans a voice in county government. But the Supreme Court majority was not willing to assume, without proof, that racial motivation underlay the plan.[42]

Paradoxically, while race-oriented redistricting may increase the numbers of racial minorities elected to office, the creation of majority-minority districts works in other ways against minority interests. When population pockets of African-American or Hispanic voters are packed into a majority-minority district, the surrounding districts are effectively "bleached" or "whitened," making them more likely to elect a Republican representative. The careful race-conscious carving of the boundaries not only creates a district likely to elect an African-American or Latino representative; it also results in the creation of more Republican districts in the surrounding areas, increasing Republican representation in Congress, decreasing the likelihood of policies favorable to central-city interests.

Race-conscious redistricting plans have also compounded intergroup tensions. In Dallas, attempts to create an additional safe African-American council district angered Hispanics who believed the plan undermined their own ability to win election. In Dallas and elsewhere, computer-generated maps allow voting rights advocates to use block-by-block census data to create minority-majority districts. Such intricately carved districts also wind up altering representational styles; council members from such districts tend to act as spokespersons for narrow racial constituencies as they have little electoral need to fashion a broader multiethnic coalition.[43]

CONTRACT COMPLIANCE AND MINORITY SET-ASIDES

Racial minorities have used their control of city hall to build minority-owned businesses and bring jobs to minority neighborhoods. **Contract compliance** programs contain affirmative action–style preferences in the award of city contracts to minority-owned firms and to firms that agree to racial hiring targets.

But here, too, Supreme Court decisions have placed important constraints on minority incorporation. In *Richmond v. Croson* (1989), the Court struck down a city of Richmond requirement that at least 30 percent of the total dollar amount of municipal contracts be awarded to minority firms. Before passage of the ordinance, black firms had received less than 1 percent of the city's business despite the fact that African Americans were more than half of the city's population. When African Americans finally gained control of city hall, the minority set-aside program was one of the first measures the city council enacted.

Richmond's downtown business leaders supported the program, recognizing the political benefits of tying development in the central business district to the African-American agenda. Contract compliance set-asides were the "glue" that allowed African Americans and whites to agree on economic development initiatives.[44]

But other white-owned businesses, especially in the construction industry, objected that the law amounted to reverse discrimination. Other critics argued that the program served only to enrich a "chosen few" in the minority community. The Supreme Court struck down Richmond's contract compliance program as a noxious racial classification.

A city cannot just allege a history of past discrimination to justify minority preferences. Instead, it must prove that the city had engaged in unconstitutional discrimination in the specific service area in question. The city must also show why more temporary and race-neutral programs cannot correct the problem. **Disparity studies**—statistical analyses pointing to the disparity between the number of minority businesses in a market area and the percentage of a city's contracts they received—can be presented to *help* establish the existence of a pattern of discrimination. A city must also demonstrate that its minority set-aside program is **narrowly tailored,** that the program does not offer special preferences willy-nilly to all minorities but only to groups who are truly the victims of discrimination.[45]

In the wake of *Croson*, many localities retreated from compliance programs. Others, however, began to amass the history of deliberate incidents of discrimination in a local industry that could be used to defend minority contracting preference programs in case of a challenge in court. Post-*Croson* judicial rulings upheld local minority business set-aside provisions that are narrowly drawn, that are enacted for a fixed period of time, and that are justified by historical and marketplace analyses that clearly document pervasive discrimination.[46]

In some states, voters have used the tools of direct democracy to limit racial preferences. Most notably, California voters in 1996 passed **Proposition 209,** which bars the use of racial and gender preferences in government contracting. San Francisco's Board of Supervisors, however, voted to continue the city's affirmative contracting plan despite Prop 209, arguing that the plan was justified by a disparity study, that it met federal constitutional standards, and that it was necessary to correct continuing discrimination.[47]

The very next year, voters in Houston bucked the national trend and voted *against* a proposed ban on affirmative action preferences. In Houston, affirmative action had the support of the city's business elite. Houston mayor

Bob Lanier, a white real estate developer, argued: "Let's not turn back the clock to the days when guys like me got all of the city's business." The large voting turnout in the city's minority communities also helped defeat the measure. Blacks were about 25 percent and Latinos 30 percent of Houston's population.[48]

RESEGREGATION AND THE FUTURE PROSPECTS FOR JUDICIAL ACTION

In the 1950s, the Supreme Court helped lead the attack on *de jure* racial segregation. But, as we have seen throughout this book, the Supreme Court has not been willing to commit to a similar assault on *de facto* segregation. Nor has the nation's highest court been willing to attack exclusionary zoning and the continuing inequalities that result from the local-based funding of public schools.

As we reported in Chapter 1, the Supreme Court's 1975 *Millikin v. Bradley* decision sharply limited school desegregation efforts. The Court effectively ruled that suburbs need not participate in interdistrict efforts to undo *de facto* the segregation of central-city schools. The decision "sent the unmistakable message—urban apartheid would not be overcome through judicial decree."[49]

In the years that followed, the Court allowed DeKalb County (Georgia), Kansas City, Charlotte-Mecklenburg (North Carolina), and a whole host of other cities across the nation, in both the north and the south, to abandon school busing and other desegregation efforts that had been pursued for a considerable length of time. The results of the Court's decision have been unmistakable; **school resegregation** is on the rise.[50] The percentage of students attending racially integrated schools declined.

School officials today must rely primarily on voluntary techniques—including magnet schools with their special curricula and the provision of a safe school environment—in an effort to persuade parents to send their children to a school other than their neighborhood school.[51] Even these programs, however, produce only relatively few pro-integration transfers.

Polling data reveals that African Americans have come to accept the reality and permanence of *de facto* segregation.[52] African Americans as well as whites no longer place any great faith in school integration.

THE FUTURE OF NATIONAL URBAN POLICY

What should be the federal government's response to urban problems? Some observers call for a more aggressive and explicit national urban policy designed to alleviate urban ills. Yet critics argue against such a policy, pointing out that federal action over the years has been ineffective, wasteful, and, at times, even counterproductive. They argue for devolution, that program and policy choices should be left to the more capable hands of states, cities, and local communities. They also argue for privatization, that the government's role be limited to allow market forces to create more results-driven urban action.

We conclude this book by presenting three radically different directions for national urban policy. We also seek to determine if there is any possibility of sustaining federal urban actions in an age in which the dispersion of political power presents a policy environment hostile to large-scale urban aid efforts.

THE CALL FOR A NATIONAL URBAN POLICY

In the 1960s, noted urban expert and then-presidential adviser (later to become senator from New York) Daniel Patrick Moynihan observed the many gaps, inconsistencies, and coordination problems in the War on Poverty's program-by-program approach to urban problems.[53] He and others called for a national urban policy.

As we saw in Chapter 14, "National and State Policy Toward Cities," Jimmy Carter was the only president ever to heed the call and attempt to formulate an explicit national urban policy. His policy, though, went nowhere, dying on the shoals of a district-protectionist and suburban-oriented Congress. Since Carter, no president has even attempted to formulate an explicit policy that would make cities the targets of coordinated federal action.

Still, despite this cautionary experience, numerous urban experts continue the call for a national urban policy. Paul Kantor argues for expanding federal social spending and the federal role in urban development in order to liberate cities from their economic dependence on private business. Kantor argues that the federal government should regulate urban development and compensate "loser" communities. To reduce the intercity competition for business, Kantor suggests reducing federal assistance to cities that award tax abatements and other subsidies to business. He also argues for enterprise zones targeted to distressed areas.[54]

A special issue of the *Journal of Urban Affairs* similarly declared the importance of a national urban policy. According to the issue's editors, only strong government intervention can remedy the problems caused by the demographic shifts, economic dislocations, and changed intergovernmental aid patterns that have buffeted American cities.[55] The authors of one article concluded: "Only a total rethinking of the nation's priorities and a reinvestment in social and human capital can transform urban life."[56] The authors viewed contemporary urban problems as interdependent and systemic, requiring interventions that are multifaceted, holistic, and broad in scope.

More recently, Janet Rothenberg Park, writing for the influential Brookings Institution, has made essentially the same argument. She argues that the ability of policy proposals "to turn urban development away from its current trajectory will require the policy community to enact major policy changes *simultaneously*, rather than piecemeal." She further emphasizes "the need for *coordinated* policy changes."[57]

The advocates of a national urban policy are right in one critical regard: Nothing short of a broad rethinking and comprehensive, holistic, coordinated action can be expected to remedy urban ills. The key problem with this solution, however, is that a broad, sweeping, national urban policy is no longer possible. Anti-tax fever, national budgetary limitations, and the swelling representation of suburban and Sunbelt constituencies in Congress all act to make the enactment of a broad-scale, systemic urban policy increasingly difficult, if not outright impossible.

The nature of Congress' decision-making system, which puts so much power in committees and subcommittees, leads to a focus on small, discrete issues rather than broad national policy concerns. The "gross overrepresentation" of smaller and less urban states in the U.S. Senate also works against the passage of effective policies focused on urban, especially big-city, communities. Add to this the United States Senate's filibuster and cloture rules, which essentially means that any major policy initiative requires the vote of 60 of the nation's 100 senators for passage, and the chances of enacting a far-reaching, comprehensive, and well-defined urban policy are nil.[58]

Recognizing these difficulties, Pietro Nivola argues for a "lite" menu of policies, that the United States adopt policies that European nations have already used to promote higher densities of development, increased use of public transportation, and the curtailment of sprawl: "Why don't most Dutch people and Danes vacate their tight towns and cities, where many commuters prefer to ride bicycles, rather than sport-utility vehicles, to work?" According to Nivola, the answer can be found partly in the sales tax on a new medium-sized car, which is nine times higher in The Netherlands than in the United States. In Denmark it is 37 times higher. The United States, in contrast, through its hidden urban policy, has continued to provide generous subsidies for suburban home ownership.[59]

But Nivola's allegedly "lite" menu of policy suggestions is not lite enough for the American public to swallow. The United States will not repeal tax provisions favorable to homeowners; the homeowner's interest deduction is politically sacrosanct. Similarly, few politicians will have the courage to endorse the steep increase in the gasoline tax that Nivola recommends. If anything, American politicians win votes by enacting policies in opposition to Nivola's recommendations, such as decreasing taxes on gasoline to offset the effects of rising fuel prices. The call for a national urban policy has little resonance outside of academic circles:

> In fact, the very idea of an "urban agenda" has lost its currency—another casualty of America's habitual despair over cities. Outside the dusty corridors of HUD and the lecture halls of graduate public policy schools, the phrase scarcely has a meaning. Or more precisely, its meaning is more and more taken to be something dreadful, like the massive utopianisms of the past: An "urban policy"—here one can detect the muttered prayer "God save us"—is what we had under Urban Renewal, the War on Poverty, and Model Cities. Spare us any more of that, if you please.[60]

The age of national urban policy is not about to begin. Its time in the United States has already passed.

REDUCING THE FEDERAL ROLE

Years of federal spending have not solved the urban problem, leading some analysts to call for a sharply reduced federal role in urban affairs. The new federalism, devolution, deregulation, and privatization are all initiatives that seek to give a more prominent role to state, local, and private-sector actors.

Subnational officials complain about **regulatory creep**, the increased regulations and constraints that are imposed as the price of accepting federal aid.[61] In many areas, project grants are narrow and specialized, denying recipient governments program flexibility. Local governments incur substantial overhead costs in applying for these grants and in meeting their accompanying paperwork, evaluation, and auditing requirements. Many small grants are not cost effective. Grant consolidation can both save on administrative costs and afford recipient governments greater flexibility.

The advocates of devolution argue that the federal government should leave many important policy decisions to the states, while maintaining the responsibility to ensure that civil rights laws and other constitutional obligations are met. These advocates observe that states and localities have modernized their governmental structures and revenue systems and are more capable than ever. Further reductions in federal taxes and regulation can also liberate the private sector to create wealth.

Yet critics of policy devolution argue that the national government has a responsibility to pick up the costs of dealing with problems that are national in scope and that are not the result of local mismanagement. These problems include the transition to a post-industrial economy, porous immigration borders, continuing racial segregation, and homeland security.

Critics of devolution also fear that states and localities, left on their own, will seek to maintain their economic competitiveness by cutting taxes and by reducing environmental safeguards and the services offered to the poor.[62] Only the federal government can afford to engage in equity programs and strong environmental protection without fearing that taxes and regulations will lead businesses to move to other states or locales.

Deregulation and privatization strategies serve to increase private initiative, entrepreneurship, and free-market competition. The competitive pressures of educational vouchers, charter schools, and other choice plans can increase the incentives for schools to perform better. Deregulation has given Chicago and other cities the freedom to tap market forces and build mixed-income housing projects close to the city's downtown, tearing down failing high-rise public housing projects in the process.

Yet whatever the utility of market-oriented solutions, increased deference to the private sector does not assure that urban ills will be cured. The free market creates winners and losers. Left on their own, declining cities, unable to win the competition for business, will continue to decline. School choice programs enable some children to get a better education but ignore the problems of children who are left behind in troubled schools that receive fewer resources as a result of choice. In the contemporary United States, high-risk children remain concentrated in inner cities; they face increasingly dim life prospects even while the conditions for children as a whole, nationwide, continue to improve.[63]

Mixed-income housing projects are able to attract market-rate tenants and buyers only if the developments contain relatively few units for the poor. The lucky few former public housing residents who gain access to the mixed-income developments gain a much-improved living environment. But such developments, shaped by the demands of the market, are expensive to build and provide little benefit for the great bulk of public housing residents.

Nor do housing vouchers enable all recipients to obtain decent, affordable housing. Vouchers are of limited value to residents in cities with a tight housing market where few units are within the financial reach of people using vouchers (or Section 8 certificates). Vouchers also do not assure a cure to housing discrimination; white households report greater success in finding acceptable units with the vouchers than do black households, especially as private landlords are also under no obligation to take Section 8 housing certificates.[64]

Even national economic growth does not bring prosperity to all cities. Chattanooga, St. Louis, Milwaukee, Gary, Detroit, Pittsburgh, Newark, Hartford, and Richmond did not "come back" during 1980–2000, a period of national economic expansion; according to a number of statistical measures, these cities fell further behind. Distressed cities during this period averaged an 8.5-percent population loss, a 6-percent drop in median income, and increases in unemployment from 9.4 to 10.7 percent.[65] A free-market policy of national economic growth does not by itself solve the urban crisis. A targeted approach to urban problems is also needed.

PICKING UP THE PIECES? URBAN POLICY FOR AN ANTI-URBAN POLICY AGE

The dream of a holistic, comprehensive, coordinated national urban policy is politically unrealistic. But the opposite policy direction, the withdrawal of federal initiatives, leaves cities and poorer communities at the mercy of market forces.

Is it possible to identify a workable middle ground? Can we identify a politically pragmatic role for federal—and state—urban policy in an anti-urban policy age?

As sociologist William Julius Wilson concluded in a discussion of social policy, "the real challenge is to develop programs that not only meaningfully address the problems of the underclass but that draw broad support."[66] The same challenge confronts the development of urban policy. How can urban advocates design strong urban programs that are capable of drawing broad political support?

Quite simply, urban analysts need to confront the fact that there is only limited support for programs that are explicitly identified as "urban." Urban advocates need to push for the enactment of effective ameliorative programs that are less obviously "urban" in nature. Such programs accomplish other laudable goals, and in the process, still provide substantial aid to cities and distressed communities.

What follows is a set of ten keys for developing more pragmatic urban strategies, urban policy pieces, and "nonurban programs"[67] that can provide real assistance to troubled urban communities and their residents. The list provides tactical advice for developing effective urban programs in a decision-making environment that is not conducive to strong urban policy:

1. **Spread program benefits. Pursue universal and "race-neutral" programs.** Programs that spread benefits have the potential for garnering a large supportive constituency. Highly targeted and race-specific programs, in contrast, are less capable of attracting a wide, stable base of support. Consequently, William Julius Wilson has argued for broad, race-neutral programs that promise assistance to white, middle-class citizens, not just to people of color and the poor.

   The recent rollback of affirmative action programs serves to underscore the vulnerability of programs that target benefits on the basis of race. Yet the history of the civil rights struggle also shows that, under certain circumstances, the United States has accepted race-specific programs that are not seen as favoritism but are justified by such universal values as equality and justice.[68]

   The American public over the years has supported education, job-training, and local economic revitalization programs that provide disproportionate benefits to the inner-city poor, as long as working- and middle-class citizens and communities are not disqualified from receiving benefits.[69] Urban constituencies will gain disproportionately from education and national health care reform programs that promise to meet the needs of middle-class citizens as well as those of the poor.

   Yet strategies that promise universal benefits also suffer important disadvantages. Spreading program benefits dilutes the assistance given to people and constituencies in need. The high cost of universal programs also eats up funds that might otherwise be available for more effective and targeted programs.

   At times, the high cost of universal benefits may also jeopardize a program's political viability. The Reagan administration terminated general revenue sharing, a program that provided aid to just about every city and county across the nation. It was precisely the wide spread of revenue sharing's benefits that made the program vulnerable; Reagan argued that the nation could no longer afford such a wasteful program that spent money in communities where there was no obvious need.

2. **Target when possible. Target within universalism.** There is no real need to choose between a strictly targeted or a strictly universal approach to urban policy. A mixed approach may provide the most satisfactory alternative. Theda Skocpol provides sound practical advice with her strategy of **targeting within universalism**, where eligibility is spread

broadly but extra benefits and special services are given to poor people and other targeted constituencies.[70]

For many urban programs, targeting within universalism entails a two-step approach. The legislative act declares that a large number of communities are eligible to participate in a program. But during the second step, a program's implementation, administrative mechanisms are used to whittle down the number of applications and target the bulk of program benefits to constituencies with greater need. During the Carter years, approximately 90 percent of the U.S. population lived in areas designated as distressed and eligible for Economic Development Administration (EDA) assistance; yet the EDA was still able to award the bulk of the program's monies to more distressed communities.

3. **Emphasize a program's middle-class constituency.** The political viability of a program is enhanced if it contains benefits for the middle class as well as for the poor. Advocates need to stress the benefits that the middle class will obtain from program reform. Education reform, for instance, promises to deal with the many problems that middle-class parents, not just the poor, have in getting public schools to be responsive to the needs of their children. Bill Clinton and George W. Bush both recognized the potential popularity of a broad-based educational reform program that promised benefits to middle-class parents as well as the poor.

   Similarly, citizen participation and community empowerment strategies can also be justified as giving middle-class citizens, not just the poor, a new voice in overly bureaucratized and irresponsive service systems. The community control movement in the 1960s faced bitter opposition as it concentrated reform on poor, minority, inner-city neighborhoods. Its leaders had neglected to bring parental empowerment efforts to working-class and middle-class portions of the city.[71] To succeed, urban advocates must build winning coalitions.

4. **Emphasize programs that tie benefits to participation in the workplace.**[72] **Where possible, distribute benefits through the tax code.** Americans are hostile to expanding "welfare." However, programs that emphasize workforce participation and the transition from welfare to work are consistent with the high value that Americans place on work. A public opposed to "welfare" may still support expanded assistance for the "deserving poor," especially the working poor. The public supports job training and job creation over welfare. There is also greater support for programs to assist private-sector job training as opposed to "make-work" government programs that provide no real training in the skills demanded by private firms.

   One of Bill Clinton's major accomplishments in office was his expansion of the **Earned Income Tax Credit (EITC)**, a program of wage supplements to the working poor. Clinton expanded EITC with virtually none of the public debate that swirled around other "welfare" and "urban" programs. Clinton knew that his EITC agenda enjoyed two great political advantages. First, Americans are willing to help "deserving" people in need, those who are willing to work. Second, because it is a credit administered through the tax system, most Americans do not really understand it well. Even if aware of the EITC, they are likely to see it only as a complicated tax code provision, not as welfare or public assistance. Sometimes it is easier to gain the enactment of urban-oriented provisions in the tax code than it is to create new, redistributive, direct spending programs.

Even in an era of tight budgets, the public can be expected to support job training programs—if they are seen as effective and not as wasteful—and child-care programs that enable the entry of mothers into the job market. The public can also be expected to subsidize minivan and other transportation programs that enable inner-city residents to reach suburban job sites. Tax credits can be offered as an incentive for private-supported job training, mentoring, and transportation programs.

5. **Focus on education. Focus on children. Focus on the elderly.** While suspicious of a great many domestic programs, the American public nonetheless continues to view education sympathetically: "Focusing on the needs of children would be more politically positive than focusing on urban needs."[73]

"Education" enjoys four distinct advantages over "urban" programs. First, children, especially young children, constitute a sympathetic constituency. Second, education is accepted as a good investment. Increased spending for education can be portrayed as a cost-efficient alternative to social spending. If schools do their jobs and children learn, there will be less in the way of costly social problems and crime for society to deal with later. The nation can either pay for education now or pay for other costly programs later in response to increased social problems. Third, the benefits of increased spending for education can be spread to increase political support. Even if the major portion of new school spending is targeted for children or districts in need, a portion of new spending can be allocated to improve educational opportunities for working-class and middle-class children as well. Finally, spending for education can also be justified in terms of increasing national economic growth and local economic development. A city's business community will support educational initiatives, including mentoring and other special programs, that provide local businesses with a technologically competent and capable workforce essential to maintaining the city's economic competitiveness.

Education and human resource development initiatives are key components of any local economic development program. One review of the economic development literature has concluded that "the evidence is clear that in the long run education and human resource policies are vastly more important to urban economic development than more narrowly and traditionally conceived development policies such as tax concessions, industrial bonds, or enterprise zones."[74]

Children are a sympathetic group. Head Start was expanded during times when other social programs faced cutbacks.

The elderly constitute another sympathetic constituency that the public is willing to help. Communities will build subsidized housing for the elderly even when they resist new construction for the nonelderly poor.

6. **Build on programs with a demonstrated record of success.** The American public will continue to oppose social spending that they view to be unnecessary and ineffective. However, the public will support social programs when there is demonstrated evidence that the programs work, that they are not a waste of money. Head Start and the supplemental food program for women, infants, and children (WIC) are two programs that not only survived the Reagan budget onslaught but actually were expanded over time. Although Reagan attempted to cut these programs, members of Congress and the various policy communities acted to save them, convinced of the programs' demonstrated records of success.[75]

The Harold Washington Single-Room Occupancy (SRO) Hotel in Chicago's Uptown neighborhood seeks to provide safe, high-quality, assisted housing as an alternative to homelessness. The Harold Washington SRO does not look like a typical single-room occupancy hotel. It respects the privacy and dignity of its residents, while at the same time providing necessary counseling services. The building, well supervised and well maintained, is not seen as a threat by it neighbors. While expensive, it is a program that continues to receive support because it works. The Harold Washington SRO is a demonstrated success story, a workable and more dignified alternative to dormitory-style shelters.[76]

7. **Play to powerful symbols and sympathetic constituencies.** Certain causes and constituencies evoke greater public sympathy than others. The plight of the homeless, people with AIDS, and battered women have all received substantial public airing in recent years; as a result, programs aimed at helping these constituencies are more likely to receive public support than programs aimed at the urban poor in general. The plight of veterans and families on the street, even if not typical of the majority of homeless individuals, can also be used to mobilize support for homelessness prevention.

"Environmentalism" is another powerful symbol that can be used to mobilize support for urban programs. Regional growth management can be framed as an approach designed to prevent sprawl and preserve disappearing greenspace and farmland, not as a policy designed to drive new development back to central cities and inner-ring suburbs. Similarly, a program to clean up and redevelop toxic, once-industrial "brownfields" can attract the support of environmentalist organizations that otherwise would have little interest in the economic fate of inner-city communities.

8. **Emphasize the economic development benefits of the "new regionalism." Pursue creative regional alliances.** In Chapters 12 and 13, we argued that cities and suburbs can find common ground for cooperative regional action. However, joint regional action is not possible in all policy areas; it is most likely to occur when cooperation promises mutual benefits to the various jurisdictions involved.

The prominence of economic development concerns provides a fruitful arena for regional cooperation. In the new interregional and global competition for business, cities and suburbs find that they are often unable to attract new businesses by "going it alone." Instead, joint efforts may succeed at marketing an entire region as a "world-class" site for business. Cities and suburbs can increase a region's chances of attracting a major new employer by working cooperatively to put together a package that includes tax abatements, infrastructure improvements, job training, and affordable housing for workers.

Numerous arrangements allow for regional cooperation. Oftentimes, extragovernmental business-led arrangements flourish as the result of the initiative taken by a region's chamber of commerce and various business and civic associations. Both regional business associations and "neutral" civic associations have initiated joint efforts to improve the regional economy.[77]

States, too, have the power to propel new regional collaborations. Governors and other state leaders have an interest in increasing the economic competitiveness and health of their metropolitan areas.[78]

The advantages of regional action are substantial, yet the prospects of a new regionalism should not be overstated. Metropolitan cooperation tends to occur most frequently on housekeeping and economic development matters. Cities and suburbs are not very likely to join in cooperative efforts to integrate schools or to help solve public housing and social welfare problems.[79]

The ISTEA/TEA-21 legislation, with its requirement for metropolitan planning organizations (MPOs) to coordinate transportation development, serves as a model for what the federal government can do to promote regional cooperation. In the future, Congress may similarly find it desirable to promote regional cooperation in such policy areas as health care, where regional planning can minimize the costly duplication of services.

Environmental protection represents another possible arena for future regional action. An activist environmentalist constituency may demand federal legislation that requires local governments to undertake coordinated, regional action to curb urban sprawl.

9. **Pursue public-private partnerships, especially in the area of economic development** As we have already observed, concerns for economic development have dominated the local arena in recent years. Urban advocates need to ride this wave. They should seek appropriate measures designed to assist entrepreneurship and job creation and remove

barriers to urban economic performance. The Atlanta Project, initiated by former President Jimmy Carter, serves as one model of what private corporate involvement can achieve; corporate CEOs committed substantial organizational resources working in partnership with grassroots organizations in such areas as education and job training.[80]

Public-private partnerships are mixed blessings. Corporations and other private actors often derive the primary benefits from growth-oriented partnerships. Corporate-led commitments also are often insufficient to alter the urban situation. Despite the noteworthy successes of the Atlanta Project, urban poverty persists in Atlanta, and the city's more distressed neighborhoods have fallen further behind. Reliance on public-private partnerships risks creating a dual city, especially if development is pursued solely on business' terms and if programs are shaped according to the vision of the city's business partners.

To avoid this prospect, tax concessions and other subsidies given to business can be predicated on the number of jobs or training slots created for the poor. Public and community participation and strict accountability measures, too, are necessary to ensure that growth is structured for public as well as for private benefit.

10. **Build cities from the bottom up through CDCs and other nonprofit and community-based organizations.** There is good news in city politics. As urban affairs journalist Neal Peirce has observed, hope for the urban future lies with community development corporations, mutual housing associations, land trusts, reinvestment corporations, and the myriad of disparate civic, neighborhood, and corporate and citizen volunteer organizations.[81] Successful federal and state urban policy needs to nurture and sustain the creative, problem-solving energies of the tens of thousands of nonprofit and community organizations that exist in urban America.

Community development corporations play an especially important role in bottom-up policy devoted to community revitalization.[82] CDCs have an enviable record of success, leveraging the investment of resources for housing and neighborhood development, building a community's "social capital" in the process.[83] Critics charge that CDCs have neglected more confrontational and political community organizing strategies as an emphasis on housing and physical development requires friendly relations with private financial and real estate actors. CDCs are also criticized for their lack of democratic control, that their boards are not generally chosen by, or answerable to, the larger community. Yet despite these criticisms, CDCs offer community-based strategies that work. In city after city, CDCs have formed community-private sector partnerships to build and rehabilitate housing and to provide new job training and local economic opportunity.

CDCs cannot work in isolation. They require corporate philanthropy and the assistance of nonprofit foundations and government programs.

Three key federal programs—Low-Income Housing Tax Credits, Community Development Block Grants, and the HOME Investment Partnership program—helped to fuel much of the revitalization that took place in lower-income neighborhoods in the 1990s. The Low-Income Housing Tax Credit (LIHTC), enacted in 1986, was especially important in providing financial incentives for corporations to invest in low-income housing construction and rehabilitation, the most noteworthy area of CDC success. LIHTC provides a notable example of how the federal government has been able to catalyze private and nonprofit action in the rebuilding of urban areas.[84]

An urban policy approach that works through community, religious, and other nonprofit organizations can enjoy great public legitimacy and tap greater public support and expertise than one that relies solely on government action. Nonprofit and community organizations know a neighborhood's needs; they have expertise as a result of their extensive experience in working with local problems over the years. Volunteer and client participation also extends the problem-solving reach of the government by supplementing limited public resources. As community and voluntary organizations promote citizen empowerment, they represent a healthy alternative to continued dependency on government. A decentralized approach to problem solving also promotes flexibility.

The limitations of the community-based approach are obvious. What voluntary and nonprofit organizations do they do very well. But they have limited resources and personnel. Voluntary, nonprofit, and faith-based organizations also can also be selective and choose whom they will aid. Government, in contrast, is more universal in its service provision.

* * *

The ten pragmatic steps just listed do *not* add up to the full-fledged national assault required to combat deep-rooted urban ills. They do not constitute anything near as perfect or as comprehensive as an ideal urban policy. But politics is the art of the possible. Barring a cataclysmic event and a fundamental change in political attitudes, the achievement of a strong national urban policy is not politically achievable in the United States.

The famous community organizer Saul Alinsky once observed that a true radical was not an idealist but a pragmatic tactician whose attack on the political and social system started from where the world is, not from where one would like it to be.[85] In the United States, advocates of a national urban policy are idealists who describe the world as they would like it to be. The advocates of more limited, discrete urban programs, in contrast, recognize the limitations imposed by power realities. They are the pragmatic radicals who attempt to ameliorate urban problems by starting from where the world is.

NOTES

1. Theresa M. Daniel, Bonnie Grohe, and Rod Hissong, "Economic Development in Texas Cities: 10 Years After" (paper presented at the annual meeting of the Urban Affairs Association, Washington, DC, April 2, 2004).

2. Harold Wolman, "Local Economic Development Policy: What Explains the Divergence between Policy Analysis and Political Behavior?" *Journal of Urban Affairs* 10, 1 (1988): 19–28.

3. Mark S. Rosentraub, *Major League Losers: The Real Costs of Sports and Who's Paying for It* (New York: Basic Books, 1997); Michael N. Danielson, *Home Team: Professional Sports and the American Metropolis* (Princeton, NY: Princeton University Press, 1997).

4. Heywood T. Sanders, "Hotel Socialism and the New Urban Politics" (paper presented at the annual convention of the Urban Affairs Association, Washington, DC, April 1, 2004). As Sanders observes, Moody's rated the bond for St. Louis' convention hotel as "speculative," yet city elites continued to push the project.

5. Robert G. Lehnen and Carlyn E. Johnson, "The Impact of Tax Increment Financing on School Districts: An Indiana Case Study," in *Tax Increment Financing and Economic Development: Uses, Structures, and Impact*, eds. Craig L. Johnson and Joyce Y. Man (Albany, NY: State University of New York Press, 2001), pp. 137–154.

6. Joan Fitzgerald and Nancey Green Leigh, *Economic Revitalization: Cases and Strategies for City and Suburb* (Thousand Oaks, CA: Sage Publications, 2002), p. 117.

7. Amy Ellen Schwartz and Ingrid Gould Ellen, "Cautionary Notes for Competitive Cities," a paper of The Brookings Institution Center on Urban and Metropolitan Policy, Washington, DC, May 2000, p. 9. Available at www.brookings.edu/es/urban/Schwartz&Ellen.pdf.

8. John D. Kasarda, "Urban Change and Minority Opportunities," in *The New Urban Reality,* ed. Paul E. Peterson (Washington, DC: The Brookings Institution, 1985), p. 64. The quotations in this paragraph are from Kasarda.

9. Dennis A. Rondinelli, James H. Johnson, Jr., and John D, Kasarda, "The Changing Forces of Urban Economic Development: Globalization and City Competitiveness in the 21st Century," *Cityscape: A Journal of Policy Development and Research*, a publication of the U.S. Department of Housing and Urban Development, 3, 3 (1998): 85–89.

10. Norman I. Fainstein and Susan S. Fainstein, "The Politics of Planning New York as a World City," in *Regenerating the Cities: The UK Crisis and the US Experience,* eds. Michael Parkinson, Bernard Foley, and Dennis R. Judd (Glenview, IL: Scott, Foresman, 1989), pp. 143–162.

11. Dennis R. Judd and Susan S. Fainstein, eds., *The Tourist City* (New Haven, CT: Yale University Press, 1999).

12. Kathryn A. Foster, *The Political Economy of Special-Purpose Government* (Washington, DC: Georgetown University Press, 1997), p. 103; David Ranney, *Global Decisions, Local Collisions: Urban Life in the New World Order* (Philadelphia: Temple University Press, 2003), pp. 106–107, 111–118.

13. David L. Imbroscio, "Overcoming the Economic Dependence of Urban America," *Journal of Urban Affairs* 15 (1993): 173–190, discusses a number of these strategies.

14. "How Important Is 'Quality of Life' in Location Decisions and Local Economic Development," in *Dilemmas of Urban Economic Development: Issues in Theory*

and Practice, Urban Affairs Annual Review, vol. 47, eds. Richard D. Bingham and Robert Mier (Thousand Oaks, CA; Sage Publications, 1997), pp. 56–73.

15. Comments of Judith Garber on the panel on "Cities and the New Era of Terrorism" at the annual meeting of the Urban Affairs Association, Washington, DC, April 2, 2004.

16. Hank V. Savitch, "An Anatomy of Urban Terror: Lessons From Jerusalem and Elsewhere" (paper presented at the annual meeting of the Urban Affairs Association, Washington, DC, April 2, 2004).

17. "Midtown Retail Rents Rise to Pre-9/11 Levels," *Crain's New York Business,* April 29, 2004, available at www.crainsny.com/news.cms?newsId-7878; Miriam Kreinin Souccar, "Broadway Chases Blues With a White-hot Streak," *Crain's New York Business,* April 26, 2004, available at www.crainsny.com/article.cms?articleId=20926&a=f.

18. Nicolai Ouroussoff, "At Ground Zero, Disarray Reigns, and an Opportunity Awaits." *The New York Times,* May 2, 2005.

19. For a moving description of women's jobs at the margins, see Barbara Ehrenreich, *Nickel and Dimed: On (Not) Getting By in America* (Henry Holt/Owl, 2002).

20. Cynthia Fuchs Epstein and Stephen R. Duncombe, "Women Clerical Workers," in *Dual City: Restructuring New York,* eds. John Hull Mollenkopf and Manuel Castells (New York: Russell Sage Foundation, 1991), pp. 177–203. Fuchs Epstein and Duncombe provide the basis for our discussion in the previous paragraph as well.

21. Transportation expert Mark Alan Hughes, quoted in Jane Gross, "Getting to Jobs in Suburbs Is Hard for Walking Poor," *The New York Times,* November 18, 1997.

22. For a readable account of the growth of political power of suburbia and its consequences, see G. Scott Thomas, *The United States of Suburbia: How the Suburbs Took Control of America and What They Plan to Do With It* (Amherst, NY: Prometheus Books, 1998). Thomas, though, may overstate suburban power, as he does not fully report the diversity of suburbia and possible fault lines that may result.

23. Rondinelli, Johnson, and Kasarda, "The Changing Forces of Urban Economic Development," p. 82.

24. Rebecca R. Sohmer and Robert E. Long, "Downtown Rebound," a paper of the Fannie Mae Foundation and The Brookings Institution Center on Urban and Metropolitan Policy, Washington, DC, May 2001. Available at www.brookings.edu/dybdocroot/es/urban/census/downtownrebound.pdf.

25. Bruce Weber, "Cities Are Fostering the Arts As a Way to Save Downtown," *The New York Times,* November 18, 1997. For a description of the steps that San Jose, California, took to build its "suburban" downtown, see Steven Jacobs, "Creating Downtown: The Capital of Silicon Valley Builds a Center Where There was None," *Metropolitics,* a publication of Columbia University's Center for Urban Research and Policy (1998), available at www.sipa.columbia.edu/CURP/ resources/metro/v01n0407.html.

26. Myron Orfield, *Metropolitics: A Regional Agenda for Community and Stability,* rev. ed. (Washington, DC: Brookings Institution Press, and Cambridge, MA: Lincoln Institute of Land Policy, 1998); Myron Orfield, *American Metropolitics: the New Suburban Reality* (Washington, DC: Brookings Institution, 2002); David Rusk, *Inside Game, Outside Game: Winning Strategies for Urban America* (Washington, DC: Brookings Institution Press, 1999).

27. Roberto E. Villarreal, "The Politics of Mexican-American Empowerment," in *Latino Empowerment: Progress, Problems, and Prospects*, eds. Roberto E. Villarreal, Norma G. Hernandez, and Howard D. Neighbor (Westport, CT: Greenwood Press, 1988), p. 6.

28. Michael Finnegan and Mark Z. Barabak, "Villaraigosa's Support Goes Beyond Latinos," *Los Angeles Times*, May 19, 2005; Harold Meyerson, "In L.A., a Pol for a Polyglot City," *The Washington Post*, May 19, 2005.

29. Roberto E. Villarreal and Howard D. Neighbor, "Conclusion: An Overview of Mexican-American Political Empowerment," in *Latino Empowerment: Progress, Problems, and Prospects*, p. 128.

30. "Racial Change in the Nation's Largest Cities: Evidence from the 2000 Census," a report of The Brookings Institution Center on urban and Metropolitan Policy, April 2001. Available at www.brook.edu/es/urban/census/citygrowth.htm. Of course, "nonwhite" refers to non-Anglo white.

31. Stacey Warren, "Migra Mouse: The Startling New Demographics of Disneyland" (paper presented at the annual meeting of the Urban Affairs Association, Washington, DC, April 1, 2004).

32. In the 1998 congressional elections, the voting turnout rate was 32.8 percent for Hispanics as compared to 41.8 percent for African Americans and 47.4 percent for whites. See the U.S. Census Bureau, "Number of Hispanics Who Vote Up 'Sharply,' Census Bureau Reports," press release, August 29, 2000. Available at www.census.gov/Press-Release/www/2000/cb00-139.html.

33. Rodolfo O. de la Garza and Louis DeSipio, "Save the Baby, Change the Bathwater, and Scrub the Tub: Latino Electoral Participation after Twenty Years of Voting Rights Act Coverage," in *Pursuing Power: Latinos and the Political System*, ed. F. Chris Garcia (Notre Dame, IN: University of Notre Dame Press, 1997), pp. 72–126.

34. Melissa R. Michelson, "Exploring Latino Political Efficacy and Electoral Participation in California and Chicago" (paper presented at the annual meeting of the American Political Science Association, Washington, DC, August 31–September 3, 2000).

35. Matt A. Barreto, Mario Villarreal, and Nathan D. Woods, "Metropolitan Latino Political Behavior: Voter Turnout and Candidate Preference in Los Angeles," *Journal of Urban Affairs* 27, 1 (2005): 71–91.

36. Alexandra Cole, "The 'Sleeping Giant' Shifts: Latinos and Orange County Politics" (paper presented at the annual meeting of the American Political Science Association, Washington, DC, August 31–September 3, 2000).

37. Ali Modarres and Greg Andranovich, "Local Context for Understanding Poverty and Segregation" (paper presented at the annual meeting of the Urban Affairs Association, Washington, DC, April 1, 2004).

38. Paula D. McClain and Steven C. Tauber, "Racial Minority Group Relations in a Multiracial Society," in *Governing American Cities: Inter-Ethnic Coalitions, Competition, and Conflict*, ed. Michael Jones-Correa (New York: Russell Sage Foundation, 2001), pp. 111–136. For a description of the polarization between Cubans and African Americans in Miami, see "Blacks and Cubans in Miami: The Negative Consequences of the Cuban Enclave on Ethnic Relations," pp. 137–157 in the same volume.

39. These issues are discussed by Karen M. Kaufmann, "Cracks in the Rainbow: Group Commonality as a Basis for Latino and African-American Political Coalitions." Also see Wilbur C. Rich, ed., *The Politics of Minority Coalitions* (Westport, CT: Praeger, 1996). For evidence from California that Latinos are

very similar to whites in their opinions on major policy questions, see Mark Baldassare, *California in the New Millennium: The Changing Social and Political Landscape* (Berkeley, CA: University of California Press, 2000), pp. 99–127.

40. Robert Courtney Smith, *Mexican New York: Transnational Lives of New Immigrants* (Berkeley: University of California Press, 2005).

41. For a case study of Latino activism in redistricting, see James A. Regalado, "Latino Representation in Los Angeles," in *Latino Empowerment: Progress, Problems, and Prospects,* pp. 94–104.

42. See David Lublin, *The Paradox of Representation: Racial Gerrymandering and Minority Interests in Congress* (Princeton, NJ: Princeton University Press, 1997) for a review of the Supreme Court's decisions on race-oriented redistricting.

43. Ruth P. Morgan, *Governance by Decree: The Impact of the Voting Rights Act in Dallas* (Lawrence, KS: University Press of Kansas, 2004), pp. 168–177 and 270–272.

44. W. Avon Drake and Robert D. Holsworth, *Affirmative Action and the Stalled Quest for Black Progress* (Urbana and Chicago: University of Illinois Press, 1996), pp. 71–79 and 120–125.

45. Mitchell F. Rice, "State and Local Government Set-Aside Programs, Disparity Studies, and Minority Business in the Post-*Croson* Era," *Journal of Urban Affairs* 15 (1993): 533. In its 1995 *Adarand* decision, the Court, in a 5-to-4 ruling, struck a further blow against minority set-aside programs, applying the *Croson* logic to federal preference programs. Even federal set-aside requirements would be subject to strict scrutiny and must be narrowly tailored. See Mitchell Rice and Maurice Mongkuo, "Did *Adarand* Kill Minority Set-Asides?" *Public Administration Review* 58, 1 (January/February 1998): 82–86.

46. Rice, "State and Local Government Set-Aside Programs," pp. 536–550; Neil Smelser, William Julius Wilson, and Faith Mitchell, eds., *America Becoming: Racial Trends and Their Consequences,* Volume II (Washington, DC: National Academic Press, 2001), pp. 216–217.

47. Rachel Gordon, "Board Votes to Extend Affirmative Action Plan," *San Francisco Examiner,* September 23, 1998.

48. Details on the defeat of Proposition A in Houston are provided by Sam Howe Verhovek, "Houston Vote Underlined Complexity of Rights Issue," *The New York Times,* November 6, 1997.

49. David L. Kirp, "Retreat into Legalism: The Little Rock School Desegregation Case in Historical Perspective," *PS: Political Science and Politics* (September 1997): 446.

50. Megan Twohey, "Desegregation Is Dead," *National Journal* (September 18, 1999): pp. 2614–2619.

51. Jennifer Hochschild, "Is School Integration Still a Viable Policy Option?" *PS: Political Science and Politics* (September 1997): 463.

52. Susan Welch, Michael Combs, Lee Sigelman, and Timothy Bledsoe, "Race or Place? Emerging Public Perspectives on Urban Education," *PS: Political Science and Politics* (September 1997): 454–458.

53. Daniel Patrick Moynihan, "Toward a National Urban Policy," *The Public Interest* 17 (Fall 1969).

54. Paul Kantor, *The Dependent City Revisited* (Boulder, CO: Westview Press, 1995), pp. 238–246, especially pp. 238–240 and 245–246.

55. David L. Ames, Nevin C. Brown, Mary Helen Callahan, Scott B. Cummings, Sue Marx Smock, and Jerome M. Ziegler, "Rethinking American Urban Policy,"

Journal of Urban Affairs 14 (1992): 197. The prestigious Brookings Institution, a Washington "think tank," also revived the call for a national urban policy. See Bruce Katz, "Enough of the Small Stuff! Toward a New Urban Agenda, "*The Brookings Review* 18, 3 (Summer 2000): 4–9.

56. Edward J. Blakely and David L. Ames, "Changing Places: American Urban Planning Policy for the 1990s," *Journal of Urban Affairs* 14 (1992): 423.

57. Janet Rothenberg Pack, "Metropolitan Development: Patterns, Problems, Causes, Policy Proposals," in Pack, ed., *Sunbelt/Frostbelt: Public Policies and Market Forces in Metropolitan Development* (Washington, DC: Brookings Institution Press), pp. 22–23 (emphasis in the original).

58. Bernard H. Ross, Cornelius M. Kerwin, and A. Lee Fritschler, *How Washington Works* (Sun Lakes, AZ: Thomas Horton and Daughters, Inc., 1996); G. Ross Stephens, "Urban Underrepresentation in the U.S. Senate," *Urban Affairs Review* 31, 3 (January 1996): 404–418.

59. Pietro Nivola, "Fit for Fat City: A 'Lite' Menu of European Policies to Improve Our Urban Form," Brookings Institution Policy Brief #44, Washington, January 1999. Available at www.brookings.edu/commlpolicy/briefs/pb044/pb44.htm.

60. Paul S. Grogan and Tony Proscio, *Comeback Cities: A Blueprint for Urban Neighborhood Revival* (Boulder, CO: Westview, 2000), pp. 246–247.

61. National laws are often necessarily imprecise and ambiguous; ambiguity is a political consensus-building strategy that allows competing parties to come together. But such compromise and vagueness leave the development of more specific program rules and regulations to federal agencies, agencies such as HUD that may earn the animosity of state and local officials who claim that new regulations are unnecessarily restrictive and that program goals are being distorted. For a review of how congressional politics, bureaucratic power, and intergovernmental relations affect the development and implementation of domestic policies, see Ross, Kerwin, and Fritschler, *How Washington Works*.

62. For a good example of this literature, see John D. Donahue, *Disunited States: What's at Stake as Washington Fades and the States Take the Lead* (New York: Basic Books, 1997).

63. Isabel Sawhill and Laura Chadwick, "Children in Cities: Uncertain Futures," a report of The Brookings Institution Center on Urban and Metropolitan Policy, Washington, DC, December 1999. Available at www.brookings.edu/dybdocroot/es/urban/sawhill.pdf.

64. For a review of the limitations of housing vouchers and other housing dispersal programs, see Edward G. Goetz, *Choosing the Way: Deconcentrating the Poor in Urban America* (Washington, DC: The Urban Institute Press, 2003), pp. 70–75 and 239–250.

65. Kimberly Furdell, Hal Wolman, and Edward W. (Ned) Hill, "Have Central Cities Come Back?" (paper presented at the annual meeting of the Urban Affairs Association, Washington, DC, April 2, 2004).

66. William Julius Wilson, "Public Policy Research and The Truly Disadvantaged," in *The Urban Underclass*, eds. Christopher Jencks and Paul E. Peterson (Washington, DC: Brookings Institution, 1991), p. 478.

67. Marshall Kaplan and Franklin James, eds., *The Future of National Urban Policy* (Durham, NC: Duke University Press, 1990).

68. Dona Cooper Hamilton and Charles V. Hamilton, *The Dual Agenda: Race and Social Welfare Policies of Civil Rights Organizations* (New York: Columbia University Press, 1997).

69. William Julius Wilson, *The Truly Disadvantaged* (Chicago: University of Chicago Press, 1981); and Wilson, "Public-Policy Research and The Truly Disadvantaged." Also see Robert Greenstein, "Universal and Targeted Programs to Relieving Poverty," in *The Urban Underclass,* eds. Jencks and Peterson, pp. 437–459.

70. Theda Skocpol, "Targeting Within Universalism: Politically Viable Policies to Combat Poverty in the United States," in *The Urban Underclass,* eds. Jencks and Peterson, p. 414.

71. Douglas Yates, *The Ungovernable City* (Cambridge, MA: MIT Press, 1977).

72. Greenstein, "Universal and Targeted Programs to Relieving Poverty."

73. Jeffrey A. Raffel et al., "Policy Dilemmas in Urban Education: Addressing the Needs of Poor, At-Risk Children," *Journal of Urban Affairs* 14 (1992): 281.

74. Hal Wolman, Royce Hanson, Edward Hill, Marie Howland, and Larry Ledebur, "National Urban Economic Development Policy," *Journal of Urban Affairs* 14 (1992): 235.

75. Greenstein, "Universal and Targeted Programs to Relieving Poverty."

76. For an interesting view as to how housing design features, big and small, can add to the dignity, safety, and political viability of housing for the homeless, see Sam Davis, *Designing for the Homeless: Architecture that Works* (Berkeley: University of California Press, 2004).

77. David K. Hamilton, "Developing Regional Regimes: A Comparison of Two Metropolitan Areas," *Journal of Urban Affairs* 26, 4 (2005): 455-477.

78. William R. Barnes and Larry C. Ledebur, The *New Regional Economies: The U.S. Common Market and the Global Economy* (Thousand Oaks, CA: Sage Publications, 1998), pp. 141–160; Frances Frisken and Donald F. Norris, "Regionalism Reconsidered," *Journal of Urban Affairs* 23, 5 (2001): 467–479.

79. See, for instance, Foster, *Political Economy of Special-Purpose Government,* pp. 223–224.

80. Dan E. Sweat and Jacquelyn A. Anthony, "The Role of Corporations in Urban Revitalization: The Experience of the Atlanta Project," *National Civic Review* (Summer–Fall 1995): 239–247.

81. Neal Peirce, "An Urban Agenda for the President," *Journal of Urban Affairs* 15 (1993): 457–467.

82. For a short summary of the accomplishments, potential, and limitations of CDCs, see Thad Williamson, David Imbroscio, and Gar Alperovitz, *Making a Place for Community: Local Democracy in a Global Era* (New York: Routledge, 2003), pp. 213–235. Grogan and Proscio, *Comeback Cities,* pp. 62–101 present more anecdotal evidence of CDC successes in cities across the country.

83. Ross Gittell and Avis Vidal, *Community Organizing: Building Social Capital as a Development Strategy* (Thousand Oaks, CA: Sage Publications, 1998), especially pp. 33–56.

84. Grogan and Proscio, *Comeback Cities,* pp. 94–95 and 248–253.

85. Saul D. Alinsky, *Rules for Radicals: A Pragmatic Primer for Realistic Radicals* (New York: Vintage Books, 1971).

CREDITS

P1.1   The Freedom Tower design—© Reuters/Landov

P2.1   The Port of Houston in Deer Park, Texas—© Ray Soto/CORBIS

P3.1   Stop Gentrification graffiti—© David Robinson/CORBIS

P3.2   Shanghai mayor greets Chicago mayor—© Claro Cortes IV/ Reuters/CORBIS

P6.1   Jewish Mayor of New York wears green—© Mark Peterson/ CORBIS

P6.2   Harold Washington with supporters—© Jacques M. Chenet/ CORBIS

P7.1   Harvey Milk by his camera shop, 1977—© Bettmann/CORBIS

P8.1   African-American women of CHA tenant patrol—© Ralf-Finn Hestoft/CORBIS

P11.1   African-American family moving into Levittown—© Bettmann/ CORBIS

P11.2   A photo showing the dramatic fall off in development at the edge of Portland's Urban Growth Boundary AP/WWP—© Associated Press/AP/Wide World Photos

P11.3   Planned community, Seaside Florida—© Richard Bickel/CORBIS

P14.1   Cabrini-Green Public Housing Project in Chicago, 1995— © Ralf-Finn Hestoft/CORBIS

P14.2   New mixed-income housing in Chicago—© Frank Polich/ Reuters/CORBIS

P15.1   *New York Daily News* Headline: "Ford to City: Drop Dead"— © 1975 *New York Daily News*.

Maps designed by World Sites Atlas, www.sitesatlas.com

NAME INDEX

SUBJECT INDEX